MONEY AND FINANCE: READINGS IN THEORY, POLICY, AND INSTITUTIONS

MONEY AND FINANCE:
READINGS IN THEORY, POLICY AND INSTITUTIONS

SECOND EDITION

DEANE CARSON, EDITOR

Professor of Banking
Graduate School of Business
Columbia University

John Wiley & Sons, Inc.
New York · London · Sydney · Toronto

Library of Congress Catalogue Card Number: 70-37643

ISBN 0-471-13712-X

Printed in the United States of America.

10 9 8 7 6 5 4 3 2 1

To David Meiselman

To David Meiselman

MONEY AND FINANCE:
READINGS IN THEORY, POLICY AND INSTITUTIONS

SECOND EDITION

DEANE CARSON, EDITOR

Professor of Banking
Graduate School of Business
Columbia University

John Wiley & Sons, Inc.
New York · London · Sydney · Toronto

Library of Congress Catalogue Card Number: 70-37643

ISBN 0-471-13712-X

Printed in the United States of America.

10 9 8 7 6 5 4 3 2 1

PREFACE

If monetary theories, policies, and institutions were static, there would be little justification for a revised volume of readings to supplement text assignments in the money and banking course. The second edition of *Money and Finance* has been prepared in light of the quite remarkable developments that have occurred since 1965, when the book was first published. I have taken account of these developments, many of which have not yet been incorporated into textbooks, in this edition.

With respect to monetary and financial institutions, both the banking system itself and the institutions of the money market have experienced rapid and significant change in the past decade. Banks have become aggressive seekers of resource inputs rather than passive acceptors of deposit flows, as the remarkable growth of the Euro-dollar market, the utilization of certificates of deposit, the issuance of commercial paper by subsidiaries, the selling of loan participation instruments, and the aggressive seeking of new kinds of capital will attest. Moreover, the structure of the banking system is undergoing substantial change, in the growth of holding companies, the establishment of foreign branches, and a widened scope of market competition, both geographically and within existing banking markets.

In Part 2, which deals in general with commercial banking, I have selected readings that would be supplementary to the standard texts in the field, a fact that accounts for the relative lack of material dealing with lending functions, which are amply covered in the typical money-and-banking text. I have emphasized three aspects of banking: (1) the theoretical and observed behavior of banks in managing their liquidity positions in response to monetary policy; (2) the variety of bank behavior that one finds in what is often treated as a monolithic banking system; and (3) the role of banking regulation in influencing banking behavior, the structure of banking markets, and economic efficiency.

The first of these aspects is represented by the Anderson-Burger article, which presents both theoretical and empirical material relating to the liquidity behavior of banks, and the articles by Delores P. Lynn and Fred H. Klopstock, who examine the observed responses of banks to liquidity pressures in 1966 and 1969. The second aspect is represented by my essay, "A Bank Is a Bank Is a Bank?," the thesis of which is that the game of banking, unlike most industry games, is played under strikingly different rules, not only in different ball parks, but also in the *same* ball park, a fact that is mainly, but not entirely, due to the irrational regulatory hodgepodge that applies to commercial banking and other financial institutions. This is logically followed by Meltzer's searching analysis of the *rationale* of the entire spectrum of regulation of financial institutions—entry, branching, merger, portfolio constraints (both on the asset and liability sides of the balance sheet), and deposit insurance, in light of their influence on economic efficiency and contribution to aggregate economic stability. Meltzer concludes that only deposit insurance is justifiable, and even here, the present insurance system should be significantly changed. Edwards' contribution, which concludes Part 2, is to examine the forces that have led to the rapid growth of one-bank holding companies, forces that, interestingly enough, he finds to have been largely generated by bank regulation itself.

Part 3 introduces the student to the Federal Reserve System—its structure, goals, indicators, and tools—in articles that hopefully add to his or her depth of understanding of the central bank. My own selection on the structure and government of the Federal Reserve System attempts to lay bare the real power center of the System and to explore the power relationships within the system and externally with Congress and the Executive. Thomas R. Saving explores the goal, target, and indicator problem—an extremely important area that is only recently finding its way into the standard texts in any systematic way. (In discussing goals, the instructor may wish to assign the first selection in Part 6). Both Meiselman and Meltzer argue for the adoption of aggregate indicators by the Federal Reserve authorities to guide their operations, while the official Federal Reserve view is discussed in "Monetary Aggregates and Money Market Conditions in Open Market Policy." Again, the instructor may find it useful to use Alan Holmes' article in Part 5 at this stage; I felt that there were informational gaps that precluded its inclusion in this Part. In any case, the controversy over whether aggregate or money-market-conditions variables give the most accurate signals to the monetary authorities is introduced at this point and might serve to introduce the larger moneterist neo-Keynesian debate.

Monetary policy tools, which are amply explained in most textbooks, are treated in Part 3 in two ways. First, the actual techniques of conducting open-market operations are emphasized; Cooper's study should supplement the student's appreciation of how purchases and sales affect bank reserves, interest rates, and the money supply with knowledge of actual trading procedures and techniques carried out in the Trading Room at the Federal Reserve Bank of New York. His discussion of long-term security operations of the Desk in the "operation-twist" period of 1961–1964 is particularly enlightening and appropriate today, when the Open Market Committee is again engaged in a similar operation. Second, the articles on discounting (an obsolete term since 1970—the Federal Reserve System does not discount paper anymore, and is struggling with the problem of finding a term to describe what it does at the window), reserve requirements, and Regulation Q are cast in terms of reform. It is quite likely that the administration of the discount window will be substantially altered by the time this volume appears; the probable nature of these changes is discussed in selections 7 and 8. Selection 9 in this part sets forth the economic arguments for abolishing legal reserve requirements as a policy instrument, which is followed by Charlotte E. Ruebling's examination of Regulation Q, an examination that clearly argues for *its* abolition.

Ideas in these selections should stimulate the student's interest in the Federal
Reserve System.

Monetary theory is treated in the selections in Part 4. In making choices in this
regard, I have reflected my monetarist bias, which is offset by the preponderance
of nonmonetarist articles in Part V, "Monetary Policy." This may seem incongruous
and requires some justification. First, with a few notable exceptions, empirical
testing of monetary hypotheses has been conducted by monetarists in recent
years, and the preponderance of advances in monetary theory have been generated by monetarists. Again, with exceptions, the Keynesian role has been largely
defensive and nonempirical. The most notable exception, in my view, has been
Tobin's work which, in published form and in manuscript is—also in my opinion—
unsuitable for the undergraduate course. Instructors may wish to supplement the
present readings with his "Post Hoc Propter Hoc" article or some other one.
Professor Fand's discussion of Keynesian monetary theory in "Keynesian Monetary Theories, Stabilization Policy and the Recent Inflation" is also worth assigning; it is not included here because his monetarist views are contained in the
selected readings. Second, with few exceptions, the standard money-and-banking
textbooks (as well as elementary-economics textbooks), are geared to the presentation of the Keynesian model and neo-Keynesian interpretation of money and
appropriate policy. In this sense, the selected readings are genuinely supplementary to textbook treatment.

On the other hand, the selections of Part 5 tend to reflect monetary policy as
it is and hence reflect neo-Keynesian analysis and prescriptions. In a sense, from
the monetarist's view, Part 4 presents the policy prescriptions that derive from
modern monetary theory and empirical evidence, while Part 5 reflects "established" theory and actual policy formulation and execution.

A further note should be taken of the content of these two parts, which applies
as well to several of the readings throughout the volume. That is, they require
modest student familiarity with the formulation and testing of economic hypotheses.
There are several ways to approach this problem when one's students are
deficient in statistics.

The first approach, and the one I find superior, is to spend a class hour or so
explaining the technique of multiple regression analysis, using one of the empirical
articles (I find Keran's in Part 4 ideal). Without going very far into statistical theory,
it is possible to explain the significance and meaning of coefficients of correlation,
R^2's, standard errors, signs, the Durbin-Watson Statistic, and "T" values. Time
thus spent is immensely valuable to the students, even to those who have had some
statistics.

Second, one may assign portions of the articles in which the empirical weather
is heavy. Almost without exception, empirical articles explain rather well what the
problem is and what hypotheses are being tested at the beginning, and at the end
summarize the major results.

Finally, the instructor may elect not to assign selections—and this will be done
in any case, perhaps, for other reasons. An alternative, of course, is to make some
outside reading assignments optional for the student.

The introduction to Part 4, "Monetary Theory," was written by Professor Richard
Zecher of the University of Chicago. He treats the demand for money as a
wealth asset subject to the usual constraints and the supply of money as a commodity produced at zero cost; and he considers the economic implications of

demand and supply, under these market conditions, for real income, employment, the general price level, and interest rates. His final section on the implications of theory for monetary policy argues for Federal Reserve attention to the growth of the money supply as an indicative variable.

Friedman and Meiselman make similar points, both arguing, in different contexts, that the rate of interest is not the "swing" variable of either monetary theory or monetary policy, as the neo-Keynesians would contend. Friedman's selection argues that monetary changes effect nominal and *real* rates in different ways over a time path, and these differences affect nominal and *real* income in very different ways. Meiselman is concerned with the term structure of rates, with special regard to recent research relating to his expectational theory and also to the segmented market hypothesis, which lays emphasis on supplies of debt assets. Meiselman is refreshingly candid in his appraisal of policy implications of research on the term structure of interest rates—in effect, he argues that policies designed to change the existing term structure involve a game of blind man's bluff, since no one, including theorists, market participants, and policy-makers, has a reasonably precise idea of where such policies will lead.

Indeed, this latter attitude is a syndrome of monetarism—skepticism in making policy decisions without reasonable certainty of the effects of government action.

Part V is specifically oriented to three aspects of monetary policy. First, I have included approximately two thirds of the Minutes of the Federal Open Market Committee of November 1965, the last date for which complete deliberations of the Committee have been published. The Committee has more recently published very attenuated versions of its meetings on a three-month lag schedule; I have included this longer piece to show how the FOMC actually conducts its deliberations, how varied are the views presented, the kind of evidence called forth, and the way in which the Committee finally comes to a decision. While the meeting took place in 1965, the format remains essentially the same.

Following this excursion into monetary-policy formulation, I have placed a reading on "The Channels of Monetary Policy," which deals with the transmission mechanism of monetary-policy actions. Unlike the St. Louis models, which employ single-equation reduced-form techniques, this selection reports results of the econometric model generated by the Board in conjunction with MIT, which incorporates a multitude of both behavioral and functional equations for the economy.

The selections by Meltzer and Holmes constitute a reasoned debate on whether the Federal Reserve System can control the supply of money. It now seems to be agreed by almost everyone in the Federal Reserve System that the System *should* employ an aggregate indicator of the thrust of past policies as a guide for future operations. Holmes argues that monolithic concern with money supply and other aggregate indicators would be unrealistic in the sense that it would result in potential and real damage to the money market *and* that the Federal Reserve System cannot proximately determine the supply of money in any event, at least in the short run. Moreover, the System cannot ignore money-market conditions—the Penn Central commercial paper crisis of 1970, for example.

Meltzer's argument is that concern for money-market crises, which occur almost daily in the eyes that behold them, are mere ripples in the smooth flow of the larger sea. The policy-maker *can* control the flow of the sea tide but may not if he's overly concerned with each and every wave.

Warren L. Smith's article, "A Neo-Keynesian View of Monetary Policy," is representative of both how Keynesian's view policy *and* how things really are in the Federal Reserve System. In a sense, it incorporates both Keynesian Theory and Policy.

Part 5 concludes with an analysis of monetary-policy impact on a particular sector of the economy, residential construction. Monetary restraint, in the form that it has taken in recent cycles, appears to have hit residential construction particularly hard, in the sense that expenditures on housing were dampened more than other forms of investment, and the residential-building industry was in dire straits, perhaps because of irrational government policy.

Part 6 contains a great deal of noncontroversial evidence that the present international monetary system requires basic reform. As this is written, the world is once again experiencing the stresses of international monetary crisis, generated by the adherence to fixed-exchange-rate arrangements devised at Bretton Woods more than a generation ago. Serious studies of the present system are currently underway in the International Monetary Fund and elsewhere, studies that hopefully will lead to reform. As of early 1972, however, it appears that the only considerable reform will be the institution of a broader band around fixed official exchange rates, thus sustaining the relevance of the selections of this part of the volume.

In preparing this edition, I am greatly indebted to the authors and publishers of the selections for permission to use their articles in the present form. I also thank my wife, Agnes Carson, and Katherine L. Watson for typing the manuscript, and Nancy Kingsley for preparing the book for publication.

Deane Carson

Columbia University
January 1972

CONTENTS

MONEY AND FINANCE: READINGS IN THEORY, POLICY, AND INSTITUTIONS

PART 1

THE SUPPLY OF MONEY

READING 1

INTRODUCTION

Deane Carson

In recent years Government stabilization policies have increasingly relied on monetary policy. Much of the burden for controlling the inflationary forces that developed in the latter half of the 1960s, and which only now, in 1971, appear to be (temporarily?) abating, has rested on the Federal Reserve monetary authorities. This reliance has stemmed from (a) the recognition that changes in the money supply exert powerful, if delayed, pressures on prices and national income and (b) the alleged or real inflexibility of national fiscal policies embracing Government expenditures and revenues.

In formulating and executing policy, the American monetary authorities have only relatively recently given major emphasis to *monetary aggregates,* including the money supply itself, as proximate indicators of the thrust and direction of their control mechanism. For many years prior to 1970, the authorities relied much more heavily on *money market conditions*—interest rates and free reserve positions of member banks—to indicate how policy was working, while not ignoring completely the monetary aggregates. The recent shift in emphasis, which should not be exaggerated,[1] has opened up a set of policy and operational questions that have been heretofore dealt with almost exclusively in the literature of monetary economics. The shift from theoretical economics to the implementation of a policy partly based on the control of monetary aggregates has not been a particularly enlightening experience; and while it is still too early to draw conclusions, it is safe to assert that the experiment in monetarism has raised more questions than it has answered.

Perhaps the most elementary ques-

[1] In late spring of 1971, an academic seminar at the Federal Reserve Bank of New York was repeatedly cautioned by Federal Reserve officials against interpreting current policy exclusively in terms of an attempt to control monetary aggregates. This was hardly necessary in light of monetary experience and official pronouncements throughout 1970. Money-market conditions still dominate the system's approach to monetary policy, modifying attempts to control money-supply growth within a fairly narrow range.

tion that faced the Federal Reserve authorities—and one that they still profess not to have an answer to—is simply: What is money? The next selection amply demonstrates that this is not as difficult to resolve as the authorities have tended to assume. It *is* important to know, of course, what financial assets bear a stable, positive, and high correlation with the Gross National Product (GNP), if the monetary authorities are to affect the latter through management of their aggregate supply.[2] The prevailing, if not unanimous, view within the Federal Reserve is one of skepticism, generated by the conflicting theoretical and empirical evidence contained in the economic literature. In effect, the Federal Reserve authorities have tended to say: If you economists cannot tell us what money is, how do you expect us to control it? This view seems less appropriate now than it might have been a decade ago; Laidler's selection below brings heavy weight to the view that it does not make much difference whether money is defined narrowly (M_1), to include demand deposits plus currency, or broadly (M_2), to include M_1 plus time and savings deposits at commercial banks, for monetary-management purposes.

A second question raised by the monetary authorities is equally fundamental. It pertains to the *ability* of the central bank to control the supply of any monetary aggregate selected for management.[3] Here again the current Federal Reserve view is highly skeptical. It is worthy of note in this regard that the manager of the Federal Reserve Open Market Account, who has direct operating responsibilities, does not believe he can control the money supply, at least within a narrow range, in the short run, and is skeptical about his ability to control other monetary aggregates. This view also permeates the policy-making levels, the Board of Governors and the Open Market Committee. These operational and policy authorities point to the experience of 1970, when month-to-month variation in the monetary aggregates was even greater than the average of 1969, the year prior to the announced shift in emphasis to the control of monetary aggregates. Furthermore, in evaluating a recent period of average two-quarter stability, the prevailing view, as expressed by the Vice Chairman of the Open Market Committee, was that this was due more to luck than good management—the errors happened to cancel out.

At least to some extent, the problem of controlling monetary aggregates has been self-imposed by the Federal Reserve System. There is no overriding commitment to such control, and target ranges are abandoned in the face of changes in money-market conditions. Primary concern with the liquidity of the banking system, the failure of particular institutions (such as the Penn Central debacle of 1970) and the alleged needs of Treasury debt management conspire to make the achievement of aggregate monetary targets difficult if not impossible. The monetary authorities apparently believe that the costs of abandoning overriding concern with the money market are too great in terms of the benefits of pursuing monetary aggregate goals. This raises an unanswered question; yet we can con-

[2] Since the monetary managers cannot control the GNP directly, they must do so by indirectly controlling *some* economic variable or variables. To be successful, this indirect variable must demonstrate a stable relationship with the GNP, operate in the *right* direction, and be as free as possible from "feedback" effects—that is, from influence by the GNP itself.

[3] Alternative monetary aggregates that might be selected include the money supply itself (M_1 or M_2), the supply of bank reserves plus currency in circulation, and the unborrowed reserves of member banks.

clude that the so-called monetarist experiment of 1970 was strongly biased against the monetarist position that monetary aggregates *can* be controlled. The results tell us very little about the capability of the System in this regard.

The third question, which is related to the two raised above, concerns the identification of forces determining the money supply. These forces are discussed in Jordan's selection, "Elements of Money Stock Determination," reprinted in this section of the volume. Mastery of this material is essential to the understanding of the monetary mechanism, as well as to the appreciation of many of the selections that follow in Parts 2, 3, and 4.

The concluding selection on "The Economics of the Money Market" is designed to supplement standard textbooks in Money and Banking that typically pass over money-market institutions and operations very lightly. I have included this for the very important reason that the Federal Reserve, as we have seen, pays a great deal of attention to conditions in the money market—liquidity and interest rates—in pursuing policy goals. Although we personally believe that this concern is responsible for a great many monetary policy errors of the past, and indeed for the present inflation, it would be a serious mistake to ignore the money market in any discussion of current monetary affairs.

READING 2
THE DEFINITION OF MONEY

Theoretical and Empirical Problems

David Laidler*

I. INTRODUCTION

Changes in the money supply can affect the economy by two distinct mechanisms. First, they may change the level of real wealth held by the community and, by way of the influence of the level of wealth on aggregate demand, they can change the levels of income, employment, and prices. Second, even if changes in the money supply leave the level of real wealth unchanged, as is usually assumed when dealing with an economy in which money is largely the liability of a privately owned banking system, these changes nevertheless alter the composition of portfolios, and hence the rates of return at which existing stocks of assets will be held. In this case, it is changes in these rates of return that influence the level of aggregate demand.

However, whether money supply changes work primarily by way of a wealth effect or a substitution effect, before the monetary authorities in any actual economy can hope to influence behaviour in a predictable way by manipulating the money supply there are a number of preconditions that must be met. Among the most important of these necessary (but not sufficient) conditions are that the authorities must be able to control the volume of that set of assets that most closely corresponds to the "money stock" of standard macroeconomics; at the same time the demand function for this stock of assets must be stable enough for the consequences of changing its volume to be predictable with a high degree of reliability.

Source: Reprinted from *Journal of Money Credit and Banking,* August 1969, pp. 508–525, with deletions.

* An earlier version of this paper was presented at the University of Essex Staff Seminar, where it was subjected to much useful criticism. I am particularly indebted to Alvin Marty and Michael Parkin, with whom I have discussed the issues dealt with in this paper, and to Harry Johnson, Robert Clower, Chung Lee, and Edgar Feige, who read and commented most helpfully on an earlier draft. All errors and omissions are nevertheless to be attributed to myself.

Whether or not these preconditions are met is a matter of the specific economy with which one is dealing and as far as the United States is concerned there has been a good deal of debate on these issues. The once quite widely held view that the demand for money would be highly unstable due to the vicissitudes of speculative behaviour is not stressed very much in recent literature. However, the question as to whether the United States monetary authorities have control over the relevant stock of assets is one that has come in for a good deal of attention, both at the theoretical and at the empirical level.

One may distinguish three broad views of what is "money" in the United States economy. First there are those who cling to the traditional concept of currency in the hands of the public and demand deposits at commercial banks, and second, there are those who argue that time deposits at commercial banks are such a close substitute for demand deposits that they should be included in the quantity of money which the authorities must manipulate in attempting to influence the level of economic activity. Proponents of both of these points of view are broadly agreed that current institutional arrangements permit the authorities to control the relevant stocks of assets as far as monetary policy is concerned, and find themselves opposed to those who argue that the liabilities of certain non-bank financial intermediaries, particularly savings and loan associations and mutual savings banks, are such close substitutes for commercial bank liabilities as to require their inclusion in the "money stock." The latter group argue that these other institutions must also be brought under the control of the monetary authorities before one can expect useful results from monetary policy.

As we shall see, the empirical element in the debate has tended to center on the question of whether a useful definition of money should include time deposits at commercial banks, or whether the more traditional concept is adequate. One suspects that this issue of time deposits has taken the center of the stage, not so much because it is obviously a more important question than the one which asks whether the liabilities of such institutions as mutual savings banks and savings and loan associations are not also money, but rather because Milton Friedman, in using this slightly broader money concept in a pioneering and influential piece of empirical work, obtained results, particularly about the apparent insensitivity of the demand for money to the interest rate, which were quite contrary to what most would have expected, and which appeared to stem largely from the definition of money he had employed.

Whatever the historical reason for its existing as an issue, it is not unreasonable to give the question of the inclusion of time deposits in the definition of money some sort of priority in the present context because the arguments that would lead to the inclusion of Saving and Loan Association shares and the like in the definition of money all point to currency plus demand deposits being an inadequate concept. If the traditional notion proves adequate in competition with a money concept that includes time deposits, the issues raised by the other arguments mentioned above are virtually settled by default and in favour of a traditional view of what is money, a view that implies that the monetary authorities can control its quantity under present institutional arrangements. Even if the traditional definition of money fails in such tests, their outcome can still throw light on the question as to whether it might be desirable to include the liabilities of non-bank financial intermediaries in the definition of money. If it turns out that a stable demand function for money, defined to exclude these assets, can be identified, then there would appear to be no pressing need to introduce them into the definition of money. Thus, even if the basic issue is a broader one, it still makes sense to pay particular attention to the question of whether or not the introduction of time deposits into the definition of money noticeably improves empirical results, because the evidence on this question is capable of throwing light on the more fundamental issue.

II. EMPIRICAL EVIDENCE

The issues at stake are as follows. First, are time deposits sufficiently close substitutes for demand deposits to warrant treating them as the same asset? Second, if the answer to the first question is yes, is it also the case that the liabilities of other financial intermediaries are sufficiently close substitutes for those of commercial banks to warrant treating them as the same asset? Now one can only define what is meant by a "sufficiently close substitute" if he will specify the problem with which he wishes to deal, and as far as the definition of money is concerned the most important issue has been the indentification and measurement of a stable aggregate demand for money function.

As was noted earlier, it is important to know about the aggregate demand for money function if one wishes to influence the level of economic activity by manipulating the money supply, for though it is not the only relationship involved in the transmission of the effects of monetary policy, it is clearly an important one. A "more stable demand function" is precisely one that permits the consequences of shifting the supply of money to be more easily and accurately predicted.

In a deterministic world, in which all functions, and their parameters, were known and unchanging, there would be no problem of this sort. One could, for example, define money to include time deposits and worry about the determination of its velocity, or define money to exclude time deposits and introduce time deposits in their role as a close substitute for money as something that might influence velocity. In either case one would get the same results. However, in a stochastic world, with less than perfect knowledge, to get a given degree of accuracy in prediction, one approach might require knowledge of fewer parameters and the values of fewer variables than another, and hence be simpler to employ.

The problem of the "right" definition of money is, in this sense, fundamentally empirical. A "more stable demand for money function" may be taken to be one that requires knowledge of fewer variables and their parameters in order to predict the demand for money with a given degree of accuracy, or, which amounts to the same thing, one that yields parameter estimates that are less subject to variation when the same arguments are included in the function and hence enables more accurate predictions of the demand for money to be made.

That time deposits be substitutes for demand deposits is a necessary condition for a money concept that includes them, but it is not a sufficient condition. The same argument obviously holds as far as the inclusion of the liabilities of other financial intermediaries in the definition of money is concerned. Most of the empirical work that has been done on the question of the definition of money has therefore concentrated on investigating the stability of the demand for money function under different definitions of money. Some work, however, has been done on directly measuring the degree of substitutability of one potential component of the money stock for another and, as we shall see below, the results of these two types of test are not altogether consistent.

It will be convenient to begin the account of the relevant evidence with Friedman's paper. First of all, Friedman found an elasticity of demand for money with respect to permanent income of about 1.8.* Second, he was unable to produce any evidence that the rate of interest was an important variable in the demand for money function. Both of these results struck many economists as anomalous, and the inclusion of time deposits in the money definition employed was held largely, though not solely, responsible for them. It was held responsible for the high permanent income elasticity of demand for money because, it was argued, theory suggested that the demand for money would rise less than in proportion to income. This prediction was based on an inventory approach to the demand for a means of exchange pure and simple. The demand for time deposits, these not being a means of exchange, was not expected to follow this prediction, and hence their inclusion in the definition of money was held responsible for the results of Friedman's test contradicting it. As to the evidence concerning the rate of interest, it was argued that, since time deposits were interest-bearing assets, variations in the demand for them, in response to changes in the rate of interest they bore, could mask the responsiveness of the demand for demand deposits to rates of interest in general. Thus the inclusion of time deposits in the definition of money automatically resulted in an underestimate of the importance of the role of interest rates in the function. Both of these arguments are now known to be false.

Numerous studies have shown quite explicitly that the rate of interest, whatever the actual series that might be used to measure it, has a statistically significant negative effect on the demand for money, however defined. One study, by the present writer, even suggests that the inclusion of time deposits in the definition of money improves the stability of the relationship. The same study also shows clearly the Friedman's inability to find a close relationship between the demand for money and the rate of interest is a result of the test procedure he followed, for it is possible to find such a relationship using Friedman's own data and with only a slight variation on his test. As to the permanent income elasticity of demand for money of 1.8, this would appear from subsequent evidence to be partly the result of omitting the rate of interest from the function fitted, but also the product of Friedman's using a time series that goes back as far as 1869.

Meltzer's study, using data going back only to 1900, finds an elasticity of demand for money with respect to nonhuman wealth, a variable that is very highly correlated with permanent income, of just a little greater than unity for both concepts of money. This writer found, for the years 1892 to 1916, a permanent income elasticity of demand for broadly defined money in the region of 1.6, but over the period 1919 to 1960 this parameter seems to have been somewhere between unity and 1.3, appearing to fall below unity in the years following the second world war. The results for the post-1919 period are not changed if a narrow definition of money is employed, so that while they present us with the problem of explaining why there might have been a fall over time in the permanent income (or wealth) elasticity of demand for money, they also rule out the explanation being

---

* Editor's note. In effect, this means that, for every dollar of increased permanent income, the public would hold $1.80 of demand deposits, time deposits, and currency.

found in any eccentricity of the definition of money employed.

All the evidence suggests that a highly stable demand for money function can be identified whether time deposits are included in the definition of money or not. Functions using wealth and an interest rate, regardless of the precise series chosen, show a high degree of explanatory power with respect to variations in the demand for money defined on either concept, whether this explanatory power is judged on the basis of T-values of the coefficients of the arguments, the amount by which these coefficients vary when the function is fitted to independent subperiods, the amount of variation in the dependent variable that the function leaves unexplained, or the accuracy with which the function predicts variations in the dependent variable when that function is extrapolated beyond the period over which it is fitted. Moreover, the differences that do exist between the results attained with different money definitions do not consistently favour one definition or another, and are not, in the writer's judgement, large enough to furnish a firm basis for deciding whether time deposits should be included in or excluded from the definition of money.

However, these functions are stable enough to warrant the conclusion that, over the period for which they have been fitted, the liabilities of other institutions do not appear to have been such close substitutes for the liabilities of commercial banks to warrant any special attention. One must be careful though about extrapolating this judgement, which is inevitably about the way things were in the past, to deal with the present. There is some evidence that circumstances have been changing. Apart from a brief but rapid period of growth in the 1920's, institutions such as savings and loan associations have been important only in the years since the second World War, and as far as these years are concerned there is some doubt about the stability of demand for money relationships that ignore this factor. Not only did the velocity of circulation rise in the late 1940's and 1950's in a fashion that was not predictable on the basis of pre-war experience, but the performance of functions fitted separately to data for these years also frequently leaves something to be desired.

Results already mentioned suggest that the permanent income elasticity of demand for money fell to a value of less than unity in the postwar period, a statistical reflection of the fact that variations in market interest rates alone are not enough to account for the post-war rise in velocity, and that the stability of the demand function is noticeably less than for earlier periods. Similarly, Motley, when dealing with the household sector's demand for money, found a marked difference in both the value and the stability of the parameters of the function he fitted for the pre- and postwar periods. All in all, the picture that emerges is of a demand function for money whose stability is largely independent of whether money is defined to include or exclude time deposits, but whose form has perhaps changed somewhat over time as the available substitutes for money have changed. In particular, it would appear that the activities of non-bank intermediaries can now affect the public's desire to hold the liabilities of commercial banks, but, to judge from [the] evidence, in a predictable way so that there seems to be no strong case for including the liabilities of these institutions in one's notion of money.[1]

[1] It is worth noting that Friedman and Schwartz consider at some length the possibility that savings and loan associations have exercised an important influence on the demand for money in the postwar period and reject it on the grounds that there is no evidence of similar influence in the 1920's when

III. SUMMARY AND CONCLUSIONS

The problem posed by this paper is that of whether the stock of assets over which the monetary authorities have control may be regarded as corresponding to what is called "money" in macroeconomics.

The basic empirical question is one of rates of substitution between assets, and there appear to be three *a priori* defensible positions that may be held. First it may be argued that demand deposits and currency are sufficiently differentiated from their closest substitute to make it desirable to treat them as a separate asset. This view is grounded on these assets' role as a means of exchange, while the view that time deposits and the liabilities of other financial intermediaries are also money seems to be based primarily on the view that the demand for money is to an important degree the demand for an asset whose capital value does not vary with the rate of interest. The intermediate view, that time deposits, but not the liabilities of other financial institutions, should be treated as money appears to stem from a judgement that time deposits are substantially cheaper assets to use as a "temporary abode of purchasing power" than are these others.

Strong *a priori* cases can be made out on all sides of the argument and the empirical evidence is also to some degree in conflict. It would appear to be the case that stable demand functions for money defined both to include and to exclude time deposits at commercial banks may be identified for the United States economy. However, there does seem to have been some change over time, particularly since the second world war, in the assets to whose rate of return the demand for money however defined is most sensitive. The apparent importance of savings and loan associations in recent years is particularly noteworthy. These conclusions must, however, be treated with care, since they are contradicted by an important study by Professor Feige.

With the evidence we have at the moment, then, it is possible to come to only tentative conclusions about what set of assets the monetary authorities should attempt to manipulate in carrying out monetary policy. These conclusions are as follows: As far as the liabilities of commercial banks are concerned it does not seem to matter much whether the authorities confine their efforts to controlling the volume of demand deposits alone, or whether they seek to control the volume of demand and time deposits together. The demand function for money defined in either way seems stable enough for changes in the supply of the appropriate set of assets to have predictable affects on the variables that appear in the demand function, given that the influence of other factors on these variables is taken into account. It would appear though, if we overlook Feige's results, that important among these "other factors" must be the activities of such institutions as savings and loan associations.

However, we are unable to make out any strong case for extending the regulatory powers of the monetary authorities to non-bank intermediaries. The liabilities of these institutions have perhaps become important substitutes for money, but the substitution relationship involved appears to be stable, so

---

these institutions underwent a similar period of spectacular growth. It may be, however, that differences in the regulations governing the activities of commercial banks in the two periods explain this difference, for the banks are certainly less able freely to meet competition from other institutions now than they were in the 1920's. There seems to be an important unsettled question in monetary history here, and one that would be well worth investigating further.

that, provided that the activities of these institutions are taken into account, the demand for the liabilities of commercial banks seems to be no more difficult to predict than it was in the years when, for example, short-term commercial paper seems to have been an important substitute for money. The case for controlling savings and loan associations and the like, inasmuch as it rests on the substitutability of their liabilities for those of commercial banks, is no stronger than was the case in earlier years for controlling the emitters of short-term commercial bills. Of course there are more elements to the case than this, for the regulations under which commercial banks operate undoubtedly make it more difficult for them to compete *qua* financial intermediary with other institutions; there is certainly a case to be made on grounds of equity for either reducing

the amount of control the authorities exercsie over commercial banks or for increasing their control over other institutions. To go into this issue any further would take us far beyond the scope of this paper, but its relevance to some of the questions at hand should not be ignored for that reason.

To return to the main problem, however, the evidence suggests that existing institutional arrangements are adequate as far as the exercise of monetary policy is concerned. It further suggests that which particular aggregate of commercial bank liabilities the authorities try to manipulate is a question which must be settled on other grounds, for example, which aggregate it is easier to control. As far as the demand function for money is concerned there seems to be nothing to choose between the alternatives considered.

READING 3
ESSENTIAL PROPERTIES OF THE MEDIUM OF EXCHANGE

Leland B. Yeager*

I. LIQUIDITY AND MONEY

The *Radcliffe Report* and many writings on nonbank financial intermediaries urged more attention to the total liquidity position of a developed economy and less to money in the old narrow sense. This advice met widespread skepticism. Something remains to be said, though, about what facts justify this skepticism and why they are crucial although banally familiar. The actual medium of exchange remains distinctive in ways seldom fully appreciated. The differences between it and other elements of liquidity may be unimportant to the individual; yet they are crucial to the system. An individual holder might consider certain near-moneys practically the same as actual money because he could readily exchange them for it whenever he wanted. But micro-exchange-ability need not mean ready exchangeability of aggregates. (Although gold and paper moneys under the gold standard meant practically the same thing to an individual holder, for example, they did not have the same functions and significance in the national economy, especially not at a time of balance-of-payments trouble.) The famous fallacy of composition warns against that.

One familiar approach to the definition of money scorns any supposedly *a priori* line between money and near-moneys. Instead, it seeks the definition that works best with statistics. One strand of that approach seeks clues to substitutabilities among assets—to how similar or different their holders regard them—by studying how sensitively holdings of currency, demand deposits, and other liquid assets have depended

Source: Excerpt reprinted from *Kyklos,* Volume XXI, 1968, pp. 45–55 and 66–68.

* The author is indebted to Dr. Daniel Edwards and Professors W. H. Hutt, Richard H. Timberlake, Jr., and James M. Waller for many helpful comments. He accepts blame for following not all but only some of their advice.

on income, wealth, and interest rates. Another strand seeks the narrowly or broadly defined quantity that correlates most closely with income in equations fitted to historical data. Information obtained from such studies can be important for some purposes. But it would be awkward if the definition of money accordingly had to change from time to time and country to country. Furthermore, even if money defined to include certain near-moneys does correlate somewhat more closely with income than money narrowly defined, that fact does not necessarily impose the broad definition. Perhaps the amount of these near-moneys depends on the level of money income and in turn on the amount of medium of exchange through the gearing process described in section III below. More generally, it is not obvious why the magnitude with which some other magnitude correlates most closely deserves overriding attention; it might be neither the most interesting nor the most controllable one. The number of bathers at a beach may correlate more closely with the number of cars parked there than with either the temperature or the price of admission, yet the former correlation may be less interesting or useful than either of the latter. The correlation with national income might be closer for either consumption or investment than for the quantity of money; yet the latter correlation could be the most interesting one to the monetary authorities.

Of course, a broad definition of money is not downright "wrong," since many definitions can be self-consistent. But no mere definition should deter us, when we are trying to understand the flow of spending in the economy, from focusing attention on the narrow category of assets that actually get spent. It is methodological prejudice to dismiss as irrelevant, without demonstrat-

ing their irrelevance, such facts as these: Certain assets do and others do not circulate as media of exchange. No reluctance of sellers to accept the medium of exchange hampers anyone's spending it. The medium of exchange can "burn holes in pockets" in a way that near-moneys do not. Supply creates its own demand (in a sense specified later) more truly for the medium of exchange than for other things. These are observed facts, or inferences from facts, not mere *a priori* truths or tautologies.

In comparing the medium of exchange with other financial assets, we must go beyond asking what determines the *amount* of each that people demand to hold. We must also consider the *manner* in which people acquire and dispose of each asset and implement a change in their demand for it. This is presumably what W. T. Newlyn meant in urging a "functional" distinction between money and near-money according to "operational effects in the economy rather than [just] according to asset status from the point of view of the owner."[1]

To recognize how nonmonetary liquidity affects total demands for money and for goods and services, we need not blur the definition of money so badly as to subvert measurement and control of its quantity. We need not blur the distinctions between supplies of and demands for assets and between influences on supply and influences on demand. We can define the supply of money narrowly, as a measurable quantity, and see it confronted by a demand for cash balances—a demand influenced, to be sure, by the availability and attractiveness of other assets.

This approach keeps two concepts of "liquidity" distinct. The first, a vague one, corresponds roughly to what New-

---

[1] "The Supply of Money and Its Control," *Economic Journal*, LXXIV, June 1964, pp. 327–46, especially pp. 335–6.

lyn has called "financial strength"—the total purchasing power that firms and individuals consider available in their asset-holdings and their possibilities of borrowing. This "essentially . . . *ex-ante* concept . . . reflects 'the amount of money people think they can get hold of'." (What they could in fact get hold of all at once is something else again.) In a second sense, liquidity means the amount of medium of exchange in existence (or perhaps, as Newlyn implies, the relation between that amount and the volume of transactions to be performed).[2] Given a fixed stock of actual medium of exchange, widespread attempts to sell liquid assets or borrow to mobilize supposed 'financial strength' for spending would partially frustrate each other through declines in the prices of financial assets, higher interest rates, tighter credit rationing, and the like.

II. THE EXAMPLE OF CLAIMS ON NONBANK INTERMEDIARIES

To highlight the properties of the medium of exchange by contrast, let us focus on the liquid liabilities of non-bank financial intermediaries. James Tobin has restated some of the issues raised by Gurley and Shaw in a helpfully clear and forceful way.[3] He questions the traditional story of how banks create money by expanding credit. If other intermediaries are mere brokers in loanable funds, then so are the banks. A savings and loan association is a creditor of the mortgage borrower and at the same time a debtor to the ultimate saver who holds its shares; similarly, the commercial bank can be a creditor because it is in debt to its depositors. Only ultimate savers can provide loanable funds. If in some

sense both types of institution do create credit by issuing their own liquid liabilities, they are alike in that respect. Bank demand deposits are unique in being actual media of exchange, Tobin concedes; but since each type of claim on a financial intermediary has its own brand of uniqueness, there is nothing unique about being unique. It is "superficial and irrelevant" to insist "that a bank can make a loan by "writing up" its deposit liabilities, while a savings and loan association . . . cannot satisfy a mortgage borrower by crediting him with a share account." Whether or not money spent by a borrower from a bank stays in the banking system as a whole depends not on how the loan was initially made but on "whether somewhere in the chain of transactions initiated by the borrower's outlays are found depositors who wish to hold new deposits equal in amount to the new loan. Similarly, the outcome for the savings and loan industry depends on whether in the chain of transactions initiated by the mortgage are found individuals who wish to acquire additional savings and loan shares."[4]

Tobin would extend our doubts in this last case to bank deposits also. He envisages "a natural economic limit to the scale of the commercial banking industry." Given their wealth and asset preferences, people will voluntarily hold additional demand deposits only if the yields thereby sacrificed on other assets fall. But beyond some point, lower yields would make further lending and investing unprofitable for the banks. "In this respect the commercial banking industry is not qualitatively different from any other financial intermediary system."[5] Even with no reserve requirements, bank credit and deposits could not expand further when

---

[2] *Ibid.* The quotation comes from p. 342, where Newlyn in turn quotes the *Radcliffe Report,* para. 390.
[3] "Commercial Banks as Creators of 'Money,' " in: Deane Carson (Ed.), *Banking and Monetary Studies* (Homewood, Irwin, 1963), pp. 408–19.
[4] *Ibid.,* pp. 412–13.
[5] *Ibid.,* p. 414.

no further loans and investments were available at yields high enough to cover the costs (among others) of attracting and holding deposits.

In so arguing, Tobin slights some familiar contrasts. The banking system as a whole *can* expand credit and deposits so far as reserves permit. There is no problem of lending and spending new demand deposits into existence. No one need be persuaded to invest in them before they can be created. No one will refuse the routine medium of exchange for fear of being stuck with too much. Unwanted savings and loan shares, in contrast, would not be accepted and so could not be created in the first place. (And if anyone did find himself somehow holding unwanted shares, he would simply cash them in for money and so make them go out of existence. He would still cash them even if he did not want to *hold* the money instead, since money is the intermediary routinely used in buying all sorts of things.)

A holder of unwanted money exchanges it *directly* for whatever he does want, without first cashing it in for something else.[6] Nothing is more ultimate than money. Instead of going out of existence, unwanted money gets passed around until it ceases to be unwanted. Supply thus creates its own demand (both expressed as nominal, not real, quantities, of course). To say this is not to assert that there is no such thing as a demand function for money or that the function always shifts to keep the quantities demanded and in existence identical.[7] Rather, an initial excess supply of money touches off a *process* that raises the nominal quantity demanded quite *in accordance with* the demand function. Initially unwanted cash balances "burn holes in pockets," with direct or indirect repercussions on the flow of spending in the economy, in a way not true of near-moneys. Although anyone holding near-money has *chosen* to hold it as a store of value at least temporarily and has not just routinely received it in payment for goods or services sold, people do receive money in this latter way. A person accepts money not necessarily because he chooses to continue holding it but precisely because it is the routine intermediary between his sales and his purchases or investments and because he knows he can get rid of it whenever he wants. People's actions to get rid of unwanted money make it ultimately wanted by changing at least two of the arguments in the demand function for money: the money values of wealth and income rise through higher prices or fuller employment and

[6] One qualification is minor in this context: when demand deposits are cashed in for currency, the drain on reserves limits banks' assets and deposits. But this limitation works on the supply-of-money side, not the demand side. If the authorities that create "high-powered dollars" and the banks, taken together, want to expand the money supply, they can do so, unhampered by any unwillingness of the public to accept or hold money.

Another minor qualification concerns commercial-bank time deposits. A shift in the public's preferences to them from demand deposits does tend to shrink the latter if the same kind of reserve money, fixed in total amount, is held against both types of deposit. The shrinkage is the smaller, the smaller the reserve ratio for time deposits is in comparison with the ratio for demand deposits. Anyway, the decline in reserves available to support demand deposits is an occurrence affecting the *supply* of demand deposits. By providing enough reserves to support them, the monetary authorities can maintain any desired amount of demand deposits in existence.

[7] J. G. Gurley and E. S. Shaw intimated that J. M. Culbertson harbored some such idea; see their "Reply" to his criticism of their theory in *American Economic Review*, XLVIII, March 1958, pp. 135–6.

The argument about how the supply of money creates its own demand applies to the aggregate of all types of the medium of exchange and not, of course, to dimes alone or currency alone or demand deposits alone. The necessary proviso about suitable proportions of different kinds and denominations of money in their total does not impair the contrast in question between money and near-moneys.

production, and interest rates may move [fall] during the adjustment process.

No such process affects near-moneys and other nonmoneys. For an ordinary asset, a discrepancy between actual and desired holdings exerts direct pressure on its price (or on its yield or similar terms on which it is acquired and offered). If the supply and demand for an asset are out of balance, "something had to give." If the something is specific and "gives" readily, the adjustment can occur without widespread and conspicuous repercussions. But the medium of exchange has no single, explicit price of its own in terms of a good other than itself, nor does it have any explicit yield of its own that can "give" readily to remove an imbalance between its supply and demand. Widespread repercussions occur instead.

Like nonmoney assets, borrowing privileges that people do not care to use also fail to touch off any such process. (I refer to the famous idea that unexhausted overdraft privileges are an important type of liquidity.) A magical doubling of all lines of credit, unaccompanied by monetary expansion, would hardly 'burn holes in pockets' in the same way a doubled money supply would. And as we have seen, people's initial unwillingness to *hold* all newly created actual money would not keep them from accepting it and would not prevent its creation.

Tobin's idea (already cited) that a decline in interest rates on loans and investments will limit profitable expansion of bank credit and deposits, even if reserves permit, forgets Wicksell's "cumulative process." As money expansion raises prices and incomes, the dollar volume of loans demanded at given interest rates rises also. Yields on bank loans and investments need

not keep falling. The great inflations of history disprove any "natural limit" posed by falling interest rates.

III. ASYMMETRICAL ASSET PREFERENCES

Let us suppose that nonbank intermediaries, at their own initiative, somehow issue more claims against themselves to acquire earning assets. (Never mind what makes people acquire these claims in the first place.) As people find themselves holding more and more near-moneys relative to both money and nonliquid assets, they exercise what Gurley and Shaw have called a "diversification demand" for actual money.[8] People have some idea of appropriate compositions of their portfolios and will not keep on indefinitely accumulating securities or near-moneys unaccompanied by additional money. And even if, understandably, people did not want additional money as a store of value, they would nevertheless want more of it to lubricate transactions in the other components of their expanded portfolios. Asset preferences thus limit the expansion of near-moneys if the money supply is constant; exclusive attention to the low (and voluntary) reserve ratios typical of nonbank intermediaries exaggerates their scope for multiple expansion. Conceivably, though, this limit could be a rubbery one if asset preferences were highly sensitive to interest rates.

Besides a portfolio-balancing or "diversification" demand and a portfolio-transactions demand for actual money, a transactions demand connected with ordinary income and expenditure would come into play. It would, anyway, if in some implausible way issuers did expand the stock of near-moneys at their own initiative, inflating prices and in-

8 "Financial Aspects of Economic Development," *American Economic Review*, XLV, September 1955, pp. 515–38, especially pp. 525–26.

comes. People would want larger holdings of the shrunken money units and might cash in some of their near-moneys as one way to get money.

Asset preferences work asymmetrically. Because of them, a constant supply of actual money can restrain the expansion of near-moneys. But no such restraint works the other way around: not even some sort of ceiling on near-moneys could keep the monetary authorities from creating as much money as they wished. In the absence of a ceiling, near-moneys tend to gear themselves to the money supply. When monetary expansion has inflated prices or incomes, the desired nominal amounts of borrowing on the one hand and of saving and financial investment on the other hand will have grown more or less in step and so, therefore, will the amounts of securities and financial intermediation in existence. To dramatize the asymmetry, however, let us suppose that some official ban on the expansion of near-moneys thwarts this gearing. As the quantity of money expanded beyond what people initially wanted to hold, competition for the fixed supply of near-moneys would drive their yields low enough to keep people indifferent at the margin between them and money. But nothing would keep prices or money incomes from rising until people desired to hold all the new money.

Much of the contrast developed so far boils down to saying that "the most important proposition in monetary theory"[9] holds true of the actual medium of exchange only. Individual economic units are free to hold as much or as little money as they see fit in view of their own circumstances; yet the total of their freely chosen cash balances is identical with the money supply, which the monetary authorities can make as big or small as they see fit. The process that resolves this paradox has no counterpart for claims on nonbank intermediaries; instead, unwanted holdings go out of existence. The proposition also fails for other near-moneys, such as securities; but instead of shrinking in actual amount to the desired level, an excessive quantity shrinks in the market appraisal of its total money value.

Expansion of claims on nonbank intermediaries promotes economy in holding cash balances—or so postwar American experience seems to illustrate. Though not entirely wrong, this proposition is loosely phrased. Near-moneys, unlike money, cannot expand unless either monetary expansion or changes in "wants, resources, or technology" make people decide to accumulate more of them. Except as reflected in the yields or other advantages that various assets offer him, the individual does not care about their total amounts in existence. If savings and loan associations, for example, have contributed to the postwar rise in the velocity of actual money, the cause is not the sheer growth in their outstanding shares; instead, it comprises whatever changes have underlain a shift of asset preferences in their favor. These underlying changes presumably include not only the 1950 improvement in insurance features and the postwar uptrend in interest rates, permitting higher rates on savings-and-loan shares, but also whatever other factors have underlain the opening of new offices in convenient places, paid and word-of-mouth advertising, and a cumulative familiarity. Savings-and-loan growth has not unambiguously helped *cause* a rise in monetary velocity; both, rather, have *resulted* from more ultimate changes. Much the same is true of ex-

---

[9] Milton Friedman in *Employment, Growth and Price Levels,* Part 4 (Hearings before the Joint Economic Committee, U.S. Congress, May 1959), p. 609.

pansion in the amounts of other near-moneys.

IV. TRANSACTIONS COSTS

Momentous consequences seem to follow from apparently slight differences between close near-moneys and actual media of exchange. Whether or not a thing serves as a general medium of exchange might even seem a mere matter of degree, as the example of traveler's checks might suggest. If sellers of goods and services become willing to accommodate buyers by accepting payment in a near-money and if this practice reaches the point where everyone accepts it with no intention of cashing it in because he knows he can simply pass it along to someone else, who in turn will not want to cash it in, then the thing has become an actual medium of exchange.

At some point, apparently, the shading or drift from the properties of close near-moneys toward those of money becomes a jump from a difference in degree to a difference in kind. Yet this really may be the way things are with money. Several assets may have low transactions costs, but the asset with the *lowest* costs of all is unique in that respect.[10] Having the lowest transactions costs and being the medium of exchange are properties so related that even a slight disturbance to existing institutions or practices could conceivably be self-reinforcing. Perhaps the shifting of a ship's cargo offers an analogy. Minor causes can sometimes have major consequences.

If savings-and-loan shares had transactions costs no higher than those of money, the associations could grant loans in the form of their own shares, confident that the borrowers would be able to spend them directly. The essence of being merely a near-money is that people have to be *persuaded* to take it—persuaded by its yield (or by the prospect of losing a sale if the seller did not thus accommodate his customer). For assets on the borderline, what would be adequate persuasion for some takers might not be adequate for others. Hence an asset cannot be a *generally* acceptable means of payment if some inducement is required not merely to persuade people to hold it for some time but even to persuade them to accept payment in that particular form in the first place.

Fortunately, our economy has no assets just on a borderline between serving and not serving as media of exchange. Not even traveler's checks circulate indefinitely without being presented for redemption. So far as this paper has any direct implications at all for policy, and not just for theory—beyond the obvious warning against confusion over a nebulous general liquidity—it warns against blurring the crucial though possibly slight distinctions that keep an awkwardly large variety of assets from coming into routine circulation. Policy should avoid creating incentives to broaden the range of such assets, as it might do if it attached excessive disadvantages to the use of money and to the demand-deposit business. Policy should beware of the institutional instability that could arise from instability in or doubt about the relative lowness of the transactions costs of different assets.

---

[10] Transactions costs may take the form of time and trouble, of course. Ambiguity about the lowest transactions costs could explain the coexistence of two or more varieties of medium of exchange. Currency has the lowest transactions costs—loosely speaking, it is the most convenient medium of exchange—in some types of transactions, and demand deposits have the lowest costs in others. But no other asset has lower transactions costs than currency and demand deposits, respectively, in the types of transaction in which each predominates.

READING 4

ELEMENTS OF MONEY STOCK DETERMINATION

Jerry L. Jordan

Recent discussion of the role of money in stabilization policy has culminated in two central issues. The first involves the strength and reliability of the relation between changes in money and changes in total spending. If this relation is sufficiently strong and reliable, changes in the money stock can be used as an indicator of the influence of monetary stabilization actions on the economy.[1] The second issue centers on whether or not the monetary authorities can determine the growth of the money stock with sufficient precision, if it is deemed desirable to do so.

This article is concerned primarily with the second issue—determination of the money stock.[2] A framework describing the factors which influence the monetary authorities' ability to determine the money stock is presented, and the behavior of these factors in recent years is illustrated. In addition, examples of ways in which these factors influence the money stock are discussed.

I. FACTORS INFLUENCING THE MONEY STOCK

The following sections present essential elements and concepts which are used to construct a "money supply model" for the U.S. economy. First, the necessary information regarding institutional aspects of the U.S. banking system are summarized. Then, the main elements of the model—the monetary base, the member bank reserve-to-deposit ratio, the currency-to-demand deposit ratio, the time deposit-to-demand deposit ratio, and the U.S. Government deposit-to-demand deposit ratio—are discussed.

Source: Reprinted from Federal Reserve Bank of St. Louis, Review, October 1969.

[1] Leonall C. Anderson and Jerry L. Jordan, "Monetary and Fiscal Actions: A Test of Their Relative Importance in Economic Stabilization," this Review, November 1968.

[2] Private demand deposits plus currency in the hands of the public.

A. Institutional Aspects of the U.S. Banking System

Students of money and banking are taught that if commercial bank reserve requirements are less than 100 per cent, the reserves of the banking system can support a "multiple" of deposits. In fact it is often said that under a fractional reserve system the banking system "creates" deposits. The familiar textbook exposition tells us that the amount of deposits (D) in the system is equal to the reciprocal of the reserve requirement ratio (r) times the amount of reserves (R):

$$D = \frac{1}{r} \cdot R.$$

Thus if the banking system has $100 of reserves, and the reserve requirement ratio is 20 per cent (.2), deposits will be $100/.2 or $500. If the banks acquire an additional $1 in reserves (for instance from the Federal Reserve), deposits will increase by $5.

There are many simplifying assumptions underlying this elementary deposit-expansion relation. First, it is assumed that all bank deposits are subject to the same reserve requirement. Second, all banks are subject to the same regulations; in other words, all banks are members of the Federal Reserve System, and the Federal Reserve does not differentiate among classes of banks. Third, banks do not hold excess reserves; they are always "loaned up". And finally, there is no "cash drain". The public desires to hold a fixed quantity of currency, and their desires for currency are not influenced by the existence of more or less deposits.

Since the above assumptions are not true, the accuracy with which a monetary analyst can estimate how many deposits will be "created" by an addition of $1 in reserves to the banking system, depends on his ability to determine:

1. how the deposits will be distributed between member and nonmember banks;
2. how the deposits will be distributed between reserve city and country banks, which are subject to different reserve requirements;
3. how the deposits will be distributed among private demand deposits, Government demand deposits, and the sub-classes of time deposits, all of which are subject to different reserve requirements;
4. how the change in deposits will affect banks' desired ratio of excess reserves to total deposits; and
5. how a change in deposits will affect the public's desired ratio of currency to demand deposits.

These questions can be answered best within the context of a "money supply model" which is constructed to include the institutional realities of the U.S. banking system, and which does not require the special assumptions of the simple deposit expansion equation. A thoroughly developed and tested money supply model has been advanced by Professors Brunner and Meltzer.[3] The following sections present the general form and essential features of this model.

B. The Monetary Base

A useful concept for monetary analysis is provided by the "monetary base" or "high-powered money".[4] The monetary base is defined as the net monetary

---

[3] Karl Brunner and Allan Meltzer, "Liquidity Traps for Money, Bank Credit, and Interest Rates," *Journal of Political Economy,* Vol. 76. January/February 1968.

[4] For further discussion of this concept, see Leonall C. Andersen and Jerry L. Jordan, "The Monetary Base: Explanation and Analytical Use," this *Review,* August 1968.

TABLE 1

MONETARY BASE (JULY 1969—BILLIONS OF DOLLARS) CONSOLIDATED TREASURY
AND FEDERAL RESERVE MONETARY ACCOUNTS

Sources of the Base		Uses of the Base	
Federal Reserve Credit:		Member Bank Deposits at	
Holding of Securities[a]	$54.3	Federal Reserve	$22.3
Discounts and Advances	1.2	Currency in Circulation	51.3
Float	2.7		
Other Federal Reserve Assets	2.7		
Gold Stock	10.4		
Treasury Currency Outstanding	6.7		
Treasury Cash Holdings	— .7		
Treasury Deposits at			
Federal Reserve	—1.1		
Foreign Deposits at			
Federal Reserve	— .1		
Other Liabilities and			
Capital Accounts	—2.0		
Other Federal Reserve Deposits	— .5		
Sources of the Base	$73.6	Uses of the Base	$73.6
Reserve Adjustment[b]	3.9	Reserve Adjustment[b]	3.9
Monetary Base	$77.5	Monetary Base	$77.5

NOTE: Data are not seasonally adjusted. Member bank deposits at Federal Reserve plus currency held by member banks equals total reserves (required reserves plus execss reserves).

[a] Includes acceptances not shown separately.

[b] Leonall C. Andersen and Jerry L. Jordan, "The Monetary Base: Explanation and Analytical Use," this *Review*, August 1968.

Source: "Member Bank Reserves. Federal Reserve Bank Credit, and Related Items," the first table appearing in the Financial and Business Statistics section of the Federal Reserve *Bulletin*.

liabilities of the Government (U.S. Treasury and Federal Reserve System) held by the public (commercial banks and nonbank public). More specifically, the monetary base is derived from a consolidated balance sheet of the Treasury and Federal Reserve "monetary" accounts. This consolidated monetary base balance sheet is illustrated in Table 1, and monthly data for the monetary base (^{B}) are shown in Chart 1.

The growth of the monetary base, that is, "base money," is determined primarily by Federal Reserve holdings of U.S. Government securities, the dominant asset or source component of the base.[5] In recent decades changes in other sources either have been small or have been offset by changes in security holdings. A change in the Treasury's gold holdings is potentially an important source of increase or decrease in the base. However, since March 1968 the size of the gold stock has been changing only by small increments. In the postwar period the influence of changes in the gold stock were generally offset by compensating changes in Federal Reserve holdings of U.S. Government securities.

The liabilities or uses of the monetary base, or net monetary liabilities of the Federal Reserve and Treasury, are

[5] For a discussion of the statistical relation among source components of the base, see Michael W. Keran and Christopher Babb, "An Explanation of Federal Reserve Actions (1933–68)," this *Review*, July 1969.

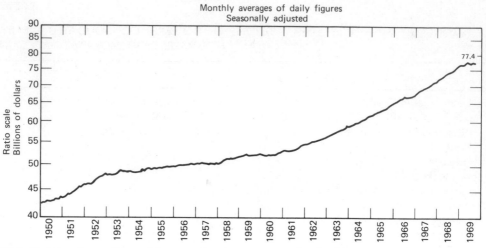

Monthly averages of daily figures
Seasonally adjusted

Chart 1. Monetary base. Uses of the monetary base are member bank reserves and currency held by the public and non member banks. Adjustments are made for reserve requirement changes and shifts in deposits among classes of banks. Data are computed by this bank. Latest data plotted: September.

shown in Table 1 to be currency in circulation plus member bank deposits at the Federal Reserve. Part of the currency in circulation is held by the public, part is held as legal reserves by member banks, and another part is held as desired contingency reserves by nonmember commercial banks. In order to relate the uses of the base to the money stock, the uses are regrouped from the *uses* side of Table 1 as currency held by the nonbank public plus reserves of all commercial banks, shown in Table 2 below.

C. Uses of Reserves

As noted above, analysis of the U.S. monetary system is complicated by the existence of both member and nonmember banks, different classes of member banks, different reserve requirements on different types of deposits (private demand, Government demand, and time), and graduated reserve requirements for different amounts of deposits. It is thus necessary to allocate the uses of bank reserves among the different types of deposits. This is illustrated by an equation showing total bank reserves (R) in terms of their uses:

$$R = RR_m + ER_m + VC_n,$$

where RR_m = required reserves of member banks,

ER_m = excess reserves of member banks,

VC_n = vault cash of nonmember banks.

TABLE 2

USES OF MONETARY BASE (JULY 1969—BILLIONS OF DOLLARS)

Currency in Circulation	$51.3	Currency Held by the Nonbank Public	$45.1
Member Bank Deposits at Federal Reserve	22.3	Commercial Bank Reserves[a]	28.5
Uses of the Base	$73.6	Uses of the Base	$73.6

NOTE: Not seasonally adjusted data.
[a] Includes vault cash of nonmember banks.

TABLE 3

RESERVE REQUIREMENTS OF MEMBER BANKS (IN EFFECT SEPTEMBER 30, 1969)

Type of Deposit	Percentage Requirement
Net demand deposits:[a]	
Reserve city banks:	
Under $5 million	17.0%
Over $5 million	17.5
Country banks:	
Under $5 million	12.5
Over $5 million	13.0
Time deposits (all classes of banks):	
Savings deposits	3.0
Other time deposits:	
Under $5 million	3.0
Over $5 million	6.0

[a] Demand deposits subject to reserve requirements are gross demand deposits minus cash items in the process of collection and demand balances due from domestic banks.

Source: Federal Reserve *Bulletin.*

In turn, required reserves of member banks are decomposed as:

$$RR_m = R^d + R^t,$$

where R^d = required reserves behind demand deposits at member banks

R^t = required reserves behind time deposits at member banks.

In turn, required reserves behind demand deposits at member banks are the sum of the amount of reserves behind demand deposits over and under $5 million at each reserve city and country bank, and similarly for time and savings deposits.[6] Present required reserve ratios for each deposit category are shown in Table 3.

Alternatively, the total amount of commercial bank reserves can be expressed as a proportion (r) of total bank deposits:

$$R = r(D + T + G),$$

where D = private demand deposits

T = time deposits

G = U.S. Government (Treasury) deposits at commercial banks.

The "r-ratio" is defined to be a weighted-average reserve ratio against all bank deposits, but is computed directly by dividing total reserves by total deposits.[7] The trend of the r-ratio in the postwar period is shown in Chart 2 on page 28. An important factor contributing to the gradual downward trend of

[6] Expanding the equation for total bank reserves,

$$R = R^d + R^t + ER_m + VC_n$$

And since R^d, for instance, is the appropriate required reserve ratio times the amount of deposits in each reserve requirement classification, the above expression is rewritten in terms of weighted average reserve ratios and deposits. See footnote No. 7.

[7] For the interested reader,

$$r = a \, \delta r^d + (1 - a) \, \tau \, r^t + e + v$$

where a = the proportion of member bank demand deposits to total deposits,

δ = the proportion of net demand deposits of member banks to total demand deposits,

r^d = a weighted-average reserve requirement ratio for member bank deposits,

τ = the proportion of net time deposits of member banks to total time deposits,

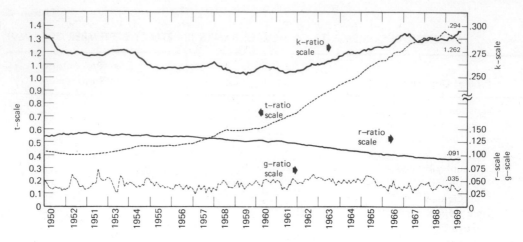

Chart 2. Monetary multiplier ratios. Latest data plotted: September.

the r-ratio is the relatively more rapid growth of time deposits (which are subject to lower reserve requirements) than demand deposits.

D. Currency Held by the Public

One of the important factors influencing the amount of money the banking system can create, given an increase in monetary base, is the proportion of currency to demand deposits the public desires to hold. For example, if the public held a fixed total *amount* of currency, all changes in the supply of base money by the Federal Reserve would remain in the banking system as reserves and would be reflected entirely in changes in deposits, the amount depending on the reserve requirement ratios for different classes and types of deposit. On the other hand, if the public always desired to hold a fixed *ratio* of currency to demand deposits (for example exactly $.25 in currency for every $.75 of demand deposits), the deposit creating potential of the banking system would be substantially less. Clearly the "currency drain" associated with an increase in the base must be taken into account in determining how much base money must be supplied to achieve a desired increase in the money stock. Currency (c) can be expressed as a proportion (k) of demand deposits (D), that is:

$$C = kD,$$
$$\text{or}$$
$$k = C/D.$$

Changes in the level of the "k-ratio" over time are influenced by such factors as income levels, utilization of credit cards, and uncertainties regarding general economic stability. The trend of the k-ratio is shown in Chart 2.[8]

r^t = a weighted average reserve requirement ratio for member bank time deposits,
e = ratio of excess reserves to total bank deposits,
v = ratio of nonmember bank vault cash to total bank deposits.

This definition is altered somewhat by the recently instituted lagged-service-requirement provisions of the Federal Reserve. It is worth emphasizing that some of the above ratios are determined by the behavior of commercial banks and the public, and others are determined primarily by the Federal Reserve. The fact that these ratios are not fixed does not impair the usefulness of the analysis.

[8] For a detailed examination of the behavior of the currency to demand deposit ratio, see Phillip Cagan, *Determinants and Effects of Changes in the U.S. Money Stock, 1785–1960* (New York: National Bureau of Economic Research, 1965), chapter 4.

TABLE 4

MAXIMUM INTEREST RATES PAYABLE ON TIME AND SAVINGS DEPOSITS
(EFFECTIVE APRIL 19, 1968)

Type of Deposit	Per Cent Per Annum
Savings deposits	4.00%
Other time deposits:	
Multiple maturity[a]:	
90 days or more	5.00
Less than 90 days (30–89 days)	4.00
Single maturity:	
Less than $100,000	5.00
$100,000 or more:	
30–59 days	5.50
60–89 days	5.75
90–179 days	6.00
180 days and over	6.25

[a] Multiple maturity time deposits include deposits that are automatically renewable at maturity without action by the depositor and deposits that are payable after written notice of withdrawal.

Source: Federal Reserve *Bulletin*.

E. Time Deposits

Time deposits are not included in the definition of the money stock discussed in this article. Nevertheless, since member banks are required to hold reserves behind time deposits, information regarding the public's desired holdings of time to demand deposits is necessary in order to determine how much the stock of money will change following a change in the stock of monetary base.

Reserve requirements are much lower against time deposits than against demand deposits as shown in Table 3, consequently a given amount of reserves would allow more time deposits to be supported than demand deposits. Time deposits (T) can be expressed as a proportion (t) of demand deposits (D), that is:

$$T = t\,D,$$
$$\text{or}$$
$$t = T/D,$$

The trend of the "t-ratio" is shown in Chart 2.

The factors influencing the t-ratio are more complex to analyze than those affecting the k-ratio. Commercial banks are permitted to pay interest on time deposits-up to ceiling rates set by the Federal Reserve and the Federal Deposit Insurance Corporation (see Table 4). Consequently, the growth of time deposits over time is influenced by competition among banks for individual and business savings within the limits permitted by the legal interest rate ceilings.

The interest rates which banks are willing to offer on time deposits (below the ceilings) are determined primarily by opportunities that are available for profitable investment of the funds in loans or securities. Similarily, the decisions by individuals and businesses to deposit their funds in banks are influenced by the interest rates available from alternative earning assets such as savings and loan shares, mutual savings bank deposits, bonds, stocks, commercial paper, and direct investments in real assets. If the interest returns from these other assets are sufficiently high that the interest rate ceilings on time deposits prevent banks from effectively competing for the public's savings, then time deposits may not grow (or may even decline) and all increases in commercial bank reserves can be used to support demand deposits. This point will be discussed in more detail below.

F. U.S. Government Deposits

Commercial bank are required to hold the same proportion of reserves against Federal Government demand deposits as against private demand deposits. Therefore, even though Government deposits are *not* included in the definition of the money stock, changes in the amount of Government deposits influence the amount of private deposits the banking system can support with a given amount of base money or reserves. Government deposits (^{G}) can be expressed as a proportion (^{g}) of private demand deposits (^{D}), that is:

$$G = g D,$$
$$\text{or}$$
$$g = G/D.$$

The amount of Government deposits in commercial banks is determined by the flow of Treasury receipts (primarily from taxes) relative to Treasury expenditures, and by the Treasury's discretion about what proportion of its balances to keep with commercial banks rather than at the Federal Reserve. Thus, short-run fluctuations in the "g-ratio" are primarily the result of actions by the U.S. Treasury. The Federal Reserve must assess, from past experience and information available from the Treasury, what will happen to Treasury balances in an impending period in order to determine the influence of changes in Treasury balances on the

money stock. The monthly pattern of the g-ratio is shown in Chart 2.

G. The Monetary Multiplier

All of the essential elements for determination of the money stock have now been discussed. The definitional relations are as follows:

(1) $M = D + C$
(2) $B = R + C$
(3) $R = r (D + T + G)$
(4) $C = k D$
(5) $T = t D$
(6) $G = g D$

By substituting (^{3}) and (^{4}) into (^{2}) we get:

(7) $B = r (D + T + G) + kD$

that is, we express the monetary base solely in terms of the various deposits. Substituting (^{5}) and (^{6}) into (^{7}), we get:

(8) $B = r (D + t D + g D) + kD,$

that is, we express the base solely in terms of private demand deposits to reduce the number of variables. Simplifying, we write (^{8}) as:

(8') $B = [r (1 + t + g) + k] \cdot D,$

from which, by simple manipulation, we can express deposits in terms of the base as follows:

(9) $D = \dfrac{1}{r (1 + t + g) + k} \cdot B.$

Since we want to find ^{D} plus ^{C}, we use (^{4}) and (^{9}) to redefine ^{C} in terms of the base:

(10) $C = \dfrac{k}{r (1 + t + g) + k} \cdot B.$

Substituting (^{9}) and (^{10}) into (^{1}) gives:

(1') $M = \dfrac{1 + k}{r (1 + t + g) + k} \cdot B,$

or the money stock defined in terms of the monetary base. We can denote the quotient as:

$$m = \dfrac{1 + k}{r (1 + t + g) + k}$$

Chart 3. Monetary multiplier. Latest data plotted: September.

where m is called the "monetary multiplier."[9]

The factors that can cause changes in the monetary multiplier are all of the factors which influence the currency (k), time deposit (t), Government deposit (g), and reserve (r) ratios, that is, the "behavioral parameters". The observed monthly values of these ratios in the past twenty years are shown in Chart 2, and the monthly values for the monetary multiplier (m) are shown in Chart 3. Quite obviously, if the monetary multiplier were perfectly constant, at say 2.5, then every $1 increase in the monetary base would result in a $2.50 increase in the money stock. On the other hand, if the monetary multiplier were subject to substantial unpredictable variation, the Federal Reserve would have difficulty in determining the money stock by controlling the base.

Since the monetary multiplier is not constant, the Federal Reserve must predict the value of the multiplier for the impending month in order to know how much to increase the monetary base to achieve a desired level of the

money stock. Techniques for predicting the monetary multiplier go beyond the scope of this paper.[10] However, examples of how changes in time deposits and Government deposits influence the stock of money will be discussed.

II. THE INFLUENCE OF TWO FACTORS ON THE MONEY STOCK

The following sections present examples of the ways changes in the growth of time deposits and U.S. Government deposits influence the money creation process. The effects are illustrated both by changes in the ratios in the monetary multiplier and with the use of commercial bank balance sheet "T-Accounts."

A. Changes in Time Deposits

The growth of time deposits relative to demand deposits is determined by many factors, including those which influence the interest rates offered by commercial banks on such deposits and those which influence the quantity of time deposits demanded by the pub-

[9] The reader should be able to demonstrate that if money is defined to include time deposits ($M_2 = D + C + T$), then

$$m_2 = \frac{1 + k + t}{r(1 + t + g) + k}$$

[10] For one straight-forward approach, see Lyle Kalish, *A Study of Money Stock Control*, Working Paper No. 11, Federal Reserve Bank of St. Louis, July 1969.

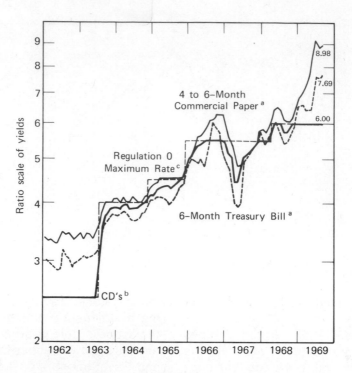

Chart 4. Short-term money market rates.

[a] Market yields converted from discount to bond equivalent basis.

[b] Average new issue rates on six month certificates of deposit of $100,000 or more. Data are estimated by the Federal Reserve Bank of St. Louis from guide rates published in the Bond Buyer and are monthly averages of Wesnesday figures.

[c] Rate on deposits in amounts of $100,000 or more maturing in 90–179 days.

Latest data plotted: September.

lic at each interest rate. Both the banks' supply of time deposits and the public's demand for them are a function of relative costs and returns of alternative sources of funds and earning assets. Thus, accuracy of predictions of the t-ratio (time deposits to demand deposits) for a future period is influenced by the ability of the forecasters to anticipate the banks' and public's behavior. Experience has shown that changes in this ratio tend to be dominated by rather long-run trends, with exceptions occurring at those times when interest rate ceilings imposed by the monetary authorities prevent banks from effec-

tively competing for deposits. It is these special cases that will be discussed.

When market interest rates rise above the ceiling rates banks are permitted to offer on time deposits, some individuals and businesses who might otherwise hold time deposits decide to buy bonds or other earning assets instead. This effect has been most pronounced on the banks' class of time deposits called "large negotiable certificates of deposit" (CD's). To depositors, these are highly liquid assets which are considered by the purchasers to be close substitutes for Treasury bills and commercial paper.[11] On at

[11] Jordan, *Deposit-Type Financial Assets,* chapter 4.

least four occasions since 1965 the yields on these substitute assets have risen above the rates banks were permitted to offer on CD's, causing the growth of CD's to slow sharply or even become negative.

To illustrate the effect on the money stock of a rise in market interest rates above Regulation Q ceilings, assume that the growth of time deposits ceases, and banks hold the same total amount of time deposits while demand deposits continue to grow. In the money supply model this is reflected in a decline in the t-ratio (time deposits divided by demand deposits), and since the t-ratio appears in the denominator of the multiplier, the multiplier would get larger as the t-ratio gets smaller.

For example, assume the following initial values for the monetary base and the parameters of the multiplier:

$$B = \$75 \text{ billion}$$
$$t = 1.3$$
$$g = .04$$
$$k = .3$$
$$r = .1$$

Since $M = \dfrac{1+k}{r(1+t+g)+k} \cdot B$,

we can solve to find $M = \$182.6$ billion.

Now suppose that in the course of several months the base increases by $1 billion, but time deposits do not grow at all as a result of the high market rates of interest relative to Regulation Q ceilings. If all of the ratios in the multiplier (including the t-ratio) had remained unchanged in this period, the money stock would have increased by about $2.4 billion to $185 billion. But, since demand deposits continued to grow, the t-ratio would fall, to 1.28 for example, which causes the multiplier to increase (still assuming the other behavioral parameters remain the same).[12]

The reader should be careful not to interpret this greater increase in money

(especially demand deposits) to mean that the banks can extend more credit than otherwise. Since the reserve requirements on demand deposits are greater than on time deposits, the $1 billion increase in monetary base would have supported a greater amount of *total* deposits (demand plus time) if time deposits grew proportionally to demand deposits, rather than only demand deposits increasing. With the assumed initial values for the parameters of the multiplier and the postulated $1 billion increase in the monetary base, money plus time deposits would have increased by almost $4.8 billion, almost twice as much as money.

To interpret the effects of this increase in money on the economy, it is necessary to analyze the increase in the supply of money compared to the demand for money to hold, and the supplies of and demands for other assets. We postulated above that market interest rates rose above the ceiling rates banks are permitted to pay on time deposits (especially CD's). In such a situation the volume of CD's (quantity supplied) is any amount depositors wish at the ceiling rates. Since the yields on good substitutes become more attractive than CD's, the *demand* for CD's declines, resulting in a decline in the outstanding volume of CD's or a slowing in the growth rate. In other words, a change in the relative yields on substitute assets causes a shift in the demand for CD's (negative), which causes a decline in the volume.

B. Disintermediation

Total deposits of banks may decline as a result of this "disintermediation" of time deposits. This means that banks must contract their assets, either loans or security holdings, as deposits decline. An understanding of the actions

---

[12] In practice, as the t-ratio falls from 1.3 to 1.28, demand deposits grow and time deposits do not, and average reserve requirement ratio (r) will rise. This will slightly attenuate the increase in the multiplier and the money stock.

ACCOUNT 1

BANKING SYSTEM

Assets		Liabilities	
TR	$ 25	DD	$100
RR $25		TD	200
ER 0			
S	100		
L	175		
Total	$300	Total	$300

of those who withdraw their deposits is important information in assessing the effects of the disintermediation caused by the interest rate ceilings.

To illustrate two possible effects of disintermediation, we will use highly simplified examples and T-accounts (commercial bank balance sheets). Account 1 shows the banking system in its initial condition having total reserves (TR) = $25, required reserves (RR) = $25, and excess reserves (ER) = O, security holdings (S) = $100 and loans outstanding (L) = $175. Bank liabilities are demand deposits (DD = $100 and time deposits (TD) = $200. We have assumed that reserve requirements against demand deposits are 15 per cent and reserve requirements against time deposits are 5 per cent.

Account 2 shows the effect of a corporation reducing its holdings of time deposits by $20 and buying $20 in securities from the banks, because of the higher return available on the latter. The immediate effect is that the ownership of the securities is changed—the corporation directly holds the securi-

ties instead of having a deposit in a bank which owns the securities, hence the term "disintermediation"—and the banks are left with $1 of excess reserves. The banking system can create loans (or buy some securities), based on the dollar of excess reserves, and increase demand deposits by a multiple of $1. In this simplified example, the effect of disintermediation resulting from relatively low interest rate ceilings is potentially expansionary on total loans, even though total deposits decrease.

For the second example, a bank, in its usual role as an intermediary, sells CD's to a corporation which wishes to invest short-term funds. With the proceeds of the sale of the CD's, the bank lends to another corporation (less the amount the bank must hold as required reserves, of course). Another simplified example of the potential effects of disintermediation on the banking system and total credit is illustrated in Account 3. For exposition, assume that the one-bank holding companies of commercial banks establish subsidiaries for the purpose of buying and selling commercial paper.

For our example, assume the first corporation does not wish to renew $20 of its CD holdings when they reach maturity, but rather, because of generally rising short-term market interest rates, seeks a yield greater than the bank is permitted to pay. Our hypothetical subsidiary of the one-bank holding company can offer to sell its own commercial paper (I.O.U.) to the

ACCOUNT 2

BANKING SYSTEM

Assets		Liabilities	
TR	$ 25	DD	$100
RR $24		TD	180
ER 1			
S	80		
L	175		
Total	$280	Total	$280

ACCOUNT 3

BANKING SYSTEM

Assets		Liabilities	
TR	$ 25	DD	$100
RR $24		TD	180
ER 1			
S	100		
L	155		
Total	$280	Total	$280

ACCOUNT 4

SUBSIDIARY OF
ONE-BANK HOLDING COMPANY

Assets		Liabilities	
Commercial Paper held	$ 20	Commercial Paper outstanding	$ 20

first corporation at competitive market interest rates (Account 4).

We assume the corporation buys the subsidiary's commercial paper. As a result of their reduced deposits the banks are forced to contract assets proportionately (as a first step in a partial analysis). Instead of selling securities, as in our previous example, the banks can contract loans outstanding by $20, as shown in Account 3 (as compared to Account 1). The subsidiary can in turn use the proceeds of its sale of commercial paper to purchase the paper of another corporation which seeks to borrow short-term money, possibly a corporation which was having difficulty getting a bank loan since bank assets and liabilities were contracting.

We find that the initial effect of the disintermediation is that the total of bank loans plus commercial paper debts of borrowing corporations is the same as the initial amount of bank loans outstanding, and that the total of time deposits plus commercial paper assets of lending corporations is the same as the initial amount of time deposits at banks. However, we also find that banks have acquired an additional $1 of excess reserves which they can lend and thereby increase demand deposits.

In summary, both of the examples of the disintermediation of time deposits caused by the interest rate ceilings show that the same initial amount of reserves in the banking system can, under certain circumstances, support a larger amount of demand deposits (and therefore money stock). In other words, if the disintermediation means

only that some funds flow through channels which are not subject to reserve requirements and interest rate ceilings, the effects of the relatively low interest rate ceilings on commercial bank time deposits are potentially expansionary on total loans.

C. U.S. Government Deposits and Money

As previously discussed, the monetary base summarizes all of the actions of the Federal Reserve which influence the money stock. However, the Treasury cannot be overlooked as an agency which can influence the money stock over at least short periods. In the money supply model, the influence of changes in the amount of Government deposits is reflected in movements in the g-ratio (Government deposits divided by private demand deposits) in the monetary multiplier.

In recent years the Government's balances at commercial banks have fluctuated from $3 billion to $9 billion within a few months time. Private demand deposits averaged about $150 billion in mid-1969. The g-ratio is therefore quite small, ranging from about .02 to about .06, but frequently doubles or falls by half over the course of a month or two.

Similar to the effect of changes in the t-ratio, increases in the g-ratio result in a fall in the multiplier since the ratio appears in the denominator. Using again the initial values we assumed for the base and multiplier, we have:

$$M = \frac{1 + .3}{.1(1 + 1.3 + .04) + .3} \cdot \$75 \text{ billion} = \$182.6 \text{ billion}$$

where .04 is the value of the g-ratio. These values imply that demand deposits (D) are about $140.5 billion and Government deposits (G) are $5.6 billion. Now suppose that individuals and businesses pay taxes of $1 billion by writing checks which draw down (D) to $139.5 billion, and Government balances rise to $6.6 billion. Assuming no change in time deposits or currency held by the public and no change in the base, we would find that the g-ratio rises to .047 (and the k- and t-ratios rise silghtly) to give us:

$$M = \frac{1 + 302}{.1\,(1 + 1.309 + .047) + .302} \cdot \$75\text{ billion} = \$181.6\text{ billion}$$

A similar example of the effects on the money stock of an increase in Government deposits at commercial banks which is associated with a change in time deposits (people pay taxes by reducing their savings or holdings of CD's) would be somewhat more complicated. In the above example, taxes were paid out of demand deposits, and the reserve ratio (r) was not changed, which implies that the distribution of the increment in Government deposits among reserve city, country and nonmember banks was the same as the distribution of the $1 billion reduction in private demand deposits.

When taxes are paid out of time deposits, the r-ratio rises, since reserve requirements against Government deposits are approximately three times the reserve requirements against time deposits. These movements are very small, and any accompanying reduction in the excess reserve ratio would attenuate the effect. Nonetheless, the effect on money is a combination of small changes in the k-, r-, t-, and g-ratios.

III. SUMMARY

The behavioral parameters of the money supply framework presented here are the currency (k), reserve (r),

time deposit (t), and Government deposit (g) ratios. The changes in these ratios reflect the actions of the Treasury, banks, and nonbank public which influence the money stock. The k-ratio is determined by the public's preferences for currency versus demand deposits; the t-ratio reflects the interaction of the banks' supply of and the public's demand for time deposits as compared to the supply of and demand for demand deposits; and the g-ratio is dominated by changes in Government balances at commercial banks. The r-ratio is the least volatile of the behavioral parameters, although it is influenced by the banks' desired holdings of excess reserves and the distribution of total deposits among all the subclasses of deposits in the various classes of banks, which are subject to a large array of reserve requirements.

The main policy actions of the monetary authorities—open market operations, changes in reserve requirements, and administration of the discount window—are summarized by the monetary base. The growth of the base summarizes the *influence* of the monetary authorities' defensive and dynamic *actions* on the growth of the money stock, regardless of the *intent* of these actions. The degree of accuracy that can be achieved by the monetary authorities in controlling the money stock is a function of their ability to determine the monetary base, and to predict the net influence of the public's and banks' behavior as summarized by changes in the money supply multiplier.

READING 5
THE ECONOMICS OF THE MONEY MARKET

Deane Carson

In the broadest sense, a market is an institutional arrangement in which demand and supply join to establish exchange of a good or service at a price. Those who have a surplus of the commodity or service offer it for sale on specified terms, and those who desire the commodity or service bid for its ownership on similar terms expressed in prices. The market serves to clear such surpluses and deficits in the ownership of the item at that price where the quantity offered is equal to the amount demanded.

Markets perform several valuable functions in an enterprise economy. As noted above, they facilitate exchange of goods and services, including not only intermediate and final products, but resource factor inputs as well. The establishment of prices in the marketplace creates a system of relative values that affords both consumers and producers a basis for rational economic choices. As one learns in elementary-economics courses, these decisions determine the ultimate allocation of resources, including what is produced, how it is produced, and how the resulting national product is shared.

First courses in economics and their textbooks quite properly devote much attention to the organization and functions of commodity and resource markets. But because the market for money is not commonly—if at all—used to illustrate market principles, the student of money and banking may be surprised to learn that money is actively bought and sold in tremendous volume every day of the work week, excluding, of course, legal holidays. The dollar money market, in terms of daily transaction volume, is by far the largest market in the world; just one of its several segments, the Federal Funds market, not uncommonly involves purchases and sales of three *billion* dollars a day. Because of its size, as well as for reasons discussed below, the money market is a very significant link in the chain of market institutions that characterize the United States economy.[1]

The essential feature of the money market is the fact that money itself is the "commodity" traded. On any given day there will exist a variety of institutions—more about these in a moment—that either (1) have more money in their asset portfolios than they desire or (2) have less money at their command than they require, given their respective cash flows, their financial and real commitments, their portfolio compositions, and the cost of money balances, principally the rate of interest. Simply stated, inequalities between actual and desired cash balances create the need for mechanisms and arrangements to bring actual and desired cash balances into equilibrium for individual institutions. The money market (perhaps more properly the money markets) serves to erase these inequalities where they exist. A good money market mechanism, by inference, is one that performs this task efficiently and at the least economic cost to the community.

If money[2] itself is the stock in trade of the money market, what is on the other side of the transaction? We find this to consist of a wide variety of financial assets, all of which share certain common characteristics that justify their classification as money-market instruments; these characteristics are outlined immediately below.

(1). Money-market instruments are unsecured short-term IOU's. Generally speaking, the time-horizon of those with cash-balance inequalities, on both the surplus and deficit side of the market, ranges from one day to one year. Somewhat arbitrarily, inequalities for which the time-horizon is longer than one year are treated, where otherwise appropriate, as capital-market needs, giving rise to capital-market instruments. Money-market IOU's are typically created for periods of one day, three months, six months, nine months, and one year, although conceivably and in fact instruments are issued for any maturity that satisfies the needs of the market participants within the specified range. In contrast to other types of debts, they are unsecured.

(2). Money-market instruments are created by institutions—chiefly financial and non-financial corporations and the Federal Government. Only those institutions with impeccable credit ratings, however, command the confidence necessary to enable them to print batches of paper debts and sell them in the money market. Examples of such issuers of money-market paper include the United States Treasury, large finance companies (G.M.A.C., C.I.T., Household Finance Corporation), large commercial banks, large nonfinancial corporations, and Government securities dealers (Salomon Brothers and Hutzler).

(3). Money-market instruments are highly liquid. By definition, a money-market instrument must possess characteristics that insure the buyer virtually riskless employment of his surplus money. While this statement is conceptually somewhat ambiguous, in practice it means that the supplier of money believes that the paper and promise he acquires will be redeemed at maturity without default and, to the extent that a secondary market for the insrument exists, that he may dispose

---

[1] Money markets exist in the financial centers of most highly developed countries although to a far smaller extent and degree than the central New York market. Some emerging nations have undertaken to establish money markets in recent years, most notably, perhaps, the Philippines.

[2] Including "high powered" bank reserves, plus the conventional moneystock, for the purposes of this discussion.

of it prior to maturity without significant (in his judgment) loss of value.

The above characteristics derive from several features of the money-market instrument itself. As noted above, such instruments are short term, a factor that minimizes fluctuations in capital value, and they are issued by very large, very sound, and very well-known institutions. While defaults are not unheard of in the money market, they are extremely rare, a fact attested to by the substantial notoriety that attends a default in the market, such as that of Penn-Central in the summer of 1970. Furthermore, the development of secondary markets for many of the instruments has contributed to their liquidity and, hence, their use and acceptability. Finally, liquidity is enhanced by the very depth and breadth of the market for the several instruments; the volume of demand and supply is such that price fluctuations are small and orderly, even in times of extreme monetary scarcity.

(4). *Money-market instruments are bought and sold in relatively large denominations.* Although minimum transaction size has tended to decline for some instruments in periods of relative scarcity of money, the smallest trades are necessarily large. Trades under $100,-000 have become more common in the Federal Funds market, for example, but a typical trade in most market segments continues to be upwards of one million dollars. This derives principally from the requirements of both buyers and sellers and secondarily from the desire to minimize transaction costs on the part of issuers of paper. Commercial paper issuers, for example, would not find it economically feasible to sell small lots of a large issue, although a commercial paper dealer, who may serve as middleman, breaks the parcel and sells it in relatively smaller pieces.

In the money market, money itself exchanges for near-monies at prices (interest rates or yields) that reflect supply and demand conditions in the several segments of the overall marketplace. These prices display differentials that reflect differences in supply and demand conditions in the several markets. These differences include (1) differences in maturity of the instruments, (2) differences in marketability prior to maturity—the existence or lack thereof of a secondary market, (3) differences in tax treatment (capital gains or ordinary income liability), (4) special features, such as the privilege of paying corporate taxes with Treasury Tax Anticipation Bills, (5) differences in the size of issues that affect transactions costs, and (6) differences in the reputation of the issuer. Table 1 gives the rates and yields which were quoted in the money market on a recent date.

While displaying spreads that reflect the sum of the factors listed above, yield differentials may and often do change in the very short run. Typically, however, money-market rates tend to

TABLE 1

Money-Market Instrument	April 7, 1971	April 8, 1970
	%	%
Federal funds	3.98	7.86
Dealer loans	4.48	8.46
Three-month Treasury Bills	3.71	6.39
Three-month Certificate of Deposit	3.94	7.21
Three-month Euro-dollar	5.64	8.59

Source: Federal Reserve Statistical Release, April 19, 1971.

move in the same direction over fairly long periods of time, for example, during a phase of the business cycle. The reasons for this similarity in money-market rate trends are not difficult to come by, and may generally be subsumed under the overall observation that the instruments are highly substitutable for each other in the minds of the buyers—that is to say, the sellers of money. This is mainly attributable to their inherent characteristics that we have considered above, and reenforced by the fact that dealers and brokers exist who make a part of their living by arbitrage operations in the various segments of the money market. Thus, for example, if the spread between a Treasury bill temporarily increases relative to bankers' acceptances of similar maturity, dealers may find it profitable to sell the overpriced acceptance and purchase the Treasury bill (yield and price bearing an inverse relationship to each other). Furthermore, sellers of money have a range of choice in the employment of surplus cash and take advantage of temporary changes in the relative return on the several instruments. This, of course, tends to increase the demand for higher-yielding instruments and decrease the demand for those with lower yields. Yields thus tend to move upward or downward together through time.

The general *level* of money-market yields fluctuates over a wide range through time. Treasury bill yields, which exceeded eight percent in early 1970, were approximately one-half as high at the beginning of the expansion phase of the business cycle in the early 1960s.[3] Yields of other money-market instruments rose in similar fashion over the period.

Fluctuations in the general level of money-market rates reflect overall sup-ply and demand. The total money supply in the economy is the theoretical maximum available to the money market, although the range of the money supply actually available to the market is much less. The total money supply in the economy *may* be determined by the Federal Reserve—our central banking authorities—if in fact it attempts to control this variable; but it may, under circumstances in which the Federal Reserve chooses to control something else (for example, interest rates), be determined by the public's desire to hold money versus other assets at the prevailing rate of interest.[4]

If we assume that the total money supply—and here we must include the "high-powered" money represented by commercial-bank reserve holdings—is in fact determined by the Federal Reserve, some part of the total will find itself lodged in the portfolios of those institutions that customarily serve as a source of funds to the money market. How large this supply will be at any given point in time depends largely on (1) the cash flow of corporations, (2) alternative uses of the cash flow, principally real investment opportunities and dividend policies, and (3) the yield on money-market instruments. Given the first two, the supply of money to the money market from corporate sources will rise with the yield on instruments in the normal fashion of a short-run supply schedule, as illustrated in Figure 1.

It should be noted that the figure assumes that the *total* amount of corporate cash balances has been determined by the cash flow (which for simplicity we take to be constant *and* outside the control of the corporate sector) and that dividend policies have been determined endogenously, leaving a maximum of *OC* for employment in the money market. Since the *cost* of

---

[3] The Treasury Bill yield at the beginning of World War II was three eighths of one percent and was pegged at that level until 1947.

[4] See the Introduction to Part 5, "Monetary Policy," below.

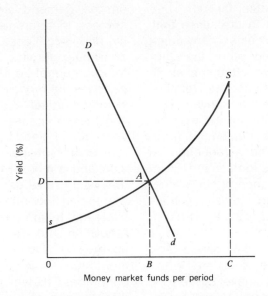

Figure 1. Supply and demand—money market funds.

holding idle cash balances rises with the yield on money-market instruments, higher yields call forth increasing amounts of funds for employment in the money market. To the corporate treasurer, the cost of holding idle money balances increases with yield; alternatively, the profit of *not* holding money likewise increases with the return on money-market instruments.

It should also be noted that we assume that yields between *Os*, although positive, call up no funds from the market; this implies that at some range of rates above zero corporate treasurers prefer idle money to any alternative— the entire available balance would be held unemployed. This would obtain if transactions cost exceed the yield on funds. On the other hand, above the equilibrium yield *OD*, corporate treasurers would prefer employment of funds to idle balances, but this amount, *BC*, must remain idle; given demand, *Dd*, only *OB* can be absorbed at the equilibrium market price.

The demand for money-market funds, as we have seen, stems from a variety of institutional sources, corporate and Governmental, and includes only those who satisfy the standards previously discussed. In general, we can assume that the aggregate demand for funds (the supply of short-term money-market paper) increases with decreasing yields, as illustrated in Figure 1. The reasons for this are perhaps too obvious to discuss in detail. The money-market analyst may, however, consider the fact that money demands can be satisfied from sources other than the issuance of short-term paper and, further, that the demand curve of Figure 1 assumes as given the costs of these alternatives. To cite only one rather obvious case, a potential corporate borrower in the money market may optionally choose to secure funds directly from commercial banks at the bank prime loan rate. If the cost of money-market funds is "too high" relative to the prime rate, he will opt for this alternative, thus confirming the negative slope of the demand curve.

Conceptually, each potential borrower in the money market—each issuer of promissary notes—can be thought to have an array of alternative sources of funds. Given prevailing costs of the alternatives, chiefly their respective interest rates, the borrower achieves equilibrium in the sense that he cannot reduce his costs by any combination of borrowing other than his present pattern. Now, let the cost of money-market funds decline relative to the cost of other alternatives. The result will obviously be an increase in the amount of funds demanded from the money market and a reduction in the amount of funds demanded from other sources, until once again, at the new set of costs and yields, the borrower is indifferent *at the margin* as to the source of his funds.[5]

We are now prepared to give a tentative answer to the question: What determines the general level of money-market yields? Obviously, demand and supply lies at the heart of the matter. Our analysis may be clarified if we ask the question somewhat differently: what causes money-market rates to rise during some periods and fall during others?

On the demand side, we can readily see that anything that increases demand will tend to increase yields and anything that decreases demand will reduce them. Such changes would include (1) a change in the cost of alternative sources of finance to the borrower, (2) a change in the requirements for short-term finance by potential issuers of money-market paper,[6] and (3) technological changes in finance that either reduce the volume of short-term finance required per unit of output or increase the number of alternative sources of such finance to potential borrowers in the money market.

In general, we may attribute short-run increases in money-market rates on the demand side *primarily* to increases in aggregate economic activity, and reductions in rates to declining aggregate demand, although the other factors cannot be ignored. In this view, changes in money-market rates most strongly reflect a derived demand for short-term finance, derived from the demand for goods and services in the real sector of the economy, both private and public. It is hardly surprising that rising rates generally occur during the expansion phase of the business cycle and falling rates during periods of recession and depression; we should observe, however, that these movements may also be affected by supply conditions, to which attention is now directed.

Rising and falling money-market yields also reflect changes in the supply of money, in the aggregate, and to the money market in particular. The causes of such changes are more difficult to sort out than are those affecting the demand side of the market equation. The complexity of the processes involved has given rise to fundamental controversies among students of monetary economics. Since these are treated elsewhere in this volume (Part 4, Monetary Theory), the remarks in this section should be considered exploratory in nature and only suggestive of possible alternative conclusions.

Our principle concern will be the impact of a change in the aggregate money supply on the supply of funds to the money market. For brevity, analysis is confined to the explanation of falling interest rates in the money market, that is, to the case of an *increasing* supply schedule and curve in Figure 1.

[5] Adopting the usual convention, the aggregate demand for money-market funds *Dd,* is the summation of individual borrower demands.

[6] Some examples: an increase or decrease in the Treasury's short-term borrowing requirements; an increase or decrease in foreign trade affecting the issuance of bankers' acceptances; an increase or decrease in automobile sales, affecting the funds requirements of finance companies; and an increase or decrease in bank-loan demand, affecting the need for "high-powered" bank reserve money.

Assume, then, an increase in the aggregate supply of money. While some difference in the result may derive from the generating source of the increase (whether from public preference or Federal Reserve operations), we will further assume that the central bank consciously increases the volume of money, and that this is accomplished by the purchase of Treasury securities in the open market.[7]

These purchases will not only increase the volume of money in the hands of the public; they will also increase bank total reserves and free reserves, reduce the floating supply of near-money,[8] and thereby immediately reduce the *yield* on short-term (government) securities. It is important to note that *all* such purchases are made from the recognized Government securities dealers, that these latter are principal factors in the New York money market whose deposits are held primarily in the large New York money-market banks, and, therefore, that the initial increase in money and reserves occurs in the center of the money market itself, New York City, and to a far lesser degree, Chicago and other money centers. The effect of the Federal Reserve purchase is to increase the money balances of dealers and the free reserves of a small group of very large money-market banks.

Now, since we must assume that neither the dealers' nor the banks' demand for money has increased, the Reserve's purchase is tantamount to an unwanted accumulation of both high-powered and ordinary money— unwanted, that is, at the previously prevailing money-market yields. Equilibrium in bank preference for reserves *vis-à-vis* other assets is upset in the sense that actual reserves exceed desired reserves at the old yield structure; dealer equilibrium is similarly upset in the sense that actual money balances now exceed desired balances at the old level of Government security yields.

Obviously, if the Federal Reserve's purchase drives short-term Government security yields down far enough to induce banks to hold the increased volume of high-powered reserve money and the dealers to hold their augmented cash balances, money-market rates will tend to settle at new lower levels without further disturbance; as we previously noted, market arbitrage will tend to bring down other money-market yields to establish former basis point differentials.

On the other hand, if yields do not initially fall far enough to induce dealers and banks to hold the new money, these holders will attempt to rid their portfolios of undesired cash: this will induce banks to purchase money-market instruments in the first instance[9] and, paradoxically, perhaps, although not necessarily, from the dealers who themselves will be actively bidding for Government securities from their customers, *including the banks.*[10] To the extent that the banks seek to purchase short-term Government securities, rather than other money-market instruments, all holders of the augmented money supply will be eager purchasers and reluctant sellers. The supply curve in Figure 1 will shift to

---

[7] See Part 3.

[8] Typically, the Federal Reserve purchases short-term Government securities—that is, Treasury debt of less than one year to maturity, which is a principal type of money-market instrument.

[9] This is a reasonable supposition, particularly if the banks look on their augmented reserves as a temporary increase.

[10] Bank purchases normally clear through the dealers. However, banks may deal directly with other money-market participants, in which case the results will be somewhat but not essentially different.

the right and yields will be marked down, reenforcing the initial impact of the Federal Reserve's removal of a part of the floating supply of near-money instruments.

This would appear to end the matter as far as initial effects of the monetary increase are concerned. Secondary effects, however, intrude to complicate and modify the results observed above. It is clear, for example, that the augmented money supply must be treated as a permanent addition to the total money supply, including in this example bank reserves, and must be held in the public's portfolios of financial assets unless, of course, the Federal Reserve authorities reverse the process—a possibility we will exclude for the sake of exposition. Furthermore, without detailed examination of the mechanics of ultimate distribution, let us note what in fact happens, namely that some part of the additional monetary supply comes to be spread beyond the initial confines of New York money-market banks and held by nonmoney-market institutions and the nondealer public.

As far as the banking system is concerned, at some point augmented reserves will be held by banks that consider the excess a permanent, rather than merely temporary, addition to the total supply. Such banks will be more willing than before to expand loans. Furthermore, since we should expect large money-market banks to retain some part of the increased reserves, eventually these latter will attempt to expand their loans. Whether this is accomplished by the relaxation of credit-rationing standards or by reduction in the prime loan rate, the result will be, *ceteris paribus,* an expansion in both credit and the money supply.

Since some part of this loan expansion will go to entrepreneurs to finance business expansion, either prices or real output, and perhaps both, will increase. Real investment, through the multiplier, will further expand income, aggregate demand, output, and, perhaps, prices. This expansion will tend further to increase loan demand. At some stage, earlier or later, the need for short-term financing will increase and hence the demand for funds from the money market; in short, the supply of money-market paper will expand along with bank loans. Eventually, too, the banking system will exhaust its power to expand the money supply, bank credit creation will become increasingly difficult, and interest rates will begin a movement upward from their former (lower) level, which was induced initially by the Federal Reserve's purchase of Government securities.

As general prices rise (inflation), nominal interest rates will be adjusted upwards; bank prime rates, which are amenable to administration by the large banks, will be increased, as banks attempt to compensate themselves for a fall in the *real* rate that the inflation generates; at the same time, suppliers of funds to the money market will wish to supply fewer funds at each nominal interest rate than before, given the fall in real rate and the consequent increase in the attractiveness of accelerated investment of cash flows in inventories and other capital goods. This latter implies that funds formerly available to the money market flow directly into real investment, not only short-term but also long-term.

This combination of events pushes nominal short-term rates even higher. The initial increase in the money supply will indeed reduce money-market yields initially, but may, by inducing changed expectations and inflation, eventually lead to rates that are higher than those that prevailed before the Federal Reserve increased the money supply. This, in effect, is what Professor Meiselman means when he challenges the prevailing orthodoxy—long held by the Federal Reserve—that easy money leads to lower interest rates. So far from doing so, easy money leads to higher interest rates! This can lead to dire central-bank policy mistakes, as Meiselman and other "monetarists" have pointed out. For, if the Federal Reserve interprets rising rates to imply tighter money, and if, (as they have in the past) the authorities use interest rates as an important indicator of the impact of their policy, they will be led to increase the money supply even further in order to validate their easy-money stance and stabilize the rate level. This, of course, merely adds more fuel to the fire.

Eventually the Federal Reserve authorities will recognize that the too large increase in the money supply is inappropriate and will reverse the process, slowing down monetary growth in the battle against the inflation that their critics attribute, in large measure, to their own prior mistakes. Unfortunately, in the past their zeal in this direction has brought monetary growth to a complete halt—the most recent example being 1969—which swing of the monetary pendulum may reasonably be expected to result in a greater slowing down of economic activity, with a considerable but unpredictable lag, than the monetary authorities would wish for.[11]

The money markets, it should be emphasized, are *credit* markets of a very special type. The interest rates that result from supply and demand forces are the prices of *near monies,* not the price of money itself. The money markets do not always accurately reflect the price of money, which is itself measured by the general price level for goods and services.

The cost of holding *money* is the loss or gain from holding money when its real value is falling or rising as the general price level, which determines the purchasing power of money, is changing. This difference can be illustrated by observing the fact that money-market credit rates can be falling (rising) when the general price level is rising (falling). Money-market rates may be falling when inflation is increasing, for short periods of time; opposite divergences can also occur. This suggests that the demand and supply for demand deposits and currency are determined by different forces from the demand and supply of near-money, money-market instruments.

The monetary authorities may, as we have seen, elect to control the cost of money-market instruments; in this case they run the risk of not being able to control the money supply and the general price level. On the other hand, the authorities may elect to control the money supply, leaving money-market rates (and by implication, long-term interest rates) to fluctuate according to demand and supply forces in the credit markets.

As we shall see in subsequent readings, the choice between these two approaches to monetary management is of profound importance. The monetarist view is that the monetary authorities have too often erred in policy—and indeed have created economic instability—by overconcern with money-market conditions on the one hand, and a consequent failure to control

---

[11] Forecasting, as all economists know, is a hazardous business. The remarks above were written in February 1970, when many signs indicated a long-anticipated and ardently desired cooling off of economic activity, if not of growth in the price level. Since I shall not avail myself of the temptation to change my forecast in galley proof, preferring principle over false infallibility, the reader will have the opportunity to chalk up one score for or against the monetarist view.

the supply of money itself on the other.

In this light, the study of money markets can be both instructive and misleading. Our monetary authorities have traditionally been "money-market experts" rather than monetary experts in the larger sense. They have conse- quently been more concerned with the tone and feel of the New York market than they have been with the supply of money itself. At best, this has led to confusion between money and credit; at worst it has led to economic instability.

READING 6
MONEY MARKET INSTRUMENTS AND RELATIONSHIPS

Parker B. Willis

I. INTRODUCTION TO FEDERAL FUNDS

Federal Funds are immediately available Federal Reserve Funds and are essentially titles to reserve balances of member banks at Federal Reserve banks. Initially, the term, as generally used, referred to the amount of reserve balances that member banks held in excess of legal requirements and were willing to lend to banks having reserve deficiencies. Currently, however, the term more accurately means simply reserve balances borrowed or loaned.

Today, some banks will deliberately run "short" on their reserve positions by lending reserve balances to other banks, thus causing or sometimes even increasing a daily deficiency that they expect to cover later in the reserve period. Usually, Funds transactions are for overnight, and the rate of interest is negotiated or determined by the demand and supply of funds in the market.

On the other hand, some banks depend on this market as a source of funds for carrying an overinvested position for varying lengths of time.

In substance, Funds transactions are borrowings or loans of reserve balances. In practice, they are described as purchases or sales. The market cannot increase or decrease total member bank reserves but only redistributes them, providing a fuller use of bank reserves and resources.

Throughout the 1920's, banks participated in Funds trading almost exclusively as a method of adjusting reserve positions. While retaining this original function in the 1950's, Funds acquired increased importance both as an outlet for short-term investment of secondary reserves and, directly or indirectly, in connection with Government securities dealer financing. In the

Source: Excerpts from *The Federal Funds Market, Its Origin and Development,* Federal Reserve Bank of Boston 1970, 4th ed.

1960's as well, an increasing number of banks sought Funds to support loans and investments.

After World War II, the practice evolved of making payment in Funds for an increasing number and variety of financial transactions. This practice was developed initially by banks when trading with dealers in U.S. Government securities. Funds payment provided banks with immediate adjustment in reserve position or portfolio arrangement. It subsequently became more convenient for the dealer to finance by the same method. Later, other customers of dealers and banks demanded settlement in Funds because it shortened the turnaround time and, consequently, the loss of interest between the sale and effective date of the new purchase by the investor.

Similarly, as business corporate structures became more fully integrated, financial officers developed methods of speeding the proceeds of collections from local and regional banks to those in major financial centers for disbursement or investment. There are now plans for automatic daily remittance in Federal Funds to the major money market banks of all balances in excess of a certain amount held outside the principal money centers.

Trading or exchanging Funds is today a more important part of the complex of interbank relationships which ties the units in the American structure into a system and provides an efficient means of distributing the volume of excess reserves according to need. Other settlements in Funds have moved financial markets toward unity in payment and away from the use of clearing house funds.

II. SOME FACTORS INFLUENCING THE FUNDS RATE

During the credit squeeze in 1966 and the period of intensive credit restraint in 1969, banks showed a strong preference for the Federal Funds market in making reserve adjustments. This was a factor contributing to increases in the rate on transactions and the volume of Funds traded. The intensity of demand was reflected in the increasing spread of the Funds rate above the discount rate. In fact, the preference for Funds over borrowing at the Federal Reserve Bank has continued to the present time.

Paying more than the discount rate for Funds reflects the elasticity of the demand for them. The market may be said to represent a marginal demand and supply schedule in which increases of demand and supply quickly result in changed rates—in contrast to some other markets where competition is less perfect. The Funds rate acts as a sensitive indicator of shifting pressures in the banking system, particularly when related to who is supplying the Funds, the volume of the flows, and the depth of the demand. The huge flow of Funds during the last five years and widespread participation of both city and country banks of all sizes underscore this characterization of the market.

Currently, Funds are bought and sold by banks at several points in each Federal Reserve district. Each local selling point is a market, but New York City still predominates as the central market. About half the transactions originate in or move through New York City, and the brokers and principal accommodating banks are located there.

Local selling points are intimately connected with the central market and with one another. They are "linked" in the sense that price differences can bring transactions from one market to another, and some of the competing buyers and competing sellers complete transactions in more than one market within a district or in several districts. In a real sense the market is national.

Transactions are accomplished rapidly and at low cost in increasing volume for increasing numbers of banks at *nearly* uniform rates. This reflects a high degree of adjustment between demand and supply and price and quantity exchanged. In each local market, the same general forces determine the rate which may exist at any given time, although the magnitude of these forces may vary from market to market.

The growth in unity and breadth and the increase in efficiency of the Federal Funds market during the 1960's have strengthened the connections between the various divisions of the money market and between those of the money market and the longer term credit markets. A given volume of Federal Funds now moves through the market with less change in rates than before, and market participants may move back and forth from one sector of the money market to another in response to shifting rate differentials without causing disruptive price changes.

Although longer run influences, such as shifts in System policy, affect the Funds rate, it is also influenced by a shift of reserves among money market and country banks and the ebb and flow resulting from banking and other financial transactions. A persistent tendency for the rate to rise indicates a greater demand for reserves relative to supply, and a persistent tendency for the rate to fall suggests a smaller demand relative to the supply of reserves. Aside from temporary problems arising from the geographical distribution of reserves, distribution among money market banks, or unusual short-term demands, such as Treasury financing, the Funds rate shows a consistent and generally stable relationship to net borrowed reserves. Longer run shifts in the relationship, however, may occur under certain conditions. The Funds rate has risen relative to net borrowed reserves when deposit drains become cumulatively large and bank liquidity becomes strained. The credit squeeze in 1966 and the intense credit restraint

in 1969 are cases in point. Demand for Funds to make reserve adjustments increases under these circumstances. The Funds rate during much of the postwar period has been considered a key variable, along with net borrowed reserves, by the Open Market Account in maintaining the desired money market conditions.

As a general rule, the Funds rate shows a distinct weekly pattern. The rate tends to be firmer on Thursdays and Fridays and to soften on Tuesdays and Wednesdays. The softening is usually most pronounced on Wednesday, the last day of the statement week. This change within the week reflects the operating practices of institutions in the market, such as those followed by different banks in determining their reserve positions. Some buyers and sellers come to the market at different times. Firmness on Thursday and Friday reflects the opening of the reserve week for all member banks. Thursday is the payment day for weekly Treasury bills, and banks most active in financing the dealers absorb Funds. Many banks usually like to develop a cushion of excess reserves which can be drawn down later in the period to meet shifts in deposits or other pressures. The position must also be established for the weekend on Friday, since these transactions carry over until Monday.

The softness of rates at the end of the statement week principally reflects lessened demand factors. Available data do not show that supplies of Funds are larger on those days. In the opinion of most market observers, lessening of demand may be attributable to several factors. Reserve requirements have been satisfied and those country banks which do not trade Funds shift excesses to city correspondents frequently. The widening use of Funds during recent years has caused country banks to compute requirements more accurately and sell excesses to city banks. When these flows from country to city banks coincide with periods of sufficiencies for Reserve city banks, the market tends to fade away.

Efforts have been made to adjust for anticipated volumes. Some banks have sold estimated excesses, and others have bought to cover estimated deficiencies a day or two prior to settlement dates. The results, however, have not always matched expectations.

It should be noted that excess Funds may appear with resulting downward pressure on rates during periods of scarcity. This has happened occasionally in the past if member banks borrow in excess of their needs prior to a long weekend or when float or other operating factors produce sizable amounts of Funds in excess of estimates.

III. MONEY MARKET INSTRUMENTS 1950–1969 AND SOME FUND RELATIONSHIPS

Chart 1 traces the continuous growth and change which have accurred during the postwar period in the composition of money market instruments. This change reflects an effort to improve the flexibility of the various institutions within the market itself and to maximize the usefulness of the existing volume of money market funds is making final adjustment between demand and supply of credit. Special techniques have been developed by both borrowers and lenders which facilitate flows between markets. Knowledge of the market also has become more widespread and internal diversity reduced, particularly since the mid-1950's.

Business corporations have become important suppliers and users of money market funds, both directly and indirectly. The activity of nonbank participants has increased partly because interest is no longer paid on demand deposits. Deposits have been redistri-

buted in the banking system to the extent that corporate treasurers have shifted from demand deposits to money market investment, and these treasurers have become increasingly active in shifting from one market to another. This activity has also been a factor in slowing deposit growth at the large money market banks and increasing the velocity of money. As all sectors of the market increased in competitiveness, the rage of fluctuations in rates has been reduced except during the recent periods of severe monetary restraint. Considerable variability in money market conditions seems to inevitably accompany such a policy. In some markets in 1969, spread between bid and asked rates was frequently widened from the characteristic one-eighth percent, to one-quarter percent, and on occasion to three-eighths percent.

Maturing instruments in the several sectors of the money market are now generally paid off in Funds as opposed to clearing house checks. Currently, unless agreed otherwise, money market instruments bought and sold in the secondary market are usually deliverable in New York the next business day following the date of the transactions, and settlements are in Funds. Banks in New York and Chicago frequently act as issuing agent and alternate paying agent when such service is required to reduce deliveries and collection expense. Banks in other principal money centers may also perform these services. U.S. securities and the majority of Federal agency securities are payable at Federal Reserve banks.

A. Federal Funds and Treasury Bill Markets

The Funds market and Treasury bill market are today the dominant sectors of the short-term money market and reflect business conducted for a widened variety of customers in substan-

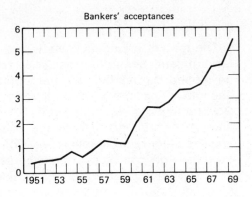

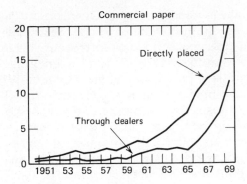

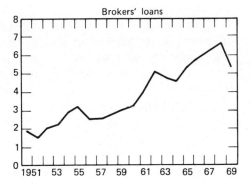

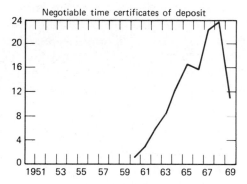

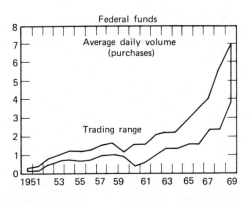

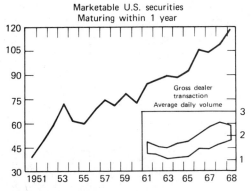

Chart 1. Money market instruments, 1950–1969, approximate amounts outstanding (billions of dollars).

Source: Federal Reserve Bulletin except Federal Funds. Funds data based on report of 250–275 banks September, 1959–September, 1962, and 46 large banks since then. Data on Federal Funds and certificates of deposit partly estimated for some years. Brokers' loan data for 1969 are June 30. All other data are year-end figures.

tially increased volume. Over two-thirds of all trading volume in U.S. securities in 1969 was conducted in Treasury bills. At the same time, Federal agency securities, up to two years in maturity, have become important in trading.

These are the markets in which the banks complete most of their reserve adjustments, and virtually all open market operations of the System Account are conducted in the U.S. Government securities market. These operations have an immediate impact on the supply of Funds and spread the effects of System monetary policy throughout the financial markets. Correspondingly, large money market banks and Government security dealers are the major participants other than the Federal Reserve. Because of different uses, the relative importance of each market to borrowers and lenders cannot be compared on the basis of absolute magnitudes.

Beyond the Funds and Treasury bill markets, other sections of the money market, some old and some new, are important not only for reserve adjustment but also for lodgement of short-term funds, and the participants link these markets to others. Some markets have changed in both function and character compared with past periods. An example of this is the brokers' loan market. Although these loans have shown a large increase in outstandings during the last several years, they are now of relatively small significance in adjusting bank reserve positions. The market is more generally used by the larger banks as a secondary reserve investment. As such, its character is considerably different from the 1920's, when working capital balances of corportions were placed in call and time loans to brokers through the agency of New York City banks.

B. Dealer Loans

The market in dealer loans with U.S. Government securities as collateral[1] developed during the postwar period, accompanying the rise in trading in Governments. It is highly specialized and closely related to both the Funds and Treasury bill markets. These loans are made on call or overnight by several of the leading New York City banks, and they help to balance out residual reserve needs in the money market as a whole.[2] In effect, the banks act as lenders of last resort for the Government security dealers. Daily volume may range from $100 million to over $1.5 billion.

This market has some aspects of a customer loan market in that most of the banks do not feel free to terminate loans without regard to the individual borrower's position. Generally the banks influence the volume of outstanding loans by making daily changes in the "posted" loan rates on new loans and renewals—announced each day after the bank has initially determined its reserve position. By varying their rates and administering the volume of loans within the framework of posted rates, these banks use dealer loans to adjust their reserve positions to reflect changes within the market itself as well as broader changes affecting the money market as a whole. Dealer loans are thus considered an important money market instrument for New York City banks. The rates on the loans are established below the call rate on other security loans, but generally one-quarter to three-quarters of 1 percent above the Federal Funds rate and frequently above the yield to dealers on the securities in their inventories.

Aside from the influence of normal operating factors, an atmosphere of

---

[1] Collateral may also include certificates of deposit, securities issued by U.S. Government agencies, acceptances, and commercial paper.

[2] One or two Chicago banks are also important sources of these loans.

ease or tightness in the general money market stems from the strength of the demand for Funds, the intensity of reserve use, bank reserve adjustments through net purchase or sale of Treasury bills, and the willingness of the banks to make dealer loans. Geographical distribution of reserves—whether concentrated in financial centers or country areas at any given time—may be a short-run underlying influence. In the final analysis, however, the degree of restraint or ease in the money market is reflected in the volume of member bank borrowing at the Reserve banks.

C. Commercial Paper

In the older markets, dealer commercial paper still serves a respectable cross section of industry. Along with the enlarged dollar volume of recent years, issuers have also increased, numbering about 500 in 1969. Although banks remain major purchasers, they now hold only one-third of outstandings. Nonfinancial corporations account for most of the balance. Agreements by the dealer to repurchase the paper from the buyer do not usually occur, but for good customers in an emergency, the dealer may try to resell the paper on a "best efforts basis."

More recent money market instruments include directly placed sales of finance company paper, and in early 1969, bank related commercial paper[3] began to grow in volume. This latter paper first appeared in small volume during the credit squeeze of 1966 and provided banks with an additional nondeposit source of Funds, enabling them to meet some of their loan demand. Both dealer and directly placed paper have maturities of three days to nine months with most carrying maturities of less than 90 days. The nine-month maximum maturity exempts commer-

cial paper from registration with the Securities and Exchange Commission, and the exemption requires that the proceeds of these notes be used for "current transactions."

The market for sales finance company paper has broadened to include nonfinancial corporate treasurers and a variety of other investors. Corporate treasurers currently account for close to 60 percent of the volume of purchases of this paper, and since the advent of the master note toward the end of the 1950's, it is estimated that bank trust departments have come to account for about 20 percent of the purchases. The master note is a device for pooling temporarily uninvested funds of a number of investors (typically the beneficiaries of trusts) under a single agreement. Bank holdings, on the other hand, are relatively small, accounting for less than 10 percent.

If need arises on the part of the buyer, the issuer of directly placed paper will generally repurchase the outstandings, often with rate adjustments, however. Since the close of the war, the dealer function—locating buyers and suiting terms to needs—has increasingly been performed by the finance companies.

About 85 percent of bank related commercial paper outstanding has been placed directly with corporate customers, and the balance sold through dealers. All kinds of commercial paper have increased significantly in volume — fourfold — since 1965, reaching a peak of $40 billion in June, 1970. Excluding bank related paper, the market has recently supplied about 25 percent of the credit represented by the combined total of commercial loans at large banks and commercial paper.

The increase reflects the extreme

---

[3] Bank related paper is commercial paper issued by bank holding companies, affiliates of bank holding companies, or affiliates of banks.

tightness of bank credit in 1966 and 1969, attempts to rebuild corporate liquidity in 1967, and the congestion and high cost in the long-term capital market. A number of utility companies used the market until the time when short debt could be funded at lower rates. In addition, certain utilities have financed current needs and accounts receivable in the market. Of particular interest is the use made of the market by nonfinancial corporations during the last several years in supplementing internal sources of funds and in providing an alternative and supplement to bank lines of credit. The market expanded so rapidly and the demand for credit was so intense during recent years in an atmosphere of general euphoria that some paper did not receive the customary scrutiny as exemplified by the bankruptcy of the Penn Central Transportation Company in June, 1970. About $87 million of this paper sold through dealers and rated prime by the National Credit Office was held by investors.[4] Commercial paper, however, will undoubtedly remain a popular alternative to bank financing. The market will be influenced by qual-

ity preference and show more caution for anything other than top rated paper. Some decline in outstandings may result.

Aggressive banks used the market through their affiliates to help hold their competitive positions. Proceeds from the sale of commercial paper by a bank holding company, its affiliate, or a bank subsidiary were generally used to supply funds to the bank through the purchase of existing loans from the bank or to finance the activities of the affiliate or subsidiary, such as mortgage servicing or factoring. In this way, the bank could make new loans, thereby accommodating its customers, or pressure on the parent bank's resources was eased.[5]

Bank related commercial paper amounted to about $4.5 billion at the end of 1969. By midyear 1970, outstandings had increased further to a level a little over $7½ billion.[6] At this level it comprised a significant share of total commercial paper. Considering the commercial paper market as a whole, corporate treasurers have succeeded the banks as major paper buyers, and the market has cut substan-

---

[4] *Wall Street Journal,* August 13, 1970, pp. 1, 16.

[5] In line with its restrictive credit policy, the Board of Governors proposed in October, 1969, that if the proceeds of the sale of bank holding company paper or that of one of its affiliates were used to supply funds to the bank, the sales would be subject to Regulation Q. At the same time, it ruled that such paper issued by subsidiaries of banks was already subject to Regulations Q and D. However, the Board suspended interest rate ceilings and waived reserve-requirement penalties on the later paper to the extent that volume did not exced the amounts outstanding on October 29. As well, it took no final action on holding company paper.

Using the authority in the Act of December 2, 1969, the Board, in January, 1970, proposed a 10 percent reserve requirement for bank related paper. Subsequently, after further discussion, the Board announced on August 17, that effective September 17, 1970, a reserve requirement of 5 percent would be imposed on a member bank affiliate's paper with a maturity of 30 days or more. Maturities of less than 30 days would be subject to the requirements on demand deposits. The authority of the Reserve banks to waive penalties for deficiencies in reserves resulting from the issue of such paper by subsidiaries was withdrawn. Simultaneously, required reserves on all time deposits in excess of $5 million were reduced one percentage, effective on the same date. The combined action was expected to release about $350 million of reserves net. This result was suited to continued moderation of the System's restraint policy inaugurated at the beginning of the year. In June, the interest rate ceiling on CD's of 30–89 day maturities was suspended. Since most commercial paper is issued in denominations of $100 thousand or more, the imposition of reserve requirements on bank related paper places instruments of this kind on practically an equal basis in terms of reserves with negotiable CD's.

[6] This class of paper will decline in anticipation of reserves to be required against it.

tially into the loan business of commercial banks with finance companies.

Businessmen's and finance companies' cost of borrowing in this market was less than at the bank counter, even at the advanced rates reached after 1965 after allowance was made for compensating balances. Similarly, bank holding companies and affiliates found it a cheaper source when measured against the cost of Euro-dollars and other nondeposit funds to their bank affiliates.

Business and finance company commercial paper market borrowers feel that the market has provided them with an alternative source of funds which is usually easily accessible and offers both flexibility in amount and terms of borrowing as well as a dependable availability of funds.

During the first half of 1969, the banks also procured additional reserves by selling over $1 billion from their portfolios under repurchase agreements to corporate customers. Such repurchases were limited to transactions between banks by a Federal Reserve Board ruling on July 25, 1969.[7] Since that date, a repurchase made by a bank with a corporate customer can be made only with U.S. Government or agency securities as collateral.

D. Bankers' Acceptances

Since 1958, the volume of bankers' acceptances has almost quadrupled, reaching $5.5 billion at the end of 1969. This reflects increasing reliance of domestic importers and exporters on acceptances as well as the rise in financing of foreign storage and shipment of goods. Acceptances for these purposes account for about 50 and 40 percent of outstandings, respectively.

It is estimated that about half of the borrowing for foreign storage and shipment is undertaken to finance Japanese trade with other nations. Acceptances are also used to cover domestic storage and shipment and to some extent to create dollar exchange. Acceptances for all purposes except dollar exchange may have maturities up to six months. Dollar exchange acceptances, however, are limited to a maturity of not more than three months.

The severe credit restraint in 1969 and the limiting effect of the Regulation Q ceiling even led some banks to create and sell "working capital" acceptances in order to continue their loan expansion. These acceptances were ineligible for purchase or discount by the Federal Reserve because they were not trade related. The volume did not exceed $200 million at year end, but by mid-summer 1970, it was estimated to have doubled.

Trading in acceptances focuses on six dealers, four of whom also trade Government securities. This market has become somewhat broader than it was in the first half of the 1950's. In part, this broadening reflects both more acceptance financing by a larger number of banks and the increasing interest of corporate and institutional treasurers in all short-term investment outlets. Foreign buyers—both commercial and central banks—although important, are today less significant participants than formerly. Domestic commercial banks and large savings banks remain the major purchasers. In 1969, acceptance rates rose to record levels and became increasingly competitive with other short-term investments. Even the small denominated bill of less than $100 thousand, heretofore considered a nuisance, was easily sold and attracted institutional odd lot

---

[7] The Board stated that the proceeds of such repurchase agreements were indistinguishable from deposit transactions except on a formalistic basis.

buyers and even individuals. Banks sold most of the "ineligible" acceptances to their customers in 1969, and in 1970, there was a limited amount of trading by one or two dealers.

In contrast to the 1920's, the market is now considerably larger in absolute size but much smaller and less important in relation to the total volumes of money market instruments. The Federal Reserve now buys only limited amounts of acceptances for its own account. Some banks continue the practice of holding their own bills for investment or accomplish transactions through dealers on a "swap" basis. Some banks sell to their correspondents and other customers from their own supply. At times, a bank will enter the market as an agent on behalf of its customers. Similarly, banks will bid for acceptances if the holder wishes to sell. These practices, however, appear to be decreasing or stabilizing, with more trading through dealers.

The acceptance market, along with the market for dealer and directly placed commercial paper, provides an important tie between the short-term money market and the bank counter. This occurs as borrowers switch from these markets to the bank counter in meeting needs. The prime rate on commercial loans has become an important part of the structure of money rates. Linkage with the long-term capital market is also provided through the bank counter as borrowers fund bank loans, depending in part upon the relationship of capital market rates to the prime rate.

E. Certificates of Deposit[8]

Although certificates of deposit have been issued in negotiable form for many years in parts of the Nation, they have become a significant money market instrument only since 1961. Earlier issuers did not expect their certificates to be traded. In fact, there was no organized secondary market.

In order to combat both the instability and shrinkage of their deposits which had been in process during the 1950's, the New York City banks announced that they would issue CD's to domestic business corporations, public bodies, and foreign sources. Issuance was expected to attract short-term corporate funds lodged elsewhere in the banking system and also provide an instrument to compete for corporate balances which were being invested in a variety of money market instruments, principally in Treasury bills. These CD's are usually issued in large denomination with minimum face value of $100,000, and maturities range from 30 days to one year or longer. Most maturities, however, are concentrated in the short-term area.

In late February, 1961, the First National City Bank of New York began to issue CD's. Two major innovations were introduced. The certificates were made negotiable, and the Discount Corporation of New York announced that it would make a market for certificates, thus broadening appeal. Competitive forces led banks in other centers to follow suit. Outstanding amounts have grown rapidly and include a variety of maturities but with considerable concentration in the short-term area.

Issuers are widespread geographically and by size of bank. Increases in outstandings have typically occurred during periods of relative ease or stability in the markets. Since rates paid are governed by Regulation Q,* banks are forced to withdraw from the issue

---

[8] Negotiable CD's are issued and traded on yield to maturity basis.

* Editor's note: Maximum interest rates that the Federal Reserve permits banks to pay depositors.

market as money market conditions firm, offering rates reach Regulation Q ceilings, and such ceilings remain unchanged. Under these conditions, market short-term rates rise relative to the Regulation's ceiling, and certificates become noncompetitive with other instruments. The rise of open market rates (not subject to the constraint of regulation) above—or their fall below—existing rate ceilings leads to the retardation or acceleration of issues as interest sensitive investors move to obtain the highest possible yields. As the market evolved, a number of the leading banks adopted the practice of varying the rate offered on certificates and, by this method, used certificates to adjust their reserve position.

Toward the end of 1968, a record high of $24 billion of outstandings was reported. Subsequently, the intensification of the System's restrictive credit policy which began to develop at the year end lifted market rates well above Regulation Q ceilings. Outstandings by the end of 1969 had dropped to about $10 billion because of net runoffs—about five times the size of the decline during the restrictive credit period in 1966. The move to a restrictive credit policy in the first half of 1969 was accompanied by a decision to leave Regulation Q ceilings on time deposits unchanged and thus below market rates. This was the first time that Regulation Q had been used by the Federal Reserve with the direct intention of restraining bank credit expansion. The decision not to change time deposit rates and the reduced availability of bank reserves interacted on the demand for bank credit throughout the year in 1969, as it had after mid-1966. Banks were forced to seek nondeposit sources of funds—such as Euro-dollars and commercial paper—and to use the Funds market more intensively as a source of funds to accommodate customers' credit demands. Prior to 1966, Regulation Q ceilings were generally accommodated to market rates.

To the holder, at least of better known names, the secondary market, centered in the principal U.S. Government security dealers, provides reasonable liquidity except during periods of tight money, such as occurred in 1968 and 1969. The mere existence of the market has broadened the acceptance of all issues by facilitating sales to third parties before maturity for most certificates. Trading volume has ranged in "good markets" from $40 to $125 million daily average, while dealer positions have ranged from $150 to over $600 million. In "poor markets," such as occurred in 1966 and 1969, dealers substantially cut their positions, as supply and consequently trading volume dried up. In 1969, both the dealer positions and trading volume were nominal, falling as low as $1 to $2 million at times. Some distress selling occurred at times of sharp rate change.

Expansion of economic activity slowed during 1969, came to a halt near the year end, and declined during the first half of 1970. System policy accordingly became less restrictive, and moderate but progressive growth in the money supply and other financial aggregates was resumed. Reflecting these developments and as adjustment in business continued, pressures in the financial markets eased gradually as 1970 progressed. Short-term interest rates declined on balance as a consequence. In this context the Board of Governors liberalized the Regulation Q ceilings toward the end of January, raising the rates for each maturity. In June, the ceiling on the 30 to 89 day maturity range was suspended indefinitely, effective June 24. As a result of the January action, as market rates adjusted, banks were able to add CD's in moderate volume in the following months. The June action was undertaken partly in recognition of possible heavy demands on commercial banks for short-term credit resulting from uncertainties in the commercial paper market arising from the bankruptcy of the Penn Central Railroad Company and partly to support the easier credit policy. The System also used the discount window and open market operations to forestall liquidity pressures. Freed from the constraint of rate ceilings in this maturity, the banks aggressively sought short-term CD's to accommodate borrowers who could not obtain funds in the paper market. Banks received a substantial inflow of funds in respone to offering rates of about 8 percent.

The June action is the first suspension of the rate ceiling which has occurred. If ceilings should eventually be discarded, the rate paid by individual banks offering CD's would become increasingly a function of the average rate prevailing in the market, the volume of CD's outstanding, and the amount of new issues proposed. This development could lead to a more even flow of marketing of issues and better balance of factors in the secondary market.

As a short-term investment, certificates of deposit compete principally with three-month Treasury bills and commercial paper, both dealer and directly placed. They are held mainly by corporations and other businesses, although state and local governments and foreign entities also hold significant amounts. Generally, banks do not frequently buy other bank certificates. Unlike other money market instruments, variation in amounts of CD's outstanding may influence the reserve position of banks because of the lower reserve required for time deposits. Issuing rates reflect the increased competitiveness of the CD's with other sectors of the money market. As the market has developed, changes in issuing rates have declined from one-quarter of 1 percent to one-eighth of 1 percent.

F. Other Market Instruments

Strong competition in the money market, characteristic of the past decade, was clearly reflected by the offering of straight, unsecured short-term notes by the First National Bank of Boston in early September, 1964. A dozen or more large banks scattered over the Nation followed suit. These notes were directly placed by issuers in multiples of $1 million at rates that competed with finance company paper, negotiable CD's, and other money-market instruments. A limited trading market centered with major U.S. security dealers subsequently developed. Only about $600 million of these notes were outstanding at any one time. In contrast to the CD's, they required no reserves or insurance and were not subject to rate and maturity restrictions imposed by Regulation Q. On the other hand, the issuance utilized some of the bank's capacity to borrow. Effective September 1, 1966, however, bank issues of short-term notes of less than 2 years in maturity were brought within the provision of Regulations D and Q, being defined as deposits in the interests of equity.

The variety of competition and money market participants' willingness to try to improve the flexibility of the institutions within the market itself have also been reflected in the issuance of short-term notes by the Federal National Mortgage Association inaugurated in April, 1960. In the private sector, the Savings Bank Trust Company also began issues of short-term notes in October, 1962.

The FNMA notes are issued at a discount and are unsecured, with maturities designated by lenders ranging from 30 to 270 days with a wide choice of denominations. The FNMA has placed increasing reliance on these notes, and along with the Federal Home Loan Bank, has during the last three years increased the number of issues with maturities up to 2 years. This use of Federal agencies as intermediaries has provided significant amounts of money for the real estate mortgage market. The Savings Bank Trust Company has an issue of three year notes outstanding, and both these and its short-term securities are largely secured by FHA and VA real estate mortgages. Like the Federal agencies, the Trust Company uses a dealer in placing its notes. The outstanding volume of the Trust Company notes, however, is relatively small as are the amounts which are likely to be issued.

PART 2
COMMERCIAL BANKING

READING 7
A BANK IS A BANK IS A BANK?

Deane Carson

The primary purpose of the selections in Part 2 is to provide information that the student of money and banking will not typically find in his textbook coverage of commercial banking. These readings will yield several insights into banks and their operations that will increase the breadth and depth of his understanding.

The title of these introductory remarks reflects, with due apologies to Gertrude Stein, my dissatisfaction with the usual textbook treatment of commercial banking in one particular respect, namely, the rather common tendency to leave the reader with the impression that commercial banks are very much alike when, in fact, their differences are considerably greater than their similarities.

Indeed, the prevalent use of the term "the banking system" fosters the impression that the business of banking is homogeneous, when the truth is that very substantial and significant variation exists in the operations of individual banking firms, My thesis is, whatever one might think of Spiro Agnew's dictum concerning slums, it is not true that "once you've seen one bank, you've seen them all."

The origins of the contrary view derive from the observation that banks do share important common features, chiefly the acceptance of deposits from the public, and the use of these funds to make loans and acquire short-term securities. Furthermore, commercial banks collectively create money in the form of demand deposits, an important economic function, to be sure, but one that accounts in part for the small amount of attention given to variations in bank operations in banking courses.

This is not to say, however, that college courses should attempt to teach you how to run a bank. Even if this were possible, and the weight of evidence is to the contrary, it would still be far more efficient to have this done in banks for graduates that are planning to be bankers, leaving to the universities and colleges the broader task of explaining the monetary system. Nevertheless, the student of money and banking ought to supplement his appreciation of the central role of banks in the money-creating process with a similar appreciation of the structure of the industry, the market characteristics of bank firms, and the various portfolio policies of these institutions. In a small way, this selection will provide an introduction to these matters, although it would really require a large volume to cover the scope of this material adequately.

We fill first look at the structure of banking in the United States; this will be followed by a review of banking markets and a short discussion of bank portfolio policies and the decision-making processes of banks in a wide variety of circumstances.

I. BANKING STRUCTURE AND REGULATION

The structure of banking in the United States is unique in the world, which accounts for the difficulty foreign students (and some from Scarsdale and Des Moines as well), experience when confronted with our commercial-banking arrangements. A Canadian student of mine recently complained in class, after a lecture on the subject, "It just does not make sense!" I agreed with his broad evaluation, while further contending that some things that do not seem to make sense can nevertheless be explained.

A Canadian, particularly, has reason to wonder at the structure of banking over the border. In Canada, there are less than ten commercial banks; these institutions, through branches that extend throughout the country, serve the banking needs of the nation. In the United States, there are some 14,000 individual bank firms, operating approximately 22,000 offices, all the latter of which, with minor exceptions, are at least confined to the state boundaries of the parent firm and often restricted to an even greater degree, depending on governing state legislation.

To be sure, there are differences between the United States and Canada that might account for this significant difference in banking structure, although neither geographical nor population differences seem to be relevant. Close inspection of the matter involves a brief excursion into the historical development of the two systems, where we find the answer to the apparent paradox.

Both Canada and the United States derive their political and commercial antecedents from England, the England of the 17th and 18th centuries. During this formative period, banking was still in a nebulous stage in England, although given the custom of royal grants of monopoly, promising to become what in fact it became, a system consisting of a very small number of large banking firms. Until relatively late in the Colonial period, there were no commercial banking institutions in the colonies. After the American Revolution, a banking structure began to evolve in the United States, which at first appeared to be following the British model (and which ultimately did so in Canada), but which soon broke away from that pattern, resulting in the present system. The Canadian colonies, which had retained political ties to England, retained English banking customs and structure as well.

What caused the break with English tradition in the United States? As noted in the preceding paragraph, the early American system began to evolve along British lines. The establishment of the Federally chartered First Bank of the United States in 1791 and its second charter granted in 1816, promised to generate a dominant national system of branch banks and an effective regulator of state-chartered commercial banks as well. Opposition to this system developed very early from the Jeffersonian democrats (who were generally opposed to any aggrandizement of Federal powers), from state legislatures that then had chartering power to establish state banks in competition with the Bank of the United States, and from farmers and merchants who resented the latter's "tight money" policies.[1]

The election to the Presidency of Andrew Jackson, who represented states' rights advocates and opposition to the extension of Federal control, sounded the death knell of the Bank of the United States and with it the possibility that the banking structure would develop along British lines. State governments chartered all banks from 1836 to 1863 and jealously guarded against intrusion of "foreign" branches and offices from outside their boundaries. In 1863, the National Banking System was established, providing for Federal charters to be granted by the Comptroller of the Currency; it was hoped that this development and a discriminating tax on state-chartered bank notes would establish a single system of National banks, an expectation that was not realized; at the present time, therefore, both the several states and the Federal Government issue charters.

Prior to 1933, bank charters were relatively easy to acquire; only minimum requirements were imposed by state bank commissioners and the Comptroller of the Currency, and, as a consequence, a very large number of commercial banks was established—the number being approximately 20,000 by 1920. The number fell thereafter, due to failures, mergers, and greater restriction on new bank formation, and has apparently stablized in recent years to approximately its present level.

To sum up, the American banking structure evolved within a political and economic system that was hostile to central government intervention in economic affairs, dominated by rural and small-business interests through political control of state legislatures, devoted to free enterprise (including enterprise banking!), and generally, although not always consistently and effectively, hostile to monopoly and a large concentration of business power. The Early American Dream that any man could own his own business extended to banking, at least in principle; furthermore, the independence generated by the frontier fostered a local pride—some would say parochialism—that soon brought a bank to practically every village and hamlet in America, and in many cases more than one. Local ownership and control of banks is still a chartering criterion of both state and Federal Government authorities.

That many of these influences on the banking structure are changing is quite clear, whatever one's views may be on the desirability of such changes. But as far as the banking structure itself is concerned, fundamental change is not likely; the *fait accompli,* together with very strong barriers to change that are built into our political and bank regulatory system, would seem to perpetuate the status quo.[2] This conclusion leads us to the consideration of bank regulation, the most pervasive influence on the banking organism.

Understandably, students are often confused, as are some bankers, by the apparent hodgepodge of banking regulatory agencies. Table 1 summarizes who is responsible for what in the reg-

[1] See Bray Hammond, "Banking Before the Civil War," in Deane Carson (Ed.), *Banking and Monetary Studies,* (Homewood, Illinois: Richard D. Irwin Inc. 1963), pp. 12–13. Jefferson himself considered banks "more insidious than standing armies," a view that is now very ably represented by the Chairman of the House Banking and Currency Committee, the Honorable Wright Patman of Texas.

[2] This is not to say that the structure is either static or immune from change. An indication of at least desire for change is found in a recent speech by the Banking Commissioner of New York, who proposed that New York and California Commissioners be empowered reciprocally to charter branches of banks in their states in cities with over 500,000 population. Under this authority, a New York bank could establish a branch, for example, in San Francisco and vice versa.

TABLE 1

BANK REGULATORY AGENCIES AND RESPONSIBILITIES

AGENCY	REGULATORY ACTIVITY			
	New Bank Charters	Charter of Branches	Merger Proposals	Examination of Banks
Comptroller of the Currency (Federal Government)	Applications for national bank charter	Applications from national banks (state laws govern the permissable locality)[a]	Where surviving bank would be a national bank[b]	All national banks and District of Columbia banks
State Bank Commissioners (50)	Applications for state bank charters	Applications from state-chartered banks		State-chartered banks that are not insured by Federal Deposit Insurance Corporation
Federal Deposit Insurance Corporation	Approves insurability only	Approves insurability only		Insured state-chartered banks that are not members of the Federal Reserve System
Federal Reserve Board	New national banks must join Federal Reserve System		Where surviving bank would be a state-chartered member of the Federal Reserve System[b]	State-chartered banks that are members of the Federal Reserve System
Federal Department of Justice			Submits advisory opinion to merging authority; may, within 30 days after merger approval, announce intention to seek injuction against the merger[c]	

[a] The Comptroller cannot approve a branch in any state where such a branch could not legally be established by a state-chartered bank.

[b] In considering merger proposals, the agency receives advisory opinions from other agencies on the competitive effect of the merger.

[c] This often is tantamount to a veto of the merger approval.

ulation of various structural aspects of America banking.

The American banking system has been described as a dual system, meaning that banks are subject to either Federal or state regulatory control, and, in some matters, both. Within the Federal structure, there are no less than four agencies with major regulatory powers, the Comptroller of the Currency, the Federal Reserve Board, the Federal Deposit Insurance Corpora-tion, and the Department of Justice.[3] In addition, other Federal agencies, such as the Securities and Exchange Commission, concern themselves with banking matters that fall within their specialized jurisdiction. On the state level, each government has an agency that is responsible for regulation of state-chartered banks.

It is not surprising, given this regulatory structure, that substantial differences exist in the supervision of banks.

[3] Conflicts between the Federal regulatory agencies are not uncommon and reached a peak in the years 1961–66 when James J. Saxon was Comptroller of the Currency. These have led to proposals to consolidate regulation on the Federal level into one agency.

Activities that are permissable in Oklahoma are not permissible across the border in Colorado, for example, even though some banks in those states are in the same competitive market.

Such differences are particularly pronounced in four major areas of banking supervision—chartering of new bank firms, approval of branches of existing banks, the legal reserve requirements to which various banks are subject, and portfolio supervision.

In the first of these areas, differences exist not only between state and Federal jurisdictions, but also between state authorities as well. Federal-state differences in new-bank chartering philosophy may at times be pronounced, for example in the period 1961–65, when the Comptroller of the Currency reversed a long trend of parsimony in the granting of new National Bank charters extending from the late 1920s,[4] a reversal that was only belatedly followed by some state banking supervisors. Among states, regulatory permissiveness varies widely; and while none of the states can be accused (or applauded in one view) of open-handedness in granting charters, some maintain standards that are considerably more difficult to meet than others.[5]

This lack of uniformity is even more pronounced in the second area of supervision, the approval of branches. State laws, which govern the permissible geographical boundaries for branches, apply not only to state banks, but also to national banks. Some states, such as Rhode Island and California, permit the approval of branches anywhere within the state; others, such as Pennsylvania, restrict branch offices to the counties contiguous to that of the home office; still others, for example Illinois, Colorado and Florida, do not permit the establishment of branches.

Even within a single state, differences in branching philosophy between the Comptroller of the Currency and the state banking supervisor may exist that change the structure of banking. In New York, for example, a change in the state's legal code in 1960 expanded branching to permit New York City banks branch offices in Westchester and Nassau Counties. The Comptroller, Mr. Saxon, quickly approved many branch applications that were submitted by the First National City Bank, which was under his supervision, while the state supervisor of banking followed a more hesitant policy with respect to Chase Manhattan, then a state-chartered institution and National City's chief competitor. As a result, the latter achieved a distinct competitive advantage in both Westchester and Nassau counties, preempting the choice locations and establishing a foothold in the market.[6] It can thus be seen that even banks that are very much alike in size, location, and other respects are quite unalike in the constraints that govern their operations.

In the third area of regulatory differences, legal reserve requirements, a similar story unfolds. National banks are by law required to be members of the Federal Reserve System; state-chartered banks on the other hand, may elect to be members of the System at their discretion. This difference gives competitive advantages to state-chartered non-members over national banks within the same banking market, since

---

[4] See Ross M. Robertson, *The Comptroller and Bank Supervision* (Washington: Office of the Comptroller of the Currency, 1968) for an excellent discussion of chartering policies.

[5] Someone once remarked that St. Paul couldn't get a state commercial bank charter in St. Paul. For many years before Mr. Saxon became Comptroller it is doubtful that a reincarnated Washington would have received a charter in the District of Columbia.

[6] Chase Manhattan became a national bank in 1965, partly because it believed it would receive greater latitude in its operations from the Comptroller of the Currency than it had under state charter and supervision.

the Federal Reserve's legal reserve requirements are almost invariably higher and more stringent than those imposed by the several states. In general, the differences derive from (1) higher levels of percentage reserve requirements imposed by the System and (2) the rather common feature of state laws that permits state-chartered banks to hold reserves either as cash with correspondents or in short-term government securities, whereas member banks must keep required reserves in cash—either in a vault or with the Federal Reserve itself. The relative lack of earning power of member bank reserves introduces a further inequality in the treatment of banks within the same competitive market and, as well, influences the portfolio and cash asset holdings of such banks.

Furthermore, since state laws vary considerably with respect to reserve requirements, state-chartered banks in different regulatory jurisdictions are unequally treated. Some states impose rather high reserve requirements, while others, notably Colorado, Illinois, and Florida, impose none at all. My research in this regard clearly demonstrates the competitive advantage of nonmember banks over national banks in Illinois (and presumably Illinois state-chartered member banks as well). This derives from the fact that cash reserves constitute a tax on the earnings of the bank on which they are imposed. The study demonstrates a significantly higher cash/deposit ratio for member banks than for nonmembers in Illinois.[7]

Finally, as referral to Table 1 indicates, banks are examined by both state and Federal authorities. Not only may Federal and state examination procedures vary; supervision in this respect varies among states as well.

The examination of banks involves, among other things, a periodic appraisal of bank assets and portfolio management. Individual assets in the bank's portfolio may be questioned by the examiners, portfolio policies criticized, and various degrees of pressure for reform imposed. The quality and quantity of examinations varies according to the general examination policies and "rules of thumb" adopted by the regulatory authorities in the several supervisory jurisdictions.

A single illustration of what may happen when two supervisory authorities differ in the regulation of bank portfolios will suffice to indicate a broad range of conflicts that exist in this area. In the early 1960s, the Comptroller of the Currency ruled that national banks could treat Federal Funds transactions as outright purchases and sales; the seller of Reserve Funds, therefore, was not restricted in the amount sold to another bank by the customary loan limit to a single *borrower,* ten percent of the bank's capital and surplus. The Federal Reserve Board ruled to the contrary, a ruling that was to apply to all member banks including national banks, holding that Federal Funds were to be treated as loans to a customer, and therefore subject to the one-borrower limitation. The donneybrook created considerable confusion for the banks that were selling Funds, although it soon became apparent that the latter would in practice adhere to the Federal Reserve's restrictive rather than the Comptroller's permissive ruling.[8]

---

[7] "Zero Reserve Requirements" (in preparation).

[8] If this result seems strange, one need only reflect on the power of the Federal Reserve System. The explanation, which cannot detain us further at this point, lies in this power. That bankers generally are not more aggressive in seeking their self-interest is also a story that must be told in detail elsewhere. Suffice it to say that regulated firms, protected by the regulators from competition and their own mistakes, may lose the killer instinct in much the same way as wolves have evolved into man's best friend.

To summarize the foregoing brief observations on the regulatory processes, banks are subject to a wide variety of regulatory authority, which is often the source of discrimination between banks even in the same competitive market area. The powers of a bank, its growth potential, its revenues and costs, and its service to the community are strongly affected by the regulatory jurisdiction to which it is subject. Banking is played under different rules, not only in widely separated regions, but also within the same market.

II. COMMERCIAL-BANKING MARKETS

The market for a bank's output, its loans and investments, may be international, national, regional, or local. Some very large banks, such as the Bank of America, Chase Manhattan, and the First National City Bank, operate in all of these sectors. Others, which are large enough to compete beyond purely local areas and yet too small to compete in the national and international arenas, serve a regional market, the extent of which may encompass one or more states.

The extent of a bank's market is a function of (1) the size of its capital funds, which determines its maximum loan to a single borrower, (2) the vigor and aggressiveness of its management within the above constraint, and (3) the legal constraints governing the geographical area of permissible branching.

Very large corporate borrowers seek bank funds in the national prime loan market. Since their borrowing requirements are very large, they can only be satisfied by those banks whose maxi-

mum loan (ten percent of bank capital and surplus) is also very large. Of the thousands of banks in the United States, only a few hundred compete for this business. Within this latter group, only a relative few are solely wholesale lenders; the large majority serve local small business needs, the local mortgage market and the local consumer loan market as well. These latter are designated as "department stores of finance."

At the other extreme, the vast majority of banks operate within a geographical periphery narrowly centered in the local community. In times past, more so than at present, each such bank thought of its market as a rigidly proscribed area spreading from its head office. Custom, tacit agreement, and more formal cartel arrangements, resulted in a division of the local loan market among the (usually) few competitor banks. Banks did not lend to borrowers outside their territory, and it was considered bad form at best and cutthroat competition at worst to violate the conventions. Regulatory agencies fostered this by looking unfavorably on new bank applications within the territories claimed by existing banks.[9]

These barriers to competition have been in the process of breaking down in the past ten years or so. The growth of branch banking and the intrusion into local markets of branches of large banks has hastened the trend toward more local banking competition and an expanding horizon for the operations of individual banks.[10] Moreover, management recently has been more aggressive in expanding the territory of banks, even where that has involved

---

[9] State laws also fostered the idea of protected franchises. For example, the New York law prevents the location of a branch of a New York City bank in any city of Nassau and Westchester counties that contains the home office of an existing bank. This protection will end, however, in 1976.

[10] For example, the expansion of New York City banks into Nassau county in the 1960s, previously referred to, led directly to the expansion of Franklin National, a Nassau-based bank, into New York City to meet that firm's growth goals.

stepping over traditional boundaries and into the implied spheres of influence of other banks. Banks that wish to grow more rapidly than the local economy allows have sought loans and deposits far afield from their former protected markets. The most vigorous of the latter type have come to serve broad regions of the United States; a bank in Kansas City, for example, may compete for business loans in St. Louis, in Chicago, and in Denver, as well as in its local metropolitan area.

The structure of markets and the nature of market competition is a broad and complex subject, which cannot be treated fully in the space we have available. It is useful to keep in mind, however, a few salient points concerning the banking industry of the United States. First, the industry, unlike most, is regulated by government authority and its structure and markets are strongly influenced by this regulation. Unlike other regulated industries, however, restriction of entry into banking is accompanied by neither specific rate (price) making[11] nor output regulation. Second, restraint of entry into the industry has fostered oligopolistic market structures in the market for some, although not all, banking services. Third, the application of antitrust laws to banking, and Federal merger legislation in the 1960s, have tended to freeze the existing banking structure into its present pattern.[12] Thus, while we may continue to have some increasing bank concentration, through the holding company device, this will come in the future from endogenous growth

of particular institutions and not from bank mergers, as it did in the period 1945–1965. These points are more fully treated in the selections which follow.

III. BANK-PORTFOLIO POLICIES

Finally, we must give recognition to the fact that a substantial amount of variation exists in the portfolio policies of individual banks. Our discussion here is of necessity general and brief, and only suggestive of the differences that exist between banks.

Loan and investment portfolios, as well as cash holdings, reflect (1) choices that have been made by bank management and (2) legal and regulatory proscriptions.

The legal and regulatory milieu in which a bank operates may influence (a) the amount of cash held relative to other assets, (b) the term structure of the loan and investment portfolios, (c) the specific instruments held in the investment portfolio (state laws usually provide that local government deposits be "backed" by a specified proportion of specified securities),[13] and (d) the kind of loans that the bank may legally make (e.g., Federal law limits the maturity of mortgage loans that National banks may acquire in their portfolios).

Within the legal and regulatory proscriptions and constraints, a bank exercises discretion with respect to the composition and quality of its assets. Thus, in addition to variations that can be ascribed to different regulatory environment, asset structures vary ac-

---

[11] The exceptions are ceilings imposed on some, but not all, bank prices (interest rates), under Regulation Q and state usury laws.

[12] This has had the somewhat paradoxical effect of preserving local competition while retarding the growth of regional and national competition. Under the present application of merger laws, it is unlikely that a merger could be consummated that substantially increased banking concentration in the *local* market, irrespective of the merger's potential impact of increasing regional or national competition.

[13] In the 1960's, the Comptroller and the Federal Reserve Board were at odds as to whether national banks could underwrite the bonds of local authorities that were unsecured by the general revenues of the state.

cording to bank preferences, philosophies, and market competition.

Within the banking industry, it is widely recognized that some banks are more conservatively managed than others, even within the same market. A conservatively managed bank will generally structure its portfolio toward liquid assets: cash, Treasury bills, and short-term business loans. A more aggressive institution will keep minimum cash balances; acquire longer-term investments; and assume a variety of loan risks, including term business loans—those with a maturity of one to ten years or more—unsecured consumer loans, and mortgages.

Banks also behave differently with respect to their deposit and capital inputs. Some, again conservative, display a liability structure that emphasizes traditional deposit forms and capital accounts. Others, in recent years, have evolved a wide range of both deposit and capital accounts, including certificates of indebtedness, consumer-type savings bonds, and loan-participation certificates on the deposit side; and debentures, unsecured capital notes, and preferred stock to augment traditional common-stock capital funds. In general, we find aggressive bank-portfolio policies associated with aggressive and imaginative management of the liability accounts.

A concluding observation is appropriate: While we have argued the position that a great amount of variation exists in commercial banking today, there appears to be a long-run tendency toward uniformity. Increased communication may partly account for this tendency; additionally, increased competition has tended to force the adoption of business practices and innovations on a wide scale. Specialization in banking seems to be losing ground and "full service banking" becoming an increasing fact as well as an advertising ploy. Even the regulatory and legal differences under which different banks conduct business are gradually diminishing.

Even so, it would appear likely that for some time to come the question mark we affixed to the title of these introductory remarks is appropriate. It is not true that a bank is a bank is a bank.

READING 8
ASSET MANAGEMENT AND COMMERCIAL BANK PORTFOLIO BEHAVIOR: THEORY AND PRACTICE

Leonall C. Andersen
and Albert E. Burger*

This paper reports the results of an investigation we have conducted regarding two aspects of commercial bank portfolio management. With regard to the first aspect, two alternative hypotheses regarding bank behavior are tested. These are the "accommodation principle" implied in the commercial loan theory of banking and the "profit maximization principle" implied in recent developments in bank portfolio theory and related research. The second aspect is an investigation into the proposition that there has been a significant change in bank portfolio behavior in recent years.*

Knowledge of the first aspect of commercial bank behavior is important for monetary management. The accommodation principle implies that the demand for bank loans determines bank portfolio behavior. On the other hand, the profit maximization principle implies that commercial bank responses to market forces determine their portfolio behavior. Expectations of bank response to actions of the Federal Reserve System differ according to which principle is accepted.

For example, under the accommodation principle, Federal Reserve open-market operations which slow growth in the reserve base could have little effect on growth in the volume of bank loans if the demand for such loans, at given interest rates, was expanding rapidly. Such would be the case if economic activity were expanding rapidly.

Source: Reprinted from *The Journal of Finance,* Vol. XXIV, No. 2, May, 1969.

* Editor's note: The second part of his study is not included in this selection.

Thus, loans could continue to rise at the previous rate or even to accelerate if demand should strengthen. Banks would tend to accommodate such demand by shifting out of investments. By comparison, in such circumstances of Federal Reserve restraint, profit maximization would induce banks to reduce the rate of growth of both loans and investments, at given interest rates, with loan growth continuing at its previous rate only if interest rates on loans rose relative to interest rates on investments.

Monetary authorities, when attempting to forecast the asset behavior of banks in response to a given change in monetary policy, must take into consideration empirical evidence bearing on these questions. If the central bank attempts to forecast bank behavior based on a set of relations estimated from past observations of dependent variables such as borrowings, excess reserves, and loans and a set of independent variables, and if the conditions under which these estimated relations are proposed to represent bank asset behavior no longer hold, then the preditcions of the response of commercial banks to monetary policy actions may be far from satisfactory. Furthermore, during different periods of time, banks may change their behavior, perhaps from accommodating business loan demand to responding more to market forces such as the relationship between short and long-term interest rates.

This report consists of three sections. First, recent literature and research into commercial bank asset behavior is surveyed with a view to delineating the accommodation and the profit maximization principles. Then, a model of bank asset behavior is constructed which provides the basis for testing these two principles. Next, the two rival hypotheses of bank asset behavior are tested.

I. REVIEW OF LITERATURE ON BANK ASSET BEHAVIOR

The study of commercial bank portfolio behavior is important for at least two major reasons:

1. Commercial bank portfolio behavior is an important explanatory factor for the magnitudes and changes in the magnitudes of the aggregate economic quantities of the money stock and bank credit.
2. At a less aggregate level, bank portfolio behavior is a key determinant of the cost and flow of credit to specific sectors of the economy.

For purposes of discussion, monetary theory is defined as the set of theories concerned with the influence of the quantity of money in the economic system, and monetary policy as policy employing the central bank's control of the stock of money as an instrument for achieving the objectives of general economic policy. If one believes that changes in the magnitude of the money stock are an important explanatory variable for changes in real output, employment, and prices which are the goals of economic policy, then the study of factors determining the money stock becomes of crucial importance. Especially, if one is interested in monetary policy, knowledge about the linkage between operations that may be performed by the monetary authorities and changes in the magnitudes of economic quantities such as the money stock and bank credit becomes primary.

Recent research in the field of monetary theory has shown that the magnitudes of the stocks of money and bank credit are determined jointly by the actions of the Federal Reserve, commercial banks, and the public.[1] The

Federal Reserve, by its actions alone, does not determine the magnitude of the money stock. The immediate impact of a Federal Reserve operation, such as a purchase or sale of Government securities, may be to increase or decrease the money stock. However, the equilibrium magnitude of the money stock is determined by the conjunction of the Federal Reserve action and the behavioral reactions of the commercial banks and the public to that action.

The behavioral responses of the banks and the public may be viewed as a portfolio adjustment process. The ability to predict the effect of a given action by the monetary authorities on the magnitudes of money and bank credit depends on being able to predict the behavioral responses of the banks and the public as they adjust their portfolios of financial and real assets.

In this section we present a summary review of some recent developments in the study of commercial bank portfolio behavior, incorporating the profit maximization principle. This summary is followed by a brief analysis of the accommodation principle. Due to limitation of space and the nature of the content of the rest of our article, we concentrate primarily on bank portfolio behavior as it affects the holdings of excess reserves, borrowings from Reserve banks, and the volume of loans outstanding.

IA. Profit Maximizing Principle

At the micro-level, the individual commercial bank is viewed as an economic unit whose goal is to maximize profits. The commercial bank holds a portfolio of assets and, given the char-

acteristics and distribution of its liabilities, the commercial bank attempts to structure its portfolio of assets in such a manner as to yield the greatest return subject to these constraints. The assets held by a bank may be divided into two broad classes, frequently called earning assets and non-earning assets. Earning assets are the two balance sheet items called loans and investments. Non-earning assets consist of the total reserves of the bank. Total reserves are then frequently partitioned into required reserves and excess reserves.

In most studies of bank portfolio behavior it is assumed that given such factors as the present and expected levels of market interest rates, loan demands and cash demands, the level of the discount rate, and actions by the Federal Reserve System, the individual commercial bank has a desired distribution of assets in its portfolio. If the existing distribution of assets held by the commercial bank is not the distribution desired, then the bank will attempt to adjust its portfolio of assets by increasing its holdings of some assets and decreasing its holdings of other assets.

Federal Reserve actions such as an open market purchase or sale of Government securities, a change in the legal reserve requirements on member bank demand and/or time deposits, or a change in the discount rate have their initial impacts in the commercial banking sector on total reserves. A purchase of Government securities by the Federal Reserve System leads to an increase in total reserves of the commercial banks. An increase in reserve requirements alters the composition of total reserves leading to an in-

---

[1] We might mention at this point that actions of the government sector, specifically actions by the Treasury in financing the debt, may enter as an explanatory variable in the actions of the monetary authorities. However, the actions of the monetary authorities determine the effect of a Treasury financing operation on the money stock.

crease in required reserves and a decrease in the actual level of excess reserves. A change in the discount rate alters the cost for member banks of borrowing reserves from the Federal Reserve Banks.

Given that, before the action by the Federal Reserve System, commercial banks were holding their desired distribution of assets, these actions by the monetary authorities lead to a portfolio adjustment process on the part of the individual banks. For example, if an individual bank finds its total reserves increased as a result of the purchase of securities from the public by the Federal Reserve System, the bank will no longer be holding its desired distribution of assets. The proportion of non-earning assets to earning assets will be greater than the desired level. The bank will have an incentive to expand its earning assets by extending additional loans and/or purchasing securities.[2]

Assuming that the proportion of assets held in the form of required reserves is determined by the existing legal reserve requirements against commercial bank demand and time deposits, a commercial bank faces the decision of allocating its portfolio of assets between earning assets (loans and investments) and non-earning assets (excess reserves). Having chosen the desired distribution between earning and non-earning assets the commercial bank then decides what portion of its non-earning assets to hold in the form of free reserves (excess reserves less borrowings from Reserve banks). For member banks this involves a decision as to the level of borrowings from the

Federal Reserves Banks they desire to maintain.

Given the dejure and de facto status of the majority of their liabilities, and given that the individual bank cannot predict with certainty future deposit flows, loan demands, interest rates, and actions by the monetary authorities, commercial banks desire to have a portion of their portfolio of assets represent a stock of liquidity to act as a buffer against changes in these factors. One form in which commercial banks may hold this stock of liquidity is excess reserves. Also available to banks are other assets, such as Treasury bills, which under most circumstances can be converted into cash with little loss of time or value, and unlike excess reserves yield an interest return to the bank. Also, member banks may borrow from Federal Reserve banks to meet reserve demands; and they also may acquire reserves in the Federal funds market.[3]

A considerable amount of research in the field of commercial bank portfolio behavior has been devoted to the question of what factors determine a banks desired holdings of excess reserves. As recent research has highlighted, there are definite costs to the individual commercial bank in adjusting its portfolio of assets to meet changes in deposit flows, loan demand, and actions by the Federal Reserve System.

Although excess reserves yield no interest return as do other assets, they implicitly have a positive yield for commercial banks. Excess reserves act as an immediate source of liquidity, and hence enable the individual bank to minimize the adjustment costs asso-

---

[2] Since interest rates are usually entered as an explanatory variable in bank demand functions for assets, the interest rate impact of the open market operation will also affect the adjustment process.

[3] The difference between these two sources of reserves is that by borrowing from the Federal Reserve Banks total reserves of all commercial banks may be increased, while by borrowing in the Federal funds market reserves of the borrowing bank are increased and reserves of the lending bank are decreased with no change in total reserves of the system.

ciated with restructuring its portfolio. Commercial banks desired holdings of excess reserves are postulated to depend on (1) the yield on Treasury bills which are the main alternative to holding excess reserves for liquidity purposes and hence represents the primary opportunity cost of excess reserves, and (2) the adjustment costs involved in restructuring the banks portfolio. Such adjustment costs are the costs of alternative sources of funds to cover reserve demands. The primary alternative sources of short-term funds are borrowings from Federal Reserve banks and borrowings in the Federal funds market. Recent research by Peter Frost indicates that banks will permit their holdings of excess reserves to fluctuate within certain limits and adjust their holdings only when the return from doing so exceeds the potential cost of not making the adjustment.[4]

Sometimes the Federal Reserve discount rate is used as a proxy for the adjustment cost. However, as pointed out by several authors, the actual level of the discount rate may not fully represent the actual cost to a member bank of using this means to make adjustments in its portfolio.[5] Federal Reserve banks do not always set the discount rate and then allow member banks to determine the volume of the borrowings at that rate. They also "administer" the discount window and subject the use of borrowings of member banks to careful surveillance. This so-called "discipline of the discount window" has probably at times made the cost of borrowing from Reserve banks less attractive and hence raised the implicit return to commercial banks from holding excess reserves.[6]

Recent research by Stephen Goldfeld and Edward Kane has brought into question the assumption that all banks react in the same manner to changes in factors such as short-term market interest rates, the discount rate, availability of reserves and new loan demand. Goldfeld investigated commercial bank portfolio behavior using a stock adjustment model.[7] He fitted the structural model with quarterly, seasonally adjusted time series data from the third quarter of 1950 to the second quarter of 1962. Goldfeld concluded that for both country and city member banks the major determinants of excess reserve holdings appeared to be interest rate considerations (the differential between the bill rate and the discount rate) and changes in the availability of reserves (as measured by a potential-deposit variable). However, the portfolio responses of the two classes of banks to changes in interest rates, deposit flows and new loan demand were markedly different. In the management of excess reserves the city bank sector was found to be more responsive to interest rate considerations than country banks. With respect to changes in borrowings to meet new loan demand, Goldfeld found that city banks increased their borrowings by

[4] Peter Frost, *Banks' Demand for Excess Reserves*, unpublished UCLA dissertation, 1966, University Microfilms: Ann Arbor, pp. XIV–XV, 279–287.

[5] See Stephen Goldfeld and Edward Kane, "Determinants of Member Bank Borrowing: An Econometric Study," *Journal of Finance*, September, 1966, pp. 499–514; and Murray E. Polakoff and William L. Silber, "Reluctance and Member-Bank Borrowing: Additional Evidence," *Journal of Finance*, March, 1967, pp. 88–92.

[6] The effect of Federal Reserve surveillance is extremely difficult to quantify. However, the existence of periods such as the middle of 1966, when the spread between the discount rate and the Federal funds rate rapidly widened while member bank borrowings did not increase, lends some credulence to the assertion of the existence of such an effect.

[7] Stephen Goldfeld, *Commercial Bank Behavior and Economic Activity: A Structural Study of Monetary Policy in the Postwar United States*, Amsterdam: New Holland Publishing Co., 1966.

$12 for each $100 of new loan demand while country banks borrowings rose only about $6 per $100.[8]

Kane and Goldfeld also estimated a model of member bank borrowing from Reserve Banks.[9] Banks were assumed to maximize utility which was postulated to be a function of the cost of acquiring reserves and borrowing. Utility declines as this cost of borrowing rises. Kane and Goldfeld suggest that, following an exogenous disturbance, banks may effect desired changes in their security portfolios through a series of partial adjustments. In the short-run a bank may prefer to borrow from the Federal Reserve rather than immediately liquidating its securities. Hence, banks may borrow more in the short-run than a static model would imply. They estimated the dynamic version of their model using weekly data on reserves and borrowings for four member bank categories from July, 1953 through December, 1965. The results using both seasonally adjusted and unadjusted data supported the importance of a distributed lag response. Also, they found that the speed of portfolio adjustment for country banks was slower than the speed of city bank portfolio adjustment.[10]

IB. Accommodation Principle

The accommodation principle of commercial bank behavior stems from an older concept of the proper role of banking in economic life. This older concept is known as the "commercial loan theory" or the "real bills doctrine" of commercial banking. According to this theory bank earning assets should be limited to short-term, self-liquidating loans related to the production and distribution of goods and services. Proper banking practice is to accommodate the "legitimate credit demands" of business, commerce, and agriculture.

This principle of banking is imbedded in the Federal Reserve Act.[11] Accordingly, the accommodation principle has been used as a basis for Federal Reserve supervision of banks, eligibility requirements for collateral for borrowing from Reserve banks, and Federal Reserve collateral for its issue of currency.

The accommodation principle has also played an important role in monetary management. The real bills debate over the proper types of securities for Federal Reserve open-market transactions points to the importance given this principle by monetary authorities.

The accommodation principle holds that commercial banks should primarily make business loans and agricultural production loans. The use of the term "accommodation" implies that the *demand* for such loans would mainly determine bank behavior regarding borrowing from Reserve banks, holdings of excess reserves, and the division of earning assets between loans and investments.[12] Thus, the response of demand for loans to such economic vari-

---

[8] Goldfeld, pp. 149–152.

[9] Goldfeld and Kane, *op. cit.,* pp. 499–514.

[10] Kane and Goldfeld, p. 512.

[11] See Clifton B. Luttrell, "Member Bank Borrowing: Its Origin and Function," *Quarterly Review of Economics and Business,* Bureau of Economic and Business Research, University of Illinois, Autumn, 1968, pp. 56–65.

[12] Some discussions of the Federal Reserve–M.I.T. Econometric Model seem to indicate that an accommodation hypothesis of bank lending behavior was assumed in constructing the model. For example, "Banks are assumed to accommodate short-run changes in loan demand by their business customers partly by changing their free reserve position." Frank de Leeuw and Edward Gramlich "The Federal Reserve–M.I.T. Econometric Model," *Federal Reserve Bulletin,* January, 1968, p. 14. Also see Robert Rasche and Harold Shapiro, "The F.R.B.–M.I.T. Econometric Model: Its Special Features," *American Economic Review,* May, 1968, p. 139, and footnote 19.

ables as interest rates and economic activity would also determine bank behavior regarding the above mentioned balance sheet accounts.

II. MODEL OF BANKING PORTFOLIO BEHAVIOR

Bank behavior regarding assets is viewed in this paper as a process of allocating a given amount of wealth (defined as total deposits) between nonearning assets (required and excess reserves) and earning assets (loans and investments). Once this allocation is determined, earning assets are allocated between loans and investments. We now proceed to set forth the factors influencing bank behavior with regard to this allocation process.

Since this study is concerned only with the behavior of member banks of the Federal Reserve System, the special considerations regarding the reserve requirements imposed on these banks will be applied. The following discussion is based on the assumption that banks are profit maximizers. Their behavior based on the accommodation principle will be presented later. Aggregate member bank behavior is used in the remainder of this article.

IIA. Bank Behavior under the Profit Maximizing Principle

TOTAL DEPOSITS

Member bank total deposits (D) are constrained by their total reserves (deposits at Reserve banks and vault cash) and the average reserve requirement ratio. This relation may be expressed by the following identity:

$$D = \frac{1}{r} R$$

In the above expression, R is member bank total reserves and r is the average reserve requirement ratio. R consists of nonborrowed reserves (NB)

and borrowings from Reserve banks (B). The term r is the average reserve requirement which takes into consideration the distribution of deposits between demand and time accounts and between reserve city and country banks.

The identity may be expanded to:

$$D = \frac{1}{r} (NB + B)$$

With r constant, borrowing from Reserve banks or a result of the Federal Reserve System increasing nonborrowed reserves, member banks as a group may expand their deposits, thereby allowing them to have more earning assets.

BORROWING

Member bank borrowing from Reserve banks, although relatively small compared with NB, is an important aspect of bank behavior. It is a liability item which allows banks some flexiblity in their asset management within the constraint imposed by nonborrowed reserves.

The desired level of borrowings from Reserve banks (B*) is postulated as follows:

$$B^* = f_1 (i_s, i_d, i_F, C_b, D)$$

In this relationship, i_s is the short-term interest rate, i_d the Federal Reserve discount rate, i_F the federal funds rate, and C_b other costs of borrowing. B* is postulated to be positively related to i_s, i_F, and D and negatively related to i_d, and C_b.

EXCESS RESERVES

Holdings of excess reserves, other things constant, results in holdings of fewer earning assets; therefore banks hold excess reserves for returns other than earnings. Holdings of excess reserves constitute a buffer stock which allows banks to meet sudden withdrawals of deposits without requiring a reduction in earning assets. The desired level of excess reserves (ER*) is given by the following function:

$$ER^* = f_2 \ (i_s, i_d, i_L, C_{er}, D)$$

ER* is postulated to be negatively related to i_s and i_L and positively related to D, i_d, and C_{er} (costs of managing excess reserves).

LOANS

Earning assets in the form of bank loans consist mainly of loans to businesses, households, and financial institutions. The desired level of loans (L*) is given by the following relationship:

$$L^* = f_3 \ (s, i_d, i_L, C_l, D)$$

L* is postulated to be negatively related to i_L and i_d, and C_l (transactions costs of lending) and positively related to i_s and D.

INVESTMENTS

Earning assets classified as investments consist mainly of holdings of government securities. The desired level (I*) is expressed as:

$$I^* = f_4 \ (i_s, i_d, i_L, C_l, D)$$

Investments are considered a residual item in this study; however, I* is postulated to be negatively related to i_s and i_d, and C_l (transaction costs of investments) and positively related to i_L and D.

IIB. Bank Behavior under Accommodation Principle

Under the accommodation principle, bank behavior would mainly reflect the demand of customers for loans. For example, a rise in the demand for loans from banks (supply of this form of earning asset) would be met, subject to the deposit constraint, by reductions in investments and excess reserves and an increase in borrowings from Reserve banks. This implies that the factors in-fluencing the demand for bank loans affect L*, I*, ER*, and B*.

The following equation is postulated as determining the supply of loans (viewed as earning assets of banks):

$$L^* = g \ (i_s, i_L, GNP, W)$$

L* is postulated to be negatively related to i_s and positively related to i_L, the level of economic activity (GNP), and to private nonbank wealth (W). These signs are the ones commonly developed on the basis of business maximization of profits and household maximization of satisfaction, subject to wealth and income constraints.

As stated above, the function g would be the relevant one for examining bank behavior under the accommodation principle. Incorporation of this principle into the functions for B*, ER*, L*, and I* in place of the profit maximization principle, introduces GNP and W into each function and reverses the signs for i_s in the B*, ER*, L* equations, and the sign for i_L in the L* equation.

IIC. Stock Adjustment Model

A stock adjustment framework is used as the basis of constructing the model of bank portfolio behavior. It is assumed that banks have a desired level of each of the balance sheet items under consideration (B*, ER*, L*, and I*) and that the stock of the item held is changed at a certain rate to close the gap between the actual and the desired level. This may be expressed as two equivalent equations:

$$X_t - X_{t-1} = \lambda (X^*_t - X_{t-1})$$

$$X_t = \lambda X^*_t + (1 - \lambda) X_{t-1}$$

In the above equation, X_t is the stock on hand at time (t); X^*_t is the desired stock, X_{t-1} is the stock in the previous period; and λ is a speed of adjustment coefficient. The desired stock depends on the economic factors spelled out in the preceding discussion. The speed of adjustment coefficient may range from zero to plus one. The closer it is to one, the faster the speed of adjustment.

III. TESTING TWO RIVAL HYPOTHESES

IIIA. Two Rival Hypotheses

Frequently, policymakers are confronted with conflicting policy advice. For example, one group of policy advisers starting from the assumption that banks passively accommodate business loan demand might predict one set of consequences for a policy action taken by the monetary authorities. Another group of advisers, assuming that banks behave as profit maximizers, might predict an alternative result for the same policy action. The policy results predicted by both policy advisers depends on whether their initial assumptions about bank portfolio behavior do in fact represent the behavior reactions of commercial banks.[13]

In this section we provide evidence on these two alternative assumptions about bank portfolio behavior. To compare the two hypotheses we first state each hypothesis so that it can be confronted with empirical evidence. Also, the two hypotheses must be stated in such a form that the available empirical evidence can discriminate between them. They must not, however, be formulated so that the empirical evidence is in good agreement with both. In Section IIIB the regression equations used in the formulation of the two hypotheses are presented. As we have formulated the two proposed explanations of commercial bank portfolio behavior, each of the two alternative hypotheses implies certain signs for the coefficients in the regression equations. These signs are presented in Exhibit I and discussed in Section IIIC. The implied signs are used as the basis for testing the hypotheses.

IIIB. Estimation Procedures

Multiple regression analysis, using monthly observations for the period 1953–1967, is used to determine which of the two alternative explanations of commercial bank asset behavior, i.e., the profit-maximization or accommodation principle, is in better agreement with the empirical evidence. Lack of suitable data resulted in dropping the wealth variable and variables reflecting transactions and other non-interest costs. Also, the Federal funds rate was omitted. Another variable, the ratio of country bank deposits (DCB) to total member bank deposits was introduced to take into consideration the possibility of differences in behavior between classes of member banks.

It was assumed that each function is homogenous with regard to deposits; hence, each variable measured in dollars was divided by D. The stock adjustment model thus becomes one involving the closing of a discrepancy between desired and actual ratios.

$$\frac{B}{D} = f_1' \left(i_s, i_d, i_L, \frac{GNP}{D}, \frac{DCB}{D}, \left[\frac{B}{D}\right]_{-1} \right)$$

$$\frac{ER}{D} = f_2' \left(i_s, i_d, i_L, \frac{GNP}{D}, \frac{DCB}{D}, \left[\frac{ER}{D}\right]_{-1} \right)$$

$$\frac{L}{D} = f_3' \left(i_s, i_d, i_L, \frac{GNP}{D}, \frac{DCB}{D}, \left[\frac{L}{D}\right]_{-1} \right)$$

In the above equations, all variables are for the current period except the lagged ratios. All of the variables are seasonally adjusted monthly averages. Monthly data for GNP was developed by a straight line interpolation of quarterly GNP centered on the mid-month of each quarter. The 91-day Treasury bill rate was used as a proxy for the

---

[13] See Albert E. Burger and Leonall C. Andersen, "The Development of Explanatory Economic Hypotheses for Monetary Management," *Southern Journal of Business* (forthcoming).

TABLE 1

REGRESSION RESULTS—MEMBER BANK BEHAVIOR BORROWED RESERVES, EXCESS RESERVES, AND LOANS (VARIABLES IN NATURAL LOGARITHMS)[a]

	Intercept	i_S	i_L	i_d	GNP/D	DCB/D	Lagged Dependent Variable	Standard Error	R^2
B/D									
1953–1960	−.715	1.717*	−1.047*	−.709*	−3.434	−2.499	.517*	.197	.94
		(.246)	(.399)	(.235)	(1.549)	(3.958)	(.069)		
1961–1967	−14.660	1.557*	−1.978	.174	1.879	−12.034	.622*	.268	.93
		(.632)	(1.032)	(.738)	(2.937)	(6.260)	(.122)		
ER/D									
1953–1960	.131	−.103	−.289*	.118	−.271	.956	.746*	.079	.89
		(.063)	(.141)	(.095)	(.849)	(1.585)	(.079)		
1961–1967	−10.704	−1.246*	−.286	.319	5.258*	−.505	.040	.094	.93
		(.223)	(.182)	(.240)	(1.033)	(2.213)	(.112)		
L/D									
1953–1960	.702	0.44*	−.041*	−.043*	−.169	.479*	1.006*	.007	.99
		(.009)	(.015)	(.011)	(1.36)	(.176)	(.033)		
1961–1967	−.038	.033*	−.019*	.015	−.008	.040	.878*	.004	.99
		(.007)	(.007)	(.013)	(0.36)	(.098)	(.030)		

[a] Numbers in parenthesis are standard errors of the regression coefficients.
* Statistically significant at 5 per cent level.

short-term interest rate, and the corporate Aaa bond rate was used for the long-term interest rate. Regressions were run using natural logarithms, thereby providing elasticity estimates. Two variables, i_S and i_L, were considered endogenous within a more complete model of bank behavior; hence, the two-stage least-squares estimation procedure was used.[14]

The regression results are reported in Table 1. The regression equations were run for the entire period 1953 through 1967. However, application of the Chow test indicated a significant structural change between the periods

1953–1960 and 1961–1967. The F-value of the Chow test was 2.83 for B/D, 9.98 for ER/D, and 3.01 for L/D. All of these values are statistically significant at the 5 per cent level. Therefore, the observation period 1953–1967 was split into two periods, 1953–1960 and 1961–1967. Only the results of the regressions for the separate periods are reported in Table 1.

IIIC. Expected Signs of the Regression Coefficients

Following the above discussions, Exhibit 1 presents the expected signs of the coefficients of the independent

---

[14] A complete model includes stock adjustment equations for demand deposits held by the public, currency in the hands of the public, and the public's holdings of time deposits. Also, there are balance sheet identities for demand deposits held by the public and bank total earning assets. In addition to the exogenous variables in the equations presented above, there are the lagged stocks of demand deposits, time deposits, and currency. Exogenous variables derived from the balance sheet identities include the factors affecting non-borrowed reserves and average reserve requirements for member banks. The balance sheet identity for private demand deposits is developed in Leonall C. Andersen's, "A Study of Factors Affecting the Money Stock: Phase One," *Staff Economic Studies,* Board of Governors of the Federal Reserve System, October 1965. The identity for earning assets is a slight alteration of the private demand deposit one.

EXHIBIT 1

	i_s	i_L	$\dfrac{GNP}{D}$
Profit—Maximizing Hypothesis			
$\dfrac{B}{D}$			
Expected sign	+	+, 0	0
Sign of Regression Coefficient			
1953–1960	+	−	0
1961–1967	+	0	0
$\dfrac{ER}{D}$			
Expected sign	−	−	0
Sign of Regression Coefficient			
1953–1960	0	−	0
1961–1967	−	0	+
$\dfrac{L}{D}$			
Expected sign	+	−	0
Sign of Regression Coefficient			
1953–1960	+	−	0
1961–1967	+	−	0
Accommodation Hypothesis			
$\dfrac{B}{D}$			
Expected sign	−	+, 0	+
Sign of Regression Coefficient			
1953–1960	+	−	0
1961–1967	+	0	0
$\dfrac{ER}{D}$			
Expected sign	+	−	−
Sign of Regression Coefficient			
1953–1960	0	−	0
1961–1967	−	0	+
$\dfrac{L}{D}$			
Expected sign	−	+	+
Sign of Regression Coefficient			
1953–1960	+	−	0
1961–1967	+	−	0

variables considered most relevant for the testing of the two hypotheses about commercial bank asset behavior. These variables are i_s, i_L, and GNP/D.

Exhibit I also presents the calculated signs of the regression coefficients. If the calculated t-value of a regression coefficient was not significant at the 5 per cent level, a zero value for that coefficient is entered in this table.

An examination of Exhibit I reveals that the results of the regression analysis do not support the hypothesis that the factors influencing the demand for bank loans are the primary determinants of bank asset behavior. In neither period is it observed that bank behavior responds in the manner described by the hypothesis that banks passively accommodate the demand for bank credit. However, the results tend to support the hypothesis that bank behavior responds to changes in i_S, i_L, and GNP/D in a manner that is consistent with the hypothesis that banks attempt to manage their asset portfolios in a way that is consistent with a profit maximizing explanation of commercial bank behavior.

In both periods, as the short-term interest rate rises, banks respond by increasing the ratio of loans to deposits. As the long-term interest rate rises, making investments more attractive relative to loans, banks restructure their asset portfolios by reducing the proportion of loans to investments in their portfolios. Lending behavior is not directly related to changes in GNP. These findings are consistent with the profit maximization hypothesis.

In both periods, as the opportunity cost of holding excess reserves increases (i.e., market interest rates rise), we find that banks respond by decreasing their holdings of excess reserves relative to deposits. This behavior is consistent with profit maximization. In the first period the long-term rate of interest is more important than the short-term rate in determining the behavior of ER/D, in the more recent period the roles of the interest rates are reversed and the short-term rate becomes a more important factor in determining changes in ER/D. In the period 1953–1960 our regression results show that GNP/D does not enter as a significant influence on banks' excess reserves to deposit ratio. In the period 1961–1967, GNP/D appears as a significant influence on excess reserve behavior. The positive sign on the coefficient of GNP/D, indicating an increase in excess reserves given an increase in GNP, is clearly not in good agreement with the expected sign under the accommodation hypothesis. However, such a large positive influence on excess reserve behavior is also surprising given the expected sign of the coefficeint under the profit-maximizing hypothesis of bank asset behavior.

With respect to borrowing behavior, we find that in both periods banks are sensitive to changes in interest rates in a manner consistent with the profit maximization hypothesis. A rise in short-term interest rates in both periods leads to a rise in borrowings by member banks from Reserve banks. Tentatively, these results indicate that banks may not be unaware of the profit opportunities inherent in a situation where the discount rate lags a rise in the short-term rate. In the period 1953–1960, as the discount rate rises, member banks reduce their ratio of borrowings to deposits. In the latter period, 1961–1967, our statistical tests indicate that the coefficient for i_d is not statistically different from zero. This may reflect the development of alternative sources of short-term funds in the more recent period. In neither period do we find that the independent variable GNP/D enters as a significant influence on commercial bank borrowing behavior.

READING 9

RESERVE ADJUSTMENTS OF THE EIGHT MAJOR NEW YORK CITY BANKS DURING 1966

Delores P. Lynn

I. INTRODUCTION

By the end of 1965 the economy had already accomplished an expansion unmatched for vigor or endurance by any other business upswing of the post-World War II period. The margin of unused productive capacity and manpower resources had narrowed considerably, and inflationary tendencies were on the rise. During the ensuing nine months, demand pressures in the economy falied to abate. Business expenditures on plant and equipment accelerated further, spending on services by states and municipalities rose, and Federal government outlays increased sharply as a result of an escalation of the Vietnam conflict and an expansion of domestic social programs. Pressures in the credit markets were intensified through September 1966 as the corporate and government sectors competed for funds in an atmosphere of increasing monetary restraint. Capital market yields soared to their highest levels in more than three decades, and demands made on the commercial banking system induced near-crisis conditions. Functioning in their traditional role of major supplier of business credit to the nation, the eight large New York City money market banks[1] were the focal point of these pressures.

II. SOURCES OF PRESSURE ON THE NEW YORK CITY MONEY MARKET BANKS

The heavy corporate demands for bank credit during 1966 reflected to a

Source: Staff Study prepared for the Treasury-Federal Reserve Study of the Government Securities Market (revised, 1968).

[1] Chase Manhattan Bank, First National City Bank, Manufacturers Hanover Trust Co., Chemical Bank New York Trust Co., Morgan Guaranty Trust Co., Bankers Trust Co., Irving Trust Co., and Marine Midland Grace Trust Co.

considerable degree an acceleration in the payment schedules for corporate Federal income taxes and employees' withheld income and social security taxes, which increased corporate working capital requirements in 1966 by an estimated $4.1 billion. These sharply expanded needs for funds occurred at a time when corporate liquidity was at low ebb and the volume of internally-generated cash flow had begun to shrink. Throughout the economic expansion that began in 1961, corporations had allowed their holdings of cash and liquid assets to run down to minimum levels in order to expand productive capacity, build up inventories, and acquire a very large volume of trade receivables. After the first quarter of 1966, moreover, the rapid growth of corporate profits came to a halt. As 1966 progressed, corporations' projections of their own cash flows proved increasingly overoptimistic in the light of actual developments, and the need for additional bank borrowing rose accordingly.

In addition to increased working capital needs of corporations, several other factors exerted pressure on the City banks during 1966. A portion of the growing number of requests for business loans represented a spillover of demand from the capital markets. With yields on new bond flotations moving rapidly to three-decade highs, many corporations sought to avoid expensive long-term borrowing by financing investment outlays temporarily at relatively favorable bank lending rates. Secondly, life insurance companies and savings banks requested loans, under lines of credit that had seldom been used in the past, in order to take up prior investment commitments. Cash inflows at both these types of financial intermediaries were seriously diminished during 1966 by the process of *disintermediation* set in motion by the sharp increase in market yields on securities relative to those available on institutional savings. Moreover, life insurance companies were subjected to heavy cash withdrawals through borrowing by policyholders at low contractual rates of interest, and for other related reasons, while savings banks experienced some loss of savings to the commercial banks, which were permitted to pay higher rates of interest on certain types of accounts.

Finally, requests for bank accommodation by businesses anticpating further interest rate increases were a constant and significant source of pressure on the banks. Throughout the first three quarters of 1966, banks were deluged with requests for business loans that were generated not only by specific investment projects or working capital needs, but also by a strong desire to obtain an adequate liquidity margin for possible future needs. In borrowing for anticipatory purposes, many businesses activated lines of credit that had been dormant for long periods in the past. Equally symptomatic of the spreading uncertainties regarding the future cost and availability of credit were the large-scale attempts by corporations to obtain additional bank lines of credit, increases in existing lines, and conversions of existing lines into formal, legally binding commitments for revolving credits or term loans in exchange for the payment of a customary commitment fee.

The prevailing belief during this period that interest rates must continue to head upward was caused by the increasing congestion in the capital markets, mounting demands for credit at commercial banks, and a step-up in military activity in Vietnam. The mood of pessimism was reinforced by the absence of fiscal measures to restrain inflation and its implication for monetary policy.

III. MONETARY POLICY ACTIONS DURING THE 1966 BOOM

Between the end of 1965 and September 1966, the Federal Reserve System utilized all of the instruments of general monetary control and also attempted to apply selective monetary pressures in its efforts to brake the boom. In December 1965 the discount rate was raised from 4 per cent to 4½ per cent, signaling a shift from the mild restraint that had prevailed during most of 1965 to a more positively restrictive policy. This increase brought the discount rate temporarily into line with other money market rates, which had been moving up rapidly. In the strong upward surge of interest rates that followed, however, the discount rate was left far behind the market. In order to avoid the possibility of a further interest rate escalation, the System refrained from raising the discount rate again in 1966, but continued to scrutinize member bank borrowings carefully as requests at the discount window mounted.

Subsequent to the discount rate change in December 1965, gradually increasing pressure was applied to member bank reserve positions through System open market operations, and aggregate net borrowed reserves of the banking system rose steadily from about $100 million in the final 1965 week to nearly $600 million in the last week of September 1966. Reserve requirements against time deposits other than savings accounts were raised to the statutory ceiling of 6 per cent in two increases of one percentage point each, the first effective in July and the second in September. Throughout the period of rising credit demands, officials of the System expressed increasing concern over the inflationary threat in the economy and the urgent need for credit restraint. Moral suasion took the form of periodic informal counsel-ing of member banks by officers of the individual Reserve Banks as well as public speeches and statements of System officials. Member banks were urged to curtail their lending and to become more selective in granting loans so as to avoid extending credit for speculative ventures, for corporate acquisitions, or for other non-productive purposes.

Maintaining the 5½ per cent interest rate ceiling on large-denomination negotiable certificates of deposit (C/D's), in the face of a sharp increase in yields on competing types of money market instruments, was one important way in which the System attempted to restrain the growth of bank credit during 1966. In refraining from raising the C/D rate ceiling, the System sought not only to affect the availability of bank credit but also to avoid stimulating further upward interest rate adjustments in the credit markets, and, thereby, to alleviate some of the pressure on mutual savings banks resulting from disintermediation. By July, the existing C/D rate ceiling posed a serious threat to the ability of the money market banks to attract new funds. Since 1961, when it first began to become an important outlet for surplus funds of corporations and other large investors, the C/D had been a major source of new funds for commercial banks, particularly the New York money market institutions. Although the rates payable on these instruments had always been subject to regulation, the ceiling under Regulation Q had been adjusted upward whenever necessary by the System in response to changes in other market rates of interest. The last such adjustment had been made in December 1965, simultaneous with the increase in the discount rate.

The accelerating business demands for credit were regarded by the System as the most threatening single element in the bank credit picture. The growing apprehension within the System over the strength of bank business lending was eventually made public in a letter issued by the System to member banks on September 1, near the peak of the financial market pressures. In this letter, which called attention to the 20 per cent annual growth rate in bank business loans over the first eight months of 1966, the System stated that "Federal Reserve credit assistance to member banks to meet appropriate seasonal or emergency needs . . . will continue to be available as in the past" and that "a greater share of member bank adjustments should take the form of moderation in the rate of expansion of loans, and particularly business loans." The letter warned that this goal would be kept in mind by the individual Reserve Banks in granting credit at the discount window and, at the same time, it offered the privilege of discount accommodation for extended periods of time to those banks cooperating in achieving this goal. The September 1 letter attracted much comment and gave rise to various interpretations. In the meantime, officers of the individual Reserve Banks continued to examine carefully trends in loans, investments, deposits and borrowings of banks that were problem or potential problem borrowers.

IV. LIQUIDITY OF THE MONEY MARKET BANKS AT THE OPENING OF 1966

A lion's share of the pressure on the banking system resulting from the combination of excessive credit demands and monetary restraint during 1966 fell on the eight large money market banks in New York City. Over the post-World War II period, the role of the New York City banks as a major supplier of business credit had hardly diminished, despite the more rapid economic growth of many regions out-side the industrial northeast and mid-Atlantic states. In 1966, the large New York City banks held about 29 per cent of total business loans outstanding at all member banks, only a slightly lesser share than the 31 per cent in 1946. Some explanation for the continued prominence of the New York City banks in business lending may lie in the widespread trend toward the integration of industry during the postwar period through mergers and consolidations. With the substantial increase in the relative size of individual business units, the City banks, possessing unusually large legal lending limits, have remained almost uniquely capable of accommodating the nation's prime borrowers. They may also have continued to be regarded by corporate business, in general, as an unfailing source of funds during periods of credit stringency.

In contrast, resources of the major New York City banks have shown a distinct tendency to decline relatively during the same era. Between 1946 and 1959, the City banks' share in total deposits of all member banks declined from 22 per cent to less than 17 per cent. Although it rose temporarily to 20 per cent during the years 1960–65 through the aggressive promotion of negotiable C/D's, this share fell to less than 18 per cent by the end of 1966 as a result of a sharp decline in C/D liabilities.

The decline in the ability of the money market banks to attract funds by means other than the issuance of negotiable certificates of deposit appears to be a secular phenomenon directly related to a revolution in the management of corporate funds that has been taking place over the postwar period. Throughout this era of generally restrictive monetary policy and rising interest rates, corporate financial managers have become increasingly aware of the cost of holding uninvested cash and of the possibility of simultaneously pursuing the goals of liquidity, safety, and income. Consequently, more corporations now hold demand balances with commercial banks to minimum working levels and invest surplus cash in a widened array of a high-quality money market instruments. During 1966, however, the banks generally demanded larger compensating balances when making loans to corporations. Although corporate programs to economize cash have had an impact throughout the banking system, their effect has been more severe at the money market banks in New York City which have traditionally relied on corporate demand deposits as a major source of loanable funds. While the negotiable C/D has enabled the major New York City banks, in effect, to recoup some portion of corporate funds previously lost to the money market. it represents an extremely volatile and expensive source of funds for these institutions. On balance, it appears that demands for loan accommodation at the City banks have tended to increase faster than the means to satisfy these demands.

The eight New York City money market banks were, at the end of 1965, less well-equipped to handle an oncoming barrage of credit requests than they had been at any previous time during the postwar period. Over the course of the cyclical expansion begun early in 1961, these banks had allowed their liquidity to fall to a historically low level. By the end of 1965, the loan-to-deposit ratio of the eight institutions, as a group, had risen to 73 per cent, compared with 63 per cent for all commercial banks. The New York City money market banks entered 1966 with their liquidity at unprecedently low levels and with a very large proportion of their deposits rather precariously

held; more specifically, highly volatile negotiable certificates of deposit accounted for nearly one-sixth of the total.

V. SOURCES OF NEW LOANABLE FUNDS

The New York City money market banks responded to the acceleration of credit demands in 1966 primarily through intensive efforts to maximize their ability to meet these demands and, secondarily, through the adoption of programs to ration demands and to scale down lending operations. At the start of the year, the negotiable certificate of deposit promised to be the major source of loanable funds for these institutions, as it had been in 1965. The maximum interest rate payable on time deposits under Regulation Q had just been raised (in December 1965, simultaneously with the discount rate increase) to a flat 5½ per cent for all maturities over 30 days, from former rates of 4 per cent on 30- to 89-day maturities and 4½ per cent on maturities of 90 days or more. The 1 to 1½ percentage point increase in the rate ceiling had restored the banks to a favorable competitive position relative to other issuers of money market instruments and had apparently allowed them ample maneuvering room in their efforts to attract funds.

As a result of the rapid upward movement in money market rates beginning early in 1966, however, the City banks raised C/D offering rates frequently, attaining the new ceiling rate within a fairly short time. As early as March, one New York City bank posted the ceiling rate of 5½ per cent on the 9- to 12-month maturity category of C/D's. Other City banks soon joined in the move to the ceiling by raising rates first on the longest maturity and then on progressively shorter maturities. By the beginning of August, an offering rate of 5½ per cent was in effect "across the board" at most New York money market banks.

Late in August, however, the negotiable C/D, except in the shortest maturity category, had little appeal for investors. Money market rates (discount basis) had risen to 5⅞ per cent on prime four- to six-month commercial paper, 5¾ per cent on 90-day bankers' acceptances, 5⅝ per cent on three- to six-month directly placed finance company paper, and about 5 per cent and 5.40 per cent, respectively, on three- and six-month Treasury bills. These rates were equivalent to investment yields ranging upward from about 5.14 per cent and 5.63 per cent, respectively, on three- and six-month Treasury bills to 6.10 per cent on prime commercial paper, compared with the 5½ per cent yield on C/D's. Subsequently yields increased further, through mid-September in the case of Treasury bills and through mid-October in the case of commercial paper; briefly during the fall, three-month Treasury bills, as well as the longer bill maturities, enjoyed a yield advantage over C/D's. Yields on commercial and finance company paper remained stable at their peak levels through the end of the year, while market yields on Treasury bills and on bankers' acceptances declined after reaching their respective peaks in mid-September and late November. Nevertheless, the longer Treasury bill maturities maintained their yield advantage relative to C/D's until the latter part of November and bankers' acceptances, along with commercial paper, continued to yield higher than C/D's through the year-end. Thus, despite a general easing of market tensions in early fall, the negotiable C/D did not become a competitive money market instrument again until just before the turn of the year.

Because of the changing structure of money market rates, the C/D performed very poorly during 1966 as a magnet for new loanable funds, contrary to indications at the end of 1965. As Chart 1 shows, this instrument drew a negligible sum into the City banks during the first eight months of the year in spite of the frequent and substantial upward rate adjustments. Increases in offering rates during January and February did attract some new money, but further increases were necessary in March in order to stem the unfavorable tide of net C/D redemptions that developed in that month and to prepare the banks for heavy seasonal credit demands during the tax period. The March rate increases led to a $0.6 billion expansion in the volume of outstanding C/D liabilities by mid-April. This improved flow of C/D funds enabled the City banks to supply without much difficulty the unusually large corporate credit demands that developed as a result of the Treasury's accelerated tax payment schedule. Borrowing needs of U.S. Government securities dealers were also heavy at this time as the dealers attempted to replace funds lost through the expiration of repurchase agreements with nonfinancial corporations around the tax date.

During May, the money market banks raised C/D offering rates again, leaving little room for further adjustments under the legal maximum, and by early August the 5½ per cent rate was quoted on all maturities by the majority of the eight banks. The rate increases during the summer permitted the City banks to hold their C/D liabilities fairly constant, but they failed to generate additional funds to enable the banks to handle renewed seasonal tax-related pressures, loan requests from nonbank financial institutions, and an extraseasonal demand for business loans.

The larger-than-seasonal demand for business loans that began to appear early in May and persisted into the fall of 1966 reflected, to a considerable

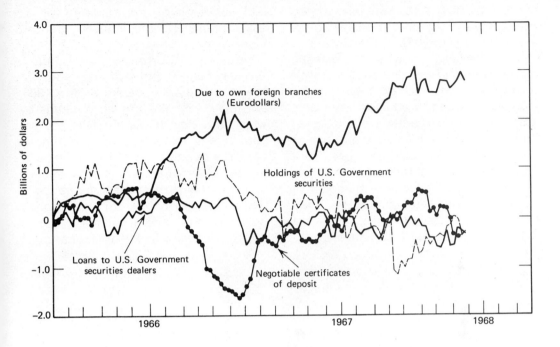

Chart 1. Cumulative gain of funds through increase in liabilities or decrease in assets, eight major New York City banks, 1966–1968.

NOTE: Data are based on Wednesday levels, except loans to U.S. Government securities dealers, which are based on the daily average amount of Federal funds and New York Clearing House funds loaned to dealers during weeks ended on Wednesday. The latter include funds supplied to dealers under repurchase agreements.

Source: Federal Reserve Bank of New York.

extent, a substantial increase in the volume of anticipatory borrowing by corporations. Over the summer, expectations of increases in interest rates and concern over the future availability of credit became widespread. These apprehensions were bolstered by evidence of increasing monetary restraint and by an awareness that the money market banks, then offering the maximum permissible rate on C/D's, would be severely limited in their ability to expand loans further. While precautionary borrowing was, thus, generated by the actual and prospective situation in the money and credit markets, it con-

tributed to existing pressures. As credit demands became increasingly urgent, the New York money market banks were subjected to rapid withdrawals of C/D funds beginning in the latter part of the summer. During the brief span between mid-August and mid-December, C/D liabilities of the large City banks fell by $2.1 billion.

In early summer of 1966, the New York City banks anticipated the large losses of funds that eventually occurred as a result of C/D redemptions. Those which had foreign branches were prepared to meet them by borrowing Eurodollars through these branches. Although the Eurodollar market is generally a costly source of funds, the relatively strong surge of money market rates in the United States toward the end of 1965 had resulted in a considerable narrowing of the differential between domestic money market and Eurodollar rates. During the first half of 1966, for instance, rates on Eurodollars were only about ⅜ of a percentage point higher than rates on comparable maturities of negotiable C/D's sold in New York City (Chart 2). This interest rate differential widened over the balance of 1966 as interest rates abroad reversed their course. Nevertheless, the cost disadvantage to the City banks of ac-

quiring Eurodollars was partly compensated for, throughout 1966, by the fact that these liabilities were not then subject to reserve requirements or to assessments by the Federal Deposit Insurance Corporation.

Eurodollar borrowings constituted the only major source of new funds for the money market banks during 1966, and they were the principal means by which the City banks survived the severe drains resulting from net runoffs of C/D's during the last four months of the year. As Chart 1 shows, liabilities to own foreign branches at the eight money market banks climbed sharply between June and December from a plateau reached in the first quarter of

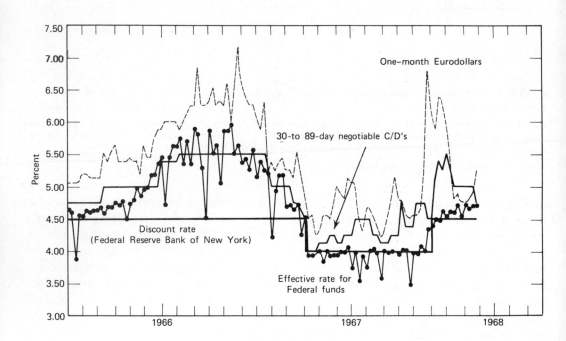

Chart 2. Selected short-term interest rates, 1966–68.

NOTE: Data plotted are the seven-day average rate on Federal funds for week ended Wednesday, the rate most often quoted on Wednesday by nine large New York City banks on new negotiable certificates of deposit, and the Wednesday rate on Eurodollar deposits.

Source: Federal Reserve Bank of New York.

1966. For the year as a whole, cumulative borrowing of Eurodollars by the City banks amounted to $1.8 billion, an amount roughly equivalent to the decline in C/D liabilities. As a group, these banks began to step up their Eurodollar borrowing fully two months before the heavy redemptions of C/D's began. Consequently, the basic reserve position of these institutions improved sharply, though temporarily, in August and early September.

Virtually all of the major money market banks used Eurodollar borrowings as an offset to C/D losses. Individual banks varied in their approach to the Eurodollar market, however. A few banks began to seek these funds after a downward trend in their C/D liabilities had become clearly visible or at the same time as C/D losses commenced. On the other hand, some borrowed Eurodollars considerably in advance of C/D runoffs. Some banks built up liabilities to foreign branches gradually over the period of C/D outflows, compensating for losses of funds as they occurred. Other money market institutions borrowed heavily initially, then allowed these foreign liabilities to remain on a plateau until the latter part of the year, when the greater part of interest-sensitive C/D funds had been withdrawn. Most of the eight banks' cumulative borrowings of Eurodollars corresponded roughly to cumulative C/D losses. At two institutions, however, Eurodollar borrowings were quite heavy relative to C/D runoffs.

Although little is known about the maturities of Eurodollars borrowed by the City banks, it may be reasonable to assume that some portion of the aggregate amount represented overnight or call money, while a relatively larger amount represented funds acquired by the foreign branches on longer-term contracts. Maturities may have varied widely from bank to bank, however, since some branches overseas characteristically seek short-term Eurodollar deposits while others seek somewhat longer maturities.

In order to increase the availability of Eurodollars for its domestic lending operations, one New York City institution in April 1966 began to sell negotiable certificates of deposit at its London office at yields slightly lower than those available for comparable maturities of regular Eurodollars. At the same time, the bank organized a secondary market for Eurodollars C/D's. Within a short time, the majority of other money market banks with branches in London had begun to sell these instruments.

The major purpose of the C/D sales abroad by the money market banks was to acquire more funds through the Eurodollar market. By offering the C/D's in relatively small denominations (the minimum of $25,000 compared with a regular Eurodollar deposit minimum of $250,000 and a New York negotiable C/D minimum of $100,000), the banks set their sights on the funds of small investors who had not previously participated in the Eurodollar market. In addition, however, the City banks hoped to benefit by acquiring Eurodollars at a reduced cost and by improving their ability to retain funds that might otherwise be lost through the redemption of domestic C/D's by foreign holders in the event of interest rate increases here or abroad. C/D's sold in London are not subject to any rate limitation such as that imposed by Regulation Q. The creation of the Eurodollar C/D market did not add significantly to the supply of Eurodollar deposits in foreign branches of the major money market banks. It is, however, illustrative of the resourcefulness of these institutions in attempting to locate new sources of funds for lending.

Although needs for new loanable funds were intense during 1966, the New York money market banks' sustained liquidation of U.S. Government securities ceased after the first quarter. Portfolio adjustments were used to tide the banks over periods of seasonal increase in loan demand, but net sales at these times tended to offset by purchases when acute pressures eased. The use of the U.S. Government securities portfolio as a temporary adjustment mechanism after the first quarter of 1966 contrasted sharply with its use as a more or less permanent source of funds earlier in the business expansion. During 1965, net sales of U.S. Governments had been a major source of new loanable funds for the City banks, second only to the issuance of negotiable C/D's, and in the first quarter of 1966 the liquidation of these investments had provided another $1.1 billion.

The reduced role of portfolio adjustments in the City banks' program to meet accelerating loan demands was primarily a reflection of the low level of holdings. By March 1966, the combined U.S. Government securities portfolio of the eight money market banks had been reduced to its lowest level of the entire postwar period as a result of the sustained liquidation which had commenced late in 1961. At this level, the bulk of securities remaining in portfolio may have been pledged against public deposits* and, hence, not saleable. Another factor tending to discourage securities sales by the City banks in the summer of 1966 was that the sharp increase in market yields raised the cost, in terms of capital losses, of liquidating coupon issues.

After September 1, moreover, the liquidation of investments by banks ran directly counter to the expressed wishes of Federal Reserve System policy makers. Through public statements, periodic counseling of individual member banks, and the administration of the discount window, System officials left no doubt that they looked with disfavor upon further reductions in bank holdings of tax-exempt securities, especially when accompanied by a sustained rate of expansion in business loans. Member banks engaging in large-scale liquidation of such securities thus tended to invite closer scrutiny when requesting discount accommodation at the Reserve Banks. This possibility of increased surveillance was not a significant restraint on liquidation, however, because of the relatively limited use of discount facilities made by the City banks during 1966. In fact, these institutions sold off tax-exempt securities at a steady pace throughout 1966, gaining about $0.5 billion from this source through June and a like amount over the latter half of the year. These sales, occurring during a period of heavy net new borrowing by state and local governments, were a significant factor in the sharp rise in yields on tax-exempt bonds to a thirty-four year high by August 1966.

VI. USE OF THE DISCOUNT WINDOW

The major New York City banks were generally in a position of deep basic reserve deficit during 1966 (see Chart 3). At times during the first eight months of the year, their reserve positions underwent some sharp, temporary improvement as a result of inflows of C/D funds, liquidations of securities, and substantial borrowing of Eurodollars during the summer months in advance of the heavy C/D runoffs. During the latter part of the year, however, the basic reserve deficit deepened to unusually high levels under the impact of the drastic decline in C/D liabilities after mid-August. As a result, the daily average basic reserve deficiency of

---

* Editor's note: State and local governments commonly require banks in which they deposit public funds to hold a percentage of such deposits in the form of Treasury bills and other short-term securities.

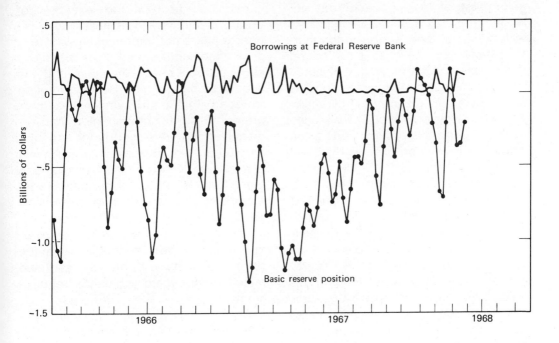

Chart 3. Basic reserve position and borrowings at the Federal Reserve Bank, eight major New York City Banks, 1966–68.

NOTE: Data are daily average levels for weeks ended on Wednesday. Figures for basic reserve position are two-week moving averages.

Source: Federal Reserve Bank of New York.

the eight banks rose to nearly $500 million in the fourth quarter of 1966 from roughly $350 million during the first three quarters of the year.

While their needs for funds to cover reserve requirements were consistently heavy during 1966, the New York money market banks made relatively little use of borrowing facilities at the Federal Reserve Bank. As shown in Chart 3, substantial increases in the basic reserve deficiency prompted only moderately increased use of the discount window. Moreover, whatever borrowing these institutions did at the Federal Reserve during 1966 was invariably the traditional overnight or short-term type of accommodation. None of the eight money market banks took advan-

tage of the privilege of extended discounting offered in the System's September 1 letter to member banks, despite the increase in their basic reserve deficits during the fall of the year.

The City banks' hesitancy to approach the Federal Reserve Bank for assistance, except at times of extreme emergency, partly reflected the unwillingness of these institutions to have their lending and portfolio adjustment practices the object of official scrutiny. It also reflected the much heavier use made of the Federal funds market by the money market banks in recent years. During the early 1960's, the City banks had begun to borrow Federal funds from other banks for the purpose of relending, particularly to Government securities dealers, as well as for the purpose of making day-to-day adjustments in their reserve positions. As the function of the Federal funds market broadened, the rate for Federal funds rose in relation to the discount rate, and had generally exceeded the latter since 1964. During 1966, however, the margin by which the effective rate for Federal funds exceeded the discount rate widened to nearly a full percentage point by mid-November from about 10 basis points throughout 1965. This sharp increase in the differential reflected the City banks' determined efforts to operate without assistance from the Federal Reserve Bank as well as their continuing use of Federal funds for dealer and other lending operations. In 1966, to an even greater extent than formerly, the City banks were permanent debtors in the Federal funds market, automatically renewing overnight loans and borrowing for periods of more than the usual one day.

VII. ATTEMPTS BY THE CITY BANKS TO CURTAIL LENDING

Between December 1965, at the time of the increase in the discount rate, and August 1966, the large New York City banks raised their prime lending rate to business borrowers in four steps from 4½ per cent to 6 per cent. These increases were largely dictated by the need to maintain profitable operations in the face of the rapid rise in the cost of loanable funds to the banks. Although the prime rate increases, and particularly those occurring in June and August, were also intended to discourage loan applications from business borrowers, they had apparently little effect on total loan demand.

Early in 1966, many of the large City banks adopted programs amounting, in effect, to voluntary credit restraint.

These programs, aimed generally at moderating the pace of business loan expansion through the exercise of greater selectivity in reviewing loan requests, were not implemented with any great vigor until the summer, when the gap between credit demands and the supply of bank funds for new lending widened significantly. Under these programs, the City banks denied loan requests which were clearly for speculative or hoarding purposes, turned down requests for term loans or formal loan commitments, and discouraged applications for loans from new customers. They also attempted to reduce loan amounts and lines of credit. Moreover, the banks reported that they made fewer loans at the prime rate and also raised compensatory balance requirements.

At the same time, however, the money market banks seemed very hesitant to turn down loan requests from old customers, or from new customers whose business they had long solicited. For competitive reasons, as well, some banks apparently went back on their original intentions not to issue formal loan commitments for a fee, even with the knowledge that the presence of a large volume of outstanding commitments would seriously limit their flexibility in time of emergency.

Despite the banks' efforts and procedures to restrain credit expansion, and the successive increases in the prime loan rate, net increases in business loans of the eight money market banks in the second and third quarters of 1966 exceeded by roughly two-fifths the amount of increase in the corresponding quarters of 1965. Not until the fourth quarter of the year did business lending fall off. In that period, the net increase in business loans declined sharply to a less-than-seasonal $0.4 billion from $1.1 billion in the fourth quarter of 1965. This rather drastic change in the pattern of business lending, however, probably reflected a slowdown in corporate demands as much as denials or scaling down of credit requests by the City banks.

During the fourth quarter of 1966, two factors which had contributed significantly to the vigorous loan demand earlier in the year were no longer present. Expectations of further increases in interest rates had largely disappeared, and corporations, whose liquidity needs were still large, had shifted part of their credit demands back to the capital markets in response to a reversal of the upward trend in bond yields. These favorable developments, in turn, had been prompted by a number of factors tending to stabilize the credit markets in the fall of 1966.

Early in September, President Johnson announced a fiscal program to combat inflation and the U.S. Treasury indicated that it would curtail certain types of Government agency financing over the balance of the year. Prospects for peace in Vietnam seemed to be improving, moreover, and hopes were high for an income tax increase after the November elections. By the end of November, the markets began to detect signs of a relaxation of credit restraint and, indeed, the record of policy directives issued by the Federal Open Market Committee shows that the New York Reserve Bank was instructed on November 22 to conduct open market operations "with a view to attaining somewhat easier conditions in the money market . . ."

READING 10

EURO-DOLLARS IN THE LIQUIDITY AND RESERVE MANAGEMENT OF UNITED STATES BANKS

Fred H. Klopstock

During the last decade, the large commercial banks in the United States have exhibited a remarkable degree of imagination and initiative in broadening their access to pools of liquid funds. Their success in attracting corporate and institutional balances through the issue of negotiable certificates of deposit (C/D's) is a case in point. Other examples are their issue of "consumer" investment certificates and the flotation of unsecured notes and debentures in the capital market. More recently this increased readiness of banks to rely on what has become known as "liability management" in the adjustment of liquidity and reserve positions has been demonstrated by their large-scale use of balances acquired through their overseas branches in the Euro-dollar market. The overseas branches became active in this market soon after it emerged in the late 1950's,

and have gradually become the most important participants. But only since the midsixties have several of the major United States banks employed large amounts of Euro-dollar balances for adjustments of their money positions in response to changing needs for funds, and more and more banks have opened overseas branches to gain access to the Euro-dollar market.

For some of the large money market banks, Euro-dollars have now become a major source of funds for loans and investments; in certain instances, the head office's dollar liabilities to overseas branches exceed or closely approach its outstanding C/D's. Altogether, liabilities of American banks to their overseas branches are now in excess of $6 billion. It is true that this total includes some funds that do not originate in the Euro-dollar market, but on the other hand the United States

Source: Reprinted from the *Federal Reserve Bank of New York Monthly Review,* July 1968, pp. 130–36.

banks' use of Euro-dollar balances in the management of their portfolios is not limited to the amounts reported as liabilities to their branches. For example, they may use such balances for transfers of loans to overseas branches; or they may conserve head-office resources by referring some loan demands to their branches for financing with Euro-dollars; and those that have no branches overseas may sell loans to foreign banks or borrow from foreign banks directly. The following pages examine the institutional and economic background of the practice of using Euro-dollars in portfolio management, a practice that has greatly increased during the last two years.

I. THE EURO-DOLLAR MARKET AS A SOURCE OF FUNDS FOR UNITED STATES BANKS

The Euro-dollar market, which centers on London with links in several other major financial centers in Western Europe and elsewhere, is a telephone and telex network through which many of the world's major banks bid for and employ dollar balances. By a generally accepted definition, Euro-dollars come into existence when a domestic or foreign holder of dollar demand deposits in the United States places them on deposit in a bank outside the United States, but the term also applies to the dollars that banks abroad acquire with their own or foreign currencies and then employ for placement in the market or for loans to customers. Compared with other markets used by American banks for adjusting their liabilities, the Euro-dollar market possesses distinctive features which both add to and detract from its usefulness as a source of funds.

By far the greatest merit of the market from the viewpoint of United States banks is that it offers the possibility of obtaining balances that are not subject to the regulatory restrictions applicable to demand and time deposits. Unlike United States banks, the overseas branches may pay interest on dollar call deposits and on time deposits with maturities of less than thirty days. Thus, United States banks can gain access, through the overseas branch route, to sizable amounts of funds that they are precluded by various regulations from acquiring directly from foreign depositors. In addition, balances payable at overseas branches are not subject to Regulation Q rate ceilings, a factor of great significance when rates for money market instruments in the United States or Euro-dollar rates rise above the ceiling rates payable on deposits. And, finally, branch balances placed in head offices are not subject to member bank reserve requirements* or to the fees of the Federal Deposit Insurance Corporation (FDIC). Indeed, especially during periods of tight money, the differential between Euro-dollar rates and time deposit rates in the United States tends to reflect this saving.

Another advantage of the market is its broad scope. Actual and potential Euro-dollar sources are diverse and widely dispersed geographically. They include countless banks and corporations in many parts of the world as well as monetary authorities and international financial institutions. When conditions in some countries restrict offerings by suppliers, conditions elsewhere typically free more resources for Euro-dollar placements. Monetary authorities and international institutions may add to their offerings when commercial banks and corporations pull back theirs. In short, there is a high degree of supply flexibility in the Euro-dollar market.

---

* Editor's note: Reserve requirements have been imposed since this was written.

It must not be thought, however, that the market is always a stable source of funds for United States banks. On the one hand, there may be problems of oversupply—because of relative ease in the money markets of major supplier countries or because foreign customers' demand for loans has been weak or their established credit lines have been filled. At such times the branches will quote defensively, but even so some of them tend on occasion to take in sizable balances from day to day, as they are loath to refuse offerings by correspondent banks and corporations among their established customers that habitually lay off temporarily excess dollar balances with them. Several of the branches of major banks are in effect the residual takers of foreign banks' liquidity reserves, which tend to converge upon them largely in the form of call deposits. If these balances cannot immediately be employed abroad, the respective head offices tend to use these balances as an alternative to Federal funds purchases. Under such conditions, branch deposits in head offices may rise above the targets set by the money-desk or portfolio-management departments.

On the other hand, there are occasionally supply stringencies, notably during periods of heavy seasonal pressures. Moreover, restrictive monetary policies in major supplier countries may reduce offerings by foreign banks. Individual branches may then be unable, at a given rate, to replace maturing deposits. If such deposits account for a sizeable proportion of a branch's aggregate balances, its deposits at the head office may drop off sharply, to be built up again when the branch has been authorized to offer more competitive rates. Timing is often important, as other branches and other banks abroad may absorb early in the day major portions of the funds offered. It is true that central banks have increasingly been prepared to supply funds to the Euro-dollar market when it is exposed to pressures, but there are still occasions when the branches are forced to withdraw balances placed in their head offices, thereby forcing the latter to seek additional funds in the United States money market.

At times, the demand for Euro-dollars for use in foreign money and loan markets is so pressing that rates rise to levels that are out of line with those quoted in markets for comparable funds in the United States, thereby inducing the head offices not to renew maturing deposits. This situation is subject to reversal, because the head offices normally absorb so large a proportion of aggregate Euro-dollar deposits that any reduction of their takings will tend to bring rates down. In any event, Euro-dollar rates, especially those for call money and other short-dated funds, which are less suited than the more distant maturities for use in commercial loan markets abroad, are highly sensitive to conditions in the United States money market.

It is true, of course, that banks must allocate a major part of their branches' aggregate Euro-dollar resources to the loan and investment transactions of the branches themselves. The banks cannot disregard the demand for branch loans that comes from the affiliates abroad of important head-office accounts. And the branches must accommodate their own customers with whom they have developed close deposit and loan relationships. But the needs of the branches themselves do not appear to have restricted head-office use of the market for its own requirements. The head offices can almost always obtain additional balances in the market, at a price, if they are pressed for funds. The market has proved to be highly interest-rate elastic, and thus, as rates escalate, offerings rise at a very rapid pace. This was demonstrated during the credit crunch in the summer and fall of 1966, when United States banks by raising their bids pulled very large additional amounts into the market. The Euro-dollar pool is not inexhaustible, but it can be replenished by a large variety of funds held in several types of assets and currencies. Therefore, relatively small shifts from other uses within and to the Euro-dollar market can satisfy a rise in the demand for funds.

There are some negative aspects of the Euro-dollar market from the viewpoint of money position management. The market is far away, and because of the time difference between London and New York (not to mention Chicago or San Francisco) opportunities for immediate and direct head-office communication with it is confined to a few hours during the morning. Moreover, due to the settlement and clearing periods involved, several days pass before a head-office decision to take on Euro-dollars is reflected in available funds in the banks' reserve accounts. Meanwhile, conditions in domestic money markets may have changed significantly. Closely connected with the distance factor is the problem of adequate information. Because of the diverse conditions prevailing in the several major areas where dollar supplies originate, it is not always easy for the branches to obtain accurate knowledge of prospective market factors that might affect rates and amounts offered. And, in turn, head-office money position managers have not always found it easy to convey to their London offices their exact needs in terms of amounts and maturities, since their desire to draw on the market is partly conditional on the rates at which balances in various maturity sectors become available, and the rates change in response to market conditions.

The large banks with overseas branches differ greatly in their ap-praisal of the merits of the market as a source of funds for head-office use. A few banks look upon the market as one of their preferred methods of portfolio adjustment and have made very heavy use of it almost continuously. For most large banks, however, Euro-dollars appear to be only a second choice. Several of these banks have used the market on a substantial scale solely during periods of severe reserve pressure.

By far the largest part of branch placements with head offices is held in New York, but several banks in other financial centers also absorb relatively sizable balances from their branches. A few New York banks—and several banks elsewhere that have only recently opened overseas branches—have not yet made any large-scale use of Euro-dollar deposits.

The bulk of Euro-deposits taken for head-office use is obtained through branches in London. These branches are of course a conduit for funds from many parts of the world. In fact, some banks have instructed their branches in other Euro-dollar centers to redeposit excess dollar balances in London offices. United States banks also obtain sizable funds directly from their Paris branches and, to a lesser extent, from their branches in Nassau. Direct placements in United States head offices by branches elsewhere are generally quite small.

II. MAJOR HEAD-OFFICE USES OF BRANCH BALANCES

Conceptually, the funds of overseas branches in head offices may be separated into three main categories: (1) balances borrowed by the head offices on a more or less continuous basis for the purpose of enlarging the banks' reserves, (2) balances acquired for short-term adjustments of reserve positions, and (3) working or operating balances to accommodate adjustments between head-office and branch accounts. The boundaries between the three categories are, at least for some banks, somewhat blurred; often the same balances serve all three functions, and clearly, whatever their maturity or the ultimate objective of their acquisition, they all add to the resources of the borrowing banks. Apart from these three categories, Euro-dollars are also used by foreign banks and overseas branches for the purchase of loans from United States banks and to finance loans that otherwise would have been made directly by American banks.

A. Continuous Borrowing For Enlarging Reserves

The major motive of United States banks in using Euro-dollar funds has been to obtain balances for enlarging or maintaining their credit potential. In their efforts to locate and solicit additional loanable funds, the banks have become increasingly attracted by the continuous availability in the Euro-dollar market of very large amounts of funds in a broad maturity range. Although a large part of these funds are call and short-dated deposits, experience has demonstrated that over extended periods even the call component remains quite steady in the aggregate. Thus the presence in, or availability to, the Euro-dollar market of very large interest-rate sensitive funds provides the banks with an attractive alternative means of meeting demands on their liquidity positions and adding to aggregate deposit stability.

Rate advantages explain, of course, much of the heavy use of Euro-dollar deposits. During recent years, they have been for extended periods less expensive, or at least not more expensive, than domestic deposits. Even when rates in the Euro-dollar market are nominally higher than those in the C/D market, it may be advantageous to increase holdings of branch balances, relative to sales of C/D's, because of their exemption from reserve requirements and FDIC fees.* A further savings associated with the acquisition of branch balances arises from technical factors. When a bank obtains Euro-dollar balances from its branch, it may benefit from reduced reserve requirements, while clearing the transaction, for at least one day—and for more if the date of the acquisition is followed by a holiday or a weekend. The reason is that the check received by a bank in connection with the transfer of a Euro-dollar deposit acquired by its branch increases cash items in the process of collection, which are deductible from demand deposits in computing reserve requirements even though the branch balance does not add to deposits subject to such requirements. This saving arises only if the Euro-dollar deposit is repaid by a so-called "bills payable" check. Outstanding checks of this type need not be included in deposits subject to reserve requirements in contrast to checks issued by banks for purposes other than borrowings. The initial saving would cancel out at maturity of the funds if they were repaid with a check not exempt from reserve requirements.*

As noted, the head offices may stand ready to accommodate important suppliers, even if Euro-dollars are offered at rates somewhat above those quoted for comparable domestic funds. Generally, the large banks are very much aware of the advantages of regular contacts and dealings in the market. Some of them have concluded that a continuous readiness to accept large

---

* Editor's note: This advantage has been reduced, but not eliminated, since the imposition of reserve requirements on Euro-dollar borrowings.

amounts irrespective of immediate needs permits the overseas branches to improve their feel of the market and their information on prospective trends. Moreover, if needs for overseas balances are less urgent at a particular time, they may well rebound in the not too distant future. Keeping a hand in the market makes it a more reliable source of funds. In short, a number of United States banks believe that complete withdrawal from the market when domestic funds can easily be substituted for Euro-dollars would not serve their longer run interest, and on occasion they have been quite willing to pay a price, albeit small, for continued participation.

The head offices issue directives to the branches concerning the amounts they wish to take and the rate limits, either for specific maturities or for a "package" of maturities. During periods of rapidly mounting or declining pressures, head-office instructions to the branches regarding targets and rates are often changed from day to day. If money market conditions in the United States are relatively stable, the directives are issued for extended and sometimes indefinite periods ahead. Because the rising yield curve for Euro-dollar deposits often makes the more distant maturities too expensive relative to C/D rates for corresponding maturities, there is a tendency for head offices to concentrate on the shorter maturities among the balances that branches tap in the Euro-dollar market. Moreover, substantial offerings in the market generally carry short maturities. On occasion, the banks have instructed their branches to reach out for rather distant maturities, so that the banks' loan and investment portfolios can be financed on a more secure basis. Sometimes, the banks acquire longer term Euro-dollars from their branches and invest them in liquid assets in order to maintain a comfortable cush-

ion against the possibility of losing C/D money if open market rates should exceed the Regulation Q ceilings.

B. Borrowing to Finance Weekend Reserve Positions

United States banks seldom use Euro-dollar balances for specifically adjusting day-to-day cash and reserve positions except over weekends. The Euro-dollar market is generally not suited to immediate reserve adjustment needs. One reason is the distance factor: In the morning hours, London time, when the branch officers would need to obtain indications of immediate head-office needs in the light of current offerings, United States banks have not yet opened for business; by noon, New York time, when the evolving cash needs of banks are becoming evident, the London market is closing up shop. Of still greater significance is the fact that the normal delivery period for Euro-dollars is two days, and even if arrangements can be made early in the morning London time to acquire dollars for same-day delivery in New York, these balances become available as bank reserves in Federal Reserve accounts only the next day (see below). Moreover, banks find it difficult to estimate changes in reserve positions for more than a few days in advance. For these reasons, banks generally consider the Federal funds market far superior to the overnight sector of the Euro-dollar market for very short-term adjustments of reserve positions. Yet, a few banks appear to be quite prepared for a variety of reasons to make continuous use of overnight deposits as a substantial core of relatively low cost funds.

An important use of the Euro-dollar market as a tool of short-term reserve management is for the financing of weekend reserve positions. In fact, most of the banks with branches employ overnight deposits each Thursday as a partial substitute for Federal funds purchases on Friday. Because of New York check-clearing practices, overnight borrowing in the Euro-dollar market value-Thursday for repayment on Friday can serve as bank reserves for three days—from Friday through Sunday. Euro-dollar transactions are generally settled through checks on New York banks. Unlike Federal funds transactions, which are recorded in Federal Reserve accounts immediately, these checks must pass through the New York Clearing House, and it is not until the following business day that they become balances in the Federal Reserve accounts of member banks. Thus, a check drawn on bank A and deposited on Friday in bank B in repayment of a Euro-dollar deposit does not draw down A's reserves until Monday; the same applies if the check is deposited on the day before a holiday.

These weekend and holiday clearing delays are reflected in the rates that head offices must pay for Euro-dollar balances. For a day Euro-dollar deposit on Thursday, a United States bank in need of funds to meet its reserve requirements will be willing to pay a rate close to three times the anticipated Federal funds rate on Friday; and it will pay a corresponding multiple when the settlement date for these overnight balances precedes any other period when the New York money market is closed for one business day or longer. Thursday-Friday transactions have become so common that the rates have adjusted themselves almost fully to the anticipated Federal funds rate on Friday. Nevertheless, the banks continue to have their London branches engage in these transactions on a large scale —often for purely defensive purposes —because any bank that does not bid for overnight dollars offered value-Thursday is likely to suffer sizable losses in its Federal Reserve account as other American banks take advan-

tage of the Thursday deposit offerings.

The money-desk managers of United States banks that wish to acquire Thursday-Friday money must make their basic decisions on amounts and rates at the end of the preceding week, or at the latest on Monday, on the basis of projections of supplies and rates in the Federal funds market the following Friday. Within limits further adjustments can be made on Tuesday or Wednesday, but the bulk of the available funds has been spoken for by that time. Actual conditions on Friday may well be and often are different from those projected. By Wednesday, however, the money-desk manager knows the amount of Euro-dollar overnight deposits that will be available on Friday, and in the light of this information he can adjust his Federal fund and dealer loan operations during the closing days of the week.

There are other categories of Euro-dollar deposit transactions that take advantage of the delay in the clearing of checks in New York. For instance, a foreign bank may accept an overnight Euro-dollar deposit on Thursday and make arrangements to sell the resulting Federal funds on Friday through its United States correspondent. For foreign banks, however, such transactions are less attractive than direct dealings with American banks' overseas branches, and have come into disuse with the branches' increasing activity in the Thursday-Friday market on behalf of their head offices.

In addition, use of the foreign exchange market to take advantage of the United States check-clearing procedure is quite common. For instance, a foreign bank, using a foreign currency, may purchase dollars in New York value-Thursday for resale value-Friday. Although the dollars it buys and sells are not "good money" until the following business day, the foreign currency is immediately available to the buyer for investment, because in foreign financial centers checks deposited before a designated hour are cleared the same day. Thus on Friday, when its Thursday dollars become available as "good money," a foreign bank can put them to weekend use in the Federal funds market and also use its Friday repurchase of local exchange for payments needs or for investment over the weekend in a foreign market. Of course, a bank engaging in such a transaction forgoes earnings on Thursday. Or a United States bank buyer of foreign exchange value-Friday can employ the funds abroad over the weekend and also retain its weekend use of the dollars with which it paid for them, since the check deposited for the settlement of the transaction is not debited against its reserve account until Monday. These and similar operations have been reflected in spot and forward exchange rate distortions and erratic flows of funds from foreign money markets.

C. Operating Balances of Branches

The third type of liabilities to overseas branches consists of balances carried with head offices for operating purposes. This item has no direct relationship to the branches' overall dollar liabilities. Actually there may be no necessity for a branch to carry an operating balance in its head office if it is authorized to overdraw its account at its head office in case of need, or if the various components of its assets carry maturities of the same length as those of its corresponding deposit liabilities. Moreover, branches are ordinarily able, at a price, to obtain additional balances in foreign currency deposit markets. But the voluntary credit restraint program has made it undesirable for head offices to expose themselves to sudden branch overdrafts for meeting deposit liabilities that cannot be replaced at the time of maturity without costly rate sacrifices. Some branches have been willing to build their asset portfolios on deposits that carry somewhat shorter maturities than loan and deposit placements abroad: it is not easy, and is at times impossible, to match dollar loans to corporations with dollar deposits of similar maturities. Branches also need operating balances to discharge obligations under letters of credit and to take care of a variety of payments orders by customers, and they need contingency reserves in view of their large outstanding loan commitments.

Dollar balances at head offices have on occasion served also as contingency reserves for the branches' deposit and loan operations in sterling. Because of the swings in confidence in the pound, sterling deposits have typically been short dated. On the other hand, the branches' commercial loans in sterling —made both to United Kingdom firms and to European affiliates of United States corporations—are usually for extended periods. At times, though less so recently, the branches have preferred to draw down and convert their dollar balances at head offices in lieu of meeting their sterling liabilities through other more costly portfolio adjustments.

D. Euro-Dollar Financing of Loan Transactions

There is, finally, the special category of Euro-dollar transactions represented by head-office loan transfers to branches. To some extent these entail the sale of outstanding loans under repurchase agreements. Such sales appear to arise mainly from efforts of head offices to maintain their outstanding claims below the quota ceilings set by the voluntary credit restraint program. The sales wipe out any simultaneous increase in branch placements in head offices that have resulted from branch acquisitions of deposits abroad for the specific purpose of purchasing the loans, but the head offices obtain funds for further loans. Of course, the head office does not acquire additional funds if the loan is paid for out of existing branch deposits. In that case the head office reduces its outstanding loans and its liabilities ("due to" branches) by the same amount. Its overall balance sheet thus contracts.

The large banks do not appear to have employed repurchase agreements with branches as a device for obtaining funds for additional domestic loans. Those banks that have considerable credit leeway under the restraint program have made several sizable sales of loans to branches. Under these circumstances, however, the purpose appears to have been to enable individual branches to acquire earning assets with funds that they had taken in to accommodate important nonbank accounts on their books.

Of greater importance than such sales, in terms of dollar amounts involved, are loans made by branches to meet loan demands on their head offices. For these loans to head-office customers the branches employ deposits obtained in the Euro-dollar or other foreign currency deposit markets. It is, of course, possible that a branch would have increased its Euro-dollar liabilities even in the absence of this particular loan demand and would have placed additional balances in its head-office account.

It should be mentioned again that many United States banks without branches sell substantial amounts of their foreign loans to foreign banks under repurchase agreements, primarily in order to hold their foreign claims below the credit restraint program ceilings; the foreign banks finance these loan purchases largely with Euro-dollars. And there are indications that an increasing number of banks without branches have made arrangements to borrow Euro-dollars directly from foreign banks. These two types of transactions are analogous to, and have the same liquidity and reserve effects as, the corresponding transactions between head offices and their overseas branches.

III. HEAD-OFFICE USE OF BRANCH BALANCES, 1964–68

Before 1964, relatively few of the banks with overseas branches made much use of the Euro-dollar market for their head-office operations. Not until the summer of that year did aggregate head-office liabilities to branches remain continuously above $1 billion. Through most of 1965, they were substantially below $2 billion. The majority of the banks with branches apparently preferred other options for obtaining funds, either because of cost considerations or because head-office portfolio managements had not yet developed a close liaison with overseas branch managements.

During the first half of 1966, as Federal Reserve pressures on the banks' reserve positions mounted, borrowing gradually increased and the aggregate due to branches approached the $2 billion level. The increased resort to the Euro-dollar market during this period represented primarily an attempt to obtain resources over and above those available in domestic deposit markets and thereby to lessen susceptibility to reserve pressures.

Toward the end of June 1966, the pace of borrowing through branches quickened even more. The large money market banks then used the Euro-dollar market to cushion the effects of another weapon in the Federal Reserve's armory of credit control—administration of Regulation Q. With the Reserve System using Q as a deliberate means of reducing the rate of credit expansion, the banks were virtually priced out of the national C/D market. But about four fifths of the loss in outstanding C/D's suffered during the summer and fall of 1966 by the twelve banks with overseas branches was offset by increased Euro-dollar takings from branches. Euro-dollars at that time were in ample supply, partly because of large-scale shifts of funds out of sterling into dollars. By mid-December, aggregate redeposits in head offices, which had then reached $4.3 billion, amounted to substantially more than half of the twelve banks' outstanding C/D's, compared with less than one fifth in mid-1966.

Thus, during the summer and fall of 1966, Euro-dollar balances played an important role in banks' efforts to meet loan demands and commitments, offset losses of other resources, and reduce the need to liquidate securities at distressingly low prices. Moreover, the banks were then experiencing an increase in demand deposits relative to time deposits, and the resultant effects on required reserves were cushioned by the acquisition of balances not subject to reserve requirements.

Late in 1966 and early in 1967, when a large movement of foreign funds into the London money market coincided with a considerable easing of money market conditions in the United States, the use of branch balances by head offices fell rapidly, and by May 1967 it had dropped by about $1.5 billion from the peak level reached in December 1966. The figure then began to rise, however, and in November 1967 it began to exceed the amount outstanding during the 1966 credit crunch. During the short span of six months beginning in the middle of May 1967, aggregate borrowings from branches rose by about $2 billion.

This 1967 surge of branch deposits occurred in a market atmosphere quite different from that prevailing in the second half of 1966. During the latter part

of 1967 the demand for business loans was relatively weak. The Federal Reserve supplied bank reserves quite liberally until late in the year, and banks were able to make considerable progress in improving their liquidity positions. There was little, if any, need to reach out for funds in Europe to compensate for shortages of funds in the United States. It appears, therefore, that there was a fundamental change in the banks' attitude with respect to taking Euro-dollars from their branches. Before the summer of 1966, several of them approached the Euro-dollar market with some hesitation, looking on it merely as a marginal source of funds. In general, they discovered the market's full potential only after having been virtually forced into it. As they became familiar with its breadth and depth, they lost their skepticism and came to regard the market as another normal source of funds to be tapped whenever the price was right.

Other factors also contributed to the

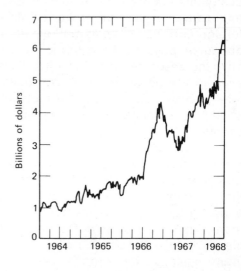

Chart 1. Liabilities of United States banks to their foreign branches.
Source: Board of Governors of the Federal Reserve System.

surge in the use of Euro-dollars during 1967. Foreign investors shifted substantial amounts of their short-term sterling investments into the Euro-dollar market in response to the Middle East crisis in June and the weakening of sterling in the fall of 1967 prior to its devaluation. In addition, market relationships had been established, with considerable effort, and the banks desired to maintain them. Several felt that a withdrawal from the market be-cause domestic funds could be easily substituted for Euro-dollars would not serve their longer run interest, even if continued participation sometimes involved a rate sacrifice.

In the spring of 1968, as money market conditions in the United States tightened, aggregate balances held for overseas branches passed the $5 billion mark, and toward the end of June they amounted to more than $6 billion. (See Chart 1.)

READING 11
EURO-DOLLARS: A CHANGING MARKET

The large increase in borrowing of Euro-dollars by banks in the United States in the past two years [1967–69] has been of major importance for borrowers and lenders in the Euro-dollar market, and has had an impact both on financial markets and on the balance of payments positions of a number of countries.

The rise in outstanding Euro-dollar liabilities of U.S. banks may be measured approximately by the rise in banks' total liabilities to their foreign branches. Such liabilities rose from $4.2 billion on December 27, 1967, to $6.9 billion on December 25, 1968. During the first 7 months of this year the increase was much more rapid, with liabilities to branches reaching $14.4 billion on July 30; in the next 2 months, however, there was only a little further net increase.

The growth in use of Euro-dollars reflected the interaction of rising demand for bank credit in the United States, reduced availability of bank reserves after late 1968, and the maintenance of ceilings on time deposit interest rates under the Board's Regulation Q. Interest rates on newly issued negotiable certificates of deposit reached the permissible ceilings under Regulation Q during the final weeks of 1968. From then until about the end of July of this year [1969], banks increased their borrowings of Euro-dollars with particular rapidity in an effort to meet both rising credit demands from customers and a run-off of maturing CD's. At times in 1968–69, U.S. banks' borrowings of Euro-dollars were also increased by speculative flows of funds out of some European currencies.

Large takings of Euro-dollars by banks in the United States through their branches occurred at a time when demands for Euro-dollars by borrowers in the rest of the world were also increasing strongly. For these reasons, interest rates on Euro-dollar deposits rose by mid-1969 to levels which would have been considered highly improbable until this year. Intense demand pressures in the Euro-dollar market helped to accelerate sharply the rapid rate of expansion already experienced by that market in previous years, a development which signaled a growing

Source: Reprinted from the *Federal Reserve Bulletin*, October 1969, pp. 765–766.

interdependence among national financial systems.

Flows of funds into the Euro-dollar market from countries other than the United States generally involve a purchase of dollars by a foreign commercial bank or nonbank investor from the central bank of the country whose currency is sold. This year, monetary authorities in some European countries have felt compelled not only to limit further placements of funds in Euro-dollars by their commercial banks, but even to reverse shifts that had already occurred, in order to bolster official reserves. In some countries, such actions were motivated by balance of payments deficits wholly or largely unrelated to Euro-dollar market developments, but even in these cases the strong pull of high Euro-dollar rates was an added consideration in the decisions to impose restrictions on banks' Euro-dollar market activities. Whatever their cause, however, all of the actions taken to force banks to reduce their net lending in the Euro-dollar market were an important additional factor contributing to the steep rise in Euro-dollar rates.

In the United States the Federal Reserve System has sought to moderate borrowings of Euro-dollars by removing a special advantage to member banks that were using Euro-dollars to adjust to domestic credit restraint. Effective September 4, a 10 per cent reserve requirement was imposed on net liabilities to foreign branches exceeding the daily-average outstanding amounts in the 4 weeks ending May 28, subject to certain qualifications.

READING 12

DETERMINANTS OF CORRESPONDENT BANKING RELATIONSHIPS

**Robert J. Lawrence and
Duane Lougee***

I. INTRODUCTION

Where state laws permit, banking structure in the United States is evolving from one of independent unit banks to one in which multi-office banking predominates. Essentially, this development involves replacing traditional correspondent relationships among banks with larger multi-office banking organizations. There have been few studies of correspondent relationships,[1] yet it appears that such studies could lead to answers to at least two important questions relating to banking structure. First, can small, independent banks compete effectively with large, geographically extensive banking organi-

zations? The answer to this question depends upon the effectiveness of correspondent banking arrangements, for it is only through services provided by its correspondents that a small unit bank is able to offer services comparable to those offered at offices of large banking organizations. Second, what is the optimum geographic form for these large banking organizations? Because they presumably improve banking operations and services by replacing correspondent ties with more direct ones, studies of the structure of correspondent relationships may yield answers to that question. It is believed

Source: Reprinted from *The Journal of Money, Credit, and Banking,* August 1970, pp. 358–369.

* The authors are indebted to Alexander Yeats, Gerald Hanweck, and Neil B. Murphy for helpful suggestions.

[1] Studies by Greenbaum and Finney deserve mention. See Stuart I. Greenbaum, "Correspondent Banking," Federal Reserve Bank of Kansas City, *Monthly Review* (March/April 1965), 9–16; and "More on Correspondent Banking," *Monthly Review* (July/August, 1965), 14–23. Also Katherine Finney, *Interbank Deposits: The Purpose and Effects of Domestic Balances 1934–54* (New York: Columbia University Press, 1958).

that this study provides some answers to the second question.

Small banks obtain many services from their correspondent banks.[2] The more important ones are check clearing, loan participations, and investment advice. In most cases payment for the services is effected through a deposit balance that the "country" bank maintains at its "city" correspondent.

The purpose of this paper is to study the demand for correspondent services from the viewpoint of spatial distribution and quantity demanded. It is known that banks have multiple correspondent relationships and that in most cases these ties are maintained in more than one city. The existence of geographic patterns to these relationships and the determinants of the patterns are investigated in this paper. Also of considerable interest is the aggregate amount of balances that banks maintain, and this aspect of the correspondent relationship will also be examined. By including both member and nonmember banks in the study, it is possible to determine the effect of Federal Reserve membership on correspondent balances as well as the total "due from banks" balances (correspondent balances plus deposits at the Federal Reserve) that banks maintain.

In Section II the factors which influence the spatial distribution of correspondent relationships are discussed, as are the determinants of total correspondent balances. The results of empirical tests are presented in Section III, and in Section IV the findings are summarized and policy implications discussed.

II. FACTORS AFFECTING CORRESPONDENT RELATIONSHIPS AND BALANCES

Two premises of this study are that correspondent relationships are established because banks need services and that correspondent balances are maintained primarily as payment for these services. This is not to suggest that correspondent balances do not serve other purposes. For nonmember banks, balances with other banks are often used to satisfy state reserve requirements. The balances are also a liquid asset and can be used to adjust to unforeseen deposit drains. Over time, however, the average balance must be sufficient to cover the costs the city correspondent incurs in providing services. Hence, while there may be daily and seasonal fluctuations in a bank's balance due to unforeseen movements in clearings, the general level of the balance is likely to be determined by the value of services demanded.[3]

The region within which the analysis of correspondent ties is to be conducted is the Denver Major Trade Area, except for minor adjustments. This region includes all of Colorado and most of Wyoming and New Mexico.[4] There are two reasons why this is a particularly good area for the study. Either unit banking or very limited branch banking prevails through-

---

[2] For a discussion of the various services and the extent to which they are used see *A Report on the Correspondent Banking System,* Committee on Banking and Currency, House, 88th Congress, Second Session, December 10, 1964.

[3] For evidence on this see *ibid.,* p. 7. If a fee system of payment for correspondent services were to become extensive, this relationship would probably no longer hold.

[4] The Denver Major Trade Area is defined in *Commercial Atlas and Marketing Guide,* 99th edition (New York: Rand McNally and Co., 1968), pp. 46–47. Only the Wyoming-Colorado-New Mexico portion of the area is to be used in the study. The small sections of Kansas, Arizona and Utah were excluded for the following reasons: the three Kansas Counties were not considered part of the area in the 98th edition, which was the one used at the time the study was planned; no banks are headquartered in the Arizona County; and only one bank is headquartered in the Utah section.

out; and the distances involved are vast, thereby granting an excellent opportunity to view the impact of distance on correspondent ties.

A. Dependent Variables

One set of dependent variables relates to the number of correspondent ties that banks maintain. The total number of correspondents is one of these variables, and the remaining variables consist of the number of correspondents in several geographic regions. These regions are Denver, outside Denver but within the Denver Major Trade Area, major commercial centers adjacent to Denver, and distant commercial centers. In this study a major commercial center is defined as one in which a Federal Reserve Bank or one of its branches is located. The adjacent commercial centers, therefore, are Salt Lake City, Helena, Omaha, Kansas City, Oklahoma City, and El Paso. The correspondent ties in the distant commercial centers are in the great majority of cases in New York, Chicago, and San Francisco.

The second set consists of two variables: (1) total balances due from domestic banks, and (2) variable 1 plus balances at the Federal Reserve Bank.

B. Independent Variables

The independent variables may be grouped into two sets: variables relating to bank characteristics and geographic variables. The first set consists of bank size, the bank's size rank in its community, the bank's ratio of demand to total deposits, and a dummy for the bank's Federal Reserve membership status. The second set includes the population of the bank's home-office city, the road-mile distance of the bank from the nearest major commercial center, and dummy variables representing the states in which the banks are located.

Country banks maintain correspond-

ent balances in order to secure services from city banks. For banks in the size range of those studied in this paper—that is, under $100 million in assets—the demand for correspondent services probably increases with bank size. It is possible that the demand for a few services would decrease with size because a larger bank could better produce its own services. For banks in this size range, however, check clearing is by far the most important service obtained; and the demand for this service is undoubtedly positively related to bank size. Therefore, both the number of correspondents and the dollar balances at correspondent banks should be positively related to bank size; indeed, it is likely that bank size is the most important of the independent variables.

A bank's size rank in its community also affects its demand for correspondent services. Generally, the larger businesses and the individuals with the most complex banking problems will patronize the largest banks in the community. Consequently, the largest banks in the community will have a greater need for assistance in providing such services.

From the point of view of the demand for services, it is clear that a higher ratio of demand to total deposits will mean a greater need for check clearing services. Hence, the higher the ratio of demand to total deposits the greater the number of correspondents and the amount of correspondent balances.

Federal Reserve Banks are alternative suppliers of some services offered by correspondent banks. System members, therefore, are likely to have fewer correspondent ties and balances. But Federal Reserve services are by no means perfect substitutes for the services of commercial bank correspondents; therefore, it is probable that the correspondent balances plus balances at the Federal Reserve Bank of member banks are greater than the correspondent balances of nonmembers. Also, state reserve requirements are generally lower than those imposed by the Federal Reserve.

The size of the town in which a bank is located probably influences the demand for correspondent services. The larger the town, the more likely it is that there will be businesses and individuals that require more sophisticated banking services. This means greater demand for correspondent services by the banks in these larger cities.

The number of correspondent ties and total correspondent balances are expected to increase with distance from the commercial center. As one moves to towns farther away from Denver the local economies become progressively less oriented to Denver and more oriented toward the adjacent commercial center or centers. Banks in the distant towns are likely to have a greater number of correspondent ties because such banks would find they had substantial clearings in more than one center and, therefore, would want a correspondent in these other centers as well as in Denver. Total correspondent balances of the distant banks are also likely to be higher. Presumably, the cost of providing services with the distance between the corresponding banks. Costs of communication increase with distance as do the costs of the city correspondent in monitoring loans in which it participated with the country bank. Thus, the amount of cor-

respondent balances a bank would have to maintain to obtain a given amount of services would increase with distance from the major commercial center. This factor, combined with the larger number of ties that such banks maintain, should yield a positive relationship between total balances and distance from Denver.

Differences in state reserve requirements undoubtedly are a factor producing variations in the amount of correspondent balances.[5] Hence, dummy variables for the three relevant states are incorporated into the "balances" regression equations.[6] These dummy variables are not included in the equations relating to the number of correspondents because there is no reason to believe that state requirements would have any effect on the number of correspondent ties.

III. EVIDENCE FROM REGRESSION ANALYSIS

Ordinary least-squares regression equations were run using the linear, double-log, and semi-log forms. With R^2 as the criterion, the semi-log forms yielded relatively poor fits. The linear and double-log forms gave about equally good results for four of the equations, but for three equations (1, 5, and 6) the coefficients of determination associated with the linear form were significantly higher (at the 95 per cent level). Consequently, the results for the linear forms are reported in this Section.

[5] These expected relationships conform to those found in a study by Lucille Stringer Mayne "Federal Reserve System-Membership, Bank Liquidity, and Bank Profitability," *Southern Economic Journal* (October, 1969), 181–84).

[6] Though the three states included in this study have different reserve requirements, it is not obvious which state has the highest. Colorado has a requirement of 15 percent of total deposits, but the requirement may be satisfied by vault cash, deposits at the Federal Reserve, demand deposits in specified commercial banks, or unpledged direct obligations of the United States. New Mexico has a 12 per cent requirement, but only cash and cash due from other banks are acceptable. Wyoming requires 20 percent of deposits to be in reserves, and the reserves must be in cash or balances at commercial banks. However, some deposits are exempted: deposits of the U.S. Government, and of the State of Wyoming and its political subdivisions.

Examination of the correlation matrix revealed that intercorrelation among the independent variables poses no serious estimation problems.

A.   The Variables

The variables used in the regression analysis are:

Dependent Variables:

C_t = total number of correspondents

C_v = number of correspondents in Denver

C_o = number of correspondents in the Denver Major Trade Area but outside Denver

C_a = number of correspondents in commercial centers adjacent to Denver

C_d = number of correspondents in distant commercial centers

B_c = balances due from domestic banks ($ millions)

B_t = B_c + balances at the Federal Reserve Bank ($ millions)

Independent Variables:

A = total assets of bank ($ millions)

R = bank's size in its community (largest = 1)

D/T = bank's ratio of demand to total deposits

M = member (1) or nonmember (0) bank

P = population of city in which bank is located (millions)

D = road mile distance of bank from Denver (hundreds of miles)

S_1 = bank located in Colorado (1), New Mexico (0), or Wyoming (0)

S_2 = bank located in Colorado (0), New Mexico (0), or Wyoming (1)

Most of the variables are adequately described above, but additional comments on P and R are required. With respect to Variable P, and SMSA is considered a "city." Thus if a bank is located in a Denver suburb which is part of the Denver SMSA, the population of the SMSA is assigned to that city. It is felt that a town of, say, 5,000 in a major metropolitan area differs significantly from an isolated town of the same population. In the former, more varied and complex banking services are likely to be demanded because of the types of business and persons in such an area.[7] In specifying a bank's size rank in its community (R), the individual town is used even though it may be part of an SMSA. Though some suburban individuals and businesses consider the "downtown" as well as their local banks as alternatives, there are many who view their local banks as the only convenient sources of banking services.

B.   The Data

In the area under consideration some banks are subsidiaries of bank holding companies. Because there is evidence of differences in correspondent banking ties of holding company banks and independent banks,[8] all banking subsidiaries of registered holding companies are excluded from the analysis. Banks may, of course, also be linked in other ways, e.g., interlocking directorates or common ownership; but such bank "chains" are not easily identified nor is there any evidence that correspondent relationships are affected by such ties. Consequently, any chain banks are included in the study.

It was recognized that the few, large, unrepresentative banks in the area could yield biased results. There were

---

[7] The regressions were run with both sets of population figures, i.e., with SMSA population and with the actual population of the town. In neither case was the coefficient of the population variable significant.

[8] Robert J. Lawrence, *The Performance of Bank Holding Companies* (Washington: Board of Governors of the Federal Reserve System, 1967), pp. 16–17.

only four banks with deposits of over $100 million, and they ranged in size from $136 to $470 million. Therefore, it was decided to exclude these four banks, making a bank with assets of $83 million the largest one in the study.

Information relating to the number and location of correspondent ties was taken from Polk's *Bank Directory* of September, 1966. Data for the various bank asset and liability items were secured from Reports of Condition. The values for these items are averages of the 1966 June and December call dates. Rand McNally's *Commercial Atlas and Marketing Guide* (1967) was the source for population data.

C. Regression Results

The regressions were run with banks ordered by asset size. This procedure permitted use of the Durbin-Watson (D-W) statistic as a check for unacceptable patterns in the residuals due to the scale variable, which was expected to be the most important one. In no equation were such patterns indicated.

In the discussion of the regression equations that follows, results are considered significant if they can be accepted at the 95 per cent confidence level.

NUMBER OF CORRESPONDENT RELATIONSHIPS

The results of the regression analyses are presented in Table 1. The T values, obtained by dividing the regression coefficients by their standard errors, are in parentheses below the coefficients. All of the F values are significant at the 1 per cent level.

The principal variables influencing the number of correspondent ties are bank size, the ratio of demand to total deposits, and the distance of the bank from Denver. The coefficients for the size of the town and the membership status of the bank are not significant. The size rank of the bank is significant in only one equation.

The total number of correspondent ties is strongly and positively related to bank size. For the banks in this study (all under $100 million in assets) there is an increase of about 1 correspondent tie for each $5 million increase in assets, other things equal. Bank size is also related to the geographic distribution of correspondents as is shown by (2–5). While the size coefficient is significant for explaining the number of ties in the major commercial center (Denver), the coefficient is small; only

TABLE 1

REGRESSION RESULTS FOR NUMBER OF CORRESPONDENT TIES[a]

| | Constant | Bank Characteristics | | | | Geographic | | R^2 | F | D-W |
		A	R	D/T	M	P	D			
(1) C_t	+.61 (.99)	+.22 (18.45)	−.05 (1.21)	+3.63 (3.77)	−.01 (.03)	−1.30 (.99)	+.33 (3.50)	.61	68.3	1.87
(2) C_v	+.92 (4.48)	+.02 (6.11)	−.03 (2.14)	+.94 (2.90)	+.13 (1.50)	+.10 (.23)	−.15 (4.89)	.24	14.8	1.91
(3) C_o	+.10 (.40)	−.00 (.92)	+.01 (.59)	+.59 (1.52)	−.10 (.97)	−.69 (1.31)	+.32 (8.56)	.29	18.8	
(4) C_a	+.01 (.03)	+.05 (8.82)	−.02 (.91)	+.65 (1.43)	+.07 (.61)	−.71 (1.15)	+.14 (3.08)	.28	18.3	1.68
(5) C_d	−.55 (1.70)	+.14 (21.45)	−.01 (.45)	+1.69 (3.32)	−.09 (.67)	+.15 (.22)	−.10 (2.08)	.67	89.3	2.09

[a] Based on 262 observations.

about 1 additional correspondent tie is established in Denver for each $50 million increase in assets. The size coefficient becomes increasingly larger as one moves to more distant commercial centers (4, 5). The relationship between size and the number of ties in distant centers is particularly pronounced. Bank size, however, has no effect upon the number of correspondents in the Denver trade area outside of Denver.

Though bank size has a relatively minor effect on the number of Denver correspondents, almost every bank has a correspondent tie in Denver: only 19 of the 262 banks do not have one. This suggests that almost every bank considers a correspondent relationship in the major commercial center of the trade area as important to effective operation. Most smaller banks, however, do not have correspondents in adjacent or distant commercial centers. Of the 131 banks below the median asset size of $4.5 million, 70 have no ties in adjacent centers and 86 have none in the distant centers.

Among the other variables representing bank characteristics, the ratio of demand to total deposits is also significantly related to the total number of correspondents. The results suggest that this variable has its greatest impact on the number of ties in distant commercial centers. A possible explanation for this is that banks with a relatively high proportion of demand deposits probably have the larger business accounts in their area; hence, these banks might have a greater need for help from banks in the nation's principal financial centers.

The coefficient of size rank of the bank in its community (R) has the expected sign in four of the five equations, but the coefficient is only significant in the equation for the number of ties in Denver. The results indicate that the larger banks in a community tend to have more ties in Denver.

Of the two geographic variables, only the distance of the bank from Denver is significantly related to the number of correspondent ties and their geographic distribution. The results for (1) show that there is an increase of one tie for about every 300 miles. The principal reason for the increase in the total number of correspondents is that the more distant banks tend to maintain ties in other cities in their trade area as well as in Denver. With increasing distance from Denver there is also a tendency to have more ties in adjacent commercial centers and fewer ties in Denver and distant centers.

AMOUNT OF DOMESTIC DUE FROM BANKS BALANCES

These equations are presented in Table 2. Two new dummy variables (S_1 and S_2), defining the state in which each bank is located, are included in the

TABLE 2

REGRESSION RESULTS FOR DOMESTIC "DUE FROM BANKS" BALANCES[a]

| | Constant | Bank Characteristics | | | | Geographic | | | | R^2 | F | D-W |
		A	R	D/T	M	P	D	S_1	S_2			
(6) B_c	−.54	+.13	+.02	+.97	−.33	+.12	+.10	+.14	+.37	.81	144.6	2.36
	(1.90)	(32.12)	(1.72)	(2.83)	(3.78)	(.26)	(2.05)	(.74)	(2.05)			
(7) B_t	−1.39	+.21	+.03	+1.66	+.46	−.67	+.10	+.14	+.38	.87	224.2	2.12
	(3.81)	(39.27)	(1.45)	(3.79)	(4.08)	(1.16)	(1.70)	(.54)	(1.64)			

[a] Based on 262 observations.

equations to test for the effects of differences in state reserve requirements. *T* values are in parentheses. Both *F* values are significant at the .01 level.

Bank size is the variable with the greatest explanatory power for the correspondent balances of the banks (6). This is to be expected; almost all bank asset categories would be closely related to total assets. The fact that the linear relation yields the best fit is important, however, because it suggests there are no important economies for larger banks with respect to the cost of correspondent services over the range of bank size considered. Further evidence is that in the log-log regression, the coefficient of *A* is not significantly different from 1 (.94 with a standard error of .05).[9]

Other variables representing bank characteristics that have the expected sign and are significant in (6) are the ratio of demand to total deposits and the membership status. With respect to the latter, the coefficient shows that the typical nonmember bank in this group has $300,000 more in correspondent balances than a member bank. Variable *R* has the expected sign, but the coefficient is not significant.[10]

Two geographic variables are significant in (6). The coefficients of the state dummies indicate that Wyoming banks tend to hold higher correspondent balances than banks in either Colorado or New Mexico, holding constant the in-fluence of all other variables. Apparently, Wyoming's effective reserve requirements are the highest of the three states. Distance of the bank from Denver is also positively related to correspondent balances.

In (7), the same variables representing bank characteristics are significant.[11] The coefficient of *M* shows that the typical member bank in the group has $500,000 more in total balances than nonmembers.[12] None of the geographic variables is significant. Apparently, the amount of balances at the Federal Reserve is not so strongly influenced by distance as correspondent balances.

IV. CONCLUSIONS

The Federal Reserve membership status of banks is not related to the number of correspondent ties or their geographic distribution, but it does explain differences in balances due from banks. Member banks have smaller correspondent balances than nonmembers; but when balances at the Federal Reserve are included, the total for member banks is higher.

Bank size is the key variable for explaining differences in the total number of correspondent ties and the geographic distribution of those ties. Evidence developed in this study also suggests that almost every bank requires correspondent services from a bank located in the commercial center of the

---

[9] The log-log regression equation with *T*-values is:

$$B_c = \underset{(19.92)}{.94A} + \underset{(3.26)}{.04R} + \underset{(3.68)}{.98D/T} - \underset{(6.49)}{.46M} - \underset{(.88)}{.02P} + \underset{(1.92)}{.06D} + \underset{(.54)}{.07S_1} + \underset{(2.19)}{.30S_2}$$

$$R^2 = .71$$
$$F = 81.1$$

[10] It was, however, significant in the double-log equation. See Footnote 9.

[11] Member banks' balances at the Federal Reserve Bank, of course, would be positively related to the ratio of demand to total deposits because of the higher reserve requirements on demand deposits.

[12] Assuming the banks could earn a net return of 8 per cent on such funds, the "cost" of Federal Reserve membership would be $40,000 per year for the typical bank in this study. Some benefits are, of course, derived from membership, e.g., access to the discount window. Whether the benefits equal the cost should be studied.

relevant major trade area; but only rather large banks (over $50 million in deposits) are likely to have more than one correspondent in the major center. On the other hand, most of the very small banks either have no need for correspondents in adjacent and distant commercial centers or do not use them if needed because of cost considerations or the difficulty of obtaining such services. The ratio of demand to total deposits and the distance of the bank from the major commercial center also influence the number and geographic distribution of correspondent relationships as well as total correspondent balances.

These conclusions have important implications for banking structure in the United States. In areas where independent unit banking prevails, correspondent ties are essential to the effective operation of the banking system. Correspondent relationships foster the interregional flow of bank credit and enable small banks to offer services which they otherwise could not. One of the prominent issues today is whether other forms of banking organization, that is holding companies and branch banks, can perform these functions better than independent unit banks linked by correspondent relationships. No position on this issue is taken in this paper except to note that the view of the majority in the academic community and in the Federal regulatory agencies appears to be that multioffice banking has advantages on balance. If this view is accepted, several conclusions seem justified given the results of this study.

Virtually all of the banks in this study have correspondents in Denver, suggesting that the correspondent relationship in the principal financial center of the region is the key one, particularly for the small banks. Therefore, if holding company or branch systems replace unit banking, it appears that the lead bank of the holding company or the main office of the branch system should be located in a major commercial center if the greatest benefit is to be obtained. In the case of the Denver region, combinations of the many rural banks in any one of the three states are unlikely to create a bank large enough to produce the required banking services. Consequently the essential link to the commercial center would still involve a correspondent relationship. These considerations further suggest that states with no major commercial center should allow at least some out-of-state holding companies or branch banks based in their area's commercial center to acquire banks or establish branches in the state. Where major commercial centers are located on state boundaries, it might also be desirable to permit limited expansion into the adjacent states by banking organizations located in such centers.

READING 13

MAJOR ISSUES IN THE REGULATION OF COMMERCIAL BANKS

Allan H. Meltzer*

All financial institutions In the United States are regulated to greater or lesser extent and are encumbered with restrictions that range from regulation of entry to restrictions on the purchase of particular assets and of the rate of interest paid on particular liabilities. The owners of financial institutions are, in part, compensated by special treatment under the tax laws. The *net* effect of governmental laws and decisions on the volume of assets invested in financial institutions—as well as the relative effect on the various specialized institutions—is difficult to calculate. The effect on resource allocation of these restrictions and tax shelters is also unknown.

The major issue about regulation is whether it achieves a desirable social purpose when both the costs and benefits of the restrictions are considered.

Broad issues of this kind cannot be resolved abstractly. They require analysis of the effect of each of the restrictions and of the combined effect, since some may partially or totally offset the effect of others, and some may impose no constraint. Unfortunately, there is no verified theory which permits a searching examination of the effect of regulation, so we must use a less satisfactory method. I have chosen to discuss the issue by examining the principal arguments for regulation.

Since many of the arguments that are used to justify regulation of non-bank financial institutions are also used to justify bank regulation or are based on a peculiar notion of equity—commercial banking is so regulated—I will deal, first, with the arguments for commercial bank regulation. Then, I will explore the principal arguments in

Source: Reprinted from "Major Issues In The Regulation of Financial Institutions," *The Journal of Political Economy,* August 1967, pp. 482–500.

* Helpful discussions with Karl Brunner, Ronald Hoffman, Alvin Marty, and E. S. Shaw, and financial assistance from the National Science Foundation are acknowledged gratefully.

more detail and reach conclusions about the regulation of commercial banking. Finally, I will consider the extent to which these conclusions furnish the basis for a policy of regulating banks and other financial institutions.

I. THE BASIS OF BANK REGULATION

Why is the number of banks or of branch banks a subject of national and state regulation? Why are banks permitted to underwrite municipal bonds but not corporate bonds? Why are banks permitted to buy municipal bonds but not stock in the American Telephone and Telegraph Company, in local utility companies, or in General Motors? Is there a rationale for a rule that permits a bank to lend money on a five-year term loan to a small unrated corporation, but prohibits the purchase of common stock in a larger more profitable corporation? Why, after all, is banking a regulated industry?

Five partly overlapping arguments are cited to justify banking regulation. Two are based on standard propositions in the theory of price: (1) a maximizing monopolist restricts output and raises price; and (2) in an industry subject to economics of scale, profit-maximizing behavior eliminates independent firms until only a monopolist remains. The first proposition is an important part of the economic justification of antitrust laws; the second furnishes a rationale for government regulation of public utilities. Banking has recently become subject to the anti-trust laws[1] and, though not a public utility, has long been a regulated industry.

The first proposition above does not apply to the banking industry. The industry produces money, or more exactly demand and time deposits, along with a by-product, bank credit. A principal factor of production [input] is the monetary base—reserves plus currency. Since the output of nominal money is proximately determined by the input of base money, the output of the industry is proximately determined by the government or its agency, the central bank. I will explore this argument in more detail in the following section.

Fear of a banking monopoly or the "money trust" has had an important influence on U.S. history. The fact that the industry's output is restricted by the government's monetary policy *does not assure* that firms in the industry would not consolidate into a monopoly, or a few dominant firms, in the absence of regulations on branching and merger. However, since the total output of the industry and the market prices of its many outputs are dominantly influenced by monetary policy, and since close substitutes for the industry's products are (or can be) produced,[2] it requires analysis to show that monopoly power can be exploited. Nevertheless, the argument that economies of scale lead to concentration and that concentration leads to monopoly has had increased influence on legislation and policy toward mergers and branching. I will consider this argument below and summarize some of the evidence on the relation of costs to output in banking.

A third justification for controls and regulations is based on an entirely different, and opposing, argument—the absence of monopoly. According to this argument, ease of entry and the prevalence of competition lead bankers to take "excessive" risks, encourage "overbanking," and thus produce an increased number of *bank failures*. To protect the public against these alleged consequences of competition in banking, restrictions have been placed on bank entry, on the type of assets that

[1] *U.S. v. Philadelphia National Bank* et al., 374 U.S. 321 (1963).

[2] Some of the industry's more important sources of revenue come from the adaptation of ideas developed by competing institutions, for example, consumer credit or term loans.

banks may purchase, on the rates of interest that they may pay on liabilities, and on a number of other details of the business. In addition, this argument has been used to justify both audit or examination of bank assets and deposit insurance.

The controls and regulations designed to prevent bank failures are often defended as a means of reducing the severity of recessions. The maintenance of inefficient banks is regarded as a small cost relative to the social benefits said to result from regulation, particularly from deposit insurance. However, Cagan's recent study suggests that there is no consistent relation between bank failures and the depth and severity of a recession.[3] His data suggest that high failure rates have occurred in mild cycles and even in periods of expansion, although bank failures have made recessions more severe at times. I will, therefore, suggest an alternative to the present system of controls, one that is designed to eliminate inefficient banks while reducing or eliminating the effect of bank failures on the severity of recessions.

The general argument for regulation based on overexpansion or "excessive risk taking" by bankers appears to rest on a misapplication of economic theory. If banks expanded output until price equals marginal cost, the value of a unit of money would fall almost to zero.[*] The economic argument for the control of money by the state rests heavily on its very low marginal cost of production and on the expected consequences of unregulated, competitive production. But this argument for controlling the nominal stock of money does not imply (or even suggest) that the *number* of producers of money

must be controlled. It seems obvious that once the determinants of a socially desirable rate of change of money are known, the desired quantity of money can be produced either by a state monopoly, by a large number of relatively small banks, or by some combination of public and private producers. The desirable number of banks can be determined on grounds of economic and social efficiency. For example, if monetary controls are used to produce a desired rate of change of money, banking regulation can be used to minimize the cost of producing or distributing money.

A separate though related argument for controls on banking assets is based on the proposition that either the venal behavior of unregulated bankers or "competitive pressures" is responsible for major inflations or depressions. In its simplest form, this argument says that, at times, unregulated bankers (1) permit the "quality of credit" to decline; (2) become fearful, call loans, and force liquidation on business; and (3) ultimately force failure of themselves or their competitors.

There are three problems with this argument as a defense of regulation and examination of bank assets. First, it presumes that bank examiners are more perceptive or more accurate judges of default risk than bankers. Second, it suggests that the quality of credit is independent of monetary policy and of the position of the economy. Third, it seeks to shift some, or all, of the responsibility of past errors and failures of public policy to banks or bankers.

This argument loses much of its force if inflation, severe contractions, and widespread bank failures are

---

[3] Approximately 15 per cent of the banks existing in 1920 closed before the end of 1928, most of them during the relatively prosperous years 1924–28. One of the most severe recessions of this century, 1937–38, came after many of the present controls of banking were in effect.

[*] Editor's note: The value of money (its price) is the reciprocal of the general price level. If marginal cost of money production is zero, or close to zero, the value of money will also be zero.

largely the result of inappropriate public policies. A strong case can be made to support the conclusion that many of the failures of monetary policy were the result of actions based on incorrect notions about the determinates of the quantity of money and incorrect assertions about the cause of changes in the quantity and "quality" of bank credit. These notions were used to shift responsibility for bank failures from the Federal Reserve to private bankers and to justify many of the controls introduced or strengthened by the Banking Act of 1935. Since it is time-consuming to deal with each of the assertions separately, I will merely point out that many of them rest on a denial of the central bank's ability to control the quantity of money and thus are contradicted by studies of the relation of central banking policy to the money supply.

Finally, there is the argument for controls designed to prevent the formation of local monopolies. It is alleged that the existence of a large number of banks in the United States and the rate of monetary expansion are irrelevant (or of little importance) to the problem of monopoly in banking. Various malefactors—city unit banks, chain banks, holding companies, branch banks—are said to threaten the survival of small, local banks and thus produce monopolies. The public interest is said to be served best by local ownership of local banks since such banks "best serve the needs of local consumers and business."

One form of this argument is based on the proposition that there are economies of scale in banking. The branch, chain, or large bank is said to eliminate competition by pricing below the average cost of the small, local bank until the local bank is forced to withdraw or become a branch. Thereafter, the larger (branch, chain) bank raises prices and exploits its local monopoly

position. In a variant of this argument, the more powerful bank enters, becomes the price leader, and permits the smaller bank to survive if it "follows the leader."

A very different version of the argument makes the small, local banker the monopolist in isolated one-bank towns. Until recently, analysis has been limited by the absence of theory and evidence, and the argument has been waged by the method of plausible assertion and counterassertion. One side has pointed to the smaller number of services and lower loan/deposit ratios of smaller banks to claim that the degree of monopoly is inversely related to bank size. Others have jumped from the assertion of increased bank concentration in local markets to a conclusion about increased monopoly power. These positions have been restated in a number of recent papers and have produced a growing literature on the effect of entry and branching on the cost of providing banking services, on the definition of bank output, and related matters. While many of the studies are concerned with fact gathering and do not present explicit theories of bank behavior (some exceptions will be noted), when combined they provide a reasonably consistent picture of the banking industry and of the effect of size and structure on output, profit, and the prices of banking services. I will discuss and interpret some of the main findings below.

To summarize, the many arguments for controls appear to fall into one of three categories which I shall call the macro, the micro, and the failure arguments. In the macro case, the output of the banking system is said to be (a) independent of—or relatively unaffected by—monetary policy, and the banking system is ssumed to expand of its own volition; or (b) the *industry* is said to behave monopolistically, restricting output and raising price. The arguments or assertions about the inability of the central bank to control the quantity of money have been discussed elsewhere and will not be repeated here. Instead, I will discuss the effect of monetary policy on the output of the banking industry on the assumption that the industry is monopolized.

The micro case for controls rests on arguments about the effects of concentration, economies of scale, and banking structure, and on the evidence supporting the claims that local monopolies exist in small towns, large cities, or both. I will summarize the evidence and draw conclusions about the relation of the benefits to the costs of controls.

The "cost of bank failure" argument for controls has both micro and macro aspects. Controls that have become a part of deposit insurance arrangements have probably become more important as a means of preventing bank failures than as a method of safeguarding deposits. The costs and benefits of reducing the number of bank failures, however, can be separated from an analysis of the role of deposit insurance. I will discuss the effects of single and multiple bank failures and the case for deposit insurance after considering the arguments for controls designed to offset industry-wide or local monopoly.

II. BANKING AS A MONOPOLIZED INDUSTRY

The theory of monopoly implies that a maximizing monopolist restricts output and raises price. The proposition applies irrespective of the source of monopoly power, so that a monopoly based on government restrictions on entry into the industry is expected to have the same effect as any other restriction that sustains a monopoly.

Entry into commercial banking is regulated by state and federal agencies. Nevertheless, this standard proposition of monopoly theory cannot be applied to banking without major qualifications.

The reason for this is that the government has a more powerful monopoly. A principal input for the production of bank deposits and earning assets is the monetary base, bank reserves plus currency, as noted above. This sum is produced by government at approximately zero marginal cost. The amount produced reflects decisions about the desired level or direction of change of output, prices, employment, or gold stock that are translated into decisions about the desired level or direction of change of interest rates, bank credit, or money. While there are important economic consequences arising from the decisions about the goal of policy and the choice of a policy target, these consequences are of limited importance for this discussion. Whatever decisions are made, the supply of base money is determined. Since the quantities of money and bank credit, the balance sheet position of the banking system, and the level of interest rates depend on the volume of base money, the equilibrium values of these variables depend on monetary policy decisions.[4]

To see this point more clearly, assume that the banking system is a monopoly firm which maximizes wealth by eliminating the difference between desired and actual reserves. (Call this difference surplus reserves). Each dollar change in the monetary base, resulting from gold flows, open market operations, etc., and any change in the public's desired holdings of currency raises or lowers the volume of surplus reserves and induces changes in money, bank credit (loans and invest-

---

[4] To simplify the discussion, I make no mention of other variables that affect market interest rates, money, or bank credit. For example, increases in the stock of interest bearing debt raise market interest rates and induces increases in money and bank credit.

ments), and market interest rates. If the monopolized banking system attempts to *restrict* output and raise interest rates by holding additions to reserves in the form of vault cash or non-interest bearing deposits at the central bank, the smaller will be changes in money, interest rates, and bank credit, per dollar change in the monetary base. To achieve its target level or rate of change of interest rates or money, the central bank can inject more base money at approximately zero marginal cost. The monopolist cannot restrict the quantity of money or raise the level of market interest rates independently of the government's policy unless it can offset the decisions of the central bank.[5] By refusing to expand, the monopoly bank will eliminate the fractional reserve system, a main source of its profits.

Frequently, it is suggested that a monopolized banking system restricts the output of loans by raising loan rates relative to other market rates rather than by restricting total earning assets and holding a larger proportion of assets as surplus reserves. Again, it is difficult to make this monopoly power effective. The government controls the outstanding stock of interest-bearing debt. The likely consequences of an attempt by banks to raise interest rates on loans is that the monopoly banks will hold a larger share of the outstanding stock of government debt and have a lower ratio of loans to earning assets or deposits. But *non-bank lenders* then hold fewer securities and make more loans. There is little reason to believe that the interest rate on loans charged by non-bank financial institutions would be affected to any important extent by the attempt of commercial banks to raise loan rates, so it is difficult to find any important economic consequences of the possible preference of monopolists for government securities rather than loans.[6] In any case, this does not happen. Branch banks and urban banks that hold a high proportion of a community's deposits generally have higher loan/deposit or loan/asset ratios, as I will note below.

These considerations of the effect of a monopoly in banking provide no basis for control of banking entry and merger. At most, they suggest that controls which prevent non-bank financial institutions from offering loans of particular types may restrict the output of particular credit instruments. But it is difficult to see how the restriction of one type of credit instrument and the expansion of another can prevent the public from achieving its desired debt position. Loans that are ostensibly made for one purpose can be used for another.

It is the government or central bank, and not the commercial banks, that has the monopoly power to restrict the output of nominal money and raise interest rates. Like any other monopolist, the government can choose a desired level of output or a desired interest rate, but not both. Suppose, for example, the central bank chooses some level of interest rates as a policy target while the private banking monopoly restricts the

---

[5] The argument is slightly more complicated than the statement in the text suggests. An open market operation changes the stock supply of government debt held by the banks and/or the non-bank public and changes the market interest rate on government debt. If the monopoly banking system attempts to restore the status quo ante, it must restore the previous rate on government securities. If there is an open market purchase from bank or non-bank holders of government debt, market interest rates fall slightly. The monopoly bank must counter this effect on interest rates by adding to excess reserves an amount larger than the addition to reserves provided by the open market operation.

[6] Of course, I assume that the monopoly is in effect and ignore the adjustment costs that occur when monopoly comes into being. I will discuss the effect of differences in cost when I consider local monopolies in the following section.

use of bank services by raising service charges or by reducing the services offered to depositors. Higher service charges on demand deposits raise the demand for currency, lower the demand for demand deposits and, as a result, change the composition of the nominal money stock, thus raising market interest rates and reducing bank credit and bank deposits.

The central bank can choose to maintain the level of market interest rates that prevailed before bank service charges were raised. Or, the central bank, can prevent prices from changing by controlling the quantity of nominal money, allowing nominal balances to fall until equilibrium is restored at the previous price level. Whether or not the banks realize profits as a result of higher service charges will, of course, depend on the policy decision of the central bank. In addition, the profitability of higher service charges to banks depends on the elasticities of the demand for deposits with respect to service charges, the interest elasticity of the public's supply of earning assets to banks, and—if prices are permitted to change—on the extent to which the banks are debtors or creditors. There is, therefore, no reason to believe that high service charges are a concomitant of monopoly.

Up to this point I have discussed the banking system as if it was a single monopoly firm. In fact, the banking system consists of more than fourteen thousand banks. However, analysis of the aggregate effect of monopoly in banking does not appear to be altered in any important way by aggregation,[7]

although the existence of a large number of banks provides an additional reason for believing that it is extremely difficult for the banking system to form a system-wide monopoly.

In short, analysis of the aggregate effects of monopoly does not provide an argument for controls on entry, branching, and merger, or support the assertions that are commonly made. If the central bank controls the monetary base, it has proximate control of the money supply and the output of the banking industry. Since proximate control of the latter quantity does not depend on the number of banks or on the number of banking offices, arguments for controls based on potential over- or underproduction of banking output appear to be unfounded. For similar reasons, restrictions on the type of assets which banks may buy, or requirements for the examination of asset portfolios, cannot be defended on the grounds that the banking system would over- or underproduce if the regulations were removed. The government has sufficient power to control the industry's output.

If this analysis is correct, and the government can, to a first approximation, control the output of money and bank credit or the market interest rate, it does not follow that the restrictions imposed on the commercial banking system have no consequences. Some regulations, for example, Federal Reserve regulation Q, influence the size of the banking system relative to the size of non-bank financial institutions, reduce the rate at which commercial banks fail, or affect the type of individ-

---

[7] In passing, it should be noted that if a monetary system has only a few monopoly banks, their average reserve ratio would be lower and the monetary multiplier would be larger than the average reserve ratio and monetary multiplier of the present banking system. The reason is that the increased concentration of deposits in the banking system reduces the expected loss of reserves per dollar of new deposits supplied by a bank. However, the increased "efficiency" that accompanies such increased concentration has little social value. The gain from producing a given money supply with a slightly lower monetary base and higher monetary multiplier is extremely small.

uals who choose to be called bankers. Still others, for example, Federal Deposit Insurance, protect the owners of deposits against the destruction of a portion of their wealth through bank failures. Although the aggregate analysis does not show the presence of benefits equal to the cost of administering the controls, some of the other possible costs and benefits remain to be considered.

III. BANKING CONTROLS AND LOCAL MONOPOLY IN BANKING

Much regulation, and much of the literature, is concerned with the problem of local monopoly in banking. Existing legislation requires the federal banking authorities to consider the effect of competition when approving or disallowing entry, branching, or merger of state or national banks. The decision in the Philadelphia-Girard case[8] and in subsequent merger cases aroused considerable interest in the problem of monopoly in banking among economists and policy makers. A series of articles discussed the courts' decisions and later spilled over into more detailed consideration of the effect of size, structure, and concentration on banking costs, profits, and services.

In the previous section, I concluded that it was government monopoly and not private monopoly that had the important influence on the prices and output of banking services. However, I noted that in principle a private monopolist could raise prices and restrict the output of deposits and bank credit by rising service charges on deposits. From this line of reasoning, it seems to follow that some useful evidence on the extent or absence of monopoly in banking can be obtained from the data on service charges and services.

Another justification for controls appears to rest on an argument similar to the following: Even if the banking system *as a whole* cannot restrict total output by raising loan rates, *local* monopolists can restrict their output of loans by charging higher rates. There may not be sufficient competition in each area or banking market to produce a competitive solution in each and every market. Small, local borrowers may have few opportunities for market search, may be inhibited by the cost of search and by the cost of providing information to bankers in distant cities. The aggregate volume of loans and securities held by the banking system may be unchanged, but in some areas monopoly banks will hold more government securities and offer fewer loans than in the absence of local monopoly; in other areas, characterized by competition in banking, financial institutions will hold more loans and fewer government securities.[9] If, in addition, long-run costs rise with output, the weighted average loan rates will be higher in the long run equilibrium position attained by the banking system.

There is no need to examine whether this argument provides a necessary or sufficient condition for higher loan rates and monopoly profits in banking or in local banking markets. One of the most frequently noted facts about the U.S. banking system is the diversity of bank size that persists in the industry. If there were significant economies or diseconomies of scale in banking, we would expect some sizes to disappear and new entrants to choose a particular size or range. Yet, more than half of the banks held de-

---

[8] *U.S. v. Philadelphia National Bank* et al., *ibid.*

[9] I ignore the problem of local monopoly banks holding larger ratios of reserves to deposits. Since such action simply lowers the average monetary and asset multiplier and can be offset by a larger monetary base, it produces results very similar to those discussed in the text. The total stock of credit (or money) is unaffected. At worst, the distribution of types of earning assets among institutions is altered.

posits of less than $5 million in the early 1960's, while one hundred large banks held approximately half of total deposits. New entrants into banking chose a range of sizes for initial capital which suggests that they expected to operate in most of the existing size groups. Similarly, the data show that more than 20 per cent of the new national banks chartered in 1962 (fourteen of sixty-four) chose areas of the country with less than ten thousand population, the same size community in which ten thousand of the approximately twelve thousand existing banks were found, while seventeen of the sixty-four new entrants chose cities with population of one million or more.

Studies of costs, profitability, or rate of return generally support the evidence obtained from examining the size distribution of new and existing banks. Costs have been found to decline until a bank reaches a size of $2 to $5 million in deposits, then remain approximately constant until a deposit size of $100 to $500 million is reached; thereafter, there is a slight further reduction in operating expenses per unit of assets as size increases. Shull and Horvitz summarized these findings: "On the basis of available evidence, it is reasonable to conclude that a well-run bank with $5 million in deposits can compete on a fairly even basis with much larger banks. . . . The data we have indicate a relatively steep decline in the long run average cost curve over the very small bank sizes. Once banks are over, say, $1 million in deposits, costs decline slowly to the minimum." A number of other studies have reached similar conclusions.

Studies of unit costs by size group do not, of course, correct for differences in the mix of output, in the mix of deposits, and in the services offered by individual banks. Some studies have attempted to control for these differences and, of these, Benston's study is particularly notable.[10] Using regression analysis, he computed the marginal cost of each of the principal banking operations and found a tendency for costs to decline slightly as *units* of output or service increased. But even this finding of slight economies of scale must be interpreted carefully, since larger banks generally make larger loans and accept larger deposits. Benston found that there were additions to cost associated with handling the same number of transactions when the average size of transaction is larger. The latter finding is consistent with the evidence, discussed below, that larger banks provide more services. It is not unlikely that large borrowers and large depositors are in a position to demand and receive more service.

In a study of loans rates, Benston found that most of the differences in the rate of interest on large and small loans could be explained by the marginal cost of lending and the marginal cost of risk. His conclusion is supported by analysis of the data from the Federal Reserve surveys of business loans. Flechsig found that "within the range of existing concentration levels . . . no identifiable relation was discovered between concentration ratios and the level of interest rates on business loans. This is true even for small borrowers who are restricted to financing within their local areas and, therefore, would be more vulnerable to non-competitive pricing practices."

If there are important economies of scale in banking, they are hard to detect and to realize. In states that do not permit branching, a bank can expand only by merging or growing.

[10] As Benston notes, the studies in which substantial economies of scale are found measure output in nominal units rather than in real units. The findings of such studies must be interpreted as showing only that it costs less per dollar to accept a fifty-dollar deposit than a ten-dollar deposit.

Merging is an expensive way to acquire new business since the acquiring bank must pay the capitalized value of a going business and cannot expect to retain all of the customers of the acquired bank when it attempts to move them to its own site. In states that permit branching a bank attempting to realize economies of scale can convert an existing bank into a branch if it obtains the approval of the banking authorities and the department of Justice.

A number of studies have attempted to isolate differences in performance, profitability, cost, etc., between branch and unit banks. A comprehensive survey of banking in New York State found that, in general, branch banks provide more services than unit banks and have higher loan-to-deposit ratios, lower or equal interest rates on loans of similar size and type. Large banks and branch banks pay higher interest rates on time and savings deposits but charge higher service charges on demand deposits. These findings have been replicated in a number of studies, including some which examined the behavior of new branches and existing banks after branching or entry restrictions were relaxed.

If banks could lower costs by branching, we would expect unit banks to be absorbed as branches in states that permit branch banking. Branch banking has grown very slowly, however. While the ratio of branch to unit plus branch banks has grown from 1 per cent to approximately 20 per cent in the past sixty years, the ratio has shown only a very slight tendency to accelerate. This finding might be interpreted as solely the result of regulation were it not for the fact that several studies show that branch banks have higher costs than unit banks of similar deposit size. Benston found that the costs are primarily occupancy costs, hence a concomitant of branching, and Schweiger and McGee concluded that on the

average, "a branch bank of $5 million to $10 million in deposits should be expected to achieve as low or lower expense rates as a unit bank of less than $2 million deposits; one of $200 million to $500 million to compare favorably with unit banks of $50 million to $100 million size, etc."

These findings are inconsistent with the view that branch banks have substantial competitive advantage over unit banks of similar or smaller size. Moreover, the data suggest that, where branching is permitted, banking services are increased at both unit and branch banks. For example, higher interest rates are paid on time deposits at unit banks when branching is permitted even when a branch does not operate in an isolated one-bank town.

A reasonable explanation of the data is that where branching is permitted, inefficient unit banks are absorbed as branches, become more efficient, or disappear. This explanation is consistent with the prediction of economic theory and the evidence that branching raises costs, since a bank could profitably purchase an inefficient unit bank and convert it into a more efficient branch. Apparently there is no expected profit to the branch bank from acquiring an efficient unit bank of moderate size.

Branching apparently improves the efficiency of the banking system without imposing social costs. Some additional benefits of branching and merger will be considered below.

Service charges and depositor services were investigated in a survey of U.S. banking conducted by Weintraub and Jessup for the House Banking and Currency Committee. Their findings are of particular interest, since my earlier argument suggests that high service charges are one means by which a banking monopoly can restrict output and raise price. Weintraub and Jessup found that (1) large banks had higher service charges than small banks, (2) branch banks generally had higher service charges than unit banks of the same size; and (3) the differences between types of banks generally declined as the size of a depositor's average and minimum balance increased. Nevertheless, on the average, small depositors pay significantly higher service charges at city banks and particularly at branch banks in large cities.

Three qualifications must be noted before these findings are interpreted as an indication of monopoly in banking. First, the banks that have the highest service charges generally offer the largest range of services to large and small depositors. The data can be interpreted as the outcome of a search, or selection, process by means of which depositors select banks that offer the package of services they desire. The higher service charges are the price of increased services. Second, the differences in average service charges, while often significant, are small. The largest cost reduction available to an average small depositor ($200 minimum balance, $300 average balance) who writes ten checks and makes two deposits per month is eighty-one cents per month and is obtained by moving his account from the (average) city unit bank with deposits of $50 to $100 million to the (average) country unit bank with deposits of less than $10 million. On the average, the maximum addition to cost of doubling the activity of an account while keeping the size and location of the balance unchanged is sixty-seven cents per month. Third, if local monopolists restrict output by raising service charges, we would expect them to increase the value of their monopoly position by raising loan rates and restricting loans. Most of the data on loan/deposit ratios point in the opposite direction. On borrowing costs, the New York banking survey found:

New York City banks, particularly the larger ones, generally charged the lowest interest rates for the three specific types of loans discussed, with large branch banks in the suburban areas around New York close behind on two of the three rates. Outside the New York City metropolitan area, unit banks charged lower rates than branch banks on new car loans and, for the last several years, possibly also on small business loans after adjusting for the effect of compensating balances. Only for conventional mortgage loans on new houses have unit banks consistently charged higher rates than branch banks throughout the period 1950 to 1962.

Furthermore, the Weintraub and Jessup data appear to reject the allegation that branch banks are reluctant to lend to local businessmen.

Taken together, these studies provide little justification for control of entry, merger and branching. Presumably, increased entry would eliminate or at least reduce, the power of existing monopolies. Increased mergers, entry, and branching would eliminate inefficient banks. These conclusions are supported by the evidence, discussed earlier, which shows that existing banks offer more services where entry or branching is permitted and that, when small unit banks become branches, banking services generally increase.

The cumulative effect of restrictions on entry and branching has been large. Between 1941 and 1950, the Comptroller's office rejected 553 applications to organize national banks and establish branches. Of the rejected applicants, 70 per cent were told that they had "unfavorable earnings prospects" or that the community had "insufficient need." The latter reason, often a euphemism for the former, was by far the most frequent reason for rejecting an application. Assuming that the Comptroller's office was not always incorrect, some of the applicants would have failed. Nevertheless, some of the banks would have remained, and it is likely that the public would now receive more banking services per dollar if all of the applications had been approved.

Additional evidence that the cumulative effect of banking regulations has been large comes from the parameter estimate of Peltzman's model of bank entry. He found that, from 1936 to 1961, the marginal effect of restrictions on entry was a reduction of more than two thousand in the number of state and national banks.

As Peltzman notes, it is more difficult to find benefits than to find costs to the public of the existing restrictions on entry. My examination of the data leads me to similar conclusions about restrictions on mergers and branching. Since entry into banking would be relatively easy in the absence of regulation, entry, mergers, and branching would eliminate inefficient banks. Repeal of legal and administrative restrictions would not produce monopoly, unless economies of scale are more substantial than those that have been found.

There are two remaining arguments for controls that have not been considered. First, if there were no restrictions on entry, the number of bank failures would increase. This argument is discussed below. Second, the number of mergers between large banks in recent years is often taken as evidence of scale economies for banks of largest size. The increased concentration of deposits after mergers is taken as evidence of actual or potential monopoly in local banking markets. The fact that approximately half of all bank deposits are in one hundred large banks is used as an argument against further concentration.

There is, however, an alternative hypothesis which does not invoke economies of scale to explain the desire of large banks to merge or to explain the concentration of deposits. This explanation makes existing regulations and restriction a principal force making for concentration in banking.

Present laws or regulations do not permit a bank to lend more than a fixed proportion of its capital—often no more than 10 per cent—to a single borrower. The average size of loans has increased over time. Unless a bank's capital increases in proportion to the size of loans, the restrictions on loans to a single borrower force a bank either to refuse to lend to large borrowers or to share such loans with other banks and financial institutions.

Inflation raised prices and increased the average size of new bank loans without increasing the capital and surplus of banks in proportion. Legal lending limits became more restrictive and forced banks to share customers that they were able to service previosly without assistance. By merging, banks increased their capital and thus were able to compete more effectively with other large banks.

The number of large borrowers is relatively small, but a large proportion of business loans is made to large borrowers. Some indication of the importance of large borrowers to large banks can be obtained from published data. At the end of 1965, only 408 of 175,000 taxpaying, manufacturing corporations had assets in excess of $100 million. These corporations, however, borrowed 45 per cent of the total volume of loans (with original maturity of one year or less) made to all manufacturing corporations. The average of such loans per corporation was in excess of $10 million for the 408 corporations. For the forty-one manufacturing corporations with assets in excess of $250 million, the average balance of loans with less than one year to maturity was $30 million.[11] Such corporations also borrow for longer-term and, of course, some borrow more than the average.

This argument assigns an important role to lending restrictions and the increased size of loans to large firms in the explanation of mergers by large banks. It suggests that competition for large loans is not reduced if mergers are permitted, and it does not invoke economies of scale as a reason for merging. However, the argument does not establish that competition in banking markets increases or that banks of largest size do not realize economies of scale by merging.

We are left with the following general conclusions. Banks of different size, structure, and location offer a variety of services at varying charges. Many of the differences can be explained adequately without using monopoly power as a part of the explanation. Indeed, in many cases, the data provide no support for the monopoly argument.

Entry into banking, in the absence of legal restrictions, would be relatively easy. To the extent that entry and branching occur, banking services increase at little additional cost to consumers and business. There is little support for the argument that existing or potential local monopoly requires government to control entry, branching, and merger. Instead, the findings suggest that monopoly in banking would be reduced if entry and branching were not regulated. The cost of restrictions seems high relative to the benefits.

IV. BANK FAILURES AND CONTROLS ON BANK PORTFOLIOS

Fear of the consequences of bank failure is invoked frequently to defend bank portfolio regulations and the numerous restrictions on the amount of risk that bankers are permitted to accept. Similar arguments are used to justify deposit insurance. There is abundant evidence that, at times, bank failures have made both the consequences of a recession and the recession itself more severe. Nevertheless, it is useful to consider the extent to which the prevention of bank failures makes it desirable to regulate the type of assets banks may buy.

There are two separable issues connected with bank failures. One is the cause and effect of multiple bank failures or, in the most extreme form, destruction of the banking system. The other is the effect of an individual bank failure.

The failure of an uninsured bank and the permanent loss of his deposit have long- and short-run effects on a depositor. The principal long-run effect is the once-and-for-all reduction in wealth which reduces consumption. In addition, the unexpected loss of wealth may affect the individual's expectations about the future or his attitude toward risk, although very little is known about the magnitude, direction, or duration of these effects. The principal short-run effect results from the unanticipated (and presumably large) change in portfolio composition which induces reallocation of a smaller stock of existing assets to obtain a desired portfolio. I find it difficult to believe that the cost of adjusting to a loss of deposits is substantially larger than the costs of adjusting to any other uninsured loss of wealth, such as the unanticipated failure of a corporation in which the individual is a stockholder, or the destruction of wealth resulting from a fire, from a natural disaster, or from some other random event.

Frequently, it is suggested that the short-term effect of a bank failure on

---

[11] Data are from *FTC-SEC Quarterly Financial Report for Manufacturing Corporations*, 4th Quarter, 1965.

the community is much larger than the sum of the effects on individual depositors. Again, the long-run effect of the failure of a single bank does not differ from the loss of an equal amount of wealth that the depositors hold in another form. However, if the bank is a principal supplier of the community's means of payment, the cost of making transactions is increased, temporarily, and remains higher until new banking services become available.

Neither laws nor regulations require that every community have a bank, so there is no reason to consider, separately, the long-run effect on a community of a bank failure (or closing) that eliminates a bank of less than minimum efficient size. Our interest here is in bank failures resulting from incorrect perceptions or risk, preference for risk, poor collection procedures by bank management, or from dishonest practices. It is in these cases that insurance and asset regulation are defended as a means of protecting bank customers. Depositors are said to be unaware of— and unlikely to pay the cost of acquiring information about—the risk position accepted by the bank or the character of the banker.

Assume that this latter argument is correct and, further, that it is undesirable for individuals to bear the costs arising from lack of information. It does not follow (1) that banks should be required to make an all-or-nothing choice —all deposits insured or all uninsured; (2) that government should offer deposit insurance; or (3) that government should select the type of assets which banks purchase. As an alternative, individuals could be permitted to purchase insurance on the fraction of their deposits they desire to safeguard at the prevailing insurance premium. Insurance companies, whether privately or publicly owned, could collect information periodically on the risk position

of banks and set premiums that depend on their estimate of expected failure.

One important economic consideration makes the system of private deposit insurance difficult to maintain: the possibility of multiple bank failures, and the destruction of a large part of the nation's means of payment in a short period of time. The probability of such an event is small, but the expected loss is large, so the cost of insurance would be high under a private system. Moreover, private insurance companies might lack the means of paying claims promptly, even if they survived the financial crisis. They, too, would be depositors.

The case for government insurance of deposits does not rest solely on the fact that government can insure deposits at lower cost. It rests on the responsibility of the government to maintain the growth rate of the money supply at a level that promotes full use of resources without inflation. Destruction of the means of payment through multiple bank failures is an indication that the government has not fulfilled its responsibility.

On this interpretation, bank failures that produce a decline in the money supply are the result of errors and misconceptions by central bankers. This view, which in one form goes back to Henry Thornton, receives strong support from recent studies of U.S. monetary history. By requiring the central bank to prevent or promptly correct errors that force the money supply to contract sharply, deposit insurance forces the central bank or the insurance agency to arrest the decline in the money supply.

Regulation of banking assets itself is much older than deposit insurance. Regulation did not prevent widespread bank failures and cannot be expected to do so unless bank examiners or banking agency officials are better judges of risk than bankers. The case for deposit insurance does not provide a rationale for restrictions on the assets banks may purchase. However, an argument can be made for audit or examination of bank assets as a part of the system of deposit insurance outlined in the following section.

V.   OUTLINE OF A SYSTEM OF INSURANCE AND REGULATION

The principal purpose of controls on banking and financial institutions is said to be protection of the public. My analysis suggests, however, that the present system of controls protects some inefficient banks against competition, protects bankers against the consequences of poor judgment, and is an inefficient means of protecting the public against the errors (or in rare cases, moral failure) of individual bankers. However, some of the present restrictions on banking protect both the public and the bankers against some of the worst consequences of errors made by the monetary authorities. Deposit insurance prevents multiple bank failures from generating a precipitous decline in the money supply, if the public is promptly compensated for losses. It seems desirable to retain the public's defense against mistakes of this kind by central bankers. In this section, I suggest changes in the deposit-insurance system and in existing controls on banking and other financial institutions. These suggestions are no more than an outline of a system of regulation, which, I believe, deserves further discussion.

The present system of deposit insurance is deficient in a number of important respects. It limits the maximum amounts of insurance on an individual account; it forces banks to make all-or-nothing decisions, in effect requiring insurance on all accounts up to the legal maximum if banks or most depositors desire insurance; it does not relate the insurance premiums to the risk position of the individual bank, but instead, is used to justify controls that limit the risks accepted by bankers; and, most important of all, it has degenerated into a system for protecting depositors by preventing bank failures and maintaining inefficient banks. These deficiencies limit the community's ability to obtain an optimal allocation of resources; thus they reduce welfare.

The following suggestions are designed to retain the most important benefits of the present system and avoid some of its weaknesses:

1. Depositors should not be required to buy insurance, but should be permitted to choose the portion of their deposit balances which they desire to insure against loss.
2. Premiums should be paid by depositors at rates based on the risk of failure by the bank of their choice and should be changed as the risk position changes.
3. FDIC (or any company that desires to sell insurance) would inspect the assets of the bank periodically and assign assets to risk classes.
4. Banks would be permitted to purchase any asset—real or financial —without any restrictions on portfolio composition and would be permitted to pay interest on demand and time deposits without restriction.

The proposal permits individuals to choose their preferred combination of risk and return and provides them with information (prices) on which to base their decisions. Computation of deposit-insurance premiums poses little difficulty. Bank examiners have established standards for judging assets and assigning them to classes that are akin to risk classes. The principal new problems that the insurance system would face arise from the wider range of assets that some banks would buy and the increased competition that banks would face if some of my other suggestions are adopted.

Elimination of controls on entry, branching, and merger appears to be desirable. There is little economic justification for present restrictions which prevent banks from branching or entering, and there are few gains to the public to offset the loss in efficiency resulting from present controls. Furthermore, there is no economic justification for present laws that permit national banks to branch only to the extent that state-chartered banks are permitted to branch, or for laws that permit U.S. banks to open branches in foreign countries but not in their own or other states. The federal government can eliminate these costly restrictions by removing controls on entry and by permitting national banks to branch nationally.

Current laws and regulations prohibit savings and loan associations and mutual savings banks from selecting the assets they choose to purchase and from issuing demand deposits. These restrictions impose costs on the public that do not appear to be offset by any comparable benefits. Recent experience provides an example of the kind of difficulties that are produced by conflicts between regulations on banks and savings institutions during a period of rising market interest rates, rising rates of interest on time and savings deposits, and a decline in the growth rate of mortgages. If savings and loan associations were permitted to buy any financial or real asset, the cost to the public of reallocating assets would be reduced and policy makers would have less reason to fear the con-

sequences of their actions or to avoid taking appropriate action.

It is worth investigating whether there is any net benefit to the public from distinguishing between banks and non-bank financial institutions. If not—and I suspect there is not—savings and loan associations should not be prevented from offering the same services as commercial banks.

Competition in financial markets would increase substantially if regulations and legal restrictions that make for arbitrary differences between types of institutions were eliminated and all institutions were permitted to offer a wider range of services. The absence of legal restrictions does not mean, however, that only large banks, offering "all" services, would survive. Acquiring information about a wide range of assets and of increasing the number of services offered raises costs. Specialization and division of labor are characteristic of financial institutions in countries that regulate far less than the United States. The benefits of removing controls come from the lower costs of adjusting to variations in the supply of specialized financial instruments and the lower costs and increased services offered to the public. The customers of all the new banks would, of course, be permitted to buy deposit insurance.

The public also gains from the proposed system through a reduction in the cost of maintaining a number of regulatory agencies. Under the suggested plan, the Federal Home Loan Banks, the Office of the Comptroller of the Currency, the Federal Savings and Loan Insurance Corporation, and a number of other state and federal agencies, departments, or divisions would be abolished. The FDIC, reduced in scope and authority, would be responsible for deposit insurance and bank examination. The Federal Reserve would be responsible for monetary, but not banking, regulation. Banking corporations would be treated like any other corporations under the tax and antitrust laws.

Even if these far-reaching changes prove undesirable after further examination, some minor but important improvements in regulatory procedures should be made. None of the regulatory agencies has produced an unambiguous statement of the criteria used to make decisions about branching, merger, or entry, or the relation of these criteria to a theory of banking markets. Decisions about what is "sufficient need" or what is regarded as a local monopoly appear to vary from time to time without any explicit statement of the reason for the variations. Decision makers use some set of criteria; arbitrary decisions can best be avoided if the rules are clearly stated and subject to public scrutiny. The Comptroller has made an effort to provide guidance to bankers about the procedures used in his office and about his philosophy of regulation. Other regulatory agencies should follow his lead.

Regulations such as Federal Reserve regulation Q and differences in reserve requirement ratios for different classes of banks do not appear to serve a useful purpose. Others—for example, lending limits, restrictions on loans to bank officers, restrictions on the type of assets banks purchase—can be replaced by less costly institutional arrangements like the deposit insurance system discussed above.

VI. CONCLUSION

If banking regulations are to serve a useful purpose, the benefits to the public must exceed the costs of the controls. The chief benefits of controls are said to be (1) the prevention of over- or under-expansion of money and bank credit through a system-wide monopoly or through "excessive" competition, (2) the elimination of local monopoly, and (3) the protection of depositors against the consequences of bank failure.

My examination of the arguments for controls, however, suggests that many of the controls imposed on banking fail to achieve their purposes, impose costs that appear to exceed the benefits or create the problem that they are said to eliminate. It would seem desirable, therefore, to eliminate many of the existing controls and to replace them with a new set of institutional arrangements. The most casual inspection of the present mass of conflicting and overlapping regulations suggests that the present system is unlikely to produce an optimal—or even improved—allocation of resources.

Attempts to regulate banking should take into account the unique features of the industry. The uniqueness results from the government's responsibility for controlling the money supply, a responsibility that gives the government an important role in the determination of the industry's output and in the pricing of the industry's products. Since the government's monopoly is more powerful than any possible private monopoly in banking, the government can force expansion or contraction on the industry.

In the past, errors by the central banks or government have caused multiple bank failures and destruction of the public's deposits. Deposit insurance is a means of protecting the industry and the public against some of the worst consequences of future errors and a repetition of past mistakes. Since private companies cannot be expected to insure the public against the widespread consequences of incorrect public policy decisions at equivalent cost, it is desirable to have government offer deposit insurance. Government insurance provides a partial safeguard against a precipitous decline in the money supply.

However, the present system of deposit insurance and the accompanying regulation of bank assets can be improved. I have outlined a proposal that encourages competition between financial institutions and which permits individuals to choose their desired combination of risk and return from money holding.

Analysis and the recent accumulation of evidence on bank behavior both suggest that present controls on entry, branching, and merger have costs that exceed their benefits. If this analysis is correct, arbitrary and costly restrictions should be eliminated along with controls on portfolios and interest payments and distinctions between banks and other financial institutions. It is to the credit of Mr. James Saxon—and perhaps the most damaging indictment of the present system—that increased competition in banking depends on the individuals chosen as regulators.

READING 14

BANK HOLDING COMPANIES

Franklin Edwards

The widespread organization of one-bank holding companies is the newest effort by banks to diversify their operations; it follows a long series of prior and unsuccessful attempts. Previously, banks attempted to expand into non-banking activities by broadly interpreting the "incidental powers" clause, which forms the heart of the basic legislation from which banks derive their powers. The National Bank Act sets forth the basic powers of national banks:

To exercise by its board of directors or duly authorized officers or agents, subject to law, all such incidental powers as shall be necessary to carry on the business of banking; by discounting and negotiating promissory notes, drafts, bills of exchange, and other evidences of debt; by receiving deposits; by buying and selling exchange, coin, and bullion; by loaning money on personal security; and by obtaining, issuing, and circulating notes according to the provisions of this chapter.

Beginning in the early sixties, banks began to construe the "incidental powers" clause as permitting them to expand their activities directly into such related activities as life insurance, travel services, commingled trust accounts, data processing services, credit cards, armored car services, and direct leasing. In addition, through wholly-owned subsidiaries, they engaged in mortgage servicing, factoring, credit reporting, warehousing, etc. Most importantly, their efforts were supported by the Comptroller of the Currency, James Saxon, who also interpreted the "incidental powers" clause in a liberal manner. In a letter on the subject of national banks acting as insurance agents, Saxon said:

Congress has consistently recognized that the business of banking covers a wide range of activities. In the National Bank Act of 1864, Congress wisely refused to define the business of banking as it then existed, foreseeing that the banking business would change and

Source: Excerpts from "The One-Bank Holding Company Conglomerate: Analysis and Evaluation," *Vanderbilt Law Review*, Vol. 22, pp. 1275–1306, 1970.

develop with the passing years. It is clear that the business of banking is advanced by financial and related services, and powers necessary to achieve and promote the fundamental purposes of banking must be regarded as powers incidental to those expressly granted by paragraph seven of 12 U.S.C. 24.

Even Saxon, however, clearly recognized that the law prohibited banks from engaging in a nonrelated, nonbanking business. In a letter on the subject of banks providing travel services, he said:

Traditionally, national banks have been excluded from direct participation in the production of raw material, manufacturing, or commerce, so as to immunize the banking system from the risks inherent in the employment of venture capital. Subject to this restriction, however, it is clear that the business of banking is the furthering by financial and related services of commerce and industry and the convenience of the public. Powers necessary to achieve the fundamental purposes of banking must be regarded as powers incidental to those expressly granted.

Comptroller Saxon nevertheless permitted national banks to provide travel services based on the broad theory that travel services are related to the banks' overall financial services.

Industry representatives in those lines of commerce threatened by bank competition struck back through the courts. One after another they filed suit to enjoin the banks from providing the newly authorized services, arguing that defendant-banks lacked statutory authority to offer such services (or that banks were engaging in *ultra vires* acts). In *Baker, Watts and Co. v. Saxon*, plaintiff sought and obtained an injunc-

tion prohibiting banks from underwriting and dealing in obligations of states or political subdivisions not secured by the general power of taxation; while in *Georgia Ass'n. of Independent Insurance Agents, Inc. v. Saxon*, banks were prohibited from acting as agents for the issuance of insurance in connection with loan transactions in any location where the population exceeds 5,000 inhabitants. More recently, *Dickinson v. First National Bank*, banks were prevented from establishing armored car services, or any off-premises activities which could be construed as contrary to states' branch banking statutes.

Banks have, however, made some gains as well, although some of these gains may be temporary. In *Arnold Tours, Inc. v. Camp*, for example, the district court found that the plaintiff lacked standing to challenge the right of a national bank to operate a travel agency and dismissed the suit. In *Wingate Corp. v. Industrial National Bank* and *Association of Data Processing Services, Inc. v. Camp*, plaintiffs were also unsuccessful in obtaining an injunction in the district court preventing national banks from providing electronic data processing services. In the *Wingate* case, however, the First Circuit Court reversed, finding that plaintiff had standing to sue under the Bank Service Corporation Act. Very recently, in *Investment Company Institute v. Camp* the Court of Appeals for the District of Columbia ruled that banks could operate commingled investment accounts, or mutual funds.*

An important point in all of these decisions, especially those won by the banks, is that in no case did the court rest its decision on section 24 of the National Bank Act, which avoided the complex problem of defining the incidental powers of commercial banks.

---

* Editor's note: This decision, however, was reversed in 1971 by the Supreme Court.

TABLE 1

	Commercial Bank Assets as Percentage of Assets of all Financial Intermediaries	Commercial Bank Assets as a Percentage of Assets of only Private Financial Intermediaries	Commercial Bank Assets as a Percentage of GNP
1900	62.5	62.5	53.8
1912	64.5	64.5	60.7
1922	59.1	65.0	65.2
1929	49.8	53.6	63.4
1933	41.6	48.5	82.3
1939	40.0	52.2	72.8
1945	46.1	63.0	75.1
1949	40.2	54.5	61.7
1952	38.8	51.8	54.8
1958	34.2	43.6	54.3
1965	31.7	38.3	52.3

The above named cases were resolved on the basis of entirely different statutes or on technical grounds such as the lack of plaintiff's standing to sue. Whether the courts will eventually be forced to tackle the difficult issue of what powers are incidental to banking remains to be seen.[1]

Hemmed in against direct expansion by a multitude of regulations and restrictive court decisions, banks turned to the holding company scheme, an old but little used device. The recent trend toward one-bank holding companies, therefore, can be partially explained by the frustration banks have encountered in pursuing their persistent desire to diversify. There remains, however, the fundamental question of why banks wish to diversify.

Reasons for Diversification

Since 1900 commercial banking as an industry has been declining in relative importance. Savings institutions, consumer lenders, and a host of other financial institutions have slowly but persistently made inroads on commercial banks. Table 1 shows that commercial bank assets, considered from several points of view, have grown less rapidly than those of competing financial institutions.[2] In 1900 commercial banks held more than three-fifths of all assets retained by financial intermediaries, but by 1965 their share had declined to roughly one-third.

This decline may be due to a lack of aggressiveness on the part of commercial banks, but this factor alone is not a complete explanation. At the turn of this century commercial banking consisted primarily of accepting short-term liabilities (demand deposits) and extending short-term business credit. In 1900 savings deposits constituted less than one-sixth of total commercial bank deposits, and the loan-to-deposit ratio was roughly 50 percent. In fact, nearly 25 percent of banks' assets were "cash assets." Since that time, savings and time deposits have continually

[1] For a possible interpretation of the incidental powers clause, see Beatty, "The Incidental Powers of National Banks," 4 Nat'l Banking Rev. 263 (1967): Huck, "What is the Banking Business?," 83 Banking L. J. 491 (1966).

[2] Burns, "The Relative Decline of Commercial Banks: A Note," 77 J. Pol. Econ. 122–28 (1969).

risen to today's level of almost 60 percent of total deposits, banks have increased their loan-to-deposits ratios to roughly 60 percent, and have moved increasingly into longer-term lending.

The drift of commercial banking away from demand deposits and short-term assets and into longer-term liabilities and assets is partially the result of changing customer tastes, partially a response to a changing economy, and partially the result of regulation. In 1946 bank customers held 50 cents in currency and demand deposits for each dollar of gross national product; today they hold less than 25 cents. This sharp change is the result of the following factors: (1) Growing confidence in the stability of our economic and financial system which reduces the need for liquidity; (2) improved credit arrangements, such as credit cards, available to large segments of the population which lessen the need for carrying large liquid balances; (3) the prohibition against banks' paying interest on demand deposits which encourages customers to switch from demand deposits to income-yielding assets; and (4) the increasingly attractive yields on substitute liquid assets, such as savings deposits, which have induced customers to shift funds from demand deposits to time and savings deposits.

As a larger proportion of banks' liabilities have taken the form of interest-bearing savings and time deposits, bank costs have increased commensurately, forcing banks to raise their loan-to-deposit ratios and to search for higher yielding assets in order to maintain acceptable profit levels. Although bank earnings (net current operating revenue) as a percent of total capital have not declined substantially during the 1950's and 1960's (ranging from 18.5 percent to about 14.5 percent), during the last few years bankers began to fear that they could no longer offset increasing costs by further increases in their already high loan-to-deposit ratios. Consequently, they began looking for alternative sources of earnings, either higher yielding assets or entirely new lines of business. Thus, slow relative growth and increasing costs combined to push bankers into attempting to diversify the scope of their operations, at first directly under a permissive Comptroller of the Currency, and then later through the device of the one-bank holding company.

The message of this discussion is clear: the one-bank holding company movement is not a sudden, unexpected, and whimsical phenomenon, but is the predictable consequence of real economic problems. As such, it demands thoughtful consideration.

Editor's Note: In 1971, Congress gave the Federal Reserve Board wide powers to determine the permissible bank-related activities of one-bank holding companies and to regulate their activities.

PART 3

THE FEDERAL RESERVE SYSTEM: STRUCTURE, GOALS, INDICATORS, AND INSTRUMENTS

READING 15

ON STRUCTURE AND GOVERNMENT OF THE FEDERAL RESERVE SYSTEM

Deane Carson

The selections contained in this part supplement the chapters in your textbook that deal with the organization, functions, and tools of the Federal Reserve System. Since these matters are covered quite extensively in most texts, I have included published articles that deal with contemporary issues in this field and materials that delve deeper into the subject that is possible in the standard textbook. Anticipating to some extent, although not entirely, the readings that follow, this brief introduction draws attention to some aspects of the structure of the Federal Reserve System.

The structure of the American central bank is more interesting than one might suppose from a casual glance at its organizational chart. (See Chart 1.) Furthermore, a great deal that has been written about the structure of the Federal Reserve System is either super-

ficially correct, or, in some fewer cases, patently wrong. The beginning of all understanding of the Federal Reserve System is the knowledge that things are not always quite what they seem.

The most interesting structural question is this: Who actually governs the System? Put another way: Where does the real power reside within the "Fed"?[1] The answer requires a very brief diversion into the history of the system.

In the beginning, that is, in 1914, the Fed was established as a System of twelve highly autonomous regional banks, each with a presiding Governor (now the District Bank President) and a Board of Directors. The stock of each District Bank was owned by the member banks in the region—and still is to this day. While enjoying considerable autonomy, the District Banks were responsible to a Board of Governors,

[1] The Federal Reserve System, and more specifically its Board of Governors, is referred to, somewhat fondly, as the Fed, just as the Bank of England, the British central bank, is "The Old Lady of Threadneedle Street." Fondly or not, its use economizes space, and I shall use this short form interchangeably with the *System* and the *Board*.

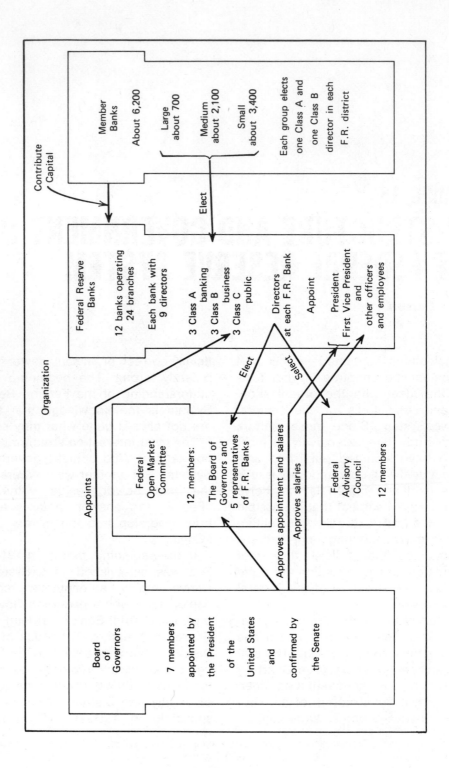

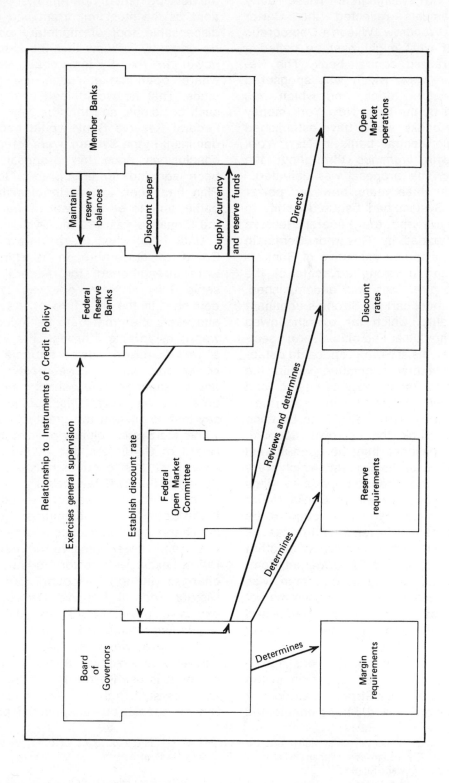

Chart 1. The Federal Reserve System.

seated in Washington. These early arrangements reflected the Carter Glass – Woodrow Wilson – Democratic view of what might best be called a decentralized central bank. The Republican view, which was sponsored by Senator Aldrich, and which was backed by the large New York money market banks, would have established a single central bank in New York City, with *branches* throughout the country. This proposal was defeated.

Within three years, however, power in the System had begun to shift to New York and the Federal Reserve Bank headed by Governor Benjamin Strong, a former executive of Bankers Trust and a strong advocate of the Aldrich plan. This was accomplished, for the most part, by Strong's dominant personality, which far overshadowed that of any other Fed official, and specifically by his shrewd proposal to establish a central committee within the System for the purpose of buying (and later selling) government securities. This had formerly been done by each District Bank for its own account. Strong reasoned that the open-market operations of the System (which were initially undertaken to provide earnings for the Federal Reserve Banks rather than for monetary control) ought to be coordinated. With remarkable ease, he succeeded in the persuasion of other Governors, and an Open Market Committee, with Strong as chairman, was formed. Henceforth, all open-market operations have been transacted through the Federal Reserve Bank of New York.

The significance of this was apparently obvious to only one man in the System, Governor Strong. A student of the Bank of England, Strong anticipated the development of open-market operations as the most important and least dispensable tool of monetary policy. He correctly foresaw that the locus of power in the System could reside where open-market decisions were made. That he would lead in making such decisions, and that the New York Federal Reserve Bank would become dominant in the System, were foregone conclusions once his proposal had been adopted. In effect, the Aldrich Plan had been lost in the legislative battle, only to be adopted *de facto* in the formative years of the System.

Until 1935, when the powers of the Board of Governors in Washington were strengthened, the Federal Reserve Bank of New York was clearly dominant in the structure of the Fed, and even after that date its influence was considerable. Through the years, a well-disguised power struggle has waxed and waned between New York and Washington.[2] We cannot pause to detail the history of this; suffice it to say that at present the greatest power within the System clearly resides in the Board of Governors; the influence of New York has been significantly reduced in the past few years.[3]

The Board now constitutes a majority in the Open Market Committee (7 of 12 members) and has exclusive power to raise and lower reserve-requirement ratios, exclusive power to approve changes in the discount rates of District Federal Reserve Banks, and exclusive power to change its own regulations, such as Regulation Q. Furthermore, when the Fed exercises "moral suasion" *vis à vis* member banks, it is usually the Board that determines such policies. And when the System speaks on fundamental policy

---

[2] At some stage in your course in money and banking you will become acquainted with the "Bills Only Doctrine." The controversy over the wisdom of "Bills Only" was at bottom a part of the New York-Washington power struggle.

[3] Without adopting a "great man" theory of history, one may reasonably attribute this in large part to the very strong leadership exercised by the Chairman of the Board of Governors, Mr. William McChesney Martin, in the years 1951–1970.

matters, it is the Board's voice that is heard and closely followed by everyone affected by central bank policies.

In touching the dominant powers of the Board, we should carefully avoid the inference that power is equally shared by its members. During the long regime of William McChesney Martin (1951–1970), power *within* the Board gravitated to the Chairman. While it would be a mistake to assert that the Board was entirely dominated by Mr. Martin, for much of this period his voice was truly the voice of the Board; only in the latter years of his tenure was his power somewhat diminished and shared.

The explanation of Martin's role in the Fed—and it is a role that is likely to be played by his successor, Dr. Arthur Burns—is rather complex. It is generally conceded that, whatever his other virtues and shortcomings, Chairman Martin was a consummate politician in the best sense. He was remarkably persuasive with his peers on the Board, he served under three Democratic and two Republican Presidents, and he managed to become a worldwide symbol of American monetary prudence and stability.

Moreover, Chairman Martin, at least in the early years, was clearly the most articulate and knowledgeable member of the Board. This dominance declined somewhat after the Kennedy-Johnson appointments, which placed a number of economists on the Board, some of whom exercised a degree of independence that had not characterized their predecessors. In dealing with the Board and with the Open Market Committee, he used his remarkable powers to persuade others to his viewpoint; failing that, he worked to achieved a policy consensus that would minimize division and split votes on major issues; and failing *that,* he always voted *last* at Board meetings, establishing his famous record for never voting on the losing side!

Finally, we may observe that the Chairman has certain inherent powers that tend to make his position dominant. He has broad powers to assign tasks to the other Board members: bank examination and supervision, personnel, and other nonmonetary policy functions. He also has the direct access to the President of the United States, although this is less a right inherent in his office than the result of the power he can accumulate if he so desires. And finally, he is in a position to magnify his image through frequent appearances before Committees of Congress, establishment of relations with central bankers and finance ministers abroad, and public speeches. All of these latter may also be cultivated by other Board members, and indeed, this has recently become increasingly the case. Yet, the very fact that he is chairman gives him an opportunity to overshadow his colleagues.

The analysis above finds the locus of Fed power in its Board of Governors, and, moreover, at least potentially, in the hands of the chairman. This should not obscure the fact that a different composition of the Board could lead to somewhat different conclusions. A weak Board or a weak chairman could well create a power vacuum for others to fill, yet it seems highly unlikely that power will shift back again to the District Banks—in the least unlikely case, specifically, to the Federal Reserve Bank of New York. The cards are now stacked against a regression of this kind.

What, then, can be said of the powers of the Federal Reserve Banks? With the exceptions noted below, these powers are primarily exercised in areas outside the sphere of monetary policy. Aside from these exceptions, the position of the District Bank President is more analogous to that of a commercial-bank branch manager than to the presiding officer of the parent institution. He (and by extension the Board of Directors) does not formulate policies, except in relatively minor housekeeping matters; rather, he is charged with executing the policies that are determined by the Board of Governors in Washington.

The most significant exception to this general description is, of course, the participation of District Bank presidents as voting members of the Open Market Committee.[4] As members of this important body, their vote has just as much weight as that of any Board member, including the chairman. Nevertheless, there are many factors that tend to reduce the relative influence of the Reserve Bank presidents in the formulation of monetary policy.

First and foremost, the presidents do not have at their command all of the decision parameters that are available to the Board. This is not to say that they do not have substantial information; they usually do, and in passing one may note that the volume of information available to all Committee members is overwhelming. The difference lies in the subtle power advantage that the Board derives from close contact with the President of the United States, Congress, the Secretary of the Treasury, the Council of Economic Advisers, and central bankers of foreign countries, all of whom are less available to non-Board members of the Committee. To some extent this advantage of contact with other centers of economic decision-making arises from the Board's location in Washington, but this is not the entire answer. More important, it is a fact that these other decision-makers have come to consider the Board as the true center of Fed power; as such they have established lines of communication with the latter that are only infrequently and sporadically, if at all, open to the Federal Reserve Bank presidents.

Secondarily, the relative influence of Reserve Bank presidents is diluted by the fact that they are not continuously members of the Committee. This is reenforced by their subordinate position to the Board in the System.[5]

In spite of these factors, one should not conclude that the presidents are completely dominated by Board views; they can, and often do, take strongly independent stances on monetary policy. This has been particularly true of the New York Bank in the past, and of the St. Louis Bank at the present time. The latter has been particularly forceful in presenting the view that the money supply, rather than interest rates, should be the variable that the central bank should control. The power of the St. Louis Bank has been instrumental in bring the Fed closer to this view of the appropriate target of monetary policy.

The role of commercial banks in the structure of the System deserves passing comment. As noted in Part 2 above, national banks must be members of the Federal Reserve, while state-chartered banks have the option of joining or not joining. Because of this, less than half of the commercial banks are members, although their deposits account for approximately four-fifths of all deposits of the banking system.

The Federal Reserve Board has nearly always acted to encourage membership in the System, and has advocated legislation that would make this mandatory for all banks. This is apparently based on the belief that monetary policy effectiveness is enhanced by

---

[4] Presidents, with the exception of the president of the New York Federal Reserve Bank, who is permanent vice-chairman of the Committee, serve as voting members on a rotating basis, five at any one time. Typically, however, all attend the meetings of the Committee.

[5] Their appointment, for example, is subject to Board approval, and they may be removed from office by Board action.

widespread membership, although the reasoning behind this view has never been adequately explained.[6]

The most interesting aspect of the commercial banks' relationship to Fed structure is the ownership of Federal Reserve Banks by the member banks in each region. This anachronism of ownership is more illusory than significant. Ownership of Federal Reserve Bank stock does give member banks voting power in the election of one third of each District Bank's Board of Directors, but it should not be assumed that ownership gives the commercial banks control over Federal Reserve monetary policy. Such influence as individual banks exercise in this regard derives from other factors.[7]

No examination of the structure and government of the Fed would be complete without reference to its relationship to the Government of which it is an integral and important part. Here we find that formal and legal ties do not provide an accurate picture of the informal and *de facto* power structure. The Federal Reserve Act and its amendments delegate Congress's Constitutional powers to "coin money and regulate the value thereof" to the Federal Reserve System. As a creature of Congress, the Fed is *de jure* responsible to the House and Senate. While the President has been given the power to appoint the Board (with Senate advice and consent), his legal powers over the Board are, by Congressional intent, severely limited.

These formal relationships mask the real power relations between the Fed and the Government. With respect to its responsibilities to Congress, several observations are pertinent. First, the very size of Congress make the exercise of responsible control the province of selected members who serve on certain committees, the House Banking and Currency Committee, the Senate Committees on Banking and Finance, and the Joint Economic Committee. For largely personality reasons, in recent years the greater responsibility for Federal Reserve supervision has been assumed by the Banking and Currency Committee of the House, rather than by the Senate Committees, and to a somewhat smaller extent by the Joint Economic Committee. Second, given the Committee system, which tends to magnify the role of the Committee Chairman, power has gravitated to a small handful of senior legislators, including, perhaps, the ranking minority committee members. Third, the real influence of even the committee chairman—and there here we are speaking of House Committee Chairman Wright Patman of Texas and Senator William Proxmire of Wisconsin on the Joint Economic Committee—is tempered by the Board's own view of its responsibilities to Congress. In brief, these leaders can advise, cajole, threaten, and harass the Board, but they cannot, except through legislation, dictate Board policies.

The Board itself has adopted the view that, while it is a creature of Congress, the powers delegated to it *cannot be shared* with Congress, either in whole or in part. Furthermore, the Board strongly feels that its public responsibilities can best be interpreted and discharged by its own members, free from the prevailing winds of public pressure.

This view of its independence, a view in which the Board makes decisions on a lofty plane insulated from the desires of the madding crowd, is one fondly nurtured by the Board itself, but it only

---

[6] See "Should Reserve Requirements Be Abolished?" in this part.

[7] It is interesting, but idle, to speculate on the precise nature of such influence, if indeed it does exist. Certainly Federal Reserve officials receive the views of private bankers on monetary policies; what weight these are given is known only to Fed officers.

partially squares with the political realities. The Fed does not want Congress to legislate policy (at least some of its reasons are valid), and the fear that Congress might do so mitigates the independence of the Board.

The power of Congress is perhaps best illustrated by the recent relations between the Joint Economic Committee and the Board. The former unanimously adopted a proposal that the Board follow a strict policy of increasing the money supply at an annual rate between 2 and 6 percent. Testimony was received from the Board, which was strongly opposed to the money-supply guideline, since it would effectively eliminate a large segment of the Board's discretionary power. Yet, in the end, the Board agreed to a plan whereby it would appear before the Joint Committee whenever, in any quarter of the year, the money supply had grown at a rate either less than two percent or more than six percent in order to explain why. These appearances would require the Board, in effect, to explain its actual monetary growth rate. This compromise effectively removed, at least temporarily, pressure for legislation, while partially satisfying the committee's desire to narrow the range of money supply fluctuations.

Finally, with respect to the Fed's relationship to the Presidency, the real power structure is markedly different from that formalized in the Federal Reserve Act. To a great degree, the former depends on the personality and economic philosophy of the President and in his self-assumed role as either an aggressive leader or a passive executor of the laws passed by Congress. The point to be made is simply this: Irrespective of legal arrangements, a President can, if he wishes, exercise considerable influence on the Board and its chairman, no matter how powerful the latter may be. This power derives from many factors, some of which are quite subtle.[8]

Nevertheless, even a strong President cannot, in the nature of things, exercise close supervision of short-run monetary policies. The secrecy that surrounds Board and Open Market Committee deliberations, together with the complexity and ambiguity of the monetary signals that spew forth in the published weekly Federal Reserve Statement, conspire against tight controls. The most that a President can expect to influence is the general drift of monetary policy; history in even this limited sphere is itself ambiguous and not easily interpreted.

A concluding and summary observation is in order. Our analysis describes the Federal Reserve System as a political structure with power relationships which, both internally and externally, are less constrained by law than by personalities. The Board, wherein the major share of power lies, is, after all, composed of human beings endowed with various degrees of intelligence, wisdom, and devotion to the public welfare. Beyond this, they are indeed fallible, and sometimes disastrously so, as an examination of monetary policy in the implosive recession of 1929–1933 will amply attest. Great power has been given to a very few men to do good or to do great injury in economic affairs. While not presently unconstrained, as we have seen, we are nevertheless impelled to ask whether further constraint on their discretion in monetary management is not now in order.

[8] Former Senator Paul Douglas asserts that the System bought long-term securities on one occasion in the late 1950s, in apparent violation of the Board's "Bills Only" policy, because it was conveyed to the chairman that he would not be reappointed at the expiration of his four-year term (Chairmen are appointed for four-year terms, even though their tenure as members is fourteen) unless he supported the long-term Treasury market.

READING 16

THE ROLE OF MONEY IN NATIONAL ECONOMIC POLICY: I

David Meiselman

I. ASSOCIATION BETWEEN CHANGES IN THE STOCK OF MONEY AND IN THE PRICE LEVEL

There is an impressive body of evidence of long standing, perhaps the most firmly established empirical association in all of economics, that there is an association between large-scale and rapid changes in the stock of money and changes in the price level. Indeed, every substantial and sustained inflation ever studied that has come to my attention has been associated with correspondingly substantial and sustained large-scale increases in the stock of money. Similarly, every important deflation ever studied has been associated with a fall in the stock of money, or, as in the case of the United States from 1869–1896, by very little or no monetary growth to match the growth in output. Of course, this is to be expected when the demand for money is relatively stable and is specified in real terms. The real value of each unit of money, given the demand for money, is related to the total nominal quantity of money. In some respects, this is an extension of the very simplest economics. Because the stock of money generally tends to be under the control of the monetary authorities, it follows that the monetary authorities can control the nominal stock of money, but the real stock of money depends on the behavior of the public.

For shorter periods, it seems that the general configuration of business cycles is similar to the general configuration of monetary change. Periods of large-scale expansion in nominal GNP are related to a corresponding large-scale expansion in the stock of money which had taken place earlier, and

Source: Reprinted from *Controlling Monetary Aggregates,* Federal Reserve Bank of Boston, 1969, pp. 15–19.

similarly for a contraction in nominal GNP, especially when related to the rate of change of the stock of money. Second, the stock of money, especially when evaluated as changes in *the rate of change* of the stock of money, tends to lead business cycle turns. But the lead of money over income does not seem to be a dependable one in the sense that there is a simple or constant lead of money over business conditions. Different investigators report different leads of money over income ranging from three to six months to three to five years. The Federal Reserve Board-MIT model seems to yield one of the longest leads of money over income. Some work at the Federal Reserve Bank of St. Louis has reported close to the shortest lead. Milton Friedman's position on this matter would seem to make him a moderate in the lag controversy.

II. THE NEED FOR CONTROL OF THE STOCK OF MONEY

In my view, monetary policy is, or should be, concerned with control of the stock of money—even though the stock of money, itself, may not be an explicit policy instrument, policy target, or policy indicator. Other things, such as interest rates, may be uppermost in the minds of the monetary authorities as targets or indicators of policy; but, as I see it, looking at interest rates, alone, is both an inefficient and self-defeating way to operate a stabilizing monetary policy. One of the reasons that it is inefficient is that interest rates are a very confusing *indicator* of monetary policy. Interest rates may also be a confusing *target* as well. Of course, traditional Keynesian analysis, which is very close to the traditional banker view, regards the rate of interest as responding inversely to changes in the

quantity of money. In this general context, recall that prices in the Keynesian analysis are given; the marginal productivity of capital also tends to be given and fixed; and that, in effect, security prices or interest rates may change, but commodity prices and perhaps the price of labor as well are also given and fixed.

The rate of interest in the traditional Keynesian analysis is the real rate of interest because price level considerations, including expectations of changing prices, are essentially ruled out. Either prices are assumed constant or the role of price expectations in affecting the nominal rate of interest is held aside. As we have all come to realize, especially in the past few years, the nominal rate of interest seen in the market is composed of the real rate of interest plus some adjustment for the expected rate of change of prices. A large increase in the stock of money ultimately affects prices, which in turn have some feedback effects on nominal rates of interest. This seems to be true not only in recent years but, as I have examined the evidence, it holds for at least the last 100 years of United States financial history, and perhaps longer in England as well.[1]

In addition to the feedback between money and interest rates through the price level effect, a change in the stock of money can also affect the real rate of interest. If by affecting aggregate demand, the change in the stock of money alters employment, then again, depending on well established elements of traditional economic analysis, the change in employment will tend to change the ratio of labor to capital in the short run, and thereby the marginal productivity of both labor and capital. Thus, for example, if there is a restrictive monetary policy which

[1] See David Meiselman, "Bond Yields and the Price Level: The Gibson Paradox Regained," in *Banking and Monetary Studies,* Deane Carson (ed.) Homewood: Richard D. Irwin, Inc., 1963.

leads to unemployment, output becomes more capital-intensive, so that the marginal product of capital falls, as does the real rate of return. This is an element in the argument that Hicks' IS curve has a positive slope.[2]

Because of these kinds of complex interactions and lags, we cannot take the marginal product of capital, or prices, or interest rates as datum. They all respond to changes in the stock of money with a very complex set of interactions and lags we know very little about. This is one of the reasons that many of us are led to focus on the stock of money as the best available indicator of monetary policy and to point to interest rates or credit market conditions as poor indicators of monetary policy. In addition, it seems to me that the stock of money can be controlled within rather narrow limits, and that this is a very important factor to consider in discusing public policy. Clearly, investment outlays cannot be controlled, and, in many respects, cannot be predicted very well. In principle, government expenditures and taxes could be controlled, but the experience of the past few years should remind us that Congress need not be sufficiently cooperative—or is the word passive?—to permit White House dictation of Federal Government expenditures and taxes, holding aside important questions about state and local government spending and taxing.

III. NEED TO RELINQUISH INTEREST RATE REGULATION

It is important to realize that, if we do emphasize monetary policy, and, with it, controlling the stock of money as the principal instrument or indicator of monetary policy, there are certain things that we will have to give up. For

example, it means that various attempts to peg or to moderate either one or a wide range of interest rates will have to go by the board. In that respect, much of the discussion about controlling the stock of money implies a need for collateral discussions regarding necessary changes in our financial structure and financial regulations. The problems posed by the savings and loans and a vast array of housing subsidies inherent in their regulation are but two of many items under this broad heading.

However, I do not think we can conclude that, because there is much doubt cast on the dependability of other factors in determining GNP, that nothing but money ever matters. I would like to ask, "If other things matter, first, what are the other things; second, how much do they matter; and third, how dependable are they?" With respect to the dependable effects of fiscal policy—and I emphasize the word dependable—at the very least I belive that the matter is very much up in the air. It seems to me that it is clear what the direction of effect on GNP would be if we have a substantial change, especially a permanent change, in income tax rates, but I think it is quite another matter to assign some specific numbers to those effects.

I have been doing some research in the past year and a half on this matter, some of which parallels the work Leonall Andersen has done at the Federal Reserve Bank of St. Louis, in which I have been trying to find some dependable statistical links between various commonly used expenditure and tax measures and measures of change in macro-aggregates. Thus far, I cannot find any of the associations traditional fiscal policy would lead us to expect.

---

[2] D. Meiselman, "Money, Factor Proportions, and the Real Cycle," presented at the Zurich meetings of Econometric Society, 1964.

READING 17

THE ROLE OF MONEY IN NATIONAL ECONOMIC POLICY: II

Allan H. Meltzer

I notice that people take various positions on monetarism. One is that Milton Friedman is completely wrong; another is that Friedman is almost completely wrong. A third is that there is a grain of truth to what Friedman says, but it is not very important; and, therefore, fiscal policy matters far more than the so-called monetarists say. Always, there is a subtle suggestion that some of us know a great deal more about the way in which the economic system operates than we have time to tell. If the argument and evidence could be presented, everyone could see that there is a considerable amount of evidence showing the sizable effect of fiscal policy operations and supporting some very detailed econometric model of the economy.

Now, I haven't seen that evidence, and I would like to see it. I do know that last November [1968], at the University of Michigan forecasting conference, the forecast of the Michigan econ-

ometric model for the first quarter of 1969 was that the GNP would increase by $4.4 billion. At about the same time, the Wharton econometric forecasting unit predicted a $5.2 billion rise in first quarter GNP and a $7.4 billion rise in second quarter GNP. We now know that these predicted changes, made only six weeks before the start of the quarter, missed from ⅔ to ¾ of the actual change. We will soon know that the second quarter GNP changes predicted by those models are considerably less than 50 percent of the actual second quarter change. Moreover, the econometric models forecast larger changes in the second and third quarters than in the first quarter, contrary to the pattern that we can now expect.

We may also recall that a year ago Arthur Okun, then Chairman of Council of Economic Advisers, warned us of the dangers of "fiscal overkill"; talked about the threat of a downturn in the third and fourth quarter of last

Source: Reprinted from *Controlling Monetary Aggregates*, Federal Reserve Bank of Boston, 1969, pp. 25–29.

year as if it were almost a certainty; and argued that the surtax and the prospective reduction in expenditures were likely to push the economy into a recession. These predictions, like the predictions of the Wharton and Michigan models, proved incorrect. The last few years have shown that it is very difficult to forecast GNP a year in advance until we know what the Federal Reserve is going to do about the quantity of money. In periods like 1961 to 1965, when the quantity of money grows at a relatively steady rate, it is easier to make accurate GNP forecasts. In periods when there are large gyrations in the stock of money, it is difficult to forecast by using models that ignore changes in the stock of money or minimize their effects. And, I believe, that piece of evidence is buttressed by the demonstrated superior predictive performance of the Andersen-Jordan model. Small and unimportant as these two facts may seem in isolation, they are two of the more important facts we have obtained from recent experiences.

If these facts were isolated, we might dismiss them or leave to the model builders to search for the source of their errors. The determinants of GNP and its components are not so well known that large forecasting errors are remarkable; and GNP predictions are not so precise that occasional large errors are either unexpected, or noteworthy. Recent errors, however, are part of a continuing sequence and follow closely the sizable errors in forecasting made in recent years by econometric models that minimize the effect of changes in money.

I. REASON FOR FORECASTING ERRORS

There is at least one important common element in the models that make for large forecasting errors. The Wharton and Michigan model builders share a common disdain for any possible influence that might be exercised by changes in the quantity of money. Professor Suits, a principal contributor to the Michigan model, has expressed his view that the neglect of changes in money has no important consequences for his model. Mr. Okun takes a similar position. He writes that the effect of monetary policy is given by the change in market interest rates. A rise in market interest rates is judged to be contractive, and a fall in interest rates is called expansive. The 1969 report of the Council of Economic Advisors, written when Okun was chairman, repeatedly takes that position and states it in terms that are too clear to be misinterpreted.

I believe that the position is incorrect, and that the cause of the error is that market interest rates are an unreliable indicator of monetary policy. That statement doesn't mean that changes in interest rates are independent of fiscal policy or real variables, and it doesn't deny that the demand for money depends on interest rates. Samuelson and Tobin raise the latter point repeatedly and force me to confess my ignorance publicly. How do you get from the fact on which we all agree—that the demand for money depends on interest rates—to the conclusion that interest rates are a reliable indicator of monetary policy?

In fact, we know very little about the determinants of short-term changes in market rates. By using interest rate changes to judge the content of current monetary policy, we are very likely to be misled. The closer the economy is to full employment, the more we are likely to be misled.

Of several different errors underlying the incorrect notion that levels or changes in the market interest rates are solely, or mainly, the result of monetary policy, two errors seem to me to be most important. One is the failure to distinguish between credit and money. Most of the changes in market interest rates that we observe are the result of activities taking place on the credit market, not on the theoretical "money market" of economic analysis. The second is the failure to distinguish between changes in interest rates that result from changes in productivity and thrift, and changes that result from inflation. The latter distinction, the distinction between nominal and real magnitudes, is one of the oldest in economics, but it has been neglected in policy discussions and in many econometric models. To understand the effect of change in money on economic activity, both distinctions have to be kept in mind: the distinction between credit and money, and the distinction between real and nominal values.

II. TWO OPPOSING VIEWS

An understanding of monetary policy, of the role of money as an indicator, and of the difference between the effects of changes in credit and money can be obtained by contrasting two frameworks. In one view, monetary and fiscal policies are seen as the means by which the public sector offsets instability in the economy resulting from changes that occur in the private sector. Fluctuations in prices and output are seen as the result primarily of real forces and changes mainly in attitude or outlook that raise or lower investment, thereby raising or lowering the nominal value of income, market interest rates, and the demand for money. The task of monetary policy, in this frame work, is to offset undesired changes in interest rates caused by the unforeseen changes in investment. The task of monetary policy, in this framework, is to offset undesired changes in interest rates caused by the unforeseen changes in investment. The task of fiscal policy is to offset the unforeseen changes in the private expenditure and maintain expenditures at the full employment level. Monetary policy is called "restrictive" if market rates are permitted to rise; "permissive" if market rates are prevented from rising; and "coordinated" if the balance of payments is in deficit, and market rates are permitted to rise so as to attract an inflow of short-term capital from abroad. With this framework, it appears reasonable to accept interest rates as the main indicator of monetary policy. If the framework were correct, the decision might be more tenable—although still not correct.

The alternative view—at least my view—does not deny that changes in market interest rates are partly the result of changes in attitude or changes in technology that shift private expenditures. The difference—and it is an important difference—is a difference of emphasis and interpretation. Not only are changes in private expenditure assigned a smaller role, but many of these so-called autonomous changes are viewed as a delayed response to past monetary and fiscal policies.

The effect of a monetary or fiscal policy is not limited to the initial change in interest rates. An expansive monetary policy raises the monetary base, stocks of money and bank credit, and initially lowers market interest rates. The expansion of money increases expenditure, increases the amount of borrowing, and reduces the amount of existing securities that individuals and bankers wish to hold at prevailing market interest rates. These changes in borrowing and in desired holdings of securities reverse the initial decline in interest rates; market rates rise until the stock of existing securities is reabsorbed into portfolios, and the banks offer the volume of loans that the public desires. If expansive operations continue, expenditures, borrowing, and interest rates rise to levels above those in the starting equilibrium. Later, prices rise under the impact of increases in the quantity of money, further reducing the desired holdings of bonds and other fixed coupon securities, and increasing desired borrowing. A rise in holdings of currency relative to demand deposits adds to the forces raising interest rates on the credit market.

In this interpretation, the effect of monetary (or fiscal policy) is not limited to the initial effect. The response to a maintained change in policy includes the effects on the credit market, the acceleration or deceleration of prices, and ultimately, if policy makers persist, the changes in attitudes and particularly in anticipation of inflation or deflation. These changes, however, are regarded as reliable consequences of maintaining an expansive or contractive monetary policy, just as much to be expected as the initial effect.

It is the temporary changes in the level of interest rates observed on the credit market that frequently mislead monetary policy makers into believing their policy is restrictive when it is expansive. Large changes in the growth rate of money become a main source of instability precisely because the credit market and price effects dominate the initial effect of monetary policy in an economy close to full employment. Misled by the change in market interest rates—or their interpretation of the change—the Federal Reserve permits or forces the stock of money to grow at too high or too low a rate for too long a time. Excessive expansion and contraction of money becomes the main cause of the fluctuations in output and of inflation or deflation. Inappropriate public policies, not changes in private expenditures, become the main cause of instability.

A portion of the second interpretation has now been accepted by the principal spokesman of the Federal Reserve System. In his March 1969 statement to the Senate Banking Committee, Chairman Martin* said:

I do not mean to argue that the interest rate developments in recent years have had no relation to monetary policy. We know that, in the short-run, expansive monetary policies tend to reduce interest rates and restrictive monetary policy to raise them. But in the long run, in a full employment economy, expansive monetary policies foster greater inflation and encourage borrowers to make even larger demands on the credit markets. Over the long run, therefore, expansive monetary policies may not lower interest rates; in fact, they may raise them appreciably. This is the clear lesson of history that has been reconfirmed by the experience of the past several years.

With that statement, Chairman Martin abandoned the framework that has guided Federal Reserve policy through most of its history and has been responsible for major errors in policy. Recognition that interest rates generally rise fastest under the impact of monetary expansion is probably the single most important step toward an understanding of the role of money that has been taken in the entire history of the Federal Reserve System.

* Editor's note: Mr. Martin retired in January 1970, and Dr. Arthur F. Burns became Chairman of the Federal Reserve Board.

READING 18

MONETARY AGGREGATES AND MONEY MARKET CONDITIONS IN OPEN MARKET POLICY: THE FEDERAL RESERVE VIEW

There has been widespread discussion over the past year or so about the emphasis given to monetary and credit aggregates, as compared with traditional operating variables such as money market conditions, in the formulation and conduct of the Federal Reserve System's open market policy. This article discusses the role—in the decision-making process of the Federal Open Market Committee (FOMC)[1] and in the day-to-day conduct of Federal Reserve open market operations—of aggregates such as the money supply and bank credit, in comparison with other financial variables. Such aggregates, of course, represent only a few of the many financial variables, including interest rates and credit flows through nonbank institutions and the market directly, that are evaluated in monetary policy decisions and their implementation. And financial conditions as a whole are evaluated against the underlying purpose of monetary policy—the encouragement of a healthily functioning economy, both domestically and in relation to the rest of the world.

The policy decisions of the FOMC are based on a full-scale evaluation by Committee members of likely tenden-

Source: Reprinted from Federal Reserve Bulletin, February 1971.

[1] The Federal Open Market Committee is the statutory body responsible for open market operations (purchase and sale of U.S. Government securities in the open market), the most flexible and frequently used instrument by which monetary policy affects bank reserves, bank credit, money supply, and ultimately over-all credit conditions. The FOMC consists of the seven members of the Board of Governors of the Federal Reserve System, the President of the Federal Reserve Bank of New York, and four of the remaining 11 Reserve Bank presidents serving in rotation. The Chairman of the Board of Governors has traditionally been elected by the Committee to serve as Chairman of the Open Market Committee, and the President of the Federal Reserve Bank of New York has traditionally been elected Vice-Chairman.

cies in critical measures of economic performance such as output, employment, prices, and the balance of payments. In deciding on the stance of monetary policy, the Committee considers whether these tendencies in domestic economic activity and the balance of payments appear desirable, and if not, how they might be influenced by changes in financial conditions—including the pace of monetary expansion, credit availability, interest rates—and by expectational factors. Once a general policy stance is adopted, guidelines are set for the day-to-day conduct of operations in the open market. During 1970 somewhat more emphasis was placed on the behavior of monetary aggregates—such as the money supply and bank credit—in providing guidance for the day-to-day conduct of open market operations.

Since it has always been recognized that the effect of monetary policy stems from its influence on bank credit, money, interest rates, and financial flows generally, the greater emphasis placed on monetary aggregates basically represented a modification of operating procedures rather than a change in the fundamental objective of policy. Under conditions of uncertainty—for example, uncertainty about the impact on interest rates of expectational factors or about the strength of future demands for goods and services—some emphasis on the aggregates helps to guard against the risk that open market operations might in the end supply either too large or too small amounts of bank reserves, credit, and money as a result of unexpected and undesired shifts in demands for goods and services and for credit.

At the same time, however, an approach that utilizes aggregates as one operating guide must take account of shifts in the demand for money and liquidity at given levels of income. Such shifts would have to be accommodated

through open market operations in order to help provide the money and liquidity demanded if interest rates and credit conditions generally were not to become unduly tight or easy. Thus, the longer-run path for monetary aggregates needs to be evaluated in relation to emerging credit conditions and tendencies in economic activity, to help determine if demands for liquidity have been properly assessed. And whatever longer-run path for the aggregates may be included as guidance for open market operations, short-run, self-correcting variations in money and credit demands need to be accommodated in order to avoid inducing unnecessary, and possibly destabilizing, fluctuations in money market conditions.

In practice, allowance has to be made—in the formulation of monetary policy and in the guides to the conduct of policy—for uncertainties with respect to both the demand for goods and the demand for money and liquidity. And trends in monetary aggregates, interest rates, and other financial variables have to be evaluated in relation to the continuing flow of evidence as to the likely course of economic activity.

I. DIRECTIVES OF THE FOMC

The monetary policy decisions of the FOMC—which in recent years has generally met about every 4 weeks—are embodied in the Committee's current economic poilcy directive, voted on near the end of each meeting. This directive is issued to the Federal Reserve Bank of New York, which, because it is located in the Nation's central money and credit market, undertakes open market operations for the Federal Reserve System. The directive is carried out by a senior officer of the Bank, who is designated by the FOMC as Manager of the System Open Market Account.

Both the form and the content of the

FOMC directive have changed over the years. Since 1961 the directive has contained two paragraphs. The first paragraph has contained statements about recent key economic and financial developments, and also a general statement of current goals of the FOMC with respect economic growth, price stability, and the balance of payments.[2] The second paragraph contains the FOMC's instructions to the Account Manager for guiding open market operations in the interval between FOMC meetings. The second paragraph is, in essence, a highly condensed summary of the Committee's discussion and conclusions as to the sort of operations that will be required to reach its longer-run policy goals. These directives are made public after a 3-month lag in a "record of policy actions," which also includes a résumé of prevailing economic and financial conditions and of the Committee's discussion of policy implications at the meeting.

The nature of the operating instructions in the second paragraph of the directive has changed from time to time. Money market conditions have remained as important guides in determining day-to-day open market activity. Though emphasis on various money market indicators has varied over the years in light of changing economic and financial circumstances, money market conditions have generally been construed to include member bank borrowings at the Federal Reserve discount window, the net reserve position of member banks (excess reserves of banks less borrowings from the Federal Reserve), the interest rate on Federal funds (essentially reserve balances of banks that are made available to other banks, usually on an overnight basis), and at times the 3-month Treasury bill rate.

At times when it was framing the operating instructions contained in the second paragraph of its directive solely in terms of money market conditions, the FOMC was nevertheless concerned with developments in monetary aggregates and financial conditions generally as they affect the broad objectives of policy. Beginning in 1966, the Committee supplemented the reference to money market conditions in the second paragraph with a reference to certain monetary aggregates, such as bank credit, and later the money supply.[3] The desired behavior of aggregates has been given increased emphasis since early 1970.

From mid-1966 through 1969 the reference to aggregates was generally to

---

[2] For illustrative purposes the first paragraph of the directive issued on Dec. 16, 1969, is quoted below:

"The information reviewed at this meeting indicates that real economic activity has expanded only moderately in recent quarters and that a further slowing of growth appears to be in process. Prices and costs, however, are continuing to rise at a rapid pace. Most market interest rates have advanced further in recent weeks partly as a result of expectational factors, including concern about the outlook for fiscal policy. Bank credit rose rapidly in November after declining on average in October, while the money supply increased moderately over the 2-month period; in the third quarter, bank credit had declined on balance and the money supply was about unchanged. The net contraction of outstanding large-denomination CD's has slowed markedly since late summer, apparently reflecting mainly an increase in foreign official time deposits. However, flows of consumer-type time and savings funds at banks and nonbank thrift institutions have remained weak, and there is considerable market concern about the potential size of net outflows expected around the year-end. In November the balance of payments deficit on the liquidity basis diminished further and the official settlements balance reverted to surplus, mainly as a result of return flows out of the German mark and renewed borrowing by U.S. banks from their foreign branches. In light of the foregoing developments, it is the policy of the Federal Open Market Committee to foster financial conditions conducive to the reduction of inflationary pressures, with a view to encouraging sustainable economic growth and attaining reasonable equilibrium in the country's balance of payments."

[3] There was also occasional reference to such aggregates in directives during the first half of the 1960's.

bank credit and was contained in a so-called proviso clause. The second paragraph of the directive issued on December 16, 1969, is illustrative:

"To implement this policy, System open market operations until the next meeting of the Committee shall be conducted with a view to maintaining the prevailing firm conditions in the money market; provided, however, that operations shall be modified if bank credit appears to be deviating significantly from current projections or if unusual liquidity pressures should develop."

In 1970 monetary aggregates came to play a more prominent role in the phrasing of the second paragraph, and references were made to the money supply as well as to bank credit. In the directive issued on March 10, 1970, the Committee stated more directly its desires with respect to the aggregates rather than referring to them in the form of a proviso clause. The second paragraph of the directive of that date read as follows:

"To implement this policy, the Committee desires to see moderate growth in money and bank credit over the months ahead. System open market operations until the next meeting of the Committee shall be conducted with a view to maintaining money market conditions consistent with the objective."

The operating instructions in the second paragraph of FOMC directives are not confined to money market conditions and a desired pattern of behavior in the monetary aggregates. The System Account Manager has also been directed, when appropriate, to take account of Treasury financings, liquidity pressures, and the possible impacts of bank regulatory changes in the process of achieving satisfactory conditions in the money market and satisfactory performance of monetary aggregates.

As the nature of economic and financial problems has altered, so has the phrasing of the second paragraph of the directive. For instance, the second paragraph of the directive issued on May 26, 1970, emphasized the need to moderate pressures on financial markets; it read as follows:

"To implement this policy, in view of current market uncertainties and liquidity strains, open market operations until the next meeting of the Committee shall be conducted with a view to moderating pressures on financial markets, while, to the extent compatible therewith, maintaining bank reserves and money market conditions consistent with the Committee's longer-run objectives of moderate growth in money and bank credit."

The short-run bulge in bank credit expansion expected to result from the Board's action around midyear in suspending ceilings on maximum interest rates payable by banks on large certificates of deposit in the 30- to 89-day maturity range was taken into consideration in the phrasing of the second paragraph of the directive issued by the FOMC on July 21, 1970:

"To implement this policy, while taking account of persisting market uncertainties, liquidity strains, and the forthcoming Treasury financing, the Committee seeks to promote moderate growth in money and bank credit over the months ahead, allowing for a possible continued shift of credit flows from market to banking channels. System open market operations until the next meeting of the Committee shall be conducted with a view to maintaining bank reserves and money market conditions consistent with that objective; provided, however, that operations shall be modified as needed to counter excessive pressures in financial markets should they develop."

And in the directive issued on August 18, 1970, an easing of conditions in credit markets was taken as an objective of open market operations parallel with desires with respect to monetary aggregates, as follows:

"To implement this policy, the Committee seeks to promote some easing of conditions in credit markets and somewhat greater growth in money over the months ahead than occurred in the second quarter, while taking account of possible liquidity problems and allowing bank credit growth to reflect any continued shift of credit flows from market to banking channels. System open market operations until the next meeting of the Committee shall be conducted with a view to maintaining bank reserves and money market conditions consistent with that objective, taking account of the effects of other monetary policy actions."

The first and second paragraphs of all directives issued from December 16, 1969, through December 15, 1970, are shown in the appendix to indicate the variety of considerations that the FOMC takes into account in formulating its policy and framing its operating instructions.

II. POLICY FORMATION

The FOMC's basic concern is with the real economy—production, employment, prices, and the balance of payments. But the Committee must translate its broader economic goals into the monetary and credit variables over which the Federal Reserve has a direct influence. Thus, whatever emphasis is given to the financial variables that influence day-to-day open market operations, it is recognized that the immediate targets of day-to-day operations are not the goals of monetary policy, but rather that those targets are set with a view to facilitating the achievement of the broader financial and economic objectives of the FOMC.

In setting its immediate operating targets, the FOMC necessarily reviews past and prospective relationships between financial conditions and economic objectives. A benchmark in this review is provided several times a year in a presentation by the staff to the Committee of an interrelated set of longer-run economic and financial projections. These exercises review in detail recent economic and financial developments, assess the outlook for and impact of fiscal policy, and trace the likely patterns of change in such measures as income, output, employment, prices, and the balance of payments for a period of about a year ahead. Provisional estimates are also presented of the flow of funds—including various monetary aggregates—and interest rates expected to be consistent with these patterns of economic development. A reappraisal of current tendencies in and prospects for economic activity, financial flows and credit market conditions, and the balance of payments is presented to the FOMC by the staff on the occasion of each meeting. Included in the regular documentation is an analysis of relationships among money market variables, paths for monetary aggregates, and interest rates broadly considered for a period several months ahead.

At each FOMC meeting, most of the time is given over to a free interchange of views by Committee members of their assessment of the current economic situation and outlook and of the related appropriate monetary policies. As the discussion proceeds, each Committee member indicates his assessment of the basic tendencies in economic activity, prices, employment, and so forth; his appraisal of recent financial developments in relation to desired economic goals; and what steps might be taken through open market operations (or other policy instruments that interact with open market operations) to help achieve financial conditions suitable to economic goals.

It may develop, for instance, that

most or all Committee members believe that economic prospects are deviating from those that had previously been expected and desired. If so, the Committee may wish to modify its objectives concerning money market conditions and desired rates of expansion in monetary and credit aggregates, so as to promote over-all financial and credit conditions that are more conducive to desired economic conditions. Or it may turn out that economic activity is developing about in line with expectations but seems to be entailing a pattern of financial flows different from that originally expected. Still another possibility is that the relationship that is developing between the variables specified for the System Account Manager for purposes of guiding day-to-day open market operations and broader financial flows and interest rates is not what was expected. Under any of such circumstances, the FOMC could react by changing its operating instructions.

The operating instructions in the second paragraph of the directive are expressed qualitatively. But the specific variables involved—money market conditions and monetary and credit aggregates—are typically indicated in terms of ranges in the discussion.

Over the past year the operating instructions embodying the Committee's policy thrust have changed in two general ways. First, as has been noted, somewhat more emphasis has been placed on monetary aggregates as a target for open market operations rather than as an outgrowth of such operations. Second, the time horizon for a path of monetary and credit aggregates (in relation to money market conditions and other financial variables) has been viewed as encompassing several months or, expressed in calendar quarters, at least one or two quarters ahead. Longer-run paths provide the Committee with a means for focusing on the emerging trend of growth in the money supply or in bank credit, while recognizing that, over very short-run periods of a week or a month or so, there may be irregular movements in rates of change in monetary aggregates because of erratic shifts in the public's demand for deposits and such factors as Treasury financings, a large change in U.S. Government deposits, or movements of funds between the U.S. and foreign countries.

III. ROLE OF MONETARY AGGREGATES

The somewhat greater use of monetary aggregates in the formulation and conduct of open market policy during the past year represents for the most part an extension of the trend of policy over the previous several years. It has always been recognized that monetary policy achieves its effects through its influence on bank credit, money supply, interest rates, and financial flows generally. But the benefits that might be expected from an increased degree of emphasis on monetary aggregates in the conduct of open market operations relate to the question of monetary control under conditions of uncertainty.

Greater emphasis on aggregates is consistent with a variety of economic theories, and it does not necessarily imply any particular judgment as to the importance for the economy of monetary flows relative to interest rates and credit conditions or relative to other influences such as fiscal policy and technological innovation. Operationally, however, by placing more emphasis on monetary aggregates in the instructions to the Account Manager, the FOMC has a greater assurance that unexpected and undesired shortfalls or excesses in the demands for goods and services in the economy, and hence in the demands for credit and money, will not lead more or less automatically to too little or too much expansion in bank reserves, bank credit, and money.

Giving more weight to monetary aggregates means, for example, that if there were an unexpected and undesired short-fall in business and consumer demand for goods and services, the Federal Reserve would continue to provide reserves to try to keep growth in money and bank credit from weakening unduly at a time when the public, with transactions demand for cash reduced, was seeking to invest excess funds in various financial assets. In the process, there would be a greater short-run decline in interest rates than would otherwise be the case. The drop in interest rates and the easing of credit conditions would help to provide financial incentives that would encourage a strengthening of demands for goods and services.

While increasing the emphasis on monetary and credit aggregates tends to increase the protection against undesired shifts in demands for goods and services, it at the same time runs the risk of reducing protection against unexpected shifts in the public's demand for cash and liquidity. Thus, for example, if the public decides to hold more liquidity relative to income than had been earlier assumed, failure to permit a faster rise in the money supply to accommodate this desire would lead to higher interest rates and tighter credit conditions as the public seeks to sell other assets to acquire cash. The tightening of credit conditions would tend to lead to a weaker GNP than desired. In contrast, the tendency toward tighter conditions could be averted if the Federal Reserve helped to meet the desire for greater liquidity by increasing its purchases of financial assets (through open market acquisitions of U.S. Government securities)—

thereby providing more bank reserves to support an increase in bank deposits and in the money supply and to keep interest rates from rising.

In practice, allowance has to be made for uncertainties about both the demand for goods and services and the demand for money and liquidity. Opinions differ among professional economists as to the relative degrees of stability of these types of demand, and practical experience over the past several years suggests that there is a good deal of variation in both. There have been periods when large increases in Federal Government purchases of goods and services and/or in private sector demands for capital goods and inventories have caused marked shifts in over-all demands for goods and services at given interest rates. But there have also been periods when liquidity strains, greatly increased financial transactions, and various international uncertainties have resulted in a sizable upward shift in the demand for cash and closely related assets at given interest rates. Furthermore, open market policy not only needs to distinguish between, and take account of, shifts in both the demand for goods and services and the demand for money and liquidity at given interest rates, but also must evaluate the extent to which such shifts are transitory or more permanent.

The late spring and the summer of 1970 are an example of a period when liquidity strains in the economy—typified by rising long-term interest rates at a time when economic activity was sluggish, by the bankruptcy of a major railroad, and by a generally cautionary attitude on the part of investors toward securities, particularly commercial paper—were giving rise to considerable uncertainty and were threatening a marked erosion in confidence. Under those circumstances Federal Reserve policy stressed the need to moderate pressures on financial markets and to accommodate liquidity needs.

In late June the Board of Governors suspended maximum ceiling rates on large CD's maturing in 30- to 89-days as part of the effort to reliquify the economy. This action made it possible for banks to compete for funds and to accommodate borrowers who were not able, in the conditions of the time, to refinance their borrowings in the commercial paper market, or were not able to do so without a bank loan commitment as back-up. And open market operations during the period were conducted in such a way as to provide the reserves to sustain the very large increase in bank credit resulting from renewed ability of banks to obtain funds through issuance of certain large CD's. The FOMC's policy directives in that period (see directives of May 26 and July 21, 1970, on pp. 179 and 180) tended to subordinate, temporarily, longer-run objectives for monetary aggregates to the shorter-run liquidity needs of the economy.

In general, in evaluating the appropriateness of particular operating guidelines at a particular time, the FOMC has to make judgments about the nature of the fundamental influences that are affecting the domestic economy and the international position of the dollar. If, for example, it developed that interest rates were higher, and over-all credit conditions tighter, than expected for a given rate of increase in bank credit or money, the FOMC would have to make a judgment as to whether GNP was stronger than anticipated, whether inflationary expectations were affecting interest rates, or whether the demands for money and closely related assets had shifted at given levels of income and interest rates. Or, as another example, interest rate movements might be undesirably affecting capital flows between the United States and foreign countries; in this case judgments might have to be made as to how the various policy instruments could be adapted to such a development.

Judgments made with respect to interrelationships among policy objectives would affect not only the open market policy instrument but also other monetary policy instruments. With respect to open market policy, types of adjustments called for in operating instructions would include, for instance, whether to change the targets for aggregates and/or whether to put more stress on money or credit market conditions. Or adjustments might be called for in other policy instruments—such as the discount rate or reserve requirements, including provisions such as those recently made affecting Eurodollar borrowings of U.S. banks—in order to achieve a variety of policy objectives more effectively.

In looking toward a desired longer-run growth rate in monetary aggregates, the FOMC has focused on money and bank credit in its operating instructions. The concept of money used for these purposes has generally been the so-called narrowly defined money supply—currency in circulation outside the banking system plus demand deposits other than U.S. Government and domestic interbank deposits—but broader definitions have also been taken into account. The determination of what rates of growth may be desired for money takes into account not only what is happening in credit markets but also the rates of growth in certain types of assets held by the public that are closely related to narrowly defined money and that the public holds as a store of value and as a source of immediate liquidity.

A number of broader concepts of the money supply and of liquidity have been utilized by economic analysts in relating money supply to economic activity. These include, in addition to the narrowly defined money supply, a concept—here termed M_2—that adds time and savings deposits other than large CD's at commercial banks to narrowly defined money; and a concept, termed M_3 that adds deposits at both mutual savings banks and savings and loan associations. And even these concepts can be broadened by adding other money-like assets, such as large marketable negotiable CD's issued by banks and other short-term marketable securities. Annual, quarterly, and monthly rates of change over the past year in the three concepts of money noted above are shown in Table 1.

As may be seen, the rates of change for the various measures may diverge noticeably, and they may show a high degree of fluctuation over the short run. Differential tendencies in the various measures of money and liquidity have been the result in large part of sharp shifts of funds by the public between deposits and market securities when market interest rates moved above and then back below ceiling rates on deposits at banks and thrift institutions. But divergent movements, particularly in the short run, may develop even when ceiling rates are not a disturbing element. This highlights the need to evaluate a variety of money and liquidity measures, among other things, in gauging the impact of monetary policy on the economy. Moreover, the relatively large month-to-month

TABLE 1

VARIOUS MEASURES OF MONEY: RATES OF CHANGE (SEASONALLY ADJUSTED ANNUAL RATES, IN PER CENT)

Period	M_1 (Currency plus demand deposits[a])	M_2 (M_1 plus coml. bank time deposits other than large CD's)	M_3 (M_2 plus deposits at S&L's and mutual savings banks)
1969	3.1	2.4	2.8
1970	5.4	8.2	7.9
1970—Q1	5.9	3.4	2.6
Q2	5.8	8.4	7.9
Q3	6.1	11.0	10.5
Q4	3.4	9.2	9.7
1970—January	9.4	2.2	1.2
February	—4.1	—1.5	—1.2
March	12.3	9.6	7.8
April	9.9	10.8	9.7
May	5.2	7.6	7.2
June	2.3	6.7	6.6
July	5.7	9.9	9.9
August	6.8	12.5	11.4
September	5.7	10.3	10.0
October	1.1	7.3	8.1
November	2.8	7.0	8.1
December	6.2	13.0	12.6

Demand deposits other than interbank and U.S. Govt.

NOTE: Monthly rates of change based on the daily-average levels outstanding. Quarterly and annual rates of changes measured from daily-average levels outstanding in end-of-period months.

variations in growth for any particular money measure—and variations are even larger from week to week—emphasize the need to evaluate data over some long period of time in judging the underlying tendency of the series.

As noted earlier, in addition to the money supply, the second paragraph of the directive has emphasized bank credit. A current measure of bank credit for the guidance of the Account Manager was provided by measuring bank credit from the liability side, since liability data are available more quickly and can be used to construct a series on a daily-average basis. This daily-average measure does not encompass all bank liabilities (it excludes non-member bank deposits and bank capital, for example) but it includes the most volatile ones. It encompasses not only the member bank component of deposits included in M_2 above, but also funds obtained by banks through large time CD's, U.S. Government deposits, and interbank deposits and through nondeposit sources such as Euro-dollars and commercial paper issued by bank-related affiliates. The sum of these deposits and nondeposit sources is called the adjusted credit proxy.

Inclusion of bank credit in the directive might be considered as recognition of a broader concept of money, since time and savings deposits at commercial banks are a key source of bank credit. In addition, however, the inclusion recognizes that bank credit is a key component of total credit availability and one that is immediately sensitive to open market operations.

The amount of bank credit that the FOMC is willing to encourage or to countenance depends, like the money supply, on over-all economic and financial conditions. When, for example, banks have been unable for an extended period to increase time and

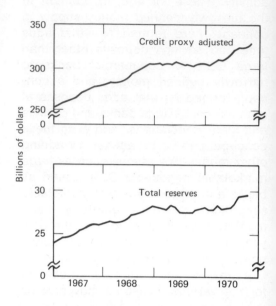

Chart 1. Credit proxy adjusted total reserves. Bank "credit proxy adjusted" is total member bank deposits plus funds provided by Euro-dollar borrowings and bank-related commercial paper. Through the first half of 1969, no data on bank-related commercial paper were available, but amounts outstanding were not thought to be growing significantly in those periods.

savings deposits because interest rate ceilings on time deposits were unrealistically low relative to market rates, it was to be expected that outstanding bank credit would grow rapidly for a time after ceiling rates again became competitive. This growth would represent mainly a shifting of credit flows from market to banking channels as banks sought to restore their previous competitive position and as the public restructured its financial asset portfolios to reflect the changed yield relationships. Federal Reserve open market operations could provide the reserves necessary to sustain the shift in the public's ability and willingness to hold time deposits relative to other assets. Chart 1 shows monthly changes in bank credit, as measured by the adjusted credit proxy, along with total bank reserves.

IV. DAY-TO-DAY OPEN MARKET OPERATIONS

The day-to-day operations in the market by the System Account Manager have continued to be guided mainly by money market conditions, in part because the information that is available daily and continuously as to the state of the money market—for example, the Federal funds rate and dealer loan rates—reflects the interaction of the demand for and existing supply of bank reserves and hence provides a basis for making daily decisions as to whether the System should be in the market providing additional or absorbing existing reserves; and if so, by how much and through what means. But the degree to which the Manager seeks to influence money market conditions has been affected by the relationship that is presumed to exist at any given time among money market conditions, reserves, and the monetary aggregates and by the Committee's desires with respect to monetary aggregates and over-all conditions in the credit market.

Changes in money market conditions, of course, may reflect factors other than efforts to influence reserve flows in accordance with longer-run targets for monetary aggregates. Some changes in money market conditions reflect no more than shifts in the distribution of reserves among banks. Others represent the short-run effects of bulges in demand for day-to-day credit at times of Treasury financings or in tax payment periods. Yet others represent unanticipated, virtually random changes in technical factors— such as float or currency in circulation —that supply to or absorb from the market more reserves than was either expected or seemed likely to be sustained. And as in the summer of 1970, open market operations in relation to money market conditions may some-times reflect primarily a concern with liquidity pressures in the economy.

Although recognizing that money market conditions are subject to a number of influences, the System Account Manager takes into consideration the relationship between money market conditions and the trends in bank credit and money that has prevailed in the recent past and the relationship that is expected to develop in the future in making decisions concerning reserve provision or absorption through open market operations. At the beginning of a statement week, for example, his operations may be aimed at a condition of tightness or ease in the money market roughly similar to that of previous weeks. This would mean that such variables as the Federal funds rate, dealer loan rates, the net reserve position of member banks, and borrowings by member banks from the Federal Reserve would generally tend to fluctuate within the range of recent experience—although there might be special, sometimes unforeseen developments (such as a mail strike) that could cause marked short-run changes in money market conditions.

If and as it becomes evident that monetary aggregates are running above or below the desired path, however, the Account Manager may aim at correspondingly tighter or easier money market conditions. Also, if it should turn out that the apparent new relationship was not long-lasting, the Account Manager would subsequently have to reverse the direction of his operations. Thus, to the extent that monetary aggregates are given more emphasis in the operating paragraph of the directive, money market conditions may be subject to a somewhat greater degree of fluctuation.

While the counterpart of greater sensitivity to monetary aggregates would be a somewhat greater tendency for actual money market conditions to change more frequently than otherwise, sharp short-run shifts in money market conditions are not likely to develop, in part because the FOMC is concerned with the state of money and credit markets as well as with tendencies in monetary aggregates. There are a number of reasons for the continuing role of money market conditions as a day-to-day guide for open market operations.

First, the money market reflects the pressure of demand for liquidity, and the nation's central bank has a unique responsibility for maintenance of orderly conditions in such a market.

Second, there are large and often unpredictable week-to-week and month-to-month swings in the economy's demand for money and bank credit. These demands are often self-correcting, and as a result there is little purpose in permitting the sharp fluctuations in money market conditions, and perhaps in credit markets generally, that would be likely to develop should the flow and ebb of these demands not be accommodated in Federal Reserve operations affecting bank reserves.

Third, because of the key role of the money market in quickly reflecting shifts in the need for and availability of liquid funds, presumably in large part as a result of the interaction of the public's spending decisions and monetary policy, sharp shifts in money market conditions may be interpreted by market participants as a harbinger of relatively permanent changes in credit demand or monetary policy. Investors, businessmen, and consumers may vary their credit outlook, and perhaps their economic outlook too, in response to the money market to the extent that they regard changes in the market as a signal of events to come. This prospect itself counsels caution in undertaking open market operations that lead to large short-run changes in money market conditions until it becomes fairly certain that longer-run tendencies in money supply, bank credit, and over-all credit conditions require such changes.

While there are reasons for emphasis on money market conditions, it should be stressed that money market conditions are only instrumental to the attainment of the main financial objectives of policy—flows of monetary aggregates and over-all credit conditions—that are appropriate to achievement of over-all economic goals. For the Account Manager, the day-to-day operations of the Account and the effect of these operations on the money market are made even more complex because he is aware that the FOMC generally has in mind not only some view concerning the desired longer-run trend in various monetary aggregates but also a view concerning what should be sought in the way of associated credit conditions.

These desires may sometimes turn out to be in conflict; for example, monetary aggregates as a group may be rising more rapidly than desirable while credit conditions may be tightening more than desirable. Meeting one desire by holding back on the provision of reserves in order to restrain growth in bank credit and money would tend, at least temporarily, to thwart the other desire by leading to even more tightening of credit conditions. Under such circumstances, the Account Manager would have to adjust his operations—thereby affecting day-to-day money market conditions—in line with the sense of priority among operating objectives given by the FOMC.

While the whole set of objectives would be reconsidered at the next FOMC meeting, the Account Manager's operations are monitored daily through a morning telephone conference call. This call involves the Trading Desk in

New York, senior officials on the staff of the Board of Governors in Washington, and one of the Reserve Bank Presidents (serving in rotation) who is a voting member of the FOMC (other than the President of the Federal Reserve Bank of New York). Individual Board members may also participate in the call from time to time, as may the President of the New York Reserve Bank. In this call the Manager explains his program for the day, and that program, or possible alternative approaches, are discussed. As part of this process, not only are current figures on bank reserve positions, money market conditions, and broader credit conditions reported, but also information on the latest deposit and bank credit figures and how these compare with FOMC desires is appraised.

In general, as the FOMC's objectives with respect to monetary aggregates, and also over-all credit conditions, have been given increased stress in the directive to the Account Manager, the timing and extent of the System's day-to-day open market operations have, of course, been altered, with consequent effects on day-to-day money market conditions. At the same time, the Manager still takes account of the emerging tightness or ease in the money market as a factor affecting the timing and extent of day-to-day open market operations. But this emerging tightness or ease is evaluated against trends in money, bank credit, and over-all credit conditions, which are, and always have been, among the basic financial objectives of monetary policy.

APPENDIX

Recent Economic Policy Directives Issued by the FOMC

MEETING HELD ON DECEMBER 16, 1969

The information reviewed at this meeting indicates that real economic activity has expanded only moderately in recent quarters and that a further slowing of growth appears to be in process. Prices and costs, however, are continuing to rise at a rapid pace. Most market interest rates have advanced further in recent weeks partly as a result of expectational factors, including concern about the outlook for fiscal policy. Bank credit rose rapidly in November after declining on average in October, while the money supply increased moderately over the 2-month period; in the third quarter, bank credit had declined on balance and the money supply was about unchanged. The net contraction of outstanding large-denomination CD's has slowed markedly since late summer, apparently reflecting mainly an increase in foreign official time deposits. However, flows of consumer-type time and savings funds at banks and nonbank thrift institutions have remained weak, and there is considerable market concern about the potential size of net outflows expected around the year-end. In November the balance of payments deficit on the liquidity basis diminished further and the official settlements balance reverted to surplus, mainly as a result of return flows out of the German mark and renewed borrowing by U.S. banks from their foreign branches. In light of the foregoing developments, it is the policy of the Federal Open Market Committee to foster financial conditions conducive to the reduction of inflationary pressures, with a view to encouraging sustainable economic growth and attaining reasonable equilibrium in the country's balance of payments.

To implement this policy, System open market operations until the next meeting of the Committee shall be conducted with a view to maintaining the prevailing firm conditions in the money market; provided, however, that operations shall be modified if bank credit appears to be deviating significantly from current projections or if unusual liquidity pressures should develop.

MEETING HELD ON JANUARY 15, 1970

The information reviewed at this meeting suggests that real economic activity leveled off in the fourth quarter of 1969 and that little change is in prospect for the early part of 1970. Prices and costs, however, are continuing to rise at a rapid pace. Most market interest rates have receded from highs reached during December. Bank credit and the money supply increased slightly on average in December and also over the fourth quarter as a whole. Outstanding large-denomination CD's held by domestic depositors have continued to contract in recent months while foreign official time deposits have expanded considerably. Flows of consumer-type time and savings funds at banks and nonbank thrift institutions have remained weak, and there apparently were sizable net outflows after year-end interest crediting. U.S. imports and exports have both grown further in recent months but through November the trade balance showed little or no further improvement from the third-quarter level. At the year-end the over-all balance of payments statistics were buoyed by large temporary inflows of U.S. corporate funds. In light of the foregoing developments, it is the policy of the Federal Open

Market Committee to foster financial conditions conducive to the orderly reduction of inflationary pressures, with a view to encouraging sustainable economic growth and attaining reasonable equilibrium in the country's balance of payments.

To implement this policy, while taking account of the forthcoming Treasury refunding, possible bank regulatory changes and the Committee's desire to see a modest growth in money and bank credit, System open market operations until the next meeting of the Committee shall be conducted with a view to maintaining firm conditions in the money market; provided, however, that operations shall be modified if money and bank credit appear to be deviating significantly from current projections.*

MEETING HELD ON FEBRUARY 10, 1970

The information reviewed at this meeting suggests that real economic activity, which leveled off in the fourth quarter of 1969, may be weakening further in early 1970. Prices and costs, however, are continuing to rise at a rapid pace. Long-term market interest rates recently have fluctuated under the competing influences of heavy demands for funds and shifts in investor attitudes regarding the outlook for monetary policy. Bank credit declined in January but the money supply increased substantially on average; both had risen slightly in the fourth quarter. Flows of time and savings funds at banks and nonbank thrift institutions have remained generally weak since year-end, and they apparently have been affected little thus far by the recent increases in maximum rates payable for such funds. The U.S. foreign trade balance improved somewhat in December, as imports fell off. The over-all balance of payments has been in substantial deficit in recent weeks. In light of the foregoing developments, it is the policy of the Federal Open Market Committee to foster financial conditions conducive to the orderly reduction of inflationary pressures, with a view to encouraging sustainable economic growth and attaining reasonable equilibrium in the country's balance of payments.

To implement this policy, while taking account of the current Treasury refunding, possible bank regulatory changes and the Committee's desire to see moderate growth in money and bank credit over the months ahead. System open market operations until the next meeting of the Committee shall be conducted with a view to moving gradually toward somewhat less firm conditions in the money market; provided, however, that operations shall be modified promptly to resist any tendency for money and bank credit to deviate significantly from a moderate growth pattern.

MEETING HELD ON MARCH 10, 1970

The information reviewed at this meeting suggests that real economic activity, which leveled off in the fourth quarter of 1969, is weakening further in early 1970. Prices and costs, however, are continuing to rise at a rapid pace. Market interest rates have declined considerably in recent weeks, partly as a result of changing investor attitudes regarding the outlook for economic activity and monetary policy. Both bank credit and the money supply declined on average in February, but both were tending upward in the latter part of the month. Outflows of time and savings funds at banks and nonbank thrift instituions, which had been sizable in January,

---

* Editor's note: Notice that *money* has been added to the proviso paragraph at this meeting.

apparenly ceased in February, reflecting advances in rates offered on such funds following the recent increases in regulatory ceilings, together with declines in short-term market interest rates. The U.S. foreign trade surplus narrowed in January and the over-all balance of payments deficit has remained large in recent weeks. In light of the foregoing developments, it is the policy of the Federal Open Market Committee to foster financial conditions conducive to orderly reduction in the rate of inflation, while encouraging the resumption of sustainable economic growth and the attainment of reasonable equilibrium in the country's balance of payments.

To implement this policy, the Committee desires to see moderate growth in money and bank credit over the months ahead. System open market operations until the next meeting of the Committee shall be conducted with a view to maintaining money market conditions consistent with that objective.*

MEETING HELD ON APRIL 7, 1970

The information reviewed at this meeting suggests that real economic activity weakened further in early 1970, while prices and costs continued to rise at a rapid pace. Fiscal stimulus, of dimensions that are still uncertain, will strengthen income expansion in the near term. Most long-term interest rates backed up during much of March under the pressure of heavy demands for funds, but then turned down in response to indications of some relaxation of monetary policy and to the reduction in the prime lending rate of banks. Short-term rates declined further on balance in recent weeks, contributing to the ability of banks and other thrift institutions to attract time and savings funds. Both bank credit and the money supply rose on average in March; over the first quarter as a whole bank credit was about unchanged on balance and the money supply increased somewhat. The U.S. foreign trade surplus increased in February, but the over-all balance of payments appears to have been in considerable deficit during the first quarter. In light of the foregoing developments, it is the policy of the Federal Open Market Committee to foster financial conditions conducive to orderly reduction in the rate of inflation, while encouraging the resumption of sustainable economic growth and the attainment of reasonable equilibrium in the country's balance of payments.

To implement this policy, the Committee desires to see moderate growth in money and bank credit over the months ahead. System open market operations until the next meeting of the Committee shall be conducted with a view to maintaining money market conditions consistent with that objective, taking account of the forthcoming Treasury financing.

MEETING HELD ON MAY 5, 1970

The information reviewed at this meeting indicates that real economic activity weakened further in the first quarter of 1970. Growth in personal income, however, is being stimulated in the second quarter by the enlargement of social security benefit payments and the Federal pay raise. Prices and costs generally are continuing to rise at a rapid pace, although some components of major price indexes recently have shown moderating tendencies. Most market interest rates have risen

---

* Editor's note: Monetary growth is now seen as a target. Compare with previous meeting.

sharply in recent weeks as a result of heavy demands for funds, possible shifts in liquidity preferences, and the disappointment of earlier expectations regarding easing of credit market conditions. Prices of common stocks have declined markedly since early April. Attitudes in financial markets generally are being affected by the expansion of military operations in Southeast Asia and by concern about the success of the Government's anti-inflationary program. Both bank credit and the money supply rose substantially from March to April on average, although during the course of April bank credit leveled off and the money supply receded sharply from the end-of-March bulge. The over-all balance of payments was in considerable deficit during the first quarter. In light of the foregoing developments, it is the policy of the Federal Open Market Committee to foster financial conditions conducive to orderly reduction in the rate of inflation, while encouraging the resumption of sustainable economic growth and the attainment of reasonable equilibrium in the Country's balance of payments.

To implement this policy, the Committee desires to see moderate growth in money and bank credit over the months ahead. System open market operations until the next meeting of the Committee shall be conducted with a view to maintaining bank reserves and money market conditions consistent with that objecive, taking account of the current Treasury financing; provided, however, that operations shall be modified as needed to moderate excessive pressures in financial markets, should they develop.*

MEETING HELD ON MAY 26, 1970

The information reviewed at this meeting indicates that real economic activity declined more than previously estimated in the first quarter of 1970, but little further change is projected in the second quarter. Prices and costs generally are continuing to rise at a rapid pace, although some components of major price indexes recently have shown moderating tendencies. Since early May most long-term interest rates have remained under upward pressure, partly as a result of continued heavy demands for funds and possible shifts in liquidity preferences, and prices of common stocks have declined further. Attitudes in financial markets generally are being affected by the widespread uncertainties arising from recent international and domestic events, including doubts about the success of the Government's anti-inflationary program. Both bank credit and the money supply rose substantially from March to April on average; in May bank credit appears to be changing little while the money supply appears to be expanding rapidly. The over-all balance of payments continued in considerable deficit in April and early May. In light of the foregoing developments, it is the policy of the Federal Open Market Committee to foster financial conditions conducive to orderly reduction in the rate of inflation, while encouraging the resumption of sustainable economic growth and the attainment of reasonable equilibrium in the country's balance of payments.

To implement this policy, in view of current market uncertainties and liquidity strains, open market operations until the next meeting of the Committee shall be conducted with a view to moderating pressures on financial markets, while, to the extent compatible therewith, maintaining bank reserves and money market con-

* Editor's note: Notice that money-market conditions has been "demoted" to the proviso clause. Compare with December 16, 1969.

ditions consistent with the Committee's longer-run objectives of moderate growth in money and bank credit.†

MEETING HELD ON JUNE 23, 1970

The information reviewed at this meeting suggests that real economic activity is changing little in the current quarter after declining appreciably earlier in the year. Prices and costs generally are continuing to rise at a rapid pace, although some components of major price indexes recently have shown moderating tendencies. Since late May market interest rates have shown mixed changes following earlier sharp advances, and prices of common stocks have recovered part of the large decline of preceding weeks. Attitudes in financial markets continue to be affected by uncertainties and conditions remain sensitive, particularly in light of the insolvency of a major railroad. In May bank credit changed little and the money supply rose moderately on average, following substantial increases in both measures in March and April. Inflows of consumer-type time and savings funds at banks and nonbank thrift institutions have been sizable in recent months, but the brief spring upturn in large-denomination CD's outstanding at banks has ceased. The over-all balance of payments was in heavy deficit in April and May. In light of the foregoing developments, it is the policy of the Federal Open Market Committee to foster financial conditions conducive to orderly reduction in the rate of inflation, while encouraging the resumption of sustainable economic growth and the attainment of reasonable equilibrium in the country's balance of payments.

To implement this policy, in view of persisting market uncertainties and liquidity strains, open market operations until the next meeting of the Committee shall continue to be conducted with a view to moderating pressures on financial markets. To the extent compatible therewith, the bank reserves and money market conditions maintained shall be consistent with the Committee's longer-run objective of moderate growth in money and bank credit, taking account of the Board's regulatory action effective June 24 and some possible consequent shifting of credit flows from market to banking channels.

MEETING HELD ON JULY 21, 1970

The information reviewed at this meeting indicates that real economic activity changed little in the second quarter after declining appreciably earlier in the year. Prices and wage rates generally are continuing to rise at a rapid pace. However, improvements in productivity appear to be slowing the rise in costs, and some major price measures are showing moderating tendencies. Since mid-June long-term interest rates have declined considerably, and prices of common stocks have fluctuated above their recent lows. Although conditions in financial markets have improved in recent weeks uncertainties persist, particularly in the commercial paper market where the volume of outstanding paper has contracted sharply. A large proportion of the funds so freed apparently was rechanneled through the banking system, as suggested by sharp increases in bank loans and in large-denomination CD's of short maturity—for which rate ceilings were suspended in late June. Consequently, in early July bank credit grew rapidly; there was also a

---

† Editor's note: Notice the change in emphasis in this final paragraph, and the final paragraph for the next meeting.

sharp increase in the money supply. Over the second quarter as awhole both bank credit and money supply rose moderately. The over-all balance of payments remained in heavy deficit in the second quarter. In light of the foregoing developments, it is the policy of the Federal Open Market Committee to foster financial conditions conducive to orderly reduction in the rate of inflation, while encouraging the resumption of sustainable economic growth and the attainment of reasonable equilibrium in the country's balance of payments.

To implement this policy, while taking account of persisting market uncertainties, liquidity strains, and the forthcoming Treasury financing, the Committee seeks to promote moderate growth in money and bank credit over the months ahead, allowing for a possible continued shift of credit flows from market to banking channels. System open market operations until the next meeting of the Committee shall be conducted with a view to maintaining bank reserves and money market conditions consistent with that objective; provided, however, that operations shall be modified as needed to counter excessive pressures in financial markets should they develop.

MEETING HELD ON AUGUST 18, 1970

The information reviewed at this meeting suggests that real economic activity, which edged up slightly in the second quarter after declining appreciably earlier in the year, may be expanding somewhat further. Prices and wage rates generally are continuing to rise at a rapid pace. However, improvements in productivity appear to be slowing the rise in costs, and some major price measures are showing moderating tendencies. Credit demands in securities markets have continued heavy, and interest rates have shown mixed changes since mid-July after declining considerably in preceding weeks. Some uncertainties persist in financial markets, particularly in connection with market instruments of less than prime grade. In July the money supply rose moderately on average and bank credit expanded substantially. Banks increased holdings of securities and loans to finance companies, some of which were experiencing difficulty in refinancing maturing commercial paper. Banks sharply expanded their oustanding large-denomination CD's of short maturity, for which rate ceilings had been suspended in late June, and both banks and nonbank thrift institutions experienced large net inflows of consumer-type time and savings funds. The over-all balance of payments remained in heavy deficit in the second quarter, despite a sizable increase in the export surplus. In July the official settlements deficit continued large, but there apparently was a marked shrinkage in the liquidity deficit. In light of the foregoing developments, it is the policy of the Federal Open Market Committee to foster financial conditions conducive to orderly reduction in the rate of inflation, while encouraging the resumption of sustainable economic growth and the attainment of reasonable equilibrium in the country's balance of payments.

To implement this policy, the Committee seeks to promote some easing of conditions in credit markets and somewhat greater growth in money over the months ahead than occurred in the second quarter, while taking account of possible liquidity problems and allowing bank credit growth to reflect any continued shift of credit flows from market to banking channels. System open market operations until the next meeting of the Committee shall be conducted with a view to maintaining bank reserves and money market conditions consistent with that objective, taking account of the effects of other monetary policy actions.

MEETING HELD ON SEPTEMBER 15, 1970

The information reviewed at this meeting suggests that real economic activity, which edged up slightly in the second quarter, is expanding somewhat further in the third quarter, led by an upturn in residential construction. Wage rates generally are continuing to rise at a rapid pace, but improvements in productivity appear to be slowing the rise in costs, and some major price measures are rising less rapidly than before. Interest rates declined in the last half of August, but most yields turned up in early September, as credit demands in securities have continued heavy; existing yield spreads continue to suggest concern with credit quality. The money supply rose rapidly in the first half of August but moved back down through early September. Bank credit expanded sharply further in August as banks continued to issue large-denomination CD's at a relatively rapid rate, while reducing their reliance on the commercial paper market after the Board of Governors acted to impose reserve requirements on bank funds obtained from that source. The balance of payments deficit on the liquidity basis diminished somewhat in July and August from the very large second-quarter rate, but the deficit on the official settlements basis remained high as banks repaid Euro-dollar liabilities. In the light of the foregoing developments, it is the policy of the Federal Open Market Committee to foster financial conditions conducive to orderly reduction in the rate of inflation, while encouraging the resumption of sustainable economic growth and the attainment of reasonable equilibrium in the country's balance of payments.

To implement this policy, the Committee seeks to promote some easing of conditions in credit markets and moderate growth in money and attendant bank credit expansion over the months ahead. System open market operations until the next meeting of the Committee shall be conducted with a view to maintaining bank reserves and money market conditions consistent with that objective.

MEETING HELD ON OCTOBER 20, 1970

The information reviewed at this meeting suggests that real output of goods and services increased slightly further in the third quarter but that employment declined and unemployment continued to rise; activity in the current quarter is being adversely affected by a major strike in the automobile industry. Wage rates generally are continuing to rise at a rapid pace, but improvements in productivity appear to be slowing the increase in costs, and some major price measures are rising less rapidly than before. Most interest rates have declined since mid-September, although yields on corporate and municipal bonds have been sustained by the continuing heavy demands for funds in capital markets. The money supply rose slightly on average in September and increased moderately over the third quarter as a whole. Bank credit expanded further in September but at a rate considerably less than the fast pace of the two preceding months. Banks continued to issue large-denomination CD's at a relatively rapid rate and experienced heavy inflows of consumer-type time and savings funds, while making substantial further reductions in their use of nondeposit sources of funds. The balance of payments deficit on the liquidity basis diminished in the third quarter from the very large second-quarter rate, but the deficit on the official settlements basis remained high as banks repaid Euro-dollar liabilities. In the light of the foregoing developments, it is the policy of the Federal Open Market Committee to foster financial conditions conducive to orderly reduction in the rate of inflation, while encouraging the resumption of sustainable economic growth and the attainment of reasonable equilibrium in the country's balance of payments.

To implement this policy, the Committee seeks to promote some easing of conditions in credit markets and moderate growth in money and attendant bank credit expansion over the months ahead. System open market operations until the next meeting of the Committee shall be conducted with a view to maintaining bank reserves and money market conditions consistent with those objectives, taking account of the forthcoming Treasury financings.

MEETING HELD ON NOVEMBER 17, 1970

The information reviewed at this meeting suggests that real output of goods and services is changing little in the current quarter and that unemployment has increased. Part but not all of the weakness in over-all activity is attributable to the strike in the automobile industry which apparently is now coming to an end. Wage rates generally are continuing to rise at a rapid pace, but gains in productivity appear to be slowing the increase in unit labor costs. Recent movements in major price measures have been erratic but the general pace of advance in these measures has tended to slow. Most interest rates declined considerably in the past few weeks, and Federal Reserve discount rates were reduced by one-quarter of a percentage point in the week of November 9. Demands for funds in capital markets have continued heavy, but business loan demands at banks have weakened. The money supply changed little on average in October for the second consecutive month; bank credit also was about unchanged, following a slowing of growth in September. The balance of payments deficit on the liquidity basis was at a lower rate in the third quarter and in October than the very high second-quarter rate, but the deficit on the official settlements basis remained high as banks repaid Euro-dollar liabilities. In light of the foregoing developments, it is the policy of the Federal Open Market Committee to foster financial conditions conducive to orderly reduction in the rate of inflation, while encouraging the resumption of sustainable economic growth and the attainment of reasonable equilibrium in the country's balance of payments.

To implement this policy, the Committee seeks to promote some easing of conditions in credit markets and moderate growth in money and attendant bank credit expansion over the months ahead, with allowance for temporary shifts in money and credit demands related to the auto strike. System open market operations until the next meeting of the Committee shall be conducted with a view to maintaining bank reserves and money market conditions consistent with those objectives.

MEETING HELD ON DECEMBER 15, 1970

The information reviewed at this meeting suggests that real output of goods and services has declined since the third quarter, largely as a consequence of the recent strike in the automobile industry, and that unemployment has increased. Resumption of higher automobile production is expected to result in a bulge in activity in early 1971. Wage rates generally are continuing to rise at a rapid pace, but gains in productivity appear to be slowing the increase in unit labor costs. Movements in major price measures have been diverse; most recently, wholesale prices have shown little change while consumer prices have advanced substantially. Market interest rates declined considerably further in the past few weeks, and Federal Reserve discount rates were reduced by an additional one-quarter of a percentage point. Demands for funds in capital markets have continued heavy, but business loan demands at banks have been weak. Growth in the money supply was somewhat more rapid on average in November than in October, although it remained below the rate prevailing in the first three quarters of the year. Banks acquired a substantial volume of securities in November, and bank credit increased moderately after changing little in October. The foreign trade balance in September and October was smaller than in any other 2-month period this year. The over-all balance of pyaments deficit on the liquidity basis remained in October and November at about its third-quarter rate. The deficit on the official settlement basis was very large as banks continued to repay Euro-dollar liabilities. In light of the foregoing developments, it is the policy of the Federal Open Market Committee to foster financial conditions conducive to orderly reduction in the rate of inflation, while encouraging the resumption of sustainable economic growth and the attainment of reasonable equilibrium in the country's balance of payments.

To implement this policy, System open market operations shall be conducted with a view to maintaining the recently attained money market conditions until the next meeting of the Committee, provided that the expected rates of growth in money and bank credit will at least be achieved.

READING 19
MONETARY POLICY TARGETS AND INDICATORS

Thomas R. Saving*

The revival of interest in monetary economics and the return to the idea that "money matters" have rekindled concern on the part of economists over the problems of monetary policy-making. As a result there has been an outpouring of research on the effectiveness of various aspects of monetary policy, including both considerable criticism of and advice to the monetary authorities. However, both the criticism and the advice often have been contradictory. As Allan Meltzer so aptly put it, "Our advice to the Fed most often took the form of nearly unanimous agreement that what they had done was wrong and nearly *zero* agreement about what they had done."

If agreement cannot be reached on what the past policy has been or on what the current policy is, it is difficult to agree on the course of future policy. A recent example will illustrate the ex-

tent of the disagreement. The July, 1966, *Federal Reserve Bulletin* characterized the monetary policy of the first six months of 1966 as one of *monetary restraint,* while the October, 1966, issue of the *Federal Reserve Bank of St. Louis Review* characterized the policy during this same period as one of rapid *monetary expansion.* The recurrence of such contradictory descriptions of past policy has led to discussion by economists of what has come to be known as the "indicator problem", that is, the problem of finding a variable or combination of variables that will best describe the effect that current monetary policy is having on economic activity. The importance of the problem arises from the fact that the choice of future policy is influenced by the policymaker's estimate of the effect of his current policy.

To illustrate how such differences in

Source: Reprinted from *Journal of Political Economy,* Aug. 1967, pp. 446–456.

* I would like to thank Karl Brunner, Jan Kmenta, William R. Russell, and Robert F. Lanzillotti for many helpful suggestions.

interpretation of past and current policy may arise, consider again the period of the first six months of 1966. For purposes of discussion define a restrictive policy as one that reduces aggregate demand and an expansionary policy as one that increases aggregate demand. Since the effect of current policy on aggregate demand is not directly observable, the monetary authority must gauge the effect of its policy by observing some proxy variable. If the chosen variable is the interest rate or free reserves, then the first six months of 1966 would be characterized as a period of restrictive monetary policy. On the other hand, if the money supply were used as the proxy, then this same period would be characterized as one of monetary expansion. Of course, how the monetary authority characterizes past policy is irrelevant as long as these policy evaluations do not affect the course of future policy. However, this is an unlikely circumstance in view of the uncertainties surrounding the policy decisions. Thus, a characterization of a given past and current policy as restrictive in a period when the monetary authority desires to reduce aggregate demand will affect the course of future policy differently than if the same policy were characterized as expansionary.

I. THE JUSTIFICATION FOR MONETARY-POLICY TARGETS AND INDICATORS

The need for monetary-policy targets and indicators is derived from the desire to pursue that particular monetary policy which is optimal in some sense. Thus, the justification for the use of targets and indicators must begin with a discussion of the choice of optimal policy. For this purpose define "monetary policy" as the manipulation of certain aspects of the economy that are under the direct control of the mone-

tary authority, usually called "policy instruments," so as to attain goals that are considered desirable. A policy is then a particular vector of the various policy instruments, for example, a given level of the discount rate, reserve requirements, and rate of change in [the Fed's] portfolio [of government securities].

Since the choice of an optimal path for policy requires that "optimal" be defined, it is assumed that the policy-maker has some objective function in mind; this is usually called a "goal function." Such a goal function may be a single-valued function of unemployment, or it may be a complicated function of many arguments, for example, employment, real income, stability of prices, rate of growth in real income, and balance of trade. Denote this function as

$$G = G(y_i), \qquad (1)$$

where y represents the levels of various endogenous variables in the economic system and will in general be a proper subset of the set of all endogenous variables in the system.

In addition to defining the objective function, the choice of optimal policy requires a specific hypothesis of the structure of the economic system. That is, if the policy maker is to choose that policy which maximizes his goal function, he must know the effects of various policies on the endogenous variables. Denote the structure as

$$Y_t = F(Y_{t-i}, X_t, X_{t-i}, Z_t, Z_{t-i}), \qquad (2)$$

where Y_t is the vector of current values of the endogenous variables; Y_{t-i} is the vector of past values of the endogenous variables; X_t is the vector of the current values of the policy-determined variables, that is, instruments; X_{t-i} is the vector of past policy variables; Z_t is the vector of current values of the non-policy-determined exogenous variables; and Z_{t-i} is the vector of past values of the non-policy-determined exogenous variables.[1]

The problem generally considered in the literature on optimal-policy choice is the maximization of (1), that is, the goal function, subject to (2), that is, the known structure of the economic system, through the manipulation of the policy instruments, that is, the vector X_t. The optimal policy is that vector X_t which yields the maximum for G. This problem has been considered in two forms: (a) when the function F in (2) is assumed non-stochastic and (b) when the function F in (2) is considered to be stochastic. The stochastic form of the optimal-policy problem has been shown to be equivalent to the non-stochastic form (that is, these two forms yield the same optimal policy vector) for the case in which the choice of policy does not affect the variance of the endogenous arguments of the goal function.

Both the stochastic and the non-stochastic forms of the optimal-policy problem usually assume the policy-maker has complete knowledge of the structure and of the current economic situation; that is, it is assumed that the function F in (2) is known and that the vectors $Y_{t-i}, X_{t-i}, Z_t, Z_{t-i}$ are all known with certainty.[2] In fact, however, the policy-maker has many different and competing hypotheses of the structure available to him. In addition, many of the important endogenous and exogenous variables are observable only after a considerable lag. Thus, the monetary policy-maker does not have complete knowledge of either the function F or the non-policy determined arguments of F. *It is the union of these two prob-*

lems that leads to the need for targets and indicators of monetary policy.

A. The Target Problem

Consider a world in which the policy-maker does not know the correct form of the structural equations or the values of all the parameters of any one form. Assume, however, that he has adequate information to determine the direction of the effect of his policy actions on the various endogenous variables; that is, he has enough information to make qualitative statements about the world. Additionally, assume that those variables that are arguments of the goal function are observable only after considerable lag. Under these conditions it can be shown that it is reasonable for the policy-maker to choose an endogenous variable, which is observable with little or no lag, and aim his policy at making this endogenous variable take on some desired value. Such a value of an endogenous variable is usually called a *monetary policy target,* that is, a value that the monetary authority shoots at in determining the policy vector.

There are two reasons for the use of target variables. First, since the structure is unknown, the exact effect of a policy cannot be obtained from the structure. However, our lack of knowledge is not uniform throughout the structure. Thus, the policy-maker may be reasonably certain of the relationship between some observable endogenous variable and the goal variables, even if he is very uncertain about the exact effect of his instruments on the goal variables. He may then choose this observable endogenous variable as

---

[1] Equation (2) can also be expressed as a system of differential equations that describes the time path of the endogenous variables. When expressed in this way the relevant goal function would be a functional of the time paths of selected endogenous variables.

[2] This complete knowledge may or may not include the knowledge of the means, variances, and covariances, of the stochastic elements. However, it is generally assumed that the probability distributions of the stochastic terms at time t are independent of the value of these terms at time $t - i$ for all i.

a target variable and adjust his instruments until this variable reaches its desired (target) level. Presumably this desired level will be the one that is consistent with the goal variables reaching their desired levels. Using this approach, the policy-maker circumvents some of the uncertainties in the effect of policy on the goal variables.[3] Second, since the goal variables are observable only after considerable lag, the effect of policy will only be seen after the policy has been pursued for some time. During this period, exogenous changes may occur, making the effect of the policy chosen larger, or smaller, than it otherwise would have been. If a target variable is used, however, then these exogenous changes may simply affect the magnitude of the operation necessary to make the target variable reach the level desired. Thus, the use of a target variable can remove some of the uncertainty resulting from unobservable goal variables.

For example, consider a situation in which (1) the goal function is an increasing function of real income, (2) the monetary authority lacks complete knowledge of the structure, (3) the level of real income is observable only after a considerable lag, and (4) policy affects the level of real income with a lag. Now the monetary authority chooses as a target variable an endogenous variable that is close to monetary policy, that is, affected rapidly by policy; readily observable; and related to the goal variable, real income. Such a target variable is the interest rate. It is close to monetary policy, readily observable, and in most structural hypotheses related to real income. The advantage of using a target such as

interest rates is that many changes in exogenous variables that affect the required magnitude of policy, such as a change in the currency-deposit ratio, will result in an adjustment in policy even though the changes in exogenous variables are unobservable. In addition, if the relationship between interest rates and income is known, the correct magnitude of policy may be achieved by simply pursuing policy until the rate of interest reaches a desired level, even if the relevant monetary parameters are unknown.

For a target variable to perform in the manner suggested above, it must be (1) readily observable with little or no lag, (2) rapidly affected by the policy instruments, and (3) related to the goal variables in the sense that policies resulting in the target variable taking on certain values must in turn result in the goal variables taking on certain values.[4] The choice of an optimal-monetary-policy target variable will require a structural hypothesis and a goal function. However, the choice will not require complete knowledge of the structure, since it is lack of knowledge of the structure that gives rise to the need for a target variable. Thus, if complete knowledge is available, and the goal variables are observable with little or no lag, then the need for a target variable disappears, since the optimal policy may now be uniquely determined.

B.   The Indicator Problem

Unfortunately, the use of an endogenous variable to adjust policy actions is not without its drawbacks. In particular, changes other than those induced by policy actions may occur in the

---

[3] In other words, part of the variance in the goal variables is due to uncertainty between the target variable and the policy. If the policy can be adjusted instantly to account for any random change between the policy and the target, then this part of the uncertainty can be removed.

[4] What is required is that the reduced-form equations for the target variable and the goal variables be such that a policy vector that results in the target variable taking on its desired magnitude will, when substituted into the reduced form for the goal variables, result in their taking on certain values.

economy resulting in changes in the target variable. Such non-policy-induced changes in the target variable may result in the attainment of the target being inconsistent with the goal. For example, assume that the policy-maker uses interest rates as a target and that his goal is to reach full employment from an initial position of unemployment. Assuming the structure is such that monetary actions which reduce the rate of interest increase aggregate demand, a target level below the current market level is chosen for the interest rate. The monetary authority then manipulates its instruments until this target level of the interest rate is attained. If, during the period of the policy action, business expectations turn more pessimistic, the investment function will shift leftward, and the equilibrium rate of interest will fall, possibly below the target level set by the monetary authority. Thus, the policy actually undertaken may be one of raising the rate of interest to the target level rather than reducing it, with the result that the policy will have reduced aggregate demand and further reduced employment.

The possibility that changes in the economy will occur during the implementation of policy raises the need for an indicator of the effect of the policy being pursued. That is, if the policy-maker is to adjust his policy to changes in his environment occuring during the implementation of a particular policy, he must have an index of the effect of current policy. Essentially, the policy-maker requires a separation of the change in his target variable into a policy effect and an exogenous effect. Since observation of the changes in the target variable yields only the total effect, some other variable or combination of variables is required to reflect the policy effect. This other variable or combination of variables, usually called a "monetary-policy indicator,"

must be distinct from the target variable in the sense of being mathematically independent; that is, the indicator must not be a scalar multiple of the target variable. In addition, since the purpose of the indicator is to measure the policy effect, it must be chosen so that either (1) exogenous changes that affect the target variable do not affect the indicator or (2) if these exogenous variables do affect the indicator their effect must be swamped by the policy effect.

Since the task of the indicator is to gauge the effect of monetary policy, the choice of an indicator requires some hypothesis concerning the structure. In addition, if the indicator is used to measure the effect of policy on the goal variables rather than the target variables, knowledge of the goal function will also be required. Even in the latter case the choice of the target variable requires the goal function, so that the choice of the indicator indirectly involves the goal function. Just as in the target case, the indicator must be (1) easily observable with little or no lag, (2) close to the policy actions in the sense that it is quickly affected by the policy undertaken, and (3) related to the target and goal variables. Because the indicator of policy gauges the effect of the immediate past policy and because the future course of policy will be influenced by the policy-maker's estimate of the effect of policy, it is crucial that the indicator yield at least qualitatively correct results. Otherwise there is a danger that a policy will continue to be pursued that amplifies rather than moderates the cyclical fluctuations in the goal variables.

To illustrate the use of an indicator, consider the previous example of a policy designed to reduce interest rates that encounters a subsequent leftward shift in the investment function. In that example it was shown that the pursuit of policy until the target is reached may result in a rate of interest that is higher than would have existed in the absence of policy. Suppose that this worst possible case occurs so that the effect of policy actually decreases aggregate demand instead of increases it. How can the policy-maker warn himself of such a contingency? If he had, for example, used the monetary base as an indicator of the effect of his policy on interest rates, the fact that policy had actually resulted in an increase in interest rates would have shown up as a decrease in the monetary base. Thus, the use of an indicator can serve to separate the exogenous effect from the policy effect in those cases where the exogenous changes affect only the target variable. The above discussion can be extended to show why the indicator must be distinct from the target. Consider the case of the interest rate being used as both target and indicator. Then the policy effect will be indistinguishable from the total effect, so that any time the target is hit, the policy will be depicted as being correct.

II. THE CHARACTERIZATION OF POLICY

Monetary economists frequently refer to monetary policy as being "expansionary" or "restrictive," "tight" or "loose," "more expansionary" or "more restrictive," "tighter" or "looser." Such terms may be interpreted in two fundamentally different ways: (1) these terms may simply involve a taxonomic scheme for classifying policy, or (2) they may describe the policy's effect on some endogenous variable or combination of endogenous variables. The taxonomic approach is useful as a summary of the policy itself, but it is important to recognize that the terms "expansionary" and "restrictive" or "tight" and "loose" are then determined by the levels of the instruments

and not by the net effect of policy. The second interpretation of policy statements involves going a step further than simple taxonomy, since it is based on the net effect of policy on some variables considered to be important, for example, aggregate demand. In this second case, policies are not restrictive or expansionary in and of themselves but are restrictive or expansionary only in terms of a specific structural hypothesis and criterion for characterization. Hence, a given policy might be expansionary under one structural hypothesis and criterion and restrictive under another.

If policy statements are of the first type, that is, purely taxonomic, then the classification of policy will have no effect on subsequent policy actions. The reason is that future policy action, whether this entails a continuation of present policy or some change in policy, depends on the policy-maker's view of the effect of policy and not on the taxonomic classification of current policy. On the other hand, if policy statements are interpreted in the second sense, that is, as descriptive of the *effect* of policy, then a particular description will affect the decision to continue or change policy because this description reflects the policy-maker's view of the effect of current policy.

III. DIVERSE ISSUES CONCERNING INDICATORS

Since the problem of monetary policy indicators was first raised by Brunner and Meltzer, considerable debate (both written and at various conferences) has ensued. During these discussions many issues were raised that still remain in the air. I shall discuss below several of these issues which I feel are as yet unresolved in the eyes of those who have raised them; I state these issues for brevity in the form of assertions.

Since the problem is essentially lack of knowledge of the structure, we should devote our time to filling this gap.

Considerable sentiment has been expressed, in various discussions of monetary policy indicators, that finding an indicator is really a "second best" solution. Since the need for targets and indicators arises because of lack of knowledge about the structure, the optimal procedure is to acquire the missing knowledge. This objection to spending time on the problem of indicator choice misses the point of the discussion entirely. True enough, the problem arises because we desire to pursue policy in spite of lack of knowledge concerning the structure. However, from this fact it does not follow that the problem is best solved by devoting all our energies to getting the missing knowledge. This solution would only be optimal if it were true that the marginal return to additional effort spent on knowledge acquisition exceeds the marginal return to additional effort spent on the choice of indicator, at any level of effort on the indicator problem. Moreover, since this form of solution requires complete knowledge, I would venture to say that even with a total effort, this complete knowledge is unobtainable in the foreseeable future. Thus, either we must (1) continue to live with the problem until such time as complete knowledge is available, or (2) discontinue policy entirely, or (3) devote some of our energy to finding ways to live better with the lack of complete knowledge. It seems to me that the third alternative is the only reasonable solution. Note that I am not suggesting that the search for new knowledge be abandoned but only that some (not all) of our efforts be devoted to the problem of optimal-policy decisions under the existing conditions of lack of complete knowledge.

The world is so complex that the choice of targets and indicators is an insurmountable problem. It is often asserted that, even though an indicator would be a useful tool, a reliable indicator cannot be found because of the complexity of the economic system. This statement may be interpreted in two ways. First, the antecedent of the proposition, that is, that the world is complex, may mean that the structural relations are many and that each is complicated, for example, non-linear. From this, however, it does not follow that a reliable indicator cannot be found, since presumably a solution for the system exists; the reduced form may be found. Using the reduced form and the goal function, targets and indicators can be constructed. Hence, in this form the statement is false. Second, the antecedent may be interpreted to mean that there are many stochastic links in the chain of effect so that the variances of the endogenous variables are large relative to the policy effect. Thus, the stochastic effect may easily swamp the policy effect for any given indicator, resulting in unreliability. In this form the argument may be valid but up to this point it merely represents an assertion about the world. Lastly, those economists who profess to hold this view continue to make comparative statements about policy, implying that they have found an indicator that at least they believe to be reliable. As long as indicators are to be used, they should be chosen in some systematic fashion.

The use of an indicator is equivalent to putting on blinders. Since an indicator of policy is essentially a proxy for the effect of policy on the target or goal variables, indicators by their nature exclude most of the other information in the economy. Thus the question arises: Instead of looking at an indicator, why not look at all the variables? There are basically two reasons for concentrating on an indicator. First, most of the information available is about endogenous variables that are of little interest, that is, not goal variables and only tenuously connected to the goal variables, so that their use simply clouds the issue. Second, the variables in which we are ultimately interested are observable with a considerable lag, so that by the time we find out what the effect of our policy has been, considerable damage may have been done. Hence, the choice of indicator does not imply that useful information is being discarded but only that all the information is not necessarily useful or available or both. With this view in mind, I believe that the use of an indicator is better characterized as the use of a *spotlight* rather than of blinders.

The characterization of policy is of secondary importance. As was noted earlier in this paper, the way current policy is characterized is unimportant if agreement can be reached on the future course of policy. As Franco Modigliani put it at the UCLA Conference on Targets and Indicators of Monetary Policy, "That is, it seems to me that the question of the terminology of tight or loose, or easy and expansionary or restrictive, is what I refer to as a matter of semantics, and of secondary importance, in the sense that I don't really care whether you want to call a situation loose or tight as long as we agree in what direction to go." I agree with Modigliani's statement, but this begs the question of the choice of indicator. It is exactly because the characterization of policy affects the future course of policy that we cannot agree on "what direction to go." For example, consider again the first six months of 1966. As pointed out earlier, the Board of Governors of the Federal Reserve System was characterizing policy during this period as tight and was pointing to interest rates and free reserves for verification (see *Federal Reserve Bulletin 1966*). If the Federal Reserve acts on the belief that their past policy was tight in the determination

of future policy then the characterization of policy becomes more than just an issue over semantics. In other words, the decision on how to revise the current policy cannot be made without evaluating the effect of the current policy. Every policy action involves in some way the interpretation of policy, that is, involves the indicator problem.

The choice of a "best" indicator is simply a matter of one's utility function. Since the choice of an indicator involves, either directly or indirectly, the assumption of a goal function, it is often asserted that this choice is entirely subjective. However, this does not imply that this choice should not be discussed in a systematic manner. Moreover, it is not at all apparent that the goal functions of various individuals differ in a way that would affect the choice of indicator. It is more likely that these differences will affect the choice of policy rather than the criterion for evaluating the effects of policy.

IV. THE PROBLEM OF INDICATOR CHOICE

Up to this point I have discussed the justification for monetary-policy targets and indicators and some of the objections that have been raised concerning the relevance of indicators and the existence of a "best" indicator. The problem of a criterion for choosing a "best" indicator still remains. Since any choice of an indicator necessarily involves only a proper subset of all information available, we must have a criterion for judging the numerous candidates for indicators. An example of the use of a criterion to solve such a problem is provided in some recent work done by Brunner and Meltzer.

Brunner and Meltzer proceed by considering a general macro-economic model with only the signs of the partial derivatives specified. Thus, their results are valid for a wide range of structural hypotheses. They further assume the goal function of the policy-makers to be a monotonically increasing function of real income. Various endogenous indicators are then compared to see how well they gauge the effect of policy on real income. A minimax strategy is then used to choose the best indicator. In this case "best" is taken to be the indicator that has the minimum-maximum deviation between the actual effect and the indicated effect, using the limited knowledge that Brunner and Meltzer assume they have of the structural parameters. For the class of hypotheses of the structure and the criterion of choice used, the money stock was judged to be the "best" indicator among those endogenous indicators considered. Brunner and Meltzer emphasize that this indicator is not ideal and does at times yield misleading results but that it is the least misleading of those considered. They also emphasize that consideration of combinations of endogenous variables rather than single variables as indicators may improve the results.

Perhaps some insight into the problem of indicator choice can be obtained by considering the behavior of several alternative indicators during both boom and downswing periods. The indicators to be considered are (1) the rate of interest, (2) the level of free reserves, (3) the money stock, and (4) the monetary base. For purposes of this discussion, assume that the goal of the policy-maker is the maximization of real income, that is, the attainment and maintenance of full employment. In addition, assume a structural hypothesis in which the level of income is affected ultimately only by the level of aggregate demand. Hence, policy may be characterized by its effect on aggregate demand. In this circumstance a good indicator should reveal the magnitude and direction of the effect that the policy being pursued is having on the level of aggregate demand. Then the relationship between aggregate demand and our goal function reveals whether this is the appropriate policy. Assume that the structural hypothesis is such that (1) the interest rate is negatively related to aggregate demand, (2) free reserves are positively related to aggregate demand, (3) the money stock is positively related to aggregate demand, and (4) the monetary base is positively related to aggregate demand. In addition, assume that inflation and deflation both result in lower real income so that during inflationary periods the aim of policy will be to reduce aggregate demand while during deflationary periods the aim of policy will be to increase aggregate demand. The four indicators of policy can now be evaluated using only the general assumptions of the goal and structure listed above.

A. The Rate of Interest

Since the rate of interest follows a pro-cyclical pattern—that is, it rises during upswings and falls during downswings—its use as an indicator will tend to show that current policy is affecting aggregate demand in the desired direction when the actual effect is just the opposite. That is, the exogenous effect has the same sign as the desired policy effect so that the actual policy effect may be in the wrong direction and the total effect still be in the right direction. Since the indicator shows only the total effect, it can be misleading. Moreover, the likelihood of this type of mistake is greater the greater the cyclical effect on the rate of interest. In particular, if the cyclical effect is greater the larger the rate of change in income, then the policy followed is more likely to be ill timed in periods of rapid inflation or deflation than in periods of slower change. For example, assume a rapid downswing so that the cyclical effect on the rate of interest is large and in the downward direction. This downward movement in the rate of interest will indicate that current policy is increasing aggregate demand, that is, current policy is expansionary, when in fact the policy may be reducing aggregate demand. What has happened, of course, is that the cyclical effect has swamped the policy effect. Thus, the difficulty with the interest rate as an indicator is that the cyclical effect cannot be easily separated from the policy effect. Of course, if the policy-maker knows what the rate of interest would have been in the absence of policy, then his problem is solved, since the policy effect may now be isolated.

B. Free Reserves

Because of its relationship to the rate of interest, the level of free reserves moves countercyclically. But, since increases in free reserves increase aggregate demand and decreases reduce aggregate demand, a free-reserve indicator suffers from the same problems as an interest-rate indicator. In particular, a downswing results in increased desired free reserves on the part of banks, both because of the decrease in the rate of interest and because of an increase in the expectation of currency drains. The use of free reserves as an indicator will then show that the policy being pursued is expansionary when in reality it may be restrictive. That is, the cyclical effect on the level of free reserves may swamp the policy effect. Again, if the monetary authority knew the level of free reserves desired by the banks at all times, then it could, of course, separate out the policy effect.

C. Money Stock

The money stock, like interest rates, moves pro-cyclically, since during the upswing the increase in the cost of holding free reserves causes the banking system to draw down its free reserves, with the result that the money stock increases. But here the similarity ends as far as the indicator problem is concerned. For a downturn, which results in a downward movement in the money stock, a money-stock indicator has a cyclical effect that makes policy appear restrictive even when it may be expansionary. Thus, the money stock when used as an indicator tends to result in policy that is either more restrictive (in time of inflationary boom) or more expansionary (in time of deflation) than the policy desired by the monetary authority. If a minimax criterion were used, this type of error would generally be preferred to an error that resulted in feeding the boom and starving the bust. Thus, the money stock would be preferred to either interest rates or free reserves on this basis.

D. The Monetary Base

The stock of base money need not move cyclically at all, and thus may be the ideal indicator, since changes in it will completely reflect changes in policy as long as that policy is confined to open-market operations. The proviso that policy actions be confined to open-market operations is necessary since a given stock of base money is consistent, given the structure, with a different level of aggregate demand for each level of the discount rate or required reserves. Thus, in a period when discount rates and required reserves are constant, the monetary base will not deviate from the ideal indicator and hence will reflect the direction of the effect of policy on aggregate demand.

V. MONETARY-POLICY TARGETS OR INDICATORS?

Much of the controversy over the indicator problem boils down to a failure to distinguish between a target and an indicator. Arguments concerning the relationship between monetary variables and policy are used to support the use of particular variables as indicators. Such arguments fail to realize that, while the indicator must be related to policy, this relationship is not sufficient for a variable to be a good indicator. Moreover, in these discussions there is a general failure to realize the necessity for the indicator to be distinct from the target.

For example, the statement that free reserves should be used as an indicator because the behavior of bankers can be controlled by making free reserves deviate from what the bankers desire them to be is not an argument for the use of free reserves as an indicator but is rather an argument for their use as a target. A free-reserve indicator, by this reasoning, must be the difference between the actual level of free reserves and the level desired by the bankers. Thus, unless a mechanism is included to estimate the desired level of free reserves, the fact that the behavior of the banking system is affected by the level of free reserves, while true, does not imply that free reserves are a good indicator of monetary policy. Similarly the argument that, because the primary effect of monetary policy occurs via changes in the rate of interest, this rate should be looked to for an indication of the effect of policy is also a non-sequitur. All that follows from the assumption that monetary policy affects aggregate demand through the rate of interest is that the rate of interest is a good candidate for a policy target. For the rate of interest to be a reliable indicator of monetary policy, the monetary authority must know what the rate of interest would have been in the absence of policy. Since this information is unavailable, the use of interest rates as an indicator of policy is questionable. Thus it appears that at least a portion of the discussion on targets and indicators has been at cross purposes simply because of a failure to distinguish clearly between a target and an indicator.

TECHNIQUES OF THE FEDERAL RESERVE TRADING DESK IN THE 1960's

Robert L. Cooper

I. BACKGROUND

The arrival of the 1960's introduced new problems and new objectives into the conduct of Federal Reserve open market operations. The most pressing problem was the persistence of a sizable deficit in the United States' balance of payments, that depleted the United States gold stock and that produced, in October of 1960, a serious run on gold in the London market. Meanwhile, in contrast with booming economic conditions abroad during the early 1960's, particularly in Britain and West Germany, the United States' economy behaved quite sluggishly, with an unpalatably high rate of unemployment, and needed whatever stimulation could be provided by an easy monetary policy. It was evident, however, that if domestic short-term interest rates were permitted to decline in response to monetary ease, higher rates abroad would attract volatile funds, aggregate capital out-flows already in progress, and increase the deficit in the balance of payments. During the two previous periods of active ease in 1954 and 1958, System operations to expand reserves had been accompanied by a decline in Treasury bill rates to the neighborhood of ⅝ of one per cent. The repetition of such a performance, or of any substantial decline in Treasury bill rates, was clearly intolerable in the context of the 1960's.*

Faced with this situation, the Federal Open Market Committee had to adopt

Source: This selection was taken from a larger study of the author *Techniques of the Federal Reserve Trading Desk in the 1960's Contrasted With the Bills Preferably Period*, a staff study conducted by the Treasury and Federal Reserve into the U.S. Government Securities Market, 1967.

* Editor's note: Mr. Cooper's view presumably reflect official views of the Federal Reserve, by which he was employed as Account Manager, Federal Reserve Bank of New York at the time this study was prepared.

and pursue some objectives, however limited, with respect to interest rates. This was in direct contrast with the Committee's policy of scrupulously avoiding any specific interest rate objectives throughout the "bills preferably" period.† Beginning in late 1960, it became an important purpose of the Committee to minimize further declines (or to foster some rise) in short-term interest rates, particularly in the rate for three-month Treasury bills, which was watched intently here and abroad as a criterion of international rate relationships.

It was readily apparent that one way to minimize downward pressures on short-term rates would be to spread System purchases of securities to supply reserves over a wider range of maturities, rather than concentrating such purchases, as in the past, in the very sector of the market where it was desired to keep rates up. Therefore, the Committee gradually abandoned its policy of restricting operations exclusively to the short-term area of the market (Treasury bills in practice). Starting late in 1960, coupon issues due within 15 months were purchased along with Treasury bills in order to provide reserves, and very short-term coupon issues, equivalent to Treasury bills in maturity, were sold on occasion in dealing with downward pressures on rates in that area. Beginning in February 1961, the Committee authorized the Desk to operate in issues maturing in up to 10 years and in March 1961, the ten-year limitation was removed. Moreover, the Desk was permitted to make offsetting purchases and sales of securities so that it could sell short-term securities in dealing with downward rate pressures in that area and purchase longer term issues simultaneously or within a very short time if monetary policy did not call for any net absorption of reserves at the time.

The Committee's intention with respect to short-term interest rates was generally understood within the System and was fairly obvious to both dealers and investors in Government securities. To the extent possible, short-term rates were to be kept competitive with comparable rates abroad and Federal Reserve open market operations were to be conducted in such a way as to encourage the accomplishment of that purpose, but without actually seeking to attain or hold any specific level of rates. On the other hand, there was considerable confusion in the market regarding possible System objectives with respect to long-term interest rates.

The Federal Open Market Committee did not publicly espouse any formal policy regarding long-term rates, largely because of the divergent and shifting opinions of the members and staff throughout the period when operations in coupon issues were being discussed, decided upon, initiated and carried out. It was generally recognized that an improved flow of long-term funds, needed to bolster the sagging domestic economy, could probably be stimulated by somewhat lower long-term interest rates. It was also recognized that System purchases of intermediate- and long-term Government securities to supply reserves or to offset sales of short-term issues would absorb some of the floating supply of coupon issues and would tend to influence prices (and rates) as would any other large-scale buying. On the other hand, there never was any clear-cut or formal agreement as to whether a reduction in long-term rates should be a deliberate aim of policy or should be passively accepted, if it occurred, merely as a desirable

---

† Editor's note: This is the period from 1953 to 1960 when System operations were confined to the short term end of the Government Securities Market.

outcome of shifting some System buying into coupon issues in order to deal with short-term rates. There was agreement on one point, however, that deliberate or not, any System influence on prices should not be permitted to degenerate into pegging rates at any specific level such as occurred during the war and postwar period. In the market, there was much misunderstanding and misinterpretation of the Desk's intentions, especially at times when the Desk was also operating for Treasury accounts. Much stronger long-term rate objectives were attributed to the System than were ever acknowledged by the Federal Open Market Committee acting for itself. The whole program was publicly nicknamed "operation twist," since the official objective was widely thought to be a simultaneous raising of short-term rates and lowering of long-term rates.

In view of the public's fixation on the rate aspects of the change in policy, Chairman Martin made a major statement on the subject in a speech on April 11, 1961 to the Reserve City Bankers in Boca Raton. Noting that *levels* of interest rates had been overemphasized, he said that the Federal Reserve's object was actually to influence flows of funds in international and domestic channels—"in respect to short-term rates, whether the outflow of funds to foreign centers is being stemmed; and in respect to long-term rates, whether the flow of capital into productive investment activities is being facilitated."

Since late 1960, therefore, the Desk has not been so limited in its choice of techniques as it was during the "bills preferably" period. The operating policies that had governed open market operations between 1953 and 1960 were first suspended and then discontinued. This enabled the Desk to operate outside the short-term area and to engage in swaps when appropriate. In practice of course, the bulk of operations over any extended period continued to be carried on in Treasury bills, because only the bill market could accommodate the large-scale transactions required to meet the reserve needs of the banking system. The Desk continued to avoid any outright trading for the System in issues involved in Treasury financings or issues of comparable maturity and, as noted above, there was no intention to support or maintain any specific level of prices or yields, especially in the intermediate- and long-term area where the new operations were being undertaken. With the Committee no longer operating solely to affect reserves, the achievement of the broader objectives required greater flexibility in the approach of the Desk to the Market. At the same time, dealers and investors had to adapt themselves to System operations throughout the maturity spectrum and to the necessary refinements and changes in the techniques employed by the Desk.

II. TECHNIQUES EMPLOYED

The methods of approach to the market during the early stages of expanding operations beyond Treasury bills were necessarily experimental and were limited by the inherent peculiarities of coupon issues as contrasted with Treasury bills. These peculiarities were not so apparent in the short-term area of the market, i.e., in issues due within 15 months but they became increasingly important as the Desk gradually extended its operations into the intermediate- and long-term area. Even in the short-term area, it was found that in contrast with the normally good two-way market for Treasury bills, purchases of coupon issues could usually be undertaken more readily than sales, confirming the meagre experience of 1957. In general, it was found that the market for coupon issues was normally quite thin and frequently one-sided, and that prices were much more responsive to official operations than were rates for Treasury bills. Moreover, the thinness and one-sidedness of the market increased markedly with the length of maturity, especially beyond the "bank" area of five or ten years. From the start, therefore, it was evident that the Desk would have to adapt its techniques to the peculiarities of the coupon market, and perhaps to develop new methods of approach to operations in those issues.

The purchases of coupon issues due within 15 months in late 1960 were mainly accomplished by responding to offerings made at the dealers' initiative. On the other hand, sales of very short-term coupon issues were undertaken mainly on "go-arounds"* either alone or in conjunction with sales of Treasury bills, in order to secure a maximum effect on short-term rates. When operations were extended into the intermediate area of the market, several "go-arounds" were conducted to buy coupon issues due within 10 years. The results were disappointing. There was an obvious tendency for dealers and investors to withdraw offerings from the market in the hope of higher prices as soon as it became known that a System "go-around" had begun. Moreover, in a typical "go-around," there was no opportunity for dealers to develop additional sources of supply, so that potential System purchases were limited to the securities immediately available at the time the Desk asked for offerings. Therefore, the Desk quickly abandoned the use of "go-arounds" for the purchase of intermediate- and long-term coupon issues except under unusual circumstances.

After a short period of experimenta-

tion, it was found that the most practical and most productive method of purchasing intermediate- and long-term issues was for the Desk to respond to offerings made at the dealers' initiative. (Since practically all System transactions in intermediate- and long-term issues involved purchases, the following discussion has been couched in terms of dealer offerings and System purchases, in order to simplify the text.) Accordingly, the Desk developed much more formal records of dealers' offerings, with greater detail as to the time each offering was made, the composite offering price for each active issue at the time, and any changes made by the dealers in amounts or prices during the day. These offerings were not "firm," i.e., they were understood to be subject to change of amount or price, or to complete withdrawal, without notice to the Desk. Therefore, before any business could be transacted, it was necessary for a trader on the Desk to contact the dealers involved and to get the offerings on a firm basis. If a dealer was still willing to sell the securities, and if prices had not changed significantly, the terms of the original offering would usually be made on a firm basis for a reasonable time so that the Desk could compare alternative issues and prices and make a selection. The traders would then go back to the dealers to either accept or reject the offerings that had been made "firm."

This method of buying coupon issues had some important advantages over the "go-around" technique especially during the early part of the 1960's when the Desk was a consistently large-scale buyer of coupon issues for System and/or Treasury account. As dealers became accustomed to the frequent buying by the Desk, most of them

---

* Editor's note: A technique whereby the Federal Reserve trading desk solicits bids and offers of securities from dealers over the phone.

offered securities to the Desk regularly throughout the day. Thus, even before the Desk indicated its intention to buy securities on a given day, there was available a realistic indication of the potential supply at or close to the current price level. This is in contrast with a typical "go-around," where the size and pricing of potential offerings is obtained only after contacting all dealers, thereby revealing the Desk's interest in buying a sizable amount of securities. Also, the frequency with which dealers increased or decreased the amounts offered, or changed the prices on their offerings, imparted valuable information as to the strength or weakness as well as the breadth or thinness of the market. Another advantage was found in the ability to spread System (and Treasury) purchases over the course of several hours, or over the entire day, instead of confining buying to the 30 or 40 minutes of a "go-around," in which case dealers had little opportunity to contact customers. It was frequently found that once the Desk had purchased some securities, perhaps most of those available at a given time, some dealers developed additional sources of supply and made subsequent offerings to the Desk, often at the same or at even lower prices. Furthermore, there was less chance that the market would be artificially strengthened by the knowledge that there was official buying, since the Desk only approached those dealers who, by their offerings, had already evidenced a willingness and ability to sell securities. In a "go-around," the Desk approaches all dealers indiscriminately and its buying interest may have a disproportionate influence on the outlook of those dealers who have no securities for sale. The dealers naturally assume that if the Desk initiates a "go-around," it definitely intends to buy a substantial amount of securities.

The usefulness and productivity of this method was, of course, dependent upon the day-to-day regularity of dealer offerings to the Desk. During periods of steady and heavy official buying, most dealers maintained a close contact with the Desk, making changes in amounts and prices of their offerings throughout the day, in order to be sure of participating in any business that might transpire. However, after a period of inactivity on the part of the Desk, some dealers tended to become discouraged, and to become lax in making offerings. Then, when the Desk suddenly bought securities, those dealers were not approached. When they subsequently learned of the System buying, they were likely to be disgruntled at having missed an opportunity to participate. For this reason, dealers were constantly encouraged by representatives of the Account Management to reflect their offerings to the Desk daily, whether or not the Desk was currently buying securities. These efforts met with varying degrees of success.

III. EFFORTS TO MINIMIZE PRICE EFFECT

As noted above, the Federal Open Market Committee did not adopt any specific goals with respect to intermediate- and long-term interest rates. Therefore, in buying coupon issues for the System, the Desk consistently tried to exert as little immediate influence on prices as possible and generally did not enter the market unless conditions would permit purchases without undue price effects.

In order to minimize any direct effect on prices, several techniques were employed. Most importantly, System buying was confined as much as possible to days or periods when there was a ready availability of securities in the market. Such availability was usually discernible in the size and frequency of dealer offerings to the Desk and/or in a downward movement of prices. In making its purchases, the Desk tried to avoid paying the full offered side of the market, i.e., the composite offering price, even if reserve objectives had to be modified in order to do so. The Desk also sought to avoid buying large amounts of securities at a given price level when to do so would even suggest an attempt to hold prices. Instead, a reasonable amount of securities (in relation to total offerings) would be purchased at a certain price level and further purchases would be made only after offering prices had been lowered. On the other hand, on a day when offerings were relatively scarce, and the general price level steady, all of the System buying might be accomplished with little or no variation in prices for individual issues. Only on rare occasions did the System buy securities for itself at rising prices—the mere fact that quotations were moving higher would in itself suggest that the possibilities of providing reserves through bond purchases were very limited and probably not worth exploiting. Finally, the Desk consciously attempted to leave some supply of securities in the market after its buying, i.e., to avoid pre-empting all of the securities available in the market at a given time. Thus, by using these techniques, the Desk sought to minimize the direct price effect of its buying to the extent possible, given the substantial size of the operations that were necessary.

Some modifications of these techniques were required in handling buying order for Treasury investment accounts. Much of this buying was undertaken in direct support of Treasury financing operations and frequently involved an attempt to exercise a constructive influence on the tone of the market even to the extent of holding price levels temporarily. On such occasions, the Desk was apt to be more aggressive in its approach than was the case when it operated to accomplish System reserve objectives. Response to dealers' offerings was still the basic method of buying, but larger amounts might be purchased at a given price level even to the point of deliberately clearing the market of certain issues such as "rights" or "when-issued" securities. At such times, the Desk might also approach dealers with a request for additional offerings and, perhaps, accept some at higher prices than had been paid earlier in the day.

When this type of buying operation occurred during a period of Treasury financing, it was readily recognizable as stemming from Treasury investment accounts rather than from the System, and its more aggressive character was generally accepted as a normal action on the part of the Treasury. At other times, market participants found it difficult, if not impossible, to distinguish between operations undertaken for the System and for the Treasury until the publication of the System's weekly statement on the following Thursday night. This was particularly true in 1961 and early 1962, when both the System and Treasury simultaneously bought a huge volume of securities. Another such period occurred in 1965, when the Treasury undertook sizable purchases for its investment accounts between, as well as during, financing periods. Despite the aggressive character of some of this buying, it was mistakenly attributed to the System, and the market became quite confused as to the real nature of the Desk's objectives.

The techniques described above were used consistently for the purchase of intermediate- and long-term issues during the period from 1961 through 1965. However, after 1963 the size and frequency of official operations in coupon issues, particularly those undertaken for the System, were greatly reduced compared with the early 1960's.* As a result, some of the advantages of the techniques described above became less important. Between September 3, 1965 and February 17, 1966 no coupon-bearing securities were purchased by the System and purchases for Treasury investment accounts were once more confined mainly to periods of Treasury financing. During this interval, the Desk began to experiment with "go-arounds" to purchase securities for the Treasury. System operations in coupon issues were again undertaken in the second half of February 1966 and since then all of these purchases have also been made through "go-arounds." Judging by the results over such a period, the market for coupon issues seems to be more conducive to this type of operation than it was earlier in the 1960's. Five years of experience with System operations outside the Treasury bill area have apparently removed much of the "shock" effect of System purchases on dealers and investors. Moreover, the size and frequency of individual operations have been greatly reduced and the Desk has recently been giving more information regarding its intentions as to the likely size of an operation. Consequently, the appearance of the Desk on a "go-around" does not seem to result automatically in the withdrawal of offerings and the raising of prices and the Desk has generally been able to accomplish its own and the Treasury's objectives by this means.

IV. IDENTIFICATION OF ACCOUNTS FOR WHICH DESK OPERATES

As suggested above, dealers have found it more difficult in the 1960's than in the 1950's to identify the account for which the Desk is conducting an operation at any given time. In the earlier period, practically all operations in coupon issues were recognized by the dealers as stemming from Treasury investment accounts, since the System Account deliberately confined its normal operations to Treasury bills. The dealers were usually also able to distinguish between operations for the System and for foreign accounts even when System buying or selling was undertaken without a "go-around." A rather dependable clue was given because the Desk immediately had to check figures with the dealers on face amount, discount (or accrued interest) and proceeds on all transactions for foreign accounts. This was necessary so that the Foreign Department could send out wires to the foreign central banks with confidence that there would be no subsequent changes due to errors of calculation.

The dealers have been much more concerned over their inability to distinguish between System and Treasury operations in coupon issues. There is no dependable clue since the same basic techniques are employed in approaching the market for either agency and it is not necessary to check figures for any of these accounts. Therefore, if the Desk buys coupon issues on a given day, the dealers normally have to await the publication of the weekly banking statistics to see if there is any change in System holdings of notes and bonds. If there is none, it may be assumed that the transactions were undertaken for Treasury investment accounts. Since mid-1966, as an outgrowth of the Treasury-Federal Reserve study of the Government securities market, the Desk has become more willing to identify, in general terms, the account for which it is operating at a

---

* Editor's note: In 1970–1971, operations were again conducted in longer-term Government securities as a part of what some analysts describe as the "new operation twist." The latter was motivated by conditions similar to those that prevailed in 1961–1963.

given time. Thus, in approaching the market on large-scale transactions, especially those involving a "go-around," the Desk has been informing the dealers whether the operation is for System or Customer Account, and the approximate size of the customer interest. However, the Desk must reserve the right to withhold such information if the nature of operations or market conditions warrant such a course of action in the opinion of the Account Manager.

V. OPERATIONS IN THE SHORT-TERM AREA

Despite the abandonment of the "bills preferably" policy, purchases and sales of Treasury bills continued to be the principal means by which the System provided and absorbed reserves during the 1960's. Operations in intermediate- and long-term issues provided a very useful supplement to open market operations, but the supply of coupon issues was never sufficiently large for them to supplant Treasury bills as the major medium of open market purchases, and no serious attempts were made to sell coupon issues. The techniques used in buying and selling Treasury bills were essentially the same as those employed in the 1950's but the attainment of the more varied objectives adopted by the Committee required greater flexibility in the choice of the particular method to be used at a given time.

The increased flexibility was evident in a less frequent use of "go-arounds" as a means of approach to the market, especially in 1961 and 1962. Given the Committee's concern over the level of short-term rates, it was very often advisable to avoid the psychological impact of a full "go-around" when purchases were involved. Therefore, the Desk responded more frequently to offerings made at the initiative of deal-

ers, provided of course that other quotations and the knowledge of market conditions obtained routinely by the Desk's traders confirmed that the prices being paid were the best obtainable for the issues involved. As in the case of coupon issues, this shift in emphasis away from "go-arounds" made it very important for dealers to keep the Desk informed of their bids for and offerings of Treasury bills and of changes in their rates during the day, in order that each dealer might be assured of an equal opportunity to compete for business transacted by the Desk. In the event that purchases of Treasury bills were decided upon, and a "go-around" was not considered appropriate, the Desk would seek to "firm-up" those offerings already made to it by dealers. Assuming that the offering sheet provided a realistic indication of the potential supply and of current rate levels—and it usually did —it was frequently not necessary for the Desk to go beyond these offerings in order to accomplish its objectives. By using this technique, the Desk bought Treasury bills from those dealers most eager to sell them, as evidenced by the persistence and pricing of their offerings, and thereby sought to reduce the rate effect of the purchases. Circumstances calling for the use of this technique have occurred much less frequently in the recent past, and during 1966 most System operations in Treasury bills were accomplished by means of "go-arounds" as were those in coupon issues as noted above.

The choice of Treasury bill issues included in each purchase or sale operation also took on added significance in the 1960's. During the "bills preferably" period when operations were undertaken solely to affect reserves, it was not usually important to concentrate buying or selling in particular areas of the bill market. "Go-arounds," and other buying programs as well, did not involve any deliberate discrimination among bill maturities unless the limited size of an operation, unusual market conditions, or the make-up of the System's portfolio suggested that it would be advisable for the Desk to do so.

In contrast, the adoption of short-term rate objectives by the Committee in the 1960's made it necessary for the Desk to pay much more attention to the particular issues of Treasury bills that were bought and sold. The rate for three-month Treasury bills became the focal point of domestic and international attention as an indicator of changing relationships between short-term interest rates in the United States and those abroad, particularly in Canada and the United Kingdom. For this reason it became an important task of the Desk to resist any decline in the three-month bill rate, and in a few surrounding maturities, even though rates of other bills, both longer and shorter, might move lower.

In carrying out this objective, the Desk concentrated its sales of Treasury bills as much as possible in the three-month area, and its purchases in other areas of the bill market. On "go-arounds" to sell bills, dealers were frequently asked to bid just for issues in the three-month area whenever it was felt that sufficient bids would be received to accomplish reserve objectives. Conversely, in buying bills, the request for offerings did not include bills in this area unless the Desk's need for bills was so large that it could not be satisfied without them. The same pattern with respect to maturities was followed, of course, in Treasury bill operations by methods other than "go-arounds." Market participants quickly became aware of this pattern and developed some resistance of their own to recurrent downward pressures on the three-month bill rate.

The securities operations of foreign accounts handled by the Desk also assumed much greater importance during the early 1960's since these transactions were mostly limited to Treasury bills. Such operations became increasingly large and more frequent, and their potential effect on Treasury bill rates had to be considered in the light of System objectives. In handling foreign account transactions the Desk policy has been to place the orders in the market unless there were overriding System objectives that would be served by handling the transactions in another manner. With System objectives closely geared to short-term interest rates there were, in the early 1960's more frequent occasions when it became desirable to keep foreign account buying out of the market, especially when it involved bills in the three-month area.

In order to accomplish this, the System Account sold bills to the foreign accounts when reserve objections and System holdings permitted, or crossed bills between foreign accounts on those occasions when purchase and sale orders of different accounts matched as to amounts, maturity areas and delivery dates. The authority to make offsetting purchases and sales for the System Account was also used when the reserve absorption resulting from System sales of bills to foreign accounts was contrary to reserve objectives. If coupon issues were readily available in the market, the System sold bills to the foreign accounts and purchased an equivalent amount of coupon issues in order to offset the reserve effect. Sales of Treasury bills by foreign accounts were also frequently kept out of the market when they coincided with a need for the System to supply reserves. To the extent that bills could be purchased from foreign accounts, the Desk could achieve a release of reserves without buying bills in the market, and thus avoid exerting a depressing influence on rates.

VI.   REPURCHASE AGREEMENTS

Throughout the entire thirteen-year period from 1953 through 1965 there was no essential change in the System's methods of handling repurchase agreements with dealers. During 1955, the Desk began to obtain and keep formal records of dealers' daily financing requirements and of the dealers' progress in obtaining funds during each day. Inquiries were made routinely each day whether or not there was any System intention of making repurchase agreements. Dealers cooperated by reporting their initial financing needs at the beginning of the day, the amount of funds obtained, rates paid, and the general sources of available funds, such as "out-of-town bank," "corporate repurchase agreement," "foreign agency funds," etc. This information enabled the Desk to measure more accurately the pressures in an extremely sensitive area of the money-market—an area where residual demands for credit tended to converge during the day. It also formed, along with many other indicators, an important basis for daily decisions whether or not to provide reserves, through outright buying as well as through repurchase agreements.

The approach of the Desk to the market in making repurchase agreements depended on the size and urgency of reserve objectives and the potential opportunity for making the agreements, as revealed by the dealers' reports to the Desk. If the Desk was not particularly anxious to make any agreements, it might follow the progress of dealers in obtaining funds from other sources until early afternoon before reaching a decision. Meanwhile, the dealers were presumably scouring the country for available funds and reporting their progress to the Desk. By early afternoon, the dealers would be informed if the System would make repurchase agreements, and if so, what part of their remaining requirements would be met. The Desk's final decision had to be made by 2:00 p.m. at the very latest. Unless repurchase agreements were consummated before that time, there was a danger that delivery problems might result.

On the other hand, there were times when the Desk was anxious to make repurchase agreements, and the first check of dealer financing needs revealed a limited opportunity to do so. On such occasions, the dealers would be contacted early, informed that repurchase agreements were available and asked how much they were interested in making. Under these circumstances, the amount to be made with each dealer might be determined by 11:00 a.m. or even earlier, although the particular issues involved might not be decided upon by the dealers until later in the day.

This method of handling repurchase agreements presented some problems for both the dealers and the Desk. On those days when the System was reluctant to provide any reserves through this channel, or when an appraisal of the reserve situation or of money market conditions could not easily be made, the Desk would delay its decision until the latest possible moment, with the hope that dealers might uncover additional sources of funds as the day progressed and perhaps satisfy their needs without recourse to the System. On the other hand, dealers were anxious to know if System repurchase agreements were likely to be available before stepping up the rates they were willing to pay elsewhere. Conversely, on days when the Desk was anxious to make repurchase agreements early in the day, dealers might be reluctant to make commitments until they had exhausted the possibilities of making cash sales and/or were sure that cheaper funds were not available elsewhere. Under most conditions, however, the general procedures worked out satisfactorily and enabled the Desk to appraise the significance of the progress reports on dealer financing, relate them to other information on money market conditions, and arrive at a decision not too long after noon.

The amount of repurchase agreements made with each dealer usually depended upon the amount of financing each dealer had left uncovered at the time the Desk was prepared to act. For example, if it was decided at 12:30 p.m. to make about $150 million repurchase agreements, and the dealers still needed about $300 million financing in the aggregate, the Desk generally provided about one-half of each dealer's remaining need—if about $225 million needs remained, about two-thirds of each dealer's needs were met, etc. This might involve some loss of opportunity to those dealers who were most aggressive in seeking funds since they were likely to have already obtained a substantial part of their financing from other lenders. At the same time, their very progress was an important guide to the Desk in measuring reserve needs and money market pressures. Consideration has been given from time to time to using other criteria such as individual dealer's over-all market performance in allotting repurchase agreements among dealers but there are some problems that would have to be overcome before such guides could be administered practically and equitably on a regular basis.

The Desk was always mindful of the credit risks involved in making repurchase agreements with dealers even though short-term Government securities were involved. Dealers regularly furnished the Desk with statements of condition and each dealer's net worth provided the principal basis for deciding the maximum amount of repurchase agreements that might appropriately be made with that firm. These internal "lines" were reviewed with the receipt of each new statement and the maximum amounts set were not considered absolute. On occasion they have been flexibly interpreted in order to attain necessary reserve objectives. On the other hand, excessive financing needs of a particular dealer were never considered alone as a reason for exceeding the dealer's "repurchase line" with the System.

The rate charged on repurchase agreements was usually the same as the prevailing discount rate of the Federal Reserve Bank of New York. In periods of credit restraint and tight money, this rate was usually lower than the dealers were paying for funds from other sources. Therefore, if the dealers had any significant position in short-term securities the Desk could count on making a moderate amount of repurchase agreements when it desired to do so. On the other hand, in periods of easy money, dealers were frequently able to secure funds at rates below the discount rate and might be reluctant to make repurchase agreements with the Reserve Bank.

On some such occasions, when repurchase agreements were the most convenient means of supplying needed reserves, the Desk made repurchase agreements below the discount rate to induce dealers to place some of their financing with the System and keep it there. However, under the continuing authority directive of the Committee, the rate charged can not be less than the most recent average issuing rate for three-month Treasury bills (assuming, of course, that the bill rate was below the discount rate). This technique was used infrequently. One occasion when it proved useful was around the close of 1960 when the System was anxious to avoid the impact of outright buying on Treasury bill rates and also to make repurchase agreements that would provide an automatic absorption of reserves when they matured in January. At the same time, dealers were not interested in making repurchase agreements with the System because rates on other funds were relatively low. In order to compete for new agreements and to discourage premature withdrawal of those that were made, the Desk made repurchase agreements at 2¾ per cent while the discount rate was at 3 per cent. Another notable occasion was in 1964 when an increase in the discount rate to 4 per cent in November was followed by an undesirable degree of upward pressure on Treasury bill rates later in the year. In dealing with this situation, the Desk made a substantial volume of repurchase agreements at 3.85 and 3⅞ per cent.

Under the continuing authority directive, repurchase agreements could also be made at rates above the discount rate of the Federal Reserve Bank of New York. This technique was used in 1955. During the late summer of that year, discount rates at various Reserve Banks were not uniform, and the rate of the New York Reserve Bank was below those in some other Districts. Meanwhile, the latest average issuing rate for three-month Treasury bills fell within the range of discount rates and appeared to be more representative of general money market rates. Accordingly, this rate, rounded to the nearest 5 basis points, was used as the rate for repurchase agreements. Also, around mid-November of 1955, repurchase agreements were made at a rate ⅛ per cent above the uniform discount rate, which was substantially below rates

charged the dealers by other lenders and on the verge of being raised.

The maturity of repurchase agreements varied according to the reserve outlook and the objectives of the Desk. Throughout the entire period under review, a maximum of 15 days was authorized by the Committee. The maximum term was generally used when a projected need for reserves extended over several weeks, at a time when outright purchases of securities were not considered to be appropriate or as easily made. In general, longer term repurchase agreements tended to be made in periods of easy credit policy, and shorter term agreements in times of tighter policy. Very short-term agreements enable the Desk to keep a tighter rein on the reserves released, and provide an early opportunity to review the situation and to decide whether to withdraw the reserves through the maturity of the agreements or to keep them out through new agreements. During periods of Treasury "exchange" refundings, repurchase agreements against rights were normally scheduled to mature on the settlement date of the refunding, even though agreements against other Treasury issues might simultaneously be made for a shorter term.

At times of Treasury refundings, the Desk, under instructions from the Committee, was normally concerned with maintaining an even keel in the money and securities markets. The period of even keel was usually considered to extend from just before the announcement of the terms of the financing to the settlement date for the securities involved, although it might extend beyond the latter date if serious problems related to secondary distribution of the new securities arose. During "exchange" refundings, repurchase agreements against "rights" were normally made to expire on the settlement date of the financing. However, the Desk was authorized to make repurchase agreements only against securities maturing within 15 months until March 6, 1962, and thereafter against securities due within two years. Consequently, on refundings involving a choice of issues maturing beyond this limitation, dealers were required to withdraw any "rights" converted into longer term issues on the day following the submission of their exchange subscriptions. This inconvenience was eliminated in March 1965, when the Desk was authorized to make repurchase agreements against securities of any maturity during periods of Treasury financing. Since June 1966 such agreements have been permissible outside periods of Treasury financing as well.

All repurchase contracts between the Reserve Bank and the dealers provided for termination at any time prior to maturity at the option of either party. Dealers regularly exercised this option by withdrawing securities that they had sold or that could be financed more cheaply elsewhere. The Reserve Bank never formally required the dealers to withdraw securities before the maturity of the agreements. However, on several occasions when an absorption of reserves was needed, and substantial amounts of repurchase agreements were outstanding, the dealers were informed that the Desk "would not be disturbed" if the dealers, at their option, terminated most or all of the contracts. Such action was taken only when alternative financing was readily available at rates favorable to the dealers.

Repurchase agreements provided a very useful tool to the Desk and also helped the dealers in financing their portfolios. However, it was always unmistakably clear to the dealers that such accommodation was only avail-

able when it was appropriate from a reserve standpoint. Dealers had no right of recourse to the Reserve Bank and repurchase agreements were not made available simply because the dealers had a heavy financing need (although this was one indicator of money market pressures and of a possible need to supply reserves). Moreever, the repurchase contracts did not permit any substitution of securities. Therefore, if a dealer had to withdraw securities in order to obtain particular issues he needed, he automatically reduced his recourse to System credit by an equivalent amount unless reserve objectives on the day of withdrawal made it appropriate for the Desk to make new repurchase agreements.

During most of the thirteen-year period, the Desk made no general announcement of its intention to make repurchase agreements on a given day. Therefore, the only way a dealer could know immediately that such action was being taken was to have a request for repurchase agreements under consideration by the Desk at the time the decision was made. If a dealer had reflected no financing need, he would have no indication from the Desk as to whether or not repurchase agreements were being made. Moreover, repurchase agreements are made only with nonbank dealers so that the dealer banks had no direct knowledge as to whether the facility was available to nonbank dealers on a given day, although the information appeared to be indirectly obtainable by the banks through market channels almost as soon as the agreements were made. Since the availability of System repurchase agreements was considered to be an important market influence, there was considerable dissatisfaction among the dealer banks, and to some extent among nonbank dealers when they had no financing need, that knowledge of the Desk's action in this area was not directly available to them. Consequently, since late 1966, the Desk has been informing all dealers, including the dealer banks, of its intention to make repurchase agreements on a given day.

VII. MATCHED SALE-PURCHASE TRANSACTIONS

During 1966, the Desk employed a new technique that had not been used either in the "bills preferable" period or in the first half of the 1960's. This technique was the matched sale-purchase transaction. It was designed to accomplish a temporary absorption of reserves, with a minimum effect on the market, in much the same way that the repurchase agreement had been used for many years to supply reserves temporarily. The new technique involved cash sales of selected issues of Treasury bills to dealers and a simultaneous commitment by the Desk to buy the same issues of bills back within a few days. By this method, redundant reserves were absorbed immediately and were automatically restored when the securities were redelivered to the System.

The matched sale-purchase transactions are all accomplished by means of "go-arounds." In a typical operation, all dealers and dealer banks are contacted simultaneously and offered an opportunity to purchase a particular issue (or issues) of Treasury bills at a specified rate of discount closely related to the current composite bid and asked quotations for the issue(s) reflected on the Trading Room quotation board. At the same time, the dealers are asked to reoffer the same bills to the Desk for future delivery at a rate to be set by the dealer. The dealers are allowed time (normally 15 to 30 minutes) to determine the extent of their interest. During this period a dealer might decide to take some of the bills himself to cover a short position or for other reasons, assuming he can arrange to finance the bills at a rate that would enable him to compete favorably for them with other dealers. Otherwise, a dealer might seek to develop temporary investment interest for the bills, in other words, to arrange with a bank or other investor a "reverse repurchase agreement" extending for the same period of time set by the Desk.

At the end of the allotted time, the dealers specify the amounts of bills they are interested in buying for cash (at the rate set by the Desk) and the rates at which they are willing to sell the bills back to the Desk for future delivery. The Desk then sells the bills to those dealers whose reoffering rates provide the best result for the Desk on the combined transaction. If only one bill issue is involved, the highest reoffering rates of discount would also provide the best result—if more than one issue is involved, further calculations are required based on the time each bills has to run to maturity and the dealers' offering rates of discount for each issue.

The matched sale-purchase transaction has enabled the Desk to absorb large amounts of reserves at times when market conditions might not have been conducive to an equivalent amount of unmatched sales for cash. Likewise, the offsetting future purchases by the Desk have little effect on the market since they are contracted for simultaneously so that the dealers have presumably completed necessary arrangements before submitting their reoffering proposals to the Desk. In most cases, the Desk has arranged to buy the bills back within 1 to 3 days after the cash sales were made.

READING 21

A REVIEW OF RECENT ACADEMIC LITERATURE ON THE DISCOUNT MECHANISM

David M. Jones

I. INTRODUCTION

After approximately two decades of disuse, the Treasury-Federal Reserve Accord of 1951 prompted renewed interest in the nature and effectiveness of the discount mechanism. Analysis since the Accord has been devoted in large part to the unresolved controversy over the nature of the relationship between discounting and monetary control.

The scope of this paper will be confined to that post-Accord academic literature which bears directly on the implications of discounting for monetary control. Special emphasis will be placed on the determinants of member bank borrowing, including a review of the major issues and related empirical findings. The responsiveness of borrowing to interest rate movements is of

particular concern in this regard. An effort will also be made to cover in some detail the wide range of proposed changes in the current discounting arrangement.

II. MAJOR ISSUES AND RELATED FINDINGS

The fundamental issue raised by post-Accord literature dealing with the Federal Reserve discount mechanism is that of whether this mechanism operates to subvert or to supplement over-all monetary control. Critics have argued that the discount function as it currently operates is fundamentally antagonistic to monetary management. Related to this position, issues have developed around a number of topics,

Source: Prepared for the steering committee for the Fundamental Reappraisal of the Discount Mechanism Appointed by the Board of Governors of the Federal Reserve System.

namely: (1) the effects of borrowing during periods of restraint; (2) the factors that determine borrowing; (3) the significance of non-price rationing; and (4) the announcement effects of discount rate changes.

A. Borrowing and Monetary Restraint

On one hand, the discount mechanism may be viewed as a sort of "safety valve" which cushions but does not offset the usually uneven impact on individual banks of restrictive shifts in monetary policy. Temporary reserves are allocated through the discount window directly to those banks coming under greatest stress, and thus the System is free to act more decisively than otherwise would be the case.

The case favoring the present discounting arrangement turns on the contention that reserves supplied through the discount "window" are by nature more restrictive in terms of credit and deposit expansion than reserves supplied through other means. Borrowing from the Federal Reserve is looked upon as only a temporary source of funds for the individual bank, usually requiring some form of asset adjustment in order to effect prompt repayment. Thus, the larger the overall volume of borrowing relative to other sources of reserves, the greater the restrictive impact on credit growth.

The academic critics of the existing discount mechanism have not sought to directly refute the points raised above. Their position is founded instead upon the following three general considerations:

1. The initiative in using the discount mechanism rests with the borrowing banks themselves rather than with those charged with the responsibility for monetary control;
2. Member bank borrowing from the Federal Reserve *adds* to total reserves, in contrast with the sale of Treasury bills or any other

means of reserve adjustment available to the banks; and
3. Member bank borrowing tends to rise during periods of monetary restraint and fall during periods of monetary ease.

In essence, the critics hold that overall monetary control is weakened to the extent that discounting counters the impact of Federal Reserve System open market operations on the reserve base. Working in the context of models linking bank reserves to the money supply, and the money supply to real economic activity, some economists have argued that borrowing accentuates cyclical swings.

B. Determinants of Member Bank Borrowing

With discounting at the banks' own initiative and, therefore, difficult to predict, post-Accord inquiry has focused on the determinants of member bank demand for borrowed reserves. To what extent are bank borrowing decision influenced by profitability considerations? How strong is the so-called "tradition against borrowing?" These questions are remnants of the old need vs. profitability issue which was debated at length in the 1920's and 1930's.

The "need" concept has never been clearly defined by its advocates, but according to common interpretation banks that borrow out of "need" do so only to meet temporary, unexpected reserve deficiencies. At the same time, the needy banks supposedly make every effort to repay these debts as quickly as possible. This view of borrowing behavior presumes a strong traditional reluctance on the part of banks to be in debt to the Federal Reserve.

On the other hand, the strict version of the "profitability" thesis posits that banks will borrow whenever additional funds can be invested in earning assets carrying yields higher than the discount rate. In short, banks borrow out of a calculated effort to profit from rate differentials, rather than simply in response to the unpredictable swings in market factors that produce temporary reserve deficits.

Expressed in these terms, "need" and "profitability" appear to be conflicting motives. In effect, the borrowing-out-of-"need" proponents postulated an interest-insensitive bank borrowings demand function, while the "profitability" school visualized a functional relationship in which borrowings were interest-sensitive.

One of the few important contributions of the post-Accord discounting literature has been that of the theoretical resolution of the "need" vs. "profitability" issue. The argument runs roughly as follows: given a reserve deficiency or the need to borrow— whether the cause is an unexpected surge in required reserves, or a sudden cash drain, or some other reserve absorbing factor—the *extent* to which a bank makes use of the discount window for its reserve adjustment depends upon the relative costs of borrowing and other means of replenishing reserves. For example, the higher the Treasury bill rate (i.e., the higher the opportunity cost of running down bill holdings) relative to the discount rate, the greater the "profitability" of borrowing to meet a given reserve deficit. Thus, a reluctant bank that borrows only to meet its immediate "needs" can be, at the same time, sensitive to the rate differentials between its alternative sources of short-term funds. Using this modified concept of profitability, it has been demonstrated with some rigor that it is possible to integrate, into a consistent theory, bank reluctance to be in debt to the Federal Reserve and the profit incentive for such borrowing.

During periods of monetary restraint, the discount rate tends to lag behind rising market rates on alternative sources of funds and borrowings rise. Conversely, the discount rate remains above falling market rates on the same sources of funds during periods of monetary ease and borrowings fall. This fact represents one basis of the contention that borrowings tend to accentuate cyclical swings.

C. Non-Price Rationing

The attitude of banks toward the non-price terms applied at the discount window has an important bearing on their borrowing decisions. Yet, these terms appear to be quite difficult to administer. A wide variation in non-price terms, between the various Federal Reserve districts and/or over time can serve to diminish significantly the predictability of borrowings. It is difficult, if not impossible, to separate the relative effects of non-price rationing from effects of bank reluctance to borrow. It has been argued that these two factors have a mutually reinforcing effect on bank borrowing. But there has been very little in the literature on this subject. Generally, there seems to be a dissatisfaction with non-price rationing, explicitly on the grounds that the price mechanism would operate more effectively.

D. Announcement Effects

A major source of contention in the literature has been the question of whether discretionary changes in the discount rate have undesired effects on expectations. On one hand, it is argued that one must make inconsistent assumptions about the behavior of lenders and borrowers in order for the announcement feature of discount rate changes not to have unintended effects. It has also been argued that, at best, the announcement effects will be unpredictable.

There are, however, those who see some merit in announcement effects. They argue that discretionary discount rate changes have two basic advantages. First, the changes are widely publicized and especially useful as a universal means of signalling the intent, for example, to stem a balance of payments drain. Secondly, discount rate adjustments, as the only major monetary instrument having no direct reserve effects, can play a unique and often helpful role as an index of the course of policy.

E. Proposals for Change

Proposals for changing the discount mechanism have run the gamut from abolishing it all together, to allegedly making it the most powerful tool of monetary policy. Elimination of the discretionary aspect of discount window administration is the object of nearly all the proposed modifications in the mechanism.

A plan frequently advanced would eliminate discretionary discount rate changes by "tying" the discount rate to the market rate on some alternative source of ready funds. This type of arrangement usually involves setting the discount rate high enough above the anchor rate to make it a "penalty" rate. Most advocates of such a scheme would rely on the price mechanism alone to allocate Federal Reserve credit and to keep borrowing in check, discarding the present borrowing "privilege" with its non-price connotations in favor of granting banks the "right" to borrow. There has been controversy, however, on the appropriate market rate.

A somewhat more radical plan calls for the payment of interest at the discount rate on member bank excess reserves. Through discount rate adjustments, the Federal Reserve would then have direct control over the opportunity cost of bank lending. Under such an arrangement, banks would be tempted to increase their excess reserves and reduce their holdings of short-term Government securities. The discount rate would take on sharply increased importance among the major instruments of monetary policy.

There are, in addition, those who would abolish the discount mechanism. Two basic reasons for such a move have been advanced. First, by doing away with borrowing at the banks' own initiative the Federal Reserve would greatly improve its control over total reserves. Secondly, it has been argued that the discounting function is no longer necessary in view of the substantial postwar growth in bank holdings of short-term Government securities which can be used to make the necessary adjustments in reserve positions. Needless to say, the latter argument is of diminished relevance under circumstances in which bank holdings of short-term Governments are minimal.

It has also been proposed, however, that the discounting terms should be fully discretionary. The basic contention is that the discretionary approach entails the power not only to control total borrowing, but also makes possible the selective control of bank lending practices.

F. Concluding Observations

Although most of the major issues raised in the course of the academic dialogue on discounting remain unresolved, it is possible to draw some general conclusions. Discounting does not, for example, appear to weaken monetary control to any significant extent during periods of monetary restraint. Indeed, the discount mechanism is, for the most part, a useful complement to open market operations. In particular, shifts in monetary policy are, as argued by those favoring the current arrangement, cushioned by the provision of temporary reserves through the discount window to those banks coming under the greatest stress. At the same time, borrowed reserves have less expansive implications for credit and deposit growth than a corresponding amount of reserves supplied through other means.

On the other hand, regardless of how limiting the effect of borrowed reserves on credit growth may be, the fact remains that monetary control is rendered less precise under conditions in which banks borrow at their own initiative. Hopefully, the predictability of borrowing can be improved by reliable quantitative measurements of the relative effects of interest rates and other factors that influence borrowing decisions.

With regard to discount window administration and general supply considerations, there is almost unanimous agreement among economists on the desirability of complete reliance on the price mechanism to control borrowing. But regardless of how appealing the "tied" rate plans may be, there has been no final agreement on the market rate to which the discount rate should be linked nor on the appropriate spread to be maintained. While experience suggests that there should be some substantial revisions in the present non-price discounting guidelines, it seems, nevertheless, that both non-price and price terms will continue to be necessary to insure effective monetary control.

Finally, the predominant view in the literature is that under present circumstances discount rate changes will have, at best, ambiguous announcement effects. At the same time, those who fear that discount rate changes will have *adverse* effects on expectations may have over-rated their case a bit. In particular, it is not likely that discount rate changes alone, whatever may be their effects on expectations, dominate the behavior of borrowers and lenders. Indeed, these rate adjustments are only one of many factors that influence expectations about the course of monetary policy and future economic conditions.

III. DISCOUNTING AND MONETARY CONTROL

A. Borrowing and Monetary Restraint

As noted above, the assumption is frequently made by those favoring the current discount procedures that borrowed reserves are less expansive in terms of credit growth than a corresponding amount of reserves provided through open market operations.[1] It is argued that banks will seek to extinguish their borrowed reserves promptly, usually through some form of asset adjustment. In Roosa's words:

In the American setting the fact that banks borrow only as a privilege means that even though any individual bank can temporarily, in effect, cause the creation of reserves by borrowing at the discount window, that same bank simultaneously takes on an obligation to find ways of extinguishing those reserves—the more promptly the better, in order to preserve its privilege for use again when unexpected reserve drains occur. Thus, as a general rule, the larger the aggregate volume of bank borrowing from the Federal Reserve, the greater will be the effort going on, through the banking system, to limit credits and bring reserves into balance with the requirements against deposits.[2]

The fact that Roosa casts his discussion in terms of the actions of an *indi-*

---

[1] See for example, Board of Governors of the Federal Reserve System, and the United States Treasury, *The Federal Reserve and the Treasury: Answers to Questions from the Commission on Money and Credit* (Englewood Cliffs, New Jersey: Prentice-Hall, Inc., 1963), p. 118.

[2] Robert V. Roosa, "Credit Policy at the Discount Window: Comment," *Quarterly Journal of Economics,* LXXIII (May, 1959), p. 334.

vidual bank is not to deny that a high or rising volume of borrowings for the banking system as a whole may persist for long periods as, for example, when an increasing number of banks turn to the discount window for temporary reserve relief. *But the key point is that aggregate borrowed reserves have a restrictive impact on credit expansion and the higher the level of such borrowing, the greater the restriction involved.* *

Apart from the special nature of borrowed reserves, Samuelson has argued that the tendency for borrowings to partially offset the reserve effects of open market operations actually strengthens monetary policy. He observes that:

While it is true that discounting often acts counter to open-market operations, there is no evidence that a unit change in open-market operations induces an opposing change in discounting large enough to reverse or substantially wipe out the original effect. So it is not really difficult for the planners of open-market operations to take all this into account; and precisely because they know that the discount window provides an escape valve, they can be more courageous in the use of open-market operations.[3]

Among the critics of the existing discounting arrangement, Milton Friedman looks upon borrowing with somewhat more alarm. He contends that with discounting at the banks' own initiative, the System is unable to exert direct control over monetary expansion.[4]

Warren Smith, another academic critic of the existing discount mechanism, asserts that those who emphasize the restrictive nature of borrowed reserves overlook the all-important fact that member bank borrowing adds to total reserves. ". . . Therefore . . . borrowing constitutes an offset to the restraint that brought it about to the extent that the supply of reserves is thereby increased."[5]

The administration of the discount window contributed both in the twenties and the fifties to the cyclical variability of the money supply. The discount rate typically lags behind the movements of the market rates. A cyclical upswing, generated or reinforced by non-monetary factors, pushes market rates ahead of the discount rate, and induces banks to expand their borrowing. The rising volume of discounts and advances increases the [reserve] base and consequently, increases the money supply. A reverse operation occurs in a downswing. The cyclical variability of the money supply is thus amplified by the operation of the discount window.[6]

B. Determinants of Member Bank Borrowing

Most of the post-Accord dialogue on the factors that influence borrowing decisions has been conditioned by the need vs. profitability issue that was debated extensively in the 1920's and 1930's. Recent attempts have been made to isolate and quantify the impact of interest rates on borrowing, and

---

* Editor's note: This statement reflects one of the great myths held by Federal Reserve officials and some economists. It simply isn't true; belief in it has led to profound monetary policy errors.

[3] Paul A. Samuelson, "Reflections on Monetary Policy," *Review of Economics and Statistics,* XLII (August, 1960), p. 266.

[4] Milton Friedman, *A Program for Monetary Stability* (New York: Fordham University Press, 1959), p. 38.

[5] Warrent L. Smith, "The Discount Rate as a Credit Control Weapon," *Journal of Political Economy,* LXVI (April, 1958), p. 172.

[6] U.S. House, Subcommittee on Domestic Finance, *An Alternative Approach to the Monetary Mechanism,* by Karl Brunner and Alan H. Meltzer, 88th Congress, 2nd Session, August 17, 1964, p. 89.

general comments on the sensitivity of borrowing to rate movements are abundant in the literature. Somewhat less attention has been devoted to the question of bank reluctance to borrow. One of the more interesting contributions in the post-Accord literature is a theoretical reconciliation of these two motives.

1. INTEREST RATES AND BORROWING

Many of those who feel that the present discount mechanism weakens monetary control are alarmed by evidence suggesting that borrowings are sensitive to interest rates and therefore work systematically against open market operations. Although the extent to which borrowings respond to rate movements is clearly an empirical question, the evidence is scanty. Typical of the casual observation in this area is the following: "No doubt it is true that banks are reluctant to borrow, but like many ordinary persons, bankers allow their reluctance to be overcome by more attractive alternatives."[7] Aschheim theorizes in a similar vein:

The Federal Reserve prefers to state that in time of monetary tightness there is a great "need" on the part of member banks for rediscounting. Economically, the more informative formulation, however, is that in times of monetary tightness it is more profitable for banks to borrow from the Federal Reserve than in other periods.[8]

Warren Smith is somewhat more specific about the way in which he feels that interest rates influence borrowing decisions, but he too stays primarily in the realm of supposition in observing that while bank demand for readily available funds to satisfy the kind of urgent needs that commonly induce banks to borrow at the discount window is probably quite interest-insensitive, the *extent* to which banks actually turn to the Federal Reserve to satisfy these needs rather than relying on other sources may be significantly affected by rate movements.

In most cases, banks have a choice of obtaining additional funds by borrowing at the Federal Reserve or by liquidating secondary reserves or other investment securities. Surely, the major factor influencing the choice will be the relevant cost of funds obtained by the various methods, and this depends chiefly on the relation between the discount rate and the expected yield on assets that the bank may consider liquidating.[9]

Meigs, who actually focuses on bank demand for free reserves (excess reserves less borrowing), concludes that "aggregate member bank borrowing is indeed influenced by the net yields obtainable on borrowed funds, within a considerable part of the range of interest rates and other conditions observed."[10] In this connection Meigs makes the point that the hypothesis that member bank borrowing is not responsive to changes in market interest rates cannot be confirmed solely by demonstrating that banks are reluctant to borrow. Rather, the characteristics of the demand schedule must be determined by direct empirical observation of borrowing and interest rates.

More recently, de Leeuw has concluded from empirical bank borrow-

---

[7] Earl Rolph, "Discussion," *American Economic Review,* Papers and Proceedings, XLV (May, 1955), pp. 413–414.

[8] *Techniques of Monetary Control,* p. 91.

[9] "The Discount Rate as a Credit-Control Weapon," *op. cit.,* p. 172.

[10] A. James Meigs, *Free Reserves and the Money Supply,* (Chicago: University of Chicago Press, 1962), p. 89.

ings demand estimates (based on quarterly data for the 1954–62 period) that the response of borrowings to the differential between the discount rate and the yield on 3-month Treasury bills is "moderate," with implied long-run elasticities with respect to the discount rate and the yield on Treasury bills of −0.7 and +0.5, respectively.[11] De Leeuw uses a stock-adjustment formulation of the borrowings demand function in deriving these results. According to the stock-adjustment principle, changes in bank borrowings in any given period are a function of the discrepancy between the *desired* level of borrowings in that period and the actual level of borrowings in the preceding period. DeLeeuw posits that *desired* amounts of borrowing are dependent, in turn, upon the differential between the Treasury bill and discount rates, the Treasury bill rate level, and the net inflow of bank funds (i.e., changes in private demand deposits plus Federal Government demand deposits plus private time deposits less member bank required reserves less holdings of loans and other private securities).

The Federal Reserve System has not always been completely clear on the importance it attributes to interest rate considerations in bank borrowing decisions. The following is among its pronouncements on the subject:

Banks are generally reluctant to become indebted to the Federal Reserve except for very short periods, and when in debt feel constrained to liquidate assets. The deterrents to borrowing are greatly weakened if market yields on securities owned become and remain substantially higher than the discount rate.[12]

Going into greater detail on the relationship between borrowings, market rates, and the discount rate under conditions of monetary restraint, the System has commented that:

. . . it is of prime importance that the general reluctance of banks to borrow at the Federal Reserve be reinforced by a discount rate with real deterrent power at times when a tempering of bank credit growth is in the public interest. In other words, in order to make the discount mechanism an effective supplement to open market operations the Federal Reserve is obliged to maintain discount rates not markedly lower than market yields on the most readily available alternative source of bank reserves, Treasury bills. If the Federal Reserve in these circumstances did not adjust its discount rates to keep them "in touch" with market rates, the task of administering the discount window to prevent excessive credit expansion would become very difficult.[13]

On the other hand, the System has more recently concluded that a comparison of the costs of alternative sources of ready funds with changing amounts of borrowed funds "does not suggest that there is a powerful borrowing response to changing cost considerations."[14]

2. RELUCTANCE TO BORROW

Attempts to discern the nature of the tradition against borrowing date back to the need vs. profitability discussions of the 1920's. Bank reluctance to bor-

[11] Frank de Leeuw, "A Model of Financial Behavior," in *The Brookings Quarterly Econometric Model of the United States,* (eds.) James S. Duesenberry, Gary Fromm, Lawrence R. Klein, and Edwin Kuh (Chicago: Rand, McNally and Company, 1965), pp. 512–513.

[12] U. S. Congress, Joint Economic Committee, *Employment Growth and Price Levels, Hearings,* "Part 4 —The Influence on Price of Changes in the Effective Supply of Money," 86th Congress, 1st Session (May 25–28, 1959), p. 775.

[13] *Ibid.,* p. 756.

[14] *The Federal Reserve and The Treasury: Answers to Questions from the Commission on Money and Credit,* p. 134.

row is commonly associated with the notion that since banks are already "in debt" to their depositors with repayment due in many cases on demand, it is imprudent to incur additional debt that is of a prior claim nature. Continued borrowing has been viewed as a confession either of weakened condition or of poor management. There is general agreement that the reluctance to borrow varies markedly in intensity among banks. Nevertheless, it has been argued that "in most cases" bank reluctance to borrow is "a deterrent sufficiently strong to prevent excessive use of discounting."[15]

At first glance, the premium in excess of the discount rate that banks have paid for Federal funds might be construed as a manifestation of bank reluctance to borrow from the Federal Reserve. In fact, however, the larger banks that are primarily responsible for bidding up the Federal funds rate are almost certainly not insensitive to rates as the traditional meaning of reluctance would imply. Rather, these banks might be viewed as adding an implicit cost factor to the discount rate in order to take account of scrutiny by the discount authorities. Under such circumstances, the effective cost of borrowing to these large banks will exceed the published discount rate and the Federal funds premium may be largely illusory.

3. NON-PRICE RATIONING

The guiding principles of Regulation A (as amended in 1955) have been interpreted and applied only with considerable difficulty. The appropriateness of borrowing under these non-price terms turns on the intent of the borrower. A bank is not, for example, to willfully borrow in order to profit from rate differentials. But this is basically a subjective determination and the uses to which borrowed reserves are put are quite difficult, if not impossible, to pinpoint.

Distinctions between appropriate and inappropriate borrowing can be quite fine, as evidenced by the following case cited by a former Federal Reserve discount officer:

. . . if a bank borrowed temporarily to meet a commitment to make a loan to a business concern at 4 per cent, with reasonable expectations of having funds at hand shortly to pay out, the bank would not be borrowing to earn a rate differential even though it was borrowing at the lower rate (in one market) and re-lending at a higher rate (in another market).[16]

With regard to the stability of discounting terms over time, Professor Whittlesey has set out to correct what he terms a "common misconception" that non-price discount window standards are adjusted to changing business conditions. He contends that: "The fact is that neither the way in which the discount window is administered nor the standards by which member bank borrowing is judged are modified to conform to over-all monetary policy.[17]

The dominant view in the literature is that there should be greater reliance on the price mechanism and less on non-price rationing in the allocation of Federal Reserve credit through the discount window. As will be seen in a subsequent section of this paper, proposals by Aschheim, Brunner and Meltzer, and Tobin all call explicitly for

[15] *The Federal Reserve and the Treasury: Answers to Questions from the Commission on Money and Credit, op. cit.*, p. 130.

[16] George W. McKinney, Jr., *The Federal Reserve Discount Window* (New Brunswick: Rutgers University Press, 1960), pp. 106–107.

[17] Charles R. Whittlesey, "Credit Policy at the Discount Window," *Quarterly Journal of Economics,* LXXIII (May, 1959), p. 209.

an "open" discount window where banks have the right to borrow all they wish at the existing discount rate.

4.   ANNOUNCEMENT EFFECTS

There has recently been a growing concern with the impact of discount rate policies on *expectations*. Apparently not everyone agrees with C. E. Walker's observation that changes in the discount rate are "a simple and easily understandable technique for informing the market of monetary authorities' views on the economic and credit situation."[18]

According to Kareken, some asymmetrical assumptions about the behavior of lenders and borrowers are necessary in order to argue that the "announcement effects" of discount rate adjustments are necessarily stabilizing. In particular, lenders must be expected to interpret an increase in the discount rate as a sign that tighter credit conditions lie ahead and react with a more conservative lending policy; while borrowers, on the other hand, must take the discount rate rise as signaling the end of good times and cut back their spending plans and loan demands accordingly.[19]

Samuelson is not so sure that the borrowers will in fact react in such a manner. He reasons that:

Today, financial men know that the Federal Reserve "leans against the breeze," tightening money when it thinks the forces of expansion are strong and easing money when deflation seems a threat. Therefore it is ra-

tional for an investor to say, "Aha!, the 'Fed' is raising interest rates; they must know that the current outlook is very bullish, and if that is going to be so, I'd better expand my operations." Conclusion: Announcement effects are often ambiguous.[20]

On the other hand, the System has observed that discretionary discount rate changes are a useful complement to the other major tools of credit policy because they are probably the most widely publicized step that a central bank can take—and yet they have no direct effect on the available supply of bank reserves.[21]

IV.   PROPOSED CHANGES IN THE DISCOUNT MECHANISM

The critics of the present discounting arrangement have offered alternative proposals that range from abolishing the practice to making it the most powerful tool in the central banker's kit.

A.   Abolition of the Discount Mechanism

Perhaps the most adamant advocate of abolishing discounting is Milton Friedman, who argues that since member banks discount at their own initiative, the Federal Reserve System cannot determine the amount of money it creates either through the discount window or by a combination of discounting and open market operations.[22] Regarding discount rate policy in particular, Friedman is highly critical of those who have looked to the level

---

[18] C. E. Walker, "Discount Policy in the Light of Recent Experience," *Journal of Finance,* XII (May, 1957), p. 229.

[19] John H. Kareken, "Federal Reserve System Discount Policy: An Appraisal," *Banca Nazionale Del Lavoro Quarterly Review,* No. 48 (March, 1959), p. 109.

[20] "Recent American Monetary Controversy," *op. cit.,* p. 10, n. 1.

[21] *The Federal Reserve and the Treasury: Answers to Questions from the Commission on Money and Credit, op. cit.,* p. 146.

[22] *A Program for Monetary Stability, op. cit.,* p. 38.

of the discount rate rather than its position relative to other rates as an indication of the tone of monetary policy.* Under a discretionary discount rate policy, an unchanged rate is, according to Friedman, accompanied by unintended shifts between monetary tightness and ease as market rates change relative to the discount rate. Moreover, the occasional but usually substantial changes in the discount rate are viewed as a source of general instability. Friedman sums up his feelings as follows:

. . . rediscounting should be eliminated. The Federal Reserve would then no longer have to announce a discount rate or to change it; it would then have direct control over the amount of high-powered money it created; it would not be a source of instability alike by its occasional changes in the discount rate and by the unintended changes in the "tightness" or "ease" of policy associated with an unchanged rate, nor would it be misled by these unintended changes; and it would be less subject to being diverted from its main task by the attention devoted to the "credit" effects of its policy.[23]

One vital qualification is, however, added by Friedman to his argument for total abolishment. He reasons that since required reserves are calculated after the fact, some discrepancies between required and actual reserves are unavoidable. As an alternative to the current charge of the discount rate plus two percentage points on realized reserve deficits, Friedman offers a fixed rate of "fine" that should be large enough to make it well above likely market rates of interest. The fine would then become the equivalent of a truly 'penalty' discount rate, no collateral, or eligibility requirements, or the like would be involved.

B. Nondiscriminatory Approach

A general dissatisfaction with the discretionary features of discount policy is reflected in nearly all of the suggested modifications in this mechanism. The proposals along this line rest on the assumption that "profitability" considerations do, in fact, bear heavily on borrowing decisions. The central feature of the proposed non-discretionary discounting arrangements is a discount rate that is "tied" to the Treasury bill rate or some other money market rate that is relevant to borrowing decisions. Such an arrangement is apparently motivated in large part by the desire to: (1) stabilize the rate differentials that influence borrowing decisions, thus hopefully stabilizing the borrowing aggregate, and (2) eliminate the threat of adverse announcement effects stemming from discretionary discount rate changes. When coupled with a penalty rate concept, this system establishes a basis for relying entirely on the price mechanism for the allocation of credit at the discount window.

The practical problem of how high to set the "penalty" rate is an important one. If the rate is set too high, borrowing from the Federal Reserve Banks might cease to be a practical alternative for banks unexpectedly in need of reserves. Many regard this lender-of-last-resort function as an important central bank responsibility, however, and the adverse effect on the attractiveness of membership in the System is also a consideration. On the other hand, if the penalty rate is set too low,

---

* Editor's note: More recently, Friedman and others have criticized the discount mechanism as an unjustifiable subsidy to individual banks. The liquidity position of *indvidual banks* is a matter to concern banking supervisors, not the monetary authority.

[23] *Ibid.,* p. 44.

the volume of borrowing might become "excessive." A perhaps even more thorny problem is created by the fact that market interest rates do not move in perfect tandem with each other. Thus if the discount rate were tied to some particular rate, movements of other market rates relative to the chosen rate could result in continued interest rate-induced instability in the aggregate volume of borrowing.

The choice of the market rate to which the discount rate would be tied and the size of the differential to be used hinges in significant part on the question of whether banks balance borrowings against rates on other sources of readily available funds or whether borrowings are related to the rate that banks can earn on loans. A penalty discount rate that is effective under conditions in which borrowings are balanced against rates on marginal assets (i.e., Treasury bills) may not inhibit borrowing decisions that are related to the higher return on earning assets.

Moreover, even if the discount window authorities effectively preclude borrowing to lend at a profit under the terms of Regulation A, a given penalty rate may become ineffective as banks shift from one short-term source of funds to another. If, for example, the discount rate is set at some specified margin above the Treasury bill rate, but if, in fact, a substantial number of banks turn to other sources of short-term funds such as CD's, the discount rate may lose its initial penalty properties.

C. Tobin's Proposals

Professor Tobin advocates a radical departure from the current discounting arrangement which would make the discount rate "the most powerful tool in the central bankers' kit."[24] He makes two basic proposals:

1. The Federal Reserve Banks should pay interest at the discount rate on member bank reserve balances in excess of requirements.
2. Banks should be released from the prohibition of interest payments on demand deposits and from the ceilings on interest rates on time and savings deposits.

According to Tobin, the purpose of the first proposal is to tighten the control of the Federal Reserve over the opportunity cost of bank lending. By raising the discount rate, the Federal Reserve would "clearly, directly, and quickly" make lending less attractive to all banks regardless of whether they are in debt to the Federal Reserve or not. The discount rate would become a floor to the rate on Treasury bills and similar short-term paper that banks might hold as secondary reserves.

The purpose of the second proposal is to tighten the Federal Reserve's control over the opportunity cost that bank depositors charge against any alternative investment of funds. "The rate that banks pay depositors will be closely geared to the discount rate since a bank will also be able to earn a fraction of the discount rate (one minus the required reserve ratio) on a new deposit."[25] Among the advantages claimed by Tobin for the second proposal, are the elimination of the "unproductive efforts" devoted to economizing cash in periods of high interest rates, and the replacement of the existing "wasteful and imperfect" non-price competition with price competition. "Better to pay depositors interest than

---

[24] James Tobin, "Towards Improving the Efficiency of the Monetary Mechanism," *Review of Economics and Statistics,* XLII (August, 1960), p. 279.
[25] *Ibid.,* p. 278.

to seek their patronage by organ music, free silverware, and plush surroundings." [26]

Another important feature of Tobin's plan is that the Federal Reserve would make a perfect Federal funds market at the discount rate. Among the impli-cations forseen by Tobin for his proposals are that much of the short-term Government debt would be transferred to the Federal Reserve from banks and corporations, leaving them to hold excess reserves and bank deposits, respectively.

[26] *Ibid.*

READING 22
REAPPRAISAL OF THE FEDERAL RESERVE DISCOUNT MECHANISM

On July 22, 1968, the Federal Reserve made public the report of a System committee which has completed an intensive, 3-year restudy of Federal Reserve lending policies. The document, entitled "Reappraisal of the Federal Reserve Discount Mechanism," reaffirms three long-established principles of Federal Reserve lending, but it also proposes several significant changes in lending policies and procedures aimed at providing more liberal and clear-cut access for member banks to Federal Reserve lending facilities. Thus re-designed, the "discount window—as the Federal Reserve Banks' lending facilities are often called—is expected to play a more active part in enabling commercial banks to more effectively meet their communities' credit needs.*

I. BASIC PRINCIPLES REAFFIRMED

First among the basic principles governing the use of Federal Reserve credit is that Federal Reserve System lending is to accommodate bank asset and liability adjustments over limited time periods and to meet essentially short-term fluctuations in member bank needs for funds. Coordinately it is intended that individual member banks shall not be continuously and permanently in debt to the Federal Reserve.

The second principle reaffirmed, however, is that Federal Reserve Banks always stand ready to lend to any of their member banks caught in special regional or local adversities—such as droughts, drastic deposit drains, or other emergencies—for as long as reasonably needed for the bank to work out of these circumstances.

Thirdly, the report recognizes that the Federal Reserve serves as "lender of last resort" to buttress the entire financial system in the event of widespread emergency. Within the limits of existing law, and lending primarily through the conduit of member banks, the Federal Reserve is prepared to

Source: From Federal Reserve Bulletin, July 1968, pp. 545–551.

* Editor's note: As of May 1971, the Federal Reserve Board has not promulgated any of the proposed changes in the administration of the discount mechanism. It seems likely that action will be taken, however, during the year.

supply liquid funds to other groups of financial institutions when such assistance is not available elsewhere and is necessary to avoid major economic disruption.

II. SIGNIFICANT NEW ELEMENTS

To provide more clear-cut access to Federal Reserve lending facilities, the report proposes that each soundly operated member bank be given a "basic borrowing privilege," enabling it to borrow limited amounts of funds from its Reserve Bank upon request in as many as half of its weekly reserve periods.

In addition, it is proposed that any member bank foreseeing large seasonal bulges in its needs for funds would be able to arrange for loans from its Reserve Bank to help meet all such needs in excess of a specified minimum. This arrangement, more explicit and more liberal than currently provided, is termed the "seasonal borrowing privilege."

Member banks experiencing drains of funds that are not of a seasonal or emergency nature, but that are bigger or longer in duration than can be accomplished under the new "basic borrowing privilege," are not precluded from short-term borrowings from their Reserve Banks pending a prompt reversal of their fund outflows or an orderly adjustment of their assets and liabilities. Such borrowings would be subject to essentially the same kinds of administrative procedures now applied to member bank borrowings from their Reserve Banks.

A final major new idea proposed by the report is to make the discount rate —the interest rate charged by Federal Reserve Banks on their loans to member banks—more flexible than heretofore. It is recommended that the discount rate be changed considerably more frequently, to keep it reasonably

closely in line with the movements in other money market rates.

III. EVOLUTION OF THE DISCOUNT MECHANISM

The proposed redesign represents the latest in a series of evolutionary changes in Federal Reserve lending policies and procedures. When first established by the Federal Reserve Act in 1913, the discount mechanism was expected to operate by member banks presenting certain types of short-term customer notes (termed "eligible paper") as collateral for borrowing at the Reserve Banks. During most of the first 20 years of Federal Reserve operation, member banks borrowed a sizable proportion of their total required reserves on the security of such customer notes. During the next 20 years, however, member banks accumulated large amounts of U.S. Government securities and other liquid assets; accordingly, they did very little borrowing from their Reserve Banks and collateralized such borrowing as they did with Government securities. This marginal role for the discount window was recognized in a formal change in 1955 in the Board's Regulation A covering loans to member banks; under that revision. bank borrowings from the Federal Reserve were to be limited to assistance over the peaks of temporary, seasonal or emergency needs for funds that exceeded the dimensions that the banks themselves were capable of reasonably meeting out of their own resources.

In the last decade or so, however, credit demands on banks have grown and loan-to-deposit ratios are much higher. Moreover, at many banks more sophisticated portfolio management has pared liquidity positions substantially. Borrowings from other sources than the Federal Reserve have expanded. In view of these developments, the proposed redesign of the discount mechanism is aimed at relating Federal Reserve lending more clearly and closely to the changing bank and community needs.

IV. BASIC BORROWING PRIVILEGE

The most commonly used of the new lending provisions for member banks in good standing would undoubtedly be the basic borrowing privilege because it would provide credit up to specified time and amount limits on a virtually no-questions-asked basis.

The size of each bank's basic borrowing privilege would be established as a proportion of that bank's capital stock and surplus. The present proposal calls for each bank to have a basic borrowing privilege equal, on a reserve-period-average basis, of between 20 per cent and 40 per cent of its capital stock and surplus, up to $1 million, between 10 per cent and 20 per cent of its capital stock and surplus between $1 million and $10 million, and 10 per cent of its capital stock and surplus in excess of $10 million. Thus a bank with $1 million of capital stock and surplus could borrow between $200,000 and $400,000 on *each* day of the 7-day reserve period or between $1,400,000 and $2,800,000 on any one day during the period.

Frequency of use of the basic borrowing privilege would also be limited. This is necessary because Federal Reserve credit is not properly a long-term or permanent addition to the loanable funds of individual member banks. The aim is to make credit available over a long enough period to cushion the bulk of short-term fluctuations or asset adjustments and in most cases permit orderly adjustment to longer-term movements of funds.

The proposed frequency limitation would allow access to credit so long as the bank is indebted in no more than half the reserve periods in the interval—that is, so long as the bank does not use adjustment credit in more than 6 (or up to 13) of the 13 (or up to 26) consecutive reserve periods ending with the current period. Thus, whether a member bank is eligible to use its basic borrowing privilege at any time is established by examining its record of borrowing at the window for adjustment purposes for the previous 12 (or up to 25) reserve periods.

Before the plan is finally made effective, choices will be made in the light of comments received as to the particular percentages within the indicated ranges which would apply to the amount and frequency limitations.

The considerations will be that individual credit access should not be so small nor so infrequently available as to be insignificant to the member banks, nor should total access be so liberal as to exceed the ability of the Federal Reserve to undertake any necessary offsetting open market operations. (Adjustment credit beyond these limits will be available, as described elsewhere, to any member bank having a justifiable need larger or longer in duration than could be accommodated within the basic borrowing privilege, and therefore the basic borrowing privilege does not represent the maximum Federal Reserve credit to which the member bank could have access and need not encompass all bank needs which may be expected to arise.)

Borrowing within the basic-borrowing-privilege limitations could, as noted, take place virtually upon request, unless the Reserve Bank has notified the member bank that its over-all condition is unsatisfactory as determined by such factors as adequacy of capital, liquidity, soundness, management, or noncompliance with law or regulation and that such unsatisfactory condition is not being corrected to the Reserve Bank's satisfaction. The only other circumscription on the actions of a qualified borrowing bank would be the avoidance of net sales in the Federal funds market during the reserve periods in which it was borrowing from the Federal Reserve. This administrative rule, already in force, is being continued in the interest of precluding retailing operations in Federal Reserve credit obtained through the discount window. It is ,of course, recognized that circumstances might occur as a result of miscalculations or large unforeseen movements in the bank's position, in which net selling of funds would be extremely difficult to avoid. In such infrequent situations this rule would be waivable.

V.   OTHER ADJUSTMENT CREDIT

It is recognized that basic borrowing privileges would not be large enough to encompass every member bank's needs for funds in all instances that justify the use of discount credit. This is particularly true in cases of the larger banks, which borrow infrequently but for rather large amounts, but it is also true in the case of smaller banks faced with sharp temporary drains of funds. Arrangements are therefore recognized as necessary to permit member bank borrowings outside the basic borrowing privilege up to the limits of appropriate needs on as convenient and understandable terms as possible. These arrangements are referred to in the report as "other adjustment credit" and are virtually identical to the arrangements presently existing for the use of discount credit on such a scale.

When a member bank uses "other adjustment credit," it should expect that the circumstances of its borrowing would come under examination in some detail. In many cases this would consist of a review of information available at the Reserve Bank. Hence it would involve no immediate contact with the member bank, especially if this review clearly showed continued credit extension to be appropriate. However, if the use of "other adjustment credit" becomes more extended in amount and time, the Reserve Bank would follow the case more closely and directly. In due course, the bank would be expected to outline its plan and timetable of adjustment and thereafter to carry it out. The circumstances surrounding individual borrowing cases will differ widely, and, as now, the precise timing and nature of these administrative actions would be related to such differences. Close contacts among the Federal Reserve Banks' discount officials will be maintained in the interest of dealing uniformly with similar cases.

VI.   SEASONAL BORROWING PRIVILEGE

The third category of credit which would be available to member banks at the proposed discount window is called the "seasonal borrowing privilege." A Reserve Bank would be prepared to establish such a "seasonal borrowing privilege" for any member bank experiencing demonstrable seasonal pressures persisting for a period of at least 4 weeks and exceeding a minimum relative size. It is expected that this borrowing privilege will be of value principally to smaller units in agricultural or resort areas in which seasonal swings have a substantial impact on the entire community and where access to the money markets or other adjustment resources is not always readily available.

The existence of seasonal pressures would be judged on the basis of past years' patterns of loan and deposit fluctuations. Totally new seasonal pressure, such as might be occasioned if a new industry with a strong seasonal pattern moved into a small town, would not justify establishment of a seasonal borrowing privilege in the first year. The resulting credit needs could be accommodated under other adjustment credit arrangements, however, with recognition that this was in fact a justifiable need, and in succeeding years a borrowing privilege could be formally established.

The establishment of a qualifying seasonal swing in net availability of funds (defined as the net of deposits minus loans to customers in the bank's market area) would ordinarily be fixed by negotiation once a year. The basic data to be used in this determination would in most cases be already on file at the Reserve Banks. The proposal suggests that where feasible the determination of a seasonal borrowing privilege might best be accomplished prior to the actual credit need, since this would permit more orderly planning on the part of both the borrowing bank and the Reserve Bank.

Once the existence of a qualifying seasonal need was established, the Reserve Banks would agree to extend discount credit up to the qualifying amount and for the length of time the need was expected to persist, up to 90 days. The 90-day maximum is imposed by statute; however, should the need extend over a longer period than this, the Reserve Banks would regard renewals of credit as in accordance with the initial seasonal credit negotiation. Seasonal credit needs would normally be expected to last for several months, but in exceptional cases could range up to as much as 9 months.

Seasonal credit obtainable at a Reserve Bank would be limited to the amount of the borrowing bank's seasonal swing in excess of a specified percentage of its average deposits in the preceding year. This "deductible" principle, requiring a bank to meet a part of its seasonal need out of its own resources, is designed to encourage individual bank maintenance of some minimum level of liquidity for purposes of flexibility. It also serves effectively to limit the aggregate amount of credit extended under the seasonal borrowing privilege to an amount consistent with over-all monetary policy, while allowing the Federal Reserve to provide this assistance to all those member banks with relatively large seasonal needs. The precise level of the deductible percentage would lie in the range of 5 to 10 per cent of average deposits, with the final choice again to be made by the Board in the light of comments received.

The amount of credit arranged for during the original negotiation of a seasonal borrowing privilege would not normally be revised in mid-season, but the proposal recognizes that unforeseen developments essentially afford the need for seasonal credit. In such unusual circumstances renegotiation would be allowed. Likewise, the Reserve Bank would, under normal circumstances, abide by the original negotiations. Only in the cases of a clear and significant change in the bank's need or flagrant abuse of the seasonal borrowing privilege would a Reserve Bank exercise its option to curtail an outstanding seasonal credit arrangement.

Borrowings under the seasonal borrowing privilege would not be counted in determining a bank's eligibility to use its basic borrowing privilege as described above.

VII. EMERGENCY CREDIT

The proposed redesign of the discount window would provide that the Federal Reserve continue to supply liberal help to its member banks in emergency situations. So long as the member bank is solvent and steps are being taken to find a solution to its problems, credit would be available on the same basis as it currently is, and, within the limits of the law, *ad hoc* arrangements would continue to be

TABLE 1

SUMMARY OF PROPOSAL FOR REDESIGN OF DISCOUNT MECHANISM

Item	Basic Borrowing Privilege (1)	Other Adjustment Credit (2)	Seasonal Borrowing Privilege (3)	Emergency Credit to Member Banks (4)	Emergency Credit to Others (5)
Definition	Member bank access to credit upon request, within precisely stated limits on amounts and frequency and on specified conditions.	Supplemental discount accommodation, subject to administrative procedures, to help a member bank meet temporary needs that prove either larger or longer in duration than could be covered by its basic borrowing privilege.	Member bank access to credit on a longer-term and, to the extent possible, prearranged basis to meet demonstrable seasonal pressures exceeding minimum duration and relative amount.	Credit extended to member banks in unusual or exigent circumstances.	Credit extended to institutions other than member banks in emergency circumstances in fulfilling role as lender of last resort to the economy.
Rate	Discount Rate.	Discount Rate.	Discount Rate.	Discount Rate.	Significantly higher rate than discount rate.
Quantity limitations	——(20–40) per cent of first $1 million capital stock & surplus plus ——(10–20) per cent of next $9 million, plus ——(10) per cent of remainder.	None specified.	Seasonal needs in excess of ——(5–10) per cent of average deposits subject to reserve requirements in preceding calendar year.	None specified.	None specified.

Frequency or duration limitations	——(6–13) of any ——(13–26) consecutive reserve computation periods.	None specified.	Need and arrangement must be for more than 4 weeks. Maximum 9 consecutive months.	None specified.	None specified.
Administrative procedures	None other than general discouragement of net selling of Federal funds by borrowing banks.	Appraisal and, where necessary, action broadly similar to procedures developed under existing discount arrangements.	Prearrangement involves discussion between discount officer and bank management concerning amount, duration, and seasonality of need. Administrative review maintained during borrowing to prevent abuse or misuse.	Continuous and thoroughgoing surveillance. Require that bank develop and pursue workable program for alleviating difficulties.	Continuous and thoroughgoing surveillance (may have to be through conduit). Require that institution develop and pursue workable program for alleviating difficulties.
Other restrictions	Must not have been found to be in unsatisfactory condition.	None specified.	None specified.	None specified.	Required to use all other practicable sources of credit first.
Method of provision	Direct.	Direct.	Direct.	Direct.	(1) through central agency; (2) direct; (3) conduit through member bank.

made where necessary. Assisting a bank in an emergency situation would generally require credit extension for periods longer than would normally be allowed at the window, but this would be expected and regarded as appropriate.

In addition, the redesigned window would recognize the possibility that the Federal Reserve, in its role as lender of last resort to other sectors of the economy, might in extreme conditions find it necessary to extend circumscribed credit assistance to institutions other than member banks. This action would be taken only when all other sources of credit had been exhausted and failure of the troubled institutions would have a significant impact on the economy's financial structure. When lending to nonmembers, the Federal Reserve would act in cooperation with the relevant supervisory authority to insure that steps are taken to find a solution to its problems. Credit would normally be extended through a conduit arrangement with a member bank and would be provided at a significantly higher rate than the prevailing discount rate.

VIII.   RELATED CONSIDERATIONS

The proposed discount window does not include the provision of inter-mediate- or long-term credit to meet the needs of banks servicing credit-deficit areas or sectors—that is, areas or sectors where the opportunities for profitable investment continuously outstrip the savings generated locally. While this is recognized as a problem of some significance, it was concluded that attempting to solve this problem through the discount window would involve socio-economic and political decisions outside the proper scope of System responsibility. It was also felt that financing the expansion of loan portfolios far beyond the limtis of deposits through the provision of long-

term discount credit would seriously and in some cases dangerously distort the normal balance sheet structure of commercial banks. The study committee concluded that an appropriate and effective solution to the problem was most likely to be found in the improvement of secondary markets for bank assets and liabilities. Detailed studies of the feasibility of actions to promote such improvement are expected to begin in the near future.

While Federal Reserve open market operations are still envisioned as the main tool of monetary policy, the proposed changes in discount operations would be expected to lead to a generally higher level of borrowing being done by a rotating group of member banks. Such a higher level of borrowing would not, however, mean a corresponding increase in total reserves, since increased borrowing would be expected to be about offset by correspondingly smaller net System purchases in the open market.

The study committee recognizes that a period of transition would undoubtedly be required before the full potential of the proposed redesign of the discount window could be realized by either the Federal Reserve or the member banks. However, it believes that this redesign can bring the mechanism into closer touch with the prevailing economic climate and lead to a more effectively functioning member banking system.

Table 1 summarizes the proposals contained in the current report. It outlines the several complementary arrangements for borrowing at the window, each designed to provide credit for a specific type of need. These are: the basic borrowing privilege, column (1); other adjustment credit, column (2); the seasonal borrowing privilege, column (3); and emergency credit assistance, both to member banks, column (4); and to other financial institutions, column (5).

READING 23

SHOULD RESERVE REQUIREMENTS BE ABOLISHED?

Deane Carson

More than six years have elapsed since I first proposed the abolition of legal cash reserve requirements.[1] Apart from a few flurries of agreement within the academic world,[2] however, my proposal has been greeted with something approaching absolute silence.

This lack of interest, let alone approval, is particularly puzzling to me where the commercial banks are concerned, since at least some of these institutions would undoubtedly profit rather handsomely from a system of zero reserve requirements.

Philosophically, I am not prepared to accept the proposition that commercial bankers are so much different from other businessmen that they cannot recognize their own self-interest when it is abundantly apparent. The answer to their indifference must lie elsewhere,

and I suspect that it lies in that broad and deep box of communication failures, for which, in this instance, I share responsibility. This article is designed to rectify, at least in part, past shortcomings in this regard.

At the outset, however, I must state that my interest in the matter of abolishing legal reserve requirements is motivated by the belief that reserve requirements impose unnecessary burdens on the efficiency of the banking system and result in a misallocation of resources to the detriment of the entire economy. If the correctness of this view happens to be consistent with higher bank profitability, which adoption of my proposal would entail, so much the better for us all.

My remarks fall into three major categories, viz., (1) the effects of legal re-

Source: Speech prepared for the Columbia Graduate School of Business' Commercial Bank Management Conference, Arden House, April 15, 1970, abridged and edited.

[1] Deane Carson, "Is the Federal Reserve System Really Necessary?" *Journal of Finance,* 1964.
[2] See Lucille Mayne, "Federal Reserve System Membership, Bank Liquidity, and Bank Profitability," pp. 181–184, *Southern Economic Review,* October 1969.

serve requirements on individual banks, (2) reserve requirements as an instrument of monetary policy, and (3) the banking system under a system of Zero Legal Reserve Requirements.

I. REQUIRED RESERVES AS A TAX ON BANK EARNINGS

Legal reserve requirements, whether those imposed by the Federal Reserve Board on member banks or those imposed by the several states on nonmembers, may be rightly considered a tax on bank earnings.[3] But one hears little or no protest against either the level of reserve requirements or the infrequent increase in reserve requirements levied by the Federal Reserve Board. Increases in reserve requirements, for example in April 1969, are met with, if not indifference, the resigned attitude that "the Board knows best; it's all for the good of the country," and no little sympathy, even, with the Board's "problem" of making the transition to higher reserves as painless for the banks—read this to include the Government securities dealer market—as possible. This statesmanship, I contend, is largely misguided, not only from the standpoint of individual banks, but also from that of the national interest as well. One can only conclude that bankers have not properly distinguished their interests from those of the Federal Reserve, and further, that the Board and the bankers have incorrectly interpreted both the level and increases in the level of reserve requirements as necessary instruments of monetary management.[4]

Familiar though they are, required reserves reduce the earning assets of member banks to the extent that actual holdings of idle cash exceed the level that individual banks would choose in the absence of legal requirements. On the basis of a preliminary study of Illinois banks, where nonmember institutions have no reserve requirements to meet whatsover, the author has estimated that *country banks* would hold significantly lower ratios of total cash to total assets in the absence of legally required reserves. Preliminary results indicate a four to five percentage point spread between small member and nonmember banks in Illinois. Whether this range of the estimated difference would hold for all banks, large and small, throughout the United States cannot de determined. It does seem reasonable, however, to assume that the level of cash ratios would be generally lower if reserve requirements were abolished. This implies that banks could generally hold larger ratios of earning to total assets and, hence, would earn larger returns on total assets.

That individual banks do derive valuable benefits, in the form of services, from Federal Reserve membership cannot be doubted. The recognition of this fact, however, should not obscure the additional one that the Federal Reserve Banks are, in this sense, correspondents, and therefore direct competitors in the sale of such services, of privately owned correspondent banking firms. Indeed, one is hard-pressed to come up with a single service that is sold by the Federal Reserve to its members that is not provided by either private correspondent banks or nonbank enterprises. Furthermore, as every banker must know, the Fed does not carry all of the

---

[3] For the sake of brevity, the analysis will be confined to the former class of reserve requirements.

[4] The defections of smaller banks from Federal Reserve membership in recent years must stand as a significant exception to this indictment. This has been recognized by the Fed, whose "graduated" reserve requirements are frankly designed to encourage small bank membership, in addition to the achievement of other objectives.

brands in its store that are found in those run by private banking correspondents—portfolio management advisory service comes immediately to mind.[5]

Professor Lucille Mayne of Pennsylvania State University has studied this matter in great detail, and her general conclusion is that Federal Reserve membership involves a net cost (expense minus revenue) that is higher than that of banks that are not members, and that the reserve tax is the most significant item of expense to the member bank.[6]

If this is indeed the case, one properly may ask why any bank that has an option—and of course national banks do not—would elect to belong to the Federal Reserve System. Bankers generally believe that it would be "out of the question politically" for a very large bank to remain outside the System. What this means precisely in terms of the implied "political" pressures has never been very clear. Someone, perhaps a member of the Reserve Board or an executive officer of one of the large "captive" banks, would render a valuable service by explicating these "political" pressures more completely than has been done in the past.

Quite aside from the above unsatisfying answer to the question, what about the smaller banks that are not subject to "political" pressure to join the system and pay the reserve tax? Within this group, I suspect that many value an implicit benefit of Fed membership at a very high level—and who is to gainsay that? I refer specifically to the prestige value that some bankers

attach to their relationship with the District Federal Reserve Bank directly and to the Board of Governors somewhat more remotely. Membership gives senior bank management the privilege of wining and dining with central bankers, the opportunity to advise them on local conditions, and the like.

This has taken us, profitably I hope, somewhat afield from the central point, which is that banks would be generally better off if legal reserve requirements were abolished. Indeed, the reserve issue and the membership issue are separable from the standpoint of maximization of bank profit, although perhaps not so from the standpoint of what the Federal Reserve considers its self-interest, and many individual bankers *their* self-interest.

II. RESERVE REQUIREMENTS AS AN INSTRUMENT OF MONETARY POLICY

If the interest of banks lies in the abolition of legal reserve requirements —that is, in adoption of a system in which each bank would be free to establish its own cash ratio—it remains to examine whether the private interest coincides with the public interest. Central to this issue is whether abolition of reserve requirements would significantly impair the effectiveness of monetary policy. If it can be demonstrated that monetary management would not be significantly impaired, the case for Zero Legal Reserve Requirements becomes unassailable on any ground. If there is any lingering doubt in anyone's mind about the impact of the plan on monetary control, these will have to be

---

[5] Some Federal Reserve Banks have developed a partial substitute for the advisory services of private correspondents, namely a format for the estimation of costs and revenues of various inputs and outputs of the bank and a report that enables the bank to compare its performance with others in like circumstances. This undoubtedly was an innovation of the Federal Reserve Banks and should be credited to their account. Obviously, however, correspondent banks have this tool at their disposal as well as the Fed, since the procedure and comparison reports are generally available. In this case, Macy does tell Gimbel.

[6] Lucille Mayne, *Costs and Benefits of Federal Reserve Membership;* monograph available from the American Bankers Association, New York City, N.Y.

weighed against its public benefits that are discussed in section III

That reserve requirements are a dispensable instrument of monetary control is quite clear in principle. Let the central bank reduce legal reserve requirements to a level equal to the cash ratio of the least prudent bank.[7] A cash reserve base continues to exist and this base is what the Fed ought to be controlling, if it is to control the money supply.[8] Now let the Fed drop legal reserve requirements altogether. The reserve base is now the cash holdings of the banking system, a quantity that can be easily increased or decreased through either purchases or sales of government securities in the open market.[9] This cash reserve base would continue to be reported to the Federal Reserve, and we could now require *all* banks to so report.

Would abolition of reserve requirements make the Fed's open-market task more difficult than it is under present reserve requirements? In responding to this it must first be noted that the banks cannot, in the aggregate, change the *total* cash base through expansion or contraction of their loans and investments. On the other hand, the ratio of cash to deposits (or to loans and investments) *can* be changed by banks. But this is true today, since banks control their excess reserves. It would seem in any case that wide swings in this ratio would present a problem to the monetary managers, although certainly not

an insurmountable one. Changes in the aggregate ratios that induce changes in the money supply can be offset, if desired, by open-market operations; and while such operations might have to be larger than at present, it is highly unlikely that this would constitute an impairment of effective monetary control.[10]

Finally, we must consider the objection that abolishing reserve requirements also abolishes favorite indicators of the Federal Reserve, the excess reserve, and free reserve levals of the banking system. If there are no reserve requirements, excess and free reserves would have to be computed from a base of zero. But they could be computed and hence used by the Fed to indicate the impact of monetary policy if desired.

III. BANKS AND BANKING UNDER ZERO RESERVE REQUIREMENTS

The abolition of legal reserve requirements would obviously benefit those banks whose actual cash holdings exceed desired balances under present regulations. In a regime of zero legal reserve requirements, these banks would hold a higher ratio of earning assets to total resources, and would thereby enjoy a higher return, other things assumed to be equal. Loans and investments would replace that part of total cash now thought to be excessive.

But this would not be the sole benefit

---

[7] In my study of Illinois banks, I find this to be about five percent. Banks cannot "get away" with much less, given their clearing needs and the minimum balances they must hold with correspondents to pay for the services they receive.

[8] Space forbids a discussion of what the targets are or should be. The question is discussed in "Monetary Policy Targets and Indicators" by Thomas R. Saving, in Part 3.

[9] As reserve requirements are lowered, the Fed would ordinarily absorb reserves through open-market sales. Reserve requirements could, however be reduced gradually enough over time to match the monetary growth requirements of the economy.

[10] It might, however, affect the Government securities market and make the task of dealers more difficult. Interest rates would show larger short-term swings (something that the Federal Reserve has been at pains to avoid in the past). My view, and that of other monetarists, is that such swings make little difference in the larger scheme of things, and the Fed has pursued wrong policies precisely because of its concern with the money market's fluctuations.

redounding to individual banks. Post-poning for the moment the potential public benefits of zero reserve require-ments, let us consider how the individ-ual bank would operate in such a world of free choice.

Left to make its own decision in the determination of cash reserves, bank management would be faced with two problems, first, *how much* cash to hold, and second, *where* to hold it.

With respect to the appropriate cash balance, the bank would be faced with a decision that is by no means entirely unfamiliar to it, but one that would re-quire greater judgment—greater in scope and greater in degree. Under legal reserve requirements, when new deposit funds become available, the bank's decision involves the disposition of that part of the funds that is in ex-cess of the known reserve requirement liability. The bank's need to meet re-quired reserves is a datum that, under present Federal Reserve regulations, is known in advance of the current ac-counting period, and that, therefore, is not subject to management discretion. Under zero reserve requirements the entire accretion to bank funds is, in a sense, comparable to the concept of excess, reserves, and, hence, subject to the discretionary decision of bank man-agement. The latter must decide, even as it now does, what part of the "ex-cess" will be held idle as a reserve against its additional deposit liabilities and potential loss of deposits in the future. Management's responsibility is thus increased, although being of the same kind that is discharged by bank officers under present arrangements.

It seems reasonable to suppose that the question of the appropriate cash balance would be one that would en-gage the close attention of bankers. Management would necessarily be faced with the problem of establishing a policy in this regard, most likely one involving a cash ratio that would serve either as a guideline or as a target ob-jective of portfolio supervision. Each bank would presumably fix this guide-line or target according to its specific requirements for cash, as determined by such things as deposit composition, volatility of deposits, asset structure and maturity, expected internal cash flow, risk preference, and rate of return on earning assets.

Once a general policy has been adopted, bank management would con-tinue to be faced with day-to-day deci-sions, since it is unlikely (if not unwise) that an inflexible target ratio would be established. Most likely, banks would fix their target in the form of a band or range of ratios, with an upper and lower boundary that could not be exceeded without a review of the policy itself. In most cases the latter would be estab-lished by the directors of the bank or an executive committee. We may suppose, therefore, that prudent bank manage-ments will establish targets that are reasonably reflective of bank needs, and cash ratios that are reasonably stable in the short run. The latter fol-lows from the presumptions, justified I believe, that (1) narrow target bands will be established and (2) bank de-mand for cash will not be subject to wide variation in the short run.[11]

It should be clear, however, that zero reserve requirements would provide additional flexibility to banks in the management of cash reserves, and that additional responsibility in this regard

---

[11] Some critics of the proposal fear that a period such as 1968–1970 would bring cash ratios to an "undesirably low" level, where yields on loans and investments are rapidly rising. This can be discounted, since one would expect ratios to be established initially near the bottom of the banks' long-run requirements, as historically estimated. But even if this is not the case, banking supervisors and examiners are charged with the responsibility for bank solvency and liquidity standards, and they tend to be conservative.

has its reward. Additional reserve needs, which are now met by borrowing from the Federal Reserve Bank or purchase of Federal Funds, can be met by a reduction in the cash ratio within the limits of the target range. Fewer trips to the discount window will be necessary, as well as fewer excursions to the market for Federal Funds.[12] As long as a bank is not at the lower boundary of its cash ratio target, it may, in effect, borrow from itself; and even where it is at the lower boundary, the bank has the option of reducing the policy ratio. Whlie the implicit interest cost advantage of this may be zero, the bank may thus avoid the costs of transactions with the Federal Reserve and the Federal Funds market.

The decision involving the location of cash reserves under the present proposal is also an extension of the decisions now made by commercial banks. The difference, of course, lies in the greater range of choice available to the bank. Freed from the necessity of holding reserves solely in vault *or* in the Federal Reserve Bank, the institution may keep its balance where it receives the highest return. The direct effect of this is to place the Federal Reserve in competition with correspondent banks for cash deposits, which should benefit the individual banks and the public as well. Cash that is now held in vault or at the Fed to meet reserve requirements (rather than day-to-day transaction needs) can be held with correspondents to pay for the services the latter render.[13]

Granted that individual banks would benefit under the zero reserve requirement proposal, what can be said for the economy as a whole? I contend, in general, that here individual interest coincides with public interest.

On the most general level, freedom of choice in economic affairs, unless some clear and overriding public interest is thwarted, yields maximum social benefit and provides the best guide to optimal resource allocation. This widely held principle is at one and the same time the foundation of the free enterprise system *and* (given the proviso) the *rationale* of government intervention in the private economy. The question that arises in the present context is, therefore, whether there *is* a public interest in legal reserve requirements that overrides the benefits of free choice in the selection of cash ratios. In section II above, we found no compelling monetary policy need for legal reserve ratios. To the writer's knowledge, there is no published statement extant that establishes that need, either in the voluminous reports of the Federal Reserve or in the abundant academic literature on the subject. If the present discussion has no other effect, one would hope that it would result in the appearance of a satisfactory defense of legal reserve requirements.

On a more specific level, freedom of choice in the selection of bank cash ratios would tend to reduce the costs of providing banking services. Assuming that cash ratios are generally lower under the proposal, the implicit tax on cash reserves, however small, that must enter into the price of bank services, is reduced. For any given level of total assets, marginal costs will be lower after the adoption of the proposal. To the extent that banking is

---

[12] Abolition of reserve requirements does not imply the abolition of the discount window. The Federal Reserve does not need the reserves of banks to make loans. Furthermore, since some banks might continue to hold cash at District Banks, for clearing purposes, the proposal would not necessarily extinguish the Federal Funds market.

[13] Cash now must be placed with correspondents beyond that which is held for legal reserve requirements.

competitive, more or less of this cost reduction will be passed on to the bank customer.

Finally, free choice in the cash ratio decision would tend to provide an economically rational allocation of banking resources. To the extent that uniform legal reserve requirements affect the profits of banks without regard to their actual cash needs, some institutions appear relatively more profitable than they really are, while others appear less so. In a free market these distortions would disappear, and bank capital would be reallocated to its highest uses.

READING 24
THE ADMINISTRATION OF REGULATION Q

Charlotte E. Ruebling

Interest rate ceilings on deposits at banks which are members of the Federal Reserve System are established under Federal Reserve Regulation Q. Ceilings at insured nonmember banks, which have been the same as for member banks, are set by a regulation of the Federal Deposit Insurance Corporation.[1] These regulations stem from Banking Acts of 1933 and 1935, respectively.[2] Some states have at times imposed ceilings for state-chartered banks which are lower than those established by the Federal agencies. There were no explicit nationwide regulations on interest and dividend rates at mutual savings banks and savings and loan associations until 1966. Legislation in September of that year brought rates paid by Federally insured mutual savings banks under the control of the Federal Deposit Insurance Corporation, and rates paid at savings and loan associations which are members of the Federal Home Loan Bank Board under its control. That legislation also required the three regulatory agencies to consult with each other when considering changes in the ceiling rates.

This article examines changes in the maximum rates payable on commercial bank time and savings deposits. The maximum rate permitted on demand deposits has been zero since 1933.[3]

Source: From Federal Reserve Bank of St. Louis Review, February, 1970, pp. 29–40.

[1] Changes in maximum rates permitted at nonmember banks are given in the Annual Reports of the Federal Deposit Insurance Corporation. See for example, in *The Annual Report of the Federal Deposit Insurance Corporation* 1968, pp. 145–147.

[2] Historical background on interest rate restrictions, including developments prior to 1933, are summarized in "Interest Rate Controls—Perspective, Purpose and Problems" by Clifton B. Luttrell in the September 1968 issue of this *Review*, also available as Reprint No. 32. See also Albert H. Cox, Jr., *Regulation of Interest Rates on Bank Deposits*, Michigan Business Studies, Vol. XVII, No. 4 (Ann Arbor: University of Michigan, 1966), pp. 1–30.

[3] The implications of this interest rate ceiling for bank behavior have been analyzed by Donald R. Hodgman in *Commercial Bank Loan and Investment Policy* (Champaign: University of Illinois, 1963).

TABLE 1

YIELD DIFFERENTIALS (PER CENT PER ANNUM)

Type of Deposit	Regulation Q Ceiling Rate	Spread between Government Security Yield and Comparable Ceiling Rate[a]	
Savings deposits	4.50	(30 days)	2.64
Other time deposits			
Multiple maturity			
30–89 days	4.50	(3-mo.)	3.57
90 days or more	5.00	(6-mo.)	3.11
Single maturity			
Less than $100,000			
30 days to 1 year	5.00	(6-mo.)	3.11
1 year	5.50	(12-mo.)	2.53
2 year	5.75	(2 yrs.)	2.40
$100,000 or more			
30–59 days	6.25	(3-mo.)	1.82
60–89 days	6.50	(3-mo.)	1.57
90–179 days	6.75	(6-mo.)	1.36
180 days to 1 year	7.00	(12-mo.)	1.03
1 year or more	7.50	(12-mo.)	0.53

[a] On January 21, 1970, yields (bond-yield equivalents, see footnote 6) were 7.14 per cent on Treasury bills maturing in 30 days, 8.07 per cent on three-month bills, 8.11 per cent on six-month bills, 8.03 per cent on twelve-month bills, and 8.15 per cent on notes maturing in approximately two years (February 1972).

Ceiling rates on time and savings deposits have been changed from time to time during the past 35 years, particularly during the 1960's. Two factors largely responsible for changes during the Sixties were the rising level of market interest rates and the growing importance of large certificates of deposit as a money market instrument. Use of negotiable certificates of deposit as a means of attracting large accumulations of money market funds began in February 1961, when the First National City Bank of New York announced it would offer large denominational negotiable CD's, and the Discount Corporation, a Government securities dealer, announced it would make a market for them.[4] The transferability of these CD's enhanced their desirability as a financial asset.

Changes in ceiling rates have usually been considered and made when ceilings were out of line with market interest rates. However, ceiling rates have sometimes remained out of touch with market conditions.[5] Changes in the structure of ceilings or in the relationship between market rates and the ceilings have, at times, been permitted in order to direct the flow of funds among financial institutions, geographical areas, or sectors of the economy, or to accomplish stabilization objectives.

[4] Helen B. O'Bannon, "Certificates of Deposit," in *Money and Finance: Readings in Theory, Policy, and Institutions,* ed. By Deane Carson (New York: John Wiley and Sons, Inc. 1966), pp. 118–124.

[5] In this article interest rates on Treasury bills and commercial paper are quoted on a bond-yield equivalent (rather than discount) basis to make them comparable to rates on time and savings deposits.

This article has three purposes:

1. to chronicle changes in ceiling rates;

2. to indicate reasons expressed by policymakers for making or dissenting from the changes; and

3. to evaluate the feasibility of achieving intended goals through deposit rate regulations.

Table 2 summarizes changes in the ceiling rates and the reasons behind them.

TABLE 2

REGULATION Q CEILING RATES

Date Effective	Ceiling Rates		Reasons for Ceilings	Dissents
Nov. 1, 1933	All time and savings deposits	3.00%	To prevent interest rate competition which might lead to bank failures.	
Feb. 1, 1935	All time and savings deposits	2.50%	Market rates had been declining. No investments suitable for banks offered ceiling rate. The increasing spread in rates being paid in different areas of the country was considered undesirable.	
Jan. 1, 1936	Savings deposits	2.50%	Market interest rates had been declining; rates offered by banks had been reduced. Time deposits with shorter maturities should earn a lower rate of return.	
	Other time deposits			
	Less than 90 days	1.00		
	90 days–6 months	2.00		
	6 months or longer	2.50		
Jan. 1, 1957	Savings deposits	3.00%	Market interest rates had risen above ceilings. Banks should have greater flexibility in competing for funds.	Robertson: Raising ceilings would impair bank liquidity and solvency as they sought higher yielding assets in order to pay higher rates.
	Other time deposits			
	Less than 90 days	1.00		
	90 days–6 months	2.50		
	6 months or longer	3.00		
Jan. 1, 1962	Savings deposits		To enable banks to attract longer-term savings and permit investment in longer-term assets needed for economic expansion. To enhance freedom of competition and efficiency of allocation. To enable banks to compete for foreign deposits.	King: Rate competition would have adverse effects on many commercial banks without making a significant contribution to solution of the U.S. Balance of Payments deficit, and present savings were adequate for economic expansion.
	Less than 12 months	3.50%		
	12 months or more	4.00		
	Other time deposits			
	Less than 90 days	1.00		
	90 days–6 months	2.50		
	6 months–12 months	3.50		
	12 months or more	4.00		
July 17, 1963	Savings deposits		To avoid outflows of funds to foreign competition. To prevent a run-off of bank time deposits, which might unduly tighten bank credit, given the discount rate increase. To elimnaite bookkeeping efficiency cause by splintered ceiling rates.	
	Less than 12 months	3.50%		
	12 months or more	4.00		
	Other time deposits			
	Less than 90 days	1.00		
	90 days or more	4.00		

TABLE 2 (Continued)

Date Effective	Ceiling Rates		Reasons for Ceilings	Dissents
Nov. 24, 1964	Savings deposits	4.00%	To insure a sufficient flow of funds through banks to finance domestic investment. To avoid outflows of funds to foreign competition. Savings deposits rate was not raised higher because it might then disturb the relationship with rates of other thrift institutions and complicate Treasury financing. A higher rate on short time deposits might compel unwise competition.	Robertson—To the 4 percent ceiling on other time deposits: This increase would aggravate volatility of deposits. Shepardson and Robertson— To a 4 percent ceiling on savings deposits: It was discriminatory to small savers in view of the 4.5 percent rate permitted on some other time deposits.
	Other time deposits			
	Less than 90 days	4.00		
	90 days or more	4.50		
Dec. 6, 1965	Savings deposits	4.00%	To enable banks to attract and retain time deposits and therefore make more effective use of funds already in the economy to finance loan expansion. Market interest rates had risen since November 1964 under demand pressure.	Robertson: It would conflict with credit restraint hoped from the discount rate increase. Larger banks would be able to attract funds from smaller banks which rely on demand and time deposits. It would force smaller banks into higher risk positions.
	Other time deposits	5.50		
July 20, 1966	Savings deposits	4.00%	To help forestall excessive interest rate competiton among financial institutions at a time when monetary policy was aimed at curbing the rate of expansion of bank credit.	
	Other time deposits			
	Multiple maturity			
	30–89 days	4.00		
	90 days or more	5.00		
	Single maturity	5.50		
Sept. 26, 1966	Savings deposits	4.00%	To limit further escalation of interest rates paid in competition for consumer savings. To keep growth of commercial bank credit to a moderate pace.	
	Other time deposits			
	Multiple maturity			
	30–89 days	4.00		
	90 days or more	5.00		
	Single maturity			
	Less than $100,000	5.00		
	$100,000 or more	5.50		
Apr. 19, 1968	Savings deposits	4.00%	To supplement policy measures of monetary restraint. To give banks some leeway to compete for interest sensitive funds. To resist reduction in CD's while not promoting expansion of bank credit.	
	Other time deposits			
	Multiple maturity			
	30–89 days	4.00		
	90 days or more	5.00		
	Single maturity			
	Less than $100,000	5.00		
	$100,000 or more			
	30–59 days	5.50		
	60–89 days	5.75		
	90 days–6 months	6.00		
	More than 6 months	6.25		

TABLE 2 (Continued)

Date Effective	Ceiling Rates		Reasons for Ceilings	Dissents
Jan. 21, 1970	Savings deposits	4.50%	To bring ceilings more in line with Market rates.	
	Other time deposits		To encourage longer-term sav-	
	Multiple maturity		ings in reinforcement of anti-	
	30–89 days	4.50	inflationary measures.	
	90 days or more	5.00	To increase the pool of savings	
	Single maturity		for investment in mortgages.	
	Less than $100,000			
	30 days to 1 year	5.00		
	1 year	5.50		
	2 years	5.75		
	$100,000 or more			
	30–59 days	6.25		
	60–89 days	6.50		
	90–179 days	6.75		
	180 days to 1 year	7.00		
	1 year or more	7.50		

I. EMPHASIS ON PREVENTION OF DESTRUCTIVE COMPETITION

November 1933. As the Federal Reserve Board implemented its authority by adopting Regulation Q on November 1, 1933, the main theme was the prevention of destructive rate competition, which members of the Senate Committee on Banking and Currency, commercial bankers, and others believed to have been one cause of bank failures in earlier years. Possible destructive rate competition was often cited in later years as a reason for objecting to higher ceilings or as a justification for a particular structure of ceiling rates.

The Federal Reserve Board set a 3 per cent maximum rate on all time and savings deposits, effective November 1, 1933. On average for the year, the ceiling was above some short-term market rates, but below the rates apparently being paid on deposits at commercial banks, savings and loan associations, and mutual savings banks. Comparing total time and savings deposits at all commercial banks with interest expense of banks suggests that they were paying an "effective" average rate of 3.4 per cent in 1933. Similar measures for savings and loan associations and mutual savings banks indicate the same rate.[6] Market interest rates on high-grade short-term securities were far below 3 per cent. The three-month Treasury bill rate averaged .53 per cent in 1933, while rates on prime four- to six-month commercial paper averaged 1.77 per cent. The average rate banks charged on commercial loans in New York City fell from a peak of 4.79 per cent in March 1933 to 2.61 per cent in December.

February 1935. In early 1935 the Board lowered the ceiling rate to 2½ percent, accepting a recommendation of the Federal Advisory Council (composed of commercial bankers):

. . . in view of the wide divergence in rates of interest now being paid on

[6] This "effective" rate is calculated by dividing interest expense of all commercial banks by average balance of time and savings deposits for the year, and is a crude, but about the only, measure of rates banks were paying. The deficiencies of this measure are brought out by Albert H. Cox Jr., *op. cit.* p. 37. For one thing, it ignores maturity. For a listing of annual effective yields from 1930 through 1968, see United States Savings and Loan League, *Savings and Loan Fact Book,* 1969, p. 17.

thrift and other time deposits in different sections of the country, and in view of the increasing difficulty of obtaining from suitable investments a yield sufficient to warrant payment of the maximum rate now fixed under provision of Regulation Q of the Federal Reserve Board, it is recommended that the Board give consideration to the advisability of lowering the present maximum rate.

In the opinion of the Council the present rate might well be lowered one-half of one per cent.[7]

January 1936. The Federal Reserve set different rates for time deposits with various maturities as of January 1, 1936, lowering the ceilings on short-term deposits. The maximum rate payable was changed to 1 per cent on time deposits maturing in less than 90 days, and to 2 per cent on those maturing in from 3 to 6 months. The Board stated "... that banks were not justified in paying as high rates of interest for time deposits having shorter maturities in view of their greater availability for withdrawals and therefore that the rates fixed by the Board should be graduated according to maturities.[8] Discussions associated with the change pointed to the general downward trend of interest rates and the fact that many banks were finding it necessary to make further reductions in rates paid depositors because of decreased earnings. This comment suggests that banks were responding rationally to market forces and that any ceiling rate may have been superfluous. The lower ceilings, nevertheless, vindicated bank actions to their depositors.

Those favoring ceilings in order to limit "destructive competition" felt that free competition for deposits would force some banks to offer rates on short-term funds which were out of line with returns obtainable on assets "suitable" for banks to hold. In order to earn a return higher than it was paying on deposits, a bank might accept higher-risk and longer-term assets, thus impairing the liquidity and solvency of that bank and the banking system.

Banks were paying an average effective rate of 3.4 per cent, about twice the rate on prime four- to six-month commercial paper. The rates banks were paying do not appear significantly different from rates they were charging on short-term business loans. It could be argued that banks were offering strongly competitive rates to improve liquidity, which had fallen because of strong demands for currency and liquidity in the rest of the economy. This might be considered corrective behavior, while restraint on competition imposed by ceiling rates simply treated symptoms rather than the cause of the financial crisis.

Regulation Q ceilings do not appear to have encouraged or safeguarded bank liquidity. On the contrary, liquidity, in terms of the ratio of loans to deposits, has often dropped (the ratio rising) during periods when Regulation Q constrained competition for funds. For example, the ratio of loans to total deposits increased from 61.1 per cent in December 1968 to 67.8 per cent in December 1969, a period in which Regulation Q was the primary cause of a $10.7 billion decline in time and savings deposits. Chart 1, a comparison of the spread between the market yield on prime four- to six-month commercial paper and the highest Regulation Q ceiling with bank liquidity ratios, suggests that ceilings, when effective, have had an adverse effect on bank liquidity by forcing a run-off of deposits at the

[7] Federal Reserve Board, *Annual Report,* 1934, p. 203.
[8] Federal Reserve Board, *Annual Report,* 1935, p. 211.

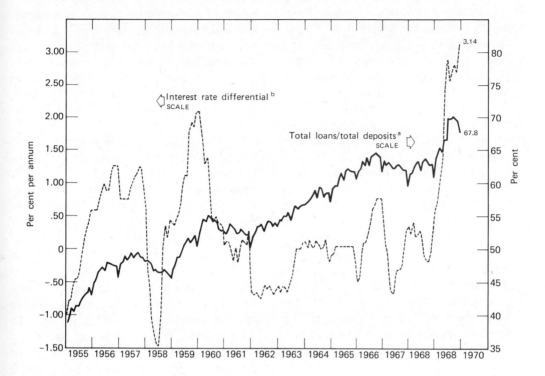

Chart 1. Interest rate differential and bank liquidity.
ᵃ All commercial banks, last Wednesday of the month.
ᵇ The spread between market yields on prime four-to six-month commercial paper, converted to bond-yield equivalent basis, and the maximum rate banks are permitted to pay on any time deposit.

very time when credit demands at banks have been strongest.

II. CEILING RATES RAISED TO PERMIT FREEDOM OF COMPETITION

The ceiling rates remained un-changed for twenty-one years from 1936 to 1957. Market rates, too, were relatively stable until the late Forties. Beginning then, market rates increased somewhat but, in general, remained below the ceilings. Therefore, during the twenty-one year period, Regulation Q ceilings were virtually forgotten by both bankers and public policymakers.

During the late Fifties and early Sixties, market yields rose and interest rate ceilings were raised in actions re-flecting the view that ceilings should be generally in line with market rates.

In deliberations on the changes, pre-vention of undue restriction on compe-tition was emphasized more than was prevention of destructive competition.

January 1957. In the mid-1950's short-term market interest rates rose above Regulation Q ceilings. The aver-age rate on prime four- to six-month commercial paper was 3.41 per cent in 1956; three-month Treasury bills were trading at an average of 2.67 per cent; and savings and loan associations were paying, on average, an "effective" rate of 3 per cent. In contrast, commercial banks were paying an "effective" rate of 1.6 per cent on time and savings deposits, while ceiling rates remained at the 1 to 2.5 per cent levels estab-lished in 1936.

Because banks were not offering competitive yields, time and savings deposits suffered a relative decline. From 1955 to 1956 time and savings deposits increased only 3.3 per cent, compared with a 7.2 per cent average annual rate in the previous four years. Deposits at savings and loan associations and at mutual savings banks rose 15.6 per cent and 6.4 per cent, respectively, during 1956, compared with rates slightly faster in the previous four years.

In view of this situation the rate ceilings on bank time and savings deposits were raised effective January 1, 1957, in order to give banks greater flexibility in competing for funds. The maximum rate payable on time deposits of less than 90 days remained 1 per cent, while rates permitted on other time and savings deposits were raised one-half of one percentage point. The specific reasoning behind the decision was that:

. . . there was insufficient reason to prevent banks, in the exercise of management discretion, from competing actively for time and savings balances by offering rates more nearly in line with other market rates. By increasing the rate limitations only on savings deposits and on time deposits with maturities longer than 90 days, the Board continued to recognize the special thrift character of savings accounts and to preserve a differential between longer-term time deposits and short-term time deposits representing essentially liquid balances.[9]

Governor Robertson voted against the change, going back to arguments presented at the hearings on the Banking Act of 1933. He held that it would increase bank operating costs, making it more difficult for banks to raise addi-

tional capital, that it would make banks seek higher yielding assets and impair the liquidity and solvency of the banking system, and that short-term funds "should be invested in open market paper, so that holders would have to bear the burden and risks of fluctuating rates and not shift that risk to the banking system."[10]

January 1962. In general the Governors took a more favorable attitude toward rate competition, and the ceilings were raised again on January 1, 1962. The change resulted in some further splintering in the classification of time and savings deposits, as the Board distinguished maturities longer than one year from shorter maturities. Ceilings on savings deposits and time deposits with maturities of six to twelve months were raised from 3 per cent to 3.5 per cent, and banks were permitted to offer a rate of 4 per cent on time and savings deposits held for twelve months or longer.

The Board of Governors felt that the resulting flexibility and freedom of competition would be useful for three reasons: (1) it would enhance economic growth; (2) it would contribute to improving the United States balance-of-payments position; and (3) it would have a healthy effect on the management of individual banks. The impact on growth was expected to come through encouraging the flow of bank funds to longer-term assets. "By permitting higher rates to be paid on deposits held for longer periods, the new limits would make it possible for banks to attract long-term savings, in contrast to volatile liquid funds, and thereby give banks greater assurance that they could invest a larger portion of their time deposits in longer-term assets."[11]

---

[9] Federal Reserve Board *Annual Report,* 1956, pp. 52–53.

[10] *Ibid,* pp. 54–55 contain a full statement by Governor Robertson, giving considerable detail on why there should be ceiling rates and why they should not be raised at certain times.

[11] Federal Reserve Board *Annual Report,* 1961, p. 103.

This possible effect on the selection of bank assets was one reason Governor King dissented and Governor Mills questioned the action.

Another reason for raising the ceilings in 1962 was that it would permit competition for foreign deposits "that might otherwise move abroad in search of higher returns, thereby intensifying an outflow of capital or gold to other countries."[12] Balance-of-payments considerations also played a part in subsequent changes of the ceilings. In October 1962, legislation was passed which exempted deposits of foreign governments, and certain international institutions in which the United States was a participant, from the deposit rate ceilings for three years. Exempting legislation and exemption under Regulation Q were renewed in 1965 and 1968.

In discussing competition, most Governors emphasized the desirable rather than the possible destructive effects. They felt that the higher ceilings would "enable each member bank to determine the rates of interest it would pay in light of the conditions prevailing in its area, the type of competition it must meet and its ability to pay."[13] Governor Robertson specifically expressed this thought—urging ceiling rates even higher than many banks might pay, in order to place responsibility for determining rates upon the individual bank. He noted that Regulation Q might impart the unintended and unwanted idea that ceilings indicated what the Federal Reserve thinks banks ought to be paying.[14] This view of competition seems to suggest that the ceilings were not essential in preventing undue concentration of funds and that, as a guide to banks, they may be undesirable.

III. RESERVATION: IMPACT OF HIGHER CEILING RATES ON OTHER SAVINGS INSTITUTIONS AND ON HOUSING

One reservation about freer competition for commercial banks was its possible impact on other savings institutions. Governor Mills voted for the increase in ceilings in 1962, but questioned going above a 3½ per cent maximum, which would retain the usual spread between rates on commercial bank deposits and rates on deposits at other savings institutions.[15] The aggregate "effective" rates paid by both banks and savings and loan associations had continued to rise in the late Fifties and early Sixties. In 1961 savings and loans were paying an average "effective" rate of 3.92 per cent, compared with 2.71 per cent for commercial banks. In 1962, after the ceilings were raised, the rate at banks jumped nearly 50 basis points, compared with a 15 basis point increase at savings and loan associations.

Concern over nonbank thrift institutions has been behind resistance to raising Regulation Q ceilings at least since 1962. It has been argued by many, including those associated with savings and loan associations and mutual savings banks, that, because these institutions enhance the availability of credit for housing, they should be given an advantage in the competition for consumer-type savings.

While it is important that there be an optimal flow of funds into the construction of housing, it should be considered whether regulation of bank interest rates accomplishes this goal, and whether this method involves costs which could be avoided.

The examples of 1966 and 1969,

---

[12] *Ibid*, p. 102.
[13] *Ibid*, p. 102.
[14] *Ibid*, p. 104.
[15] *Ibid*, p. 103.

when interest rate ceilings effectively prevented both banks and other thrift institutions from competing for funds, seem to suggest that the ceilings alone cannot accomplish an optimal flow of funds into housing. From May to November 1966, growth of deposits at savings and loan associations was only a 2.3 per cent annual rate compared with an 11 per cent rate in the previous 4½ years. In the last half of 1969 the increase was at a 1.6 per cent rate, compared with 5.4 per cent in the previous year.

It has sometimes been argued that because savings and loan associations invest in longer-term assets than banks, they cannot adjust so easily as banks to changes in interest rates. Therefore, without differential ceiling rates, held stable even when market rates vary, savings and loan associations could not operate profitably. However, longer-term assets only imply that a savings and loan association requires a relatively large amount of reserves in order to pay a higher rate on deposits than the average rate earned on assets during a period of transition. As savings and loan associations adjust the rates charged on loans, they should be able to restore a workable relation between interest expense and interest earnings.[16]

Inability to attract and retain deposited funds is potentially as dangerous to savings and loan associations as is paying higher rates in the short-run than they are able to earn. During 1969, Government agencies tried to supplement savings and loan sources of funds by selling securities in the capital market at competitive rates and lending the proceeds to savings and loan associations. As a result savings and loan associations pay the higher competitive yield only on marginal funds, with fewer funds directed away from the housing market because of the rate ceilings than in 1966.

It appears that the interest rate ceilings have not accomplished the goal of encouraging housing. In fact, they probably have made credit for housing more difficult to obtain. On the other hand, they have encouraged the Government to protect a specific set of institutions and to provide services which regulations hinder private markets from providing.

IV. CHANGES IN CEILING RATES TO INFLUENCE GROWTH OF BANK CREDIT

Beginning with the change of ceilings in 1963, the influence of Regulation Q on the growth of bank credit has gradually become the focus in discussions of changing ceilings. The flow of deposits into banks is one factor influencing the ability of banks to expand loans and investments. The relation of interest rate ceilings to market rates is, in turn, an important factor influencing the amount of time and savings deposits which banks are able to attract. Therefore, through its influence on bank credit, Regulation Q has come to be considered a major tool of monetary stabilization policy.

July 1963. The change which took place in July 1963 raised the ceiling rates on all time deposits held longer than 90 days to 4 per cent, eliminating some of the previous splintering in the rates. While the balance-of-payments was cited as the primary reason for the change, Governor Robertson, who dissented from the concurrent discount rate increase in ceilings was necessary to offset any restrictive impact of the discount rate increase on bank credit.[17]

[16] See Norman N. Bowsher and Lionell Kalish, "Does Slower Monetary Expansion Discriminate Against Housing? in the June 1968 issue of this *Review,* also available as Reprint No. 29.

[17] Federal Reserve Board, *Annual Report,* 1963, pp. 39–40.

November 1964. In November 1964 ceiling rates were raised again, after some further increases in market interest rates and in conjunction with a discount rate increase to 4 per cent. The action adjusted the maximum rate on time deposits held less than 90 days from 1 per cent to 4 per cent, while raising that on longer maturities to 4.5 per cent. The differential ceiling rates on savings deposits were also eliminated by permitting a rate of 4 per cent on any savings deposit held longer than 30 days.

The principal reasons for raising the ceilings were to insure a sufficient flow of funds through banks to finance domestic investment and to avoid an outflow of funds which might worsen the balance-of-payments deficit. Again, Governor Robertson thought that some change in the maximum interest rates permitted under Regulation Q was warranted by the need to prevent a run-off of time deposits. He dissented from raising the ceiling to 4 per cent on time deposits with maturities less than 90 days, however, because he expected it to "encourage the replacement of maturing certificates of deposit with new certificates of shorter original maturities, thus aggravating bank deposit volatility and pressures upon bank liquidity positions.[18]

Both Governor Robertson and Governor Shepardson thought that a 4.5 per cent maximum on savings deposits would be appropriate in that it would treat small savers more equitably. The majority of the Board of Governors, however, felt a 4 per cent rate would preserve the prevailing relationship between rates paid on savings deposits by commercial banks and those paid by savings institutions such as mutual savings banks and savings and loan associations, whereas a higher ceiling might encourage unwise competition and possible complicate Treasury financing problems.[19]

December 1965. In December 1965 an increase in ceiling rates was intended to permit some continued orderly expansion in bank credit while other policy instruments exercised restraint. The maximum rate payable on time deposits, regardless of maturity, was raised to 5.5 per cent, while the ceiling on savings deposits remained 4 per cent. The discount rate was again raised—this time to 4.5 per cent. Most of the discussion reported concerned the discount rate action and the majority view that monetary policy should move promptly against inflationary credit expansion, at a time when market rates had been rising under demand pressures, resource-use had been intensifying, and the pace of Government expenditures was accelerating.

The increase in Regulation Q ceiling rates was intended to help stabilize the growth of bank time deposits and thereby permit banks to make more effective use of funds than when they are uncertain about retaining deposits. The general idea that regulated rates should be in line with market rates is reflected in the statement: "In addition, a pattern of interest rates that was accepted by borrowers and lenders as fully reflecting market forces should, it was thought, add assurance of a smooth flow of funds to all sectors of the economy."[20]

Governor Robertson, however, dissented on the grounds that the increase in ceilings would conflict with the credit restraint hoped for from the discount rate increase. The alternative action he suggested was to dampen bank issu-

[18] Federal Reserve Board, *Annual Report,* 1964, p. 48.
[19] *Ibid,* p. 48.
[20] Federal Reserve Board, *Annual Report,* 1965, pp. 64–65.

ance of promissory notes by defining them as deposits, while maintaining the current discount rate and interest rate ceilings on deposits. He also felt that higher ceilings would shift deposits from smaller to larger banks or force smaller banks into higher-risk assets.[21]

July 1966. The ceiling rate structure of 4 per cent on savings deposits and 5.5 per cent on time deposits lasted little more than six months. In July 1966 the Board of Governors took two actions influencing ceiling rates. For one thing they lowered the ceiling rate on multiple maturity deposits. A multiple maturity deposit was distinguished from single maturity as one: (1) payable at the depositor's option on more than one date; or (2) payable after written notice; or (3) subject to automatic renewal at maturity. Maximum rates on multiple maturity deposits were lowered to 5 per cent if held more than 90 days and to 4 per cent if held only 30–89 days. This lowering of rates was intended to inhibit competition between banks and thrift institutions "at a time when monetary policy was aimed at curbing the expansion of bank credit."[22]

The other action was to recommend legislation to facilitate distinction between consumer-type deposits and money market CD's. The Board considered the previous action of defining multiple maturity deposits only a partial attempt at this. They recommended that Congress broaden the authority of the Federal Reserve by allowing them to distinguish deposits by amount in regulating rates, and that it extend similar authority to the Federal Home Loan Bank Board to determine maximum rates at savings and loan associations.

September 1966. Public Law 89-597, passed September 1966, permitted time deposits under $100,000 to be treated differently from larger ones in regu-

lating maximum rates and authorized national regulation of maximum rates paid by savings and loan associations and mutual savings banks. On the same day the law was signed, the maximum rate on any time deposit less than $100,000 (excluding passbook savings deposits) was set at 5 per cent. Like the previous reduction, this one was intended to limit rate increases caused by competition for household savings, and to keep the growth of bank credit at a moderate pace.[23]

During 1966 market interest rates continued their upward trend, culminating in the so-called "credit crunch." Yields on prime four- to six-month commercial paper reached 6.11 per cent and yields on three-month Treasury bills reached 5.08 per cent in August 1966. Rates paid at banks and savings and loan associations were not competitive with these other market instruments. As a result, the growth of time and savings deposits slowed substantially. In early 1967 market interest rates subsided somewhat, financial institutions could again attract funds, and growth of deposits quickly moved to the previous rapid trends.

April 1968. In the spring of 1968, market interest rates climbed into the range at which ceilings prevented banks from competing for funds as effectively as before. In April the ceiling rates on large denomination CD's were raised "in order to give banks some leeway to compete for interest-sensitive funds." Rates on single maturity CD's in denominations larger than $100,000 were raised to 5.75 per cent if held 60 to 89 days, to 6 per cent if held 90 days to 6 months, and to 6.25 per cent if held longer than 6 months. Ceiling rates on other time deposits were not raised; the resulting structure was considered sufficient to resist the

[21] *Ibid,* p. 70.
[22] Federal Reserve Board, *Annual Report,* 1966, pp. 97–98.
[23] Federal Reserve Board, *Annual Report,* 1966, pp. 104–106.

run-off of CD's, while not promoting expansion of bank credit.[24]

1969. While the relationship between ceiling rates and market interest rates changed significantly in 1969, no change was made in ceiling rates. For example, the spread between yields on four- to six-month commercial paper and the ceiling rate on three- to six-month CD's was over 3 percentage points at the end of 1969. Prior to the last time ceiling rates were raised, in 1968, the spread was about one-half of one percentage point. As a result of the change in relative yields, by December 1969 banks had lost over half of the $24 billion in CD's held in December 1968. Other time and savings deposits, savings and loan capital, and mutual savings bank deposits also stopped increasing or increased at substantially slower rates than in 1968.

Bank credit increased only 2.5 per cent in 1969, after rising 11 per cent in 1968. This slowing was due partly to slower growth of the monetary base and partly due to the impact of Regulation Q.

January 1970. The disintermediation in 1969 led to an upward revision in the ceiling rates effective January 21. The maximum rate on bank savings deposits became 4.5 per cent. Small certificates (less than $100,000) are now permitted to yield 5.50 per cent if they mature in one year, and 5.75 per cent if they mature in two years. The ceiling on each maturity classification of large CD's was raised ¾ of a percentage point, and a new classification, large CD's maturing in a year or more, is permitted to yield 7.50 per cent.

The changes were made to bring the structure of ceiling rates ". . . somewhat more in line with going yields on market securities," to permit a more equitable rate on small savings, and ". . . to encourage longer-term savings

in reinforcement of anti-inflationary measures." Along with these reasons was the belief that higher rates on savings at institutions would increase the amount of funds available for mortgages. On the following day the Federal Home Loan Bank Board raised the maximum rates savings and loan associations are permitted to pay.

There was no explicit mention of bank credit in the press release which announced the change. However, it was pointed out that:

The revisions in the Board's Regulation Q ceiling rates were held to moderate size, so as not to foster sudden and large movements of funds into the banking system that could cause distortions in traditional financial flows or lead to an upsurge in bank lending.

During the Sixties the idea that Regulation Q is a major instrument for controlling bank credit became the predominant rationale behind the structure of the ceilings. Implicit in this view was the importance of bank credit as a target variable in monetary stabilization policy. It does appear reasonable that the growth of spending in the economy, and that appropriate stabilization policy during a period of excessive spending would be restricting the growth of bank credit. It should be recognized, however, that there are alternative channels through which funds flow from savers to borrowers.

Savers, who are discouraged from putting their funds in banks or other thrift institutions because of low yields, have had alternative, higher earning assets available. Therefore, any slowing in the growth of bank deposits and hence bank credit, which is caused by restricting competition, is probably offset by a rise in the flow of funds through unregulated markets, leaving

---

[24] Federal Reserve Board, *Annual Report,* 1968, pp. 69–70.

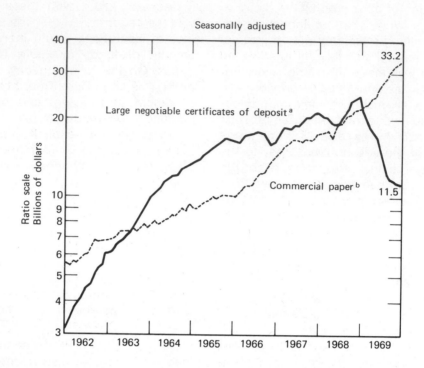

Seasonally adjusted

Chart 2. Certificates of Deposits and commercial paper, outstanding volume.
a Large commercial banks, last Wednesday of the month figures, seasonally adjusted by the Federal Reserve Bank of St. Louis.
b Seasonally adjusted by the Federal Reserve Bank of New York, end of month figures.
Latest data plotted: December.

the growth of total credit unaffected. In 1969, for example, at the same time that the outstanding volume of large negotiable CD's declined $13 billion, the outstanding volume of commercial paper increased by $11.5 billion. A stronger demand by individuals for small denomination ($1,000 and $5,000) Treasury bills also developed, as savers sought higher returns than banks were permitted to pay.

The impact of Regulation Q has encouraged banks to find nondeposit sources of funds. During the past two years, they found supplemental sources of funds in the sale of commercial paper by bank subsidiaries and holding companies and in Euro-dollar transactions. The channelling of dollars through Europe to avoid interest rate restrictions increased the cost and dis-

tance of flows of funds and led to new regulations imposing reserve requirements on such borrowing. Regulations concerning the sale of commercial paper are pending, while commercial banks continue to seek ways to avoid the discriminatory impact of Regulation Q.

V. SUMMARY AND CONCLUSIONS

The Banking Act of 1933 authorized the Federal Reserve Board to establish maximum rates which banks may pay for funds. In November of that year, the Federal Reserve Board adopted Regulation Q, which imposed a ceiling rate of 3 per cent on member bank time and savings deposits. The action was taken to help avoid unwise competition among banks and its detrimental effects on the soundness of banks. This reason has gradually received less attention.

While the ceilings have been raised on occasion in order to permit some competition for funds, changes in the spreads between the ceiling rates and market rates sometimes have been allowed to occur with the intention of increasing the flow of funds toward nonbank thrift institutions or influencing the growth of bank credit. The primary justification for the current structure of Regulation Q ceilings has been its presumed control on bank credit for purposes of economic stabilization. Given this goal, the adverse impact of Regulation Q ceilings on bank liquidity at certain times has probably been intended. However, Regulation Q cannot control total credit in the economy, since funds leaving bank time deposits are channelled through unregulated markets or return to banks through nondeposit sources of funds.

Though the growth of total credit probably is unaffected by Regulation Q, the allocation of credit is affected. At times when ceilings restrict the amount of funds available to financial intermediaries, borrowers in the unregulated markets are able to obtain funds more cheaply than if all markets were freely competitive, while borrowers who rely on banks or other thrift institutions are forced to pay a higher price or may find funds simply unavailable. The situation is analogous for savers. Holders of large amounts of liquid funds with knowledge of capital markets can receive the highest return available, while those who must rely on regulated institutions to hold and accumulate savings receive a lower return than if banks were free to compete.

It appears that interest rate restrictions on financial intermediaries impose inequities on our economy, discriminating against housing, small savers, and the regulated financial institutions. They encourage inefficiencies as banks try to reroute funds, intermediaries try to compete through premiums, and Government agencies have to find both new regulations and ways to ease the burden on those most severely hurt. It further appears that interest rate restrictions are of little consequence in the control of total credit or total spending in the economy. At the same time, there is no evidence that the absence of Regulation Q would be detrimental to the equity of the economy, the solvency of the banking system, or the control of total spending.

PART 4

MONETARY THEORY

READING 25

ON THE CONTENT AND ISSUES OF CURRENT MONETARY ECONOMICS*

Richard Zecher

I. INTRODUCTION

What makes the study of money so interesting is the apparent paradoxes surrounding its creation and use. In one sense it is only a veil obscuring what *really* is happening. Yet it is real in the sense that people derive utility from it—they are willing to give up goods and services to hold money—and firms derive productive services from it—they are willing to reduce other assets to hold money. While money is real in the sense that it yields utility and productive services, fiat money, such as dollar bills in the United States, can be produced by the government at essentially zero cost. Now if the government could produce cars, education, or any other good at zero cost, it would be socially desirable for it to do so—to the point where additional amounts of these goods would not make anyone any happier. Unfortunately, only money can be produced at

zero social cost. Noting this, some governments, whether from altruistic or other motives, have greatly increased the supplies of fiat money at zero cost by simply printing bigger numbers on the new currency. Paradoxically, the result of this policy was to *reduce* the quantity of money services, both per dollar bill and in total, accruing to each individual and firm.

Monetary theory addresses itself to these and to other problems surrounding the creation of, and economic behavior toward, money. This article is divided into six sections. In section II money is viewed as an asset in the portfolios of individuals and firms. This discussion is centered on the description of portfolio equilibrium, determinants of marginal expected rates of return on money and other assets, and the effects of various changes on prices and rates of return. Section III deals

* Editor's note: This discussion is an original contribution to this volume.

with the production of nominal money balances in the United States, or the theory of money supply. In this section the definition of money is quite explicit. In the rest of the article, however, unless otherwise indicated, the term money refers only to government fiat money, and not to commodity money or commercial bank deposit money. In section IV we take a closer look at the relationship between portfolio equilibrium and expenditure flows, and particularly at the implications of this relationship for the flow of real income, the rate of unemployment, and the price level. In section V there is an attempt to explain, in terms of the theory, some of the obvious and important differences of opinion among economists concerning the conduct of monetary policy, and the general importance of money in determining income, employment, and prices.

II. DEMAND FOR REAL MONEY BALANCES

Modern monetary theory treats the demand for money much like the demand for any other asset in an individual's or firm's portfolio. Given the size of the portfolio, assets are adjusted so that the expected return from an additional dollars worth of any asset in the portfolio is identical. If an individual holds two assets A_1 and A_2, and the expected return on an additional dollars worth of A_1 exceeds that for A_2, then he will expand his holdings of A_1 and diminish his holdings of A_2. For reasons that we will go into shortly, these actions will reduce the marginal expected return (MER) from A_1 and increase MER for A_2. When the individual has adjusted his portfolio so that the MER is equal for A_1 and A_2, his portfolio is efficient. Efficiency here means that our individual, given the size of his portfolio, could not increase his flow of income by further adjustments.

Even if the individual has an efficient

portfolio, it may not be of optimal size. To understand this we introduce the concept of internal rate of discount. For each individual, given his income-generating potential (or simply his wealth), there exists an internal rate of discount (IRD) that expresses the rate of exchange between present and future goods that would leave him indifferent. An IRD $= 5\%$ means that the individual is indifferent between one unit of good X today and 1.05 X in the next period. If he were given the opportunity to exchange one X today for 1.1 X tomorrow he would make the exchange, and if he were offered one X tomorrow for one X today, he would reject the exchange. In fact, this second offer would cause him to make the counter offer of paying anything up to 1.05X tomorrow in exchange for one X today. So long as the rate at which individuals can exchange present for future consumption (MER) differs from the rate at which they are indifferent between present and future consumption (IRD), individuals will continue to adjust their consumption patterns. If MER exceeds IRD, then individuals will reduce current consumption in order to obtain future consumption (they will save), and if IRD exceeds MER they will dissave or consume part of their wealth. In the process of changing portfolio size each individual will change his MER and IRD in opposite directions, and adjustments will cease when IRD $=$ MER.

Having defined a portfolio that is efficient and of optimal size, it remains to specify the determinants of MER and IRD. For each individual the MER for additional amounts of any asset may be thought to consist of two parts, a pecuniary return and a nonpecuniary return. Examples of pecuniary returns are the expected interest yield of bonds, dividend yield of equities, and wage yield from human capital. (For the moment we shall ignore any expected changes in either relative prices or the general price level.) Two types of nonpecuniary yields are of particular importance here. One rationalizes diversified portfolios in the presence of unequal expected pecuniary returns, and the other rationalizes the fact that money is held in portfolios even though its pecuniary return is lower than on other assets, and frequently even negative.

Looking only at pecuniary yields, it is clear that most portfolios do not have the property that an additional dollar of any asset will yield the same expected *pecuniary* yield. Professor Tobin explains this phenomena through individuals' behavior toward risk. He notes the statistical property that, in the presence of randomly and independently changing relative asset prices and yields, a portfolio containing only one asset is subject to more short-run fluctuations in value than one composed of two or more assets. Thus, given the choice of two portfolios with the same expected pecuniary yield, individuals will in general prefer a diversified portfolio to a single-asset portfolio. This is consistent with the notion that individuals are generally risk-averse.

Averting risk probably accounts for a considerable fraction of the expected nonpecuniary yields of assets. Particularly in adding the first few units of some asset to a portfolio, the expected (risk-averting) nonpecuniary returns may be very large relative to the expected pecuniary returns. As more units are added, the expected nonpecuniary returns *from risk aversion* diminish. This phenomena explains how an individual facing fixed pecuniary yields in the market can affect his MER for each asset by changing the quantity held of that asset. The efficient portfolio, as before, is one in which MER, including expected nonpecuniary returns, is the same for each asset in the portfolio.

Risk aversion rationalizes much of observed portfolio behavior, but as defined above it is surely a minor source of nonpecuniary returns to money. Such returns are associated with the property that money is widely used in transactions in many markets. This property makes money an inexpensive source of information about relative prices, and an inexpensive way to transact when all transactions cannot be foreseen with certainty. To select an efficient portfolio, the individual must have correct information about all relative prices (including relative prices of present and future goods). No one collects all that information in a changing economy because it is too costly. However, more information can be obtained for the same outlay if some goods are more efficient in producing this information than are others. In addition, the fact that money exchanges on many markets tends to make it a good abode of generalized purchasing power to draw on in the event of unexpected opportunities or crises.

Firms, like individuals, have portfolios containing many assets and including money. Portfolio equilibrium for firms similarly consists of adjusting to a position where the MER for each asset in the portfolio is the same (efficiency of production), and to where the portfolio is of optimal size (scale of production). The firm, however, is not guided to optimal size by the relationship between IRD and MER, but rather by the relationship between the MER of the firm (same for all assets in the efficient portfolio) and the marginal expected rate of raising new capital (the expected cost of borrowing or of issuing equities, which should be the same). Nonpecuniary returns are definitionally the same for firms as for individuals, except that the flow of services from money held by firms is a factor of production instead of a final consumption good.

This brief description of efficient and optimal portfolios specifies that money is held, like any other asset, because it yields a flow of utility or productive services. *The amount of money demanded, like the amount of any other asset demanded, depends on marginal expected yields (efficiency) and on portfolio size or wealth (optimal scale).*

An additional and very important property of the theory is that it makes real balances, not the number of pieces of paper in circulation, yield the utility and productive services. This follows from the description of money as a form of *generalized purchasing power,* with a yield determined mainly by its ability to effect transactions now or in the future, expected or unexpected, more efficiently than any other asset. Thus utility and productive services flow from real and not nominal balances.

Changes in yields and relative prices affect the amount of real money services demanded even for a given level of wealth. One particularly important relative price for money demand is the own price, that is, the price of money in terms of goods, or *simply the inverse of the general price level.*

III. CAUSES AND EFFECTS OF CHANGES IN THE GENERAL PRICE LEVEL, AND A DISAGREEMENT ABOUT THE BEST RATE OF PRICE CHANGE

Assume that a nonchanging economy satisfies the general equilibrium conditions described in section II, and that nothing will change this equilibrium except at our command. What could be changed to make the general-price-level rise (the relative price of money in terms of all other assets fall)? Let asset number one, A_1, be real money balances, and let the marginal expected return on A_2 rise for each individual and firm in the economy. Portfolios are now out of equilibrium because the MER on A_2 exceeds that on any other asset. For simplicity, consider the adjustment to new equilibrium for

the case of only two assets, A_1 and A_2. Individuals and firms will attempt to adjust by increasing their holdings of A_2. Each economic unit will believe that he can reduce his holdings of money (A_1) by increasing his expenditures on A_2, but since the number of units of currency is fixed and someone has to hold the existing currency, the economy as a whole cannot change its holdings of nominal money. What happens is that the price level, the price of A_2 in this example, rises. A rising price level means falling *real* money balances and increasing MER of real money balances. Eventually the MER for A_1 and A_2 will be equal at a higher price level and a lower level of real balances. In the longer run portfolios will be expanded, both A_1 and A_2, to bring the new, higher MER into line with the IRD.

A disturbance to the system that will result in price-level increases can be imposed by changing the nominal quantity of money. For the moment assume that this money is simply dropped from airplanes and that everyone receives an amount proportional to his previous cash balance. The immediate results are that (1) everyone is wealthier because he has his previous portfolio plus the new (real) cash balances, and (2) everyone is in portfolio disequilibrium because larger real cash balances mean a lower MER on cash balances, and all other MERs are unchanged. In the process of attempting to reduce money holdings by spending at a faster rate, prices rise and real balances fall. Ultimately real balances return to their previous level, and all real magnitudes are unchanged.

Changes in the nominal money stock would receive considerable attention as a source of price change even if it were proved not to be the major cause of price changes. This is because, unlike MERs, it is easy to measure and easy to control (by the monetary authorities, as discussed in section IV). However, the evidence runs in the other direction. Every major recorded price inflation or deflation has been accompanied by major changes in nominal money in the same direction. The implication is clear. To avoid major price upheavals, avoid major monetary upheavals. For minor price changes of less than two or three percent per year, many other factors, such as the first change in MER considered above or even measurement error, become important.

The welfare aspects of price changes were discussed in considerable detail by John Maynard Keynes in his *Tract on Monetary Reform* (1924). He concluded at that time, after the major price changes during and following World War I, that the best monetary policy would be one that kept prices more or less constant. Two modern theories, however, disagree with this policy prescription. The neo-Keynesian theory, rationalizing an empirical relationship between prices and unemployment first discovered by Phillips, argues that an increasing price level will reduce unemployment and increase welfare. A very different argument, forwarded by Milton Friedman, is that a decreasing price level will increase real balances, hence wealth, hence welfare.

One argument rationalizing the Phillips-curve relationship is that increasing prices and money wages reflect excess demand in the commodity sector. Since output (and hence welfare) is demand determined over a large range, say up to full employment, in the Keynesian system, excess commodity demand and rising prices cause increases in demand for labor and falling unemployment. Friedman's argument is quite different. He observes that changes in the price level constitute an important return or cost of holding real money balances. Inflation increases this cost

and causes individuals to reduce their real money demanded, and deflation reduces this cost, or increases the return, and causes an increase in real money demanded. In an economy with only fiat money it costs nothing to produce or destroy nominal money, so the increase in real-money balances, wealth, and welfare costs no real resources. This is one of the unusual "free good" cases in economic analysis.

To a large extent these two arguments may be reconciled by treating one as applying to the short run, and the other to the long run. In this context the Phillips curve argues for an inflationary policy that gains employment and welfare in the short run at the expense of reduced real money balances in the long run (this assumes that in the long run unemployment is determined not by price change, but by the underlying "real" conditions such as the production function and capital stock). Friedman's argument suggests the alternative policy of price decline to gain wealth and welfare in the long run at the expense of higher but temporary unemployment in the short run. This is only one of many examples where the period of analysis leads to very different results. Several other issues in monetary economies that arise partly because of differences in the analytical period will be discussed in a later section.

IV. PRODUCTION OF NOMINAL MONEY IN THE UNITED STATES

The production of nominal money balances has been analyzed most extensively by Friedman, and Schwartz, and Brunner and Meltzer. Their analytical framework begins by dividing the economy into three behavioral groups, commercial banks, monetary authorities, and firms and individuals. Each of these groups, in turn, has a dominant influence on certain aspects of the money creation process. One version of the single-equation money-supply hypothesis is developed here.

$$M = C + D + T \qquad (1)$$

where C, D, T, and M are currency, demand deposits, time deposits, and total money holding of the *public*.

$$B = C + R \qquad (2)$$

where R and B are total member bank reserves and total non-interest-bearing debt of the monetary authorities to the public.

$$\frac{M}{B} = \frac{C + D + T}{C + R} \qquad (3)$$

$$\text{or } M = \left(\frac{C/D + 1 + T/D}{C/D + R/D} \right) B$$

The ratios C/D, T/D, and R/D are behavioral parameters. Determination of behavioral parameters C/D and T/D is dominated by demands of the public, R/D by demands of commercial banks, and B by the monetary authorities. A brief discussion of what affects these variables will clarify how the interaction of the three classes of economic actors determines the nominal money stock. For each individual and firm there is some decomposition of nominal money holdings into C, D, and T that equalize the marginal expected return MER for all three forms of money. Furthermore, whether or not actual total money holdings are equal to desired total money holdings, the decomposition into C, D, and T can be in equilibrium with equal MER. Anything that affects the MER of C, D, and T, such as changes in service costs or interest payments on deposits, will cause adjustments in the composition of money holdings. This adjustment will affect the ratios C/D and T/D and hence the stock of *nominal* money balances in a way is obvious from equation 3.

The value of R/D is the result of profit-maximizing behavior by commercial banks in producing money services. View the bank's output as the flow of money services to the public associated with the stock of demand deposits D, and one of the production inputs as the flow of money services to banks associated with the stock of reserves R. A major portion of the cost of money-service inputs is the opportunity cost of foregone interest. That is, since reserves do not yield interest payments and other bank assets do yield interest payments, each dollar of reserves held has an opportunity cost equal to the interest rate. If the yield on earning assets rises, banks may be expected to produce a given D with fewer reserves and more of some or all other inputs.

A major portion of the expected yield of reserves (in production of D) is associated with expected deposit flows. If deposit flows are expected to become more variable, and if this increases the marginal productivity of reserves, then more reserves will be held per dollar of deposits. An extreme case is when a bank expects a run on its deposits, and desires more reserves per dollar of deposits.

Technically, banks can make R/D take a wide range of values. They can reach a desired R/D by selling earning assets (R/D rises) or buying earning assets (R/D falls). As an empirical observation, banks generally choose to hold R/D close to the minimum required reserve ratio imposed on member banks by the Federal Reserve System. A notable exception was the middle and late 1930s when R/D was well above the legal minimum. The interest opportunity cost of holding reserves in that period was low by historical standards, and it is likely that the expected yield, given the traumatic monetary events of 1929–1933, was very high. Also in the late 1930s the inflow of R was too rapid to be immediately absorbed as output.

Once the public has adjusted to desired values for C/D and T/D and banks have attained their desired R/D, it remains only for the monetary authorities to set B for the nominal stock of money to be determined. One set of actions by monetary authorities that affects B includes conditions under which deposits will be accepted, mechanics of check clearing, conditions for buying and selling gold, and conditions for making loans to member banks and others. These are passive policy actions because their effect on B depends on how the rest of the world responds. Active monetary policy actions concern the open-market portfolio of the monetary authority. By selling or buying interest-bearing government debt in exchange for non-interest-bearing government debt, the monetary authorities directly affect B and can move B to any desired positive level.

The modern money-supply theory outlined above summarizes how, in the current U.S. economy, the interaction of the public, commercial banks, and monetary authorities determine nominal money supply. Individuals and firms choose efficient and optimal portfolios, banks maximize profits in money production, and monetary authorities choose a level of base money B. It should be clear that very similar theories can be constructed for other definitions of money such as currency, currency plus demand deposits, currency plus total bank deposits plus savings and loan shares, and the like.

Before leaving money-supply theory, it should be noted that the decision criteria to be used by monetary authorities in choosing a level or rate of change for B continues to be a subject of debate. Some argue that interest rates are the best indicator of the thrust of monetary policy. High and rising interest rates by this argument reflect excess demand for money and indicate that nominal money-stock expansion is

appropriate policy. Others argue that interest rates are likely to be misleading indicators of the effect of changes in money on rates of expenditures. A much more reliable indicator, they argue, is the rate of growth of monetary aggregates, where rapid growth indicates expansive policy and slow growth indicates restrictive policy. Unfortunately, it frequently happens that both interest rates and money stocks are either rising or falling together. In these cases monetary policy will move in the wrong direction if it chooses the wrong indicator (only one of them can be giving correct information).

V. HOW MONEY AND OTHER THINGS AFFECT EXPENDITURES AND UNEMPLOYMENT

Macro economic policies are designed to achieve high levels of expenditures and employment along with a stable price level. In section III the effects on prices of changes in the nominal money stock, and other changes affecting relative marginal expected returns on assets, were derived from the model. In order to affect the price level, changes in nominal money or other shocks to the system have to change rates of expenditures according to this model. This section is concerned with these expenditure flows, and in particular with their response to various shocks, including changes in nominal money supply.

To facilitate this discussion, we continue to assume an economy that is not growing. Loosely speaking, we assume no changes in utility or production functions and no change in population. The starting point for this discussion is one of complete equilibrium as described in sections II and III. Two shocks are introduced into this system: (1) a decrease in the marginal expected yield on real capital and (2) a decrease in the nominal stock of money. The focus of the discussion is on how these shocks affect the flow of expenditures and the rate of unemployment.

At the outset each individual's portfolio is efficient and of optimal size. Thus, each individual consumes all of the nonpecuniary (service) flows and pecuniary flows from his portfolio, and neither saves nor dissaves. Firms have efficient and optimal size portfolios, maximize profits, and operate in competitive markets.

The first shock introduced is a decrease in the marginal expected yield on real capital. Little is known about the formation of expected yields, but it seems clear that such a change might derive from a variety of different sources, including actual or expected changes in government policies or change in consumer preferences. The initial effect of a reduced MER for real capital is to cause portfolio disequilibrium. Individuals and firms desire to reduce their holdings of real capital and thus will act to increase its MER, and to increase their holdings of all other assets. If it is assumed that these transactions proceed very rapidly after the initial change in MER is perceived, then the main effect is to lower the price of the existing real capital stock (raise its MER) and to raise the price of all other existing assets (lower their yields). In fact, we will assume that these prices adjust instantaneously to the levels where MER on all assets are once again equalized.

The new equilibrium point for portfolios is characterized by a lower price for the existing stock of capital. With nothing else changed, this lowers the price of existing capital goods relative to their new supply price, and hence decreases demand for new capital goods. If input prices in the capital-goods industry are not flexible downwards (in the short run), then production of new capital goods will be cut

back and unemployment will rise. The other side of this coin is that the prices of existing stocks of all other assets have risen relative to their new supply prices. If industries producing these (noncapital) assets can expand production by hiring the workers and capital released from capital goods production, the effect on total expenditure flows and unemployment should be small or zero. However, to the extent that resources are not perfectly mobile, at least part of the increased demand for new assets other than real capital goods will be accommodated by price rises. This is certainly true of the increased demand for real balances, which is accommodated by the change in the price level and absorbs no real resources.

The important feature of this adjustment process is that the lower MER on real capital led to a lowering of the price of existing capital goods relative to their new supply price, and the resulting decreased flow demand for new capital led to a contraction in new capital-goods production and in employment. We can call this the Tobin mechanism relating the prices of existing stocks of assets and the new supply prices of assets to the rate of production of new assets and employment.

If the system is shocked by changes in nominal money supply instead of changes in MER, the sequence of events is altered little. A decreased stock of nominal *and real* balances initially increases the MER for real-balances. Prices of nonmoney assets fall and the price of money, the inverse of the price level, rises. As before, the Tobin mechanism operates to reduce flow demand for new assets and results in reduced production and increased unemployment.

These events take place in what can be termed the intermediate—run period. In the long run, involuntary unemployment must disappear if all prices are flexible. But the long run can be a period of several years if the shocks to the system are sufficiently large, so this intermediate-run period becomes one of great importance to policy-makers.

VI. SOME ISSUES IN CURRENT MONETARY ANALYSIS

It would take something less than an astute observer to note that eminent economists have strong disagreements about the proper conduct of monetary policy and about the general importance of monetary phenomena for income, prices, and employment. Assume that these economists agree with the general outlines of the portfolio theory developed in sections II, III, and IV. Specifically, assume that they agree (1) that the equilibrium conditions set out are in fact valid equilibrium conditions, (2) that changes in nominal money supply affect marginal expected yields, relative prices of assets, and flows of expenditures as described above, and (3) that changes in taxing policy, government expenditures, population growth, technological changes, consumer preference changes, and the like, can all be analyzed from a portfolio point of view, and their effects on marginal expected yields, relative asset prices, and flows of expenditures similarly derived. Even with agreement on all of these basic points, it is still possible to have strong disagreements about the appropriate conduct of monetary policy and about the importance of monetary shocks on income, employment, and the price level. One way to see this is to examine various positions taken by participants in monetary debates. In setting out these representative positions, I have relied on testimony by economists before various Congressional committees, and other public statements, as well as professional papers.

Consider first the issues surrounding determination of the general price level. From our model it was seen that any change affecting the marginal expected return for any asset would affect demand for real-money balances and, with a fixed nominal stock of money, the price level. Actual or expected changes in taxing or government expenditures, technology, consumer preferences, or foreign relations, among many other things, would affect marginal expected returns, expenditure flows, and the price level. In addition, as we saw earlier, changes in the nominal money supply initially change real-money balances and hence marginal expected returns on money, relative prices of assets, expenditure flows, and ultimately the price level.

One group of economists, the monetarists, argue that of all these possible sources of price-level change, shocks provided by changes in the nominal stock of money are by far the most important. It costs very little in real resources to increase or decrease the nominal supply of money, and monetary authorities have caused, or at least allowed to occur, very substantial movements in nominal money from time to time. Each of these large movements, as pointed out in section II, has been accompanied by large movements in the price level. Thus monetarists argue that nominal money supply can be changed relatively costlessly; hence money is sometimes changed by large amounts, and on these occasions the price level also changes by large amounts.

Another group of economists, Neo-Keynesians or nonmonetarists, place much less importance on money as a determinant of price change, particularly for smaller changes in prices. They tend to stress the effects of fiscal-policy actions on the price level.

It may occur to you that these positions are not really inconsistent with each other. For instance, nonmonetarists may agree that *very large* changes in nominal money supply are always accompanied by very large changes in the price level, and monetarists may concede that small changes in the price level of 2% to 3% may result primarily from fiscal-policy actions or any of a variety of other sources. But unfortunately, this does not resolve all the price-level issues, since many periods, such as 1965 to 1970, have moderately high price changes and hence are somewhere between the areas of agreement. For this period, monetarists argue that even with much expansionary fiscal policy, the price level would have increased rapidly because of the rapid growth in the nominal money supply. Nonmonetarists respond that the generally expansive fiscal policy over this period would have caused prices to move up significantly even with little change in the money supply. The issue of the relative importance of monetary policy, fiscal policy, and other things on prices thus is reduced to a disagreement about the *relative empirical importance,* not theoretical existence, of monetary- and fiscal-policy shocks of intermediate size.

In the shorter run, say less than one year, the disagreement between monetarists and nonmonetarists is very similar to that outlined above, but in this case concerns rates of real output and levels of employment. Monetarists argue that in the short run, changes in nominal money supply have a large and frequently dominant effect on income and employment. Large changes in nominal money supply are followed by large changes in the same direction of real income and employment. In the longer run, after the economy is completely adjusted to this shock, the initial change in money will be reflected in prices and real income, and employment will return to the levels they would have taken without the monetary shock.

To return to the short run, however, the monetarists' position implies that there is a great potential for good or for evil in using monetary policy to iron out or cause fluctuations in real output and employment. A monetary policy that could offset destabilizing shocks to income and employment from all other sources, including the effects of past monetary policy actions, would make business cycles obsolete. In addition, it could accomplish this feat at close to zero real cost. On the other hand, if monetary policy has such powerful effects on the current level of economic activity, and monetary-policy actions are inappropriate for whatever reason, these actions would reinfore or initiate fluctuations in income and employment.

Nonmonetarists differ from monetarists mainly in the importance they place on the money supply relative to fiscal-policy effects and other shocks to the system. Since they view money as less important, and frequently very much less important, they contend that its potential for either counteracting or causing business cycles is limited.

A final and very important disagreement between monetarists and nonmonetarists concerns our ability, at our current state of knowledge, to use monetary policy to actively offset other destabilizing effects on income and employment in the short run. Here monetarists argue that since changes in nominal money supply will have their major impact on expenditures and employment six months to a year following the change, and since we do not know at our present state of knowledge what impact monetary policy *should* have that far in the future, the best policy is to never change the rate of growth of money very much. If we could only know what monetary shocks would be appropriate six months to a year from now, then current policy actions could be actively designed to provide the desired impulses. But monetarists despair that we can currently predict that far into the future. Hence monetarists recommend a more or less steady rate of growth in the nominal money stock, not because this is an optimal policy in a world with perfect information, but because it minimizes the chance of tragic monetary mistakes in a world of very imperfect information about future events. The steady-growth rule would also assure, under reasonable assumptions, that monetary effects would be stimulative if real income were growing at less than its long-run average, and restrictive if real income were growing at a rate too high to be sustained indefinitely.

There are many other issues separating monetarists and nonmonetarists, but I believe those mentioned above to be by far the most important. It should be clear that all the issues mentioned are empirical issues that, at least in principle, can ultimately be decided by appealing to real-world events. Much empirical work relating to these issues is now available or in progress, including studies by Friedman, Meiselman, Schwartz, Modigliani, Ando, the many contributors to the Brookings and Federal Reserve MIT econometric models, Andersen, Jordan, Brunner, Meltzer, and many, many others. My reading of this evidence from both single- and multiequation models suggests that changes in the nominal money stock are very important in determining short-run levels of real income and employment. This interpretation implies that, at the very least, money should not be assigned a minor role in theoretical and policy discussions concerning the determination of real income, employment, and the price level.

READING 26
A MONETARIST MODEL OF THE MONETARY PROCESS

David I. Fand

INTRODUCTION

Important differences in stabilization policy have emerged in recent years between those who seek to stabilize the economy through discretionary fiscal policies, and those who favor a stabilization framework defined in terms of guidelines (or rules) for the money stock. For lack of better terms, I shall refer to these two points of view as the Monetarist and Fiscalist schools. Fiscalists are those who follow the Income-Expenditure theory and place chief reliance on the government's taxing and spending powers to stabilize the economy, while Monetarists follow the Quantity theory and emphasize the central banking system's control of the money stock.[1;2]

Source: Reprinted from The Journal of Finance, May 1970, pp. 275–289. The author gratefully acknowledges financial support from Wayne State University and the National Science Foundation.

[1] The term Fiscalist is not a particularly good one. It is intended to cover the large group of modern Keynesians ranging from the neo-stagnationists to the neo-classicists, who advocate fiscal policies on theoretical growths, but also including some who may favor fiscal policy for pragmatic reasons. Note too that the Keynesian neo-classicists are, in many analytical respects, closer to the Monetarists than to the neo-stagnationists. Nevertheless, in spite of these obvious limitations, the term Fiscalist does probably convey the range of views we are trying to analyze. The term Monetarist is intended to cover the group who base their macro-economic policies on the modern Quantity theory.

[2] For influential statements of the Fiscalist position as applied to the U.S. economy in the early 1960's see Council of Economic Advisers, The American Economy in 1961: Problems and Policies (Washington, 1961, and P. A. Samuelson, Stability and Growth in the American Economy, 1962 Wicksell Lectures (Stockholm, 1962). For an articulate statement of the "New Economics" Fiscalist approach to stabilization emphasizing discretionary changes in the full-employment surplus, see W. W. Heller, New Dimensions of Political Economy (Norton, 1966). See also W. W. Heller (ed.), Perspectives on Economic Growth (Random House, 1968), and A. Okun, The Political Economy of Prosperity (Brookings, 1970). For a cogent statement of the neo-classical synthesis and its application to stabilization policy in the U.S. in the early 1960's, see J. Tobin, The Intellectual Revolution in U.S. Economic Policy Making (The University of Essex, 1966).

A popular view of the two schools stresses the following differences: Monetarists define stabilization policy in terms of the money stock, favor either fixed rules or a set of guidelines for the monetary aggregates, and seemingly uphold extremist views that "only money matters"; Fiscalists implement stabilization policy in terms of the full-employment surplus, take a more positive view of discretionary budgetary changes, and emphasize—and possibly exaggerate—the short run stabilization potentials of temporary changes in taxes and expenditures. This summary does not point to any analytical basis for their different views; it therefore leaves open the possibility that their respective stabilization policies may reflect differences in temperament, emphasis, judgment, or political affiliation.

In this paper we shall argue that the stabilization differences between Monetarists and Fiscalists reflect substantially different models of the monetary process, and is not just a question of emphasis, judgment, or temperament. We shall also suggest that a classification of monetary theories in terms of "does money matter" or "only money matters" does not highlight the distinctive analytical aspects of these monetary models. We illustrate some of these aspects by considering the following substantive features of the modern Quantity theory—the Monetarists' model of the monetary process: the Monetarist distinction between nominal money, a policy variable, and real cash balances, an endogenous variable; the Monetarist distinction between high and rising interest rates, and between nominal and real interest rates; and the Monetarist distinction between *ceteris paribus* and *mutatis mutandis* fiscal effects—defined in terms of the monetary growth rates. In our concluding section we summarize some essential features of the Monetarists' model.

I.   THE CLASSIFICATION OF MONETARY THEORIES: MONETARY EXTREMISM RE-EXAMINED

In a recent paper on "The Role of Money in National Economic Policy," Samuelson states that monetarism is "the central issue that is debated these days in connection with macro-economic aggregate demand—whether there will be unemployment, whether there will be inflation—is money, M_1 or M_2, and more specifically, perhaps, its various rates of change." He adds that if we can define a spectrum of remarks from "money doesn't matter," to "money alone matters," monetarism is somewhere between "money matters most" to "money alone matters"—at the right end of the spectrum.[3]

This view of monetarism has some validity: Monetarists do attribute the Great Depression, and the subsequent terrible debacle of the 1930's, to the precipitous fall (between 25–35 per cent) in the money stock—explaining these great disasters in terms of erratic money stock behavior. Finding few exceptions to this generalization, they

The classic statement of the pre-Keynesian Monetarist theory is, of course, in I. Fisher, *The Purchasing Power of Money* (Macmillan, 1911). For statements of the modern Quantity theory see L. W. Mints, *History of Banking Theory* (Chicago, 1945) and *Monetary Policy in a Competitive Society* (McGraw-Hill, 1951). See also Clark Warburton's selected papers for 1945–1953 in *Depression, Inflation, and Monetary Policy* (Johns Hopkins Press, 1966); M. Friedman (ed.) *Studies in the Quantity Theory of Money* (Chicago, 1958); M. Friedman, *A Program for Monetary Stability* (Fordham, 1959); M. Friedman and A. Schwartz, *A Monetary History of the United States* (Princeton, 1963); and M. Friedman, *The Optimum Quantity of Money* (Aldine, 1969); D. Patinkin, *Money Interest and Prices*, 2nd ed. (Harper, 1965); and H. G. Johnson, *Essays in Monetary Economics* (Harvard, 1967).
[3] See P. A. Samuelson's "The Role of Money in National Economic Policy" in *Controlling Monetary Aggregates* (Federal Reserve Bank of Boston, 1969), pp. 7–13.

accept the hypothesis that the money stock is the key policy variable for avoiding inflations and for preventing severe depressions. The Fiscalist, in contrast, seeking to explain the twin scourges of depressions and inflations, is apt to be more eclectic and highlights either fundamental (or structural) changes in the economy, or overpowering external forces, such as a war. Monetarists thus often do appear either as extremists—in asserting that a major disaster such as the Great Depression could be averted by good monetary policy—or as naive in overlooking, or dismissing, many of the fundamental changes in the real economy emphasized by the Fiscalists.

If we move on to consider the impact of monetary policy on economic growth, there is a significant change in their respective views. Many Fiscalists believe that the central bank can stimulate capital formation and the growth rate of real output by adopting a monetary-fiscal policy mix of easy money and tight budgets. Monetarists, in contrast, are more inclined to the view that changes in monetary policy affect prices rather than interest rates and rates of return. One could therefore argue that the Fiscalists may be taking an extreme position and exaggerating the monetary impact on the real rate of interest, on rates of return, on capital formation, and on economic growth.

"Monetary extremism" may serve as a mnemonic symbol for calling attention to the strategic role assigned by the Monetarists to money policy in avoiding deep depressions and inflations; it may also highlight the Fiscalists' position that monetary policy may play a key role in facilitating capital formation and economic growth. But it does not focus on the theoretical basis for the policies recommended by Monetarists and Fiscalists for dealing with ordinary business cycle fluctuations, with mild inflations, or with the sluggish performance of the American economy in the late 1950's.

Theories said to contain extreme views of money are, in effect, being classified with respect to singular, and very specific, issues. Accordingly, this is meaningful if we limit analysis to deep depressions or galloping inflations, to the so-called "Keynesian Case" (absolute liquidity preference and zero elasticities) where "money doesn't matter," to "Radcliffe" type theories where "money hardly matters," and to the contribution of easy money policies to economic growth. Barring these special cases, both the Monetarist and Fiscalist schools clearly believe that "money matters," and neither school believes that "only money matters." Far more important are the substantive differences between Monetarists and Fiscalists concerning the precise manner in which money matters—the theory of the transmission mechanism explaining how changes in the nominal money stock may affect real output, employment, the price level, capital formation, and economic growth.[4]

The monetary models used by the Monetarists and Fiscalists contain substantively different assumptions with respect to the following technical questions: Can the Federal Reserve control the (nominal) money stock within fairly close limits, or should we treat it as an endogenous variable?[5] Is it possible for the Federal Reserve, acting through the FOMC, to lower (or raise) interest rates if such a change is thought to be either

---

[4] The statement that a theory is extreme is always somewhat arbitrary, and depends partly on the classification principle that it used. Thus, a theory with any new result, whether the result is important substantively, or is merely a trivial addition to previous results, can be viewed as an extremist theory, if all theories are classified on the basis of whether they contain this new result.

[5] See D. I. Fand, "Some Issues in Monetary Economics," *Banca Nazionale del Lavoro Quarterly Review*, 90, September 1969, and *Review*, Federal Reserve Bank of St. Louis, January 1970.

desirable or necessary? Should the Federal Reserve formulate the directive to the account manager in terms of the monetary aggregates and scrap its present money market strategy?[6] And would the stabilization performance of recent years have been better if the authorities were required by statute to keep monetary growth within a given set of guidelines?[7]

Substantive differences in the monetary models used by Monetarists and Fiscalists led, in turn, to substantially different conclusions concerning the following policy issues: Is the post-1965 inflation the result of extraordinary expansion in the monetary aggregates, or of an excessively lax, and inappropriate, fiscal policy? Is the transmission mechanism, as conceived in the income theory, too restrictive or may changes in the nominal money stock

directly affect private expenditures, aggergate demand, and the price level? Does the theory of fiscal policy often assume an elastic (or accommodating) monetary policy, and does it therefore fail to distinguish between a pure fiscal deficit excluding any money stock effects (a *ceteris paribus* effect) and an increase in the monetary aggregates accompanied by a fiscal deficit (a *mutatis mutandis* effect)?[8] And do temporary changes (discretionary or automatic) in the full-employment surplus have quantitatively predictable effects on aggregate demand?[9]

Differences in the assumptions implicit in the monetary models used by Monetarists and Fiscalists help explain some of their substantive differences on policy issues. And until we are able to clarify and resolve these differences, the controversy over the relative merits

[6] For an explanation of the Federal Reserve's money market strategy, and an interpretation of the proviso clause as a device for correcting errors in the projected relation between money market variables and the monetary aggregates, see the recent paper by Governor Sherman Maisel, "Controlling Monetary Aggregates" in Federal Reserve Bank of Boston, *Controlling Monetary Aggregates* (September 1969). See J. M. Guttentag, "The Strategy of Open Market Operations," *Quarterly Journal of Economics* (February 1966). See also the paper by A. Meltzer and the joint paper by G. Horwich and P. Hendershott on "The Appropriate Indicators of Monetary Policy" in *Savings and Residential Financing,* 1969 Conference Proceedings (U.S. League, 1969).

[7] M. Friedman, "The Role of Monetary Policy," *American Economic Review,* March 1968; P. Hendershott, *The Neutralized Money Stock—An Unbiased Measure of Federal Reserve Policy Actions* (Richard D. Irwin, 1968); the Joint Economic Committee *Hearings on Standards for Guiding Monetary Action* (Washington, 1968); D. I. Fand, "Comment: The Impact of Monetary Policy in 1966," *Journal of Political Economy,* August 1968; the House Committee on Banking and Currency *Compendium on Monetary Policy Guidelines and Federal Reserve Structure* (Washington, 1968); T. Mayer, *Monetary Policy in the United States* (Random House, 1968); K. Brunner (ed), *Targets and Indicators of Monetary Policy* (Chandler Publishing Co., 1969).

[8] See L. Andersen and J. Jordan, "Monetary and Fiscal Actions: A Test of Their Relative Importance in Economic Stabilization," November 1968 issue of the *Review,* Federal Reserve Bank of St. Louis; the Comment by F. DeLeeuw and J. Kalchbrenner, and Reply by Andersen and Jordan in the April 1969 *Review* of the Federal Reserve Bank of St. Louis; M. Levy, "Monetary Pilot Policy Growth and Inflation," and W. Lewis, "Money is Everything Economics—A Tempest in a Teapot" in the *Conference Board Record* for January and April 1969; R. Davis, "How Much Does Money Matter? A Look at Some Recent Evidence" in the June 1969 *Monthly Review,* Federal Reserve Bank of New York; and L. C. Andersen, "The Influence of Economic Activity on the Money Stock: Some Additional Evidence," August 1969 issue of the *Review,* Federal Reserve Bank of St. Louis.

[9] The American Enterprise Institute's symposium volume, *Fiscal Policy and Business Capital Formation* (Washington, 1967) contains an informed discussion of this subject. See especially the papers by P. McCracken, C. Harriss, S. Fabricant, and R. Musgrave, and the comments by G. Haberler and N. Ture.

The key stabilization role assigned to changes in the full-employment surplus is critically reviewed by G. Terborgh in his *The New Economics* (MAPI, 1968). For a discussion of the stabilization roles to be assigned to monetary and fiscal policy see the Friedman-Heller dialogue, *Monetary vs. Fiscal Policy* (Norton, 1969).

of monetary and fiscal policy, as it is emerging in the current dialogue, will necessarily continue. We shall now take up three distinctive features of the Monetarists' model: their theory of money, their theory of interest rates and prices, and their analysis of fiscal policy.

II. A MONETARIST VIEW OF MONEY: NOMINAL MONEY VS. REAL BALANCES

The Monetarist position is often misunderstood, and they are often interpreted as advocating extremist views about money. This failure to communicate effectively may be due to the fact that Monetarists seem to be advocating two contradictory propositions at the same time: on the one hand, their theoretical analysis views the nominal money stock as a kind of veil (as in the classical tradition) and stresses real variables as opposed to nominal variables; on the other hand, their historical and applied analysis suggests that movements in the money stock are the key to curbing inflation and to preventing depressions. As we move from monetary theory into the analysis of stabilization policy, the money stock is somehow transformed from an innocuous veil into an extremely powerful force for determining income, employment, and the price level. Monetarists may have experienced difficulties in obtaining a wider understanding of their model, and in communicating the theoretical basis of their monetary theory because it seems to include, in one category, both the money veil of theory and the extremely potent high-powered money of stabilization policy.[10]

There is an apparent paradox, striking some as a contradiction, between the theoretical proposition that the quantity of nominal money will not, substantially, affect any of the real endogenous variables, and a policy recommendation to impose either fixed rules or policy guidelines on monetary growth, in order to stabilize the economy. The first proposition implies that monetary changes will only affect nominal variables; the second, that monetary policy is, in fact, the key to obtaining the desired values for the important real endogenous variables of macroeconomics (i.e., the real wage, employment, real output, and the rate of economic growth).

The puzzle may be resolved by noting first that the nominal money stock may affect nominal variables while exerting very little *direct* influence on the real variables. Thus, when an increase in nominal money raises money income, the level of money wages and the price level, without affecting any of the real endogenous variables—when nominal money stock changes affect only nominal variables—money is properly viewed as a veil. Second, nominal money stock changes may significantly affect the real endogenous variables, in an economy where output can easily expand and where quantities adjust faster than prices. The money veil of theory can become an extremely powerful stimulus to increase real output and employment in the world of stabilization policy. Third, in an economy where output can no longer expand and where prices adjust rather than quantities, control of the nominal money stock is the key to controlling the rise in prices. And it is in these latter cases the Monetarists focus on the growth rate of nominal money as the key policy for preventing both depressions and inflations.

To emphasize this distinction be-

---

[10] In saying that Monetarists view nominal money as a veil we do not wish to rule out the possibility that in a growth model context, alternative policies with respect to nominal money may affect some of the equilibrium values of the endogenous variables in the real economy. But even with this property, nominal money is still almost like a veil in a comparative static sense.

tween the money veil of monetary theory and the potent money of stabilization policy, Monetarists distinguish between nominal money—a supply-determined policy variable—and the real (value of the) money stock—a demand-determined endogenous variable. Monetarists treat the quantity of nominal money as a variable determined primarily by the supply condition, postulating a fairly close link between the monetary base (or high-powered money) supplied by the central bank, and the quantity of nominal money available to the public. In contrast, the real money stock is an endogenous variable, determined by the interaction of the financial and real sectors, and satisfying the demand function for real balances. Thus, while the nominal money stock may be varied as a policy variable, the real money stock is an endogenous variable with an equilibrium solution value, given by the demand function for real balances.[11]

The Monetarist therefore postulates (1) that the nominal money stock can be controlled by the monetary authorities and used for policy purposes, (2) that the real money stock is determined by the general equilibrium of the real and monetary sectors, and cannot generally be controlled by the authorities. This model therefore implies (3) that the authorities cannot increase real balances by printing nominal money, and that they will ultimately fail and serve only to raise prices, unless there is a substantial volume of unused resources. The relation between money and prices in (3) serves to emphasize

(4) that an increase in nominal money will generally bring about permanently higher prices, rather than lower interest rates. The Monetarists' linking of nominal money with prices contrasts sharply with the Fiscalists' linking of nominal money with interest rates.

The sharp distinction drawn between the nominal money stock, treated as a supply-determined policy variable, and the real money stock, treated as a demand-determined endogenous variable (with an equilibrium solution value), is a striking feature of monetarism. It is also a paradoxical feature, since the Monetarists' model allows the authorities effective control over the nominal stock, while simultaneously severely limiting the circumstances where they influence the stock of real balances.[12]

The Monetarist emphasis on the endogenity of real cash balances, suggesting a close relation between nominal money and the price level, is the basis for their rejection of the liquidity preference theory as a general theory of money and interest rates. We shall now consider the Monetarist theory relating money and prices with nominal and real interest rates.

III. A MONETARIST VIEW OF MONEY, INTEREST RATES AND PRICES

The Income-Expenditure theory of the Fiscalists adopts a particular transmission mechanism to analyze the effects of a change in the money stock (or its growth rate) on the real economy. It assumes that money changes will affect output or prices only

---

[11] The proposition that the quantity of nominal money is determined by conditions of supply is not intended to rule out the possibility that the money supply function has some interest elasticity, or that some variation in the quantity of money may result from shifts in the demand for money. What it does say is that through its control over the monetary base the central bank can exercise effective control over the nominal money stock.

[12] The Fiscalist does not usually distinguish between nominal and real balances. The Fiscalist model may allow the authorities less control over nominal balances and greater control over real balances, as compared to the Monetarists' model.

through its effect on a set of conventional yields—on the market interest rate of a small group of financial assets, such as government or corporate bonds. A given change in the money stock will have a calculable effect on these interest rates (this set of conventional yields) given by the liquidity preference analysis, and the interest rate changes are then used to derive the change in investment spending, the induced effects on income and consumption, etc.

Monetarists, following the Quantity theory, do not accept this transmission mechanism and this liquidity preference theory of interest rates for several reasons: First, they suggest that an increase in money may directly affect expenditures, prices, and a wide variety of implicit yields on physical assets, and need not be restricted to a small set of conventional yields on financial assets.[13] Second, they view the demand for money as determining the desired quantity of real balances, and not the level of interest rates. Third, and most fundamentally, they reject the notion that the authorities can change the stock of real balances—an endogenous variable—and thereby bring about a permanent change in interest rates, except [under] very special circumstances.[14]

Monetarists reject the liquidity preference interest rate theory because it applies only as long as we can equate an increase in nominal money with a permanent increase in real balances. This suggests that the liquidity preference theory may be useful as a theory of the short run interest rate changes—the liquidity effect—associated with the impact effects of nominal money changes. But Monetarists also insist that this liquidity effect is temporary and will disappear as aggregate demand, output, and/or prices rise. Monetarists therefore depart from the Income theory and conclude that the liquidity effect will spend itself, and that market interest rates will return to their former level. They argue that the rise in income increases the demand for money, causing market interest rates to rise, and that any tendency for prices to rise with output will lower the real value of the money stock, and thus hasten the return of interest rates to their former level. The income and the price level effects thus reinforce each other to raise interest rates, offsetting

---

[13] Monetarists favor a transmission mechanism in which an increase in money may driectly affect expenditures, prices, and implicit yields on physical assets. They suggest that money may be substituted not only for bonds but also for other assets, and that individuals may re-establish portfolio equilibrium by purchasing either a financial or a physical asset. Note that when money is used to acquire physical assets the interest rate effect no longer precedes the price effect, since it is only through an increase in the price of assets that the reduction in yield is effectuated. Moreover, if we define assets to include consumer durables (e.g., cars, appliances) it would be reasonable to suppose that these expenditures—which are now classified as consumption—can be directly stimulated by an increase in money. In a period of rising prices, inflationary expectations raise the cost of holding money and the public has an incentive to reduce the quantity of desired real balances by increasing expenditures. The link between money and prices is likely to be strengthened during an inflation. See D. I. Fand, "A Monetary Interpretation of the Post-1965 Inflation in the U.S.," *Banca Nazionale del Lavoro Quarterly Review*, 89, June 1969. See also W. J. Yohe and D. S. Karnosky, "Interest Rates and Price Level Changes," December 1969 *Review*, Federal Reserve Bank of St. Louis.

[14] Thus, if prices are given in the short run, and if real and nominal balances do move together, the money demand function may be used as a liquidity preference function to analyze the initial *changes* in the level of interest rates. Moreover, if an increase in real balance does not affect aggregate demand, income, and prices, the initial effect is also the total effect on interest rates. See D. I. Fand, "Keynesian Monetary Theories, Stabilization Policy and the Recent Inflation," *Journal of Money, Credit and Banking*, August 1969.

the initial decline due to the liquidity effect. Some recent estimates suggest that market rates will, on the average, return to their initial level within a year, so that a one-time increase in nominal money will have no lasting effect on the level of interest rates.[15]

An additional price expectation effect may also become operative if accelerated monetary growth generates *rising* prices, and if the public expects the price rise to continue. Anticipated price increases—inflationary expectations—may indeed cause market interests rates to rise above their initial level, if the rate of monetary growth is sufficiently large to bring in the price expectation effect. When this occurs, market rates will rise above their initial level.[16]

Monetarists and Fiscalists both acknowledge that an increase in nominal money may have a permanent effect on output, on prices, on interest rates, or on some combination of these. Monetarists, nevertheless, emphasize the permanent effects on the price level and/or output, while Fiscalists emphasize the effect on interest rates and/or output, and treat the initial liquidity effect as if it were the permanent interest rate effect. Monetarists thus envision the price level as equilibrating the demand for, and supply of, real balances,

so that the nominal money stock is a determinant of the price level; Fiscalists view the interest rate as equilibrating the demand for, and supply of, money and explain the price level in terms of money wages, unit labor costs, markup factors, etc.[17]

The interest rate and price level theories of the Monetarists and the Fiscalists are thus mutually exclusive: if an increase (or accelerated growth) in nominal money permanently lowers interest rates and/or raises output, its effect on prices is lessened; alternatively, if its permanent effect is to raise prices and/or output, its effect on real interest rates is lessened. The transmission mechanism of the Income theory in which an increase in nominal money directly affects interest rates but not prices is thus a crucial link in developing the negative *ceteris paribus* association between money and interest rate movements. The opposite assumption, that the real value of the money stock is an endogenous variable—relating the stock of nominal money and the absolute price level—is the basis for rationalizing a positive relation between money and interest rates. The historical association between interest rates and prices may be interpreted as a *mutatis mutandis* relation, where the initial liquidity effect of an increase in

---

[15] See W. Gibson, "Effects of Money on Interest Rates," Federal Reserve *Staff Economic Studies #43*, January 1968; P. Cagan, "The Channels of Monetary Effects on Interest Rates" (M.S., 1966); W. Gibson and G. Kaufman, "The Sensitivity of Interest Rates to Changes in Money and Income," *Journal of Political Economy*, May 1968; M. Friedman, "Factors Affecting the Level of Interest Rates" in *Savings and Residential Financing*, 1968 Conference Proceedings (U.S. League, 1968); P. Cagan and A. Gandolfi, "The Lag in Monetary Policy as Implied by the Time Pattern of Monetary Effects on Interest Rates," *American Economic Review*, May 1969.

[16] The Keynesian liquidity effect is the permanent interest rate effect if, and only if, there are no offsetting income, price level, and price expectations effects. But this requires an economy in which money does not affect demand, real output or prices—an extreme case that would be rejected by both Monetarists and Fiscalists.

[17] The price level theory incorporated in the FRB-MIT model is described as follows:
Prices are assumed to be a variable markup over wages, with excise taxes completely shifted onto consumers. The variables determining the markup are the productivity trend which allows producers to maintain profit shares even though wages rise faster than prices, farm and import prices, which measure other costs, and the ratio of unfilled orders to shipments, which indicates demand shifts.
See F. DeLeeuw and E. Gramlich, "The Channels of Monetary Policy," *Federal Reserve Bulletin*, June 1969.

nominal money is subsequently offset by the induced income and price expectation effects.[18]

The Monetarist theory of interest rates utilizes the close link between nominal money and prices to rationalize the positive association between monetary growth and the level of market rates. It helps motivate the distinction emphasized by the Monetarists between *high* and *rising* rates, that has become increasingly relevant in recent years. In a fully anticipated inflation, we expect that market interest rates will be high, reflecting the rate of inflation, even if *real* rates (or rates of return) remain constant. Thus, if the real rate, r, is 5 per cent and stays at that level, and if the rate of inflation, i, is expected to continue indefinitely at a 20 per cent annual rate, the market rate, m, should start to rise. It will continue to rise for an indefinite period until the rate of inflation is fully anticipated, when it will settle at 26%, as shown in equation (1):

$$m = r + i + ri. \qquad (1)$$

This important distinction between high (low) rates and rising (falling) interest rates, and their relation to rising (falling) prices was developed by Irving Fisher in the 1890's.

Fisher's theory, relating monetary growth, price level changes, and market interest rates helps rationalize the puzzling, though well documented, empirical association between high interest rates and high prices—the Gibson Paradox. The Fisher model postulates: that market rates are high (low) when prices are rising (falling); that market rates lag behind price level changes; that market rates are highly correlated with a weighted average of past price level changes. Gibson's empirical finding that *high* rates accompany *high* prices and *low* rates accompany *low* prices may then be explained if there is a fairly long lag between interest rates and prices. The Fisher theory thus clearly suggests a sequence in which (excessive) growth in the money stock causes first a rise in prices and, ultimately, higher market rates (nominal interest rates).[19]

Monetarists following the Fisher model thus relate monetary expansion, rising prices, with rising (and high) market interest rates. They distinguish

---

[18] The statement that the Fiscalists have a monetary theory of the interest rate and a non-monetary theory of the price level needs to be modified somewhat when we consider the large scale econometric models. But while the larger models do allow for some feedback from money to prices, they still retain the negative association between money and interest rates, even allowing for the price level effects. Thus, in the FRB-MIT model, an increase in money will lower interest rates and these rates do not return to their former level even in simulation that extend for several years (20 quarters). In this sense even the large scale models retain the main features of the simpler Fiscalist models, and do not approximate the more classical results. See G. Kaufman and R. Laurent, "Simulating Policy Strategies on the FRB-MIT Model Under Two Alternative Monetary Policy Regimes," a staff memorandum, Federal Reserve Bank of Chicago, Oct. 1969.

[19] For an analysis of the Gibson Paradox see I. Fisher, *Appreciation and Interest* (Macmillan, 1930); *The Theory of Interest* (Macmillan, 1930); J. M. Keynes, *A Treatise on Money* (Macmillan, 1930); D. Meiselman, "Bond Yield and the Price Level: The Gibson Paradox Regained" in D. Carson (ed) *Banking and Monetary Studies* (Irwin, 1963), and his "Money and Factor Proportions" (M.S. 1964). See also the summary of the Wicksell and Keynes Analysis in P. Cagan's *Determination and Effect of Changes in the Stock of Money* (Columbia University Press, 1965); M. Friedman and A. Schwartz, *Trends in Money, Income and Prices* (M.S.); and D. I. Fand, "Keynesian Monetary Theories, . . .," *op. cit.*

W. J. Yohe and D. S. Karnosky in their comprehensive article on "Interest Rates and Price Level Changes 1952–1969," *op. cit.*, provide a succinct statement of the Fisher theory and an illuminating discussion of the theoretical aspects of the Gibson Paradox. They summarize their experiments with several weighting patterns for the price expectation effect, derive alternative estimates of the real rate, and relate this analysis to explain interest rate movements in recent years.

therefore among the following concepts: (1) *rising* rates, when inflationary expectations have not yet caught up with the actual rise in prices; (2) *high* (though stable) rates, when inflation is fully anticipated; (3) market rates, nominal interest rates incorporating inflationary expectations; and (4) real rates, interest rates corrected for the rate of inflation. Monetarists therefore postulate a sequence of monetary expansion, rising prices, and high interest rates, distinguish between nominal and real rates, and introduce a price expectation variable in order to rationalize a rise in market rates (relative to the real rate) when prices are rising.

Fiscalists, following the liquidity preference theory, abstract (1) from any direct link of monetary growth on prices, (2) from any direct link of rising prices on rising (or high) market rates, and (3) from the resulting divergence between market rates (nominal interest rates) and real rates. They do not distinguish between *rising* rates and *high* rates, between market rates (nominal interest rates) and real rates, and do not accept the Fisher rationalization of the *mutatis mutandis* positive association between monetary expansion and high (or rising) interest rates. Accordingly, to explain empirical data suggesting a positive association of interest rates and prices, they must necessarily assume increases in the demand for money—or an increase in the natural rate relative to the market rate—causing market rates to rise; and in the absence of monetary growth would leave market rates at even higher levels.

The implications of the Monetarists' theory is best seen if we consider the consequences of the Fiscalists' reluctance to distinguish between market rates and real rates, and to bring in a price expectations variable in the analysis of interest rate movements. This has two subtle, but important and far reaching, consequences: first, they

must postulate successive upward shifts in the demand for money—or in the natural rate—in order to explain a continuing rise in market interest rates since they are reluctant, *ex hypothesi*, to explain rising (or high) market rates in terms of rising prices and price expectations; second, by assuming that the variability in market rate movements corresponds to changes in real rates, the Fiscalists' theory necessarily carries an implication that real interest rates, or rates of return, the marginal productivity of capital, and the real sector of the economy are highly volatile. But this substantively important conclusion about the instability of the real economy is clearly inappropriate if market rates are responding to and reflecting, past and present price level changes.

The significance of the Monetarist theory, explaining the association of rising rates with inflation, of high rates with high prices, and of high rates with excessive monetary growth—a rationalization not available to the Fiscalists —is thus clear. The Fiscalist, seeking to explain the positive association of interest rates and prices, must hypothesize shifts in the demand for money, or increases in the natural rate, to explain rising market rates. The assumption that the variability in market rates corresponds to the volatility of real rates, and the far reaching implications concerning the instability of the real economy, are therefore directly related to the Fiscalists' analytical framework— his liquidity preference theory of interest rates. They serve, therefore, to highlight and emphasize the extraordinary contribution of Fisher's theory relating money and prices to interest rates.

IV. A MONETARIST VIEW OF FISCAL POLICY

Monetarists and Fiscalists disagree, by definition, on the relative roles of monetary and fiscal policy in stabilization: Monetarists analyze the taxing and spending decisions in the budget—in older pre-Keynesian public-finance tradition—as having their primary effect on the allocation of resources from the private to the public sectors, and conclude that budget policy should not be the major instrument for stabilizing aggregate demand. This is, of course, in sharp contrast to the Fiscalists—in the post-Keynesian tradition—who emphasize fiscal policy as the key variable in controlling aggregate demand.

Monetarists are sometimes interpreted as denying that fiscal surpluses (or deficits)—e.g., a rise (or cut) in taxes holding government expenditures constant—have any substantial effects on aggregate demand. This inference is, in my opinion, incorrect. Monetarists must surely acknowledge that an increase in taxes, with constant government expenditures, will certainly depress private expenditures if the Treasury impounds the revenue. They will also agree that an increase in taxes, with both government expenditures and the monetary aggregates (or their rate of growth) constant, will also depress aggregate demand. The rise in taxes will raise the surplus (or reduce the deficit), causing interest rates to fall, and bring about a reduction in private spending if desired real money balances respond to changes in interest rates. What the Monetarists do question is whether a *mutatis mutandis* increase in taxes, allowing both government expenditures and the monetary aggregates to rise, will necessarily reduce either private spending or aggregate demand.

A Monetarist—focussing on the monetary aggregates—distinguishes between a *mutatis mutandis* increase in taxes, where both government expenditures and the money stock may vary, and a *ceteris paribus* tax action, where government expenditure and monetary growth are held constant. That an increase in taxes, matched by an equivalent increase in expenditures, will be stimulative rather than restrictive is, of course, an accepted theorem in the Fiscalist theory, and they take account of this by measuring fiscal policy changes in terms of the full-employment surplus. But while the full-employment surplus nets out the taxes against the expenditures, it does not specify any requirements for the money stock, nor is it adjusted for the size of the real GNP, or for price level changes.

The notion that fiscal restraint can be offset by easy money is not unique to the Monetarist. What may be unique about the Monetarist view is his further statement that this offset will occur even if market interest rates are rising. To the Monetarist, the thrust of monetary policy is defined by the aggregate rather than by market rates, and easy money (accelerated growth in the monetary aggregates) is not necessarily inconsistent with rising interest rates. The admitted failure of the Revenue and Control Act of June 1968 to cool down the economy seems to support the Monetarist view. It has brought about greater agreement, if not a consensus, that an increase in the monetary aggregates may be expansionary and offset a rise in taxes, even if market interest rates are rising. But this is all that the Monetarist needs to question about fiscal policy, and it is surely not equivalent to saying that fiscal policy actions do not affect aggregate demand. To deny any short run stabilization effects to fiscal actions, one must be prepared to argue that surpluses (or deficits), irrespective of magnitude, have no direct effect on spending through changes in disposable income; and that they have no indirect effect through changes in desired real money balances or desired liquidity, and on velocity. But this can be true only in the exceptional case of a completely (interest) inelastic demand for money.

The Monetarist analysis of the stabilization effects of fiscal actions is directly related to calibration of the posture of monetary policy in terms of monetary aggregates, and which, as recent events have indicated, may differ substantially from the Fiscalist calibration based on interest rates.[20] The Fiscalist calibration of monetary policy will therefore associate tight money with high (or rising) interest rates, stable monetary policy with stable rates, etc. As a consequence, a fiscal deficit, accompanied by stable interest rates, is accordingly defined as a *ceteris paribus* action—as a fiscal stimulus with monetary policy constant. On this calibration it is natural to attribute the entire rise in income to the deficit. But a fiscal deficit with stable interest rates implies money creation (financing through the banking system), and (accelerated) growth in the monetary aggregates. Using the Monetarist calibration, this very same action is necessarily defined as a mon-etary stimulus—an expansive monetary action. The *ceteris paribus* fiscal stimulus, when interest rates serve to define the posture of monetary policy, is thus necessarily a (*mutatis mutandis*) monetary stimulus, when the monetary aggregates serve to define the monetary posture.

Because deficits are associated with money creation and surpluses with decelerated monetary growth, much of the evidence can be rationalized by both the Income theory as well as the Quantity theory.[21] On the basis of experience in the 1930's and 1950's, Fiscalists have accepted the multiplier analysis of the Income theory; accordingly, they focus on the full-employment surplus as the key to controlling aggregate demand, and de-emphasize the allocative function of the budget relative to its stabilization function. This approach to budget policy assumes that monetary policy cannot serve effectively as a major instrument of stabilization, a view that was widespread among Fiscalists until very recently.[22]

[20] The relevance of this point is apparent when we consider the June 1968 tax action where fiscal restraint was accompanied by rising interest rates. To a Fiscalist this is a case of a *joint* action, since the increase in the full-employment surplus—fiscal restraint—was compounded by high interest rates—monetary restraint. The combination of high interest rates, together with the rise in the full-employment surplus, helps rationalize the articulated fears of overkill in the summer of 1968 and constitute a case of an offsetting action, since the increase in the full-employment surplus—fiscal restraint—was associated with an accelerated growth in the money stock—monetary ease. Moreover, the offsetting monetary action was, apparently, stronger than the enacted, and presumed massive, dose of fiscal restraint.

[21] Deficits (and surpluses) are usually associated with acceleration (deceleration) in money stock growth, and it is therefore possible for Fiscalists and Monetarists to cite the same evidence to support their respective views. Fiscal deficits associated with rising income, employment and prices, seem to support the Multiplier theory of Fiscalists. But when a period of fiscal stimulus is characterized by monetary expansion—e.g., the 1964 tax cut—it also supports the Monetarist theory. It is only when movements in the money stock and in the full-employment surplus go in opposite directions, as in 1966 and in 1968, that we can get any real test of their relative effects. See D. I. Fand, "Some Issues in Monetary Economics," *op. cit.*

[22] Although the stagnationist fears of the 1930's receded somewhat in the early fifties, the revival of monetary policy was interrupted when it appeared ineffective in stopping the mild inflations of the 1950's. Many Fiscalists concluded that the monetary policy was ineffective in dealing with mild inflations associated with wage or cost push, markup, administered price, demand shift, and sectoral inflation. The Fiscalist's interpretation of our recent history, as manifest in the early 1960's, seem to conclude that monetary policy was not only ineffective in the deep depression of the 1930's, but almost equally ineffective in dealing with the mild inflations experienced by the advanced industrialized countries in the 1950's. For a useful summary of these views see the Joint Economic Committee *Staff Report on Employment, Growth, and Price Level* (Washington, 1959).

Monetarists have challenged the interpretation of the 1930's and of the 1950's which played such a major role in shaping the stabilization theories of the Fiscalists; and their re-examination of the evidence leads them to conclude that the Fiscalists' earlier pessimism is unjustified, and that monetary policy can indeed play a major, and decisive, role in stabilization.[23] Monetarists have also challenged the Fiscalist stabilization theory and the key role assigned to the full-employment surplus. They question whether discretionary fiscal policy actions will affect private spending without a fairly long lag, whether these spending effects do come about very quickly, and whether temporary budget changes have effects that are dependable, and easily predictable. They question whether the Multiplier theory and the econometric estimates of the multiplier adequately distinguishes between the *ceteris paribus* and *mutatis mutandis* fiscal effects; they also question whether the important priorities implied by the budget decisions—the determination of the relative size and the resources allocated to the public sector—should be constrained with short run stabilization goals. Taken together, these questions raise doubts whether discretionary fiscal policy can, in fact, serve effectively as a short run stabilization tool.

The Monetarist concludes that discretionary budgetary changes are not an efficient means for short run stabilization purposes, and that fiscal policy changes are likely to have permanent effects on the relative sizes of the private and public sectors. Accordingly, they stress the crucial importance of a stabilizing monetary policy. Monetarists do not deny that discretionary fiscal policy actions may affect aggregate demand in the short run, although their analysis of the effects may differ from the Fiscalist analysis. Perhaps the most fundamental difference between Monetarists and Fiscalists is in choosing those policies which are most likely to succeed in keeping the economy on a course of high employment with stable prices. Monetarists believe that stable monetary growth is the most effective policy for stabilizing the economy, while Fiscalists place their hopes on discretionary changes in the full-employment surplus.[24]

CONCLUSION

This paper assesses the Monetarists' model of money, emphasizing those analytical aspects which differentiate it from the Fiscalists' monetary model. Although these two models are sometimes categorized in terms of "money matters" or "only money matters," this mnemonic classification does not highlight the analytical distinctiveness of their respective monetary theories. To

---

[23] A recent study concludes with the following comments:

A historical investigation of the past fifty years reveals that in every case where the monetary variable and the fiscal variable moved in opposite directions, economic activity moved in the direction of the monetary variable and opposite in direction to the fiscal variable. Every cyclical movement in the money stock since 1919 has been followed by a proportional cyclical movement in economic activity.

Both the statistical results and the historical investigation provide strong support for the case that monetary influences have a significant impact on economic activity over the business cycle. An important implication of these results is that monetary policy should be given a central role in any economic stabilization program.

See M. W. Keran, "Monetary and Fiscal Influences on Economic Activity—The Historical Evidence," November 1969 Review Reserve Bank of St. Louis.

[24] The monetary lag surfaced in the 1950's before the relatively recent (post-1968 tax action) discovery of a possible similar lag in fiscal policy. Differences between Monetarists and Fiscalists based on, or at least presuming, the non-existence of a fiscal lag, may disappear in time. See J. M. Duesenberry, "Tactics and Targets of Monetary Policy" in *Controlling Monetary Aggregates*.

obtain a better understanding of the Monetarists' model we also need to distinguish the money veil of theory and the extremely potent, and high-powered, money of stabilization policy, and between nominal money and the real money stock.

The monetary model (Quantity theory) of the Monetarists incorporate a theory of money, prices and interest rates that differs substantially from the liquidity preference analysis of interest rates of the Fiscalists. Monetarists have a monetary theory of the price level, a non-monetary theory of the (real) interest rate, and a theory relating rising (or high) market rates (nominal interest rates) to rising prices: they postulate, following Fisher, a sequence leading from monetary expansion to rising prices and high market rates; they distinguish, therefore, between rising rates and high rates, and between market rates and real (interest) rates; and they rationalize a rise in market rates (relative to real rates) by introducing a price expectation variable in their model to capture the impact of rising prices on nominal interest rates. The Fiscalists, in contrast, have a monetary theory of the interest rate, a non-monetary theory of the price level, and do not distinguish either between rising and high rates or between nominal and real rates: they assume that high (or rising) market rates reflect corresponding changes in real rates; and they associate the variability of market rates with volatility in real rates. The implication concerning the instability of the real economy is, in this sense, related to this particular analytical framework.[25]

The Monetarists' view of fiscal policy may also be somewhat misunderstood, because it is closely tied to the manner in which they calibrate and measure the posture of monetary policy. An action defined by Fiscalists as one of fiscal stimulus may also be defined by Monetarists as one of monetary stimulus, so that clear-cut discriminating tests of the two theories are not readily available. Thus, it is only when movements in the money stock and in the full-employment surplus go in opposite directions—as in 1966 and in 1968—that we get any real tests of their relative effects.

The Monetarist advocacy of stable monetary growth does not necessarily imply that discretionary fiscal policy actions have no short run aggregate demand effects. It is sufficient for Monetarists to argue that the effects of temporary budgetary changes are uncertain, that they have long and variable lags, that they are not superior (and may be inferior) to monetary actions in terms of effectiveness, and that budgetary changes should be instituted primarily for their important allocative effects. The post-1968 experiences, and the discovery that some fiscal effects may also be subject to a lag, should serve to re-open theoretical and policy discussions of the relative roles of Monetary and Fiscal policy in stabilization.

---

[25] The income-expenditure theory of money, interest rates and prices may explain several of the troublesome features of recent stabilization policy: a tendency to use market interest rates as an indicator of monetary policy; a tendency to minimize the price level consequences of excessive monetary growth; a tendency to abstract from the impact of inflationary expectations on market interest rates; a tendency to treat nominal variables as if they were real quantities; and a tendency to explain the rising market interest rates in the U.S. since 1965 as reflecting an increased demand for money, and not as the result of accelerated growth in the monetary aggregates.

READING 27

MONETARY AND FISCAL INFLUENCES ON ECONOMIC ACTIVITY—THE HISTORICAL EVIDENCE

Michael W. Keran*

A subject of continuing interest in professional and recently in popular economic writing is the relative role of monetary and fiscal influences in determining economic activity.[1] This debate has been renewed by Leonall Andersen and Jerry Jordan (AJ) in an article published in this *Review*.[2] That article presented evidence which indicated that monetary influences had a larger, more predictable, and faster effect on economic activity than fiscal influences in the period from 1953 to 1968.

These results have stimulated considerable interest and discussion.[3] The

Source: Reprinted from Federal Reserve Bank of St. Louis Review, November 1969, pp. 5–23.

* The content and presentation in this article have been substantially improved by the suggestions of the author's colleagues in the Research Department of the Federal Reserve Bank of St. Louis: Homer Jones, Leonall Andersen, Christopher Babb, Denis Karnosky, and William Yohe. In addition, he received valuable comments and criticisms from Oswald Brownlee, Karl Brunner, Philip Cagan, Albert Cox, Milton Friedman, Harry Johnson, John Kalchbrenner, Thomas Mayer, David Meiselman, and Allan Meltzer.

[1] This issue was first raised in a somewhat different context by Milton Friedman and David Meiselman in "The Relative Stability of Monetary Velocity and the Investment Multiplier in the U.S." *Stabilization Policies,* The Commission on Money and Credit, Prentice-Hall, 1963.

[2] Leonall C. Andersen and Jerry Jordan: "Monetary and Fiscal Actions: A Test of Their Relative Importance in Economic Stabilization," this *Review,* November 1968.

[3] Richard G. Davis, "How Much Does Money Matter?" *Monthly Review,* Federal Reserve Bank of New York, June 1969; Edward M. Gramlich, "The Role of Money in Economic Activity: Complicated or Simple?," *Business Economics,* September 1969; "The Usefulness of Monetary and Fiscal Policy as Discretionary Stabilization Tools," (presented at the American Bankers Association, Conference of University Professors, Milwaukee, September 1969); Frank de Leeuw and John Kalchbrenner, "Monetary and Fiscal Actions: A Test of Their Relative Importance in Economic Stabilization—Comment,"

ensuing debate has mainly confined it-self, however, to the time period used in the original AJ article (1953–68). Since other economic experiences might suggest a different assessment of monetary and fiscal influences, it seems useful to expand the testing periods to include a longer period in United States economic history.

It is reasonable to assume that tests obtained from a wider range of experi-ence would go a long way toward an-swering some of the questions raised about the AJ article. If the dominance of monetary influences prevailed in earlier periods, then confidence in the reliability and stability of the original results and their continued applicability is enhanced. On the other hand, if the dominance of monetary influences is shown to be confined to only the most recent time period, then it could be as-serted that special circumstances are at work in the present period which could not be relied upon to continue. The intent of this article is to test the relative impact of monetary and fiscal influences on economic activity in the United States on a quarterly basis from 1919 to 1969 and for selected sub-periods.

This article is organized in the follow-ing way. First, a brief and highly simpli-fied review is given of some of the theoretical and statistical issues which have been raised in connection with the type of tests used by AJ. This review will allow us to see what can and can-not be deduced from any results. Sec-ond, the test results for the 50-year period from 1919 to 1969, with 200 quar-terly observations, will be presented,

together with a historical review and comparison. Finally, the statistical re-liability of the results will be considered.

I. THEORETICAL AND STATISTICAL ISSUES

There are two primary ways to study the relative importance of monetary and fiscal influences on economic activity. First, their effects can be inferred with-in the context of a fully specified and statistically estimated structural model of the economy, as in the FRB-MIT model.[4] The monetary and fiscal vari-ables are introduced in the structural model at those points where their func-tional roles are indicated by economic theory. The measured impact on eco-nomic activity of the monetary and fis-cal variables is dependent upon the ex-plicit transmission mechanism which is postulated and built into the structural model. Second, monetary and fiscal in-fluences can be measured by direct estimation of a single regression equa-tion. In this case, some measure of eco-nomic activity is regressed directly against the monetary and fiscal vari-ables without specification of a trans-mission mechanism.

A. The Large Structural Model Approach

There are advantages and disadvan-tages associated with each of these ap-proaches. An important advantage of the large structural model is that it allows one to distinguish between di-rect and indirect monetary and fiscal influences, and to see how subsectors of the economy are affected. In formal terms a structural model is essentially a

---

this *Review*, April 1969; Paul S. Anderson, "Monetary Velocity in Empirical Analysis," *Controlling Monetary Aggregates*, prepared by the Federal Reserve Bank of Boston, September 1969; M. J. Artis and A. R. Nobay, "Two Aspects of the Monetary Debate," National Institute *Economic Review*, Vol. XLIX (August 1969), pp. 33–51; and Wilfred Lewis, Jr., " 'Money is Everything' Economics—A Tempest in a Teapot," National Conference Board *Record*, Vol. VI, No. 4 (April, 1969), pp. 32–35.

[4] See Frank de Leeuw and Edward M. Gramlich, "The Channels of Monetary Policy," Federal Reserve *Bulletin*, June 1969. A structural model is one in which the major behavioral assumptions of a theory are explicitly included in the statistical estimates. It is fully specified if there are as many equations as there are endogenous variables.

hypothesis of the model builders about the interrelations in the economy. The statistically estimated equations represent components of that hypothesis. If it turns out that the model builders' view of the economic mechanism is reasonably correct, then the "structural richness" of the large models permits a wider range of questions to be answered.

The major disadvantage of structural models is that the model builder may have omitted an important channel of transmission and, consequently, incorrectly estimated the magnitude of the monetary or fiscal influences. Indeed, even if the model builder has a good idea of the transmission channels, it may be technically impossible to estimate them because the channels have not or cannot be quantified. For example, assuming that the cost of borrowing is an important link in the monetary transmission mechanism, it is quite possible that this is not accurately measured by market interest rates. Both changes in credit rationing and compensating balance requirements, for which there are no available quantified measures, could affect the cost of borrowing yet not be reflected in changes in market interest rates.

B. The Single Equation Approach

An advantage of the single equation approach is that if the monetary and fiscal variables are correctly specified, and if they are not themselves determined by economic activity, they will capture the direct and indirect impact of monetary and fiscal influences on economic activity, irrespective of the transmission channels. The single equation approach avoids the problem of specifying and measuring specific links between monetary and fiscal influences and economic activity, and will gener-

ally be consistent with a wide range of theories (hypotheses) about the structural interrelations in the economy.

One major disadvantage of the single equation approach used here is that it can deal with only a single question, the relative impact of monetary and fiscal influences on economic activity. It does not distinguish between the direct and indirect impact of the monetary and fiscal influences on economic activity or how subsectors of the economy are affected.[5] In addition, both the structural model approach and the single equation approach face the same problem of selecting measures of monetary and fiscal influences which are exogenous in a statistical sense.

In order to derive results which are comparable with AJ's work, the single equation approach (the so-called St. Louis equation) is used here. However, before presenting the test results, it would be useful to consider what can and cannot be implied by using this approach. First, as was previously noted, the single equation approach restricts us to considering just one question—the relative impact of monetary and fiscal influences on economic activity. We cannot say what the channels of the influence are.

Second, the single equation approach used here does not allow us to discriminate between economic theories. Take the generalized statement of the single equation which is used in this article:

$$\Delta Y = \alpha_0 + \alpha_1 \Delta M + \alpha_2 \Delta F$$

where ΔY = changes in economic activity,
ΔM = changes in monetary influences.
ΔF = changes in fiscal influences.

The parameters, α_1 and α_2, indicate the magnitude of the impact of monetary and fiscal influences, respectively, on economic activity, and α_0 is a proxy for the net trend of all other influences on

---

[5] One way to handle this disadvantage is to regress the monetary and fiscal variables against the components of GNP to see which broad sectors of the economy are affected. See Leonall C. Andersen, "Money and Economic Forecasting," *Business Economics,* September 1969, for the results of such a test.

economic activity. Assume for the moment that the statistical results of a test using this format subsantially favor monetary influences (ΔM) over fiscal influences (ΔF) in determining economic activity (ΔY). These results do not provide clear-cut evidence to help answer the question of whether the Keynesian Income-Expenditure Theory or the Modern Quantity Theory is a better representation of the economic world. Both theories provide an operational rule for monetary influences, and thus the dominance of the monetary variable does not discriminate between them.[6] A test of competing economic theories can be conducted only if the alternative behavioral assumptions are made explicit.[7]

Third, the single equation approach does not necessarily tell us anything about monetary and fiscal policy decisions of the authorities. If the independent variables have been chosen properly, they will indicate monetary and fiscal influences on the economy. One can assert that such influences are simultaneously a measure of the policy intentions of the authorities only if additional external evidence is provided, which indicates that the policy-makers have acted either consciously or otherwise to systematically control the monetary and fiscal variables used in the equation.[8]

The third point can be clarified with an example: Assuming there are two countries, A and B. Statistical tests indicate that the monetary variable dominates the fiscal variable in influencing economic activity in each country. However, it is also known that Country A does not have a central bank, while Country B does. Obviously, we can only talk about discretionary monetary *policy* in Country B, but we can talk about monetary *influence* in both countries. In Country A, the monetary variable is dominated by factors other than by the actions of a central bank—perhaps by the domestic gold supply. In Country B (with a central bank), the monetary variable could be dominated by the central bank; however, our statistical results do not provide any evidence with respect to that issue. Such evidence can be derived only by an explicit investigation of the behavior of the central bank in Country B. Thus, discretionary monetary policy and monetary influences are not necessarily measured by the same variable.[9]

---

[6] There are a number of empirically estimated Keynesian economic models which have a "weak" monetary sector. Evidence that monetary influences are important would tend to cast doubt on the usefulness of those models. However, this is more a criticism of the particular model and not the underlying Keynesian theory. Within the context of standard Keynesian theory, there are circumstances where strong monetary and weak fiscal influences could exist.

[7] A test of competing economic theories conceptually could be conducted either wtih a single reduced-form equation or with a more fully specified structural model. When Friedman and Meiselman, "The Relative Stability . . ." attempted such a test using the single equation reduced-form approach, a considerable controversy occurred within the economics profession. To the best of the author's knowledge, no one has attempted to compare competing theories by a test of alternative structural models.

[8] Such information would come from studies of the "reaction function" of the policy-making authorities. There have been a number of such studies of the monetary authorities. For example: (1) William Dewald and Harry Johnson, "An Objective Analysis of the Objectives of American Monetary Policy, 1952–1961," *Banking and Monetary Studies,* ed. Deane Carson (Homewood, Illinois: Richard D. Irwin, 1963); (2) James W. Christian, "A Further Analysis of the Objectives of American Monetary Policy," *The Journal of Finance,* volume XXIII, June 1968; (3) Michael W. Keran, and Christopher T. Babb, "An Explanation of Federal Reserve Actions (1933–68)," this *Review,* July 1969; (4) John Wood, "A Model of Federal Reserve Behavior," *Staff Economic Study No. 17,* Board of Governors of the Federal Reserve System.

[9] This point is quite important and open to some misunderstanding. To link monetary policy with the indicator of monetary influence, it is not necessary that the authorities consciously control the value of the monetary variable. All that is required is that in controlling some monetary variable the

Given this array of caveats with respect to the single equation approach, it is nevertheless highly useful in indicating monetary and fiscal influences on economic activity. The key reason has already been discussed. An economy is an extremely complex array of interrelated and interdependent markets tied together by the price mechanism. Millions of individual decision-making units participate in these markets. In this complex web of inter-relationships, attempts at specific and detailed measurement of the channels through which monetary and fiscal influences operate on economic activity are quite hazardous.

Given the complexities of the economy and the existing uncertainty about the transmission mechanism, it is useful to measure the monetary and fiscal influences directly, without constraining them to operate within our imperfect notions about how they operate. Freedom from this type of specification error is perhaps the principal virtue of the single equation approach.

C. Problems of the Single Equation Approach

The key methodological and statistical problems with the single equation approach are related to selection of appropriate indicators of monetary and fiscal influences. First, a theoretical justification for using particular variables is required. Such justification naturally evolves from the various economic theories (hypotheses) which have been developed to explain the determination of aggregate economic activity. For example, bank credit or free reserves are unlikely indicators of monetary influence because there is no well-specified economic theory from which these variables are a derivable

consequence. Even if statistical results indicate a close relation between bank credit and economic activity, it is difficult to interpret the results. On the other hand, the money stock is a good choice as an indicator of monetary influence because it plays an important role in both the Keynesian Income-Expenditure Theory and the Modern Quantity Theory of Money.

Second, there must be evidence that the actions of monetary and fiscal authorities determine the movements in the variables selected. It is not necessary that the policymakers have acted consciously to control the specific variables used; it is only necessary that policy actions systematically dominate movements in the indicated variable.

This leads naturally to the third and final condition. To be able to interpret the regression coefficients meaningfully in the single equation approach, the monetary and fiscal variables must be statistically exogenous. The economic meaning behind this condition is that the variables selected to represent monetary and fiscal influences should not be contemporaneously determined by the behavior of the public, as measured by changes in economic activity. If this exogeneity assumption is not satisfied, the direction of causality is uncertain, and a close statistical association with economic activity does not provide any evidence of the magnitude of the impact from monetary and fiscal influences. This is the so-called "reverse-causation argument" against the single equation approach.

The next section presents the results of various statistical tests of monetary and fiscal influences on economic activity. The last section will consider the reverse-causation argument and whether movements in the monetary

---

authorities in the process also dominate movements in the variable used to indicate monetary influences. If the authorities have not deliberately attempted to control the variable which is the best indicator of monetary influence, then their policy actions could be criticized. However, this is not necessarily an argument against using that variable as an indicator of monetary influence.

variables are dominated by the monetary authorities or by the public. Because the theoretical justification for the monetary and fiscal variables used in this article has already been considered in the AJ article, it will be presented here.

II. MONETARY AND FISCAL INFLUENCES

The test procedure used in this article is to regress quarter-to-quarter changes in a measure of economic activity against quarter-to-quarter changes in the indicators of monetary and fiscal influence. Because of the length of the test period (1919–69), data problems were encountered. For example, the most widely used measure of economic activity (nominal GNP), and the most widely used measure of fiscal policy (high-employment receipts and expenditures of the Federal Government), are not available on a quarterly basis before 1946. These deficiencies in the data necessitated developing proxies for these measures.

A proxy for nominal GNP was constructed to measure economic activity. The proxy consists of the scaled product of the Industrial Production Index (IPI) and the Consumer Price Index (CPI), both of which are available on a monthly basis in continuous time series back to February 1919. Each is the broadest available measure of real output and prices, and their scaled product is an index of economic activity. To convert this value index into a dollar measure, it was multiplied by the value of nominal GNP in the base years of the value index (1957–59).[10] By this method an index of quarterly economic activity, measured in billions of dollars, was constructed for the period II/1919 to II/1969.

This proxy for economic activity clearly has a number of defects. The service industries, levels of government and agriculture are excluded. In addition, industrial production traditionally grows at a faster trend rate than overall real output because it is more responsive to increases in productivity. Also, it shows larger swings over the business cycle than does nominal GNP. However, for the purpose of measuring the *changes* in economic activity from one quarter to the next, this proxy appears to be both useful and reasonably accurate.[11] Chart 1 shows the quarter-to-quarter rates of change in nominal GNP and in our proxy from 1947 to 1969.

As a measure of fiscal influence, changes in the national debt (ΔD) and actual Federal Government expenditures (ΔE) (purchases of goods and services plus transfer payments) were used. Data on tax receipts are available, but because of the strong influence which economic activity has on the value of tax receipts, it was not used.

Because ΔD is also influenced by changes in tax receipts, only the results using Government spending are reported. The use of Federal Government spending as our single measure of

---

[10] The formula used to compute this measure of economic activity (Y) is:

$$Y = \frac{IPI \cdot CPI}{10,000} \cdot (\$457.4 \text{ billion})$$

[11] The regressions between rates of change of nominal GNP (G$\dot{N}$P) and our proxy variable ($\dot{Y}$) appear as follows:

I/1947 — IV/1952

G$\dot{N}$P = 3.78 + .45 $\dot{Y}$ R^2 = .74
     (3.53) (8.24)   D-W = 1.82

I/1953 — I/1969

G$\dot{N}$P = 3.42 +   .40 $\dot{Y}$ R^2 = .80
    (11.44) (15.80)   D-W = 1.55

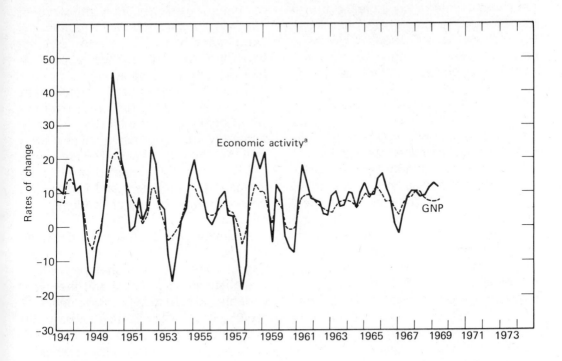

Chart 1. Nominal GNP and economic activity. Quarterly data at annual rates.

a Economic Activity is measured by the scaled product of the Consumer Price Index (CPI) and the Industrial Production Index (IPI) multiplied by Gross National Product (GNP) in the base years 1957–1959:

$$\frac{CPI \cdot IPI}{10,000} \cdot \$457.4 \text{ billion} = \text{Economic Activity.}$$

Sources: GNP—U.S. Department of Commerce; *Economic Activity*—Industrial Production Index, Board of Governors of the Federal Reserve System; Consumer Price Index, U.S. Department of Labor.

fiscal influence is not as serious a drawback as it might first appear. Andersen and Jordan (AJ) found that the strongest measure of fiscal influence was achieved by using Federal Government expenditures alone. The observed level of Government spending which is used from 1919 to 1945 is not significantly different from the high-employment level of Government spending which AJ used, and which is used here for the subperiods from 1946 to 1969.[12]

As measures of monetary influence, three variables were tested: total reserves of member banks, the monetary base, and the narrowly defined money stock (currency holdings of the non-bank public and private demand deposits). The separate use of monetary and fiscal variables in these regressions implies that one can think of monetary and fiscal influences as having separate impacts on economic activity. This may not be the case. One well-known fiscal influence on monetary actions can occur because of "even-keel" actions. "Even-keel" is the policy of the Federal Reserve to stabilize money market conditions during periods when the United States Treasury is floating a new issue of securities. Thus, an increase in Government

[12] The only difference between the observed levels of Government spending and the high-employment level of Government spending is an adjustment for unemployment compensation payments. These payments did not start until 1937 and did not amount to a significant figure until after World War II. See Chart 3 for sources of data for Government spending, money stock, and economic activity.

spending financed by an increase in debt could induce an increase in the money stock because of Federal Reserve "even-keel" actions. This issue can be dealt with only by asserting that all factors which affect the money stock are monetary and all factors which affect Government spending are fiscal. This is not unreasonable, since the Federal Reserve could stop even-keel actions if it chose to do so.

The tests of monetary and fiscal influences were run using four measures of change: quarterly first differences, quarterly central differences, quarterly first rates of change, and quarterly central rates of change. Only the results with quarterly first differences of the money stock and Government expenditures are reported in this article. However, alternative measures of change and alternative measures of monetary and fiscal influences give substantially similar results.[13]

In each test the form of the equation was estimated with money alone, fiscal alone, and a combination of the two. Alternative time lags between t-1 and t-10 were tried using the Almon distributed-lag technique.[14] The form of the equation selected and the time lags to represent each time period were chosen on the basis of minimum standard error of estimate adjusted for degrees of freedom.[15]

The total period was divided into five subperiods: 1919–29, when economic conditions were generally prosperous; 1929–39, when economic conditions were generally depressed; 1939–46, when the United States was approaching or was in a total war situation; 1947–52, the early postwar adjustment period and finally, 1953–69, a period when economic conditions were again generally prosperous. These subperiods cover a sufficiently wide range of economic conditions to provide an indication of monetary and fiscal influences under a variety of economic circumstances.

A summary of the regression results is reported in Table I. For the total period 1919–69, the monetary variable is statistically significant and the fiscal variable is statistically insignificant at the 95 per cent confidence level. In the five subperiods, the monetary variable is significant in all but the subperiod covering the war years, 1939–46. The absence of a statistically significant monetary variable in this period is probably due more to the inadequacies of the data than to a lack of a relationship. Because of price controls, the measure of economic activity was substantially understated between 1939 and 1946. Therefore, it is not surprising that the variables measuring the influences of stabilization actions were not statistically significant in that period.

The fiscal influence was statistically

---

[13] The other results are available upon request.

[14] The Almon lag technique, by constraining the distribution of coefficients to fit a polynomial curve of n degree, is designed to avoid the bias in estimating distributed-lag coefficients which may arise from multicollinearity in the lag values of the independent variables. The theoretical justification for this procedure is that the Almon constrained estimate is superior to the unconstrained estimate because it will create a distribution of coefficients which more closely approximates the distribution derived from a sample of infinite size. In order to minimize the severity of the Almon constraint, the maximum degree of the polynomial was used in each case. The maximum degree is equal to the number of lags plus one of the independent variables up to five lags. Following the convention established by Shirley Almon, "The Distributed Lag Between Capital Appropriations and Expenditures," *Econometrica*, Vol. XXXII, No. 1 (January 1965), if there are n lags, $t + 1$ and $t - n - 1$ are both constrained to zero. The regressions were also run without constraining the beginning and ending values to zero, and the results are virtually identical.

[15] For a discussion of this criteria for selecting lags, see Leonall Andersen, "An Evaluation of the Impact of Monetary and Fiscal Policy on Economic Activity," *Papers and Proceedings,* Business and Economic Statistics Section, American Statistical Association, August 1969.

TABLE 1

INDICATORS OF MONETARY (ΔM) AND FISCAL (ΔE) INFLUENCES ON ECONOMIC (ΔY)

$$\Delta Y = a_0 + a_1 \Delta M + a_2 \Delta E$$

(Quarterly First Differences—Billions of Dollars)

Time Periods	Lags[a]	a_0	$a_1 \Delta M$ (sum)	$a_2 \Delta E$ (sum)	R^2 D-W
II/1919—I/69	t-6	1.92	2.89	—.07	.32
		(2.34)	(4.31)	(.28)	1.15
II/1919—II/29	t-3	.36	5.62	b	.35
		(.51)	(3.16)		1.58
III/1929—II/39	t-5	—.51	5.40	—7.97	.39
		(.54)	(3.41)	(1.95)	1.86
III/1939—IV/46	t-5	6.32	—1.21	.35	.66
		(1.39)	(.59)	(.81)	1.60
I/1947—IV/52	t-10	3.65	13.82	—3.37	.72
		(.84)	(3.51)	(4.12)	2.74
I/1953—I/69	t-4	1.42	8.85	—.84	.47
		(.74)	(4.70)	(1.07)	1.71

NOTE: Regression coefficients are the top figures; their "t" statistics appear below each coefficient, enclosed by parentheses. R^2 is the percent of variations in the dependent variable which is explained by varaitions in the independent variable. D-W is the Durbin-Watson statistic.

[a] Lags are selected on the basis of minimum standard error, adjusted for degrees of freedom.

[b] Fiscal variable omitted for 1919–29 because it increased the standard error of the estimate.

significant in only one of the five subperiods, 1947–52. However, the sign of the coefficient is negative due to special factors which are explained below.

In general, the results with respect to both monetary and fiscal variables for the period 1919–69 and the subperiods conform closely to the results reported in the AJ article for the period 1953–68. The coefficient of determination (R^2), which measures the per cent of variations in ΔY due to variations in ΔM and ΔE, is lower than that reported by AJ. This result is not surprising considering that our proxy is probably inferior to nominal GNP as a measure of economic activity.

Because of the major importance of the monetary influence, it is useful to look at the estimated coefficients of the monetary variable during the various subperiods. In both of the prewar subperiods, 1919–29 and 1929–39, the estimated coefficients on the monetary variable are almost the same, around 5.50. This implies that for every $1 increase in the money stock there will

be a $5.50 increase in economic activity after three to five quarters. These are remarkably stable coefficients. In the postwar subperiods, however, the coefficients are substantially larger, and they are also different with respect to each other. In the 1947–52 period the coefficient on the monetary variable is 13.82 with a ten-quarter lag in its impact. In the 1953–69 period the coefficient is 8.85 with a four-quarter lag. What does this variation in the value of the monetary coefficients imply?

The difference in the values of the coefficients between postwar subperiods is due to the different length of lags. These lags are selected on the basis of minimum standard error of estimate, adjusted for degrees of freedom. The results for the 1947–52 subperiod with a four-quarter, rather than a ten-quarter lag, had a monetary variable coefficient of 7.24. This value is quite close to the 8.85 value for the 1953–69 subperiod where the minimum standard error estimate was with a four-quarter lag.

The higher average value of the monetary coeffiicents in the postwar subperiods over the prewar subperiods is due to the weakness in the proxy selected to measure economic activity. The most complete measure of economic activity is nominal GNP. However, it is available on a quarterly basis only since 1946. As previously indicated, our proxy for economic activity tends on the average to grow more rapidly than nominal GNP because its "real" component is measured by industrial production. This factor did not bias the value of the coefficients in the prewar subperiods, because the Great Depression insured that our proxy did not grow significantly between 1919–29 and 1929–39. For the postwar subperiods, however, the substantial and continuous increases in economic activity probably have caused an upward bias in the size of the monetary variable coefficient presented in Table 1. For the 1953–69 period, AJ had a monetary variable coefficient with a four-quarter lag of 5.63, using nominal GNP. This value is almost identical to prewar subperiods when economic activity is measured with our proxy.

Thus, it is quite possible that if quarterly nominal GNP figures were available back to 1919, the estimated value of the monetary coefficients would have been close to 5.50 in all subperiods.

A. Testing Propositions

The propositions which AJ tested were whether monetary or fiscal influences were (1) stronger, (2) more predictable, and (3) faster in their impact on economic activity. They concluded that the evidence for the 1953–1968 period strongly favored the dominance of monetary over fiscal influences. These same propositions are tested in this article and provide additional evidence that monetary influences consistently have been stronger, more predictable, and faster in their effect on economic activity than have fiscal influences. The results are detailed below.

1.   WHICH IS STRONGER?

To measure the relative strength of monetary and fiscal influences, we need to know which has the largest impact on economic activity. This question can be answered by making an appropriate comparison of the coefficients of the monetary and fiscal variables. If the variables on which these coefficients are estimated have the same dimension and magnitude of variation, then the comparison can be made directly. These conditions, however, are not satisfied with these data. Money is a stock variable measured as first differences, and Federal Government spending is a flow variable measured as first differences at annual rates. Also, the degree of variation in the two variables differs substantially. In general, the fiscal variable has fluctuated more than the monetary variable (see Chart 3 on pages 298 and 299).

To make the *estimated coefficients* of the monetary and fiscal variables comparable for an assessment of their relative impact on economic activity, they were transformed into *beta coefficients*. The "sum" beta coefficients are presented in Table 2. For the whole period the monetary influence is large and statistically significant, while the fiscal influence is negative and statistically insignificant. This result also applies to each of the subperiods, except for World War II and the early postwar periods (1939–52). During the World War II years the monetary influence is statistically insignificant and negative, and the fiscal influence is insignificant and positive. For the early post-World War II years the fiscal influence is statistically significant and negative.

TABLE 2

BETA COEFFICIENTS

	ΔM (sum)	ΔE (sum)
II/1919—I/69	.331*	—.026
II/1919—II/29	.515*	—
III/1929—II/39	.593*	—.803
III/1939—IV/46	—.153	.219
I/1947—IV/52	1.768*	—2.347*
I/1953—I/69	.726*	—.159

NOTE: "Beta coefficients" are equal to the estimated coefficient times the standard deviation of the independent variable over the standard deviation of the dependent variable. See Arthur S. Goldberger, *Economic Theory* (John Wiley & Sons, 1964) pp. 197–98.

* Significant at the 95% level of confidence.

TABLE 3

t VALUES

	ΔM (sum)	ΔE (sum)
II/1919—I/69	4.31	— .28
II/1919—II/29	3.16	0
III/1929—II/39	3.41	—1.95
III/1939—IV/46	— .59	.81
I/1947—IV/52	3.51	—4.12
I/1953—I/1969	4.70	—1.07

NOTE: A *t* value is a statistical indicator of the confidence one may have that the "true relationship" between the independent and dependent variable has the same sign as the statistically estimated coefficient of that relationship.

This postwar regression result seems to be due to special factors which are outlined below.

2. WHICH IS MORE PREDICTABLE?

The monetary or fiscal variable with the more statistically significant coefficient is also more reliable in that its relationship to economic activity is more predictable. Statistical significance is measured by the *t* values of the coefficients of the monetary and fiscal variables when measured against the same dependent variable, which in this case was ΔY. A *t* value is a statistical indicator of the confidence one may have that the "true relationship" between the independent and dependent variable has the same sign as the statistically estimated coefficient of that relationship. The larger a *t* value, the more confidence we have that the monetary and fiscal variables are related to economic activity. The *t* values of the sum coefficients are presented in Table 3. For the whole period, the *t* value of the monetary variable is substantially larger than the *t* value of the fiscal variable. The same statement also holds with respect to the *t* values of the monetary and fiscal variables in the subperiods, with the exception of the war and early postwar periods (1939–52). Thus, in general, the monetary variable has a more predictable effect on economic activity than the fiscal variable.

3. WHICH WORKS FASTER?

The relative promptness of monetary or fiscal influences can be measured by observing which variable has a shorter time lag in influencing economic activity. This can be seen in the quarterly patterns of the regression coefficients after they have been transformed into beta coefficients. The latter are plotted in Chart 2 and are derived from the same set of statistical results summarized in Table 1. The fiscal variable has about the same impact as the monetary variable in the contemporaneous quarter during the total period 1919–1969. However, in the succeeding quarters the fiscal influence declines and becomes negative, while the monetary influence continues to be positive through the third lagged quarter. The quarterly pattern of the monetary influence in the subperiods is quite similar to that of the total period. The pattern of the fiscal influence varies irregularly over subperiods. However, in all subperiods except the war period 1939–46, the monetary variable has a consistently faster influ-

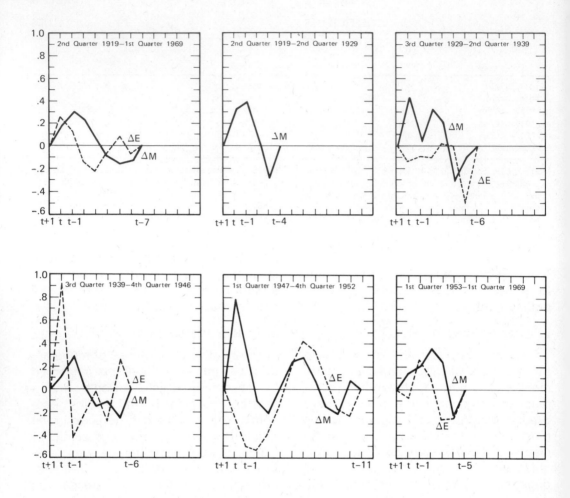

Chart 2. Beta coefficients of Monetary and fiscal influences, first differences.

NOTE: Beta coefficients are for the Money Stock (ΔM) and Government Expenditures (ΔE), and are calculated as the products of the regression coefficients for the respective variables times the ratio of the standard deviation of the independent variables to the standard deviation of Economic Activity (ΔY). Lags were selected on the basis of the minimum standard error of estimate. These charts are derived from the statistical results which are summarized in Table 1.

ence on economic activity than the fiscal variable.

B. Historical Review

The statistical results reported above are estimated on the basis of the average response of economic activity to monetary and fiscal influences within each of the periods selected. A different way of looking at monetary and fiscal influences on economic activity

is to investigate specific historic episodes. Chart 3 on pages 298 and 299 is designed to assist in that investigation. In the lower tier of the chart the monetary and fiscal variables are plotted as rates of change on a common axis. In the upper tier of the chart economic activity is also plotted in its rate-of-change form.[16]

The most interesting comparisons are to be found where the monetary

[16] Rates of change are used to allow comparisons over long time periods on a similar basis.

and fiscal influences are operating in opposite directions. In those periods the movement in economic activity will indicate which influence is dominant. The monetary and fiscal variables move in opposite directions in the periods 1919–21, 1931–32, 1939, 1948–50, and 1966–67. In each of these years economic activity, after a short lag, moved in the same direction as the monetary variable and in the opposite direction to the fiscal variable. As a matter of fact, all cyclical movements in the money stock were followed by proportional cyclical movements in economic activity. Of the *twelve* cyclical movements in economic activity from 1919 to 1969, *eleven* are preceded by corresponding movements in the money stock.[17] The single exception is the deceleration in economic activity in 1951, which is discussed below.

1.   1919–1929

Although this period was one of general economic prosperity, there were three cyclical declines in this ten-year period. The first and most severe occurred in late 1920 and early 1921. During the remainder of the 1920's two shorter and milder declines occurred; in late 1923 to early 1924, and in 1927.

Each of these cyclical movements in economic activity is matched by a corresponding movement in the money stock. Money switched from a 15 per cent rate of increase in the fourth quarter of 1919 to a 16 per cent rate of decline in the first quarter of 1921. This was the sharpest five-quarter deceleration in the money stock recorded during our fifty-year period. The money stock had pronounced, though milder, decelerations in 1923 and late 1926.

Federal Government spending showed substantial fluctuation in the earlier part of the period and very little

movement in the middle and latter part of the period. This experience reflected the demobilization after World War I and the conservative spending policies of the Harding and Coolidge administrations.

The statistical results reported in Table 1, page 293, omit the fiscal variable entirely for this subperiod, because its inclusion raises the standard error of the estimate (adjusted for degrees of freedom) and thus contributes nothing to the explanation of movements in economic activity. This is not true of any other subperiod in this study.

2.   1929–1939

The first part of this period is undoubtedly the most depressed in the entire economic history of the United States. It was not the sharpness of the decline that was so disastrous. There were more rapid declines in both 1920 and 1937. Its duration was disastrous. Economic activity declined at an annual rate of 20 percent or more for ten of the eleven quarters between late 1929 and late 1932. Sustained recovery did not start until the middle of 1933, when 25 per cent of the labor force was unemployed and the price level was 24 per cent below its 1929 level. This recovery lasted, with one significant interruption in 1937, through the end of the period.

Monetary influences during this period have been characterized by a number of observers as being especially ineffective. The results presented in this article indicate that quite the opposite was the case. Monetary influences played an important role in the declines in economic activity in 1929–33 and 1937–38, and in the recovery in the intervening years.

Although the initial decline in the third quarter of 1929 apparently was

---

[17] Milton Friedman and Anna Schwartz made a similar observation in "Money and Business Cycles," *Review of Economics and Statistics,* February 1963.

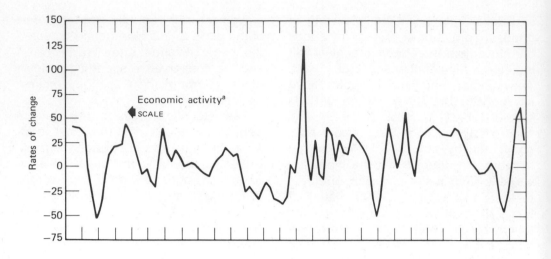

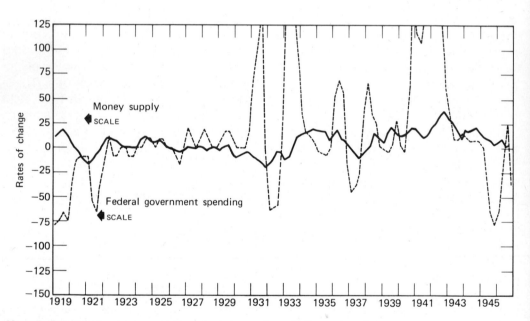

Chart 3. Changes in money supply and government expenditures in relation to changes in economic activity. Quarterly data at annual rates.

* The magnitude of fluctuations in the three series plotted decreased considerably after World War II. The rate of change scale for the postwar years (1947–74) consequently has been enlarged to facilitate comparisons among the three series.

a Economic activity is measured by the scaled product of the Consumer Price Index (CPI) and the Industrial Production Index (IPI) multiplied by Gross National Product (GNP) in the base years 1957–59:

$$\frac{CPI \cdot IPI}{10,000} \cdot \$457.4 \text{ billion} = \text{Economic activity.}$$

not due to tight money influence (the money stock did not decline until the fourth quarter of 1929), the fact that the economic decline lasted for more than three years is associated with a decline in the money stock.[18] The initial

---

[18] Milton Friedman and Anna Schwartz, *A Monetary History of the United States*, (Princeton, New Jersey: Princeton University Press, 1963), chapter 7, go into considerable detail describing how Federal Reserve actions dominated movements in the money stock during this period.

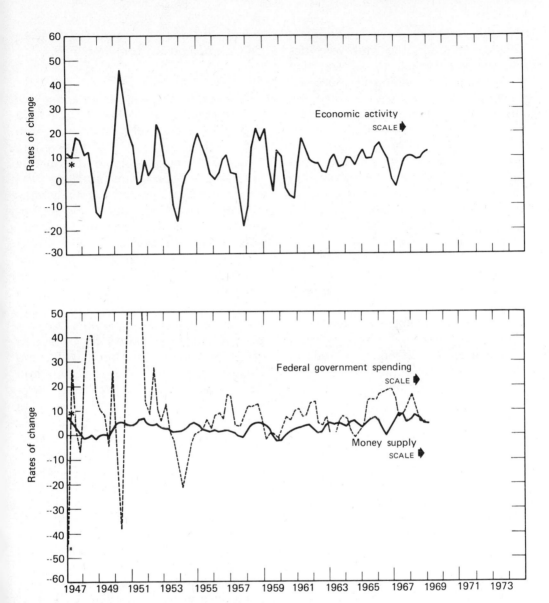

Sources: Money Supply: 1919–46, Milton Friedman & Anna J. Schwartz, "A Monetary History of the United States; 1947–1969," Board of Governors of the Federal Reserve System; Federal Government Spending: 1917–28, estimated from U.S. Historical Statistics, Bureau of Census; 1929–1945, estimated from National Income & Products Supplement, U.S. Department of Commerce; 1946–69, Federal Reserve Bank of St. Louis; Economic Activity: Industrial Production Index, Board of Governors of the Federal Reserve System; Consumer Price Index, U.S. Department of Labor.

five quarters of decline in the money stock were relatively mild. After reaching an annual 9 per cent rate of decline in the first quarter of 1930, it slowed to a 3 per cent rate of decline in the fourth quarter of 1930. Then, for the next four quarters, the money stock decelerated substantially and reached an annual rate of decline of 18 per cent in the fourth quarter of 1931. For the next six quarters the declines became progressively smaller. Finally, at the end of 1933 the money stock registered the first quarterly increase since the third quarter of 1929. The money stock had shown continual quarterly declines for almost four years.

Economic activity moved parallel

with the money stock pattern in 1929–33. Although the first year decline was substantial, it was less than the four-quarter decline in 1920–21, and only moderately greater than the four-quarter decline in 1923–24. In the first half of 1931 the rate of decline actually slowed, responding to the less restrictive monetary influences. However, in the next year the decline in economic activity increased sharply. In the year ending June 1932, it declined by 37 per cent. In late 1932, economic activity finally stopped declining, and in early 1933 it started to increase. This increase generally continued until the middle of 1937, when it was temporarily reversed by the tight money influence which developed in late 1936.

During this period fiscal influences, as measured by changes in Federal Government expenditures, were quite erratic. They were highly expansionary in the years 1931, 1933 to early 1934, 1936, and 1938. On the other hand, they were restrictive in the years 1932, 1935, and 1937. This pattern sometimes conformed with and sometimes opposed monetary influences. But in every case economic activity moved consistently with the direction and magnitude of monetary influences.

3. 1939–1946

Data for the war years are presented to make the series complete. However, with comprehensive price controls tending to create a discrepancy between the equilibrium and observed growth rate in economic activity, there is little to be learned about monetary and fiscal influences from this period. Our results indicate that the monetary variable was not statistically significant during this period. The fiscal variable had a strong positive influence in the quarter in which the Government spending took place, but tended to

"washout" after five quarters, leaving only a small positive net influence.

4. 1947–1952

There were three cyclical expansions in this period: early 1947–48, late 1949 and 1950, and in 1952. There were cyclical contractions in the intervening years. The movements in the money stock did a good job of "tracking" the movements of economic activity during this period, with the single exception of the deceleration in economic activity which occurred in 1951. This is the only deceleration in economic activity in the fifty-year period which was not anticipated by movements in the money stock.

A quite plausible expanation for this phenomena is provided by Friedman and Schwartz.[19] In March 1951 the United States Treasury Department and the Federal Reserve reached an "Accord," which permitted the latter to abandon its war-induced policy of pegging the price of Government bonds. Even though the Federal Reserve did not take advantage of this increased flexibility in policy actions immediately, the public act of abandoning support of the Government bond market greatly reduced the apparent liquidity of the public. The public was no longer assured that conversions between Government bonds and money could take place at a fixed and known price. This caused a substantial, one-time increase in the liquidity demand for money balances relative to income, and a decrease in the velocity of money in a period when velocity had typically been rising.

This experience suggests not only that permanent changes in the demand for money independent of changes in income can weaken the observed relation between money and income, but that such changes in money demand

[19] Friedman and Schwartz, pp. 598 and 612.

are relatively rare. Such changes generally have been associated with some
specific historic event which changes
the previous institutional relations
with respect to the liquidity of nonmoney assets.

The other unique factor about this
subperiod is that the fiscal variable is
statistically significant and negative.
Weidenbaum has provided a plausible
explanation for this.[20] He has shown
that Government spending influences
economic activity not when the bills
are paid and the goods are delivered
to the Government, but when the orders
are placed with industry, which must
then hire employees and open plants
to produce the products.

This discrepancy does not lead to
serious bias in measuring Government
spending except when there in a sharp
acceleration or deceleration in this
variable. This was clearly the case in
the Korean War, when Government
spending went from an annual rate of
decline of 38 per cent in the second
quarter of 1950 to an annual rate of
increase of 83 per cent in the first
quarter of 1951 and then fell to an annual rate of increase of 13 per cent in
1952. This "whiplash" movement in
Government spending follows by about
two or three quarters an equally sharp
movement in economic activity. As a

result, ΔY and ΔE moved in opposite
directions in this period. This is the
cause of the statistically significant
negative coefficient of ΔE with respect
to ΔY.

If we had chosen a somewhat longer
time period in which to measure the
impact of monetary and fiscal influences, the strong negative offset estimated with respect to ΔE would have
lost its statistical significance. We
would have had results for the early
post-World War II subperiod which
were comparable to the results of the
other subperiods.[21]

5.   1953–1969

This is the period which was covered
in the original AJ study. While their
measure of economic activity, nominal
GNP, differs from the proxy used here
and described in footnote 10, their
results and ours are similar in most
respects, as can be seen in the
comparison of summary results in
Table 4.

In each case the monetary and fiscal
measures are the same (the money
stock and government spending). Only
the measure of economic activity differs. The first equation is based on our
proxy of economic activity and is
drawn from Table 1. The second equation is based on nominal GNP.[22] In each

---

[20] Murray L. Weidenbaum, "The Federal Government Expending Process," *Federal Expenditure Policy
for Economic Growth and Stability,* (Washington, D.C.: Joint Economic Committee of Congress, U.S.
Government Printing Office, November 1957), pp. 493–506.

[21] This is shown by the following regression:

I/1947 — IV/1956

(Quarterly First Differences)

$$\Delta Y = 1.11 + 7.82 \overset{3}{\Sigma} \Delta M_{t-i} - 1.13 \overset{3}{\Sigma} \Delta E_{t-i} \qquad R^2 = .27$$
$$\quad\;\; (.48) \quad (3.31)\; i = o \qquad (1.76)\; i = o \qquad D\text{-}W = .98$$

where Σ stands for sum of monetary or fiscal influence from period t to period t-3. Lags were
selected on the basis of minimum standard error of estimate adjusted for degrees of freedom.

[22] The results with respect to nominal GNP differ slightly from the original Andersen-Jordan results
because of the different lag structure. The lag structure in their original article (contemporaneous
and three-lag values) was selected on the basis of minimum standard error of the coefficient attached
to the monetary variable. The present lag structure (contemporaneous and four-lag values) was
selected on the basis of minimum standard error of the entire equation adjusted for degrees of
freedom. In this case, the different criteria did not change the results in any significant way.

TABLE 4

MONETARY AND FISCAL INFLUENCES ON ECONOMIC ACTIVITY, MEASURED AS A
PROXY (ΔY) AND AS NOMINAL GNP (ΔGNP) (I/1953—I/1969)

Dependent Variable	Lags	Constant Term	Monetary Influence	Fiscal Influence	R^2 D-W
		a_0	$a_1 \Delta M$	$a_2 \Delta E$	
ΔY	t-4	1.42	8.85	—.84	.47
		(.72)	(4.70)	(1.07)	1.71
ΔGNP	t-4	2.59	5.63	.08	.65
		(3.19)	(6.94)	(.24)	1.78

NOTE: Regression coefficients are the top figures; their "t" values appear below each coefficient, enclosed by parentheses. R^2 is the percent of variations in the dependent variable which is explained by variations in the independent variable. D-W is the Durbin-Watson statistic.

case the monetary variable has a positive coefficient which is statistically significant and the fiscal variable has a coefficient which is statistically insignificant and close to zero in value. Both equations are sufficiently well specified to pass the Durbin-Watson (D-W) test for autocorrelation, and the lag structures are the same when selected on the basis of minimum standard error of estimate. The value of the monetary coefficient is greater with the proxy measure of economic activity (ΔY) than with nominal GNP (ΔGNP), which is due to the greater average value and amplitude of the proxy. The coefficient of determination (R^2) is larger with ΔGNP than with ΔY. This is as would be expected if, as seems reasonable, nominal GNP is superior to our proxy as an indicator of economic activity.

There were four cyclical declines in this period, each of which was led by a decline in the money stock. Government spending registered three cyclical declines, two of which corresponded to periods of decline in the money stock and one (in 1967) which did not. As noted in our investigation of earlier pe-

riods, economic activity declined following a decline in Government spending only when accompanied by a decline in the money stock.

III. DETERMINING THE VALUES OF THE MONETARY AND FISCAL VARIABLES

An assessment of the reliability of the relations presented above will depend upon whether the estimated coefficients for the monetary and fiscal variables are exogenous. This problem arises in all statistical work, and no fully satisfactory solution has been found to test for exogeneity in either single equation or in large structural models.[23] However, in the single equation test of monetary and fiscal influences on economic activity employed here, one potential source of bias is found in the so-called "reverse-causation" argument. This asserts that the observed correlation between M and Y is not because changes in M cause changes in Y, but because changes in Y cause changes in M. If this possibility cannot be rejected, then a more elaborate statistical test is needed to com-

[23] In statistical theory, a variable is exogenous if it is uncorrelated with the "true" error term of the equation. Unfortunately, only the measured error term in any equation is observable, so this test cannot be made.

pare monetary and fiscal influence on economic activity.[24]

The fiscal variable used here (total Federal Government spending, including transfer payments) is generally accepted as being determined by the fiscal authorities and not by the behavior of the public in the marketplace. For the purposes of our test we will assume that the fiscal variable is statistically independent or exogenous. With respect to the monetary variable (the narrowly defined money stock), there is considerable controversy as to whether its value is determined by the monetary authorities or by the public. For this reason we will concentrate our empirical investigation on the money variable. It will be shown that the reverse-causation argument is not supported by the evidence. In addition, the available evidence indicates that the actions of the monetary authorities dominate the movements in the money stock.

A. Does Economic Activity Affect Money?

In order to evaluate the significance of the reverse-causation argument, we need some indicator of the public's potential influence on the money stock. The indicator chosen is our proxy variable for economic activity (Y). This proxy has two adavntages: first, it is the broadest available measure of aggregate economic activity and, as such, most actions of private decision-making units in the economy are reflected in it. Second, it allows us to consider

directly the important statistical question of whether movements in Y lead to movements in M.

In order for economic activity to affect the money stock, it must operate through some transmission mechanism.[25] The Brunner-Meltzer money stock identity provides a useful structure within which to consider the several ways that economic activity could affect the money stock.[26] In this context the money stock (M) is defined as the product of the money multiplier (m) and monetary base (B):

$$M = mB$$

The sources of the monetary base consist of various kinds of credit extended by the monetary authorities to the rest of the economy. The use of the monetary base is divided between currency holdings of the nonbank public and reserves of commercial banks.

The money multiplier, which is defined as

$$m = \frac{1 + k}{r(1 + \tau + g) + k},$$

is largely determined by the behavior of the public, including commercial banks; k represents the ratio of private currency holdings to private demand deposits; τ represents the ratio of private time deposits to private demand deposits; g represents the ratio of Government deposits in commercial banks to private demand deposits; and r represents the ratio of total bank reserves and total bank deposits.[27]

---

[24] At the least, one would need an equation to. explain the monetary and fiscal variables by factors which themselves were independent of income.

[25] The approach used here to test for the influence of the public on the money stock was suggested by the work of Leonall C. Andersen, "Additional Empirical Evidence on the Reverse-Causation Argument," this *Review*, August 1969.

[26] For a systematic exposition of this approach, see Albert Burger, "An Analysis and Development of the Brunner-Meltzer Nonlinear Money Supply Hypothesis," Working Paper No. 7, Federal Reserve Bank of St. Louis, May 1969.

[27] For a detailed discussion of the determinants of the multiplier and its influence on the money stock, see Philip Cagan, *Determinants and Effects of Changes in the U.S. Money Stock, 1875–1960*, (New York: National Bureau of Economic Research, 1965); and Jerry L. Jordan, "Elements of Money Stock Determination," this *Review*, October 1969.

TABLE 5

THE INFLUENCE OF ECONOMIC ACTIVITY (ΔY) ON THE MONETARY BASE (ΔB)

$$\Delta B_t = b_0 + b_1 \Delta Y_t$$

(Quarterly First Differences—Billions of Dollars)

Time Periods	b_0	$b_1 \Delta Y$	R^2	D-W
II/1919—I/1969	.31 (8.17)	.008 (2.98)	.04	.58
III/1919—II/1929	−.012 (.68)	.009 (2.42)	.12	.64
III/1929—II/1939	.20 (3.39)	.004 (.41)	.02	.85
III/1939—IV/1946	.99 (7.30)	−.012 (1.14)	.01	1.09
I/1947—IV/1952	.12 (1.45)	.012 (1.76)	.08	.87
I/1953—I/1969	.34 (6.24)	.012 (3.45)	.15	.87

NOTE: Regression coefficients are the top figures: their t values appear below each coefficient, enclosed by parentheses. R^2 is the percent of variations in the dependent variable which is explained by variations in the independent variable. D-W is the Durbin-Watson statistic.

1. ECONOMIC ACTIVITY AND THE MONETARY BASE

The influence of economic activity on the money stock could operate either through the monetary base (B) or the money multiplier (m). To test whether economic activity has influenced the monetary base, regressions were run for the total period (1919–69), and for each of the five subperiods reported above. The results are presented in Table 5. For the entire 50-year period changes in the monetary base have a statistically significant relation with changes in economic activity. However, economic activity explains at most only 4 percent of the variance of the changes in the monetary base; that is, the R^2 was .04. For every $1 *billion* increase in economic activity, there is associated only an $8 *million* increase in the base in the same quarter.

Equally weak relations between ΔY and ΔB were found in the subperiods. Only the first (1919–29) and the last (1953–69) subperiods had statistically significant coefficients, while the R^2 varied between .01 and .15.

These results imply that the public, operating through economic activity, has only a small effect on the monetary base, and that this effect has varied substantially over time in both degree and significance. Allowing for the influence of lagged values of ΔY on ΔB does not change the results presented in Table 5, except for 1947–52 when the R^2 increases to .24 and the coefficient becomes statistically significant.

2. MONETARY AUTHORITIES AND THE MONETARY BASE

Another potential source of control of the monetary base is through the actions of the monetary authorities. There have been a number of studies which have related policy targets of the monetary authorities, such as income stabilization, to various indicators of monetary actions, such as the money stock (Dewald and Johnson),

TABLE 6

THE INFLUENCE OF STABILIZATION (FR), EVEN-KEEL (Δ) AND FINANCIAL (r-r_n)
OBJECTIVES OF THE MONETARY AUTHORITIES ON THE MONETARY BASE (ΔB)

$$\Delta B_t = c_1 \, FR + c_2 \, \Delta D + c_3 \, (r\text{-}r_n)$$

(Quarterly First Differences—Billions of Dollars)

Time Periods	Stabilization Objective	Even-Keel Objective	Financial Objective	Dummy Variable[a]	R^2	D-W
	$c_1 \, FR$	$c_2 \, \Delta D$	$c_3 \, (r\text{-}r_n)$			
II/1929—IV/1939	.33	−.219	.401	.553	.59	1.75
	(6.76)	(2.86)	(3.65)	(1.95)		
I/1940—IV/1952	.01	.070	.469	—	.46	1.90
	(.37)	(6.32)	(.81)			
I/1953—IV/1968	.19	.018	.123	.415	.69	1.84
	(2.28)	(1.73)	(2.69)	(5.58)		

NOTE: Regression coefficients are the top figures; their "t" values appear below each coefficient, enclosed by parentheses. R^2 is the percent of variations in the dependent variable which is explained by variations in the independent variable. D-W is the Durbin-Watson statistic.

[a] In 1929–39 the Dummy Variable is designed to account for the impact on the monetary base of the rise in the price of gold in February 1934. It assumes the value of 1 for the first and second quarters of 1934 and zero for all other quarters. In 1953–68 the Dummy Variable accounts for the change in presidential administration. It assumes a value of zero from I/1953 to II/1962 and a value of one from III/1962 to IV/1968.

total member bank reserves (Dewald), free reserves (Wood), and the monetary base (Keran and Babb). All these studies conclude that the monetary authorities have dominated movements in the money stock or some closely allied variable. The last named study will be briefly reviewed here because it deals explicitly with control of the monetary base by the authorities.

Keran and Babb found that a large proportion of the movements in the monetary base can be explained by the desire of the monetary authorities to achieve three objectives: a stabilization objective with respect to income, employment, and prices, reflected in the Federal Reserve Open Market Committee policy statements as proxied by the level of free reserves (FR); an even-keel objective with respect to Government debt financing, measured by changes in the national debt (ΔD); and a financial objective with respect to

stability of the financial system, measured by deviations of Corporate Aaa bond yields from "normal" yield levels (r-r_n).[28] In addition, economically "random" events, such as changes in the price of gold in 1934 and changes in presidential administrations, have also influenced the actions of the monetary authorities with respect to changes in the monetary base (ΔB). These events are represented by "dummy variables" in Table 6.

Two of the three subperiods considered by Keran and Babb were approximately the same as subperiods in the present study (I/1953 to IV/1968) and I/1940 to IV/1952). Another subperiod in that study was reestimated to match the 1929–39 subperiod in this study. The results are presented in Table 6. In each case, fifty percent or more of the variations in ΔB are explained by the actions of the monetary authorities. In contrast, where the actions of the

[28] They have also shown that in the 1953–68 period, Federal Reserve open market operations (adjusted for changes in reserve requirements) were also explained by the same three objectives plus an additional money market objective, which in effect offset the noncontrolled sources of the monetary base.

TABLE 7

RELATIVE INFLUENCE OF ECONOMIC ACTIVITY (ΔY) AND THE MONETARY BASE (ΔB)
ON THE MONEY STOCK (ΔM) $\Delta M_t = d_0 + d_1 \Delta Y_t + d_2 \Delta B_t$

(Quarterly First Differences—Billions of Dollars)

Time Periods	d_0	$d_1 \Delta Y_t$	$d_2 \Delta B_t$	R^2	D-W	Beta Coefficients ΔY	Beta Coefficients ΔB
II/1919—I/1969	.094 (1.44)	.023 (4.61)	1.89 (17.78)	.67	1.32	.198	.755
II/1919—II/1929	.075 (1.72)	.025 (2.49)	2.41 (5.57)	.61	1.43	.288	.640
III/1929—II/1939	.064 (.63)	.063 (4.45)	.71 (2.86)	.42	1.21	.546	.351
III/1939—IV/1946	.82 (2.52)	.022 (1.45)	1.69 (6.35)	.57	1.73	.181	.791
I/1947—IV/1952	.37 (2.27)	.019 (1.41)	1.46 (3.63)	.46	.97	.230	.598
I/1953—I/1969	.032 (.24)	.014 (1.92)	1.94 (8.00)	.59	1.56	.166	.696

NOTE: Regression coefficients are the top figures; their "t" values appear below each coefficient, enclosed by parentheses. R^2 is the percent of variations in the dependent variable which is explained by variations in the independent variable. D-W is the Durbin-Watson statistic.

public were assumed to operate, the best results explained fifteen percent or less of the variance in ΔB (see Table 5). The acceptable Durbin-Watson statistics in Table 6 suggest that no important explanatory variables have been omitted from the monetary authorities' explanation of ΔB. On the other hand, low Durbin-Watson statistics in Table V imply that important explanatory variables have been omitted from an economic activity explanation of ΔB.

The values of the coefficients in Table 6 for the prewar (1929–39) and postwar (1953–68) subperiods were similar with respect to the income stabilization objective (FR) and the financial stabilization objective $(r-r_n)$,[29] supporting the hypothesis that the monetary authorities have acted in a largely consistent manner in controlling the monetary base (ΔB). During the war and early postwar period (1940–52), the Federal Reserve followed a single-minded policy of supporting the Government bond market. The results in Table 6 reflect this, with only the even-keel variable statistically significant in that subperiod.

The results presented here indicate that it is the behavior of the monetary authorities (Table 6) rather than economic activity (Table 5) which have dominated movements in the monetary base (ΔB). There is no evidence that the reverse-causation argument holds with respect to ΔB.

3. ECONOMIC ACTIVITY AND THE MONEY MULTIPLIER

Another channel through which economic activity could influence the money stock would be through its influence on the money multiplier. As indicated above, most of the ratios which are involved in determining the multiplier depend upon the behavior of the public, including commercial banks.

Table 7 presents the results relating

[29] For an explanation of all variables used in Table 6 and of the difference in the even-keel sign between (1929–39) and (1953–68), see Keran and Babb, pp. 9–15.

changes in the money stock (ΔM) to changes in the monetary base (ΔB) and economic activity (ΔY). Assuming that the monetary authorities determine movements in the base, and that the public operating through economic activity influences the money multiplier, our results indicate that for the total period (1919–69) both the monetary authorities (ΔB) and economic activity (ΔY explain 67 per cent of the variance in ΔM. However, the beta coefficients, which indicate the "typical" influence of each independent variable on the dependent variable, show that the monetary authorities operating through the base (ΔB) have an impact on the money stock (ΔM) which is 3½ times as large as the public influence operating through economic activity (ΔY). The results for the subperiods are substantially the same as for the total period. The coefficient for the monetary base is statistically significant in all subperiods, while that for economic activity is statistically significant in only the first two subperiods (from 1919 to 1939). There was one subperiod (1929–39) where the beta coefficients indicated that economic activity was more important than the monetary base in determining movements in the money stock. The strength of the economic activity variable in that period reflects the substantial decline in the multiplier. The multiplier declined during the early part of that period (1929–33) due to a change in the currency-deposit ratio (k), which reflected the run on banks by households as they attempted to convert their bank deposits into currency.

These results are not changed when lagged values of ΔY and ΔB are added to explain ΔM. With four lags the statistical significance of the coefficient for ΔY disappears in 1919–29, while in 1953–69 the coefficient for ΔY becomes negative. This latter result is inconsistent with the usual reverse-causation

argument, which asserts a positive relationship.

The results presented in Table 7 imply that economic activity has had some influence on changes in the money stock, presumably through its influence on the money multiplier, especially in the important 1929–39 period. However, the observed influence of economic activity on the money stock would overstate its true influence if offset by the actions of the monetary authorities operating through the monetary base. For example, if part of the actions of the monetary authorities had been desgined to offset the influence of economic activity on the money multiplier, then the observed association of economic activity and the money stock would be, at least, statistically ambiguous.

Table 8 indicates this is the case. It shows the relative impact of the public operating through economic activity (ΔY), and the monetary authorities operating through the monetary base (ΔB), on the money multiplier (Δm). In the total period and in all subperiods the influence of economic activity (ΔY) is positive and the influence of the monetary base (ΔB) is negative. The beta coefficients indicate that in all subperiods (including 1929–39), the monetary authorities offset or more than offset the influence of the public on the money multiplier. Thus, the significance of the association of economic activity and the money stock reported in Table 8 is weakened, because those movements in the money multiplier induced by economic activity have been offset by changes in the monetary base.

The conclusions which can be drawn from these statistical tests are (1) that the monetary base is the dominant factor in determining movements in the money stock, both directly (Table 7) and indirectly (Table 8), by offsetting other influences on the money stock;

TABLE 8

RELATIVE INFLUENCE OF ECONOMIC ACTIVITY (ΔY) AND THE MONETARY BASE (ΔB)
ON THE MONEY MULTIPLIER (Δm) $\Delta m_t = e_0 + e_1 \Delta Y_t + e_2 \Delta B_t$

(Quarterly First Differences—Billions of Dollars)

Time Periods	e_0	$e_1 \Delta Y_t$	$e_2 \Delta B_t$	R^2	D-W	Beta Coefficients	
						ΔY	ΔB
II/1919—I/1969	.001	.001	−.03	.12	.96	.194	−.288
	(.14)	(4.03)	(4.20)				
II/1919—II/1929	.011	.004	−.16	.16	1.45	.438	−.403
	(1.62)	(2.53)	(2.37)				
III/1929—II/1939	−.004	.007	−.16	.50	.98	.441	−.575
	(.31)	(4.04)	(5.16)				
III/1939—IV/1946	.038	.001	−.034	.32	1.27	.274	−.528
	(3.05)	(1.32)	(3.34)				
I/1947—IV/1952	.008	.0001	−.028	.24	.95	.062	−.308
	(2.24)	(1.45)	(2.98)				
I/1953—I/1969	.0001	.0001	−.011	.09	1.56	.100	−.332
	(.15)	(2.18)	(2.66)				

NOTE: Regression coefficients are the top figures; their "t" values appear below each coefficient, enclosed by parentheses. R^2 is the percent of variations in the dependent variable which is explained by variations in the independent variable. D-W is the Durbin-Watson statistic.

and (2) that the monetary authorities are the dominant factor in determining movements in the monetary base (Table 6). Thus, for the purposes of the single equation regressions used in this article, there are no statistical reasons for not treating the money stock as substantially controlled by the monetary authorities in all subperiods (including 1929–39).

IV. SUMMARY

The intent of this article is to measure the impact of monetary and fiscal influences on economic activity over as long a period of American history as available data permit (1919–69), and for selected subperiods. This was done to see if different financial institutions, Government involvement in the econ-

omy and general economic conditions which existed during this long period have substantially affected the relative impacts that monetary and fiscal influences have had on economic activity.

For the whole period and for each of the subperiods (except the war years 1939–46), the relative impacts of monetary and fiscal influences have been remarkably stable. Changes in the money stock (the indicator of monetary influence) have consistenlty had a larger, more predictable, and faster impact on changes in economic activity than have changes in Federal Government spending (the indicator of fiscal influence). This basic relationship is observed in the economically depressed period of 1929–39 and in the prosperous periods 1919–29 and 1953–69.[30]

[30] The author was surprised at the consistency of the monetary influence during the various subperiods. Before conducting the research reported in this article, he considered that monetary influences on economic activity were strongly significant only during periods of generally strong business conditions like the 1920's and 1960's, while fiscal influences were dominant in periods of generally weak business conditions like the 1930's. In the March 1967 issue of this *Review* (page 14), he said: "during the 1930's business expectations of the future were so badly impaired by the depression experience that even large change in financial variables like money, . . . would not be sufficient to induce new investment and consumption." In the November 1967 issue (page 8) he made the same

A historical investigation of the past fifty years reveals that in every case where the monetary variable and the fiscal variable moved in opposite directions, economic activity moved in the direction of the monetary variable and opposite in direction to the fiscal variable. Every cyclical movement in the money stock since 1919 has been followed by a proportional cyclical movement in economic activity.

Both the statistical results and the historical investigation provide strong support for the case that monetary influences have a significant impact on economic activity over the business cycle. An important implication of these results is that monetary policy should be given a central role in any economic stabilization program.

statement in a slightly different context: "If the forces which create strong private demand should disappear, i.e., loss of optimistic expectations by firms and households, the rate at which money is made available to the economy may not result in a predictable change in income."

The results reported in this article do not support the above quotations. Monetary influences have dominated fiscal influences on economic activity in both periods of secular boom and periods of secular recession.

MONETARY POLICY AND CONSUMER EXPENDITURES: THE HISTORICAL EVIDENCE

David Meiselman and Thomas Simpson

I. INTRODUCTION

The Quantity Theory in its current state seeks to explain a more limited range of economic phenomena than many alternative hypotheses, which ought not dull the lustre of its performance in predicting nominal aggregate income or the price level, neither easy nor trivial tasks. Widening the range of implications of the effects of monetary change would, however, enhance the usefulness of the stock of money as a predictor of short-period economic change, including whether there are dependable associations between money and specific expenditures. If dependable associations between money and specific expenditures do exist, they may suggest some elements of the process by which the economy adjusts to a change in the stock of money to add to our rather meager tested knowledge of the channels through which monetary policy affects the economy.

II. SUMMARY

The main purpose of this paper is to provide some evidence about the empirical association between monetary policy and both the aggregate of consumer (or household, as distinct from government or business) spending and some of its principal components, including expenditures for residential housing construction. The paper first updates some of the regressions done in the original Friedman-Meiselman study[1] on the relationship

Source: From Federal Reserve Bank of Boston, *Consumer Spending And Monetary Policy*, Boston: 1972.

[1] Milton Friedman and David Meiselman, "The Relative Stability of Monetary Velocity and the Investment Multiplier in the U.S., 1897–1958," in *Stabilization Policies*, A Series of Research Studies prepared for the Commission on Money and Credit (New Jersey: Prentice Hall, 1963).

between money and consumer demand and improves on these estimates for the 1952–1969 period mainly by the use of the Almon lag technique. The most important finding is that there is a strong association between monetary policy, evaluated as changes in either of two measures of the stock of money or the monetary base on the one hand, and both consumer spending and G.N.P. on the other. The paper reports on experiments with disaggregating the main components of household spending and of G.N.P. and reports some interesting regularities which are highly suggestive of the adjustment process.

One of the most interesting regularities is that the more durable the class of expenditures, the shorter the lag, and correspondingly, the less durable the class of expenditures, the longer the lag. The change in money affects expenditures for housing construction first, and consumer services last. This suggests two main channels by which monetary change affects aggregate demand. The first effect may be considered a capital stock effect but mainly influencing household capital, because money alters outlays for capital goods first. The second effect may be considered a service flow effect because money later alters outlays for services.

The capital stock effect may be the result of substitutions, either directly between money and tangible capital, or, alternatively, a longer chain of substitutions which starts with an initial substitution between money and credit instruments leading to changes in credit market and interest rate conditions, which in turn affects capital outlays. In housing, expenditures are related to money, accelerating at first, and later decelerating, with an overall impact that is more fully described in the following section. The service flow effect may essentially reflect the impact of monetary change on permanent income, perhaps as the consequence of the earlier impact of money on household capita. The resulting change in permanent income may be the link between money and the demand for consumption services, an income rather than substitution effect. It may explain why the lag of services is significantly longer, and more substained.

This suggests that many of the apparent differences between the quantity theory and income-expenditure theory with respect to the adjustment process may hinge critically on definitions of the variables involved. For example, our results indicate that investment expenditures are the first private outlays for goods and services that respond to monetary policy as the Keynesian analysis has asserted, but that the empirically relevant investment expenditures are for household rather than business capital, for housing more than plant, and consumer durables more than equipment. Similarly, the service flow effect suggests that money affects consumption by altering income, but that the relevant measure of income is permanent rather than measured income and that the relevant measure of consumption is the flow of consumption services rather than what statisticians have come to measure as Personal Consumption Expenditures. In other words, these results suggest that when the variables are properly defined and measured, there may well be great merit to the empirical presumption of the income-expenditure theory analysis that the chain of causation resulting from monetary change may indeed be from money to capital goods to income to consumption.

Because of the evidence we present about the strong association between money and consumer spending, we also tested whether a change in monetary policy leads to a corresponding change in consumer spending or the other way around. The paper reports some interesting and impressive results of attempting to resolve the long standing chicken-egg problem. It concludes that a change in the stock of money (or the monetary base) is followed by a change in consumer spending or total GNP, *but not the reverse.* As is generally the case in the use of timing evidence to adduce causality, this evidence is highly suggestive of the direction of effect but is not conclusive by itself.

III. EXPERIMENTS WITH THE ALMON LAG PROCEDURE ON THE IMPACT OF MONEY ON HOUSEHOLD SPENDING AND ITS MAJOR COMPONENTS

These and other statistical problems led us to experiment with the use of the Almon lag procedure to estimate distributed lag relationships between first differences of monetary change and first differences of consumption outlay and its major components or GNP and some of its major components.

We experimented with alternative periods of lag for each set of calculations reported in this paper. We settled on the best lag on the basis of whether adding additional periods of lag altered the regression coefficients and whether the regression coefficients of additional periods of lag were statistically significant. We initially experimented with up to eight quarters of lag. It turned out that in most cases, and for all three monetary variables we examined, the best distributed lag spanned contemporaneous through five consecutive earlier quarters. In several cases, however, notably in the case of the service component of personal consumption expenditures, still longer lags appeared best. For services, we experimented with distributed lags of up to 12 quarters and found that the best lags were either 9 or 10 quar-

ters. These are estimates of lags where it appeared to us that the best relations involved periods of lag greater than five quarters. In the distributed lag estimations involving first differences of M_1 as the independent variable and personal consumption expenditures as the dependent variable, the best lag pattern is found when there are six rather than five quarters of lag.

Table 1 contains the distributed lag regression equations between (1) first differences of nominal GNP, nominal consumer spending and housing and (2) first differences of the nominal stock of the M_1 definition of money.

To illustrate the use of the table, consider the effects of a once-for-all unit change in M_1 on GNP. To do so, read down the column. It shows that an increase in M_1 of $1 billion leads to an increase in GNP of $1.388 billion in the same quarter. The regression coefficient of $1.388 is highly significant and has a t-value of 3.58. In addition, the effects of a once-for-all increase in the quantity of money continue for several quarters more. One quarter later, the first difference of GNP will increase still more, and by $1.681 billion. Two quarters later, the first difference of GNP will increase again, but at a decreasing amount ($1.315 billion), and so forth. The entire effect will be exhausted after a lag of three additional quarters. Four and five quarters after the initial increase in the stock of money, there is essentially no further impact on aggregate GNP. Considering the total effect over the period as a whole, the $1 billion increase in M_1 leads to an increase in GNP of $4,892 billion. For some indication of relative scale, this is approximately 0.87 percent of the mean value of GNP for this period of $560.9 billion.

Personal consumption expenditures, its principal components, and housing can also be analyzed in the same way. A $1 billion increase in M_1 leads to an

TABLE 1

DISTRIBUTED LAG REGRESSION EQUATIONS OF FIRST DIFFERENCES OF NOMINAL GNP, NOMINAL CONSUMER SPENDING, AND SOME PRINCIPAL COMPONENTS ON FIRST DIFFERENCES OF THE NOMINAL STOCK OF MONEY (M_1 = Currency plus Demand Deposits Adjusted) FOR THE SAME AND 5 EARLIER QUARTERS, 1952–1969[a]

	Pers. Cons. Exp.	Dur.	Auto.	Furn.	Other	Non-Dur.	Serv.	Housing	C + H	Y
M_{1t}	0.620	0.186	0.088	0.059	0.049	0.173	0.260	0.395	1.015	1.388
	(2.94)	(1.27)	(0.66)	(1.59)	(2.17)	(1.42)	(4.58)	(5.86)	(4.64)	(3.58)
M_{1t-1}	0.732	0.288	0.162	0.096	0.034	0.257	0.187	0.291	1.023	1.681
	(5.76)	(3.24)	(2.02)	(4.28)	(2.48)	(3.48)	(5.46)	(7.17)	(7.76)	(7.19)
M_{1t-2}	0.612	0.259	0.162	0.089	0.003	0.264	0.088	0.019	0.631	1.315
	(3.64)	(2.21)	(1.53)	(3.01)	(0.15)	(2.71)	(1.95)	(0.35)	(3.61)	(4.25)
M_{1t-3}	0.441	0.114	0.080	0.041	−0.016	0.215	0.112	−0.202	0.239	0.669
	(2.68)	(0.99)	(0.77)	(1.41)	(−0.89)	(2.25)	(2.52)	(−3.84)	(1.40)	(2.21)
M_{1t-4}	0.305	−0.075	−0.043	−0.025	−0.012	0.134	0.246	−0.261	0.044	0.066
	(2.30)	(−0.81)	(−0.51)	(−1.08)	(−0.85)	(1.74)	(6.88)	(−6.16)	(0.32)	(0.27)
M_{1t-5}	0.193	−0.177	−0.116	−0.062	0.003	0.051	0.319	−0.157	0.036	−0.227
	(0.87)	(−1.13)	(−0.83)	(−1.58)	(0.13)	(0.39)	(5.30)	(−2.20)	(0.15)	(−0.55)
Sum	2.903	0.595	0.333	0.198	0.061	1.094	1.214	0.084	2.987	4.892
	(8.31)	(2.44)	(1.52)	(3.21)	(1.62)	(5.40)	(12.87)	(0.75)	(8.24)	(7.61)
Constant	2.092	0.181	0.036	0.089	0.058	0.746	1.164	0.085	2.176	3.032
	(4.30)	(0.53)	(0.12)	(1.04)	(1.11)	(2.64)	(8.87)	(0.54)	(4.31)	(3.39)
Mean Dep. Var.	354.6	51.8	22.6	22.1	7.2	162.8	140.0	23.9	378.5	560.9
Sum/Mean (%)	0.82	1.15	1.48	0.90	0.84	0.67	8.87	0.35	0.79	0.87
R^2	0.52	0.13	0.03	0.23	0.05	0.31	0.70	0.46	0.56	0.53
SE	2.45	1.71	1.54	0.43	0.26	1.42	0.66	0.78	2.54	4.51
D-W	2.21	2.44	2.47	2.28	2.71	2.39	0.94	1.54	2.16	1.36

[a]Quarterly, seasonally adjusted data.

NOTE: t-values in parentheses.

increase in personal consumption expenditures of $.620 billion in the same quarter, $.732 billion a quarter later, and so forth, with the total effect on personal consumption expenditures summing to $2.903 billion, or 0.82 percent of the mean value of $354.6 billion for the period. These figures suggest that personal consumption expenditures tend to be relatively less responsive than gross national product when considering *total* effects. Note also that the coefficient for concurrent personal consumption expenditures of 0.620 relative to the sum of the coefficients of 2.903 suggests that only about 20 percent of the total effect of monetary change on C takes place during the same quarter. Similarly, almost 25 percent of the total effect takes place one quarter later, its peak effect, and roughly 20 percent of the total effect is two quarters later, approximately 15 percent three quarters later, and so forth. All regression coefficients for the synchronous and the first four quarters of lagged changes in M_l are highly significant and the coefficient of multiple determination (R^2) is 0.52, especially impressive for a regression using first differences of quarterly and seasonally adjusted data. The Durbin-Watson statistic of 2.21 indicates essentially no serial correlation of the residuals.

Because of the coefficients of a set of components sum to the coefficient of the aggregate of the components, another set of comparisons is also possible with the use of this table. For example, the coefficient of GNP in each period can be interpreted as the marginal total of individual components that sum to GNP. Thus, we can see that the coefficient for synchronous personal consumption expenditures is approximately 45 percent of the coefficient of GNP. This indicates that 45 percent of the change in aggregate demand brought about by a change in the stock of money will come from personal consumption expenditures. The proportions of the components of personal consumption expenditures will be given by the relative weights of their separate coefficients. Thus, a $1 increase in M_l will cause expenditures for services to increase by 26¢ in the same quarter, or approximately 18.5 percent of the total change in GNP in that quarter attributed to a concurrent increase in the stock of money, and 41 percent of the change in personal consumption expenditures. Similarly, the sum of the coefficients for each of the components taken separately can also be interpreted as a marginal total summed vertically. Thus, the sum of the coefficients for GNP can be interpreted as the grand total of all the cells.

Finally, expressing the sum as a percent of the mean level value within the 1952_4–1969_4 period suggests the responsiveness or sensitivity of each component to monetary change. This procedure is analogous to deflating the sum of the coefficients for each component by its own mean in order to correct for scale differences. Thus, even though the sum of the coefficients for personal consumption expenditures is 2.9, several times greater than that for the durables component of .595, when deflated by their respective means it turns out that expenditures for consumer durables are relatively more responsive to changes in the stock of money than is the aggregate of personal consumption expenditures. For the moment, holding aside questions about the statistical significance of the sum for the automobile component of consumer durable, if we use this index as a reflection of the responsiveness of the component to monetary change, it can easily be seen that the 1.48 percent for the automobile component of durables is substantially greater than the 0.90 percent for the furniture component. Indeed, the sum of the coefficients for automobiles is larger relative to its own mean than any of the other components contained in Table 1. Of other GNP components that we have examined thus far, it turns out that only the plant and equipment component of gross private domestic investment is more responsive to changes in M_1 than automobiles, and but slightly so. (The sum of its coefficients is 1.51 percent of its mean.)

IV. MONEY AND HOUSING CONSTRUCTION EXPENDITURES

The responsiveness of expenditures for residential construction, H, to changes in M_1 is one of the most interesting aspects of Table 1. According to these estimates, monetary policy has a relatively great impact on housing expenditures in the same quarter. The coefficient of 0.395 indicates that when M_1 increases by $1, housing expenditures in the same quarter increase by 39.5 cents, which is about 28 percent of the synchronous change in GNP explained by the change in M_1. One quarter later the effect is still large but is decreasing, as housing expenditures continue to increase at the rate of 29.1 cents for every dollar of increase in M_1 the quarter before. One quarter later, at t-2, the effect has reached a peak. By the third quarter, the strong positive effect has started to slow down, as housing expenditures *decrease* by 20 cents. One quarter later at (t-4) housing expenditures continue to fall and at a still greater pace, with the decline leveling off somewhat in the fifth quarter of lag. The later showing effects come close to offsetting all of the earlier positive ones, and the sum of all the coefficients turns out to be close to zero and statistically insignificant.

This suggests that an increase in the stock of money has a relatively rapid and sizeable impact on housing expenditures, which in turn is a large pro-

portion of the initial impact of monetary change on aggregate demand but that the early acceleration in housing expenditures is not maintained.

The lag pattern of the response of housing to monetary change suggests a mechanism for the transmission of monetary policy to housing and perhaps to consumer (and producer) durables, and through these expenditures to the rest of the economy, as well as the later negative feedback of the economy on housing and durables. If the demand for housing is related to interest rates, as is generally conceded, the initial increase in the stock of money, by lowering interest rates, quickly causes a sharp increase in housing expenditures. However, once the effects of monetary change result in an increase in aggregate demand, interest rates start to rise, moderating the increase in housing. (Note that the lag patterns for consumer durables suggest a response similar to housing but somewhat weaker and slower.) The U.S. financial structure and regulation would appear to accentuate these tendencies.

If one looks at the timing of response to monetary change, the results in Table 1 suggest that an increase in the stock of money has a strong impact on housing in the same quarter. It also affects personal consumption expenditures in the same quarter, but this effect is small indeed when one compares the size of personal consumption expenditures. Effects on the durable and nondurable components are relatively small and are not statistically significant. The greatest impact of changes in M_1 on personal consumption expenditures occurs one quarter after the monetary change has taken place. The same holds true for the durables component of personal consumption expenditures as well as its principal sub-components, automobiles and furniture. The peak impact on nondurables is in (t-2). Spending for consumer services also peaks in period (t-2). Thereafter, coefficients tend to decline and many of them lose significance. Some of the coefficients become negative, as in the case of housing. The coefficients for durables also become negative at (t-5), but the coefficients are not statistically significant.

READING 29
FACTORS AFFECTING THE LEVEL OF INTEREST RATES

Milton Friedman

There is a problem in terminology that is worth commenting on at the outset. In all sorts of monetary discussions, there is a tendency to use the word "money" in three different senses. We speak of a man making money when we mean that he is earning income. We speak of a man borrowing money when we mean that he is engaging in a credit transaction. Similarly, we speak of the money market in the sense of a credit market. Finally, we talk about money when we mean those green pieces of paper we carry in our pocket or the deposits to our credit at banks.

I. CONFUSION OF CREDIT WITH MONEY

Much of the misunderstanding about the relationship between money and interest rates comes from a failure to keep those three senses of the term "money distinct," in particular to keep "credit" distinct from "quantity of money." In discussing credit, it is natural and correct to say that the interest rate is the price of credit. General price theory tells us that the price of anything will be lowered by an increase in supply and will be raised by a reduction in supply. Therefore it is natural to say that an increase in credit will reduce the rate of interest. That is correct. A shift to the right of the supply curve of loanable funds—that is, an increase in the supply of loanable funds at each interest rate—will, other things being the same, tend to reduce the interest rate. A decrease in supply will tend to raise it.

The tendency to confuse credit with money leads to the further belief that an increase in the *quantity of money* will tend to reduce interest rates, and a reduction in the *quantity of money* will tend to increase interest rates.

Because of this confusion, there is also a tendency to regard the term

Source: Reprinted from Donald Jacobs and Richard Pratt (Eds.), *1968 Conference Proceedings,* Savings and Residential Financing Conference, U.S. Savings and Loan League, Chicago, 1968.

"monetary ease" as unambiguous, as meaning either a more rapid increase in the quantity of money or lower interest rates and, similarly, monetary tightness as meaning either a reduction in the quantity of money or higher interest rates.

II. INTEREST RATE THE PRICE OF CREDIT, NOT MONEY

My main thesis is that this is wrong, that the relation between the quantity of money and the level and movement of interest is much more complicated than the relation that is suggested by the identification of money with credit. It is more complicated because the interest rate is not the price of money. The interest rate is the price of credit. The price level or the inverse of the price level is the price of money. What is to be expected from general price theory is what the quantity theory says, namely, that a rapid increase in the quantity of money means an increase in prices of goods and services, and that a decrease in the quantity of money means a decrease in the price of goods and services. Therefore, to see what effect changes in the quantity of money have on interest rates, it is necessary to look more deeply beneath the surface.

Before going into the detailed analysis, let me prepare the groundwork by discussing some facts. If you ask most economists, or most noneconomists for that matter, certainly if you ask most people at savings and loan institutions or in banks, whether an increased quantity of money will mean higher or lower interest rates, everybody will say lower interest rates; but looking at broad facts shows the reverse.

If I ask in what countries in the world are interest rates high, there will be widespread agreement that they are high in Brazil, Argentina and Chile. If I say, "I take it that in those countries

there are very low rates of increase in the quantity of money and that interest rates are high because money has been tight," you will laugh at me. Those are countries which have had very rapid increase in the quantity of money and inflation.

If I ask in what countries of the world are interest rates low, you will tell me in countries like Switzerland. On the usual view, this would imply that they have been having rapid increases in the quantity of money. Yet we all know that the situation is precisely the reverse. Switzerland is a country which has held down the quantity of money.

Let us turn to the United States. Suppose I said, "What is the period in the United States when interest rates fell most rapidly?" There is not the slightest doubt when that was. It was the period from about 1929 to the mid-1930s. Would you then say, "That must have been the period when the quantity of money was increasing." Obviously not. We all know that it is the opposite. From 1929 to 1933, the quantity of money fell by one-third and, as I shall proceed later to say, therefore interest rates fell, although in terms of the usual presumptions that economists have and which are enshrined in our elementary textbooks, one would say precisely the opposite.

Similarly, interest rates are high now in the United States in nominal terms. Nominal interest rates are far higher than they were in the mid-'30s, far higher than they were just after the war. Yet, in the past five or six years, the quantity of money has been increasing relatively rapidly.

The point of this crude and rough survey of experience is to bring home that the broadest factual evidence runs precisely contrary to what most of us teach our students and what is accepted almost without question by the Federal Reserve System, by bankers, and by the savings and loan business.

So far I have mentioned one set of broad facts, namely, the relation between the level of interest rates and the rate of change in the quantity of money. When the quantity of money has been increasing very rapidly, there is a tendency to have high interest rates; when it has been decreasing very rapidly or increasing slowly, there is a tendency to have low interest rates.

III. GIBSON PARADOX: PRICES, INTEREST RATES MOVE TOGETHER

Another empirical regularity, which was pointed out many years ago, exists not between money and interest rates but between prices and interest rates. The Gibson paradox is the observed empirical tendency for prices and interest rates to move together. When prices are rising, interest rates tend to be rising; when prices are falling, interest rates tend to be falling.

This was regarded as a paradox because of the orthodox view I have been questioning. Ordinarily, prices would be expected to be rising because the quantity of money is increasing. If the quantity of money is increasing, the orthodox view is that interest rates should be falling. Yet we find that when prices are rising, interest rates are rising, and when prices are falling, interest rates are falling.

That is another piece of empirical evidence which needs to be interpreted by any theory which tries to explain the relationship between the changes in the quantity of money on the one hand and the level or direction of movement in interest rates on the other hand.

Let me turn from this background to a theoretical analysis of the relationship between money and interest rates.

This analysis is one which has been developed over the past few years, and in that period three different empirical pieces of work have been done which I am going to summarize for you.

The first is work that Anna Schwartz and I have done in studying the relationships between longer term movements in the quantity of money and in interest rates. The second is some work that Phillip Cagan has done at the National Bureau on shorter term movements in interest rates within the cycle. Mrs. Schwartz's and my work uses as the basic unit a half-cycle, so it has to do with the inter-cycle movement. Professor Cagan's work has to do with the intra-cycle movement.

The third is a doctoral dissertation just recently completed at the University of Chicago by William Gibson, which also deals with the shorter period relationships between money and interest rates.

The new work in this area is an interesting phenomenon because it reflects a very long cycle. Irving Fisher worked on this problem back in the '20s and '30s. What the three of us have done is to redo Fisher and find that he was right after all. While there has been considerable work done in these past three years, it owes a great deal to the much earlier work done by Fisher. This is particularly true of the analysis of the Gibson paradox.*

IV. ANALYSIS OF CHANGES IN MONEY AND INTEREST RATES

I should like to present to you what seems to me now to be the correct theoretical analysis of the relationship between changes in the quantity of money and interest rates. I shall argue that there are three sets of effects which have to be distinguished. The first is

* Editor's note: The Gibson Paradox refers to an earlier Gibson, not the William Gibson previously referred to in the preceding paragraph.

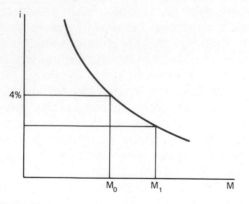

Figure 1

the liquidity effect. The second is what I shall call the income effect. The third is the price anticipations éffect. I shall argue that, of these three effects, the first one works in the direction which has been generally expected, but the second and the third work in the opposite direction. If the effect of monetary change on interest rates is to be understood, all three have to be taken into account.

The liquidity effect in its simplest form is the usual textbook relationship between the quantity of money and the interest rate which says that the larger the quantity of money, the lower the interest rate will have to be to induce people to hold it. I have drawn it in that form in Figure 1, but no one who is careful writes it in that form and this is one of the slips in the analysis. What

really should be measured on the horizontal axis is not M, the nominal quantity of money, but M/P, the real quantity of money.

Part of the story of tracing the effect of a change in money is going from a change in the nominal quantity of money to what happens to the real quantity of money. For the moment, however, let us waive that. We shall come back to it because it is in the second set of effects—the income effect or income-and-price effect. Let us stay here for the moment with the liquidity effect.

Consider now Figure 2, in which time is measured on the horizontal axis. Let us suppose that up to some moment of time, t_0, there has been a constant rate of increase in the quantity of money, say 3% per year. At a certain time it suddenly starts increasing at 5% a year. Let us suppose that interest rates prior to t_0 have been 4%, as shown on Figure 2. What should we expect to be the pattern of behavior of interest rates as a result of this one-shot change in monetary growth as it works itself out through time? That is the central theoretical problem.

The first tendency of any economist, in terms of our present literature, is to stress the fact that in order to get people to hold the larger quantity of money, interest rates will have to go down. As

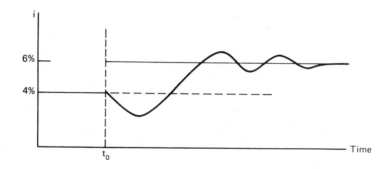

Figure 2

shown in Figure 1, people were willing to hold M_0 at a rate of interest of 4%. To get them to hold more, there will have to be a movement along the curve to lower interest rates. There is an implicit assumption in that analysis that needs to be brought to the surface. The implicit assumption is that prices are not in the first instance affected by the change in the quantity of money.

Let us suppose that prior to this time, prices were stable. Let us suppose for a moment that 3% corresponds to the rate of output increase in the economy and that velocity is constant, just to keep matters simple. None of these assumptions really affects the essence of what I am saying. If, when the quantity of money started increasing at 5% per year instead of 3%, prices suddenly started increasing at 2% per year, you would stay exactly in the same place on the curve in Figure 1 (if the horizontal axis is interpreted as M/P), and there would be no tendency for interest rates to go down. The implicit assumption that, in the first instance, the effect is not likely to be on prices, is consistent with much empirical evidence. I should qualify this statement. The implicit assumption seems correct if this jump from 3% to 5% is an unanticipated jump. If it were announced that the jump was going to occur, it would be more plausible that it would have an immediate effect on prices.

A.   Liquidity Effect: Price of Securities Up, Interest Rate Down

If this is an unanticipated jump in the rate of monetary increase, it is reasonable to suppose that its first impact will be that people will find the composition of their portfolios disturbed. Holders of cash will find that they have more cash than they planned to have. Their first impulse will be to attempt to readjust the portfolios by replacing cash with other securities. This will bid up the price of other securities and lower the rate of interest. This would be the liquidity effect.

This is the effect which explains why academic economists in general will say offhand that an increase in the quantity of money will lower interest rates. In economic terminology, we would call this an effect through stocks. The financial economist or Federal Reserve economist will argue a little differently. He would expect an immediate effect through flows. He would say, "How is the rate of increase in the quantity of money stepped up?" He would say that in our kind of financial system ordinarily it will be stepped up by an increased rate of purchase of securities by the central banks, which in turn will add to the reserves of commercial banks which will expand by making additional loans. He would say that the very process of stepping up the quantity of money in our kind of financial system operates to raise the supply of loanable funds. That is entirely true for our kind of financial system.

These two factors—the effect on stocks and the effect through flows—would work in the same direction. However, the title "liquidity effect" under which I have included both is not an entirely descriptive term. Both factors tend to make for an initial decline in the rate of interest—the stock effect because of a movement along the liquidity curve and the flow effect because of a movement to the right in the supply of loanable funds. There is a difference. The flow effect would produce a decline in the interest rate which might be expected to happen immediately. As long as prices do not react, the effect through stocks will exert a continuing downward pressure on the interest rate. So it is not clear whether the liquidity effect would produce simply a sudden drop to a new level, or a period during which interest rates fall, as I have shown it on Figure 2. That is the first effect—a liquidity effect.

B. Income-and-Price Level Effect

The next effect is the income-and-price level effect. As cash balances are built up, people's attempts to acquire other assets raise the prices of assets and drive down the interest rate. That will tend to produce an increase in spending. Along standard income and expenditure lines, it will tend to increase business investment. Alternatively, to look at it more broadly, the prices of sources of services will be raised relative to the prices of the service flows themselves. This leads to an increase in spending on the service flow, and therefore to an increase in current income. In addition, it leads to an increase in spending on producing sources of services in response to the higher price which can now be obtained for them.

The existence and character of this effect does not depend on any doctrinal position about the way in which monetary forces affect the economy. Whether monetary forces are considered as affecting the economy through the interest rate and thence through investment spending or whether, as I believe, reported interest rates are only a few of a large set of rates of interest and the effect of monetary change is exerted much more broadly, in either case the effect of the more rapid rate of monetary growth will tend to be a rise in nominal income.

For the moment, let us hold prices constant and suppose that the rise in nominal income is entirely a result of rising output. What effect will that have? It will raise the demand curve for loanable funds. A business expansion is in process and the increasing level of income will raise the demand for loanable funds. This will exert a force tending to raise interest rates or at least to counteract the downward pressure from the increasing stock of money. In addition, the rising incomes will tend to shift to the right the liquidity preference curve of Figure 1, since the higher the income, the larger the quantity of money demanded at each interest rate. (Strictly speaking, under our assumptions that the initial position was one of a 3% per year rate of growth in real income, the effect will be a still more rapid shift of the liquidity preference curve. Alternatively, we can interpret Figure 1 as representing a trend-corrected curve.)

Suppose the expansion in income takes the form in part of rising prices. This will not alter the tendency for the demand for loanable funds, expressed in nominal terms, to rise. But, if we measure the real quantity of money (M/P) on the horizontal axis of Figure 1, this tendency will affect that figure. Suppose prices go up as rapidly as the increased rate of monetary growth, in our assumed case, 2%. The real quantity of money will remain constant. If prices go up more rapidly than that, you will tend to move back along the curve. As income rises, whether or not prices rise, interest rates will turn around and go up, as a result of the rising demand for loanable funds, the shift of the liquidity preference curve and the possible movement along it.

There are many reasons to believe that this rise in interest rates will go too far. It will overshoot. I cannot cover this point in full here but let me suggest some reasons to expect even this short-run effect to overshoot.

In the first place, we started out by saying that prices will be slow to react and that the initial effect is the disturbance of portfolios. That means that there is some caching up to do. We can see what is involved most readily by looking at the ultimate long-run position.

If the rate of monetary growth stayed at 5%, the long-run equilibrium posi-

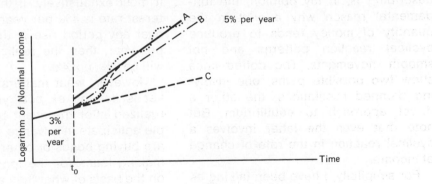

Figure 3

tion would involve nominal income rising at 2% per year more than it did prior to the increase in the monetary growth rate. In Figure 3, Line C is a continuation of the original trend of rising income, let us say, at 3% a year. Line B shows a trend linked to the initial trend but with a rate of rise of 5%. If at first income proceeds along C but ultimately has to proceed along B, then for some period income will have risen more rapidly in order to catch up. That is one reason for a tendency to overshoot.

A second reason is a little more complicated. The true long-run equilibrium position of income will not be Line B but a higher line, say Line A. It will be a higher line because the amount of real balances that people want to hold will be smaller when prices are rising at 2% per year than when they are stable.

C. Price Anticipation Effect

This brings us to our third effect, the price anticipation effect. When prices are rising at 2% a year and people come to anticipate that they will continue to, this raises the cost of holding cash. Consequently, they will want to hold smaller balances relative to income. This is clearly the case and has been well-documented for hyper-in-

flation and substantial inflation. Cagan's study on hyper-inflation, which is by now a classic, documents very clearly that in such episodes, the higher the rate of change of prices, the higher is monetary velocity or the lower are real balances.

Studies for countries like Argentina and Brazil and Chile, countries that have had very substantial inflation, show the same phenomenon. For the United States, it has been much harder to pin down that phenomenon because our price movements have been mild.

In the study by Anna Schwartz and me, using averages for half-cycles, we have been able for the first time to extract from the American data the same kind of response to the rate of change in prices as had been extracted for the more extreme inflationary episodes.

As a theoretical matter, the higher the rate of change of prices, the higher the velocity expected. This shows up as an empirical phenomenon. This is why the long period equilibrium will be a path like A in Figure 3 rather than like B. Therefore, even if there were no lag in the initial adjustment, at some time or other income or prices have to rise faster than the ultimate equilibrium rate of 2% per year in order to get up to this higher level. To digress for a moment, the phenomenon I have been describing is, in my opinion, the fundamental reason why a shift in the quantity of money tends to produce cyclical reaction patterns and not smooth movements. The dotted lines show two possible paths, one involving damped oscillations, the other a direct approach to equilibrium. But note that even the latter involves a cyclical reaction in the rate of change of income.

For simplicity, I have been talking as if the initial position we started from was one where there was reasonably full employment, so that while in the interim there can be a period with income increasing and prices stable, sooner or later the higher rate of rise in income will be translated into a higher rate of price increase. That really is not essential for my story at all.

It may be that part of the effect will be taken up in output rather than in prices. All that is essential is that there be some tendency for prices to rise somewhat more than they otherwise would, although I may say that, as an empirical matter, I would expect a shift from one fairly steady rate of monetary growth to another to be reflected fully, sooner or later, in prices.

V. DISTINGUISH BETWEEN NOMINAL AND REAL RATE OF INTEREST

As long as there is some tendency for part of the increase in the rate of growth of the quantity of money to end up in a higher rate of price rise, sooner or later people will come to anticipate it. As people come to anticipate it, we introduce a distinction that I have so far kept out of the picture, namely, the distinction between the nominal rate of interest and the real rate of interest.

We are all very much aware of the distinction right now. It is also a distinction that goes back in our literature,

at least to Irving Fisher who analyzed it most exhaustively. If the nominal interest rate is 4% per year and if prices over any period rise at the rate of 2% per year, then the realized real yield will be 2%, not 4%.

However, what matters for the market is not the *ex post* yield which is realized after the event but what people anticipate in advance. People today are buying bonds or other securities or making loans for the long-term future on the basis of what they anticipate will happen.

Let us designate the nominal interest rate by R_B (the B for bonds) and the real rate by R_E (E for equity). Now $\left(\frac{1}{P}\frac{dP}{dt}\right)$ is the percentage rate of which prices are changing at time t. Let an asterisk attached to it stand for an anticipated rate, so $\left(\frac{1}{P}\frac{dP}{dt}\right)^*$ is the anticipated rate of change in prices. Then, the relation Fisher developed is $R_B = R_E + \left(\frac{1}{P}\frac{dP}{dt}\right)^*$. In other words, the nominal rate of interest on the market will be equal to the real rate of interest plus the anticipated rate of price change. Therefore, if R_E stays the same but the anticipated rate of price change goes up, the nominal interest rate will also go up. That is the third effect.

Returning to Figure 2, we see that if the whole of this 2% higher rate of monetary growth goes into prices, and if the initial equilibrium interest rate was 4%, then the new long-run equilibrium rate will be 6%. The interest rate pattern then will be something like that shown in Figure 2 and will ultimately get up to 6%.

That is the whole of the theoretical analysis that leads to tracing out a path of reaction in interest rates. I have exaggerated what can be traced out from the theoretical analysis alone since the fluctuations I have put in are not well determined. What is really determined by the theoretical analysis is an initial decline, a subsequent rise and an ultimate attainment of a level higher than the initial one.

VI. DURATION OF RESPONSE OF INTEREST RATE TO MONETARY CHANGE

Let me give this theoretical analysis some empirical content. How long are these periods? What is their duration? Of the three studies that I have described, the one that Mrs. Schwartz and I have done traces out the time pattern at the end, while Cagan's and Gibson's studies trace out the time pattern at the beginning. So far we have a missing link in between. The empirical work all three of us have done is entirely consistent with the pattern traced out in Figure 2. Empirically, there is a tendency for a rapid rate of monetary growth to be followed by a decline in interest rates and, after a lag, by a rise, and then a final ultimate movement to a level higher than the starting point. The major patterns are recorded in the empirical evidence and do come out very clearly.

i have been talking about an increase in the rate of monetary expansion. Obviously, everything is reversed for a decrease, and our empirical studies, of course, cover both increases and decreases.

It turns out that the initial decline in interest rates after an acceleration of monetary growth lasts about six months. Clearly, there is variation but the average period is about six months. The time it takes to get back to the initial level is something like 18 months.

A. Long Period to Final Equilibrium Level

The period it takes to get to the final equilibrium level is very long. Fisher came out with a period of something like 20 years. He did a number of different studies which gave him estimates of 20 or 30 years. Our own estimates are about the same. They make a distinction which Fisher's did not. They suggest that the period is different for short rates than it is for long rates. Fisher did his studies for long rates and did not make that distinction.

As a purely theoretical matter, one would expect that it would take longer for long rates than for short rates. When you are buying a security with a short life, you are really interested in extrapolating price movements over a shorter future period of time than when you are buying a very long-term security. It seems not unreasonable that if you are extrapolating for a short period, you will look back for a shorter period than when you are extrapolating for a longer period.

I regard it as very strong empirical confirmation of this interpretation of the evidence that it does turn out that the period it takes to get full adjustment tends to be much longer for long rates than it does for short rates.

In Figure 2, the time it takes to get to the final equilibrium level depends on how long it takes for a change in the rate of monetary change to produce general anticipation of further price rises. That implicitly means that it depends on how far back people look in forming their anticipations. The mean period of price anticipation turns out to be something like 10 years for short rates and 20 years for long rates. Since these are the average periods, they imply that people may take an even longer period of past history into account. These results are wholly consistent with Fisher's.

VII. RELATIONSHIP BETWEEN ANALYSIS AND GIBSON PARADOX

Let me tie this in to the Gibson paradox. The explanation that Fisher offered for the Gibson paradox was the

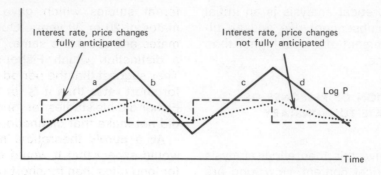

Figure 4

same as what I have called the third effect, but it hinges very much on how long it takes for people to form their anticipations. If price change were perfectly anticipated, if people instantaneously anticipated what was actually going to happen, high interest rates would be associated with rapid rates of price rise, and low interest rates would be associated with low rates of price rise or with price declines, but there would be no reason to expect a connection between rising prices and rising interest rates.

To clarify this point, suppose that the historical record of prices was like that plotted in Figure 4, where the ordinate is the logarithm of the price, so that straight lines correspond to constant rates of price increase or decrease. If people fully anticipated this, the result would be that for periods a and c the interest rate would be high, for periods b and d the interest rate would be low— as shown by the dashed steps. There is no reason why rising prices would be associated with *rising* interest rates. Rising prices would be associated with *high* interest rates; falling prices with *low* interest rates. Yet the Gibson paradox is that rising prices are associated with *rising* interest rates and falling prices with *falling* interest rates.

In order to explain the Gibson paradox on this basis, Fisher says that if prices start to rise, people do not really

believe it. It takes a long time before they accept the idea that prices are rising. Therefore, if we plot on Figure 4 not what the actual rate of change of prices is but what the anticipated rate of change of prices is, we find that it behaves like the wavy dotted line; the anticipated rate of change of prices starts low, and only gradually rises, and keeps on rising for a time after actual prices start declining. Only after a lag, will it start to decline and then it will decline only gradually.

So, said Fisher, let prices start to rise when those prices have been stable. As prices rise, people gradually come to anticipate the rise. Only after prices have been rising for a long time will people take full account of the actual rate of rise.

VIII.   RECENT EXPERIENCE ILLUSTRATES ANALYSIS

Let me conclude simply by applying this analysis to recent experience because it applies beautifully. When I say this analysis, I really am talking mostly about the short period analysis, not Fisher's long period analysis. Consider what happened in 1966 and 1967, because it was almost a perfect representation of the relationship I have shown in Figure 2.

There was rapid rate of growth in money until April 1966. (The exact date depends on whether you use a narrow or a broad definition of money but nothing I say will be affected by that, because the patterns of behavior of the different rates are the same although the quantitative rates of change are different.) From April 1966 to about December 1966 there was a brief but sharp decline in the rate of monetary change.

From December 1966 or January 1967 through most of 1967, to something like October or November of 1967, there was an even more rapid rate of increase than before April 1966. Since about November 1967, there has been a tapering off in the rate of growth to the present.*

What happened to interest rates during that period? Prior to April 1966 interest rates were rising. Why were they rising? This was the delayed impact of the earlier high rate of monetary growth.

Suddenly there was a tightening of money—a sharp decrease in the rate of growth of the quantity of money. What does our theory say? Turn Figure 2 upside down. It says a rapid increase in interest rates would be expected because the delayed effect of earlier monetary ease is reinforced by the impact effect of monetary tightness. That, of course, is what happened. There was a very sharp rise in interest rates culminating in the so-called credit crunch.

The interesting question is, when did that culminate? In September or October 1966, several months before the reversal in monetary growth. That is exactly what our analysis would lead you to expect—a turnaround about six months after the shift in monetary growth.

At this point the tight money was having a depressing effect on interest rates.

The liquidity effect had shot its bolt, the income effect was beginning to take over. That income effect resulted in a slowdown in the economy in the first half of 1967 which reduced the demand for loanable funds and so interest rates fell.

Then what happened? After monetary growth accelerated in January 1967, the short-term effects of easy money reinforced the delayed effect of the tighter money and so interest rates continued to fall. But this time the short-term effect was abnormally short —less than six months. Interest rates turned around some time in March or April that year and started to go up. These delayed effects of easy money were then reinforced in November 1967 by the tapering off of monetary growth.

IX. MANY FACTORS AFFECT INTEREST RATES

Obviously, I would not contend for a moment that monetary change is the only thing that affects interest rates. I have merely isolated that part of the interest rate movement which is determined by monetary change. Many other things affect interest rates. Our squared correlations are perhaps on the order of about .5 which means they account for half of the fluctuations in nominal interest rates. I do not for a moment want to suggest that if you understand the effect of monetary change on interest rates, you therefore have a theory of interest rates. In the first place, there are other forces which will change real interest rates. In the second place, there are undoubtedly other forces changing nominal interest rates, but it so happens that the major movements of nominal interest rates in 1966 and 1967 seem to have been dominated by the monetary effects so they serve to

* Editor's note: May 1968.

bring out very clearly the relations I have described.

One more word about the longer term relations. If this analysis is right, our present interest rates of 6% or 6½% are still on the way up because they are still reflecting the building up of antici-pations of price increases. Our present interest rates are extremely low—if you subtract the rate of price change, you have very low real interest rates. There-fore, if this analysis is right, the long-term trend of interest rates ought still to be up.*

* Editors note: In the months after Professor Friedman made this forecast, rates did rise appreciably, and Treasury bills, a basic rate, yielded more than 8% by late 1969.

READING 30
THE POLICY IMPLICATIONS OF CURRENT RESEARCH IN THE TERM STRUCTURE OF INTEREST RATES

David Meiselman

I. INTRODUCTION

The discussion of the policy implications of current research in the term structure of interest rates logically follows discussion of factors affecting the level of interest rates because it turns out that one of the main findings of a large number of independent researchers in the last 10 years has been that the only dependable way to change the relationship between short-term and long-term interest rates is to change the level of rates. This is the consequence of two empirical regularities: first, that all default-free interest rates tend to move in the same direction, and second, that the longer the maturity the less the amplitude of change. Thus, the term structure itself tends to be related to the level of interest rates. When rates are high relative to historic norms, as has generally been the case in recent years, short-term rates are high relative to long-term rates, and the yield curve tends to be negatively sloped (a falling curve). When, as in the 1930s, rates are low relative to historic norms, short-term rates are low relative to long-term rates, and the yield curve tends to be positively sloped (a rising curve). A yield curve describes the structure of default-free interest rates at a point in time as a function of term to maturity. It is typically drawn with term to maturity along the horizontal axis and interest rates along the vertical axis. Thus, if interest rates are higher when the term to maturity is longer, the yield curve has a positive slope, or is a rising curve. Of course, it does not mean that the curve itself rises through time.

A vague understanding of these rela-

Source: Excerpts from "The Policy Implications of Current Research In The Term Structure of Interest Rates," Conference on Savings and Residential Housing *Proceedings*, D. Jacobs and R. Pratt (Eds.), U.S. Savings and Loan League, 1968.

tionships has been an important consideration leading to policy proposals for varying the so-called "mix" of monetary and fiscal policies in order to achieve "desirable" interest rates, which many interpret as a desirable term structure of interest rates. This is widely taken to be where short-term rates are below long-term rates because there is a presumption that a rising yield curve has at least two "desirable" consequences. First, it permits financial institutions which borrow short-term and lend long-term, such as savings and loan associations and mutual savings banks, to profit by trading on the difference between the two ends of the yield curve or to avoid the dangers of having the profit potential eliminated. Second, a positively sloped yield curve helps to augment the supply of mortgage funds and thereby assists residential construction.

For purposes of discussing policy implications, the state of knowledge of the term structure is easily summarized. It turns out that the bulk of research since my own study[1] has been consistent with my findings that expectations have been a dominant factor determining the yield curve and, correspondingly, that the relative quantities of short-term and long-term debt have but a minor or nonexistent role in explaining short- and long-term interest rates. Moreover, I do not believe that it has been unambiguously demonstrated that a short-term claim is any more "liquid" than a long-term claim, in the sense that a short-term claim is often understood to be a composite security, part money and part debt, perhaps along a continuum of liquidity or "moneyness." Even if one were to accept the conclusion of some studies that a long-term rate of interest is a biased estimate of expected short-term rates, a long-term rate being higher than the average of

expected short-term rates by either a risk premium, a liquidity premium, or some measure of differential transaction costs, I know of no serious attempts to estimate the proportions of money and of debt in such short-term instruments as a 90-day Treasury bill or a 138-day piece of GMAC commercial paper, along the lines of Roy Elliott's frequently cited[2] but unpublished study in which he estimated mutual savings bank deposits to be something like 35% money.

This means that we have very little solid ground for making responsible public policy recommendations that depend crucially on the presumption of so-called liquidity effects—precisely because these effects have never been quantified.

Another implication of recent term structure research is that the segmented market hypothesis is contradicted by the data. The most convincing body of evidence is the systematic variation of the yield curve as a whole which suggests that there are *many* market connections among different maturities, that financial markets are indeed "fluid" and fungible. The implied high degree of substitutibility, where so many borrowers and lenders can readily shift to alternative sources or uses of funds, points to an added danger of pegging individual rates or tampering with particular financial instruments or transactor groups.

II. LONG-TERM INTEREST AVERAGE OF EXPECTED SHORT-TERM RATES

Regarding the dominant role of expectations, the bulk of the evidence has been consistent with the hypothesis that a long-term rate of interest, and of course we are discussing default-free nominal interest rates, is an average of expected short-term rates.

[1] David Meiselman, *The Term Structure of Interest Rates,* 1962.
[2] Roy Elliott, "Savings Deposits as Money," unpublished Ph.D. dissertation, University of Chicago, (1964).

Because the explanatory power of expectations decreases as the term to maturity lengthens, this suggests that either other factors become progressively more important or that the simple kinds of theories that we have been using to explain expectations formation are systematically less relevant to more distant phenomena. Despite the room available for improving on expectations alone as an explanation of the yield curve, thus far the several attempts that have been made to estimate the effects of changes in the *maturity composition** of either the public debt alone or the public debt and the private debt taken together have shown little if any effects on the yield curve. This conclusion has held whether researchers have used my hypothesis of expectations formation or some other.

These findings are crucially important for debt management and for other public policies. Lest we make too much of the evidence, it should be pointed out that the general proposition that relative quantities of debt do make a difference has never really been satisfactorily tested, either by an explicit real world experiment or by appropriate statistical analysis. Nor, for that matter, has there been a satisfactory formal theoretical analysis of this approach, which depends on a general equilibrium, multi-sector, multi-asset model. In this model separate classes of transactors have separate preferences and opportunities for borrowing and lending at different maturities as well as their own institutional and eco-nomic restraints. Market interest rates are determined by the interaction among a large number of transactors, many of whose decisions are based on expectations. Such a general equilibrium, multi-sector, multi-asset model also may have to consider a wide variety of behavioral responses to uncertainty which would seem to have a crucial role in shaping apparent transactor preferences.

Following this general analytical orientation, investigators[3] have attempted to test the yield curve consequences of (1) changes in either the maturity composition of the U.S. Treasury debt alone—to which some have added the debt of other agencies of the U.S. government and subtracted the holdings of the Federal Reserve System in order to measure the federal debt in the hands of the public; or (2) changes in private debt as well. Several investigators have also tried to distinguish some of the major transactor groups. In this general equilibrium context, treating the maturity composition of the debt as if it consisted solely of the debt of the federal government ignores the bulk of the factors determining the term structure, especially since most of the tests of the effects of changes in the maturity composition of the federal government debt covered periods of time when changes in both the volume and composition of federal debt appear to have been relatively minor compared with developments in the private sector.[4]

There are also several identification

---

* Editor's note: Read "maturity composition" to mean the quantities of debt in various maturity classes along the yield curve.

[3] For example, see Neil Wallace, "The Term Structure of Interest Rates and Maturity Composition of the Federal Debt," unpublished doctoral dissertation, Department of Economics, University of Chicago, 1964.

[4] I recall my own experience as an economist in the U.S. Treasury in 1962–3 when there would be much comment inside the Treasury itself, as well as in the press, whenever the Treasury decided to change the weekly bill auction by as much as $100 million. This sum, although quit large on an absolute basis, is still small indeed compared with some rather ordinary week-to-week switching that goes on in the market for short-term funds stemming from variations in automobile sales, the volume of brokers loans, or shifting among alternative sources of funds by important borrowers in this market such as commercial banks or large corporations.

problems to consider. No doubt there were some periods when the maturity composition of the federal government debt was independent of relative interest rates in the sense that Treasury and Federal Reserve policy with respect to the maturity composition of the federal debt was independent of the structure of rates. Yet, in addition, there clearly have been circumstances under the federal law—which limits the coupon on long-term Treasury bonds to 4½%—when bond yields have been above 4½%, the maturity composition of the Treasury debt tended to respond to market rates instead of shaping them because the Treasury was required to issue only short- and intermediate-term securities.

There are other identification problems in considering private debt. For example, if the quantity of private short-term debt should rise relative to the quantity of private long-term debt this may be the result of shifts of either supply or demand. Thus, at the very least, this kind of general equilibrium approach also requires a detailed specification of supply and demand schedules for debts of different maturities which incorporates some theory of preferences on both supply and demand sides. It is not correct merely to sum several series on debt outstanding.

Perhaps the more perplexing measurement and analytical problems revolve about the appropriate treatment of the private sector. Regarding the measurement of maturity composition, in my own work I tried some tests using figures for aggregate private short- and long-term debt estimated by the Department of Commerce. I have my doubts about the meaning of those data because the numerical values for the aggregate debt figures depend on the degree of consolidation of the private sector. The consolidation criteria are not uniformly applied to different transactor groups, and the degree of consolidation which is taken for purposes of collecting these data are largely arbitrary and often vary through time.

Even if the term to final maturity of each dollar of debt were known and conveniently recorded and classified, which is not the case, still more trying are the problems of separating debt into meaningful maturity classes, if only because large amounts of both public and private debt do not have fixed maturities. Much debt may be prepaid at the option of the debtor, as in the case of bonds with call provisions or mortgages with prepayment clauses. Alternatively, debt may be repaid before final maturity at the option of the creditor as in the case of Series E bonds.

Another difficulty with the general equilibrium approach is that individual transactors are often both borrowers and lenders. Thus, to answer the central question, Which pattern of rates would clear all markets so that all excess demands are zero? we may well need an excess demand schedule for each separate transactor or for homogeneous classes of transactors, holding aside the difficult problem of establishing criteria for grouping individuals into homogeneous classes. This is a staggering task I leave to heartier souls than I.

A general equilibrium approach also requires a theory of preferences by both borrowers and lenders with respect to maturities. This is why, before I came to a more fruitful view of expectations in my own work, I thought that I might be able to derive transactor preferences from considerations of risk aversion, where risk aversion led transactors to attempt to hedge against the contingency of changing interest rates by balancing the maturities of their assets and of their liabilities. This led to an hypothesis, for example, that an increase in the demand for inventories, short-term assets, would tend to lead to an increase in the demand for short-term funds to finance the inventory acquisition because both are short-term. Or, an increase in the demand for residential construction would tend to increase the demand for long-term funds because both are long-term. Of course, there is still the difficult data problem of estimating the maturity distribution of both assets and liabilities. In addition, some classes of transactors such as savings and loans tend to speculate, not hedge.

To return to policy implications, they can be summarized briefly. The most important policy implication of recent research is that although there has been much fruitful and provocative research in the term structure area in recent years, there is still very little known of any precision about the relationships between the structure of rates and other important economic variables such as expenditures for important classes of goods and services or the demand for money, how to change interest rates themselves, or the lags of the system. Public policies that ignore our ignorance and presume more knowledge than we possess run the danger of serious loss of economic welfare, especially when major instruments of monetary and fiscal policy are brought into play for their hoped for interest rate effects.

III. DEBT MANAGEMENT UNIMPORTANT TOOL

Regarding implications of recent research for specific policy areas, it turns out that debt management becomes an unimportant tool of macro economic policy. It seems to make little differences for the level and structure of rates whether there is a "bills only" or "bonds only" policy, or what-

ever, given the volume of interest bearing debt in the hands of the public. Another way of putting this is that changes in maturity composition cannot be depended upon to have any impact on relative interest rates that persist. No doubt, if in one day $1 billion of bills are retired and $1 billion of bonds are issued, short-term rates will temporarily rise and long-term rates temporarily fall. Let some time pass, and it appears that the disturbance erodes away and rates tend to return to where they had been before. If changes in maturity composition do have a permanent effect at some scale they would apparently have to be massive enough to lie well outside the range of past observations. There is no way of telling a priori where this may be.

Rates can be pegged, but with the high degree of substitutibility among maturities for given expectations this suggests the likelihood that pegging any one maturity obviously runs the risks of having to peg the whole yield curve. Nominal rates can be pegged, but real interest rates cannot also be concurrently fixed because the price level effects of the pegging can neither be ignored nor effectively predicted. Alternately, real interest rates can be pegged but nominal interest rates cannot also be concurrently fixed. Consistent with these findings, perhaps the Treasury and/or the Federal Reserve should manage the composition of the debt with an eye towards minimizing disturbances to the market as well as minimizing the anticipated interest expense of the public debt.

Consistent with the limited impact of debt management, it appears that the late "Operation Twist" to raise the short end of the yield curve and lower the long achieved little, if anything, of substance. Nobody has found that it made much of a difference. Many investigators even question whether any serious efforts were ever made to twist the yield curve by means of important shifts in the maturity composition of the federal government debt in the hands of the public.

There is at least one important evaluation of Operation Twist that questions whether the hoped-for results would follow even if the yield curve were twisted.[5] The purpose of the twist was simultaneously (1) to lower the long-term rate of interest in order to stimulate aggregate demand by means of encouraging private investment outlays, and (2) to raise short-term interest rates in order to reduce short-term capital flows abroad for balance of payments purposes. The presumption was that changes in short-term rates had little effect on aggregate spending.

Ross questions this presumption, citing evidence reported by Ando and others on the interest elasticities of the demand for desired inventory stocks and the demand for fixed investment. The demand for inventory stocks is taken to be related to short-term rates; for the demand for fixed investment, the long-term rate is relevant. Ross concludes that if a twist operation raised short-term rates as much as it lowered long-term rates—it is not at all clear that this rate relationship would hold—the depressing effect on inventory holdings would be likely to more than offset the expansion in fixed investment spending, thereby causing total spending to fall. Because consumer durable outlays may also be affected by a rise in short-term rates, the "perverse" result may be even more pronounced.

In addition, a maturity swap, if effective in changing relative interest rates, may well alter short-term rates by more

basis points than it does long-term interest rates because of the general tendency for short-term rates to be more volatile than long-term rates, which would make the perverse results still more marked. I hasten to add that very little confidence attaches to these estimates because we know so little about interest elasticities and lags, unavoidable technical shortcomings which stand in the way of successful public policy to alter market rates.

IV. LITTLE RELIABLE INFORMATION ABOUT USING INSTRUMENTS SEPARATELY

Some of the same technical problems must be considered in any rigorous analysis of proposals to change the mix of monetary and fiscal policy, whether designed to affect the level of rates itself, change the level of rates in order to alter the yield curve, or for a variety of other purposes. There is little reliable information about the precise consequences for income, prices and interest rates, including lag effects, of using individual taxing, spending and monetary policy instruments separately.[6] The error of our unavoidable ignorance may be especially great with respect to interest rates, if only because of the expectational and speculative elements interest rates incorporate. Using combinations of instruments tends to magnify the problem, reducing the probability that any set of policy goals will be achieved by the set of policy instruments. Although the contrary is possible, it appears unlikely that errors associated with particular instruments will neatly offset each other or that the net unanticipated disturbances will be beneficial.

---

[5] See Myron Ross, "Operation Twist: A Mistake in Policy?" *Journal of Political Economy,* April, 1966.

[6] For several recent attempts to estimate the lagged effects of changes in the stock of money on income and interest rates see W. E. Gibson, "Effects of Money on Interest Rates," Federal Reserve System, *Staff Economic Studies* #43 (1968), and P. Cagan, "The Channels of Monetary Effects on Interest Rates," NBER ms.

Although recent research largely tells us that there is very little that is dependable to be gained on a macro level from debt management or from changing the mix of monetary and fiscal policy or other fine tuning adjustments, recent research does suggest that there are other areas where there do seem to be substantial problems on a micro level, many of which are directly related to public policy with respect to the regulation of financial institutions. To be more specific on this point, the savings and loan business is clearly an outstanding example of a business beset with financial problems inadvertently created by inept government regulation motivated by and designed to protect the industry. In turn, the poor regulation appears to provide still another basis for hobbling attempts to pursue a monetary policy which seeks to stabilize *aggregate* economic activity.

Consider the essential nature of the financial practices of savings and loan associations. Unlike other financial institutions that respond to yield curve uncertainty by hedging their balance sheets against the consequences of changing interest rates, using the hedging mechanism of matching the maturity distributions of both assets and liabilities, savings and loan associations tend to borrow short-term and lend long-term, thereby speculating on interest rates. Thus, in a period where short-term rates are very low relative to long-term rates, a sharply rising yield curve, the profit possibilities for savings and loan associations are very substantial. It is as if savings and loans acquire bonds and finance the purchase by short-term loans, and where the rate paid for the short-term funds is less than the coupon on the bonds. In other words, the savings and loans earn a profit on the "carry." I would also expect that the periods characterized by sharply rising yield curves are

the ones in which savings and loans would tend to grow rather rapidly in response to the profits of a large positive carry.

Given the typical behavior of the yield curve, if the level of interest rates should rise, all rates increase but short-term rates rise systematically more than long-term rates. For savings and loans, this means that profits on the carry are reduced. In addition, the rise in long-term rates means that the savings and loans have also essentially incurred a capital loss on outstanding mortgages, even if book values do not reflect the loss. One way some people in the business view this phenomenon is that they see savings and loans being forced to increase the rates paid on their shares, essentially all outstanding shares, but on the earning asset side of the balance sheet only the new mortgages bear higher mortgage rates.

Let rates rise further; once more short-term rates rise relative to long-term rates. The carry is reduced even more. If rates continue to rise, short-term rates will end up higher than long-term rates, a negatively sloped (declining) yield curve. What had been a positive carry will surely turn into a negative carry. Profits are replaced by losses.

V. HEDGE BALANCE SHEETS AGAINST INTEREST RATE CHANGES

There have been several general Government and private strategies for coping with problems stemming from these losses (or reduction in profits). One has been to lower the level of interest rates either by changing the mix of monetary and fiscal policy or by monetary policy alone. Another strategy has depended on a widening range of selective controls. Still another strategy has essentially sought to make savings and loan balance sheets more nearly hedged against the consequences of interest rate changes. This appears to be the only strategy offering hope of a successful solution.

Regarding the use of macro instruments to alter market interest rates, the events of the past two years strongly suggest the very limited short period efficacy of changing the mix of monetary and fiscal policies by switching among important monetary and fiscal policy instruments, especially in view of long and variable lags, both political and economic. The typical view of using monetary policy to lower interest rates involves having the Federal Reserve follow a more expansionary policy than it otherwise would, expansionary evaluated in terms of the money supply or the monetary base, in the hope that easy money would lower interest rates and thereby improve the savings and loans' carry. A growing body of research[7] indicates that this works only in the very short run. With a longer period horizon, one which considers a wider range of responses to the easy money, rates move in quite the opposite direction. The yield curve tends to end up higher than before the easy money, causing short-term rates to be still higher relative to long-term rates. The time the Federal Reserve action "buys" would seem to be expensive indeed, especially when such myopic policies also tend to have perverse effects on the general stabilization goals of stable prices and full employment as well as on the balance of payments. By pumping in so many reserves the first nine months of 1967, the Federal Reserve did manage to keep rates down temporarily, but since then the lagged effect of the excessively expansionary policy of 1967 has been to contribute to the recent acceleration of inflation as well as in the rise in rates. Especially important for the savings and loan business, with rising rates, short-term rates have increased more than long-term rates.

An alternative and potentially more promising policy route essentially involves accepting the facts of the market, and seeking means of coping with market rates. One incentive to follow this route is the current milieu of high interest rates and the likelihood that rates will continue to rise in the future. To live in the world of high and rising rates as well as negatively sloped yield curves, it is clear that the savings and loan business must be able to live with a yield curve in which short-term rates may frequently be higher than long-term rates as well as to hedge balance sheets against variations in interest rates. If the effort is successful and the losses of a negative carry are avoided, the savings and loan business may correspondingly forego the substantial profit it earns when there is a sharply rising yield curve. There have been many suggestions along these lines, especially since the 1966 "crunch," and some of these would seem to be well taken.[8] The painful alternative to hedging would seem to be a widening range of selective controls as well as an erosion of the savings and loan business.

Much of the nature of the financing

---

[7] See the extended discussion in D. Meiselman, "Bond Yields and the Price Level: The Gibson Paradox Regained," in *Banking and Monetary Studies in Commemoration of the Centennial of the National Banking System,* ed. D. Carson (1963); "The New Economics and Monetary Policy," *Financial Analysts Journal,* Nov. 1967; and "Money, Factor Proportions and the Real Cycle," *J.P.E.* forthcoming; as well as P. Cagan, *Determinants and Effects of Changes in the Stock of Money,* (1965); M. Friedman, "The Role of Monetary Policy," *A.E.R.,* March 1968; and W. Gibson, *op. cit.* All build on Irving Fisher, *Appreciation and Interest* (1913) *and The Theory of Interest* (1930).

[8] See Sherman J. Maisel, "Protecting Against Risks as Interest Rates Shift," address at the 75th Convention of the U.S. Savings and Loan League, November 16, 1967.

practices in the savings and loan business leaves it very vulnerable to important shifts in the level and structure of interest rates. Perhaps the word responsive should be substituted for the word vulnerable because under some circumstances there are substantial opportunities for profits, which, in other circumstances, lead to correspondingly substantial losses.

Unless there is a return to an era when yield curves are rising ones most of the time, which now seems unlikely because of the general inflationary bias in the U.S. economy and abroad, the financial practices of the business, whether permitted by regulation or not, will have to move in the direction of hedging the maturity composition of the savings and loans' balance sheets. To correct their unhedged balance sheets, they must essentially shorten the typical term to maturity of assets and/or lengthen the typical maturity of liabilities. Thus, on the assets side of the balance sheet, one possibility is that savings and loans be permitted to acquire earning assets that are of shorter maturity than the typical mortgage. One obvious candidate is consumer loans of various kinds; personal loans, loans to finance automobiles and other durables, and so forth. Another possibility is the escalation of mortgage payments by the level of short-term rates, making mortgages effectively more like short-term loans. There may be other devices to change or renegotiate mortgage rates, or to shorten the maturity of mortgages.

On the sources of funds side, the corresponding shift to lengthening the term to maturity of sources of funds would be facilitated if savings and loans were given permission to sell a wider variety of of long-term obligations, as commercial banks have been doing in recent years (following changes in bank regulation). The savings associations themselves have been experimenting with paying modest premiums for the acquisition of somewhat longer term funds but my impression is that they have had very limited success in this direction, no doubt because the premiums they have offered have been too low.

VI. REGULATION SMACKS OF PRICE DISCRIMINATION

Regarding regulation in general, it is distressingly clear that attempts to regulate rates paid on savings and loan shares or deposits not only smack of price discrimination against the elderly, families of modest means and the small or financially unsophisticated savers who appear to be the main suppliers of funds to the savings associations, but in an increasingly sophisticated world with increasingly mobile funds, the price fixing creates a large number of problems for the associations themselves, as well as for the mortgage market and the construction industry that depends on savings and loan financing. For another example of the perverse consequences of poorly conceived regulation, consider that one of the main effects of rate ceilings has been to raise, not lower, mortgage rates, to penalize rather than subsidize home construction. Mortgage rates are no simple markup over the stated rate paid on savings and loan shares even though it may be a favorite, if erroneous, theory of some regulators of the business and of some legislators, too. If savings and loans cannot compete for funds because of ceilings imposed by regulation, they will lose funds as individuals shift to higher yielding assets. With fewer funds available in the mortgage market, mortgage rates, at least in the short-run, will tend to end up higher rather than lower as a consequence of the regulation. Withdrawals will also complicate the un-hedged balance sheet problem.

VII. ELIMINATE RATE CEILINGS ON SHARES, MORTGAGES

A reform package in this area should include eliminating all ceilings on rates payable on shares as well as all ceilings on mortgage rates, just as a corresponding reform package for commercial banks should include eliminating all ceilings on rates payable on time deposits as well as the elimination of the prohibition of payment of interest on demand deposits. Competition it-self would currently be compelling the savings and loan business to move in the direction of these modifications of portfolio and financing practices if the industry were not prevented from doing so by financial regulation.

Finally, a still more radical implication of this discussion is that savings and loan associations be permitted to merge with commercial banks. Combining the two institutions may be undesirable on other grounds, but the move would effectively broaden the maturity range of earning assets, and perhaps also broaden the maturity range of sources of funds.

PART 5
MONETARY POLICY

READING 31

INTRODUCTION

Deane Carson

If one accepts the monetarist view that changes in the money supply exert powerful effects on output and the price level, *and* that the lags in the effect of money supply change are both long and highly unpredictable, it is difficult for one to accept the traditional role of the monetary authorities that, by and large, places great reliance on the flexible and discretionary exercise of money management. This holds true whether the authority seeks to control (or modify) interest rates and money market conditions or seeks to control the money supply.

The weight of evidence suggests that the bases of monetarism are valid— changes in the money supply are indeed both powerful in effect and unpredictably lagged. Such observations have led monetarists to advocate constraints on the exercise of policy, either through the establishment of a fixed rule of constant money supply growth or the less rigid but still constraining adoption of a narrowly prescribed band of monetary expansion.

Such prescriptions are reenforced by evidence derived from the published Minutes of the Federal Open Market Committee, the major arm of monetary policy, one example of which is contained in the selection immediately following. It is impossible to read Open Market Committee Minutes without developing a sense of the great difficulty that these monetary authorities have in (a) assessing *where* the economy is at the current moment of their deliberations; (b) assessing the *direction* in which the economy is heading; (c) weighing the often conflicting evidence of both (a) and (b); and (d) estimating how, when, and where their policy actions will bear upon the economy.

Of these uncertainties, the latter, (d), is the greatest cause of apprehension to monetarists. It is perhaps too much to say, as some indeed do, that the authorities do not know what they are doing; it is safe to say, however, and some authorities frankly admit it, that they have no clear idea of the time impact of their policies, which ought to counsel a policy of restraint in and of itself. That is, large, short-run swings in monetary aggregates ought to be avoided as normal procedure and policy.

There is some evidence that the

monetary authorities, in recent years, have recognized the inherent dangers of marked period-to-period changes in monetary growth rates. The quality of their understanding has improved substantially from the days when mystical appraisal of the "tone and feel of the market" was the hallmark of a good central banker. Federal Reserve policymakers are far more sophisticated today, I believe, than even ten years ago: I think it is significant that they are uneasy today about their policies, in marked contrast to the aura of rectitude that once characterized their pronouncements.

A great deal of the Federal Reserve's policy dilemmas appear to derive from the structure of the money market, the Government securities dealer organization through which open-market operations are exclusively conducted, and traditional system attitudes vis-à-vis these market institutions. A kind of schizophrenia has developed out of historic attitudes with regard to system responsibilities for maintaining the viability of particular market segments (microresponsibility) on the one hand, and responsibility for economic stabilization (macroresponsibility) on the other. The system grew up in an era when the former responsibility was considered most important and when maintaining the liquidity of banks was considered not incompatible with economic stability. Micro- and macroresponsibilities *need not* conflict, but that they sometimes may is the source of some considerable difficulty in policy formulation and execution. Concern for particular market liquidity, such as was the case in the Penn Central episode of 1970, may lead to 'stop and go" money growth and attendant impact of a perverse nature on the real economy. This area of policy effects deserves more attention than it has received.

READING 32

MINUTES OF THE OPEN MARKET COMMITTEE*

Ralph Young, Secretary

A meeting of the Federal Open Market Committee was held in the offices of the Board of Governors of the Federal Reserve System in Washington, D. C., on Tuesday, November 23, 1965, at 9:30 a.m.

PRESENT:
Mr. Martin, Chairman (Chairman of the Board of Governors)
Mr. Hayes, Vice Chairman (New York)
Mr. Balderston (Board)
Mr. Daane (Board)
Mr. Ellis (Boston)
Mr. Galusha (Minneapolis)
Mr. Maisel (Board)
Mr. Mitchell (Board)
Mr. Patterson (Richmond)
Mr. Robertson (Board)
Mr. Scanlon (Chicago)
Mr. Shepardson (Board)

Messrs. Bopp (Philadelphia), Hickman (Cleveland), Clay (Kansas City), and Irons (San Francisco), Alternate Members of the Federal Open Market Committee

Messrs. Wayne, Shuford, and Swan, Presidents of the Federal Reserve Banks of Richmond, St. Louis, and San Francisco, respectively

Mr. Young, Secretary
Mr. Sherman, Assistant Secretary
Mr. Kenyon, Assistant Secretary
Mr. Hackley, General Counsel
Mr. Brill, Economist
Messrs. Baughman, Garvy, Holland, Koch, and Willis, Associate Economists
Mr. Holmes, Manager, System Open Market Account

* Editor's note: The Federal Open Market Committee has recently adopted the practice of publishing, with a three-month lag, the essence of the Committee's deliberations, in greatly abbreviated form. *Full minutes* have been published up to the end of 1965. This selection is drawn from the minutes of the meeting of November 23, 1965. The central issue was whether or not an increase in the discount rate was desirable. Shortly after the meeting, the Board of Governors approved such an increase. The entire minutes of this meeting cover 94 typewritten pages. I have omitted material that would be less interesting and instructive to the student.

Mr. Solomon, Adviser to the Board of Governors

Mr. Molony, Assistant to the Board of Governors

Mr. Cardon, Legislative Counsel, Board of Governors

Mr. Partee, Associate Director, Division of Research and Statistics, Board of Governors

Messrs. Garfield and Williams, Advisers, Division of Research and Statistics, Board of Governors

Mr. Hersey, Adviser, Division of International Finance, Board of Governors

Mr. Axilrod, Associate Adviser, Division of Research and Statistics, Board of Governors

Miss Eaton, General Assistant, Office of the Secretary, Board of Governors

Messrs. Eastburn, Mann, Parthemos, Brandt, Jones, Tow, Green, and Craven, Vice Presidents of the Federal Reserve Banks of Philadelphia, Cleveland, Richmond, Atlanta, St. Louis, Kansas City, Dallas, and San Francisco, respectively.

Mr. MacLaury, Assistant Vice President, Federal Reserve Bank of New York

Mr. Geng, Manager, Securities Department, Federal Reserve Bank of New York

Mr. Kareken, Consultant, Federal Reserve Bank of Minneapolis

* . . .

Upon motion duly made and seconded, and by unanimous vote, the minutes of the meetings of the Federal Open Market Committee held on November 2 and 4, 1965, were approved.

Chairman Martin then called for the go-around of comments and views on economic conditions and monetary policy. Mr. Hayes, who spoke first, made the following statement:

The set of economic conditions on which our policy must be based is largely unchanged since three weeks ago. Such minor changes as have occurred in the over-all economic picture have tended to confirm even greater strength in the domestic economy than at the time of our last meeting and an even less satisfactory balance of payments situation than was apparent at that time. Finally, it is becoming ever clearer than artificial rigidities in the interest rate structure are handicapping the efficient flow of funds in the economy. In my judgment the time has come for monetary policy to make a significant further contribution to more balanced and sustainable growth in the domestic economy and a strengthening of the dollar's international standing.

I recognize that the Treasury is in the process of completing its November fi-

Editors' note: The meeting first considered Treasury and Federal Reserve operations in foreign currencies, particularly the lira, which at that time was having difficulty. Following this, the manager of the trading desk, Mr. Holmes of the Federal Reserve Bank of New York, reported on his operations since the previous meeting of the Open Market Committee. This was followed by visual-aural presentations by the Board staff of the domestic and foreign economic developments that should be considered by the Committee. These include analyses of real demand and supply as well as thorough discussion of developments in financial markets. The quantity and quality of these data are impressive; the Committee has before it what is the most thorough array of facts and projections available anywhere in the world.

At the November, 1965 meeting, the Committee met in an economic environment in which the economy had reached near-capacity levels, unemployment was falling (although still above four percent), prices were rising very moderately, and balance-of-payments problems were still large. Interest rates were rising, bank credit expanding, and the money supply growing at a rate of approximately nine percent annually. The Board was faced with a decision with respect to an increase in both its discount rate and the maximum rates that banks were permitted to pay on time and savings deposits and certificates of indebtedness under Regulation Q. Although only the Board could change these, they were thoroughly discussed by the FOMC at this meeting.

nancing schedule, but I believe that we are at last able to reach policy decisions without the constraint of even keel considerations.*

With respect to the domestic economy, the longer-term outlook remains strong, and business optimism seems more firmly based than a few weeks ago. The prospective buoyancy of plant and equipment spending is especially impressive. With the likelihood that GNP will be growing at a rate of around $11–12 billion per quarter in 1966, the gap between actual and potential levels of activity will probably narrow further; and this should mean continued pressure on industrial capacity and on the labor market. The over-all unemployment rate over the year ahead is, at worst, likely to be no higher than the October 1965 figure of 4.3 per cent and may well decline below 4 per cent. If so, increased shortages of skilled and even other workers will probably develop, and wage rates may be subject to excessive upward pressure. Economic prospects also seem conducive to price increases.

Our international problem remains decidedly serious, with balance-of-payments statistics continuing to make disappointing reading. Prospects are that the regular deficit for 1965 will exceed $1.8 billion and may possibly be as high as $2 billion.

Turning to credit developments, we find that bank credit showed renewed and pervasive strength in October after a weak September. In the first ten months of 1965 bank credit was growing at the rate of 9.7 per cent per annum, well ahead of the 1964 rate. While there has been some slackening in business loan growth since mid-year, as corporations were able to tap other sources more effectively, there has been renewed strength in early November, and most banks look for continuing strong general loan demand. Money supply and time deposits grew in the first ten months at an annual rate

of 9.6 per cent, as compared with 7.9 per cent for all of 1964. An examination of broader indicators of credit growth reveals that while banks accounted for a larger share of the total than in 1964, there was also a substantial rise in the rate of total credit growth. Reduced corporate liquidity, combined with the prospect of heavy business spending, points to the likelihood of further heavy demand for credit from all available sources.

A final factor of great importance is, as I mentioned at the last meeting, the distortions in the interest rate structure resulting from a combination of heavy credit demands throughout the maturity range and rate rigidities introduced by regulatory or statutory ceilings and political pressures. For example, now that the leading city banks are paying the ceiling rate on 3-month certificates of deposit, any further upward movement of market interest rates could bring a severe loss of bank deposits and a consequent shrinkage of bank assets. The prime rate is out of line with rising rates in the corporate bond market and with the rising cost of money to the banks. The 4¼ per cent ceiling on the coupon rate applicable to new Treasury bond issues is now proving to be a major obstacle to the continued flow of savings into the Treasury. And finally, the discount rate is becoming more and more out of line with market rates of interest.

In my judgment this combination of circumstances points to a clear policy conclusion. The time has come for an overt move to signal a firmer monetary policy, and an increase in the discount rate by ½ per cent is the appropriate means of effecting such a change. It seems to me imperative that the System take this action to lend additional support to the voluntary foreign credit restraint program. That program may well prove increasingly difficult to administer in the absence of such additional support, and in any case it is not

---

* Editor's note: "Even keel" refers to Federal Reserve policies during periods of Treasury debt management operations; for the most part, it means a policy of neutrality and the avoidance of operations that would interfere with success of Treasury financing.

too early to be striving for a more basic improvement in our payments position. Not only is the economy amply strong to withstand any effects of firmer interest rates, but we are probably very close to the point where continued sustainable domestic expansion depends on greater effort to keep inflationary pressures under control—and of course this is of vital importance in connection with the maintenance of a large external trade surplus. In view of these considerations, it seems no more than prudent to try once again to slow the recent excessive rate of bank credit expansion. Finally, a discount rate increase, with an accompanying increase in Regulation Q ceilings, would permit greater reliance on market forces and interest rates in channeling the flow of funds.

Most of the directors of the New York Bank have felt for some time that an increase in the discount rate is overdue. Indeed, on a number of occasions some of them have urged that the Bank take the initiative in this area. I am now prepared to recommend that they vote a ½ per cent discount rate increase within the next week or so.

As for open market operations, it seems to me that we would be well advised to avoid any significant change until we have had time to observe the effects on the market of a discount rate rise. An overt change in System policy before the end of the year is apt to come as something of a shock to the market. While the technical position of the market is much better than a month or so ago, we have to be prepared for a rather strong initial reaction to a discount rate change. No doubt market interest rates will move higher, and I believe it would be wise, for the time being at least, to keep reserve availability about unchanged while meeting the seasonal reserve needs expected in the weeks ahead. I think the Manager should be allowed fairly wide discretion to keep the market adjustment as orderly as possible, and we should be prepared to tolerate some increase in net reserve availability if this turns out to be necessary. For the moment I should think we might instruct the Manager to maintain about the same money market conditions as have prevailed in the past three weeks. Accordingly, draft directive A, as proposed by the staff, seems quite satisfactory, except that I would add the words "reflecting strong credit demand" after the words "firmer financial conditions."*

Mr. Ellis reported that the Boston Bank's regular business outlook conference last week confirmed, as expected, the standard forecast of continuing GNP growth at about $10 billion per quarter through next June. Among the varied reports, two items drew his attention as evidence of the narrowed margin of unemployed resources: an aircraft corporation was attempting to expand its Hartford workforce by 1,000 persons per week for 8 weeks; another Connecticut employer was offering a $50 "finder's fee" to present employees for each new worker hired as a result of their personal recruiting efforts. Another conference participant indicated that insurance company current commitments were running at 93 per cent of cash flow—a record high for the industry. In anticipation of further needs for funds, a larger number of companies had established lines of credit at commercial banks, a number of which had not been used as yet.

In Mr. Ellis' judgment, it would be difficult to fault the economy and its progress when appraising it in real terms. Real growth was substantial, but not so rapid or distorted as to have caused production bottlenecks. Expansion and modernization was being concentrated where capacity was tightest. Unemployment had been and continued to be reduced. The outlook was universally conceded to be for further

---

* Editor's note: The two alternative directives suggested by the Staff are appended to these minutes as Attachment A.

such growth, with no widespread convictions that rapid price inflation was inevitable. Economic strength seemed firmly based, not weakly balanced.

When described in financial terms, however, the current picture was less reassuring. It was difficult to feel secure when the money supply was expanding at 7.6 per cent (on a three-month average) while GNP was expanding 4.7 per cent in real terms. Even given the substantial expansion of intermediation by commercial banks, it was disturbing to contemplate a 20 per cent year-to-year increase in business loans, against a 9 per cent parallel gain in industrial production.

Without being able to measure the degree, Mr. Ellis said, it was nevertheless apparent to him that the quality of credit extended had declined. Without being able to assess its full potential, it was evident that banks had greatly reduced their liquidity and their capacity to withstand financial shock. While the balance of payments had improved over the past year, it was evident that further measures would be required to restrain capital outflows. One such measure, a move toward lesser ease would not only buttress the special credit restraint measures being employed but would serve as a widely understood monetary signal that would strengthen the willingness to hold dollars abroad.

Mr. Ellis said he used the phrase "lesser ease" because in retrospect the record suggested that the Federal Reserve had eased its reserve availability and allowed an accelerated expansion of reserves while limiting rate increases.

Looking ahead, however, the Committee must contend with the historical fact that in years of strong credit demands bill rates normally rose 8 or 10 basis points in response to seasonal

pressures alone in the next several weeks. In Mr. Ellis' judgment, the Committee should not pour out reserves in an effort to enforce a rate ceiling against seasonal pressures. While it could quite properly seek to insure that rate movements did not become disorderly, it should not seek to enforce a ceiling at any level. The result would be to destroy the market's ability to set its own rates and the Committee's ability to judge true demand and supply relationships in the market. Interest rates were too important to be left to arbitrary judgments from any source.

At the meeting yesterday of the Boston Bank's directors, Mr. Ellis said, he took the position that this was not the proper moment to raise the discount rate. Although he agreed with Mr. Hayes' analysis, he would reverse the sequence of moves. He would move on reserves first and the discount rate later. His choice would be to *restore reserve objectives to primary positions as targets of policy.** The underlying philosophy of such an approach was to throw onto the market the responsibility for revealing the degree of pressure for credit expansion. If higher rates, including higher discount rates, were to eventuate, they should result from increased credit demands *against a steadily growing reserve base.**

Mr. Irons reported that the latest estimates in regard to Eleventh District economic activity continued to reflect expansion and growth, particularly in the major areas of activity. There had been an increase in manufacturing output, both of durables and nondurables. The petroleum situation showed improvement, as did the chemical situation. Construction continued strong. Employment continued to set new records, with increases in both the manufacturing and nonmanufacturing

* Editor's note: Emphasis supplied.

sectors. The unemployment rate stood at 3.2 per cent. Automobile sales were exceptionally good, and the agricultural situation was very strong this year as compared with preceding years.

Bankers reported that the pressure for loans continued unabated, although the loan figures showed relatively little change from the high levels that had prevailed. In fact, the banks had reduced their loans a bit in the recent period, while disposing of some Governments and increasing their holdings of other secuirties. Although they were not borrowing from the Reserve Bank heavily, they were active in the Federal funds market, with substantial net purchases. The discount window had about cleared out the seasonal type of agricultural lending.

On the national side, he agreed with the data in the green book and the supplement to it. His appraisal was that it confirmed the strength of the economy, with continuing expansion on a broad basis. He anticipated a substantial rise in final demand through the fourth quarter and on into next year. Most economic indexes seemed likely to rise further. Demand was beginning to press on capacity, and cost presures seemed likely to increase as labor markets continued to tighten.

Money and credit markets reflected firmness, with demands placing pressure on the supply of available credit. Apparently there was some uncertainty in the market as to the probable cost and availability of credit, and perhaps as to the position the Federal Reserve would take on credit availability. This raised the question whether a more positive position would be desirable.

Mr. Irons said his thinking was somewhat along the lines of that expressed by Mr. Hayes. It seemed to him that

there might be some advantage in a confirmation of recent rate movements in the market through a discount rate change. But he was not sure it would be necessary to raise the discount rate to 4½ per cent. The present market rate structure was roughly compatible with a 4¼ per cent discount rate, so a change in the rate to that level would be a confirmation of the market rate structure and an indication of the System's policy thinking. Such a move might in the long run be more effective than either deferring a discount rate change or taking a stronger action at this particular time.

Mr. Irons thought in terms of directive alternative B, but he did not have strong feelings one way or the other. Either A or B of the draft alternatives would seem compatible with a policy approach such as he had outlined.*

Mr. Swan reported that employment in the Pacific Coast States increased somewhat in October in all sectors except construction and mining. But with the labor force growing the unemployment rate remained unchanged at 5.6 per cent. Employment in defense-related manufacturing had improved slightly further. Construction contract awards increased in September—the latest month for which statistics were available—and for the first time the cumulative figure for the year to date was above that of the comparable period in 1964. But the increase was only 1½ per cent, compared with an increase of 4 per cent for the country as a whole.

In the three weeks through November 10, total credit of Twelfth District weekly reporting banks declined as the loan increase was more than offset by a decrease in securities holdings. The reserve position of the Twelfth District banks in recent weeks had been rela-

---

* Editor's note: See Attachment A below for statement of the alternatives.

tively easy, and their borrowings from the Reserve Bank had been extremely low.

In terms of the national picture, Mr. Swan was inclined to agree with the analysis in the green book. The situation was not appreciably different than at the time of the last meeting of the Committee, but it certainly remained a strong one.

In terms of policy, Mr. Swan said, the situation was quite difficult, but it seemed to him the Committee ought to maintain its current posture. He recognized that the need for overt action might be somewhat closer. He noted the relationship discussed in the blue book[1] as between net borrowed reserves and interest rates and the prospective basic provision of nonborrowed reserves, seasonally adjusted, at about a 2½ per cent annual rate for November. If those relationships continued, the Committee could live with the situation. However, he agreed with Mr. Ellis that emphasis should be placed on the provision of reserves to take care of seasonal needs. But the situation should be allowed to develop first. He would stay for the moment with net borrowed reserves of $100–$150 million rather than to raise the sights slightly in those terms. Consequently, he would accept alternative A of the draft directives.

Mr. Galusha said all indications were that economic activity in the Ninth District was continuing to expand at a satisfactory rate. Although the dollar figures showed a significant expansion, the ratio of classified loans* was more favorable than for the preceding two years. No major price shifts had come to his attention except in the area of packaging materials.

As for the national economy, a bear-ish cast could be put on some recent economic news. For instance, it could be argued that next year's revision of the November 1965 McGraw-Hill plant and equipment spending forecast would not be anything like the revisions of 1964 and 1965—the reason being that this November's accompanying sales forecast seemed so much more reasonable than those made in November 1963 and, even more, in November 1964. And it could be argued—on the basis of recent auto sales—that the industry would not do quite as well in 1966 as it did in 1965. Yet the fact remained that it was difficult to make the outlook for 1966 anything but bullish. That apparently was the most prudent assumption upon which to base current decisions about monetary policy.

The issue, therefore, was whether coming quarters would not find business a shade too good. In that connection, the information about the behavior of money wages and industrial prices contained in the green book was encouraging. So was the staff's judgment that a fourth quarter increase in GNP of $10 to $12 billion would not change the average utilization rate or, presumably, bring on an acceleration of the moderate price creep that had been experienced.

Mr. Galusha observed that evidently no one was expecting an average quarter-to-quarter increase in GNP for 1966 of more than $12 billion. The most optimistic forecasts, which by the way probably did not take full account of the most recent increases in long-term interest rates, implied something rather less than this average increase. Thus, however justified the recent increases in interest rates were, further increases in rates might be unwarranted unless the stand was taken that an increase

---

[1] A document entitled Money Market and Reserve Relationships prepared by the staff and distributed under date of November 19, 1965. A copy has been placed in the files of the Committee.

* Editor's note: Loans that bank examiners criticize in making reports to the regulatory agencies.

in prices, even if extremely modest and not at all likely to accelerate, should not be permitted.

Nor, Mr. Galusha continued, could an increase in the discount rate be accepted as merely a technical adjustment. There was no basis, whether in theory or experience, for thinking that such an increase would leave open market rates unaffected. The thought that an increase in the discount rate would not bring on an increase in bank loan rates—the prime rate included— was hardly credible. Such an increase might be desirable, but if so the bankers ought to be able to bring it off without help from a "price leader."

Finally, Mr. Galusha said, recent developments suggested that financial markets now believed current rates to be maintainable, so an increase in the discount rate no longer appeared "necessary," if it ever did.*

He would be less than candid, Mr. Galusha commented, if the impression was conveyed by his comments that he was not uneasy. His hunch was that the Committee was approaching a moment of truth. Hunches were an important part of professional decision making, but not until experience justified some credibility. Without that experience he must rely on such evidence as came to hand, and the evidence did not appear to warrant a significant change in policy.

Mr. Scanlon reported that the economic atmosphere in the Seventh District could be characterized as ebullient. Activity was at a high level and was expected to rise further. The financial indicators confirmed the buoyant business conditions. Although the growth of business loans at Seventh District banks had slowed somewhat in recent weeks, due primarily to repayments by durable goods manufacturers,

the increase for the year to date remained well above all recent experience and slightly greater than the record increase for the country as a whole. District banks had continued to liquidate Treasury securities and gave evidence of becoming less aggressive in purchasing other securities. They continued to make less use of the discount window than in past periods of similar rate relationships. In the absence of a change in Regulation Q, reserve pressures on the banks might be expected to increase, *culminating on the December corporate tax date when a large volume of CD's was scheduled to run off.*

As to policy, Mr. Scanlon said that, like Mr. Ellis, he would not want to resist a modest seasonal rise in rates by invoking a rigid rate objective in the coming period. He would defer any change in the discount rate, although he believed there was considerable merit in Mr. Irons' suggestion. For the immediate future, he favored a policy that would imply slower growth in money and credit and, assuming continued strengthening of credit demand, modestly higher interest rates.

If market forces pressed in that direction, he would expect that in view of seasonal pressures the 3-month bill rate would rise somewhat further, perhaps as high as 4.15 or 4.20 per cent. He would hope that it might be possible to ride with such a policy during the remainder of 1965 and through the early weeks of 1966 while observing economic developments and getting a better line on Federal budget prospects. He continued to feel that any consideration of an increase in the discount rate must be accompanied by consideration of an increase in the rates banks were permitted to pay on time deposits. While he could accept

* Editor's note: While the Open Market Committee discusses the need for a change in the discount rate and Regulation Q, the Board of Governors makes the final decisions. Both the discount rate and Regualtion Q ceilings were raised shortly after this meeting.

alternative B of the draft directives, he believed that a policy such as he favored could be carried out under alternative A.

Mr. Clay commented that the national economy continued to expand faster than anticipated earlier and its prospective performance also appeared to exceed earlier expectations. There was little evidence to suggest any lessening of economic activity in the months ahead. Except for residential construction, activity in all major sectors of the economy was increasing. The scale of prospective Government spending, notably defense outlays, remained of unknown proportions, but military developments strongly suggested that that factor would be expansive beyond present indications.

With the margin of unutilized manpower and other resources smaller than earlier, however, prices were more sensitive than heretofore. Resource utilization could be expected to continue to grow and, despite expanding resources, the margin of unutilized resources probably would narrow still further in the months ahead.

As the shape of those forces would have to await further developments, Mr. Clay felt that monetary policy could justifiably continue essentially unchanged. Looking further ahead, there was ample reason to wonder whether money and capital market developments might not make the present discount rate and the current degree of reserve availability incompatible. In that event the Committee would need to choose between higher money market rates with current reserve availability, the present level of money market rates with increased reserve availability, or some other combination of those alternatives. Alternative A of the draft directives appeared to Mr. Clay satisfactory at this time, and he did not think that a change should be made in the discount rate.

Mr. Wayne reported that Fifth District business continued to improve and showed evidence of acceleration in some sectors.

Meanwhile, the national economy continued to show moderate gains from high levels of activity. Substantially all of the changes in October were favorable, indicating that the effects of lower steel production were more than offset by strength in other sectors of the economy. Additional reports of labor scarcity and the rise of overtime in manufacturing in October indicated that the pressure on manpower was rising. With the prospect of high and rising outlays on equipment next year, it would seem that there was a real possibility of a serious imbalance between productive capacity and the output of consumer goods.

In the international area, Mr. Wayne continued, the threat to sterling now appeared less acute than at any time in recent months. Some of the recent improvement had come, however, at a cost to the U.S. balance of payments.

There were some indications that the seasonal demand for credit for the remainder of the year might not be as great as expected earlier. If this was correct, the Committee might be able to get by for the rest of the year without further measures of restraint. In Mr. Wayne's judgment, that was greatly to be desired if it was feasible, since any substantial firming would require action on the discount rate and bring additional pressure for an increase in Regulation Q ceilings. He did not think that the System should resort at this time to an overt action, such as an increase of ½ per cent in the discount rate, designed to produce a sharp impact on expectations.

Mr. Robertson made the following statement:

The last three weeks have provided us with more confirming evidence that we should go no further in tightening monetary policy at this juncture.

On the price front, the gradual upcreep in the general industrial commodity index has slowed down, and certainly the latest aluminum and copper price rollbacks—whatever their broader social implications—will give a little more pause to any other administered price increases that might have been in the offing.

In financial markets, conditions also seem a little better balanced. Perhaps the most constructive thing that has happened is that market expectations of an imminent discount rate increase have been quieted somewhat. In this calmer atmosphere, funds seem to be flowing fairly well through both the money and bond markets. I see no evidence of any "knots" that need untying by official action.

In the next few weeks the seasonal pressures in the money market will mount to their usual annual peak. If feasible, I would like to avoid allowing such technical presures to force us into a basic change of monetary policy that might more appropriately wait until the impact of next year's Federal budget can be judged. Some bankers have been insisting that something must be done to resolve interest rate and Regulation Q ceiling questions before the December squeeze, but I think the availability of the Federal Reserve discount window and the Board's capability of revising pertinent Regulation Q provisions quickly, if necessary, combine to give any well-run bank all the safety valves it ought to need for this period. This particular CD squeeze does not seem to me to be the kind of development that should be dealt with by general monetary policy. That, I maintain, should be addressed to the broad performance of the economy, which I regard as too strong to warrant any easing, but not yet so clearly inflationary as to call for further tightening.

Our directions to the Manager, therefore, should be to walk a tightrope between now and year end, keeping money market rates as a group from either rising or falling significantly, and letting net borrowed reserves move where necessary in order to preserve such a money market tone. I would vote in favor of alternative A of the draft directives submitted by the staff.

Mr. Shepardson commented that every available indication pointed toward a strengthening economy. Not only were people talking about good business the rest of this year and in 1966 but some recent statements projected a continuing rise in 1967. He thought there was *clear evidence of increasing over-expectations, and that the rate of money growth and credit expansion was clearly beyond sustainable levels.* The Committee had spoken for some time in its directives about a moderate growth, but it did not seem to him that the present rate of expansion could be defined as moderate.

The reports around the table, Mr. Shepardson pointed out, all indicated an increasing shortage of labor, and that was bound to bring pressure [on prices]. Higher prices would not improve the balance of payments situation, nor would they improve the prospect of long-run economic growth.

It seemed to Mr. Shepardson that all indicators showed sufficient strength in the economy to withstand some restraint. If seasonal demands were as strong as appeared likely, this probably would result in some further pressure on the discount rate, and he would expect a move on the discount rate to be called for in the near future. When it came to the change in the rate, he did not think an increase of ¼ per cent would settle the matter. If the System was going to move, it might just as well move the rate up ½ per cent and give itself leeway to operate for some time into the future.

Mr. Shepardson favored alternative

B of the draft directives. He also felt that the System should be prepared for a discount rate increase in the near future.

Mr. Mitchell said the economy was performing better than he had expected it would at this point, and as well as he had hoped. At the moment, Mr. Mitchell did not see a threat to stability in the present and prospective rates of resource utilization. Therefore, he saw no basic reason for any further firming action on the part of the Committee at this time. Possibly there would be some disclosure when the Federal budget was presented that would provide a clue for action, but in the meantime he would supply reserves adequately and ungrudgingly to cover seasonal requirements reasonably related to the present level of GNP. He hoped that this course would be adequate to get through the rest of the year.

Mr. Mitchell said the requirement from the standpoint of the balance of payments was to contain inflation within the U.S. More should not be expected from monetary policy. If it was necessary to go beyond that, selective measures should be used; he would not want to take measures that would restrict the domestic economy generally. It seemed to him the information in the "chart show" suggested quite persuasively that the price rises that had taken place were not pervasive. They were not the type that resulted from excessive demand. For those who were worried about the money supply growth, he would point out that this year there had been no change in velocity in New York, and little change in the other six money centers. In this situation there was only one change that could occur —the money supply had to grow.

Mr. Mitchell agreed with Mr. Hayes that the rate pattern had been distorted for some time. He hoped that before too long these distortions could be more or less unraveled. But he would not like to see this done in a period when there were seasonal pressures on the whole rate structure. The Committee had lived with the distortions for a long time, and he hoped in the year ahead something could be done, but not right now.

Mr. Mitchell favored alternative A of the draft directives but proposed certain language changes. At the beginning of the first paragraph, he would say: "The economic and financial developments reviewed at this meeting indicate that over-all domestic economic activity is continuing a rate of expansion comparable to that of the third quarter despite the contractive effect of a reduction in steel inventories. Business sentiment continues optimistic and financial resources are in shorter supply." This would call attention to the fact that the contractive effect of the steel inventory adjustment had been absorbed and the economy continued to grow at the same rate as before.

Mr. Daane argued the case on economic grounds for a discount rate increase this December as follows:

1. Persisting gradual upward price pressures—with the wholesale price index rising at an annual rate of 1 per cent since June, following a 2 per cent rate of rise over the previous 9 months.
2. Continuing rapid expansion of business fixed investment at a pace disproportionate to the rise in final products—in the past 10 months, business equipment production was up 10 per cent; consumer goods production up 2 per cent.
3. A shrinking margin of unused resources — average manufacturing output at 90 per cent of capacity (and more in lines other than steel) and unemployment down to 2.9 per cent of adult males, with signs of a

beginning slowdown of productivity and rise in unit labor cost.

4. A persisting balance of payments deficit—at roughly a $400 million per quarter rate on a regular transactions basis.

On the financial side, Mr. Daane said a policy change was indicated by the following:

1. Credit demands were large and growing, especially business demands for external financing partly to pay for disproportionate expenditures on fixed investment.

2. Despite big business capital market flotations, and some bank efforts to push more borrowers into the capital markets, a stable 4½ per cent prime loan rate kept drawing in business loan demands. To the extent that resultant demands taxed bank resources, resultant rationing actions pressed most against fewer and smaller borrowers.

3. Seasonal pressures would be pushing up bill rates between now and mid-December—perhaps to in the neighborhood of 4.15 per cent on the 3-month bill. An accompanying seasonal tightening of other rates would increase pressures on discount administration and might trigger new disturbing uncertainties concerning discount rate action.

4. Higher short-term market rates would squeeze hard on bank ability to sell CD's to replace big December maturities. Such maturities were by now probably as big as September, when the post-tax-date squeeze pinched banks for several weeks and led to sharp rate run-ups.

5. Prime-name banks were already being led to merchandise promissory notes at shorter maturities and higher interest rates than allowable on CD's under Regulation Q. Unless Q ceilings were raised, promissory note issuance was likely to balloon in December, pushing up rates and complicating the Treasury's intended turn-of-year bill financing. If promissory notes were redefined as deposits to halt Regulation Q avoidance, Q ceilings would have to be raised to give banks relief, and this would trigger renewed strong expectations of a discount rate increase—expectations that could inhibit market flows.

6. Higher interest rates could increase market capacity to handle flows, as had happened in the corporate market in the past two weeks. A higher discount rate could clear the air and improve the reception for unexpectedly large Treasury financing needs in January. That would be particularly true if at the same time open market operations reduced somewhat the need for member banks to borrow.

While Mr. Daane still felt the case could be made along the lines he had indicated, he was today less certain about the timing and sequence of System actions. It seemed to him the market was now poised precariously, having been buffeted by oral suasion and shifting expectations to the point where an overt move in the form of a discount rate change might set off a chain of over-reactions that could go far beyond the sort of modest tightening he had had in mind.

Thus, the Committee faced a choice of two courses. First, it could move back on net borrowed reserves to the high side of the $150 million mark and accept, not resist, market forces that in all likelihood would produce somewhat higher rates in the days and weeks ahead. Under that course he would at that point consider a change in the discount rate. To be specific, following that particular course at this juncture argued that it would be better for the System to follow than to lead the market. The alternative course was to go ahead with an overt move on the discount rate as quickly as possible, with the cushioning action on reserves he had already suggested. Those two courses might not really be far apart in point of time, but his own preference would be, he believed, to follow rather than lead the market.

On the directive, Mr. Daane said that while philosophically he would favor alternative B of the draft directives, he could live with alternative A, provided somewhat firmer market conditions were restored along the lines he had advocated.

Mr. Maisel said he disagreed strongly with the first and last parts of Mr. Daane's analysis. He did, however, agree that there was a major problem in the likelihood of market over-reaction. He was pleased to see the feeling of both the Account Manager and the staff that this was a period of balance both in the economy and in the credit markets. The present situation was dangerous and worrisome because the economy was balanced at a high level of employment and output, but it was a very satisfactory level and one that he hoped could be maintained.

He did feel, Mr. Maisel continued, that a real danger of a sudden change in sentiment existed as a result of a misreading of the Committee's intent. This would cause the markets to react far more than anyone considered desirable.

It was fortunate at this time that a balance existed and that the Committee had an opportunity to wait and see. *No change in policy was required.* The main pressures appeared to be off with respect to the price-wage situation. The rising rate of increases in industrial commodity prices had slackened off. There was no indication of any acceleration of growth in the near term

that would lead to a deterioration in wages or prices.

Even more important, Mr. Maisel added, was the fact that the country was now in the midst of a national emergency or war. Major industries had been asked, with no uncertainty in the request, to hold the price line. Without far stronger reasons than existed, a move on the System's part at this time to help raise the price of the major commodity it influenced—money—would be taken as a sign that banks wanted to opt out of the national effort and that the System approved of such action. This would directly contravene the Administration's request to labor, industry, and the banks to hold the line.

It seemed desirable to him to hold to present policy based on the actual price-wage situation, the national effort, and the need to maintain the present level in expectations and sentiment. The Manager should completely meet seasonal needs as they worked out in the market.

Mr. Maisel concluded by saying that he opposed a discount rate change and that he supported alternative A of the draft directives.

Mr. Hickman[2] said it seemed to him the Committee had little room to maneuver, even if it wanted to, insofar as policy action today was concerned. With the last Treasury financing of the year still in progress, it would be highly disruptive to change policy at this time, particularly since the new tax bills would have to be redistributed by the banks and dealers. Moreover, financial markets continued to be unstable, with the market for U.S. Government securities still highly sensitive to rumors and expectations.

So far as commodity prices were concerned, Mr. Hickman felt that the chance of serious price inflation was now greater than at any time in the past

---

[2] President, Federal Reserve Bank of Cleveland, an alternate member of the Open Market Committee.

four years. But it could not be known that this would happen. For one thing, the standard price indexes, while drifting upward, had still not accelerated. For another, the increased capacity now coming on stream and the increase in the civilian labor force (barring unexpected draft calls) should reduce the likelihood of price inflation.

Insofar as overheating was concerned, Mr. Hickman believed the key question was the Federal budget. The normal revenue throw-off from an expanding GNP would permit a noninflationary rise in Federal spending for defense and the Great Society on the order of $5–$7 billion. On the other hand, a budgeted increase on a GNP basis much beyond that would clearly be inflationary and should be offset by tighter money.

Mr. Hickman therefore recommended no change in policy at this time, no change in the discount rate, and no change in Regulation Q. He favored alternative A of the draft directives, amended along the lines suggested by Mr. Mitchell.

Mr. Bopp[3] recalled having noted three weeks ago that it was becoming increasingly difficult for him to determine the appropriate stance for policy. Events since then and the outlook for the future certainly did not make the determination any easier.

Although the upcreep in prices had slowed and capacity limitations still did not appear to block further gains in output, many forecasts now emerging suggested a growth rate that could move the economy very close to full employment levels as 1966 unfolded. Before considering how monetary policy should react, however, it was necessary to recognize that the System was operating in a new environment of monetary, fiscal, and wage-price constraints. At present it was difficult to forecast how business would react to the more vigorous action on the guideposts and hence to determine precisely how monetary policy would fit into the new over-all mix of public policy.

As Mr. Bopp felt that this was not the time to tighten further. Also, considering that the first quarter of 1966 might be less buoyant than some expected he would be inclined to wait until seasonal pressures passed and a clearer outline of 1966 emerged before deciding whether additional monetary restraint was called for. He favored alternative A of the draft directives, with Mr. Mitchell's suggested modification.

Mr. Patterson said the Atlanta Reserve Bank's tabulation of announcements of new and expanded manufacturing plants indicated that half way through the fourth quarter the announcements of investments in that part of the country were already approaching the record third-quarter volume. This would fit in with the national McGraw-Hill findings, although the two series obviously were not comparable.

Having talked with some of the Sixth District's leading bankers, Mr. Patterson was more than ever convinced that liquidity had much deteriorated for banks generally, although he would agree that a bank-by-bank analysis was necessary to determine over-all liquidity. District banks were relying on Federal funds more than ever. But there were limits to that supply, and some banks were becoming increasingly worried about what would happen if they had to tap that source simultaneously. Some Atlanta banks had started to issue small amounts of unsecured notes, primarily to test the market. With loan demand showing no signs of letting up and Governments being used

---

[3] President of the Federal Reserve Bank of Philadelphia, an alternate member of the Open Market Committee.

for collateral rather than liquidity purposes, Mr. Patterson had the uneasy feeling that banks were looking to the discount window as their source of liquidity. Resort to the discount window obviously should not be the banks' principal line of protection, and it was restricted in any case by the fact that banks held limited amounts of eligible assets. As bankers generally woke up to that state of affairs, he would expect them to react by restricting any rapid loan expansion.

Anticipating such self-tightening— which might already be taking place if changes in interest rates were any indication—Mr. Patterson believed that the System should not tighten its reins, at least for the time being. He would adopt alternative A of the draft directives.

Mr. Patterson added that, as he had already noted, some of the Sixth District's banks—cramped by the ceiling on CD rates—were beginning to solicit funds in a way that he considered subterfuge. *Would it not be preferable, he asked, to allow banks to compete freely for time deposits?* Personally, he would favor lifting the time deposit rate ceiling. And if that were done, he would be prepared to support some compensating open market operations and a technical change in the discount rate, because it was known from previous experience that a change in Regulation Q might lead to an acceleration in deposit expansion, which he would consider unwarranted in the present economic climate.

Mr. Shuford thought the economy might be approaching the point where such a rapid expansion in aggregate demand as was occurring would result in less increase in real product and more price rises. In his appraisal, prices had risen significantly during the past year. In view of the continued rapid increase in aggregate demand and a possible limit on the ability of production to match such an expansion, price increases might accelerate. There was a great deal of official concern with price increases, and that concern seemed to him to be well taken. But he was puzzled that the treatment most discussed and followed was administrative control.

Taking into consideration the strength in total demand, which was exerting upward pressure on prices, as well as an apparent escalation of the U.S. commitment in Vietnam, which might add further to total demand, Mr. Shuford thought a tightening in monetary policy was desirable. He was not sure how this could best be accomplished. The problem of timing was always of concern, but he was persuaded that action should be taken promptly to raise the discount rate. He had been thinking in terms of a ½ per cent increase, but the analysis by Mr. Irons had much to support it. It seemed to him that a little further discussion on that score might be needed, and perhaps additional discussion on the matter of timing. But it occurred to him that hardly ever was a completely desirable time found for a move of this kind. He was not sure it would be any easier to reach a decision in January than in December. Since it was his opinion that action was needed, he would favor moving without undue delay sometime in the first part of December.

Mr. Balderston recalled that at the meeting of the Committee on October 12 he sought to state the case for reexamining current monetary policy. Among the points he had made at that time were the following: Wage pressures, combined with Government spending for war and welfare activities, suggested to businessmen that things would cost more later on. In addition, business forecasts for the coming year were favorable. As a result of those rising expectations, both actual and projected plant investment volumes were strong. Thus business loan activity had been exceptionally heavy throughout the year, even though the current annual rate of increase in business loans was only one-half of the 20 per cent rate of increase for the first nine months, because long-term credit demands had been diverted from the open market to the banks.

The bind in which the bankers now found themselves would not have been so tight, Mr. Balderston commented, if the bankers had had the courage to utilize the pricing mechanism in guiding or forcing customers to secure their funds through channels appropriate to the use of the funds. But that did not happen, and now the Federal Reserve in its supervisory capacity faced the responsibility of remedying the chaotic rate structure. System action would have been more effective at an earlier date. But there had been a succession of Treasury financings, and it was probably better to act late than never. If the System acted—and there was not much time left before the next Treasury financing operation—the appropriate open market policy probably would be represented by alternative A of the draft directives. If the System did not act with respect to the discount rate and Regulation Q, then he would favor some other policy.

Mr. Shepardson remarked that the bulk of the criticism he had read of System policy over the past 10 years was to the effect that the System usually moved too late. It was said that the System could not arrive quickly enough at a decision. It was too late to tighten, when tightening was appropriate, and too late to ease when that was appropriate. This, in his opinion, was one of the problems with which the System had to deal.

Chairman Martin commented that over the past two years he had been proud to preside over the Federal Reserve System because, despite continuing differences of opinion, the debates had been on a consistently high level. Having said this, he would also say that he considered it unfortunate that the System had been divided and continued to be divided. He had always felt that when the System was united it occupied a strong position within the ranks of the Government. When divided, the System was in a less strong position.

As long as a high level of unemployment prevailed and resource utilization was clearly below any reasonable level, he did not think there was too much trouble in debating the "easy money" and the "not-so-easy money" schools of thought, and that was fundamentally what the debate had been about over most of the past two years. The "easy money" school had thought that some moves the Committee made were mistakes, when the Committee made them, and he respected that view.

But, Chairman Martin said, he wanted to make his own point of view clear this morning. He thought *the time for decision had arrived,* and he wanted the record to reflect his opinion that it was not possible to run away continually from making a decision. It could be debated at length whether a situation of full employment existed and whether the resource utilization level was entirely adequate. It could also be debated whether a monetary policy move at this juncture would have any impact from the balance of payments standpoint. He happened to think that it would, and he had thought so for a good while, but this was certainly a debatable point. But he thought the financial problem was acute when conditions reached a point where, regardless of the decisions made by the Open Market Committee, it was necessary to support a Treasury financing operation in order to make it successful. While there might be some who would disagree with him, he did not think there was any doubt that except for official purchases for Treasury accounts and except for System support the latest offering of the Treasury would not have been successful.

Talk about market expectations, Chairman Martin noted, could work both ways. In the market today the expectations were just as much that the President would not allow any interest rate changes as to the contrary. That created a very real problem. The Treasury expected to announce another financing on the 16th of December. Therefore, if the System was going to make any move now, it must do so before that time. He did think, however, that this week would be too early.

Chairman Martin observed that it was necessary to make fundamental judgments at this stage. It was easy for him to make a judgment because he believed the country was in a period of creeping inflation already. And he believed the balance of payments situation would be benefited by more restraint in the over-all economy. In short, he thought the economy was going too fast at the moment. This was where one came up against the basic problem—to which he did not know the answer—relating to the economics of full employment. Here there were different schools of thought. Personally he felt that at some point, if the economy went too fast, the possibility of achieving sustainable full employment would be destroyed. And he thought the situation was about at that point now.

Accordingly, he did not have any real difficulty with his line of approach. When it came to the implementation, though, he would hesitate to move in the manner that he understood Messrs. Ellis and Daane were suggesting, that is, to pursue a firmer policy by reducing the level of reserves in the reservoir. He thought that the demand forces in the economy were so strong that even

with a slight increase in the amount of reserves in the reservoir there would still be a rise in interest rates. Therefore, the Committee was in the relatively fortunate position of not having to tighten money per se.

The difficulty of the moment, the Chairman added, had been compounded by the banks' unwillingness to deal with their own problem; in his judgment they had let themselves become bound into the prime rate in a ridiculous way. But the situation had to be unraveled at some point. It some point. It could be unraveled by a decline in business, although he hoped it would not. The other way—the only way that he felt would be effective—would be to move on Regulation Q and the discount rate and to continue the level of reserves during the period of transition, or perhaps even to increase the level slightly during the period of transition so as to make the adjustment less difficult in terms of the over-all economy.

That was where he came out, Chairman Martin said. *As to the directive, he thought the Committee probably could agree on alternative A and probably could not agree on alternative B.* There seemed to be a clear majority in favor of alternative A.

In this framework, Chairman Martin continued, he would personally be prepared to approve a discount rate action, if taken by any Reserve Bank, prior to mid-December. To run too close to the next Treasury financing would, of course, be a mistake. He would expect, also, that if the Board approved a discount rate change it would make a change in the Regulation Q ceiling.

Chairman Martin commented additionally that it must be remembered that the Open Market Committee did not set the discount rate, just as it did not fix reserve requirements or margin requirements. The Committee meetings were used as a forum for discussion of System policy generally, but no commitment could be made with respect to the discount rate. The Board would have to act on that, and he could not anticipate how the Board would act. He had merely wanted to make it clear that for his part, as one member of the Board—and assuming a continuation of present conditions—if any Reserve Bank should come in with an increase in the discount rate he would be prepared to approve. He would not vote to approve, however, without an increase in the Regulation Q ceiling also. He was not suggesting that anyone act on the discount rate; he was merely expressing his present position and indicating how he would react, as one member of the Board, if such action were taken by a Reserve Bank.

Chairman Martin repeated that a majority of the Committee appeared to favor alternative A of the draft directives. He would be willing to go along with that directive himself. If, however, some members favored alternative B there was no reason why they should not so record themselves.

Chairman Martin then alluded to the modification suggested earlier by Mr. Mitchell in the language of the first paragraph of alternative A of the draft directives, and he inquired as to the wishes of the Committee members. Mr. Hayes expressed a preference for the original language of the draft directive, particularly since he felt that the introduction of the phrase "financial resources were in shorter supply" was troublesome. Others who spoke on the matter indicated that they would be agreeable to the proposed modification except for the phrase to which Mr. Hayes had referred.

Thereupon, upon motion duly made and seconded, and by unanimous vote, the Federal Reserve Bank of New York was authorized and directed, until otherwise directed by the Committee, to execute transactions in the System Account in accordance with the following current economic policy directive:

The economic and financial developments reviewed at this meeting indicate that over-all domestic economic activity is continuing a rate of expansion comparable to that of the third quarter despite the contractive effect of a reduction in steel inventories. Business sentiment continues optimistic and financial conditions are firmer. Meanwhile, our international payments have remained in deficit. In this situation, it remains the Federal Open Market Committee's current policy to strengthen the international position of the dollar, and to avoid the emergence of inflationary pressures, while accommodating moderate growth in the reserve base, bank credit, and the money supply.

To implement this policy, System open market operations until the next meeting of the Committee shall be conducted with a view to maintaining about the same conditions in the money market that have prevailed since the last meeting of the Committee.

It was agreed that the next meeting of the Committee would be held on Tuesday, December 14, 1965, at 9:30 a.m.

Thereupon the meeting adjourned.

Ralph A. Young
Secretary

ATTACHMENT A
November 22, 1965

CONFIDENTIAL (FR)

Drafts of Current Economic Policy Directive for Consideration by the Federal Open Market Committee at its Meeting on November 23, 1965

ALTERNATIVE A (NO CHANGE)

The economic and financial developments reviewed at this meeting indicate that over-all domestic economic activity is expanding strongly in a continuing climate of optimistic business sentiment and firmer financial conditions. Meanwhile, our international payments have remained in deficit. In this situation, it remains the Federal Open Market Committee's current policy to strengthen the international position of the dollar, and to avoid the emergence of inflationary pressures, while accommodating moderate growth in the reserve base, bank credit, and the money supply.

To implement this policy, System open market operations until the next meeting of the Committee shall be conducted with a view to maintaining about the same conditions in the money market that have prevailed since the last meeting of the Committee.

ALTERNATIVE B (FIRMER)

The economic and financial developments reviewed at this meeting indicate strong further domestic economic expansion in a climate of optimistic business sentiment, with strong credit demand and some continuing upward creep in prices. Meanwhile, our international payments have remained in deficit. In this situation, it is the Federal Open Market Committee's current policy to strengthen the international position of the dollar, and to resist the emergence of inflationary pressures by moderating growth in the reserve base, bank credit, and the money supply.

To implement this policy, System open market operations until the next meeting of the Committee shall be conducted with a view to achieving somewhat firmer conditions in the money market than have prevailed since the last meeting of the Committee.

READING 33

THE CHANNELS OF MONETARY POLICY

Frank de Leeuw and Edward M. Gramlich[1]

One of the most perplexing questions in macroeconomics is the importance of financial variables in influencing the real economy. Opinions on this question have varied greatly from decade to decade, and still vary from economist to economist. Whereas classical economists felt that monetary forces were quite important—indeed the only long-run determinant of the price level—the standard Keynesian view during and after the Great Depression tended to deemphasize the role of money. The period since World War II has seen a definite revival of interest in monetary phenomena, but this revival has by no means generated a consensus on the importance of money in influencing economic activity.

A basic reason for differences of opinion on the importance of money has been the difficulty in obtaining convincing empirical evidence on the sensitivity of aggregate demand to exogenous monetary and fiscal forces. Historical evidence suggests that such autonomous monetary forces as gold discoveries and reserve requirement decisions played an important role in such major economic swings as the inflation of 1900–10, the Great Depression, and the contraction of 1936–37. These findings are buttressed by the studies of Friedman-Meiselman, the staff of the Federal Reserve Bank of St. Louis, and others who find monetary variables to be much more important than fiscal variables in explaining subsequent movements in gross national product. On the other hand, the evidence from several of the large econometric models—the Wharton School model, the Commerce Department model, the Michigan model, and to a lesser extent the Brookings model—is that monetary forces are rather unimportant in influencing total demand.

Behind different assessments of the

Source: Reprinted, with deletions, from *Federal Reserve Bulletin*, June, 1969, pp. 472–490.

[1] Note: While the authors take full responsibility for statements in this staff study, they stress that credit for the ideas it contains belongs to the entire Federal Reserve-Mit group of which they are only two members. Franco Modigliani, Albert Ando, Charles Bishoff, George de Menil, Dwight Jaffee, and Enid Miller have made especially important contributions to the results reported here; many others have made important contributions to other aspects of the model.

role of monetary factors lie differences of opinion regarding the number and significance of the channels through which monetary forces operate. Many econometric models include only one channel: namely, the effects of financial yields on the opportunity cost of holding durable goods and structures, with the cost in turn influencing tangible investment. Even within this one channel there is room for a wide range of empirical estimates of the strength of the forces at work, and further research is still urgently needed. At the same time, however, the possibility should be investigated that the conflict stems partly from the existence of other channels through which monetary forces work, channels which have been either inadequately treated or completely ignored in previous econometric work.

The Federal Reserve–MIT econometric model project attempted to examine these ideas. The aim was to bulid a model which, though not necessarily larger than most other existing models, would focus more intensively on monetary forces and how they affect the economy. The format of an econometric model was chosen because it seemed to be the best way to take advantage of recent work in areas such as household and producer behavior, financial behavior, and price-wage determination; of recent econometric advances in techniques for dealing with distributed lags, autocorrelation, and constraints on parameters; and of advances in computer technology that make possible rapid estimation and solution of large non-linear systems. It was also felt that only through a model could one surmount problems involving the large number of exogenous monetary and fiscal variables, variable policy multipliers and time lags, and

other difficulties which the one-equation approach to explaining GNP necessarily oversimplifies or ignores.*

This article concentrates on the channels through which monetary forces influence the real economy. Previous reports have dealt with other aspects of the model—its over-all structure, its theoretical innovations, the characteristics of its multiplier-accelerator mechanism—and we will touch on these points to only a minor extent.

The paper first sets out the theoretical and institutional bases for the three channels of monetary policy currently represented in the model. Cost-of-capital influences constitute one channel, affecting single- and multifamily housing, plant and equipment, State and local construction, and investment in consumer durable goods. The transmission of rates of return on bonds to the value of wealth held in the form of equities constitutes a second channel, one that affects household net worth and consumption. Finally, credit rationing constitutes a third channel which we have so far found to be important only in the housing market. As yet, we have found that neither the cost of capital nor credit rationing is important for inventory investment, though we have tested these possibilities extensively.

Next the paper presents estimates of the quantitative importance of each channel. Simulation of different groups of equations of the model and of the full model under varying sets of initial conditions illustrates direct effects and complete-system effects of monetary policy alone and in comparison with fiscal policy. The results of these simulations are still subject to large uncertainties, and we will make changes as work on the model continues. For what

---

* Editor's note: Compare this view with the discussion of the single equation approach found in Keran's article in Part 4, pp. 287–89.

they are worth, however, the current results imply 1- or 2-year fiscal policy effects that are roughly comparable to results for other models and monetary policy effects that are appreciably larger than results for other models though smaller than what a simple quantity theory of money would imply. Financial variables are seen to operate with a somewhat longer lag than fiscal variables, and both monetary and fiscal multipliers vary depending on the initial state of the economy.

*

The flow diagram (Chart 1) exhibits the direct effects of monetary policy. Financial yields shown at the left affect the various categories of final demand on the right through the three channels—cost of capital, wealth effect, and credit rationing. Cost-of-capital variables affect all categories of expenditure listed on the right. The combination of these cost-of-capital linkages, the effect of financial yields on net worth and consumption, and the effect of the credit rationing variable in housing cause for the entire model a very complicated response to monetary forces. The following section estimates the quantitative importance and timing pattern of this response by simulation experiments.

For this report we are using a version of the Federal Reserve-MIT econometric model which contains 75 behavioral equations, identities for 35 other endogenous variables, and 70 exogenous variables. Many of the equations are nonlinear, many depend importantly on initial conditions, and many have complicated internal dynamics. The response patterns of the entire model are thus quite complex, with a great many oscillatory and nonoscillatory mechanisms superimposed on each other. The following results are designed to illustrate just the essential elements of the response of aggregate demand to monetary and fiscal policy measures.

The properties of this large and complicated model are best illustrated by simulation experiments. We made a series of such experiments that measured the effects of step changes in key policy variables by computing differences between two simulation runs. The first run in every case is a dynamic simulation of the model over some time period. By dynamic we mean that, while we use actual values for all current and lagged exogenous variables, we use only initial actual values for endogenous variables. The model generates solutions for the endogenous variables during the first simulation period, then uses these in generating solutions for the second period, and so forth for each succeeding period. The second run in each experiment is another dynamic simulation that is identical to the first in all respects except that one of the policy variables is altered by a specified amount beginning in a specified quarter and continuing for all subsequent quarters of the simulation period. The final step—computing differences between the control and

Editor's note: The authors set out, in this section, the theoretical and institutional bases for the three channels through which they assume monetary policy operates to affect final expenditures and Gross National Product (GNP). These channels are, as they note, (1) the cost of capital, which affects investment spending, (2) the wealth effect, which affects consumption spending, and (3) credit rationing by lenders (including banks), which may affect both investment and consumption.

While some students may find it profitable to refer to the Federal Reserve Bulletin from which this article is excerpted, the editor had deleted much of the technical material of this section on the grounds that the theoretical and institutional discussion assumes a great deal of prior knowledge which the typical reader will not possess at this stage of his study. For the general reader, however, the authors flow diagram, Chart 1, will make clear the linkages between changes in the basic interest rate (which is initially affected by changes in monetary policy) and final expenditures on GNP

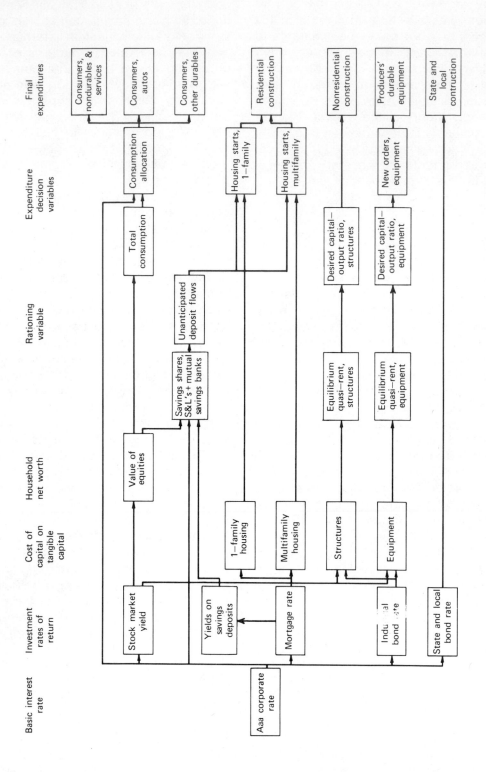

Chart 1. First-round effects of monetary policy.

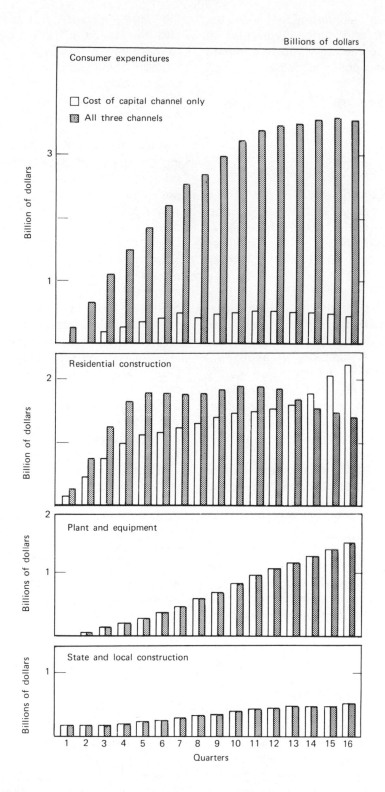

Chart 2. Direct effects on final demand of a billion-dollar step increase in unborrowed reserves, initial conditions of 1964 Q I.

experimental simulations—gives the response of endogenous variables in the model to the specified maintained change in the policy variable.

I. MONETARY POLICY SIMULATIONS

Two simulations of monetary policy were made.

A. Direct Effects of Monetary Policy

We measure the effect of our central monetary policy instrument—unborrowed reserves—by examining the response of the model to a maintained reserve increase of $1 billion. That is, we assume that the Federal Reserve made $1 billion more unborrowed reserves available than the actual historical amount in the initial quarter and maintained the billion-dollar excess over historical amounts in each succeeding quarter. While actual monetary policy changes rarely follow this step-change pattern, nevertheless it is a useful experiment because it enables us to compute the multiplier over time for this policy change.

We first conduct this experiment for a subset of the equations of the model including only the financial sector and demand equations for categories of goods and services affected directly by monetary policy. This simulation gives us only the direct effects of monetary policy on financial markets and— through financial markets—on final spending, uncomplicated by feedbacks of output and prices back to the financial sector or by multiplier-accelerator responses within nonfinancial markets. The results are presented in Chart 2 and summarized in Table 1.

The table shows that the direct effect of the $1 billion open market operations is to stimulate final demand by $3.5 billion by the end of 1 year, by $5.4 billion after 2 years, and on up to $7.0 billion after 4 years. These amounts are appreciably smaller than the total effect over the first few years including the multiplier-accelerator mechanism and the feedback from the real sector to the financial sector.

Table 1b shows that while residential construction is responsible for much of the early effect, its importance gradually declines over time. This pattern can be attributed largely to the rationing channel. In periods immediately following the policy change, market rates of interest fall relative to the sluggish deposit rates of savings institutions. There follows a sharp rise in savings deposit inflows, which in turn stimulates housing starts and expenditures. Thus the credit-rationing channel alone comprises 17 per cent of the total direct monetary effect by the end of four quarters. But as time goes on, the normal relation between deposit rates and market rates is restored and savings inflows fall relative to their recent high levels. As this happens, the importance of the rationing effect is reduced. In fact, by the end of 4 years deposit rates have adjusted completely, savings funds are returning to their pre-policy-change allocation, and a reverse credit-rationing process is at work. In the longer run, this process too dies out as deposit inflows settle down to a steady rate of growth.

The cost of capital channel operates strongly throughout the 4-year simulation period. Initial effects are important for housing and ultimate effects both for housing and for plant and equipment. As mentioned earlier, cost-of-capital effects on expenditures last only until actual capital stocks have reached their desired levels; in the model this process is not complete by the end of 4 years. One reason for this long lag is the time it takes short-term market interest rates to affect long-term rates. The simulations in Table 1 are not carried on for a long enough period to see expenditures induced by changes in the cost of capital recede towards zero. The beginnings of this pattern are visible for consumer durables, but invest-

TABLE 1

DIRECT EFFECTS OF A BILLION-DOLLAR STEP INCREASE IN UNBORROWED RESERVES
Initial conditions of 1964, Q1

a. Billions of Current Dollars

Quarter	Personal Consumption Expenditures			Residential Construction Expenditures			Plant and Equip- ment	State and Local Con- struction	Total			
	Cost of Capital	Wealth	Total	Cost of Capital	Credit Rating	Total	Cost of Capital	Cost of Capital	Cost of Capital	Wealth	Credit Rating	Total
4	.3	1.2	1.5	1.0	.6	1.6	.2	.2	1.7	1.2	.6	3.5
8	.4	2.3	2.7	1.3	.5	1.8	.6	.3	2.6	2.3	.5	5.4
12	.5	3.0	3.5	1.5	.3	1.8	1.1	.4	3.5	3.0	.3	6.8
16	.4	3.2	3.6	2.2	—.8	1.4	1.5	.5	4.6	3.2	—.8	7.0

b. Percentages of Total Effect

Quarter	Construction	Residential Construction	Plant and Equipment	State and Local	Channel		
					Cost of capital	Wealth	Credit Rationing
4	43	45	6	6	49	34	17
8	50	33	11	6	48	43	9
12	51	26	16	7	51	44	5
16	51	20	21	8	66	45	—11

NOTE: The results shown describe only the effect of unborrowed reserves in financial markets and, through financial markets, on final demand for goods and services. They do not include multiplier-accelerator interactions or feedbacks from goods markets to financial markets.

ment in plant and equipment, multi-family housing, and State and local construction is still building up after 4 years.

The wealth effect also operates strongly throughout the period. Since the change in wealth affects consumption promptly, this wealth effect accounts for 35 per cent of the total effect by the end of the first year. It builds up gradually to 45 per cent by the end of 4 years, and in the very long run when the other channels fade out of the picture—aside from the permanent replacement effect of the cost of capital—the wealth effect would comprise the entire direct monetary effect.

B. Full-model Effects of Monetary Policy

We turn now to the full-model effects of a change in unborrowed reserves.

These are different from the direct effects we have described earlier because we now allow these direct effects to set in motion a multiplier-accelerator process and because we also permit the real sector to feed back into the monetary sector. The former inclusion expands the effects of monetary policy changes in early years, whereas the latter inclusion, by allowing the rise in money income to increase interest rates and partially reverse initial rate movements, gradually dampens the long-run effects.

The results of the full-model simulation beginning in the first quarter of 1964 are shown in Table 2. Here the effects on real GNP build up to $5.4 billion in 1 year and $10.0 billion in 2 years, but after that they decline so rapidly that by the end of 4 years there is scarcely any effect on real income.

TABLE 2

EFFECTS OF A BILLION-DOLLAR STEP INCREASE IN UNBORROWED RESERVES, FULL
MODEL EFFECTS

Initial conditions of 1964, Q1

In percentage points unless otherwise indicated

Quarter	Real GNP (Billions of 1958 Dollars)	GNP Deflator	Money GNP (Billions of Current Dollars)	Corporate Aaa Bond Rate	Unemploy- ment Rate
1	.7	—	.8	—.27	—
2	2.0	—	2.3	—.14	—.1
3	3.6	.1	4.3	—.12	—.2
4	5.4	.1	6.6	—.16	—.3
5	7.0	.2	8.9	—.19	—.4
6	8.3	.3	11.1	—.22	—.5
7	9.3	.4	13.2	—.22	—.6
8	10.0	.6	15.1	—.24	—.6
9	10.5	.8	16.9	—.25	—.7
10	10.7	.9	18.6	—.26	—.7
11	10.3	1.2	19.9	—.24	—.7
12	9.4	1.4	20.6	—.25	—.6
13	7.9	1.7	20.6	—.25	—.6
14	6.1	1.9	20.1	—.23	—.5
15	3.9	2.1	19.0	—.23	—.3
16	1.4	2.2	17.2	—.23	—.2

The 4-year effect of the monetary change on money GNP is thus almost entirely in the form of higher prices. For the first 2 years the full-system response for real GNP is much larger than the direct effect shown in Table 1 because of the multiplier-accelerator mechanism. But after that the full system real response dies out because of the oscillations inherent in the accelerator system as well as because of the rises in interest rates stimulated by the rise in money GNP. By way of illustration of this interest-rate feedback, in the direct-effect simulations underlying Table 1, the corporate Aaa rate declined by 46 basis points after 4 years, whereas in the full-model simulations underlying Table 2 the corporate rate declined by only 23 basis points.

We see that initial real income effects in the 1964 (Table 2) simulation are moderately larger than in the 1958 (Table 3) simulation. The price response is substantially higher in 1964, even allowing for the bigger initial real income response, because of the lower initial unemployment rate. But it is interesting to note that the much higher 1964 money GNP response leads to a greater reversal of initial interest-rate movement; this means that by the end of 4 years the real GNP response is much less in the 1964 simulations. In the very long run of, say, 15 or 20 years, the real GNP response would die out in both cases—but this happens more quickly the faster prices respond.

C. Comparison of Monetary and Fiscal Policy Multipliers

Finally these monetary policy multipliers are compared with multipliers for common fiscal policy stabilization

TABLE 3

EFFECTS OF A BILLION-DOLLAR STEP DECREASE IN UNBORROWED RESERVES, FULL
MODEL EFFECTS

Initial conditions of 1958, Q2

In percentage points unless otherwise indicated

Quarter	Real GNP (Billions of 1958 Dollars)	GNP Deflator	Money GNP (Billions of Current Dollars)	Corporate Aaa Bond Rate	Unemploy- ment Rate
1	—.5	—	—.5	.27	—
2	—1.3	—.1	—1.5	.14	.1
3	—3.7	—.1	—2.9	.13	.2
4	—4.2	—.1	—4.6	.17	.3
5	—5.4	—.2	—6.1	.20	.4
6	—6.5	—.2	—7.5	.24	.5
7	—7.3	—.3	—8.8	.27	.6
8	—7.9	—.4	—9.8	.28	.7
9	—8.3	—.5	—10.7	.29	.7
10	—8.5	—.6	—11.5	.29	.7
11	—8.6	—.7	—12.1	.29	.7
12	—8.4	—.8	—12.5	.30	.7
13	—8.1	—.9	—12.8	.30	.7
14	—7.7	—1.0	—13.1	.30	.7
15	—7.2	—1.1	—13.2	.30	.6
16	—6.6	—1.2	—13.4	.29	.6

tools. The comparisons are given in Table 4, which shows the full-model response to a $1 billion increase in unborrowed reserves, a $5 billion increase in real Federal compensation of employees, and a 0.02 decrease in the personal income tax rate. The last implies an initial revenue loss of $4.5 billion at levels in the first quarter of 1964.

The size of these policy changes, and hence of the real GNP and price results, is arbitrary; there is nothing "natural" about comparing a $1 billion reserve change with a $5 billion expenditure change or any other specific amount. Of interest are the dynamic paths—which show a much more rapid approach to peak real GNP effects for Federal spending than for monetary policy—and tax rates in between the two. We have noted before that these

findings imply that it is difficult for monetary and fiscal authorities to conduct "fine-tuning" stabilization policy operations though stabilization operations could be successful against more persistent exogenous swings.

Monetary policy works more slowly than fiscal policy in our model because it takes time for the open market operations to be reflected in changes in long-term interest rates and even more time for these rate changes to be reflected in investment decisions. The latter delay can be attributed to the putty-clay behavior of equipment investment expenditures and the long decision lag for producers' and State and local construction expenditures. If we had found these decision lags to be shorter, or if we had found the more quick-acting credit rationing and wealth effects of monetary policy to be more impor-

TABLE 4

EFFECTS OF THREE EXPANSIONARY POLICIES

Initial conditions of 1964, Q1

In percentage points unless otherwise indicated

Quarter	Real GNP (Billions of 1958 Dollars)			GNP Deflator			Money GNP (Billions of Current Dollars)			Corporate Aaa Bond Rate			Unemployment Rate		
	A	B	C	A	B	C	A	B	C	A	B	C	A	B	C
1	.7	6.6	1.4	—	—	—	.8	7.3	1.6	-.27	.06	.03	—	-.2	—
2	2.0	8.3	2.9	—	—	—	2.3	9.4	3.4	-.14	.05	.02	-.1	-.5	-.2
3	3.6	8.7	3.6	.1	.2	.1	4.3	10.3	4.4	-.12	.05	.02	-.2	-.6	-.2
4	5.4	8.9	4.0	.1	.2	.1	6.6	11.2	5.2	-.16	.06	.03	-.3	-.6	-.3
5	7.0	9.0	4.5	.2	.4	.2	8.9	12.0	6.1	-.19	.08	.04	-.4	-.6	-.3
6	8.3	8.7	4.8	.3	.4	.2	11.1	12.4	6.8	-.22	.09	.05	-.5	-.6	-.3
7	9.3	8.0	5.0	.4	.6	.3	13.2	12.6	7.6	-.23	.10	.06	-.6	-.6	-.3
8	10.0	7.9	5.2	.6	.7	.4	15.1	13.5	8.5	-.24	.12	.07	-.6	-.6	-.3
9	10.4	7.6	5.3	.8	.9	.5	16.9	14.1	9.3	-.25	.14	.09	-.7	-.5	-.4
10	10.7	6.8	5.4	.9	1.0	.6	18.6	14.3	10.1	-.26	.16	.10	-.7	-.5	-.4
11	10.3	6.1	5.4	1.2	1.1	.7	19.9	14.5	10.9	-.24	.17	.12	-.7	-.4	-.4
12	9.4	5.6	5.2	1.4	1.3	.8	20.6	15.2	11.6	-.25	.19	.14	-.6	-.4	-.3
13	7.9	5.8	4.7	1.7	1.4	.9	20.6	16.5	11.8	-.25	.20	.14	-.6	-.4	-.3
14	6.1	6.2	3.9	1.9	1.6	1.1	20.1	18.2	11.7	-.23	.22	.15	-.5	-.4	-.3
15	3.9	5.7	2.8	2.1	1.8	1.2	19.0	18.8	11.3	-.23	.24	.16	-.3	-.4	-.2
16	1.4	5.0	1.6	2.2	1.9	1.2	17.2	19.2	10.6	-.23	.25	.18	-.2	-.3	-.2

NOTE: A indicates step increase in unborrowed reserves of $1.0 billion; B indicates step increase in real Federal wage payments of $5.0 billion; and C indicates step decrease in personal tax rate of .02 (about $4.5 billion in revenue).

tant in the first year, the model would have implied a more rapid operation of monetary policy.

Comparisons of these results with those of other models reveal a mixture of similarities and differences. Although the fiscal policy multipliers in Table 4 roughly agree with those of other econometric models, the monetary multipliers are much larger. On the other hand, the monetary multipliers are appreciably smaller than those obtained by the staff of the St. Louis Federal Reserve Bank recently in a regression of GNP on monetary and fiscal variables. In addition, the timing patterns and the effect of fiscal policy computed by the two studies are radically different.

We would like, in conclusion, to encourage the use of the Federal Reserve —MIT model as a framework for resolving these puzzling differences among estimates of monetary and fiscal policy effects. Most of the estimates suggest properties of the economy which can be translated into assertions about equations and parameters in our model. The structure of the model is flexible enough to permit monetary policy to be either a dominant or a rather minor force and to permit the income-expenditure approach with its implication of important fiscal policy effects to be either completely overshadowed or largely valid. Monetary policy is permitted to work through a number of channels, including carefully developed measures of the cost of capital, wealth effect, and credit rationing. We have presented one set of estimates of the model in this paper, suggesting important roles for a wide range of policy instruments. Further work on the specification and estimation of the model should be a useful way to analyze and ultimately reconcile different views about how our major fiscal and monetary policy tools operate.

READING 34
CONTROLLING MONEY

Allan H. Meltzer*

Three questions recur frequently in current discussions of monetary policy: (1) Can the Federal Reserve control the stock of money if it chooses to do so? (2) What are some main consequences of choosing the stock of money as opposed to some other variable as the focus of control? (3) Which stock of money can be controlled best; or stated in another way, how should we define and measure the stock of money that is to be controlled?

These questions are distinct from the larger question: Should the stock of money, somehow defined, receive the main attention of policymakers when they seek to translate some broad national or international objective, or combination of objectives—such as balance-of-payments equilibrium, reduced inflation, high level employment of resources—into an operating monetary policy? Although I do not bypass this question completely, in most of my discussion I assume that the larger question has been answered affirma-

tively and that there is general agreement on the following four propositions.

First, the stock of money is a main—indeed *the* main—objective of monetary policy operations. This statement means either that directives are written or monetary policy actions are judged in terms of some level, change or rate of change of one or another monetary aggregate.

Second, control of the stock of "money" is a means and not an end. Given our limited and uncertain knowledge of the timing and magnitude of the effects of policy changes, the growth rate of the stock of money is used to indicate the effects that are likely to be achieved, at some sequence of dates in the future, as a result of monetary policy operations that have been taken up to the present.

Third, monetary policy is not the only means of achieving the broad national or international objectives mentioned above, although it may be the most important means. Other policy opera-

Source: Reprinted from Federal Reserve Bank of St. Louis *Review*, May 1969, pp. 16–24.

* I am as always indebted to Karl Brunner for the benefits derived from years of joint research, which provided the background for this paper and most of what I know about money.

tions (tax and spending decisions or changes in the size of the government deficit, and changes in tastes and opportunities for example) have short- or long-term effects on output, employment, prices and interest rates that are independent of the effects on these variables of changes in one or another measure of the stock of money.

Fourth, "money" is used to assess the relative and not the absolute effects of monetary policy. A maintained increase in the growth rate of money is interpreted as a more expansive action; a maintained decrease is interpreted as contractive. The terms "expansive" and "contractive," however, compare the size of monetary changes to the changes that have gone before and not to some absolute or ideal rate of monetary expansion.

The questions posed at the outset, though more narrow and technical, are no less important than the larger question. If the term "money" cannot be defined, money cannot be controlled. Even if there is an acceptable or accepted definition, the decision to control money is said to have unacceptable consequences. Two types of objections to controlling money are generally raised, one broad, the other more narrow and technical. Separating the two permits a far more meaningful discussion of the short-term consequences of monetary policy and gives more precision to the role that money can play and the various ways in which the stock of money can be used as an instrument of monetary policy. In the next section, I comment on several of the issues briefly. Then I discuss some of the more technical problems and in the process, define money and suggest an appropriate role.

I. SORTING OUT THE ISSUES

Many, if not most, of the criticisms of assigning money a more important role either rest on a misconception or attack a "straw man." The misconception is that any decision to assign a larger role to money means that discretionary monetary policy must be abandoned and replaced by a monetary rule. The attack on the monetary rule—a law of constant monetary growth—is an attack on a straw man because the critics of the rule generally fail to deal with any of the relevant issues. Choices need not be limited to decisions between extreme points. Abandoning the present policy of high variability does not require a move to the other extreme: a constant growth rate.

In this section, I distinguish three separable issues. One is the role assigned to money. A second is the ability to control the stock of money. A third is the ever-important, but often neglected, distinction between nominal and real changes in money and interest rates.

A. The Role of Money in Monetary Policy

Money may be used as an *indicator,* as a *target,* or as both *indicator* and *target.* Broadly speaking, when money is used as an indicator, changes in the growth rate of the stock of money become the principal means of deciding whether monetary policy is more or less expansive. When money is used as a target, policy decisions are directed toward providing a particular stock or growth rate of money, or perhaps maintaining the growth rate of money within certain limits. The limits within which such policies may be carried out are set by the extent to which money or its growth rate can be controlled. For short-term movements, the degree of control depends very much on the definition of money.

The same problem exists, of course, for any variable chosen as a target. Neither the level of free reserves nor the Treasury bill rate are now controlled completely. The relevant issues here are not whether money or some other variable can be completely controlled, but whether the degree of control exercised by the Federal Reserve is increased or decreased, and the effectiveness of monetary policy in carrying out its assigned tasks enhanced or weakened, by the substitution of some money stock target for some money market target. I return to this subject in a later section, where I suggest an appropriate target and discuss the degree of control.

The use of money as an *indicator* of monetary policy does not presuppose and does not require *any* reduction in the variability of the growth rate of money. In principal and in practice, money can be used as an indicator while the Manager of the System Open Market Account conducts his daily operations in precisely the same way he does now. He can continue to use free reserves, interest rates or money market conditions as his targets. He can offset, or fail to offset, any of the changes in float, currency, or Treasury deposits, that he wishes. Discussion of the appropriate amount of variability in the growth rate of money can and should be separated from the decision to accept money as a reliable indicator of changes in the size of policy operations and of the future effect of policy. Here, the relevant choice is not between a rule and complete discretion but between various indicators that provide more rather than less accurate information about the future effects of policy.

The reason that choosing money as an indicator has no necessary consequence for the variability of the stock of money is recognized in the distinction between so-called defensive and dynamic operations. The Manager can continue to offset money market changes, conduct defensive operations

while the Open Market Committee or its staff uses some monetary aggregate to judge the direction in which monetary policy has changed and the future effects of policy operations. If the Open Market Committee decides to make policy less inflationary, the growth rate of the stock of money is reduced. While carrying out the defensive operations, the Manager sells more on balance, and both the Committee and the Manager determine how much to sell by comparing the maintained and desired average growth rates of money.

The question arises as to whether this minimal step is feasible. Can money be used as an indicator even if daily operations are conducted with as much variability as in the recent past? The answer seems obvious. Those who used money as an indicator in recent years correctly predicted the inflation of 1966, the slowing of economic activity in 1967, the renewed inflation in 1967 and the increased rate of inflation in 1968. Despite the high variability of the monetary growth rate, it was possible to predict the longer-term consequences of monetary policy with reasonable accuracy. Since some of the predictions were made at meetings with the Board of Governors and rejected, it seems reasonable to conclude that the Open Market Committee and its staff relied on less accurate indicators. It is hard to avoid the conclusion that monetary policy would have achieved more of the policy-makers' announced and frequently repeated aims, if changes in the maintained growth rate of money had been used as an indicator in recent years and in earlier periods as well.

B. The Ability to Control Money

Critics of the use of money as an indicator of monetary policy delight in pointing out that there is less than unanimous agreement on the most appropriate definition of money. The critics hardly ever mention that there are very few times when it would have made much difference whether one or another of the commonly accepted definitions had been used. The maintained growth rates of currency plus demand deposits and currency plus total deposits—the most common definitions—are almost always in the same direction, and changes in the growth rates generally occur at about the same time. There are very few periods in which the qualitative judgment reached about the future effect of monetary policy depended importantly on the definition chosen. Among the exceptions are several recent periods in which changes in market rates relative to Regulation Q ceiling rates caused large, temporary changes in time deposits and in the relative growth rates of time and demand deposits. In these periods, I believe the narrower definition—currency and demand deposits—generally provided the more accurate indicator.

If policy operations retain their short-term focus and some measure of money replaces market rates or free reserves as a target of the Manager's operations, it becomes important to choose between the various measures. One difficulty in using money (currency and demand deposits) or money plus time deposits as a target of monetary policy is that reliable information is not available daily or even weekly. Another difficulty is that when information becomes available, it is imprecise.

Both of these objections apply to the use of money as a target of monetary policy; neither applies with much force to the use of money as an indicator. Both objections are overcome by choosing the monetary base as a tar-

get. The monetary base can be measured, weekly, with greater reliability than some of the operating targets now in use, such as the level of free reserves. Weekly data on the base are now available from the Federal Reserve Bank of St. Louis. If the Manager of the Open Market Committee wishes to combine control of money with defensive operations, the directives written to the Manager should specify a desired change or level of the monetary base.[1]

Evidence from past periods suggests that the monetary base is the most important determinant of the money supply and that there is a high degree of association between the base and the money stock. The degree of association and the extent to which money can be controlled by controlling the base varies with the length of the period. Our analysis suggests that even if policy retains its short-term focus, month to month changes in money can still be kept within a very narrow range. In the past, 85 per cent of the variance of the monthly change in money—currency and demand deposits—resulted from changes in the monetary base and changes in Treasury deposits at commercial banks in the current and previous month. Even in periods of substantial variability in the growth rate of money and sizable defensive operations, monthly changes in money were dominated by current and past changes in the base. The relation between monthly changes in the monetary base and money plus time deposits is not as good. Nevertheless, more than 75 per cent of the variance of the monthly changes in this monetary aggregate can be controlled by using the base as a target and estimating Treasury deposits as accurately as in the past. Table 1 shows some of the evidence

[1] In a later section and in Table 2, I compare the information required to control the monetary base to the information collected daily at the Federal Reserve Bank of New York.

TABLE 1

CORRELATIONS BETWEEN MONTHLY CHANGES IN "MONEY" AND SOME
EXPLANATORY VARIABLES

Time Period	Definition of Money	Explanatory Variables and Their Coefficients (Constant Term Omitted)	R^2
March 1947 to March 1965	ΔM_1	2.38 ΔB_t — .85 ΔD_t (24.6) (—18.0)	.80
	ΔM_1	2.23 ΔB_t — .74 ΔD_t + .78 ΔB_{t-1} — .02 ΔD_t (26.0) (—17.3) (8.84) (—.58)	.86
	ΔM_2	2.15 ΔB_t — .82 ΔD_t (17.7) (—14.2)	.70
	ΔM_2	1.98 ΔB_t — .70 ΔD_t + .91 ΔB_{t-1} — .05 ΔD_{t-1} (18.3) (—13.0) (8.15) (—.86)	.77
Feb. 1947 to Dec. 1964	ΔM_1	1.39 ΔB_t and 11 dummy variables to (5.88) adjust for seasonal variation	.80

NOTE: "t" statistics are in parentheses.
None of the data were seasonally adjusted.
Explanation of Symbols
  ΔM_1 = Monthly Change in Currency and Demand Deposits
  ΔM_2 = Monthly Change in Currency and Total Deposits.
  ΔB_t = Monthly Change in Monetary Base.
  ΔD_t = Monthly Change in Deposits of the Treasury at Commercial Banks.

on which these conclusions are based, giving the correlations between money and some explanatory variables.

A related but very different argument raised against the use of any monetary aggregate is that, even if these variables can be measured accurately and promptly, they cannot be controlled. Changes in the composition of deposits between demand and time account, changes in the composition of money between currency and deposits, gold flows and changes in the proportion of deposits held by foreigners are cited as sources of changes in the monetary base or the stock of money that are not controlled and are said to be outside the control of the Federal Reserve. Since the evidence cited above (and a substantial body of additional evidence) makes clear that if the Federal Reserve controls the size of changes in the monetary base, it controls by far the larger portion of the changes in the stock of money, I shall discuss this argument with reference to the monetary base and compare the degree of control over the base to the control of short-term market rates or free reserves.

To a very large extent, arguments suggesting that the base cannot be controlled are a play on the use of the word "control" that fail to separate short- and long-term changes and do not distinguish between the sources and the uses of the base. The problem of controlling short-term changes arises whether the Committee uses free reserves or the monetary base (or almost any variable worth mentioning) as the target of monetary policy. The reason is that monthly or weekly changes in both free reserves and the monetary base are the result of (1) actions taken by the Manager, for example, purchases and sales of securities (2) changes resulting from market forces that the Manager observes, but chooses not to offset, and (3) changes that are unforeseen because of errors in reporting or errors of measurement. I see no point in describing the changes that the Manager makes as "controlled" and the changes he permits as "uncontrolled." The more relevant question is the extent to which the Manager has more accurate and reliable information, within a given time span following the change, about one target variable rather than another. As I indicated, the weekly change in the monetary base can be known more reliably than the weekly change in free reserves. This is one important reason for choosing the base as a target. I return to this point below.

Whether the target variable is the level of free reserves, the short-term market interest rate or the monetary base, changes in the target during any period are the result of both current and past policy and nonpolicy changes. Suppose a policy of reducing the rate of inflation is translated into a policy target of forcing or permitting higher market interest rates or a lower growth rate of the monetary base. If the policy is maintained and begins to take effect, weeks or months after the policy is initiated the inflow of gold or foreign exchange rises, and with fixed ceiling rates of interest paid on time deposits, time deposits decline relative to demand deposits. Gold is a source of base money, so the inflow of gold raises the base and lowers market interest rates; the redistribution of deposits from time to demand accounts raises the weighted average reserve requirement ratio, lowers the base, and raises interest rates. There is no reason to expect these effects to occur at the same time, to be offsetting on any particular day or over any particular span, or to cancel the effects of changes in tastes, opportunities, and actual or expected rates of inflation. Nor is cancellation

essential for the conduct of monetary policy.

The Committee and the Manager require: (1) an accurate estimate of the size of the current change in the target variable (the base or interest rates, or free reserves); (2) a clear idea of the desired value of the target variable; and (3) an ability to translate the longer-term goals of monetary policy into a desired current value of the target and to translate changes in the target into changes in the rate of inflation, level of employment, or balance of payments.

The crucial problem in the example, as in practice is not one of measuring the so-called noncontrolled changes in the target but of deciding how large the change in the target should be to achieve longer-term objectives. The Federal Reserve can observe and record current changes in the base, free reserves, or short-term interest rates shortly after they occur. If they could translate these changes into future levels of employment and rates of inflation, they could decide how much to buy or sell to achieve the level of interest rates, free reserves or base that are consistent with the long-term aims of economic policy. The difficult problem is not the measurement of short-term changes but the interpretation of these changes—for example, knowing whether a given level or change in market interest rates is too low or too high, too large or too small, to prevent inflation or unemployment.

I see no way of resolving this problem, given the present or forseeable future state of knowledge, other than by choosing a reliable and readily available *indicator* of the future of policy. The reason is well known: the effect of current changes in policy on output, prices and the balance of payments are not observable for months and in some cases are not recognized for years. Equally important, errors generally cannot be offset or reversed without forcing large and sudden changes in policy that have destabilizing effects. There is, perhaps, little reason to dwell on this point. Too many of the current problems of monetary policy are now recognized as the result of errors in judging the expected effects of past policies or justifiable fears of the consequences of suddenly reversing previous policies.

The above discussion should not suggest that the choice of the target is a subsidiary and unimportant matter. The choice depends very much on the information reliably possessed and the ability to measure, control and interpret short-term changes. My remarks are misread if they appear to downgrade the problem or to suggest that one target is as useful as another. They should be read instead as an attempt to sort out some of the meanings of "controlling money."

In discussing the meaning of "control," I found it useful to make three distinctions. One is the degree to which monetary aggregates can be measured and manipulated during a particular time span. The monetary base can be controlled weekly and perhaps daily with as much accuracy as other variables now used as targets. In the past, we found that most of the monthly changes in money can be controlled by controlling the monetary base. The base is, therefore, a more useful target than the stock of money (or other monetary aggregates) if policy retains its short-term focus. A second distinction is between controlled and noncontrolled changes in a target variable (such as the base) and the degree to which controlled changes can be used to offset the changes resulting from past policy and nonpolicy decisions. A third is the distinction between measuring the change in a target variable and interpreting the change. By controlling the growth rate of the base the

Federal Reserve can contain the short-term growth rate of money within narrow limits. Since the stock of money is a useful and reliable indicator of changes in the thrust of monetary policy, I believe the Federal Reserve should use the stock of money—currency and demand deposits—as an indicator.

To this point, I have discussed the ability of the central bank to use monetary aggregates as useful targets and reliable indicators of monetary policy and to offset the effects of past policy changes and noncontrolled changes on current nominal values of the monetary base, money, market, market interest rates or free reserves. The Federal Reserve, and any other modern central bank, can offset and hence control the size of current changes in free reserves, short-term market interest rates or the monetary base, and to a very large extent can determine the size of changes in money if it chooses to do so. However, there is a very important sense in which a central bank cannot control either money or interest rates. To discuss this meaning of control, we need an additional distinction—the distinction between nominal and real changes in money and interest rates.

C. Nominal and Real Changes

Perhaps the oldest and best established proposition in monetary theory states that the government or central bank controls the nominal stock of money while the public decides on the price level at which it willingly holds the nominal stock. In our day, the nominal stock is the amount of currency and demand deposits issued by commercial banks and Federal Reserve banks. The real stock of money is the nominal amount deflated by some representative index of prices.

The distinction between nominal and real applies with equal force to every monetary aggregate and to interest rates as well. To compute the real rate of interest from the nominal or market rate, we have to subtract the *anticipated* rate of price change. One major problem in interpreting changes in market interest rates and using levels or changes in market rates as indicators of monetary policy is separating the effects of anticipations from other forces affecting market rates. Without reliable estimates of the anticipated rate of price change, it is impossible to interpret changes in market rates or to use market rates as indicators of monetary policy. Recent monetary history suggests the type of error that is likely to be made if high or rising market interest rates are interpreted as a sign of restrictive, anti-inflationary policy. The same or opposite error has been repeated throughout monetary history.

Just as the Federal Reserve cannot control the value of real money balances, it cannot control the long-run market rate of interest. A brief description of some links between money, interest rates, actual and anticipated price changes may explain the reasons.

Let the Federal Reserve increase the growth rate of the nominal stock of money. Initially market interest rates fall, but the initial reduction is temporary and is followed by a rise in market rates as consumers and business attempt to borrow more so as to accumulate inventories and increase expenditures. The Federal Reserve can, if it chooses, increase the amount of open market purchases and more than offset the rise in market rates resulting from the increased demand for loans and increased expenditures. However, with technology and real resources fixed or changing more slowly than the quantity of money, the continued expansion in the public's expenditures causes prices to rise.

If the higher growth rate of money is maintained, eventually consumers and businessmen are confronted with fre-

quent announcements of price increases. They are led to examine the prices they change for the goods or services they sell and to consider whether their prices should be adjusted upward. Gradually, they learn to anticipate price increases.

Individuals and businessmen attempt to protect themselves against the consequences of inflation or to profit from those consequences. They sell bonds and spend money to reduce their holdings of claims fixed in nominal value. They seek to borrow to increase liabilities with fixed nominal values. They switch, at the margin, from assets with fixed nominal value to assets that rise in price during inflation.

All these responses can be summarized by saying that if the Federal Reserve maintains the higher rate of increase in the nominal stock of money, market interest rates rise with the spreading anticipation of future inflation. To maintain the previously prevailing market rate, the Federal Reserve must supply an ever-increasing amount of base money and permit the money supply to increase at an increasing rate. Attempts to lower or maintain the market rate however, implant the anticipation of inflation more firmly and force still higher actual and anticipated rates of inflation.

The process I have described as an adjustment of nominal rates could be described just as well as an attempt by moneyholders to reduce the amount of money they hold. As before, the attempt causes prices to rise and, as prices rise, the real amount of money corresponding to any nominal stock falls. Attempts to maintain the higher growth rate of money eventually produce a higher actual and anticipated rate of inflation and a higher market rate of interest. If tastes and productive opportunities remain unchanged, equilibrium is restored when the public is willing to hold an unchanged real amount of money at the higher market rate of interest.

One frequently repeated form of the argument just made confuses the Federal Reserve's inability to control the long-run real value of the stock of money with an inability to control the nominal amount of money if exchange rates are fixed. This line of reasoning starts by showing that among the consequences of the inflationary increase in the nominal stock of money (or reduction in market interest rates) are increases in imports and declines in exports, an increased deficit in the balance of payments. The (increased) deficit on current account causes an outflow of gold that reduces the nominal stock of money and raises market interest rates. This portion of the argument is correct. However, the Federal Reserve can offset or more than offset the effect of the gold outflow on money and interest rates, if it chooses to do so. In the past decade, we have elected to raise the growth rate of the stock of money in an attempt to hold market interest rates below the level they would have reached in the absence of inflationary monetary policies. Gold outflows have not prevented the Federal Reserve from maintaining one of the highest rates of monetary expansion in United States history.

If foreign countries inflate at a slower rate than the U.S., one ultimate consequence of our higher rate of inflation is a change in the dollar price of gold or in the fixed exchange rate system. Neither these consequences nor the outflow of gold should suggest that the Federal Reserve is unable to control the nominal stock of money. On the contrary, inflation and the balance of payments deficit are consequences of the system of fixed exchange rates and of an over-production of nominal money—production of more nominal money than the public is willing to absorb at the anticipated rate of price change. The public's ability to reduce its holdings of real money balances, not the inability of the Federal Reserve to control the nominal stock, should be seen as the means by which excessive expansion of nominal money is translated into inflation and a balance-of-payments deficit.

A related argument is used to suggest that the stock of money cannot be controlled because an increase in money or its growth rate reduces interest rates and causes a short-term capital outflow. I have dealt with one part of the argument above and suggested that the Account Manager can observe the outflow and offset the effect on interest rates or money, if the Committee desires to do so. Public policy may dictate that open market operations be used to offset the gold outflow or prevent it. The latter decision should not be confused, however, with an inability to control the nominal stock of money since the identical problem arises whether the Federal Reserve uses money, interest rates or some other variable as an indicator or target of monetary policy. The core of the problem is a conflict between a relatively high rate of inflation (or deflation) and a fixed exchange rate. At the present time, conflicts of this kind are of little practical importance, since policies designed to reduce the rate of inflation would help to maintain the prevailing exchange rate.

II. TECHNICALITIES AND TECHNIQUES

Several of the arguments I discussed in the previous section reflect a lack of understanding of the means by which the monetary base can be manipulated to control the stock of money. In this section, I first discuss the sources and uses of the base, pointing out the information available to the Manager and comparing the available information on sources of the base to the information now collected on the sources of free reserves. Then I discuss, briefly, the validity of some of the criticisms of the use of money in monetary control.

A. Data on Sources and Uses

The data for computing the monetary base is obtained from the table "Member Bank Reserves, Reserve Bank Credit, and Related Items" in the Federal Reserve *Bulletin*. The table also serves as the basis for computing free reserves and other reserve measures. There is, therefore, a similarity about the basic input data used for the computation of the base and other measures. Many of the computational differences result from the way items are grouped or classified. Table 2 compares the components of the base to the components of free reserves.

The *uses* of the base are bank reserves plus total currency held by the public and by nonmember banks plus the amount of reserves liberated or impounded by changes in reserve requirements or redistributions of deposits between classes of banks. Accurate weekly estimates of each of these uses are not available directly. A more reliable method is to compute the sum of the *sources* of base money; the sum of the sources is, of course, equal to the uses and can be computed daily or weekly from the information now collected at the Federal Reserve Bank of New York. As Table 2 shows, there are two main differences between the computations now prepared and the data required to compute the base. One is the way in which the items are combined. The other is that the estimates of a few items such as excess reserves and vault cash held by banks are not required for the computation of the base. Computation of these two important sources of error can be eliminated.

B. Instability of Interest Rates

One of the main arguments against controlling the stock of money is that the variability of interest rates would increase—that interest rates would be "unstable." This is not a necessary consequence of the use of money as an, indicator or the use of the monetary base as a target. As I noted earlier, the use of money as an indicator of monetary policy and the use of the base as a target should not be confused with acceptance of a monetary rule.

There are several strands to the argument and I attempt to deal with the most common versions. One version concerns the usefulness of defensive operations. This is an issue that is best resolved by measuring, or attempting to assess, the cost and benefits of more rather than less variability in money. However, the decision about variability is independent of the decision to control money. Any of the defensive operations that the Manager now undertakes to smooth market interest rates can be carried out just as effectively if the base is the target and the stock of money is the indicator.[2]

A second version concerns the level around which interest rates fluctuate. Again, this has little to do with the decision to control money rather than interest rates. The level of market interest rates, or the average around which rates fluctuate during any three- or six-month period, is determined—in the one case as in the other—by a combination of market forces and policy decisions.

However, there is one important reason to expect a change in the average level of market interest rates if money replaces interest rates as an indicator of monetary policy. Since money is a more accurate indicator, the Federal

[2] This leaves aside the desirability of these operations or the desirability of institutional changes that would remove some of the sources of instability. Recent practice has been to make institutional arrangements more complex and thus adds to the variability.

TABLE 2

SOURCES AND USES OF FREE RESERVES AND THE MONETARY BASE

(Illustrative Calculation—Billions of dollars)

SOURCES

	Monetary Base	Free Reserves
Factors Supplying Sources		
Reserve Bank Credit net of Discounts and Advances	55.0	55.0
Reserve Adjustment (cumulated sum of Reserves liberated by Reserve Requirement Changes)	4.8	——
Discounts & Advances	0.8	——
Gold Stock	10.4	10.4
Treasury Currency Outstanding	6.8	6.8
Total Factors Supplying Sources	77.8	72.2
Factors Absorbing Sources		
Treasury Cash	0.8	0.8
Treasury Deposits at Federal Reserve	0.6	0.6
Foreign and other Deposits	0.6	0.6
Other Federal Reserve Accounts	—0.8	—0.9
Required Reserves	——	27.1
Currency in Circulation	——	49.2
Less Currency held as Reserve	——	—4.6
Total Factors Absorbing Sources	1.2	72.8
Total Sources (Factors Supplying Sources minus Factors Absorbing Sources)	76.6	—0.6

USES

	Monetary Base	Free Reserves
Reserve Adjustment (cumulated sum of Reserves liberated by Reserve Requirement Changes)	4.8	——
Total Reserves	22.6	——
Currency in Circulation	49.2	——
Excess Reserves	——	0.2
Less Discounts and Advances	——	—0.8
Total Uses	76.6	—0.6

Reserve obtains a more accurate assessment of the thrust of current policy. It avoids misinterpretations of policy that cause acceleration or deceleration of prices and eventually large changes in the anticipated rate of inflation or deflation. Recent policy provides an example. The highest rates in a century are in part a result of misinterpreting the thrust of monetary policy. If money had been used as an indicator, policy—guided by this indicator—would have been less inflationary; the high rates would have been avoided; the average market rate would have been lower, and monetary policy would have contributed more to economic stability and less to inflation.

A basic error lies behind the notion that the average level of interest rates would change if money replaced interest rates as the indicator. The source of the error is the belief that the Federal Reserve is able to control market interest rates, and the cause of the error is the neglect of the role of changes in the actual and anticipated rate of price change in the determination of market interest rates. There is no reason to doubt the Federal Reserve's ability to reduce or increase the level of market interest rates temporarily. However, there is also no reason to believe that the Federal Reserve can maintain rates above or below their equilibrium level, if it is unwilling to produce an ever-increasing rate of inflation or deflation. As before, it is important to recognize the roles of anticipations in the determination of market rates and to separate nominal and real changes.

A third issue requires a distinction between the size of interest rate changes and the time rate of change. Many of the fears of market participants and Treasury department officials reflect concern about the size of cyclical or monthly changes in interest rates. On closer examination, the focus of the concern is on the effects of large changes in interest rates during periods of Treasury (or private) financing.

As before, there is no incompatibility between the use of money as an indicator, the use of the monetary base as a target, and the maintenance of defensive operations. The critical question is whether defensive operations and so-called "even keel" policies designed to assist the Treasury to sell debt issues should be permitted to interfere with the attainment of longer-term aims of monetary policy. In the recent past, the base money supplied during periods of even keel has remained in the system and has been used to produce the increases in money

that have maintained or increased the rate of inflation.

III. CONCLUSION

The main practical issues about controlling money concern the role or roles assigned to money, the speed with which information on monetary aggregates becomes available, the degree to which unforeseen or unanticipated changes in monetary aggregates can be offset and the extent to which monetary aggregates can be controlled during short and longer time spans. By discussing these issues and avoiding the more abstract discussion of rules, I was able to compare some operating consequences of controlling money to the results of present policies which are based on control of interest rates and money market variables.

As in previous work with Karl Brunner, I distinguished between the role of money as an indicator, or measure of the thrust of monetary policy, and as a target of monetary operations. As an indicator, money provides a relatively accurate measure of changes in the degree to which monetary policy has become more or less expansive. Used as a target, money becomes the variable that the Manager attempts to control when carrying out the policies agreed upon by the Open Market Committee. Unlike previous work and despite my own predilections, I assumed, throughout, that defensive operations would be retained, that the short-term focus of policy operations would continue, and that the principal difference between future and past policies would be the use of monetary aggregates in place of free reserves and interest rates.

My main recommendations can be summarized succinctly. The Federal Reserve should translate the longer-term goals of monetary policy into a desired growth rate of money, defined as currency and demand deposits. The growth rate of the stock of money is then used as the indicator of monetary policy. The desired growth rate of money is translated in turn into a desired growth rate of the monetary base and a desired weekly or daily change in the monetary base. The Manager is instructed to obtain the target change or rate of change of the base.

The Committee is able to audit the Manager's performance by observing the change or rate of change in the base. More importantly, the Committee is able to assess the extent to which monetary policy is too expansive or too contractive by observing the size of changes in the indicator, the growth rate of money, and can change the degree to which monetary policy is expansive by changing the rate of change of the base. Nothing in the proposal requires the Federal Reserve to adopt a rule as a condition of con-

trolling money. The desirable size and frequency of changes in money can and should be separated from the use of money as an indicator.

Since the Manager can control changes in the base more accurately than he now controls money market variables such as free reserves, there is no difficulty in using the base as a target. Data from past periods suggest that by controlling changes in the base and obtaining estimates of the change in Treasury deposits at commercial banks, the Federal Reserve is able to control more than 85% of the monthly changes in money.

Past policy errors were very often the result of misinterpretations of the effect of policy and reliance on misleading indicators. Acceptance of a more reliable indicator and more appropriate target can go a long way toward improving the conduct of monetary policy and avoiding some of the more serious errors of the past.

READING 35

OPERATIONAL CONSTRAINTS ON THE STABILIZATION OF MONEY SUPPLY GROWTH*

Alan R. Holmes

The debate over whether the Federal Reserve should rely exclusively on the money stock—somehow defined—as an indicator or a target of monetary policy, or both, continues unabated. While the debate has shed some light on the role of money in monetary policy and the role of monetary policy in the overall mix of policies that affect the real economy, there has been perhaps as much heat as light. And the light that is being generated from the many research studies that have stemmed from the debate is very often dim indeed.

This paper does not attempt to contribute to the controversy. Instead it tries to sketch out briefly current practices of the FOMC in establishing guidelines for the conduct of open market operations—guidelines that involve a blend of interest rates and monetary aggregates. It then turns to the operational constraints and problems that would be involved if the Federal Reserve were to rely exclusively on the money supply as the guideline for day-to-day operations.

The approach taken in the paper is essentially practical rather than theoretical. The views expressed should be taken as those of the author, and not as representative of the Federal Reserve System. It will probably not come as much of a surprise, however, that the conclusions find much in favor of current FOMC practices and procedures.

Source: From Controlling Monetary Aggregates, Federal Reserve Bank of Boston, 1969.

* Editor's note: The preceding selection gave a view on money supply control by a leading monetarist. Contrast it with this selection by the manager of the Federal Open Market Account, who is responsible for carrying out the policy directives of the Open Market Committee.

I. CURRENT FOMC PRACTICES

The Federal Reserve has frequently been accused of money market myopia. This is a false charge usually made by economists affected in some degree by a peculiar myopia of their own. The charge stems, or so it seems to me, in the first instance from a confusion between monetary policy decisions *per se* and the operational instructions given by the FOMC for the day-to-day conduct of open market operations.

The Federal Reserve has always maintained that money matters just as it believes that interest rates matter too, particularly given the institutional framework of our financial system. In reaching policy decisions, the Committee not only pays attention to the real economy—to current and prospective developments in employment, prices, GNP and the balance of payments—but it also considers a broad range of interest rates and monetary measures. Among the monetary measures, there are the various reserve measures—total reserves, nonborrowed reserves, excess reserves, and free or net borrowed reserves. Next are the measures of money ranging from M_1 on out. Finally, there are the credit measures, bank credit, the credit proxy—ranging on out to total credit in the economy and the flow of funds.

Is the Federal Reserve wrong in its eclectic approach? Is it wrong to consider a broad range of interest rates and aggregates and to reach a judgment as to the combination of rates and aggregates (and the resultant impact of that mix on market psychology and the expectations of consumers, savers, and investors) that is compatible with desirable movements in the real economy and the balance of payments? Should it instead adopt a single aggregate variable—the money supply —and devote its entire attention to stabilizing that variable no matter what

happens to other aggregates or to interest rates?

Despite the empirical claims of the monetary school, there appears to be little conclusive evidence to support their case that such a course of action would give the desired overall economic results. Both the St. Louis equations and correlation analysis at the Federal Reserve Bank of New York, for example, give slightly better marks to bank credit than to money supply. Moreover, the analyses suggest that significantly different results can be attained by relatively small changes in the time period covered.

While I do not believe that research results to date justify adopting an operating policy designed solely to stabilize the monetary growth rate, I nevertheless believe that the research efforts stimulated by the monetary school have a real value. Out of it all, there is bound to develop a better understanding of the relationships between monetary aggregates, interest rates, and the real economy. I suspect, however, that the underlying relationships are so complex that no simple formula can be found as an unerring guide to monetary policy. The psychology and expectations involved in private decision making are probably too complicated to compress into any such simple formula.

Thus, I think, the FOMC is right in paying attention to a broad range of reserve, money, and credit aggregates; in trying to understand why they are behaving as they are; and in assessing the implications of their past and prospective behavior for employment, prices, and GNP. Further, I think the Federal Reserve is right in not restricting itself to a single theory of money, and in choosing the best from a number of theories.

In reaching a policy decision, the Committee pays close attention to a wide spectrum of interest rates, ranging from the Federal funds rate, through the short and intermediate term rates, out to rates in the long-term capital markets. One obvious problem with interest rates as either an indicator or target of monetary policy is that they may be measuring not only the available supply of money and credit but also the demand for money and credit. Obviously, a policy aimed at stabilizing interest rates in the face of rising demand will give rise to greater increases in the monetary aggregates than would be the case if demand were stable. Interest rates can also be misleading indicators of underlying conditions at times of special short-lived supply and demand relationships—of some fiscal policy development or of prospects for war or peace in Vietnam, to take some recent examples. But interest rates have the decided advantage of being instantaneously available, and they can often be excellent indicators that estimates of monetary aggregates, particularly reserve estimates, are wrong. The judicious use of interest rates as correctors of poor aggregative forecasting should not be underestimated.

Thus, when the FOMC reaches a policy decision, it is not thinking exclusively in terms of rates or of monetary aggregates, but of a combination of the two. A move towards a tighter policy would normally involve a decline in the rate of growth of the aggregates and an increase in rates. And a move towards an easier policy would normally involve an increase in aggregate growth rates and a decline in interest rates.

But, unfortunately, given the nature of our commercial banking system, money and credit flows cannot be turned off and on instantaneously. At any given point in time, banks have on their boks a large volume of firm commitments to lend money. Also, potential borrowers may, if they surmise that the Federal Reserve is tightening policy,

decide *en masse* to take down loans in anticipation of future needs. Hence there may be, for a time, an undeterred growth in bank credit and the money supply. But this, in turn, should involve a more rapid and larger rise in interest rates than would otherwise have been the case. The point is that the Federal Reserve is always making a trade-off between aggregates and rates. It has, and takes, the opportunity at its FOMC meetings every three or four weeks to assess what has developed, what the impact has been on the real economy and on private expectations of the future, and to determine whether another turn of the screw—towards tightness or ease—is called for.

The moral of the story, if there is one, is that Federal Reserve policy should not be judged exclusively in terms of interest rates or in terms of monetary aggregates but by the combination of the two—and by the resultant impact of this combination on market psychology and expectations about the future and, ultimately, on the real economy. The weights placed on aggregates and rates, including those placed on individual components of either group, can and do vary from time to time. It is important to recognize that there is nothing in the present framework of Federal Reserve policymaking, or policy implementation, that would prevent placing still greater weight on aggregates if that should be considered desirable. I think it is obvious that aggregate measures of money and credit are getting their full share of attention at the present time.

Rates and aggregates, along with real economic developments and prospects, are the basic ingredients of any FOMC policy decision. They are also involved in the instructions that the FOMC gives to the Federal Reserve Bank of New York for the day-to-day conduct of operations in the interval between Committee meetings. Obviously, it would make little sense for the Committee to issue directives to the Desk in terms of the real economy with which it is basically concerned. Not only are open market operations in the very short run unlikely to have a major impact on the real economy, but adequate measures of economic change are unavailable in the short time span involved.

Thus the Committee, in its instructions to the Manager, focuses on a set of money market conditions—a blend of interest rates and rates of growth of various reserve and credit measures—the Committee believes is compatible with its longer run goals. At each FOMC meeting, the Committee has before it staff estimates of ranges for the Federal funds rate, the Treasury bill rate, bank borrowings from the Federal Reserve, and net borrowed reserves that the Staff believes compatible with an overall policy of no change, or of greater tightness or ease, as the case may be. Additionally, the Staff prepares estimates of the money supply and the bank credit proxy that it believes likely to correspond to a given set of money market conditions. Needless to say, these forecasting techniques fall short of being an exact science, but their existence tends to focus attention on the vital interrelationships between interest rates and aggregates that will ensue from any policy decision.

As is well known, since the spring of 1966 the Open Market Committee has usually included in the directive a proviso clause with an explicit reference to one aggregate measure—the bank credit proxy—with specific instructions to modify open market operations if the proxy is tending to move outside a predicted or desired range. Thus the Committee expects to see money market conditions moving to the tighter end of the scale if the proxy is expanding too rapidly, or towards the

easier end of the scale if the proxy is falling short.

How does this all work out in practice? First of all, the money and capital markets send out a constant stream of signals of interest rate developments that we can and do measure from day-to-day and hour-to-hour. If there are deviations from past patterns or levels (or from anticipated patterns or levels) of interest rates, we can usually find out a good deal about the source and meaning of the deviations.

Second, we have forecasts of the factors, affecting bank reserves apart from open market operations—estimates of float, currency in circulation, gold and foreign exchange operations, and the level of Treasury balances at the Federal Reserve. These factors can and do supply or absorb hundreds of millions in bank reserves from day-to-day or week-to-week. The estimates are made at the Board and at the New York bank for the current statement week and for three weeks ahead, and they are revised daily on the basis of the inflow of reserve information available within the System each day.

Third, we have available an estimate once a week (on Friday) of the bank credit proxy and of the money supply for the current month; and, as we get towards the middle of the month, for the next month as well. And this estimate can be revised—at least informally—by the middle of a calendar week, after there has been time to analyze weekend deposit performance at Reserve City banks and a weekly sample of deposit data at country banks. We can then use these aggregate data—available less frequently and with a greater time lag than interest rate or reserve data—to modify subsequent open market operations with an impact on interest rates and the reserve supply.

I should add that we are fairly cautious about over-interpreting any short-run wriggle in the credit proxy. While forecasts of the proxy have generally proved to be more stable than money supply forecasts—perhaps mainly because the proxy avoids the large and erratic shifts between Treasury deposits in commercial banks and private demand deposits—they, too, have proved to be somewhat undependable on a week-to-week basis. Thus we have felt it desirable—particularly early in the month when firm data are scant—to wait for some confirmation of any suggested movement of the proxy before beginning to shade operations towards somewhat greater firmness or ease.

Nevertheless, the proxy has been a useful adjunct to the directive, modifying reserve and rate objectives on a number of occasions and tending to flag aggregate problems for the Committee's attention at subsequent FOMC meetings.

It should, of course, be noted that, at times like the present, when Regulation Q ceilings are pressing hard on bank CD positions, the credit proxy loses much of its value as a continuous series. It does not, however, necessarily lose its value as a short-run guide— provided that it is understood that much lower growth rates may be required to allow for the shift of intermediate credit away from the commercial banking system. Despite all the talk about disintermediation and intermediation, we need to know much more about the process and its implications for monetary policy. The problem is that commercial banks are at the same time creators of money and credit and intermediaries between savers and borrowers in competition with other nonbank financial institutions. Worthwhile research remains to be done in this area, particularly in light of the dramatic changes that are occurring in our financial institutions.

In summary, there are four main points that I would like to draw from this abbreviated review of monetary policy formulation and implementation. First, monetary policymakers have always paid close attention to monetary aggregates—along with interest rates —in the formulation of policy decisions. It has been the interaction of the two on the real economy—on employment, prices, the GNP, and the balance of payments—that has been the focus of concern. Reluctance to adopt money supply as the sole guide to policy decisions has not stemmed from lack of concern about money but from the lack of evidence that the adoption of such a guide would give the desired results. Empirical research to date does not supply that evidence.

Second, it is incorrect to characterize monetary policy in terms of money supply alone. A rise in money supply— outside some specified range—does not necessarily mean easy money nor a decline of tight money. Policy has to be judged by a combined pattern of interest rates and monetary aggregates —and money supply is only one of those aggregates.

Third, since the spring of 1966 the FOMC has included an aggregate measure—the bank credit proxy—in its directive covering day-to-day open market operations. While use of the aggregates to shape interest rates and reserve measures has probably not been as aggressive as the monetarists would like to see (and, besides, it is the wrong aggregate according to some of them), it has been a useful adjunct to the directive.

Fourth, information on the performance of monetary aggregates (e.g., credit proxy and money supply) is available only with a time lag, and week-to-week forecasts of monthly data have tended to be erratic. This suggests that, in the short run, interest rate movements may provide a very useful indication of forecasting errors. It further suggests that aggregates can contribute more to the process of policy formulation—when there are opportunities to take a long-range view—than to the process of policy implementation as exemplified by the second paragraph of the directive. But current procedures for both policy formulation and policy implementation provide room for as much attention to monetary aggregates as may be required, and it is apparent that the aggregates are receiving a full measure of attention at the present time.

II. OPERATIONAL PROBLEMS IN STABILIZING MONEY SUPPLY

In the absence of a concrete proposal, there are major difficulties in attempting to isolate the operational problems that would be involved in stabilizing the monetary growth rate to some targeted level. Much would depend on the definition of the money supply used, the time span over which the growth rate was to be stabilized, and whether the money supply was to be the sole indicator and/or target of monetary policy or mainly a primary indicator or target.

It obviously makes a great deal of difference whether the proposal is for a rigid monetary rule or whether there is room—and how much—for discretion. Some of the proposals for moving to the money supply as a target and indicator have been coupled with the complete abandonment of so-called "defensive" open market operations—a suggestion that raises a host of other problems that are not relevant to the main point at issue.

There is, of course, a strong temptation to pick and choose among the various suggestions, and to erect a money supply target as a "straw man" that can be readily demolished. I shall try to resist that temptation and consider in more general terms the operational problems that would be involved if the FOMC were to move to money supply as the principal indicator of policy or target for open market operations.

But before setting straw men aside, it might be worthwhile to consider the proposition that open market operations should be limited to the injection of a fixed amount of reserves at regular intervals—say $20 million a week. So-called defensive operations—the offsetting of net reserve supply or absorption through movements in float, currency in circulation, gold or foreign exchange operations, etc.—would be abandoned, leaving the banking system to make its own adjustments to these outside movements. While such a system would certainly reduce the level of operations at the Trading Desk, it has never been quite clear how the banking system would make the adjustments to the huge ebb and flow of reserves stemming from movements in the so-called market factors. Either banks would have to operate with excess reserves amounting to many billion dollars at periods of maximum reserve supply by market factors, or they would have to have practically unlimited access to the discount window. Neither possibility seems very desirable, if one is really interested in maintaining a steady growth rate in some monetary aggregate.

There is no reason to suppose that banks would, in fact, hold idle excess reserves in the amounts required. At times of reserve supply by market factors, attempts to dispose of excesses through the Federal funds market would drive the Federal funds rate down and generally lower dealer borrowing costs and the interest rate level. At other times, the reverse would happen. As a result, there would be either feast or famine in the money market, inducing changes in bank loan and investment behavior that would make it impossible to achieve the steady growth of financial aggregates that was presumably desired to begin with. The resultant uncertainty would undermine the ability of the money and capital markets to underwrite and to provide a means of cash and liquidity adjustment among individuals and firms.

The opening of the discount window, on the other hand, runs the risk that reserves acquired at the initiative of the commercial banks would be used to expand the total supply of money and credit and not solely to meet the ebb and flow of reserves through movement of market factors. As a result, the Federal Reserve would have to institute the same controls—in a decentralized fashion—at the various discount windows to limit the supply of reserves that are now provided in a more impersonal way through open market operations.

Consequently, it would appear wise to disassociate the debate over money supply from the problem of so-called defensive open market operations. There seems to be no reason why a seasonal movement of currency, a random movement of float, or a temporary bulge in Federal Reserve foreign currency holdings should automatically be allowed to affect the money market or bank reserve positions. There would seem to be no point in consciously reducing our efficient and integrated money and capital markets to the status of a primitive market where the central bank lacks the means and/or the ability to prevent sharp fluctuations in the availability of reserves—in the misguided attempt to hold "steady" the central bank's provision of reserves.

But the point remains that the ebb and flow of reserves through market factors is very large. While defensive operations are generally successful in smoothing out the impact of these movements on reserves, even a 3 percent margin of error in judging these movements would exceed a $20 million reserve injection in many weeks. Hence

the small, regular injection of reserves, week by week, is not really a very practical approach.

The idea of a regular injection of reserves—in some approaches at least— also suffers from a naive assumption that the banking system only expands loans after the System (or market factors) have put reserves in the banking system. In the real world, banks extend credit, creating deposits in the process, and look for the reserves later. The question then becomes one of whether and how the Federal Reserve will accommodate the demand for reserves. In the very short run, the Federal Reserve has little or no choice about accommodating that demand; over time, its influence can obviously be felt.

In any given statement week, the reserves required to be maintained by the banking system are predetermined by the level of deposits existing two weeks earlier. Since excess reserves in the banking system normally run at frictional levels—exceptions relate mainly to carryover excess or deficit positions reached in the previous week or errors by banks in managing their reserve positions—the level of total reserves in any given statement week is also pretty well determined in advance. Since banks have to meet their reserve requirements each week (after allowance for carryover privileges), and since they can do nothing within that week to affect required reserves, that total amount of reserves has to be available to the banking system.

The Federal Reserve does have discretion as to how the banks can acquire this predetermined level of needed reserves. The reserves can be supplied from the combination of open market operations and the movement of other reserve factors, or they can come from member bank borrowing at the discount window. In this context, it might be noted that the suggestion that open market operations should be used in the short run to prevent a rise in total reserves through member bank borrowing is completely illogical. Within a statement week, the reserves have to be there; and, in one way or another, the Federal Reserve will have to accommodate the need for them.

This does not mean that the way that reserves are supplied makes no difference, nor that aggregate indicators cannot be used to influence the decision as to whether reserves will be supplied through open market operations or whether banks will be required to use the discount window. A decision to provide less reserves through open market operations in any given week, thereby forcing banks to borrow more at the window, could be triggered by a prior FOMC decision (based partly on a review of aggregate money and credit measures) to move to tighter money market conditions, or it might be occasioned by the implementation of the proviso clause if the bank credit proxy was exhibiting a tendency to expand more rapidly than the Committee deemed to be warranted.

No individual bank, of course, has unlimited access to the discount window. Borrowing from the Federal Reserve involves the use of adjustment credit that is limited in both amount and in frequency of use. Eventually, as the aggregate level of borrowing is built up, the discount officers' disciplinary counseling of individual banks that have made excessive use of the window will force the banks to make the necessary asset adjustments. Other banks, desirous of maintaining their access to the discount window intact for use in their own emergency situations, will try to avoid use of the window by bidding up for Federal funds or by making other adjustments in their reserve positions. In the process, interest rates, spreading out from the Federal funds rate, will have been on the rise. As pressure on the banks is maintained or intensified, the banking system as a whole is forced to adjust its lending and investment policies with corresponding effects on money and credit—and eventually on the real economy.

A switch to money supply as the target of monetary policy would, of course, make no difference in the process through which open market operations work on the banking system to affect monetary aggregates. But, depending on the time span over which it was desired to stabilize the rate of monetary growth and on whether money were to become the exclusive indicator and/or target, there would be a significant difference in the rate of interest rate variations. How great that variation might be would be a matter of concern for the Federal Reserve in the conduct of open market operations. I would like to return to that subject in just a few minutes.

First, however, it may be worthwhile to touch on the extensively debated subject whether the Federal Reserve, if it wanted to, could control the rate of money supply growth. In my view, this lies well within the power of the Federal Reserve to accomplish provided one does not require hair-splitting precision and is thinking in terms of a time span long enough to avoid the erratic, and largely meaningless, movements of money supply over short periods.

This does not mean that the money supply could be used efficiently as a target for day-to-day operations. Given the facts that adequate money supply data are not available without a time lag and that there may be more statistical noise in daily or weekly figures than evidence of trend, we would be forced to rely on our monthly estimates for guidance in conducting day-to-day operations. Projections of money supply—and other monetary aggregates—are, of course, an important ingredient of monetary policymaking. While I believe we have made considerable progress in perfecting techniques, forecasting is far from an exact science. Money supply forecasting is especially hazardous because of the noise in the daily data and because of the massive movements in and out of Treasury Tax and Loan accounts at commercial banks.

Let me illustrate the sort of problem that might be faced by citing some numbers representing successive weekly forecasts of annual rates of money supply growth for a recent month—admittedly not a good month for our projectors. The projections cited begin with the one made in the last week of the preceding month and end with the projection made in the last week of the then current month. The numbers are: −0.5 percent, +4 percent, +9 percent, +14 percent, +7 percent and +4.5 percent. I might also note that, in the middle of that then-current month, the projections for the following month were for a 14 percent rate of growth. By the end of the month, the projection was −2.5 percent.

Assuming that the Desk had been assigned a target of a 5 percent growth rate for money supply, it seems quite obvious that, at mid-month, when the forecast was for a 14 percent growth rate for both the current and the following month, we would have been required to act vigorously to absorb reserves. Two weeks later, on the other hand, if the estimates had held up, we would have been required to reverse direction rather violently.

The foregoing should suggest that short-run measures of monetary growth do not provide a good target for the day-to-day conduct of open market operations. Use of such a target runs the serious risk that open market operations would be trying to offset random movements in money supply, faulty short-run seasonal adjustments, or errors of forecasting. In the process, offensive open market operations might have been increased substantially—and I have the uneasy feeling that financial markets might find such operations offensive in more than one sense.

While short-term measures of money supply growth appear to be too erratic to use as a primary target of open market operations, there are times when cumulative short-term evidence begins to build up—even between meetings of the FOMC—that strongly suggests that a deviation from past trends has gotten under way. Such evidence could of course be used, if interpreted cautiously, to modify operations in much the same way that the bank credit proxy is now used.

To return to the question of interest rate variation, there appears to be general agreement that variations would be greater with money supply as a guideline than they have been while the System was using multiple guidelines involving both monetary aggregates and interest rates. How great interest rate variations would be, would depend very much on how rigid the guideline was and how short the time horizon in which it was supposed to operate might be. The question of how great variations might be can probably never be resolved in the absence of any concrete experience.

Some exponents of the monetary school, however, seem to imply that interest rate variations make no difference at all—somehow the market is supposed to work everything out. It seems to me that there are serious risks in the assumption that the financial markets of the real world—in contrast to the markets of a theoretical model— can readily handle any range of interest rate variation. Pushing too hard on money supply control in the face of rapid interest rate adjustment could wind up by destroying the very financial mechanism which the monetary authority must use if it expects to have any impact on the real economy. Psychology and expectations play too great a role in the operations of these markets to permit the monetary authority to ignore the interpretations that the market may place on current central bank operations.

Thus, in the real world of day-to-day open market operations—theoretical considerations aside—the use of money supply as a target would appear to be too mechanistic and, in the short-run, too erratic to be of much use. The use of money market conditions—a blend of interest rates and reserve and credit measures—is a more realistic short-run guide, providing opportunities for trade-offs between interest rates and aggregates in the light of market psychology and expectations. Aggregate measures, including the money supply, are, of course, indispensable indicators for the monetary authorities as they reach policy decisions. But exclusive reliance on—or blind faith in—any single indicator does not appear justified by the current state of the arts.

READING 36
A NEO-KEYNESIAN VIEW OF MONETARY POLICY

Warren L. Smith

Those of us who take an essentially Keynesian view in macroeconomics are often accused, somewhat unjustly, I believe, of minimizing the importance of monetary forces. That contention was probably true 20 years ago for a variety of historical and institutional reasons. But much water has passed over the dam since that time, and I believe it would now be difficult to find an example of the popular stereotype of the Keynesian economist who thinks fiscal policy is all-important and monetary policy is of no consequence. After all, in Keynesian analysis the power of monetary policy depends on the values of certain parameters, and if one is open-minded, he must be prepared to alter his views as empirical evidence accumulates. In some respects, this process has already proceeded quite far—some of the simulations performed with the FRB-MIT model, which is decidedly Keynesian in spirit, show monetary policy having very powerful effects

indeed, albeit operating with somewhat disconcerting lags.

Thus, there is nothing inherent in the Keynesian view of the world that commits its adherents to the belief that monetary policy is weak. What is, it seems to me, distinctive about Keynesianism is the view that fiscal policy is capable of exerting very significant independent effects—that there are, broadly speaking, two instruments of stabilization policy, fiscal policy and monetary policy, and that the mix of the two is important. Indeed, I suppose most Keynesians would assign primacy to fiscal policy, although even this need not inevitably be the case. But in a certain fundamental sense, I believe the issue separating the Keynesians and the so-called Monetarist School relates more to fiscal than to monetary policy, since some Monetarists seem to deny that fiscal policy is capable of exerting any significant independent effects. In addition, the neo-Keynesian view

Source: From Controlling Monetary Aggregates Federal Reserve Bank of Boston, 1969.

seems to differ significantly from that of the Monetarists with respect to the role played by the stock of money in the process by which monetary policy affects the economy.

In this paper, I shall attempt to sketch what I would describe as a neo-Keynesian view of the process by which monetary and fiscal policy produce their effects on the economy and to evaluate some aspects of the recent controversy regarding stabilization policy in the context of this view. I shall then advance some suggestions concerning the conduct of monetary policy.

I. THE TRANSMISSION MECHANISM OF MONETARY POLICY

There appear to be several elements involved in the mechanism by which the effects of changes in monetary policy are transmitted to income, employment, and prices.

A. Portfolio Adjustments

The major advance in monetary theory in recent years has been the development of a systematic theory of portfolio adjustments involving financial and physical assets. This theory of portfolio adjustments fits very comfortably within a Keynesian framework and indeed greatly enriches Keynesian analysis and increases its explanatory power. The General Theory, itself, embodied a rudimentary theory of portfolio adjustments: the way in which the public divided its financial wealth between bonds and speculative cash balances depended on "the" rate of interest. The interest rate then affected investment expenditure, but Keynes failed to incorporate the stock of real capital into his analysis and relate it to the flow of investment spending. Indeed, many of the undoubted shortcomings of the General Theory stem

from the failure to take account of capital accumulation.

The way in which monetary policy induces portfolio adjustments which will, in due course, affect income and employment may be described briefly as follows: A purchase of say, Treasury bills by the Federal Reserve will directly lower the yield on bills and, by a process of arbitrage involving a chain of portfolio substitutions, will exert downward pressure on interest rates on financial assets generally. Moreover—and more important—the expansion of bank reserves will enable the banking system to expand its assets. If the discount rate is unchanged, the banks can be expected to use some portion of the addition to their reserves to strengthen their free reserve position by repaying borrowings at the Federal Reserve and perhaps by adding to their excess reserves. But the bulk of the addition to reserves will ordinarily be used to make loan accommodation available on more favorable terms, and to buy securities, thereby exerting a further downward effect on security yields.

With the expected yield on a unit of real capital initially unchanged, the decline in the yields on financial assets, and the more favorable terms on which new debt can be issued, the balance sheets of households and businesses will be thrown out of equilibrium. The adjustment toward a new equilibrium will take the form of a sale of existing financial assets and the issuance of new debt to acquire real capital and claims thereto. This will raise the price of existing units of real capital—or equity claims against these units—relative to the (initially unchanged) cost of producing new units, thereby opening up a gap between desired and actual stocks of capital, a gap that will gradually be closed by the production of new capital goods.

This stock adjustment approach is readily applicable, with some variations to suit the circumstances, to the demands for a wide variety of both business and consumer capital—including plant and equipment, inventories, residential construction, and consumer durable goods.

B. Wealth Effects

Since monetary policy operates entirely through voluntary transactions involving swaps of one financial asset for another, it does not add to wealth by creating assets to which there are no corresponding liabilities. Nevertheless, monetary policy does have wealth effects, which may be of considerable importance. An expansionary monetary policy lowers the capitalization rates employed in valuing expected income streams, thereby raising the market value of outstanding bonds as well as real wealth and equity claims thereto. In part, this strengthens the impact on economic activity of the portfolio adjustments, already referred to, by increasing the size of the net portfolios available for allocation. In addition, the increase in household wealth may significantly stimulate consumption. Indeed, in a recent version of the FRB-MIT model, the effect on consumption resulting from the induced change in the value of common stock equities held by households accounts for 35 to 45 percent of the initial impact of monetary policy in some simulations.

C. Credit Availability Effects

The portfolio and wealth effects appear to constitute the basic channels through which monetary policy has its initial impact on economic activity. In addition, however, the institutional arrangements for providing financing to certain sectors of the economy may be such as to give monetary policy a special leverage over the availability of credit to these sectors, thereby affecting their ability to spend. It is perhaps most illuminating to discuss changes in credit availability in the context of a restritcive monetary policy.

No doubt changes in credit availability affect many categories of expenditures to some degree. But the sector in which they are most clearly of major importance is homebuilding. Even in the absence of the rather unique institutional arrangements for its financing, housing demand might be significantly affected by monetary policy as changes in mortgage interest rates altered the desired housing stock. But as postwar experience has repeatedly shown, most dramatically in the "credit crunch" of 1966, changes in mortgage credit availability may greatly strengthen the impact of restrictive monetary policy on homebuilding and cause the effects to occur much more rapidly than the stock-adjustment mechanism would imply. There are three different ways in which mortgage credit availability may be affected by a restrictive monetary policy.

First, commercial banks may raise interest rates on consumer-type time deposits to attract funds to meet the demands of their customers. If savings and loan associations do not raise the rates paid to their depositors or raise them less than the banks raise their rates, households may rechannel their saving flows away from the savings and loan associations and toward the banks—or may even withdraw existing savings from savings and loan associations and shift them to banks. Even if, as has recently been the case, the Regulation Q ceilings are used to prevent the banks from attracting household saving away from savings and loan associations, a rise in short- and intermediate-term open-market interest rates may set in motion a process of "disintermediation," with savers channelling their funds away from fixed-value redeemable claims generally and directly into the securities markets. Either of these processes which cut down the flows of funds to savings and loan associations can have, of course, a powerful effect on housing activity. With frozen portfolios of older mortgages made at lower interest rates than currently prevail, these institutions may find it difficult to pay substantially higher interest rates to attract or hold funds even if the Home Loan Bank Board will allow them to.

Second, when commercial banks feel the effects of credit restraint, they normally reduce their mortgage lending in order to be able to accommodate the needs of their business borrowers.

Third, as interest rates rise, yields on corporate bonds typically rise relative to mortgage interest rates, and some institutional investors, such as life insurance companies, shift the composition of their investment flows away from mortgages and toward corporate bonds, which, in any case, have investment properties which make them more attractive than mortgages at equivalent yields. This tendency may be exacerbated by unrealistically low interest rate ceilings on FHA and VA mortgages and by State usury laws applicable to conventional mortgages.

The way in which mortgage credit availability impinges on homebuilding has changed with the passage of time. In the 1950's, when FHA and VA financing was more important than it has been recently and when the FHA and VA interest rate ceilings were more rigid than they are now, restrictive monetary policy affected housing mainly by diverting the flows of funds coming from investors having diversified portfolios away from mortgages and toward corporate securities. That is, the third effect listed above was the most important. In 1966, when home-building was drastically curtailed by monetary restraint, all of the effects were operating, but the first—the drain of funds away from savings and loan associations—was by far the most important. In 1968 and 1969, interest rates have risen sufficiently to arouse concern about a repetition of the 1966 experience. But while housing seems currently to be feeling the effects of tight money, it has proved to be much less vulnerable than was generally expected. There are several reasons for this, but the one most worthy of mention is the adoption by the Federal Reserve and the various Federal housing agencies of a number of measures designed to cushion or offset the effects of high interest rates on housing activity.

D.   Secondary Effects

Working through portfolio effects, wealth effects, and credit availability effects, the initial impacts of monetary policy will generate additional income, and this will further increase the demand for consumer nondurable goods and services. It will also expand the demand for the services of durable goods, thereby giving a further boost to the desired stocks of these goods. Thus, the familiar magnification of demand through multiplier and accelerator effects comes into play. It is often overlooked that the sharp reduction in the multiplier since the 1930's as a result of the greatly increased income-sensitivity of the tax-transfer system has presumably and important effects on the working of monetary as well as fiscal policy. Indeed, I would judge this increase in "built-in stability" through the fiscal system to be a major factor making monetary policy less potent today than in earlier times.

A further chain of secondary effects is set in motion as the rise in income increases demands for demand deposits and currency for transactions purposes, thereby reversing the initial decline in interest rates. This induced rise in interest rates will exert a dampening effect on the expansion by a partial reversal of the forces that initially triggered the rise in income. Whether or not this secondary effect will carry interest rates all the way back to their initial level (or higher) is an open question, concerning which I shall have some comments later on in this paper.

E. Effects on Real Output vs. Prices

I think almost all economists of a Keynesian persuasion would accept the proposition that the way in which the effect of an increase in demand is divided between output response and price-level response depends on the way it impinges on productive capacity. Thus, expansion caused by monetary policy is generally no more or no less inflationary than expansion caused by fiscal policy (or, for that matter, by an autonomous increase in private demand). This statement needs to be qualified in a couple of minor respects. First, monetary expansion might be less inflationary than an equivalent amount of fiscal expansion over the longer run if it resulted in more investment, thereby causing labor productivity to increase more rapidly. Second, the impacts of monetary policy are distributed among sectors in a different way from those of fiscal policy; and, with less than perfect mobility of resources, the inflationary effect might depend to some degree on this distribution.

II. SOME CONTROVERSIAL ISSUES

I would now like to discuss several of the issues that seem to be at the heart of the recent controversy regarding monetary and fiscal policy.

A. The Effectiveness of Fiscal Policy

For the purpose of isolating the effects of fiscal policy from those of monetary policy, I believe a "pure" fiscal policy action should be defined as a change in government expenditures or a change in tax rates without any accompanying change in the instruments of monetary policy. Under our present institutional set-up, the instruments of monetary policy are open-market operations, changes in reserve requirements, and changes in the Federal Reserve discount rate. Open-market operations may be viewed as governing unborrowed reserves plus currency, with defensive operations offsetting undesired changes in this total that would result from erratic variations in float, gold stock, etc.

An increase in government purchases of goods and services, with tax rates constant, would affect the economy by three different routes. First, there would be a direct expansionary *income effect* resulting from the purchase of output by the government. Second, there would be an expansionary *wealth effect* as the private sector, experiencing an increment to its wealth entirely in the form of net claims against the government, increased its demand for real capital in an effort to diversify its portfolios.[1] These income and wealth effects would set off a multiplier-accelerator process of economic expansion. This expansion, in turn, would activate a partially offsetting monetary effect as the rise in income increased the demand for money. If the dial settings of the monetary instruments remained unchanged, this would drive up interest rates. The rise

[1] For an extensive theoretical treatment of the wealth effect, see James Tobin, "An Essay on the Principles of Debt Management," in *Fiscal and Debt Management Policies* (Englewood Cliffs, N.J.: Prentice-Hall, Inc., 1963), pp. 142–218.

in interest rates would cause some reductions in those types of expenditures that were sensitive to interest rates through portfolio, wealth, and availability effects.

The wealth effect of fiscal policy may be quite powerful, particularly because it is cumulative—that is, it continues to operate until the budget has been brought back into balance, thereby shutting off the increase in net claims against the government. But, unfortunately, no effort that I know of has been made to incorporate it in an empirical model; consequently there is no way to formulate even a crude estimate of its importance.

If we neglect the wealth effect simply because we do not know how much weight to give it, we are left with the income effect and the offsetting monetary effect. The monetary effect will be greater (a) the greater the proportion of expenditures in GNP that are affected by interest rates, (b) the greater (in absolute value) is the average interest elasticity of these expenditures, (c) the greater is the income elasticity of demand for money, (d) the smaller (in absolute value) is the interest elas-

ticity of demand for money and (e) the smaller is the interest elasticity of the supply of money.[2]

Only if the interest elasticities of both the demand for and supply of money are zero will the monetary effect completely cancel out the income effect.[3] That is, there will be some leeway for fiscal policy to increase income if a rise in interest rates either induces economization in the use of demand deposits and currency or causes the supply of such monetary assets to expand (for example, by inducing banks to increase their borrowings at the Federal Reserve). Since the empirical evidence is overwhelming that both money demand and money supply possess some degree of interest elasticity, it seems clear that fiscal policy is capable of exerting an independent effect on income. This conclusion is heavily supported by evidence derived from large structural models of the U.S. economy. For example, while there is no unique multiplier for fiscal policy in the FRB-MIT model, a number of simulations with that model show fiscal policy to have very substantial independent effects on economic activity.

---

[2] It is possible to derive a more elaborate version of the static Keynesian multiplier incorporating the monetary effect. The following is such a multipler equation.

$$\frac{dY}{dG} = \frac{1}{1 - e + \dfrac{\dfrac{I}{Y}\eta_{Ir}\eta_{LY}}{\eta_{Lr} - \eta_{Mr}}}$$

Here Y is GNP; G is government purchases; e is the marginal propensity to spend out of GNP; I/Y is the proportion of GNP that is sensitive to interest rates; η_{Ir} (<0) is the average interest elasticity of interest-sensitive expenditures; η_{Lr} (<0) is the interest elasticity of demand for money; η_{Mr} (>0) is the interest elasticity of supply of money; and η_{LY} (>0) is the income elasticity of demand for money. The usual simple Keynesian multiplier without allowance for monetary effect is $1/(1-e)$. The monetary effect is incorporated in the third term (taking the form of a fraction) in the denominator of the equation above. Since this term is positive, its presence reduces the size of the multiplier. The statement in the text above regarding the factors determining the size of the monetary effect is based on this expression.

[3] In this case, the supply of money may be regarded as exogenously determined. If the demand for money depends only on income, income will have to change sufficiently to eliminate any discrepancies that arise between the demand for and supply of money. Thus, money controls income, and fiscal policy is incapable of affecting it. The reader will note that both η_{Mr} and η_{Lr} are zero, the multiplier for fiscal policy given in footnote 2 above becomes zero.

It is often pointed out, especially by those who emphasize the role of money in the economy, that the effect produced by a stimulative fiscal action is dependent on the way in which the resulting deficit is financed. This is in a sense true, but this way of putting it is somewhat misleading. For example, it is sometimes stated that, in order to achieve the full Keynesian multiplier effect, the entire deficit must be financed by creating money—some statements even say high-powered money. What is necessary to achieve this result is to create enough money to satisfy the demand for money at the new higher level of income and the initial level of interest rates.

Ordinarily, the required increase in the supply of money will be only a fraction of the deficit, and the required increase in high-powered money will be an even smaller fraction. Moreover, there is a serious stock-flow problem. When income reaches its new equilibrium in a stable economy, the increased deficit (a flow) will be financed out of the excess of saving over investment generated by the rise in income. Additional demand deposits and currency are needed to meet the increased transaction demand at the higher income level, but this requires only a single increase in the money stock. In reality, there may be further complexities that require a modification of this principle—for example, if the demand for money depends on wealth as well as income or if the price level is determined by a Phillips Curve mechanism

so that prices are not merely higher but are increasing more rapidly at higher levels of income.

Nevertheless, the principle is, I believe, basically correct. Rather than saying that the multiplier depends on how the deficit is financed, I think it is more accurate to say that it depends on the kind of monetary policy that accompanies the fiscal action. If monetary policy is such as to hold interest rates approximately constant, something analogous to the full Keynesian multiplier (with no monetary feedback) will be realized; if it allows interest rates to rise, the multiplier will be somewhat smaller; if it causes interest rates to fall, the multiplier will be somewhat greater.[4]

B. The Role of Money

Although I have used the term "money" in my discussion above, I am not sure the term is a very useful or meaningful one. Money (in the sense of means of payment) has two components, demand deposits and currency. Those two components are not, however, perfect substitutes—they are held, by and large, by different kinds of spending units; demand for them responds in different ways to different stimuli; and, because they are subject to markedly different reserve requirements, shifts between them alter the total amount of credit that can be supplied by the financial system. They are best regarded as two different financial assets and treated as such.

Moreover, there is no apparent rea-

---

[4] If fiscal policy has a wealth effect working through changes in the public's holdings of net claims against the government, it seems quite likely that the magnitude of this effect will depend on the form taken by the change in net claims. For example, a change in public holdings of short-term debt may have a larger effect on aggregate demand than an equal change in holdings of long-term debt. To the extent that this is the case, debt management policies which change the maturity composition of the public's holdings of government debt may have important economic effects. But there is no reason to focus special attention on the composition of increments to the debt resulting from deficits, since the increment to the debt in any year is only a tiny fraction of the total debt to be managed. In any case, as indicated earlier, we are entirely neglecting the wealth effect because in the present state of knowledge there is no way of forming a judgment concerning its importance.

son why "money"—whether in the form of currency or demand deposits—is more or less important than any of the myriad other financial assets that exist. It is now generally agreed that the demands for demand deposits and currency depend on the yields available on alternative assets and on income or related measures (and possibly, but by no means certainly, on wealth). Thus, the quantities of currency and demand deposits held by the public are generally agreed to be endogenous variables determined in a general equilibrium setting along with the prices and quantities of other financial and real assets.

Nor is there any appreciable evidence that money—whether in the form of demand deposits or currency—affects peoples' spending on goods and services directly. Such empirical evidence as there is suggests that people change their expenditures on goods and services because (a) their income changes; (b) their wealth changes; (c) their portfolios are thrown out of equilibrium by changes in relative yields on real and financial assets by actions taken by the monetary or fiscal authorities; (d) credit availability changes for institutional reasons altering in one direction or the other their ability to finance expenditures they want to make; or (e) their propensities to spend or their preferences for different kinds of assets change for essentially exogenous reasons, such as changes in tastes, changes in technology, and so on. That changes in the stock of money *per se* would affect spending seems to me highly improbable.

Of course, if changes in stocks of demand deposits and currency—or the combination of the two—were tightly linked to those changes in yields, in wealth, and in credit availability through which monetary policy operates, changes in the stocks of these monetary assets might be highly useful measures of the thrust of policy even though they played no part in the causal nexus. But this, too, I think is unlikely. In a highly sophisticated financial system such as ours, in which new financial instruments and practices are constantly being introduced, it seems highly improbable that the demands for monetary assets are simple and stable functions of a few unchanging variables.

The many empirical studies of the demand for money that have been made in recent years have generally proved incapable of differentiating among alternative hypotheses. Consequently, one is free to choose among a variety of possible theories of the demand for money. The one that appeals to me is the hypothesis that money (i.e., demand deposits and currency) is dominated by time deposits and very short-dated securities, with the result that it is not a significant portion of permanent portfolios. This leaves the demand for monetary assets as an interest-elastic transactions demand along the lines postulated by Baumol and by Tobin.[5]

Such an explanation, however, makes sense only for relatively large business firms and wealthy individuals. It does not seem applicable to smaller units. Among such units, I suspect that the general rise in interest rates that has been going on for the past two decades has pushed these rates successively above the thresholds of awareness of different groups of people, causing them to abandon their careless habit

[5] See W. J. Baumol, "The Transactions Demand for Cash: An Inventory Theoretic Approach," *Quarterly Journal of Economics,* LXVII, November 1952, pp. 545–56; James Tobin, "The Interest Elasticity of the Transactions Demand for Cash," *Review of Economics and Statistics,* XXXVIII, August 1956, pp. 241–47.

of foregoing income by holding excessive cash balances. If I am right, this behavior is probably not readily reversible if interest rates should fall. It seems to me that there is still a substantial element of mystery about the demand for monetary assets—mystery that will probably be resolved, if at all, only on the basis of extensive study of the behavior of the cash-holdings of micro-units.

C.   Relationship Between Changes in Money and Changes in Income

None of the above should be taken to mean that there is no relation between changes in demand deposits and currency and changes in income. Indeed, I believe there are three such relationships, which are very difficult to disentangle.

First, an expansionary monetary policy that stimulated increased spending and income through portfolio effects, wealth effects, and credit availability effects would bring in its wake an increase in supplies of demand deposits and currency. This would be a sideshow rather than the main event, but it would nevertheless occur. But the size of the increase associated with a given stimulus might vary considerably from one situation to another.

Second, a rise in income caused by fiscal policy or by an autonomous shift of private demand, with the monetary dials unchanged, would react back on the money supply in three different ways.[6] (1) The rise in interest rates caused by the rise in income would cause the banks to increase their borrowings from the Federal Reserve and perhaps to economize on excess reserves. (2) The rise in market interest rates would cause investors to shift funds from time deposits and similar claims into securities if, as is likely, the interest rates on these claims did not rise fully in pace with market rates. This would cause the quantity of demand deposits to increase as investors withdrew funds from time accounts and paid them over to sellers of securities for deposit in demand accounts. (3) If banks and related institutions raised rates on time-deposit type claims, some holders of noninterest-bearing demand deposits would be induced to shift funds to time accounts. To the extent that issuers of these claims held cash reserves against them, the amount of reserves available to support demand deposits would be reduced, requiring a contraction in these deposits. Effects (1) and (2) would cause the money supply to increase, while effect (3) would cause it to fall. It seems likely that (1) and (2) would outweigh (3), leading to an increase in the supply of monetary assets. The probability of this outcome would be increased if the Federal Reserve was laggard in adjusting Regulation Q ceilings. Indeed, a rigid Regula-Q ceiling would completely immobilize effect (3) while maximizing the size of effect (2).

Third, under the rubric of "meeting the needs of trade" or "leaning against the wind," the Federal Reserve has, at times, adjusted the supply of reserves to accommodate, or partially accommodate, changes in the demand for money brought about by changes in income, thereby creating a third chain of causation running from income to money supply.

With perhaps three relations between money and income present at the same time—one running from money to income and two running from income to money—it is likely to be almost im-

6 This discussion is based on an analysis developed in W. L. Smith, "Time Deposits, Free Reserves, and Monetary Policy," in Giulio Pontecoroo, R. P. Shay, and A. G. Hart (eds.), *Issues in Banking and Monetary Analysis* (New York: Holt, Rinehart and Winston, Inc., 1967), pp. 79–113.

possible to tell what is going on by direct observation. And, as Tobin has shown, in such a complex dynamic situation, it is almost impossible to infer anything conclusive about causation by studying the lags.[7]

D.   Does Easy Money Cause Interest Rates to Rise?

One of the supposedly startling propositions that has been advanced recently is the notion that an easing of monetary policy—commonly measured in terms of the rate of increase in the money stock—will cause interest rates to rise and, conversely, that a tightening of monetary policy will cause interest rates to fall. To be sure, if the rate of growth of the money stock is accelerated, interest rates will decline at first. But before long, money income will begin to grow so rapidly that the resulting increase in the demand for money will, it is contended, pull interest rates back up above the level from which they originally started.

In the first place, this possibility has long been recognized in Keynesian economics. In a static Keynesian model it is possible for the IS curve to have a positive slope, with stability conditions requiring only that this slope be less than that of the LM curve. This could happen, for example, if income had a strong effect on investment.[8] In such a situation, a shift to the right of the LM curve, which might be caused by an increase in the money stock, would cause the equilibrium interest rate to rise. A more realistic possibility is that

the economy contains endogenous cycle-generators of the accelerator or stock-adjustment type, which cause income to respond so vigorously to a stimulative monetary policy that interest rates rise above their original level at an ensuing cyclical peak.

There is another chain of causation, working through the effects of inflation on nominal interest rates, which might cause a decline in real interest rates to be associated with a rise in nominal interest rates. This possibility has generally been neglected by Keynesians, but it is in no way inconsistent with Keynesian analysis. An expansionary monetary policy, which lowers nominal interest rates (and real interest rates) initially, will push the economy up the Phillips Curve, thus causing prices to rise more rapidly. As the increase in the actual rate of inflation generates a rise in the anticipated future rate of inflation, an inflation premium may get built into interest rates, causing nominal interest rates to rise. It seems possible that nominal rates could be pushed above their original level even though real interest rates remain below this level. This outcome would be more likely (a) the greater the expansionary effect of a given fall in the real rate of interest on real income, (b) the greater the decline in unemployment caused by a given increase in real income, (c) the greater the increase in the rate of inflation caused by a given decline in unemployment, and (d) the more sensitive the response of the anticipated rate of inflation to a change

---

[7] James Tobin, "Money and Income: Post Hoc Propter Hoc?" (mimeographed); also W. C. Brainard and James Tobin, "Pitfalls in Financial Model Building," *American Economic Review,* LVIII, May 1968, pp. 99–122.

[8] The actual condition required is that the sum of the marginal propensities to consume and invest must exceed one, but (as a condition for stability) be less than one plus a term measuring the size of the monetary feedback. (Even if the two propensities totaled less than unity, the IS curve could slope upward if a rise in interest rates caused total spending to rise. But this could occur only on the remote chance that the income effect dominated the substitution effect in saving behavior so powerfully that a rise in interest rates caused consumption to increase by more than it caused investment to decline.)

in the actual rate of inflation.[9] The probability that nominal interest rates would be pushed above their initial level by this mechanism is very difficult to evaluate, however, primarily because we know very little about the extent to which, and the speed with which, an incerase in the actual rate of inflation gets translated into an increase in the anticipated rate of inflation.

Thus, the notion that an expansionary monetary policy would ultimately cause nominal interest rates to rise above their initial level is in no way inconsistent with Keynesian views. Whether such a phenomenon actually occurs is a different matter. With fiscal policy changing and with the strength of private demand changing, it is not safe to conclude that, because an easing of monetary policy was followed at some later time by a rise of interest rates above their initial level, the easing of monetary policy *caused* the rise in interest rates. The best evidence I have seen is from simulations with the FRB-MIT model which show that an injection of bank reserves causes interest rates to fall sharply at first and then rise gradually but only part of the way back to their original level. But, of course, simulations starting from a different initial position might show different results. In all probability, the phenomenon in question occurs under some conditions but not under others.

III. SUGGESTIONS REGARDING POLICY

At the very beginning of this discussion of the conduct of monetary policy, let me make clear that I am not talking about the issue of rules versus discretion. That is a different subject, which I will discuss briefly at the conclusion of my paper. Assuming that the Federal Reserve will continue to conduct a discretionary policy, let us consider what is the best way to proceed with that task.

It seems to me that much of the recent literature on monetary policy has been obsessed with a search for a magic touchstone—some measure of the impact of monetary forces that can be used as the sole guide in the conduct of policy. Unfortunately, I don't believe there is such a touchstone—the world is too complicated and we know too little about it for that. There is a second related obsession with the problem of characterizing monetary policy. Is it "tight" or "easy"? Is it "tighter" or "easier" today than it was, say, six months ago?

The first of these questions is clearly a matter of judgment and opinion. The second, comparative form of the question sounds more capable of a scientific answer, but in fact I think it is equally unanswerable. Does it mean, "Is monetary policy contributing more to aggregate demand today than it was

---

[9] Beginning with the equation $r = r' + p_e$, which expresses the relation between the nominal interest rate (r), the real interest rate (r') and the anticipated rate of inflation (p_e), the following expression can be rather easily derived.

$$\frac{dr}{dr'} = 1 + m \frac{dl}{dr'} \frac{du}{dY} \frac{dp}{du} \frac{dp_e}{dp}$$

Here m is the multiplier; dl/dr' is the response of interest-sensitive expenditure to a change in the real rate of interest; du/dY is the response of the unemployment rate to a change in real GNP; dp/du is the response of the rate of inflation to a change in the unemployment rate (i.e., the slope of the Phillips Curve); and dp_e/dp is the response of the anticipated rate of inflation to a change in the actual rate of inflation. Since three of the components of the second term on the right-hand side of the equation (dl/dr', du/dY, and dp/du) take on negative values, the second term as a whole is negative. Whether a fall in the real rate of interest will cause the nominal rate of interest or fall depends on whether the scond term on the right is larger or smaller than unity.

six months ago?" If it does mean that—and I can think of no other interpretation—I wouldn't have the faintest idea how to go about answering it. The problem facing the Federal Reserve, however, is not how to characterize monetary policy but how to carry it out, and this puts things in a somewhat different light.

Since monetary policy affects economic activity with substantial lags, policy must clearly be based on forecasts of future economic conditions. While our knowledge has improved considerably, we still cannot be very sure about the lags, which undoubtedly depend upon underlying conditions. Moreover, the lags vary from sector to sector. It seems quite clear that monetary policy can affect homebuilding quite rapidly, at least under some conditions, if the dials of policy are adjusted in the right way. The lags in the effects on the other sectors appear to be considerably longer. Forecasting is also a difficult task, but there is no way to escape the need for it. Not the least of the difficulties of monetary policy, as has been demonstrated several times in the last three years or so, is the forecasting of fiscal policy.

While the ultimate goals of policy are high employment, price stability, the rate of growth of output, and so on, these cannot be used as immediate guides to policy, because it takes so long for policy measures to affect them. The authorities must choose as guides to policy some more immediate and more specifically monetary variables that appear to be related to the goals they are trying to achieve.

There are a number of monetary aggregates that the Federal Reserve can control with varying degrees of precision if it chooses to do so. It can obviously control its portfolio of securities exactly, and it can control unborrowed reserves plus currency outside member banks quite closely by employ-

ing defensive open-market operations to offset changes in uncontrollable factors affecting reserves, such as float, gold stock, Treasury deposits at Federal Reserve banks, etc. It can probably control total reserves plus currency (the monetary base) fairly accurately either by using open-market operations to offset changes in member bank borrowing or by changing the administration of discount policy to reduce the fluctuations in borrowing. The stock of demand deposits and currency would be more difficult to control, but I suspect that its average value over a quarter's time could be controlled fairly satisfactorily.

Alternatively, policy could be directed at regulating interest rates, although some interest rates would be easier to control than others. The Treasury bill rate could be controlled with any desired degree of accuracy under present operating procedures, because the Federal Reserve deals directly in the Treasury bill market. By a shift in its operating procedures, the Federal Reserve could control the yield on some other maturity of Federal debt. I believe it could, instead, maintain fairly close control of a variety of alternative interest rates on private debt—such as the Aaa corporate bond yield—although it would have to influence such rates indirectly unless it were to deal in private debt.

The basic issue of monetary policy is: Should the Federal Reserve focus primarily on controlling some monetary aggregate or should it focus on controlling interest rates? I believe there is a very strong *prima facie* case for a policy that is oriented toward interest rates. The reason is that the portfolio effects, wealth effects, and credit availability effects through which the impacts of monetary policy are transmitted to the economy are better measured by changes in interest rates than by changes in monetary aggregates. The vast bulk of the empirical evidence supports this view, indicating that it is through interest rates that monetary policy affects expenditures on goods and services. Indeed, I know of no evidence that any monetary aggregate that the Federal Reserve could control has an effect on expenditures.

Of course, if there were tight and well understood linkages between some monetary aggregate—say, the stock of demand deposits and currency—and interest rates, it would matter little which the Federal Reserve attempted to control, because a money target would imply an interest rate target. There are indeed linkages between monetary aggregates and interest rates—these linkages are, in my judgment, sufficient to prevent the Federal Reserve from controlling both monetary aggregates and interest rates except to a very limited extent. But the linkages are not well understood and are subject to change as a result of financial innovations and changes in patterns of financial behavior. Consequently, it does make a difference whether the Federal Reserve selects a monetary aggregate or an interest rate as a guide to policy.

A. Advantages of Treasury Bill Rate as a Guide to Policy

My specific suggestion is that the Federal Reserve focus on the Treasury bill rate as its basic guide for monetary policy. There are several advantages in this approach. First, the Federal Reserve can, without any basic change in its operating procedures, control the Treasury bill rate with virtually any degree of accuracy it desires. Second, there are many occasions on which the bill rate must be a focus of attention anyway, because it is the key short-term rate affecting international capital flows. Third, the bill rate is closely related to market interest rates on those forms of short- and intermediate-term

debt that compete with fixed-value redeemable claims and are therefore of critical importance for the availability of mortgage funds. Fourth, there is considerable evidence that the bill rate works through an expectational mechanism to affect those long-term rates that are important in determining the cost of capital to business firms, State and local governments, and home buyers. Moreover, the wealth effect of monetary policy works through capitalization rates that would be indirectly affetced by a policy aimed in the first instance at the Treasury bill rate.

Of course, the bill rate target would have to be selected on the basis of a forecast of economic activity several quarters ahead, including a forecast of fiscal policy. One could, for example, use a model such as the FRB-MIT model to estimate a pattern of behavior of the bill rate that could be expected to achieve the desired performance of the economy over the next three or four quarters, given the anticipated fiscal policy. This target could then be adjusted on the basis of special factors or judgmental considerations. I would not propose to peg the bill rate exactly but to establish a range of, say, 20 basis points within which it would be permitted to fluctuate. The bill rate target would, of course, be reexamined at each meeting of the FOMC on the basis of the latest forecast of the economic outlook.

I would not, however, adhere dogmatically to such a "bills-only" policy. If long-term rates should fail to respond in the anticipated way to a change in the bill rate target, I would not hesitate to nudge them along by open-market operations in long-term Treasury securities. Nor would I entirely neglect monetary aggregates. I would want to supplement the bill rate target with some kind of quantitative guideline to prevent gross mistakes in policy. In the case of a non-growing economy, using the stock of demand deposits and currency as the quantitative guideline, the matter is relatively simple—one should be sure that this stock increases when the economy is below full employment and declines when it is above full employment. The problem here is one of distinguishing between automatic and discretionary elements of policy—similar to the problem in fiscal policy that gave rise to the full-employment surplus concept. When the economy is weak, for example, interest rates decline automatically even if the monetary authorities do nothing, and it is desirable to be sure that the authorities are reinforcing this tendency by discretionary measures rather than offsetting it as they sometimes appear to have done in the past.

The problem of developing a suitable monetary guideline is considerably more complicated in the case of a growing economy. My procedure would be to begin by estimating a "normal" rate of monetary growth. For example, if the target point on the Phillips Curve is 4 percent unemployment which is judged to be associated with 2 percent inflation, if the rate of growth of productive capacity under full employment conditions is estimated to be 4 percent per year, and if the income elasticity of demand for monetary assets is judged to be unity, the "normal" rate of monetary growth would be estimated at 6 percent per year. At any particular time, if the objective of policy was to restrain the economy, growth should be less than 6 percent; if the objective was to stimulate the economy, growth should be more than 6 percent.

There is a problem of deciding what aggregate to use as an index of monetary growth. Should it be the monetary base as calculated by the Federal Reserve Bank of St. Louis, the money supply, total bank credit, or some other aggregate? Unfortunately, the signif-

icance of a change in the rate of growth of any of the commonly used aggregates depends upon the public's preferences for different categories of financial assets, including currency, demand deposits, time deposits, and securities. Since these preferences appear to change for reasons that we do not yet fully understand, problems of interpretation are bound to arise. My quite tentative suggestion would be to use the monetary base as the index of monetary growth. But I would also monitor the behavior of the other aggregates closely. If the selected bill rate target resulted in growth of the base inconsistent with the guideline for several weeks and if the behavior of the other aggregates seemed to support the conclusion that monetary growth was too slow or too fast, the whole situation, including the bill rate target, should be carefully reexamined.

B. Other Dimensions to be Considered

I think an approach along the lines developed above would make sense in providing an overall rationale for monetary policy. But there are important dimensions that are omitted in the above discussion. It has long been my contention that those responsible for the conduct of monetary policy must pay close attention to its impacts on particulars sectors of the economy, especially when a restrictive policy is being followed. An example of this dimension of monetary policy is the variety of measures that have been taken by the Federal Reserve and a number of other Federal Government agencies during the past year to cushion the impact of high interest rates on homebuilding.

The Federal Reserve has attempted to shield the savings and loan associations from bank competition by maintaining low ceiling rates on savings deposits and those forms of time deposits that compete most directly with savings and loan shares. The Federal Home Loan Bank Board has acted to encourage continued mortgage lending by savings and loan associations by reducing the liquidity requirement applicable to the associations and by making advances available to them. In addition, the Home Loan Banks have attempted to manage their own borrowings in the capital market in such a way as to minimize the possible impact on deposit flows. The Federal National Mortgage Association increased its mortgage holdings by $1.6 billion in 1968, and increased the scope and flexibility of its stabilizing activities in the mortgage market by introducing a new program of weekly auctions of mortgage commitments, beginning in May 1968. The ceiling rate applicable to FHA and VA mortgages was raised from 6 percent to 6¾ percent in May and was raised further to 7½ percent in January 1969. Finally, in its general conduct of monetary policy, the Federal Reserve has kept its eye on the flows of funds to savings and loan associations with a view to avoiding, if possible, a rise in short- and intermediate-term interest rates sufficient to set off a "disintermediation crises" of the type that occurred in 1966.

The impact of monetary policy on the economy would, I believe, have been substantially different in 1968, and thus far in 1969, in the absence of these precautionary actions by the Federal Reserve and by the various agencies with responsibilities in the housing field. In all probability, we would long since have experienced a sharp decline in housing starts and residential construction expenditures similar to that which occurred in 1966. There are a number of reforms which might be adopted to increase the efficiency and flexibility of the mortgage market and to reduce the excessive

impact that monetary policy now tends to have on homebuilding. Unless and until such reforms are implemented, however, I believe it is appropriate for the monetary authorities to concern themselves specifically with the effects of their policies on the housing sector. Indeed, I believe structural measures of the kind employed in 1968–69 should be thought of as part of monetary policy and should be applied as the situation seems to warrant on the basis of close cooperation between the Federal Reserve and the other agencies involved.

No matter how skillfully monetary policy is conducted, things are bound to go wrong from time to time. The underlying strength of private demand will sometimes prove to be stronger or weaker than was anticipated; fiscal policy will depart from its expected path; and the timing and magnitude of the economy's response to monetary actions will seldom be exactly as anticipated. I do not count myself among the group of economists who believe the business cycle is dead. If we seriously attempt to keep the economy moving along a selected high-employment growth path, resisting departures from that path in either direction, I believe we can still expect some economic fluctuations. The hope is that we can keep these fluctuations mild. But our success in that respect is much more critically dependent on improving the performance of fiscal policy than it is on changing the techniques of monetary management. Improved fiscal policy would relieve the Federal Reserve of its recent impossible task of offsetting the effects of profoundly destabilizing movements of the Federal budget. Even operating within the framework established by a reasonably well-designed fiscal policy, the Federal Reserve is bound to make occasional mistakes, but it should be able to make an effective contribution to economic stabilization and do so without the sharp gyrations in monetary variables that we have witnessed recently.

IV. RULES VERSUS AUTHORITIES

There is no reason, in principle, why one holding Keynesian views must necessarily favor discretion over a monetary rule. One could believe that our knowledge of the responses and the lags in the system is so poor that efforts to conduct a discretionary policy add to instability rather than subtract from it. I think discretion conducted on the basis of the best information available can do a better job than a rule, but I find the question a very complex one, and I do not see how anyone can be sure of the answer.

Before a rule involving steady growth of some aggregate such as the monetary base could be seriously considered, however, it seems to me there would have to be procedural or institutional changes in three areas.

First, there would have to be some assurance of better fiscal policy than we have had recently. Our problems of the last three years are primarily the result of inaction and inordinate delay in fiscal policy, and discretionary monetary policy has helped by either taking the place of needed fiscal restraint or supplementing it when it was too-long delayed.

Second, if monetary policy is to disregard interest rates entirely, I believe we need an overhaul of the arrangement for financing housing.

And, third, interest rates cannot be disregarded until the international monetary system has been reformed in some way to remove the balance-of-payments constraint on domestic interest rates.

Having said all of this, let me add that I believe the discussion of monetary rules is largely academic anyway. Even assuming that a rule were adopted, I feel certain that there would be overwhelming pressure to abandon it the first time it appeared that discretion would enable us to acheve a better performance—and that, I believe, would occur quite soon after the rule was adopted.

READING 37
MONETARY POLICY AND THE RESIDENTIAL MORTGAGE MARKET

I. RESIDENTIAL MORTGAGE CREDIT AND THE ACTIVITIES OF THE FEDERAL RESERVE BOARD IN CARRYING OUT ITS MONETARY POLICY

The ultimate goals of monetary policy are general in nature—to contribute toward achieving high employment with sustainable growth, a stable dollar at home, and overall balance in our financial transactions with other nations. The primary instruments through which monetary policy strives to further these objectives include changes in the cost and availability of credit through open market operations in Government securities for the account of the Federal Reserve Banks, changes in reserve requirements of member commercial banks, and changes in the rates and conditions under which member banks can borrow from the Federal Reserve Banks. With these general goals and instruments as given, the monetary policy of the Federal Reserve has been and must continue to be oriented toward the broad domestic and international economic scene.

But Federal Reserve actions to influence the ultimate aggregate targets of monetary policy—maximum employment, economic growth, and price stability—must always take into account the impact of monetary developments on current and prospective conditions within particular sectors of the economy. Critical difficulties emerging in any one sector could affect the sustainability of over-all growth. Or they could affect the liquidity and solvency of major segments of our financial system.

One sector that the Federal Reserve follows closely in carrying out monetary policy is the residential mortgage market—the nation's largest single net user of individual savings. Developments within this sector have obvious implications for our ability to improve living standards, for the sustainability of aggregate demands for goods and services, and for prices of a major service—shelter. They also have a direct bearing on the viability of private financial institutions that held some

Source: Reprinted from Federal Reserve Bulletin, May 1967.

$225 billion in loans secured by residential real estate at the end of last year. Indirectly, developments in residential finance—and through this market to residential construction—have widespread effects on other types of credit, on production, and on employment.

A.   Periods of Credit Restraint

In periods when aggregate demands for goods and services tend to run ahead of the supply of resources available to meet these demands, the task of general economic policy is to initiate actions that will discourage enough spending to head off an upward spiral in prices and wages. Monetary instruments are used toward this end by reducing the availability of credit and by raising its cost. But the intensity of the monetary attack on inflation in any given period will depend on the extent to which fiscal policy is also helping to check spending.

For economic policy to be effective under these circumstances, it is clear that aggregate spending has to be cut somewhere, to levels below those that would otherwise prevail. In practice, the types of spending most affected by monetary restraint are those in sectors where demand is postponable and credit financing accounts for a large share of total outlays. Such characteristics are, of course, most typical of outlays for durable goods, and among these housing is a prime example.

Use of long-term credit is unusually large in the financing of housing, reflecting not only the extreme durability and the relatively large unit price of the structures involved, but also the substantial number of dwellings built or traded in any one year. Buyers of both new and used residential properties rely heavily on long-term mortgage financing. In the case of new, 1-family homes built for sale, for example, an average of 95 out of every 100 dwell-

ings sold in 1965 used mortgage credit to some degree, with the average credit transaction involving a loan of nearly $19,000 (excluding finance charges), or almost 88 per cent of the average purchase price. Homebuilders rely perhaps even more heavily on short-term construction financing, which is ordinarily available only if commitments for permanent mortgage financing can also be obtained. Altogether, demands for residential mortgage credit accounted for as much as three-tenths of total net short-term and long-term funds raised in all credit markets in 1965.

These special characteristics of housing outlays and their financing make residential construction as well as used-home transactions inherently vulnerable to cyclical fluctuations. For this reason, unless monetary actions are to be abandoned as an instrument of economic policy, housing is likely to continue to show larger variations between periods of monetary ease and restraint than most other types of spending.

B.   Monetary Policy and Housing Markets in 1966

In 1966, however, the cyclical impact of economic events was unusually marked on residential construction and on the exchange of used houses. While policy-induced pressures to reduce spending were widely felt throughout the economy, the weight of these constraints on the housing market was particularly severe. The magnitude of the contraction in outlays for housing reflected the interaction of several factors.

With the escalation of U.S. participation in the Vietnamese war, aggregate spending—already at a high level as a result of the ongoing business capital boom—began to intensify upward pressures on prices and wages. Although a number of fiscal actions were initiated in the first half of 1966 to limit the growth of business and consumer spending, the lion's share of the responsibility for checking inflationary tendencies was placed on monetary policy. In these circumstances, with business demands for credit remaining very heavy, interest rates rose sharply. The resulting intense competition for funds created special pressures on the nonbank thrift institutions that traditionally finance the bulk of housing activity. As interest rates rose generally, these institutions found an increasing share of total savings flows being allocated directly to securities markets. Consequently, funds available for housing were substantially curtailed.

As these unusual pressures on thrift institutions—and through them on the housing market—became apparent, the Federal Reserve took a number of actions designed to moderate their impact. These steps were intended to redistribute some of the burden on thrift institutions to other sectors of the economy, in part by dampening the interest rate competition that was contributing to the highest rates paid for savings in many decades.

In July the Board of Governors lowered the Regulation Q ceiling on maximum interest rates that member commercial banks could pay on new multiple-maturity time deposits. In the same month the Board raised reserve requirements on time deposits held by each member bank in excess of $5 million. Another increase in reserve requirements was made in September, when bank issues of promissory short-term notes were also brought under reserve-requirement and interest-ceiling regulations. These actions, along with retention of the 4 per cent ceiling on rates that banks could pay for savings deposits, exerted limits on the capacity and incentive of banks to compete for savings with other types of depository institutions that ordinarily invest a larger share of their resources in mortgages than banks do.

Early in September the Presidents of the Federal Reserve Banks sent a letter to all member banks asking for their cooperation in curtailing expansion in loans to businesses, which had been growing at an unusually rapid rate. Faced with substantial potential run-offs in large-denomination certificates of deposit as market yields rose above the rate ceiling on CD's banks might otherwise have sold securities instead of cutting back on business lending in order to adjust their positions. The adverse impact on interest rates of heavy bank liquidations of securities, in turn, would have spilled over into other financial markets, including the residential mortgage market. Toward the end of the year the September 1 letter was rescinded when it became evident that underlying economic conditions had changed.

In late September the Board—acting under new temporary authority that broadened the basis for setting interest rate ceilings on time and savings deposits—lowered the maximum interest rate that member banks could pay on individual time deposits of under $100,-000. Federal agencies that regulate savings and loan associations and mutual savings banks also established similar ceilings under this new authority. These joint actions prevented further acceleration in the maximum interest rates paid on savings, although some lenders that had been below the new ceilings initiated additional rate increases.

Finally, during the period of market stringency that developed last summer, the Board of Governors made temporary arrangements under which the Federal Reserve Banks could provide emergency credit facilities, under specified conditions, to nonmember commercial banks or to nonbank depository-type institutions, including savings and loan associations and mutual savings banks. While this emergency facility was not expected to be needed and was never used, it offered assurance that aid could be made available against the remote possibility of exceptional outflows of funds that could not be met through usual adjustment procedures. The temporary arrangement, which later expired, was not intended to be a long-run source of Government credit for the residential mortgage market. However, the System has indicated its willingness to reinstitute this arrangement if it should become desirable to do so at some future date.

Looking back on the events of 1966, it seems clear that a different mix of monetary and fiscal policy—which placed more reliance on an increase in tax rates or a cutback in Federal spending than on monetary restraint—would have helped to moderate the steepness of the general advance in interest rates. This in turn would have created less extreme pressures on savings flows to thrift institutions. At the same time, however, it is also clear that even if increases in interest rates had been more moderate, the close traditional tie between housing and credit advanced by the specialized depositary-type lenders would have contributed to a significant cutback in the supply of credit available for both new and used housing. Because thrift institutions lend long and borrow short, they are peculiarly vulnerable to general increases in interest rate levels. The relative rigidity of earnings on their essentially long-term assets limits the ability of these institutions to compete for funds in the short run by raising rates paid for new and existing savings.

Typically in the postwar period, the relative share of depositary-type savings in total savings flows has declined during phases of strong economic growth and high and rising market interest rates, as in 1955, 1959, and 1966. This behavior has emphasized that an important, if marginal, portion of depositary flows always comes from yield-conscious savers who are in a position to consider direct market investment as a convenient alternative. Market instruments, such as U.S. Treasury obligations, commercial paper, Federal agency securities, and corporate and municipal bonds, may lack the degree of protection assured to holders of insured savings accounts and shares. But they offer the immediate attraction of higher yields over a range of maturity terms and—on longer maturities—the prospect of capital gains if going market rates should eventually decline. Stocks, of course, usually provide some current yield plus the chance of rapid accruals in capital value.

In addition to these long-standing structural peculiarities of residential finance, the impact of credit restraint on housing in 1966 was affected by special mortgage market conditions, which had developed as an outgrowth of tendencies begun earlier in the 1960's when the supply of mortgage credit was abundant. Before turning to a consideration of the types of reforms that might be adopted to lessen the disproportionate cyclical vulnerability of housing in the future, a more detailed review—illustrating how both the traditional and the special peculiarities of residential finance complicated the picture in 1966—will help to highlight the need for reform.

II. FACTORS AFFECTING THE AVAILABILITY AND PRICE OF RESIDENTIAL MORTGAGE CREDIT IN 1966

Last year's combination of intense general credit demands and greater than usual emphasis on monetary restraint in lieu of stronger fiscal policy affected the availability of credit in residential mortgage markets more than in most other types of credit markets. Net growth in outstanding residential mortgage debt during the second half of the year was down by two-fifths from the record pace in the second half of 1965. New commitments for mortgage loans probably fell by somewhat more. For the year as a whole, net extensions of residential mortgage credit declined by $6.5 billion, or by three-tenths.

A. Nonbank Thrift Institutions

As has been indicated, the bulk of the reduction in mortgage credit reflected the marked decline in net savings flows to the nonbank depositary-type institutions that specialize in mortgage lending. Net acquisitions of deposits at mutual savings banks dropped to the lowest level in 5 years, and net acquisitions of shares at savings and loan associations fell to the lowest level in 13 years. Funds available for expansion of their residential mortgage portfolios were curtailed accordingly.

The reduced inflow to these thrift institutions reflected in part high and rising yields on competitive market instruments, as noted earlier, and continued aggressive competition of commercial banks for savings. It also reflected a general reluctance or inability of these thrift institutions to increase the rates paid on their own deposits or shares, at least through midyear, because their earning assets consisted chiefly of long-term mortgages bearing yields that had largely been fixed earlier when mortgage rates were generally appreciably lower. Also, savings and loan associations during much of 1966 were inhibited from raising rates on share accounts by regulatory restrictions on advances from the Federal home loan banks. These constraints were part of a continuing policy intended to achieve a sounder basis for growth than had taken place at some savings and loan associations earlier in the 1960's, when they had promoted high dividend rates and had greatly increased borrowings from the Federal home loan banks.

Over the first half of 1966, savers found a growing incentive to shift funds out of the thrift institutions that offered lower yields on fixed-value claims. In that period, savings accounts then in effect generally permitted savings withdrawals to be made virtually on demand. The resulting large outflows reduced sharply the net growth in savings shares and deposits. After midyear most large savings banks and some savings and loan associations in West Coast States raised their savings rates to a point where their net inflows began to improve. After late September, once the new ceiling rates on share accounts had been established and modifications had been made in previous regulations on Federal home loan bank advances, other savings and loan associations that were below the ceiling also raised their rates.

By the fourth quarter market rates of interest had reached a peak and had begun to decline. Accordingly, growth of savings and loan association share capital picked up, and growth in deposits at mutual savings banks improved further.

The reduction in net savings received by thrift institutions last year was compounded by a drop in cash inflows resulting from prepayments on outstanding mortgage loans. Return flows from such prepayments fell off sharply as the reduced volume of new lending slowed turnover in older properties and as more buyers were obliged to assume outstanding loans in order to finance real estate transactions. For savings and loan associations—the dominant mortgage lender—loan retirements (as measured by new loans made minus changes in loans held) were down $2.1 billion over the record level of the preceding year, with most of the decline taking place in the second half of 1966. Cash flows from both loan retirements and net growth in share capital declined by nearly $5.8 billion.

The relatively limited degree of liquidity at the thrift institutions further restricted their ability to meet demands for residential mortgage credit in 1966. During the early 1960's when credit conditions were easier, the liquidity of these lenders had been built up more slowly than their total resources. By the end of 1965—just before entering a period that would test their liquidity severely—savings and loan associations reported that their holdings of cash plus U.S. Government securities of all maturities accounted for the smallest share of their total assets (8.7 per cent) in 24 years. The average liquidity of mutual savings banks was the lowest in several decades. Ratios of reserves to total liabilities for both savings and loan associations and mutual savings banks were also comparatively low.

Also, the easier credit conditions of the early 1960's, coupled with the elimination of earlier housing shortages dating from World War II, had left some savings and loan associations with a large volume of troubled or foreclosed real estate on their hands. While the origination of these loans may have initially added high-yielding assets to their mortgage portfolios, the subsequent acquisition of the collateral through foreclosure (or the equivalent) later depressed net earnings by increasing servicing costs. It also reduced cash flows scheduled from principal and interest payments and reduced holdings of potentially salable loan collateral. By the end of 1965, savings and loan associations probably owned in excess of $1 billion in real estate other than association premises, compared with about $290 million 4 years earlier, thus further constricting their investment flexibility.

Finally, member savings and loan associations borrowed heavily from the Federal home loan banks during the early 1960's, mainly to finance additional expansion of their portfolios during a period of rapid though decelerating growth in their net savings inflows and net mortgage acquisitions. By the end of 1965, home loan bank advances outstanding were nearly $6 billion, more than double the figure only 4 years earlier. Since nearly all the open market borrowing of the Federal home loan banks was short term, virtually all their outstanding debt had to be refinanced each year. This practice limited the degree to which those banks could provide new money for additional advances later when general conditions tightened. As it was, the home loan banks went to the money market in 1966 for $7.2 billion in order to refinance outstanding obligations and to raise $1.6 billion in new money. The higher interest rates payable on these obligations were passed on to all borrowing member associations in higher costs of operation, since rates on outstanding advances were changed in line with rates on new advances.

Faced with the need to roll over most outstanding debt and to raise some new funds in an already congested market, the Federal Home Loan Bank Board felt constrained to husband the lending power of the Federal home loan banks in order to cover withdrawals of share capital at member associations. For this reason, advances for purposes of expanding mortgage credit were discontinued after early spring. Member associations after midyear were required to draw down their own liquid assets to some extent before borrowing from the System to cover withdrawals. Both changes, of course, restricted the degree to which savings and loan associations could extend additional mortgage credit at a time when their own internal resources were under pressure.

All these combined factors resulted

in a sharp slowdown in net acquisitions of residential mortgages during 1966 by savings and loan associations and by mutual savings banks. Net residential mortgage takings of savings and loan associations dropped some $5.0 billion, or by more than half, below the already reduced 1965 figure. Net takings by mutual savings banks declined by nearly $1.4 billion, or by a third, below the near-record total a year earlier. Taken together, the reduced pace of lending of these two lender groups accounted for the bulk of the $7.6 billion net decline in residential mortgage debt extended by the four major types of private institutional lenders, including commercial banks and life insurance companies in addition to savings and loan associations and mutual savings banks (see table).

B.   Commercial Banks

While commercial banks experienced a modest slowing of savings growth during the first half of 1966, the com-

position of their inflows changed sharply toward higher-cost funds, as in the case of other depository institutions. As banks began to compete more actively for time deposits of individuals and businesses, many promoted new instruments, such as savings certificates and savings bonds, with higher yields and longer maturities than regular passbook accounts. Part of the funds flowing into these time deposits merely represented transfers from passbook savings, and some came from nonbank depository institutions. But commercial banks also suffered from the aggregate shift in savings toward direct investment in market securities. Thus, even though bank time and savings deposits rose at an annual rate of 10 per cent during the first half of 1966, this rate was a third below the pace of expansion during the record preceding year.

After mid-1966, banks found it increasingly difficult to add to their time and savings deposits, in view of rising

TABLE 1

INCREASES IN NONFARM RESIDENTIAL MORTGAGE DEBT OUTSTANDING BY TYPE OF HOLDER AND TYPE OF PROPERTY

(Billions of dollars, without seasonal adjustment)

	1964	1965	1966	1965				1966			
				I	II	III	IV	I	II	III	IV
Total	21.3	21.5	15.1	4.4	5.7	5.9	5.6	4.2	4.6	3.4	2.8
Type of holder:											
Financial institution—Total	18.5	18.5	10.9	3.8	5.0	5.1	4.6	3.3	3.5	2.3	1.8
Commercial banks	2.5	3.5	2.7	.5	1.0	1.2	.8	.4	1.0	.8	.5
Savings banks	3.8	3.6	2.2	.9	.9	.9	.9	.6	.4	.6	.6
Savings and loan assns.	9.3	8.7	3.7	1.8	2.6	2.4	2.0	1.6	1.6	.4	.1
Life insurance companies	2.9	2.7	2.2	.7	.5	.6	.9	.7	.5	.5	.6
Federal agencies	—.2	.4	2.8	*	—.1	.1	.4	1.0	.6	.6	.6
All others	3.2	2.7	1.4	.6	.9	.7	.6	—.1	.5	.5	.5
Type of property:											
1- to 4-family	15.4	16.1	11.6	3.1	4.4	4.4	4.1	3.1	3.7	2.7	2.0
Multifamily	6.1	5.4	3.6	1.2	1.3	1.4	1.4	1.1	.9	.8	.8

* Less than $50 million.

Source: Board of Governors of the Federal Reserve System, new series. Details may not add to totals because of rounding, which also affects comparisons between quarters and years.

market yields on competitive investments, the unchanged ceiling on time deposits of $100,000 and over, and the reduction in ceiling rates on time deposits of less than $100,000, made in September. In fact, total time and savings deposits of commercial banks remained almost unchanged on a seasonally adjusted basis from the end of August through November, but improved in December as general credit conditions eased again.

Commercial banks allocated a larger share of their net increase in loans and investments to residential mortgages in 1966 than in any of the previous 5 years. But their net takings of residential mortgages (including construction loans) were reduced sharply in the second half of 1966, after holding close to their year-earlier pace during the first 6 months. For the year as a whole the net decline in bank acquisitions of residential mortgages came to about $700 million, a fifth below the record 1965 level.

C. Life Insurance Companies

As general credit conditions tightened during most of 1966 and interest rates rose, life insurance companies came under increasing pressure from growth in policy loans, which upset earlier projections of cash flows available for investment. Slowing in mortgage prepayments furhter contributed to a reduction in cash flows. This led life insurance companies to reduce their net acquisitions of residential loans by about $400 million, or by a sixth, although their net takings of higher-yielding nonresidential mortgages increased by about as much as their residential acquisitions declined.

For insurance companies as well as for depositary lenders, a potential source of loanable funds through the sale of existing seasoned mortgages was severely limited in 1966, despite the variable impact of tighter credit conditions both geographically and in terms of timing. In part, this limitation reflected the fact that no effective secondary market mechanism exists for the ready transfer of seasoned residential mortgages, especially conventional loans, at going prices. The sale of seasoned, Federally underwritten home loans to the Federal National Mortgage Association was ruled out, of course, by FNMA regulations, issued in mid-January, that confined its secondary-market purchases to newly made mortgages in order to conserve its resources within statutory limits.

D. FNMA Activity

A record net increase in FNMA acquisitions of unseasoned residential mortgages during 1966 helped to offset in part the large aggregate decline in takings by the four major types of private financial institutions. FNMA added $2.3 billion to its residential mortgage portfolio, chiefly through purchases from mortgage companies.

Not all this total, however, represented a net addition to the over-all availability of residential mortgage credit. Some funds raised by FNMA through its borrowings from the Treasury or through the open market undoubtedly attracted savings that might otherwise have been placed with depositary institutions that also invest in mortgages. Also, some mortgages purchased by FNMA provided funds that mortgage sellers reinvested elsewhere than in the mortgage market. Even so, FNMA's net support to the residential mortgage market was probably quite large, although its increased volume of open market borrowings helped to raise general market rates, which encouraged the shift in savings from direct lending institutions.

E. New Commitments on Residential Mortgages

The nature of the process of financing residential properties usually requires a mortgage commitment by the lender in advance of the actual disbursement of funds. This practice means that cutbacks in new commitments that have an immediate impact on plans for the construction of new houses or the transfer of used homes may show up only after some time has passed in a reduced pace of new loans closed and funds disbursed. They may be evidenced even later in declines in net acquisitions of mortgages, if loan repayments also fall off.

Fragmentary evidence suggests that new commitments on residential mortgages were cut back even more sharply than net loan acquisitions for all major types of private lenders. Lenders were obliged to cut back heavily on new commitments in order to honor outstanding commitments that bulked increasingly large in view of reduced cash flows below earlier projections. Such projections, in turn, had been based on extrapolations of favorable cash-flow trends earlier in the 1960's. They led many lenders by the end of 1965 to commit themselves farther ahead than they had done at any time in the recent past.

Greater lender selectivity — along with higher construction costs and housing prices—apparently worked to increase the average amount of mortgage credit used per loan commitment last year, continuing a long trend in this direction. Thus the number of new residential mortgage commitments was probably cut back by even more than the dollar volume of funds committed for additional lending. This factor further constrained the number of new housing starts and the number of sales of used dwellings.

Builders of new homes as well as buyers of new and used homes were hit by these cutbacks in new commitments, since both largely depend on the same credit sources and instruments. Production of new housing and transfers of used homes declined sharply after the early part of 1966.

Other influences also contributed to a minor extent to the decline in starts; these included the aftermath of earlier overbuilding in some areas and the dampening effects on demand of continuing increases in costs of land, materials, and wages.

By late fall, general credit conditions eased and interest rates in nonmortgage sectors declined. Since rates on savings at depositary institutions remained at or close to the record levels reached earlier, the pressures that produced large net savings outflows during much of 1966 began to work in reverse to generate large savings inflows toward the end of the year. Rate ceilings imposed under new legislative authority worked to direct a larger share of the total toward nonbank thrift institutions.

Not all these net savings inflows, however, were translated at once into a sharply higher volume of new residential mortgage commitments at this usually slack season in the real estate market. Many lenders first went about rebuilding their depleted liquidity positions and reducing their indebtedness. Many potential borrowers held back in expectation of still further easing. Others were not immediately aware that mortgage credit had become more readily available at lower costs. Or they were not yet in a position to seek out new commitments.

F. The Cost of Credit

The cost of new home mortgage loans rose sharply in late 1965 and through most of 1966, as did rates on all other types of market instruments. Yields on newly made, multifamily mortgages apparently increased rapidly, too. Toward the end of last year, home mortgage rates peaked and then began to decline at a pace that accelerated in the early months of 1967. In both their up and down phases, returns on home mortgages appear to have changed more rapidly than in any earlier postwar period when they gained a reputation for stickiness. Their greater sensitivity last year seems to have reflected largely the unusual degree of tightness that developed in the availability of funds for such loans.

In some eastern States where going yields on residential mortgages rose above usury ceilings, lending within local markets was said to have been cut back more than might otherwise have been the case. And in regions where interest rates on mortgages had risen most, discounts on Federally underwritten loans with fixed contract rates had increased dramatically, despite several upward adjustments, before finally reaching the statutory ceiling of 6 per cent. Discounts on FHA-insured and VA-guaranteed home mortgages—which are largely borne initially by new-home builders and used-home sellers—reached levels that discouraged offerings of new or used houses even where financing commitments were available at the advanced yields then prevailing. Even 6 per cent FHA home loans carried secondary-market discounts averaging as many as 7.3 percentage points in the Southwest last November, according to the series published by the FHA. Indirectly, the large discounts inhibited demand for new houses, since the resale market for used homes provides strong support for the new-house market.

Some potential borrowers—faced with a sharp cutback in the supply of new residential mortgage commitments and the unwillingness of many would-be sellers to absorb large discounts on Federally underwritten loans—turned to less usual financing practices in order to consummate transactions. Assumed loans, purchase money mortgages, and instalment land contracts were said to have been often involved. So too were junior loans carrying negotiated rates that may reflect the inferior bargaining position of the borrower and the inferior legal position of the creditor in foreclosure.

III. SUGGESTED APPROACHES TO REFORM

Corrective actions designed to lessen cyclical fluctuations in the availability and price of residential mortgage funds need to be addressed to the special structural problems of the mortgage market that were highlighted by the 1966 experience. The preceding review of that experience suggests many of the changes that might be considered. Among these are the restructuring of nonbank depositary institutions that specialize in mortgage lending, improvements in the marketability of the mortgage instrument, reductions in barriers to the free flow of mortgage funds among geographic regions and among types of structures, and changes in the policies and powers of Federal agencies that specialize in mortgage and housing markets. Such reforms would help to lessen the impact of credit restraint on the residential mortgage market. But even if all these changes were made, the residential mortgage market and housing would undoubtedly still prove to be more sensitive than most other sectors to sharp cyclical changes in credit availability and credit costs.

The reports of the Presidential Committees on Federal Credit Programs and on Financial Institutions, made in 1963, included numerous proposals for reform; the Board of Governors continues to endorse the general principles set forth in those two reports. Some time earlier, in 1961, the Board submitted a requested report to the Senate Banking and Currency Subcommittee on Housing that contained several observations about how instability in residential construction might be lessened in the future.

In recommending what should be

considered now, the Board of Governors believes that the following broad guidelines are of crucial importance:

A flexible fiscal policy should play a greater part than it did in 1966 in acting, when needed, to restrain aggregate economic activity. Timely reductions in income tax rates earlier in the 1960's contributed greatly to the sustained economic growth that developed after the 1960–61 recession. If, with the added economic stimulus provided by escalation of the Vietnamese war, an income-tax increase had been enacted early in 1966, the burden of restraining general economic activity would have fallen less heavily on monetary policy and hence less severely on the residential mortgage market and on housing.

The residential mortgage market— both primary and secondary—should be integrated closely with the general capital market, not insulated from it. But at the same time, certain institutional changes should be made to enhance the ability of the residential mortgage market to compete prudently for the limited aggregate supply of available credit. It should be recognized that the result would involve payment of higher rates at certain times for savings funds and for mortgage credit.

If special public measures appear warranted to ease the impact of tightening general credit conditions on the availability or price of residential mortgage credit, such actions should be taken without sacrificing the objectives of monetary restraint. Moreover, the extent of the subsidy element involved should be revealed clearly, and the substitution of public for private credit should be minimized.

Specifically, the Board of Governors suggests, without necessarily endorsing them at this time, that the feasibility of the following proposals be considered as a means of promoting greater cyclical stability in the flow of new commitments for residential mortgages and in their direct and indirect costs:

1. Improve the liquidity of thrift institutions so as to withstand better the pressures that develop when general credit conditions tighten.

First, encourage the thrift institutions to issue a greater variety of longer-term liabilities, including savings certificates and other instruments designed to retain rate-conscious funds for a considerable period of time. Greater use of longer-term savings instruments would provide a better balance against the maturity structure of the assets of these institutions. It would help to limit the extreme volatility of savings flows such as those that developed in 1966. This approach would also have the advantage of permitting payment of higher returns marginally to longer-term accounts without increasing the yield to every depositor or shareholder.

Second, establish flexible secondary-reserve requirements for nonbank thrift institutions. These reserve requirements should be implemented so as to encourage a cushion of funds to be built up in appropriate periods of sustained general credit ease that could become available later when credit tightened. Reserve requirements would also provide a margin of relief against excessive reliance on advances from the Federal home loan banks as a supplementary means of expanding credit under conditions of monetary restraint. Experience during 1966 suggested that even the resources of the home loan banks can become particularly limited when general capital markets become congested. Finally, such reserve requirements would tend to maintain loan quality by discouraging excessive mortgage lending in easy-money periods. Excessive expansion of mortgage credit in one period can lead subsequently to a large, accumulated volume of illiquid foreclosed real estate.

Third, study the question of whether an increase in the investment options available to nonbank depositary institutions specializing in mortgage investment would enhance their mortgage lending potential at times when general interest rate levels are rising. An important aspect to be considered is the extent to which broader investment powers might facilitate greater flexibility in portfolio earning power and liquidity. Improved flexibility in earnings might permit lenders to limit savings outflows during periods of general credit tightness by making more rapid upward adjustments in their rates payable on new and existing savings accounts. Improved liquidity might permit the liquidation of short-term assets to provide additional funds for relending. Both, in turn, could allow these lenders to maintain a more stable flow of new mortgage commitments at such times.

A related subject to be studied in this connection is the Federal chartering of mutual savings banks and the broadening of their lending powers. Consideration of this subject would, of course, require attention to ways in which institutions set up as Federal savings banks—or converted to them—can bear in an appropriate manner the types of burdens applicable to commercial banks insofar as reserve-type requirements and taxation are concerned.

Fourth, increase the statutory and financial capacity of the Federal Home Loan Bank System to assist its members, by providing the home loan banks with greater flexibility to change rates on advances without relating them directly to the current cost of funds. Administrative consideration might also be given to achieving a better-balanced debt structure of the home loan banks

—thereby lessening the need to refinance outstanding indebtedness during periods of credit tightness, as was required in 1966.

2. Improve the marketability of residential mortgages so as to make them more attractive and to permit lenders to adjust their portfolio positions more readily to conditions of general credit restraint.

First, provide greater flexibility in setting maximum contract interest rates on FHA-insured and VA-guaranteed mortgages, if not eliminate these ceilings entirely. Authority should at least be provided to set rates so as to keep discounts on new loans within reasonable amounts at all times, subject only to the limits of State usury laws. If substantial discounts such as those that developed during 1966 could be avoided in the primary market, lenders would be more prone to invest in Federally underwritten loans when credit conditions tightened rather than in conventional mortgages or in other types of assets. Home sellers would be more willing to offer their dwellings on the market if there were no need to absorb substantial discounts, as in 1966, and home buyers would be obliged to resort less often to costlier methods of financing.

Second, explore through the FNMA the feasibility of setting up a trading desk so as to act as a dealer in residential mortgages. In this capacity FNMA would try to maintain a continuous market on both the buying and the selling side. If a trading desk operation should ultimately prove to be workable, it would help, among other things, to keep in daily, if not hourly, touch with market prices and yields, thereby facilitating the administration of flexible ceiling rates on new FHA and VA mortgages as well as providing a source of needed information for all mortgage brokers and investors. A more viable secondary market in general would help to facilitate portfolio adjustments that were difficult, at best, to arrange during 1966 in the absence of such a centralized exchange.

Third, study through the FHA the possibility of enhancing the marketability of FHA-insured mortgages so that they would trade more like corporate and municipal securities or Treasury obligations. In part, this step could involve reducing further, if not eliminating altogether, the residual non-insured risks now attached to Federally underwritten mortgages, insofar as ultimate holders other than originators are concerned.

3. Improve the allocation of residential mortgage funds so as to assure a more efficient distribution of credit during periods of general credit restraint.

Reexamine geographical and other barriers to mortgage investment so that appropriate steps can be taken to make them more nearly comparable or to do away with them altogether. This approach, subject to appropriate safeguards of loan quality, would involve a review of the mortgage investment powers and origination practices of financial institutions. It would also involve a consideration of what the Federal Government could do positively to encourage the States to bring their mortgage and foreclosure codes as close as possible to uniformity and to adopt more realistic usury statutes, where appropriate. All these differential institutional restrictions worked to inhibit both primary and secondary mortgage investment during 1966.

Among the two most important measures to examine are the possibility of modifying, if not eliminating, geographical and type-of-structure restrictions on mortgage lending by Federal- and State-chartered depositary institutions, and the achievement of closer uniformity in maximum statutory or regulatory loan-to-value ratios and loan maturities among different types of lenders.

4. Broaden sources of funds available for residential mortgage investment, thereby relying less on depositary institutions that tend to be vulnerable to conditions accompanying general credit restraint.

Encourage more sales of participation certificates or other instruments against pools of residential mortgages, subject to appropriate safeguards. Additional efforts in this direction, by Federal agencies or by large private lenders, should help to attract savings from such investors as pension funds or trusts that are reluctant to purchase and service individual mortgages outright and prefer to invest large blocks of funds in instruments payable only at maturity. Small investors, too, could be attracted to certificates that substitute the superior credit of the issuer for that of the mortgage borrower, and provide for investment in minimum amounts well below the $15,000-plus average now required for a single, newly made first mortgage.

PART 6

INTERNATIONAL MONETARY ARRANGEMENTS AND PROBLEMS

READING 38
ON THE INTERNATIONAL GOALS OF FEDERAL RESERVE POLICY

Deane Carson

The selections in this section give broad and deep coverage to the major financial problems facing the world in establishing viable and vigorous trade. As the first selection points out, these problems fall into two major categories: first, the provision of adequate supplies of liquid reserve assets to provide clearing funds for deficit and surplus nations; and second, the provision of a workable mechanism by which the exchange valves of various national currencies can adjust to market realities.

In the past few years, rather strong steps have been taken to resolve the problems associated with providing international liquidity *within the present international system of fixed exchange rates.*[1] This has been accomplished by changes in the International Monetary Fund Agreement to provide for additional paper reserves—the Spe-

cial Drawing Rights—to supplement gold reserves, dollar reserves, and the traditional IMF lending lines to individual countries.

Progress toward achieving a more viable solution to the second problem has also been made in the past few years. This progress has been principally intellectual rather than concrete. Not so long ago, for example, it was an act of gross heresy to suggest, within established central banking circles, that exchange rates should be made more flexible (let alone free) than the small degree of flexibility provided for in the original Bretton Woods Agreement. Today, central bankers and finance ministers are at least discussing the possibility of mechanisms to provide greater freedom of movement of exchange rates, a topic formerly considered only fit for ivory tower economists.[2] Professor Machlup, in his ar-

---

[1] The term fixed exchange rates is a misleading one, given the frequent, and often large, changes in exchange parities. Perhaps a more descriptively accurate term would be *managed* exchange rates.

[2] Wider bands around new exchange parities were agreed to in December, 1971.

ticle reprinted below, discusses some of the semantic as well as real differences in the various approaches to the solution of this part of the international financial problem.

As the title of this introductory article suggests, my concern is with the goal of the Federal Reserve System in the area of international financial arrangements. In large measure, the burden of my thesis also involves a semantic problem that nevertheless has very real implications for the role of the System.

If you will refer to your textbook on elementary economics, as well as to the money and banking text that you are currently using, the odds are that the discussion of the major goals of the Federal Reserve System include a statement to the effect that the international goal of the Fed is to maintain a reasonable equilibrium in the U.S. balance of payments. The wording may vary somewhat from the above specification, but the chances are that the author's statement is very close to it. This usage is extremely common, perhaps for no other reason than that the Federal Reserve authorities themselves use this terminology in official releases and reports to describe their goal in the international sector.

My quarrels with this terminology are (1) that it is an inaccurate specification of the real goal of the system; (2) that it confuses an *indicator*[3] with an ultimate goal; and (3) the above inaccuracy and confusion serve to hide some extremely important economic issues relating to the real goal of the system in this sphere.

Having asserted these points against the "balance of payments equilibrium" statement of the Fed's goal, my own specification of the goal is in order. Essentially, I contend this goal is in

reality one of "preserving, maintaining, and strengthening the present international monetary system in which the dollar serves as a major component of world currency reserves under International Monetary Fund rules, including managed exchange rates."

In my view, the U.S. balance-of-payments position in relation to the above specified goal bears an indicator role rather than a goal role. The balance of payments equilibrium, far from being a goal in itself, is simply one convenient indicator statistic to measure the impact of Federal Reserve policy actions on the ultimate viability of present monetary arrangements and mechanisms that rest on the external value of the dollar as a reserve currency. Balance-of-payments movements stand in relation to the real goal in analogous fashion to the role of the member-bank reserve base (or Treasury bill rates) as an indicator of the thrust of monetary policy toward the achievement of domestic goals of price-level stability and full employment. Certainly no one within or without the Federal Reserve System would specify the reserve base or interest rates as an ultimate goal, yet this is precisely equivalent to what has occurred in the international area.

If this were just a semantic problem, or the result of some convenient use of shorthand to express what everyone understands to be the real goal, the need for such clarification would be less compelling. The problem is not so simply resolved, however. By the confusion of an indicator for a goal in official pronouncements, not only students are misled about some very important allocative effects of the real goal, but also bankers in Iowa, lumber dealers in New Jersey, and newspaper editors in New York City.[4]

---

[3] Refer, for a discussion of the indicator problem to Thomas R. Saving, "Monetary Policy Targets and Indicators" in Part 3.

[4] I think it is safe to say, fortunately, that the Federal Reserve authorities are not confusing themselves by using the balance-of-payment equilibrium specification in their official publications. They are

Essentially, defense of the present international monetary system involves the protection of the United States as the world's banker. The cornerstone of this system is the willingness of the rest of the world to accumulate dollar assets—dollars per se and paper claims against the U.S. banks and government denominated in dollars—which they treat as liquid reserves to meet actual and potential balance of payments deficits. Our banks and government issue these liabilities in much the same way that they create claims on themselves to the account of domestic depositors. This business is quite profitable to the issuers of claims. As long as the market value of these claims does not significantly depreciate, foreign institutions and individuals will accept them as assets and international reserves.

The major source of these claims (assets of foreigners) is the U.S. balance-of-payments deficit. If this deficit were to become too large, in the sense that foreigners valued these assets below the official conversion rate, they would attempt to convert them to assets denominated in other currencies, leading to pressures on the entire international monetary system as now constituted. The total value of existing claims far exceeds the ability of the U.S. to redeem them under present exchange rates and reserve holdings; thus, confidence is the major key to the present system.

Obviously the banks that have issued claims to foreigners have a large stake in the maintenance of the present system. These are, by and large, the great money market banks. It is not surprising, then, that they are leading supporters of the present system and the Fed's emphasis on the balance-of-payments position of the U.S. As the world's bankers, they profit from the status quo.

The benefits derived from the position of the dollar as a reserve currency are not equally distributed. Aside from the nebulous prestige value of the arrangement that may accrue to all who value world financial leadership as a symbol of world power, the pecuniary benefits devolve largely on the money-market banks. New York City as the foremost financial center of the world depends on the dollar as a reserve currency, and the business this brings to Wall Street is not inconsiderable. Smaller banks in outlying areas do not benefit commensurately.

On the other side of the coin, the costs of the system are spread rather widely. Take for example the case in which the efforts of the Federal Reserve to defend the dollar require it to take action that depresses domestic employment and growth. The costs of unemployment and underutilization of capacity are not borne by all in equal measure. Generally speaking, these costs will fall most heavily on the young, the unskilled, and the minority workers—although this is a gross simplification. The general point, however, seems valid: Costs and benefits of the present system of world finance are unevenly distributed. Recognition of this fact casts a somewhat different light on the goal of the Federal Reserve System.*

---

prone to justify their little deceit, however, on the grounds that the public can understand the necessity of balance-of-payments equilibrium, but could not be expected to appreciate the sophisticated intricacies of international monetary arrangements.

* Editor's Note: Since this was written, the U.S. has abrogated its commitment to purchase gold from central banks at a fixed rate of $35 an ounce, and during the late summer and early fall of 1971, exchange rates have floated. In December, the Treasury agreed to seek Congressional approval of a new gold price of $38 an oz. The system itself is, therefore, much the same, with new fixed exchange rates.

READING 39

THE PROBLEM OF INTERNATIONAL EQUILIBRIUM

Council of Economic Advisers

The rapid growth of international trade and capital flows has brought into sharper focus two essential requirements for an adequate world monetary system. In the first place, there must be sufficient official liquidity to finance temporary imbalances. Second, the terms of exchange between national currencies should be sufficiently stable to foster confidence in international dealings, but not so rigid that they preclude the adjustments that may be needed from time to time as trading patterns and terms of trade undergo inevitable change. The urgency of progress in both these directions has been underlined in recent years by the increasing frequency of international financial disturbances. The *ad hoc* solutions for these have often been to impose various restraints that now threaten to obstruct further advances in the efficiency of the international economy.

The past year has seen important improvements, especially in the direction of greater liquidity. Years of discussion and negotiations culminated in final agreement to create Special Drawing Rights, a new international reserve asset. Now, for the first time in history, there is an international arrangement for systematically creating reserves. Also, the official parities of two important currencies were adjusted during 1969. France reduced the exchange value of the French franc in August. Following repeated inflows of speculative capital—most notably, the flood of between $4 billion and $5 billion in May and over $1.5 billion in September—the Germans allowed the mark to float upward at the end of September, and a new, higher parity was chosen in October. These two parity adjustments, together with the devaluation of the British pound in November 1967, have resulted in a pattern of exchange rates that is more closely in line with international competitive positions. A lessening of strains and instability in the international financial

Source: From Council of Economic Advisers, *Annual Report*, 1970, pp. 131–142.

situation has followed, and the effects are apparent in the exchange markets. Most notable, perhaps, has been the narrowing of the discounts and premiums on forward exchange, which had become abnormally large before these adjustments in parities were made.

The agreement to create Special Drawing Rights provides a fundamental and lasting method for dealing with the liquidity question, but the changes in exchange rates during the past year do not assure an equally permanent solution to the adjustment problem. Some of the major maladjustments have been relieved for the time being, but basic forces that could produce new disequilibria continue to operate. Nations attach different degrees of importance to different objectives for economic policy. Changes in technology and demands have varying effects among countries. We should use the period of reduced tensions, which recent currency realignments and advances in providing for needed liquidity have granted us, to consider how the international financial system might be made more capable of adjusting to possible future shifts in the world economy.

I. INTERNATIONAL LIQUIDITY: SPECIAL DRAWING RIGHTS

Consideration of how the international economic system might become better able to cope with changes in the relative positions of individual economies must begin with the landmark decision to establish Special Drawing Rights (SDR's). As trade and investment grow, countries tend to need higher reserves. If the reserves coming into the system are insufficient, general success in meeting goals for national reserves becomes impossible, and the outcome is destructive competition for reserves. Domestic and international policies are warped by a preoccupation with the balance of payments. Reductions In barriers to trade and investment become ever more difficult; indeed, international barriers may be increased as a result of the desire to protect national reserves.

To avoid these undesirable consequences international studies were started in 1964, focusing on the possibilities of creating a new reserve asset. The establishment of Special Drawing Rights resulted from these studies and from protracted negotiations later on involving the Group of Ten and the International Monetary Fund. SDR's are created by the IMF and allocated among the member countries in proportion to their Fund quotas. Because they are counted as an increase in reserves of the member countries, incentives to compete for reserves should be correspondingly lessened.

The preliminary steps to create the SDR's were discussed in the Council's *Annual Reports* for 1968 and 1969. During the past year, two final steps were taken in preparation for activation in January 1970. The amendment to the Articles of Agreement of the International Monetary Fund creating Special Drawing Rights was ratified during August by the required 67 member countries having 80 percent of the voting power of the IMF. The next step resolved the important question of the appropriate amounts of SDR's. The deficient growth of international reserves made it desirable that initial allocations of Special Drawing Rights should be substantial. The decision by the International Monetary Fund to create $9.5 billion in Special Drawing Rights between 1970 and 1972 should permit an adequate but not excessive growth of official reserves.

In using SDR's, countries are expected to fulfill the "requirement of need." SDR's are to be transferred to meet balance-of-payments needs and cover reserve losses, but not solely to change the composition of reserves. A country may use SDR's to purchase balances of its own currency from another participant, if the other participant agrees. Another set of provisions enables the Fund to guide SDR transactions from using countries to countries designated as eligible recipients on the basis of a number of criteria, including their balance-of-payments and reserve position. No country is bound to accept additional SDR's if its holdings already amount to three times its cumulative allocations.

During 1969 the Executive Board of the International Monetary Fund also agreed to recommend an increase in quotas in the Fund by a total of $7.6 billion, or 35.5 percent. While an increase in IMF quotas does not, in itself, result in an increase in "owned" international reserves, it does create a larger pool of international credit, which acts as a partial substitute for reserves. (When countries can borrow to finance temporary balance-of-payments deficits, they are under less pressure to acquire and hold reserves.) As part of the general increase in quotas, the U.S. quota will, if Congress approves, rise from $5,160 million to $6,700 million, an increase of 29.8 percent. Special arrangements were made in order that the proportion of the quotas held by less developed countries should not fall as much as they would with a mechanical application of the usual criteria based on trade and GNP. These countries' share of the total quotas will decrease only from 28.3 percent to 27.7 percent, and in absolute terms they will rise from $6,032 million to $8,014 million.

II.   INTERNATIONAL ADJUSTMENT

Creating the Special Drawing Rights and increasing the IMF quotas will give nations more time to redress their balance-of-payments disequilibria in an orderly fashion, but the question of the most effective way to correct imbalances is still open. In principle, they can be corrected by three basic measures applied singly or in combination. First, domestic policy can be altered. Countries with a surplus can adopt more expansive policies and thereby increase their imports and reduce their exports. Countries with deficits can restrict domestic demand, thereby reducing their imports and increasing their exports. Second, governments can take direct action by adopting certain selective measures. To correct deficits, countries can increase tariff rates, or institute import quotas or controls on capital movements and tourist expenditures. In countries where a surplus exists, governments can reduce tariffs, remove other obstructions to imports, or encourage the outflow of capital. Third, exchange rates can be altered (although, as a practical matter, the United States cannot adjust its exchange rate). Countries may aim to correct deficits by adjusting the exchange rate of their currencies downward, a move that will discourage imports and encourage exports. Surplus countries can appreciate the exchange rate of their currencies, thereby encouraging imports and discouraging exports. The measures a country selects and its quickness in applying them will depend on its willingness and ability to finance deficits out of reserves and borrowings, or to permit surpluses to build up reserves.

Each of the three general methods for redressing balance-of-payments disequilibria has its advantages and disadvantages. How much international synchronization of domestic policies is desirable depends partly on whether policies to achieve internal stabilization will also restore a balance-of-payments equilibrium. It has been argued, for instance, that maintaining fixed exchange rates encourages countries to keep inflationary pressures under control, thus reinforcing "discipline." There is no automatic assurance, however, that the internal adjustment required to correct a country's balance of payments will also contribute to domestic stability. A balance-of-payments surplus might coincide with a domestic boom, in which case the restrictive policies needed by the domestic economy would further enlarge the surplus in the country's external payments. Another country might face the reverse of that situation, with underemployment at home and a deficit in its external payments. In such instances, there will be strong pressure to adopt direct action affecting international transactions, and, in some cases, to alter the exchange rate.

A. Direct Actions

International adjustment may be attempted through direct actions aimed at any of the components of the balance of payments, but the nature and limitations of such controls must be fully recognized. Although at times they may relieve an urgent situation, their function is essentially palliative. Once established, moreover, it often proves difficult either to deactivate them or to integrate them effectively into longer range solutions.

At the time the International Monetary Fund was established, capital transactions were believed to be a possible source of international disequilibrium, and capital controls were therefore considered preferable to current account controls as a means of correcting the balance of payments. Capital controls, however, also have their costs. The case for free international investment is similar to that for free international trade. Broader and freer markets for both capital and goods contribute to economic efficiency, the growth of the world economy, and a more rapid improvement of living standards generally. Capital controls create serious administrative difficulties and are likely to inspire a search for loopholes in their provisions. Once set up, they have a tendency to enmesh the economy in an ever-widening circle of restrictions rather than to develop conditions that would obviate the need for curbs. Furthermore, they are inconsistent with a liberal approach to economic policy and are irksome to business.

In his message of April 4, 1969, the President affirmed the Administration's intention to move away from controls on capital movements. The program to restrict direct investment abroad was relaxed; the minimum amount of investment, that is, the leeway before restraints are applicable, was raised from $200,000 to $1 million. This measure reduced the number of firms required to furnish quarterly reports under the program from 3,400 to 650. Furthermore, an optional earnings quota was established which allows companies to reinvest up to 30 percent of their foreign earnings. The Federal Reserve guidelines for banks were revised to give them more flexibility in financing U.S. exports and to resolve some equity problems. For 1970, further changes were made in the Federal Reserve program to encourage the financing of exports. The former minimum of $1 million under the Foreign Direct Investment Program was raised to $5 million, so long as investment over $1 million is used in the less developed countries.

On the trade side, temporary quantitative restrictions on imports are sanctioned under the GATT as a method for protecting the balance of payments. Since quantitative restrictions are particularly likely to disrupt trade, however, there has been some tendency to use import surcharges or a combination of import surcharges and export subsidies in their place. In theory, the imposition of a uniform import surcharge combined with an equivalent export subsidy is close to a change in the exchange rate in its effects on the trade balance, and therefore almost as neutral as an exchange rate adjustment with respect to the allocation of resources. In one important respect, however, these measures are not equivalent to an adjustment in the exchange rate. The latter applies to all international transactions, including tourist expenditures and other invisibles, as well as capital items. In contrast, the combination of import surcharges and export grants applies only to merchandise trade. Furthermore, almost inevitably there are pressures to exclude certain items from the surcharge-grant system, with the consequence that specified industries enjoy a degree of protection not granted to others.

It is appropriate for countries having a surplus to reduce their restrictions on imports and on capital flows, and a number of countries have taken such steps. (Countries may also undertake unilateral reduction in import barriers, or a speedup of reductions already agreed upon, to reduce domestic inflationary pressures, as Austria and Canada did during 1969, and as Switzerland plans to do in early 1970.) Although direct restrictions on imports or capital flows to correct deficits will normally have the undesirable side effect of inhibiting mutually advantageous international exchange, direct action to deal with a country's surplus by reducing barriers to trade or capital flows will have favorable side effects and will also lessen the likelihood of restrictive measures by deficit nations. Where possible, therefore, direct actions should take the form of a relaxation of controls and restraints by countries with a surplus rather than the introduction or tightening of such measures by deficit countries.

B. Exchange Rate Adjustments

Proper management of domestic economic policy, as indicated above, will always be sufficient to avoid balance-of-payments difficulties. Other factors besides improper demand management may create imbalances. Where the economic policies required for external equilibrium differ greatly from those that promote price stability and high employment at home, the Bretton Woods system provides for discrete adjustments in exchange parities. In practice, however, countries have been reluctant to make such adjustments promptly, and their delays have often generated speculative movements of funds and use of restrictionist measures. The frequency of international financial crises in recent years has focused attention on the possibility of adjusting exchange rates in a calmer and more orderly manner.

At the Annual Meeting of the Governors of the International Monetary Fund in September, the Managing Director announced that the Fund will continue its study and appraisal of proposals for "limited flexibility" in exchange rates. The Secretary of the Treasury made it clear that the United States will actively participate in and contribute to this study. Although the results of such studies cannot be foreseen, it is possible to point out some of the technical and policy problems that will need clarification.

Within the general framework of the Bretton Woods system there is scope for greater flexibility of exchange rates than has been evident in practice. It has been suggested that parity adjustments could be made more frequently and hence in smaller amounts. Some official interest has also focused on proposals to widen the band within which exchange rates would be permitted to fluctuate around parities, and to provide mechanisms, like the so-called crawling peg or sliding parity, that would make movements in parity more gradual than they have been in the past.

C. Wider Bands

Interest in proposals for wider bands has concentrated on the possible effects of a modest widening—perhaps changing the present maximum range of 1 percent on each side of parity to permit a range of 2 percent. In itself this would do little to improve the adjustment mechanism. What it might do is to help insulate domestic money markets from movements of interest-sensitive short-term funds and reduce the largely one-sided speculative options that occur under the present system. However, a modest widening of the band can have no substantial effect in reducing troublesome flows of short-term money unless abrupt changes in parities are considered unlikely. If people commonly believe that the equilibrium exchange rate falls well outside the band, the broader band in itself can do little to discourage movements of short-term funds.*

For a number of reasons, widening of the present bands cannot wholly guard against international imbalances sufficiently severe to throw established parities into question. As already pointed out, countries do not attach equal weight to the different objectives of economic policy. Some nations are more tolerant of inflation—or of increases in unemployment—than others. Governments also differ in their ability to influence the trend of costs and prices effectively. And, even if general price trends were identical in all countries, balance could be disturbed by changes in demand and supply patterns for internationally traded goods, or differing trends in government purchases and receipts. This situation has encouraged some to ask whether sta-

bility of the international monetary system would be improved if smaller and more frequent changes in parity were made in the hope of avoiding large discrete jumps.

D. Smoothly Moving Parities

A number of proposals have been made for smooth and gradual adjustments in parity of up to 2 or 3 percent per year. While these proposals for "crawling pegs" differ in technical detail, they present in common a number of the fundamental questions that figure in debates on this subject. One important issue turns on the degree of national discretion to be encouraged or permitted in altering exchange rates. Another question is whether smoothly moving parities would tie interest rates more closely to international developments and thus reduce the independence of domestic monetary policies. It is also feared that parity movements would weaken the external discipline on domestic policies. And there has been concern about whether these movements might complicate the conditions under which international business transactions take place.

The various proposals for slowly moving parities range from a completely permissive, discretionary authority to a completely automatic, mandatory system. A purely discretionary system might be no more successful than present arrangements in preventing fundamental imbalances that require abrupt changes in parity. Experience suggests that, left to their own discretion, individual countries might postpone parity changes until political or financial developments made them imperative. On the other hand, a fully automatic system might be unacceptable to nations that regard control over their exchange rate as an established prerogative of national sovereignty.

* Ed. note: In December, 1971, the maximum range was set at 2.25 percent on either side of official rates.

A possible compromise may lie between complete discretion and binding rules. One solution might be to develop presumptive rules that, with a degree of multilateral surveillance, would guide countries in making appropriate adjustments in parities.

The objective criteria most frequently recommended for incorporation into such presumptive rules are based on the behavior of spot and forward exchange rates, and on the changes in reserve levels, defined in various ways —for example, to include or not include short-term funds held by commercial banks. Typical proposals have urged that desirable parity changes be indicated by a moving average of past spot rates or by reserve movements. An advantage of including some measure of reserve movements in the criteria is that rules on direct official intervention in the spot or forward market might then be unnecessary. (If exchange rates were the only criterion, such rules might be deemed necessary, since exchange rates can be influenced by official intervention.) Much technical work remains to be done, however, before satisfactory criteria for parity changes can be established.

A number of other questions about the most desirable form of a moving parity system also require further study. For instance, how general would participation in the system need to be? An initial step, should one or a few countries be encouraged to experiment with greater flexibility? Would slowly moving parities work best if they were accompanied by a widening of the band around parity? What special problems might arise for regional economic groupings?

In addition to these technical points, questions have been asked about the fundamental value of any form of slowly moving parities or widening of the band in improving the operation of the international monetary system. A full discussion of all of these issues would go beyond the scope of this chapter, but five of the most commonly raised questions about the desirability of greater exchange rate flexibility will be considered briefly. These ask what effects a greater flexibility in exchange rates would have on monetary independence; whether internal discipline would suffer; what provision would be made for forward cover on exchange transactions; whether small but frequent exchange rate adjustments would actually be effective; and what the implications of greater exchange-rate flexibility would be for the U.S. dollar.

One criticism of smoothly moving parities has been that they would bind monetary policy too closely to international conditions. If, for example, it was generally believed that a country's parity would move downward at the maximum permitted annual rate—say, 2 percent—for an extended time and that its spot rate would move down accordingly, there would be an incentive for capital to move out of the country unless domestic interest rates were 2-percent higher than foreign rates.

This criticism assumes that movements in the spot rate are predictable. Under certain conditions they might be. If sliding parities were used in an attempt to overcome an already existing and sizable disequilibrium, the direction of future movements in the exchange rate would be clear. This, however, is a purpose for which sliding parities are not particularly well suited. Alternatively, movement of the spot rate might be predictable if the equilibrium rate were gradually rising or falling over time. If a downward crawl in the exchange rate resulted from a more rapid rate of inflation in one country than in others, that country's domestic capital markets would tend to reflect these inflationary pressures, and the higher interest rates could exist for domestic reasons. The need to have higher interest rates because of the crawling peg might not, therefore, represent a restraint on domestic policy. Similarly, in countries with less inflation, there would be a tendency for interest rates to be lower whether there was a crawling peg or not.

Different rates of inflation are not, of course, the only forces that would cause a crawling peg to move. If the par value of a country's currency were too high for other reasons, a predictable one-way downward crawl might raise complications, with international capital flows impelling the monetary authorities to keep interest rates above the level that they consider desirable for domestic reasons, perhaps over fairly long periods. In any event, the important comparison lies between the policy restraint that might result from the crawl and the policy restraint that now occurs when an exchange rate is generally considered out of line, and when capital flows may consequently be stimulated by the expectation of a large discreet adjustment in the exchange rate. Because such adjustments offer the prospect of immediate sizeable gains, the expectation that they will occur has often been an important motive behind short-term capital flows.

Furthermore, the initial capital flows in response to expected movements in the exchange rate will greatly overstate the magnitude of continuing flows. Once financial positions adjust to these changed incentives, capital movements would probably become much smaller, and the cessation of the crawl in due course would eliminate the incentives. Finally, the reversible nature of most liquid capital movements means that problems arising from short-term capital flows under a sliding parity could to some extent be dealt with by official financing instead of adjustments in interest rates.

Another concern about slowly moving parities centers on whether they would reduce the disciplinary effects that reserve losses may have on nations needing to deal with domestic inflation. Since upward movements in the par value would have no such effects, it has been suggested that greater flexibility be allowed only in moving exchange rates upward. Indeed, an upward movement of the exchange rate would reduce inflationary pressures and facilitate the maintenance of domestic price stability in countries having a surplus. For countries with deficits, the validity of the discipline argument is difficult to assess in general terms. The response of countries to reserve losses varies considerably. Most countries have been reluctant to devalue. Some have adopted more restrained domestic policies as well as imposing restrictions on international transactions. The problems that might be caused by permitting a downward crawl therefore do not lend themselves to easy generalization.

A third question has to do with the operation of the forward market when there is greater flexibility in exchange rates. A change in the international financial system that, whatever its merits, aroused even more uncertainty about exchange rates, might have an adverse effect on trade and investment. On the other hand, to the extent that greater flexibility in the exchange rate promoted better adjustment and that speculative expectations became more stabilized, demands by international traders to cover their exchange risk in the forward market actually fluctuate less than they do at present. Moreover, as the chances of an abrupt and large adjustment in the exchange rate are reduced, the consequences of being caught without forward cover become correspondingly less serious.

Another question is whether small but frequent changes in parity would be an effective means of promoting adjustments, since the evidence suggests that it takes time for trade to respond fully to a change in exchange rates; that is, elasticities in international trade are generally higher in the long run than in the short run. This lag is, of course, more relevant in situations where small changes in the exchange rate are used to correct already existing imbalances than where such changes are used to prevent a disequilibrium from developing. That being so, small but frequent adjustments of parity would probably be more useful in maintaining approximate equilibrium than in restoring a balance after a substantial disequilibrium has been allowed to develop.

Because of the central role of the U.S. dollar in the international monetary system, the United States cannot move its own parity with respect to other currencies. This implies that the United States would be particularly concerned with the direction in which other countries were moving their parities. A bias in one direction or the other could lead to an overvaluation or undervaluation of the dollar. Historically, devaluations of currencies with respect to the dollar have been more frequent and on average larger than revaluations. While to some extent this may reflect greater price stability in the United States than in many foreign countries, the danger of systematic overvaluation as a result of greater flexibility should be guarded against. This could be done by appropriate specification of the presumptive rules mentioned earlier.

III. THE DOLLAR AND INTERNATIONAL EQUILIBRIUM

The United States has the world's largest economy, and its exports and imports are larger than those of any other nation. These facts alone would make economic developments and policy here a matter of great concern to the world economy. A further point, however, is that the dollar has become the principal international currency. Much of the world's trade is denominated in dollars, and throughout the world dollars are widely held as reserves and as working balances to accommodate trade and investment.

Because the dollar plays a central role in the international monetary system, the United States is more constrained in its adjustment policies than other countries. Since the United States does not have primary control over any market exchange rate, other nations in effect determine the exchange value of the dollar. It is generally recognized that exchange rates are a matter of international concern, and the United States is consulted through the IMF and other organizations regarding the appropriateness of exchange rate adjustments. Yet the United States clearly exercises only indirect influence over the exchange value of its currency, in contrast to the more direct control exercised by other countries.

The central position of the dollar in the international system was not the result of any conscious decision or strategy on the part of the U.S. Government. It was the natural consequence of the size, strength, and stability of the U.S. economy, traits which were especially evident during the early years after the Second World War. This central role provides benefits for the United States, but it also entails problems and responsibilities.

For some years now, concern over the state of the U.S. balance of payments has been evident. The discussions of a dollar shortage in the 1950's have given way to discussions of the U.S. payments deficits. Nevertheless, in this same interval the predominant change in the exchange parities of other currencies has been downward (not upward) in relation to the dollar.

There have been only three upward changes in the past decade—the revaluations of the German mark by 5 percent in 1961 and 9.3 percent in 1969, and the revaluation of the Dutch guilder by 5 percent in 1961.

In part—perhaps in large part—this paradox can be attributed to the fact that international liquidity needed to grow, and a large part of this growth has been through official accumulation of dollars. To be sure, not every payments imbalance is an indication of a low overall level of liquidity. But when many countries simultaneously begin to feel that their balance-of-payments positions are too weak, it is evident that there is a general shortage of liquidity. It was precisely to eliminate this shortage and the resultant danger of a destructive competition for reserves that the Special Drawing Rights were instituted. The introduction of SDR's should moderate the general tendency to consider that official reserves are too low.

It is also important to the United States and to the international community that the international adjustment mechanism be strengthened. Failure to achieve this could have serious consequences. New strains on the world monetary system could develop unless our payments position assures foreign monetary authorities and private traders that the dollar will remain strong. The present situation, in which we maintain an official settlements surplus only because of large-scale foreign borrowing by U.S. corporations and banks at high interest rates, creates a feeling of some uneasiness here and abroad, and observers generally regard the present structure of the U.S. international accounts as abnormal and temporary.

Whatever the United States does is felt in other countries. We, therefore, have every reason to consider the effects that our economic policies will have on them. Continuing prosperity and economic stability abroad depends in part on stable growth in the United States. Because of our size, other countries feel the influence of inflationary or deflationary pressures originating in this country. If U.S. inflation were to continue at its recent levels, some countries might face the painful necessity of choosing between the inflationary consequences of a large export surplus or an upward adjustment of their exchange rates. For international as well as domestic reasons, it is most important that the United States restore internal balance and achieve sustainable, noninflationary growth. This responsibility, along with reasonably free access to U.S. markets, constitutes our predominant obligation toward international economic well-being.

ON TERMS, CONCEPTS, THEORIES AND STRATEGIES IN THE DISCUSSION OF GREATER FLEXIBILITY OF EXCHANGE RATES

Fritz Machlup

I am known, or even perhaps notorious, for my fondness of semantic exercises. Some of my friends will probably wince at reading this lead sentence and will mutter under their breath, "There he goes again!" Fear not! I shall not unravel 57 varieties of meaning of flexibility, 15 of band, 14 of crawl, and 13 of peg. I shall try to do only the most necessary cleaning-up job preparatory for a discussion in which the participants will not want to waste time by misunderstanding one another as they use words in ambiguous ways.

Not that I shall attempt to dictate to anyone in which of the possible meanings he should use an ambiguous term. There should be freedom of speech, even freedom of vague and ambiguous speech. Still, it may help if we know where some of the semantic traps are hidden; for we can then be on guard and, if we *want* to be understood, we can steer clear of the most likely confusions.

Besides these objectives, my comments are intended to serve still other purposes. In some instances I shall propose distinctions that seem helpful in getting a sharper focus on the issues before us. Finally, I shall warn against exaggerated claims which partisans sometimes make for the faultless working of a recommended system, new or old. The question is not of perfection but only of comparative troublesomeness.

I. PEGS AND PARITIES

Since a great deal is said in the current discussions about pegs and pari-

Source: Reprinted from *Banca Nazionale del Lavoro, Quarterly Review,* March 1970, pp. 3–22.

ties, we ought to decide whether we understand these words to mean the same thing or different things.

Since John Williamson spoke about crawling pegs where James Meade spoke about sliding parities, one would be justified in regarding the two terms as synonymous. Yet, there are many currencies (more than 20) for which no par value (parity) has been established but whose exchange value in terms of the dollar has been "pegged" by the respective monetary authorities; and there are other currencies (about 15) for which the par value agreed with the International Monetary Fund has been disregarded, yet the dollar exchange rate has been "pegged" (though the peg was changed from time to time). Thus, we had better accept the fact that in many situations the peg is not a parity and the parity is not the peg.

If we use the word peg to denote the intervention rate, that is, the exchange rate at which the monetary authorities of a country intervene in the market in order to keep the currency from falling or rising in the foreign-exchange market, then we should really speak of two pegs: a selling price and a buying price of the dollar. Where the band between the maximum selling price and the minimum buying price is narrow— say, 2 per cent, as stipulated in the Fund Agreement—it would perhaps be excessive pedantry to speak of the "two pegs" around the parity. But if the band is widened, it may be quite practical to speak of the two extreme official intervention rates as a pair of pegs.

We cannot legislate about the "correct" use of these words. In most instances we shall not be greatly mistaken if we understand pegs to be parities or close to parities, and parities to be maintained by means of pegs. But we ought to be on guard for exceptional situations in which pegs and parities are not the same. In what follows here I shall go slow on the word "peg" and speak mostly of parities. But I want it to be understood that these need not be par values agreed with the Fund, but may be average intervention rates fixed for longer or shorter periods.

For a certain class of countries a very particular system of adjusting the exchange rate has developed. In countries in which the rate of price inflation has been so fast that long delays in exchange-rate alignment would lead to intolerable misallocations of productive resources, frequent readjustments of exchange rates are strongly indicated. Some of these countries have no fixed parities (or have disregarded what was once announced as the "par value" of their currencies). They may, however, have official exchange rates, pegged temporarily and changed periodically, perhaps as often as once or twice a month. Such a change cannot be described as a glide (or crawl) of the peg, because it is too big to qualify for these descriptions. On the other hand, the designation "jumping peg" is also out of place, since "jump" has the connotation of a sudden abrupt change after a long delay. Borrowing from the vocabulary employed to characterize the rate of price increase as creeping, trotting, and galloping price inflations, some commentators speak of the "trotting peg" as descriptive of the system that provides for fast movements of the official exchange rate for currencies in a process of trotting inflation.

The trotting peg will not concern us much in a discussion that is chiefly designed to deal with the currencies of countries with only creeping price inflations. These countries usually have valid official par values of their currencies and for these countries the choice is between jumping or gliding parities.

II. ALTERNATIVE EXCHANGE-RATE SYSTEMS

It will be helpful to have terminological consistency in talking about alternative exchange-rate systems. I propose that we distinguish systems with *unchangeable* parities, *abruptly adjustable* parities, *gradually adjustable* parities, and *no* parities. The phrase "fixed parities" ought to be avoided, because it covers both unchangeable and adjustable parities, and is therefore ambiguous. Alternative designations would be "jumping parities" for abruptly (or discretely) adjustable parities, and "gliding parities" for gradually adjustable. The category of no parities includes freely flexible (floating) exchange rates, but it includes also exchange rates influenced by unsystematic official interventions in the exchange market and by restrictions on certain types of transactions, so that the absence of official parities is not equivalent to "free flexibility."

Perhaps a comment on unchangeable parities is in order. Parities are unchangeable only under gold-coin standards where gold coins comprise a substantial part of the monetary circulation. Under the gold-bullion standard, where gold does not circulate as currency but is bought and sold only by the monetary authorities, the official price of gold can be changed and parities are no longer unchangeable. To be sure, there can be systems that prescribe, by means of unchangeable legal requirements, fixed ratios between the supply of money and the official gold holdings (with an unchangeable price of gold). Such orthodox gold-standard systems would be compatible with unchangeable exchange rates, but could endure only if the people in the countries concerned were willing to forget about stable rates of employment, economic growth, and several other national objectives. It is a waste of time to discuss this theoretical possibility. Whether we like it or not, it is not in the cards. This reduces the choices to three: jumping, gliding, or no parities.

III. RATE OF CRAWL AND WIDTH OF BAND

When is a change a *jump* and when is it a *glide?* Or, in more formal language, what is a *discrete* adjustment of the parity and what is a *gradual* one?

There is no historical precedent to guide our terminological decision. Economic theory suggests that we call changes in foreign-exchange rates *gradual* if the effects that confident expectations of such changes would have upon the foreign-exchange market could be offset by relatively modest differentials between the interest rates prevailing in the countries concerned. I propose to use 3 per cent per year and 1 per cent at a time as the watershed and to call adjustments of exchange rates that exceed these limits discrete or abrupt. In a stricter sense, adjustment of a parity can be called gradual only if the upper limit of the rate of change is a small fraction of 1 per cent per week or month. The most widely cited plan for a gliding parity proposes as an upper limit for adjustments 1/26 of 1 per cent per week (which, if continued in the same direction, would cumulate to a little over 2 per cent a year). A recent variant would set the upper limit at 1/10 of 1 per cent for any half-month (which would cumulate to a maximum change of about 2½ per cent per year).

Discrete changes in the parities of major currencies, under the Bretton Woods rules, have varied from the 5 per cent upvaluations of the German mark and the Dutch guilder in 1961 to the 38.7 per cent devaluation of the French franc in 1949. Most of the parity jumps came as weekend gambols, usually after months of persistent rumors, private speculations, and official disavowals.

Both with discrete and with gradual adjustments of the parity, the exchange rates may be allowed to deviate from parity to some extent. The band of permissible or permitted fluctuations may be wide or narrow. These adjectives call for specification. Since the Fund Agreement permits fluctuations of up to 1 per cent on either side of parity, that is, a band of 2 per cent of parity vis-à-vis the dollar, one might speak of a "wider" band whenever its total width exceeds 2 per cent. Since Switzerland, however, permits—on paper, though usually not in practice—fluctuations within a band of 3 per cent, it is more convenient to take this as the starting point for any "widening" of the band. A wider band will mean, therefore, one with a total width of more than 3 per cent. Most discussions of a wider band visualize spreads of 4, 5, 6, 8, or 10 per cent.

To define the band in terms of total width rather than in such phrases as "x per cent either side of parity" is preferable, because it would be possible to have asymmetrical distances from parity. Some monetary authorities may wish to allow the price of the dollar in their own exchange market to fall by 4 per cent, but to rise by only 2 per cent from parity. This would still be a band 6 per cent wide, but the parity would not be in its center.

On what kind of considerations would one favor a band with the parity off center, that is, a band with asymmetrical distances of the edges from the parity? Evidently such an arrangement would appeal only to a monetary authority that regards deviations of the exchange rates of its currency from parity more likely to be in one direction than in the other. German economic experts, for example, would probably not think that the market rates of the German mark will fall below parity so often and stay there for so long a time as they may rise and stay above parity. If then, because of comparative rates of demand inflation at home and abroad, the pressure of the free market is expected to be far more consistently in the direction of a strong posture of the German mark, there is sense in providing more leeway for the market value of the mark to rise than to fall.

If the differences in the rates of demand inflation persist for several years, a band around parity, however wide and however asymmetrical, would not provide flexibility for very long. The exchange rate of the German mark would reach the upper edge of the band and stay there, forcing the German monetary authorities to accept "imported inflation." The only escape would be a crawl, or glide, of the parity. With the differences in inflation rates always in the same direction, the glide would be in one direction only: upward.

The idea of a gliding parity has little appeal to bank and Treasury officials in countries with consistently higher-than-average rates of inflation. They fear the downward glide of the parity might accelerate the price inflation and create a lasting inflationary bias in the policies of business and organized labor. If the system of the gliding parity is more readily acceptable in countries with strong aversion to price inflation than in countries unable to avoid higher speeds of creeping inflation, the one-way crawl may have better chances of realization than two-way variability of the parity.

If the parities of various currencies are expressed in terms of the dollar, a band of x per cent for fluctuations of the dollar-exchange rate of any currency implies that the exchange rates between any two other currencies can fluctuate by 2x per cent. If, for example, at some date the French franc were at the upper edge of the band vis-à-vis the dollar, and the Italian lira at the lower edge, and subsequently the franc were to fall to the lower edge and the lira to rise to the upper edge, each therefore moving across the entire band, the cross-rate between franc and lira would have changed by a percentage twice the width of the band for dollar-rate fluctuations. This large spread in permissible cross-rates makes some practitioners shudder when they hear proposals to widen the band for the dollar-rate to 10 per cent: it would mean 20 per cent for the exchange rates between any two currencies for which the 10 per cent band vis-à-vis the dollar is used.

IV. GREATER FLEXIBILITY

"Greater" in the expression "greater flexibility" is intended to mean "more than exists at present" but "less than unlimited." If variations of exchange rates are to be limited, this implies the need for interventions by the monetary authorities through buying or selling the chosen "intervention currency," usually the dollar, whenever its price threatens to rise above or fall below the chosen limits. These limits would be set by the upper and lower edges of the band around the parity or by the maximum allowable adjustment of the parity, or both. Some monetary authorities believe that it is expedient, or even necessary, for them to intervene in the exchange market even well within the limits. Other authorities disagree, and both sides claim that their views (theories) are firmly based on practical experience. Without attempting here to argue one or the other side of the controversial question, I want to explain an expression used by economists: they speak of "managed flexibility" if the monetary authorities intervene in the market by buying or selling foreign

exchange before the edges of the band or the limit to an allowed change of parity are reached.

A compromise regarding the scope of market interventions has been proposed in the form of a band within a band. The inner band, say, 3 per cent of parity, would be entirely unmanaged, a range for free-market forces to operate, without any official sales or purchases; the two surrounding rims or border-bands, each, say, 1½ per cent wide, would be the ranges in which the monetary authorities could play in the market in order to meet their obligation to keep the market "orderly" (or to satisfy their feeling of importance, as the free-marketeers would put it). This would represent managed flexibility around a core of unmanaged flexibility.

Changes in parity would always be managed in the sense that only market interventions would assure that the change is of a particular magnitude, not more and not less. In a system that combines a wider band with a crawl of the parity, the move of the parity may be within the band around the previous parity, so that it would be possible for the actual exchange rate to remain unchanged despite the official adjustment of the parity. In such a case the authorities would not have to intervene at all, unless they wanted to for some reason, real or apparent. In any case, an adjustment of the parity, however small, would move the band of *permissible* exchange-rate fluctuations, even if the *actual* exchange rate, being well inside the band, were unchanged.

I have said that greater flexibility still meant limited flexibility and, therefore, implied a scope for official interventions in the exchange market through buying or selling foreign currency. The limits to the exchange-rate variations thus far discussed would be set by the width of the band and/or by the maximum crawl-rate of the parity.

A very different system of greater flexibility would not limit the variations of exchange rates but would, instead, limit the authority of monetary authorities to prevent variations of exchange rates through interventions in the market. This limitation of official buying or selling in the foreign-exchange market could take the form of setting limits to the changes in the monetary reserves held by the authorities. If the authorities have intervened by selling foreign currency and have thus prevented an excess demand for foreign exchange from reducing the exchange value of the domestic currency, their net reserves would have declined. A limit to the extent of permissible depletion of reserves would stop further official sales of foreign exchange. If the authorities have intervened by purchasing foreign currency and have thus prevented an excess supply of foreign exchange from raising the exchange value of the domestic currency, net reserves would have increased. A limit to the extent of permissible accumulation of reserves would stop further official purchases of foreign exchange.

A system of this sort was used for several years in Canada, and successfully so, according to the testimony of the most qualified analysts. The limits to permissible changes in official reserves were set by the monetary authorities themselves, not by any international agreement. With appropriate institutional provisions this kind of "limited invariability" of exchange rates might well work on an international scale. The basic idea is relatively simple: since continuing large accumulations or decumulations of foreign reserves are indications of misaligned exchange rates (fundamental disequilibrium), countries should be committed to stop these accumulations or decumulations; as they stop intervening in the exchange market, exchange rates will be allowed to adjust themselves to the market forces. The scheme is properly regarded as one of "greater flexibility of exchange rates" in that it prevents the authorities from keeping exchange rates for too long a time rigidly misaligned.

V. TYPES OF GLIDING-PARITY SYSTEMS

Formerly I used to distinguish two types of gliding-parity systems: one with discretionary adjustments, the other with formula-determined adjustments. Recent discussions have taught me that clearer exposition required four sets of distinctions: the changes in parities could be:

1. Either prophylactic or therapeutic,
2. Either discretionary or formula-determined,
3. Either equilibrating or disequilibrating, and finally
4. Spontaneous, presumptive without sanctions for nonconformance, presumptive with sanctions for nonconformance, or mandatory.

A change in parity, or rather a sequence of small and continuous changes in parity, is prophylactic if it is intended to prevent imbalances of payments from arising or from worsening; it is therapeutic if it is designed to remove or reduce existing imbalances. When the German Council of Economic Experts proposed a few years ago that the German mark be upvalued by 2 per cent a year, this glide of the parity was meant to be prophylactic. For, as the Germans were planning to limit the rate of their price inflation to 2 per cent a year but expected most of their important trading partners to inflate by at least 4 per cent a year, an unchanged exchange rate would produce a payments surplus with a consequent expansion of effective demand resulting in a higher rate of domestic price inflation than had been planned—a socalled "adjustment inflation." The proposal was not accepted and the German mark became badly undervalued. The upvaluation in October 1969 was primarily therapeutic.

A change in parity is discretionary if the decision is made on the basis of an *ad hoc* judgment by the authorities and not on the basis of a rule or formula adopted in advance. (A prophylactic change is always discretionary in that it involves a judgment of future developments, not a reliance on recorded data of the past. A therapeutic change may be discretionary or formula-determined.) A formula-determined change in parity is guided by a set of rules that tell which statistical data should be taken into account to indicate when, in what direction, and by how much the parity should be changed. The indicators most widely discussed for this purpose are the spot rates in the foreign-exchange market recorded during the preceding period (six months or more), the movements of forward-exchange rates, changes in net foreign reserves, changes in the basic balance of payments, and the trend in the current account. There are many strong reasons why formulas confined to these data may at certain times lead to very wrong results. More studies of past performance and of hypothetical cues given by various alternative formulas (rules of thumb) will probably improve the instruments of navigation in these still insufficiently explored waters. My hunch is that exchange-rate variations within a wider band will be better indicators than variations within the narrow band permitted in the past; they must be combined, of course, with data on official interventions, which may have concealed the effects of free-market forces, and possibly also with data on presumably temporary (or even reversible) movements of private capital funds.

The third set of distinctions, between equilibrating and disequilibrating changes of parity, may apply either to intentions or to actual effects. Some intentionally equilibrating changes may turn out to be disequilibrating in their actual effects. This can happen even in formula-determined adjustments, where the data used as indicators are unreliable, incomplete, or ill-chosen. It is easy to imagine a situation in which the adopted formula dictates a change in the wrong direction or to a wrong extent, or indeed a change when none is "indicated" in the actual circumstances. Unintentional disequilibration can of course occur also through discretionary changes in parity, where the insight or judgment of the authorities is faulty. All therapeutic changes are intended to be equilibrating; they attempt an adjustment of an existing disequilibrium. Prophylactic changes are likewise intended to be equilibrating, not with reference to an existing but rather to an incipient disequilibrium, that is, to one that would emerge if the parity were not adjusted to an ongoing change in relative incomes and prices. Parity changes that are disequilibrating by intention could conceivably be the result of pressures by export industries and industries competing with imports. These changes would be in the nature of competitive devaluations, designed to create a payments surplus, to accumulate foreign reserves, to increase domestic employment or to "export unemployment." Operational criteria for the distinction may be found in the balance sheets of the banking system, especially the central bank. A downward adjustment of the parity may be intended to adjust for a past or ongoing expansion of the portfolio of domestic assets acquired by the banks and thus to stop or avoid the resulting loss of foreign assets; on the other hand, it may be intended to produce an increase in foreign assets. In the former case, the change is equilibrating, an adjustment to an overexpansion of domestic credit; in the latter case, the change is disequilibrating, designed to engineer an expansion of domestic liquidity and effective demand by means of a more active foreign balance (more exports, fewer imports).

The fourth set of distinctions refers to the voluntary or involuntary character of parity adjustments, all of the intentionally equilibrating kind. (A formula-determined change may still be entirely voluntary if it is neither imposed nor strongly urged by foreign or international bodies.) We may distinguish four degrees of outside influence, ranging from zero to 100 per cent. The parity adjustment is spontaneous if no foreign influence has been exerted in its favor. The adjustment is presumptive—this is Cooper's term—if, on the basis of previous agreements or understandings, this move can be expected as the appropriate reaction to the performance of certain indices and indicators. The presumption may be backed only by moral force, the adjustment being "the right thing to do," or it may be backed by certain sanctions imposed by other countries or international agencies in order to make nonconformance more unpleasant. Finally, the adjustment may be mandatory, perhaps not only in the sense that the country in question is firmly committed to it under international rules but also that other countries or an international agency have ways and means to enforce the move, for example, by interventions in the foreign-exchange markets.[1]

VI.   FLEXIBLE, STABLE, INVARIANT

Flexibility is often confused with instability. This is understandable since, if flexibility is the opposite of inflexibil-ity or rigidity, it means that it permits variations, and wide variations represent instability. Two illegitimate steps are contained here: one, from permissible potential variations to actually occurring variations; the other, from variations to wide variations. Moreover, two ideas are missing: one, the distinction between variations around a point —oscillations—and trend-like variations in one direction, and, secondly, the indispensable reference to the time period involved—changes from day to day, year to year, or over several years.

Civil engineers know the difference between rigidity and flexibility of materials for use in the construction of high buildings exposed to winds of variable strength, and they must provide flexibility in order to avoid the eventual collapse of the structure. While such analogies may contribute to the comprehension of word meanings, they do not settle the question whether flexible or rigid exchange rates will be more stable in the long run. And this, after all, is one of the questions before us.

History tells us little about the relationship between flexibility and instability of exchange rates. Of course, many countries had very unstable exchange rates in periods when they had flexible rates, but in these periods fixed rates would not have worked at all. History provides examples of very stable flexible rates, and many examples of very unstable rates fixed and refixed over time. Certainly, in the long run, fixed rates need not be stable, and flexible rates need not be unstable. Confusion between flexibility and instability must not be tolerated.

This prohibition does not rule out speculation about the effects of greater flexibility in exchange rates upon the psychology, determination, and diplo-

---

[1] The international reserve pool (settlements account or conversion account) that I proposed elsewhere was to be empowered to adjust the exchange rates of currencies according to continuous and large accumulations or decumulations of the deposits that the countries in question hold in the pool. See Fritz Machlup, *Remaking the International Monetary System* (Baltimore: John Hopkins Press, 1968), pp. 117–118.

macy of central bankers. Some hold that heavy losses of foreign reserves under inflexible exchange rates serve as effective warning signals to monetary authorities hard pressed by spendthrift governments and investment-minded businessmen, and that these signals are indispensable for monetary discipline. Others, however, hold that depreciations of the currency in the foreign-exchange market serve as even better warning signals, coming on sooner (if rates are flexible) and more conspicuously. Unfortunately, neither reading the record of the past nor analyzing views and attitudes expressed at present will solve the argument about the future comparative effectiveness of the two kinds of warning signals in inducing greater discipline in monetary and fiscal policy. The question, nevertheless, remains meaningful and relevant even if we cannot answer it now.

A purely semantic question regarding flexibility can and should be cleared up here. Since a foreign-exchange rate necessarily involves two currencies, and since the fixing and pegging of a rate may be the concern of only one of the two countries involved while the other country perhaps does not care whether the rate is held invariant or not, it is logically permissible to say that the exchange rate is fixed from one country's point of view, but flexible from the other country's point of view. This other country, as for example, the United States, does neither intervene nor hold the rate-pegging country to its interventions in the exchange market; the exchange rate could therefore vary as far as the United States is concerned. Not doing anything to keep the rate from varying, the United States may regard the rate as flexible even if it is in fact inflexible as a result of the pegging operations of the fixed-rate country.

This subjective interpretation of flexibility has probably more often confused than elucidated the issue. It is simpler to regard an exchange rate as flexible only if neither of the two countries in question undertakes to keep it invariant within narrow limits. Since the dollar is the most widely used intervention currency, one should understand, of course, that the decisions about greater flexibility are up to the countries other than the United States. It should also be understood that a system of greater flexibility does not imply universal flexibility; it means merely that countries are not discouraged from opting for greater flexibility of their dollar-exchange rates. Perhaps only a few countries would find it advantageous to do so. Too many participants in the worldwide discussion of the issue seem to assume that a system of greater flexibility would *compel* their own countries to give up the exchange practices to which they have become accustomed. This is neither implied nor presumed. Countries would be free to fix or flex their exchange rates as they pleased.

VII.   OVEREVALUATION, UNDEREVALUATION

The reason why some countries may prefer to opt for greater flexibility of the exchange rate of their currency is the realization that a rate fixed at one time at an equilibrium level is unlikely to remain an equilibrium rate very long. All sorts of things happen to transform a correct exchange rate into an incorrect one, at which the balance of payments is chronically in surplus or in deficit—unless adjustment is engineered through inflating or deflating effective demand.

An exchange rate at which a country's balance of payments is chronically in surplus may be said to undervalue its currency; an exchange rate at which its basic balance of payments is chronically in deficit may be said to overvalue its currency. Undervaluation is most quickly corrected by means of upvaluation, overvaluation by means of devaluation; but an abrupt change of parity is unlikely to hit upon the correct rate. Moreover, since upvaluations and devaluations involve difficult political decisions, they are usually deferred for too long a time, causing the basic disalignment and imbalance to worsen. Gliding adjustments of the parity are supposed to be easier, causing fewer political difficulties and smaller economic shocks, but this is not my concern at this juncture. The question to which I seek an answer is whether there are any clear criteria of undervaluation and overvaluation, apart from payments surpluses and deficits.

Let us immediately reject as useless the merely impressionistic contentions of so-called experts who give us their own intuitive judgments of the relative values of currencies. Next we must reject the naive valuations by tourists based on their experiences in shopping, dining, and lodging abroad and at home; the price comparisons of tourists are badly biased and have, in any case, very limited relevance for the balances of payments of large countries. Next in line for rejection are the price-index comparisons by economists who have misunderstood the purchasing-power-parity theory; they have not learned or have forgotten, that the relative prices of internationally traded goods reflect the actual exchange rates, however disaligned, and that the relative prices of consumer goods, the cost of living, do not reflect the relative competitiveness of the countries' industries in foreign trade. Even very special indices, such as wholesale prices of domestic products, labor cost per unit of output, or unit cost of export articles, may tell little about changes in relative competitiveness. Indeed, even if all the price indices of all the countries in question had remained unchanged or had in-

creased by an equal proportion, this would say nothing about the competitiveness of the industries that are most important in the trade of the nations.

The search for criteria is perhaps hopeless, since the concept of competitiveness is not adequate for our purpose as long as it is silent on the attainable sales volumes. At particular prices and exchange rates, a country may be able to "push out" a certain quantum of exports and "pull in" a certain quantum of imports, but its net export surplus may or may not be sufficient to finance the country's capital outflows and unilateral payments. A country's currency may at the same time be regarded as "undervalued," if the country needs no more than an even balance of trade, and "overvalued," if the country needs a surplus sufficiently large to meet payments due on its foreign debts or to finance its direct investments abroad. Any change in net financial transfers (capital balance and balance of unilateral payments) changes the equilibrium value of the currency and therefore transforms a "correct" valuation into an over- or under-valuation.

Several respected theorists in international economics object to this formulation. They prefer to develop definitions under which over- and undervaluation of a country's currency, and under- and overcompetitiveness of its industry, are independent of the financial transfers made and received (or payable and receivable). If there is no agreement on the meanings of these terms, it may be best to forego their use. As a matter of fact, some of us tried hard in our discussions to avoid using any of the ambiguous expressions, but we did not always succeed. Questions came up: "Is the pound sterling still (or again) overvalued?," "Can the overvaluation of the French franc be remedied, at a tolerable social cost, through adjustment of effective demand?," "Would gradual upvaluations of the German mark suffice to take care of its present undervaluation?" In these and similar questions, the blacklisted expressions popped up and proved irrepressible. (The discussions took place before the franc and the mark were re-aligned.)

Believers in the definitiveness of the verdicts of the free market can point to rather simple criteria: Whenever the supply of foreign currencies is such that a country's monetary authorities have to buy them in order to prevent their prices from falling, these prices evidently overvalue the foreign currencies; for, at the given exchange rates, private demand is not sufficient to take all that is offered in the market. Whenever the demand for foreign currencies is such that a country's monetary authorities have to sell out of their foreign reserves in order to prevent their prices from rising, these prices evidently undervalue the foreign currencies; for, at the given exchange rates, supply from private sources is not sufficient to satisfy the private demand.

The verdict "disequilibrium" on the evidence that the monetary authorities have to buy or sell foreign currencies in order to keep the rates from falling or rising, and thus on the ground of official reserves increasing or decreasing, suggests the kind of evidence that would support a verdict of "equilibrium." The suggestion, however, is wrong. If the exchange rates stay at the announced level while the monetary authorities neither buy nor sell in the foreign-exchange market and their reserves, therefore, remain unchanged, this is not sufficient evidence that the exchange rates are equilibrium rates. For there are several auxiliary techniques that can be used to hide excess supply or excess demand in the market, for example, corrective measures that are taken in the hope that adjustment of effective demand as well as

adjustment of exchange rates can be avoided. These corrective measures are ordinarily regarded as only temporary or stop-gap measures, either because they could not be continued very long, or because their continuance would be deemed undesirable. Examples are special intergovernmental transactions and arrangements among central banks; tax incentives or disincentives affecting private capital movements; regulations requiring discrimination in interest rates payable on foreign and domestic accounts; swap agreements (repurchase agreements) between central banks and commercial banks, shifting foreign currencies from official to private holdings and back; various other devices to attract or repel the inflow of funds, or to encourage or discourage outflows; restrictions or prohibitions of capital exports; restrictions and controls of imports of goods and services.

In resorting to measures of this sort, a government implicitly recognizes that the official exchange rate overvalues or undervalues its currency. For several years I have characterized some of the restrictive measures taken by the United States as "concealed partial devaluations" of the dollar. German government officials have spoken of the border-tax arrangements enacted at the end of 1968 as *Ersatzaufwertung* (substitute upvaluation) of the German mark. Still, the spot rates in the foreign-exchange market remain unchanged and accretions or losses of foreign reserves are avoided or reduced below the volume that would correspond to the extent of the overvaluation or undervaluation.

If then the recorded changes in official foreign reserves do not—as long as corrective measures, restrictions and controls are employed to affect supply and demand in the foreign-exchange market—fully reflect existing over- or undervaluations of the currency in question, what statistical adjustments can be made to get a more reliable picture of the situation?

For a country with an undervalued currency one begins, of course, with the reported increase in official net reserves (minus any new allocations of unearned reserves such as Special Drawing Rights), but has to add the following items: any increase in liquid foreign balances held by commercial banks under swap arrangements with the central bank; all special intergovernmental transactions that made use of official reserves (such as prepayments of foreign loans); outflows of private capital induced by special incentives and inflows averted by special disincentives; imports of goods and services induced by special tax or tariff abatements and exports prevented by special tax levies. (The last items can only be estimated, but such estimates should periodically be furnished by the governments appraising the assumed effectiveness of their balance-of-payments measures.)

For a country with an overvalued currency one has to add to the decrease in official net reserves any new allocations of unearned reserves; any decrease in liquid foreign balances held by commercial banks under swap arrangements with the central bank; all special intergovernmental transactions that augmented official reserves; private capital inflows induced by special incentives and outflows averted by special disincentives; outflows of capital prevented by prohibitions and controls; exports of goods and services induced by special tax incentives or other forms of subsidies, and imports prevented by special taxes, tariff increases or surcharges, quota restrictions, or foreign-exchange controls. (Again, several of these items would be estimates, but a requirement for governments to furnish estimates of the effectiveness of their balance-of-payments measures would be very wholesome: if the estimates were low, the restrictive measures would obviously not be justified; if they were high, however, the degree of overvaluation of the currency would be made a matter of record and the fundamental disequilibrium calling for exchange-rate adjustment would become manifest.)

This is still not all. If one recognizes that the balance of payments can be affected by temporary (or even reversible) changes, one will attempt to separate ephemeral items from recurring ones and adjust the balance of official sales and purchases of foreign exchange by the net balance of presumably non-recurring transactions. The verdict of over- or undervaluation of particular currencies will then depend on the experts' judgments as to which items and what amounts can be expected to continue and, thus, to make up the long-run supply and demand in the foreign-exchange market. Of course, such judgments have to be supported by reasoned argument.

The comments on the problem of sizing up the over- or undervaluation of a currency should be relevant for considerations of any kind of exchange-rate adjustment, discrete or gliding, discretionary or formula-determined. However, if so much estimating, guessing, and judging goes into some of the variables employed, the distinction between discretion and formula becomes rather questionable.

VIII. THE DILEMMA OF ADVOCACY: HARD-SELL OR MODESTY

The advocates of greater flexibility of exchange rates are faced with a dilemma. If they want to "sell" their plans, they must present them with enthusiasm and describe in glowing terms how well they would work; at the same time they may have to make compromises and be satisfied with stripped-down versions of greater flexibility so little different from the inflexible system of today that they cannot achieve what is promised. On the other hand, if the advocates refrain from making exaggerated claims, if they promise neither perfection nor solution of all pressing problems and, moreover, if they insist on sufficient flexibility to have it contribute decisively to real adjustment in cases of hitherto chronic deficits and surpluses in the balances of payments, then they may not be able to win acceptance for their plans.

Believers in price flexibility thus have a difficult choice to make. Either they encourage the adoption of an insufficiently flexible system, which will consequently disappoint their clients and compromise the theory of flexible exchange rates, or if they are unwilling to make exaggerated claims for their system and to make concessions, they will be unable to get their ideas across. It takes no courage to choose the second alternative: the uncompromising and therefore unsuccessful advocate will always be able to take pride in his fidelity to principles; he will not be blamed for having promised more than could have been delivered; and he can at every crisis tell the world how short-sighted the authorities had been in rejecting his advice. To choose the first alternative is to take several calculated risks, for only with a good deal of luck will the system with less inflexible, but still insufficiently flexible, exchange rates avert some of the crises that would have occurred under the system of "fixed" (abruptly adjustable) rates; regarding any crisis that is averted, it will be impossible to prove that there would have been a crisis had exchange rates been even less flexible; and regarding any crisis that is not averted, it will be impossible to convince the critics that the crisis is the consequence of too little flexibility and not of too much.

Assume, to illustrate the point, that the men in charge of international monetary arrangements are willing to accept a band of a total width of 4 per cent with no glide of parity. What are the chances for such a system of "greater flexibility" to work? Since the effects of such small variations in exchange rates upon the flow of goods and services (real adjustment) are probably not very large and only some effects upon capital flows (financial correctives) can be expected, the slightly widened band would be only a minor improvement. It would be ineffective in preventing progressive disalignments that result from a consistent divergence in the rates of price inflation in different countries. Thus, while a few difficulties arising from minor disturbances might be mitigated or avoided, the problem of fundamental disequilibrium unadjusted for many years would remain. When then the inevitable crisis of confidence arrives, some "authorities" would no doubt blame the crisis on the departure from the good old system of the narrow band.

Is this risk worth taking? The advantages of a band only silghtly widened are probably too small relative to the risk of having the "experiment" wrongly interpreted. What degree of flexibility should the believer in greater flexibility of rates regard as the minimum acceptable? To decide how flexible he ought to be in accepting a compromise, he might consider the relative probabilities of disequilibrating changes to be large or small, continuing or reversible, reinforced or offset by policy measures.

It must be taken for granted that there will always be disequilibrating changes. To mention the most likely ones, there will be discrepancies between national rates of demand inflation as well as price inflation;[2] there will also be different rates of growth, with different income elasticities of demand for imports and with different biases toward import-competing, export-oriented, and foreign-trade-indifferent industries; in addition, there will be shifts in demand, in labor supply, and several other things affecting the flow of goods and services at given exchange rates; and, last not least, there will be changes in the international flow of capital. All these changes can be countered by monetary and fiscal policies adjusting aggregate demand. However, adjustment through absolute deflation of effective demand in deficit countries is practically impossible for social and political reasons, and adjustment through price inflation in surplus countries is not very popular either. The question is now whether in most instances the effects of the disequilibrating changes can be effectively countered by alterations in exchange rates within the range of flexibility afforded by the band or crawl conceded by the monetary authorities. If the bulk of the rate adjustments that would be required by the disequilibrating changes can with ease be accommodated by the compromise arrangement, the system will work almost as well as if it allowed even greater flexibility. If, however, most of the required rate adjustments would be too big to be accommodated by the permitted flexibility, there will be troubles similar to those arising at inflexible (abruptly adjustable) rates. The troubles under more flexible rates may be just a little less severe, because of the greater risk for speculators and the modicum of

adjustment achieved in the more elastic fringes of the current account.

The relative importance of wider band or gliding parity depends on which type of disequilibrating change will be dominating. If we believe that discrepancies in the rates of demand inflation will be the most persistent causes of imbalance and that the inequality in the tempo of inflation will be consistent—say, that there will be consistently less inflation in Germany than in France—then a gliding parity would be more important than a much wider band. If we believe, on the other hand, the disequilibrating changes will take turns in pushing particular economies first one way and then another, a wide band would be the thing to have.

Judging from the experience of the past few years, one may say that a realist should vote for a glide of parity with a wider band, that is, a gliding widened band. And, to be more specific, he should vote for a glide of about 1/26 of 1 per cent a week, which would add up to some 2 per cent a year, and for a band of a total width of no less than 5 per cent of parity. In explaining his vote, he should make clear that even this degree of flexibility cannot take care of all eventualities. Revolutionary wage boosts, ratified by a policy of demand expansion, cannot be fully countered by exchange rate variations within the voted limits, unless they are followed by a wage stop at home and demand expansions abroad. Likewise, it may not be possible by means of exchange-rate adjustments of the specified extent to equilibrate the foreign-exchange markets in the case of sudden large shifts in international capital movements.

[2] I stress the distinction because demand inflation may be much more effective in causing deficits in the balance of payments than price inflation, which in fact is mitigated by the deterioration of the the balance of trade. In open economies prices need not rise as the excess demand spills over into other countries.

READING 41
THE CASE FOR FLEXIBLE EXCHANGE RATES

Harry G. Johnson*

I. INTRODUCTION

By "flexible exchange rates" is meant rates of foreign exchange that are determined daily in the markets for foreign exchange by the forces of demand and supply, without restrictions imposed by governmental policy on the extent to which rates can move. Flexible exchange rates are thus to be distinguished from the present system (the International Monetary Fund system) of international monetary organization, under which countries commit themselves to maintain the foreign values of their currencies within a narrow margin of a fixed par value by acting as residual buyers or sellers of currency in the foreign exchange market, subject to the possibility of effecting a change in the par value itself in case of "fundamental disequilibrium." This system is frequently described as the "adjustable peg" system. Flexible exchange rates should also be distinguished from a spectral system frequently conjured up by opponents of rate flexibility—wildly fluctuating or "unstable" exchange rates. The freedom of rates to move in response to market forces does not imply that they will in fact move significantly or erratically; they will do so only if the underlying forces governing demand and supply are themselves erratic—and in that case any international monetary

Source: From Hobart Papers No. 46, "UK and Floating Exchanges," (London: The Institute of Economic Affairs), May 1969. Reprinted in Federal Reserve Bank of St. Louis Review, June 1969.

* The title acknowledges the indebtedness of all serious writers on this subject to Milton Friedman's modern classic essay, "The Case for Flexible Exchange Rates," written in 1950, and published in 1953 (M. Friedman, Essays in Positive Economics (Chicago: University of Chicago Press, 1953), pp. 157–203, abridged in R. E. Caves and H. G. Johnson (eds.), Readings in International Economics (Homewood, Illinois: Richard D. Irwin, for the American Economic Association, 1968), chapter 25, pp. 413–37.

system would be in serious difficulty. Finally, flexible exchange rates do not necessarily imply that the national monetary authorities must refrain from any intervention in the exchange markets; whether they should intervene or not depends on whether the authorities are likely to be more or less intelligent and efficient speculators than the private speculators in foreign exchange—a matter on which empirical judgment is frequently inseparable from fundamental political attitudes.

The fundamental argument for flexible exchange rates is that they would allow countries autonomy with respect to their use of monetary, fiscal, and other poilcy instruments, consistent with the maintenance of whatever degree of freedom in international transactions they chose to allow their citizens by automatically ensuring the preservation of external equilibrium. Since in the absence of balance-of-payments reasons for interfering in international trade and payments, and given autonomy of domestic policy, there is an overwhelmingly strong case for the maximum possible freedom of international transactions to permit exploitation of the economies of international specialization and division of labour, the argument for flexible exchange rates can be put more strongly still: flexible exchange rates are essential to the preservation of national autonomy and independence consistent with efficient organization and development of the world economy.

The case for flexible exchange rates on these grounds has been understood and propounded by economists since the work of Keynes and others on the monetary disturbances that followed the First World War. Yet that case is consistently ridiculed, if not dismissed out of hand, by "practical" men concerned with international monetary affalrs, and there is a strong revealed preference for the fixed exchange rate system. For this one might suggest two reasons: First, successful men of affairs are successful because they understand and can work with the intricacies of the prevalent fixed rate system, but being "practical" find it almost impossible to conceive how a hypothetical alternative system would, or even could, work in practice; Second, the fixed exchange rate system gives considerble prestige and, more important, political power over national governments to the central banks entrusted with managing the system, power which they naturally credit themselves with exercising more "responsibly" than the politicians would do, and which they naturally resist surrendering. Consequently, public interest in and discussion of flexible exchange rates generally appears only when the fixed rate system is obviously under serious strain and the capacity of the central bankers and other responsible officials to avoid a crisis is losing credibility.

The present period has this character, from two points of view. On the one hand, from the point of view of the international economy, the long-sustained sterling crisis that culminated in the devaluation of November 1967, the speculative doubts about the dollar that culminated in the gold crisis of March 1968, and the franc-mark crisis that was left unresolved by the Bonn meeting of November 1968 and still hangs over the system, have all emphasized a serious defect of the present international monetary system.[1] This is the lack of an adequate adjustment mechanism—a mechanism for adjusting international imbalances of payments towards equilibrium sufficiently rapidly as not to put intolerable strains

[1] The exchange speculation in favor of the Deutsche Mark in early May 1969 is only the latest example of instability in the present fixed exchange rate system.

on the willingness of the central banks to supplement existing international reserves with additional credits, while not requiring countries to deflate or inflate their economies beyond politically tolerable limits. The obviously available mechanism is greater automatic flexibility of exchange rates (as distinct from adjustments of the "pegs"). Consequently, there has been a rapidly growing interest in techniques for achieving greater automatic flexibility while retaining the form and assumed advantages of a fixed rate system. The chief contenders in this connection are the "band" proposal, under which the permitted range of exchange rate variation around parity would be widened from the present one per cent or less to, say, five per cent each way, and the so-called "crawling peg" proposal, under which the parity for any day would be determined by an average of past rates established in the market. The actual rate each day could diverge from the parity within the present or a widened band, and the parity would thus crawl in the direction in which a fully flexible rate would move more rapidly.

Either of these proposals, if adopted, would constitute a move towards a flexible rate system for the world economy as a whole. On the other hand, from the point of view of the British economy alone, there has been growing interest in the possibility of a floating rate for the pound. This interest has been prompted by the shock of devaluation, doubts about whether the devaluation was sufficient or may need to be repeated, resentment of the increasing subordination of domestic policy to international requirements since 1964, and general discontent with the policies into which the commitment to maintain a fixed exchange rate has driven successive Governments—"stop-go policies," higher average unemployment policies, income policies, and a host of other domestic and international interventions.

From both the international and the purely domestic point of view, therefore, it is appropriate to re-examine the case for flexible exchange rates. That is the purpose of this essay. For reasons of space, the argument will be conducted at a general level of principle, with minimum attention to technical details and complexities. It is convenient to begin with the case for fixed exchange rates; this case has to be constructed, since little reasoned defense of it has been produced beyond the fact that it exists and functions after a fashion, and the contention that any change would be for the worse. Consideration of the case for fixed rates leads into the contrary case for flexible rates. Certain common objections to flexible rates are then discussed. Finally, some comments are offered on the specific questions mentioned above, of providing for greater rate flexibility in the frame work of the I M F system and of floating the pound by itself.

II. THE CASE FOR FIXED EXCHANGE RATES

A reasoned case for fixed international rates of exchange must run from analogy with the case for a common national currency, since the effect of fixing the rate at which one currency can be converted into another is, subject to qualifications to be discussed later, to establish the eqiuvalent of a single currency for those countries of the world economy adhering to fixed exchange rates. The advantages of a single currency within a nation's frontiers are, broadly, that it simplifies the profit-maximizing computations of producers and traders, facilitates competition among producers located in different parts of the country, and promotes the integration of the economy into a connected series of markets, these markets including both the markets for products and the markets for the factors of production (capital and labour). The argument for fixed exchange rates, by analogy, is that they will similarly encourage the integration of the national markets that compose the world economy into an international network of connected markets, with similarly beneficial effects on economic efficiency and growth. In other words, the case for fixed rates is part of a more general argument for national economic policies conducive to international economic integration.

A. International Immobility

The argument by analogy with the domestic economy, however, is seriously defective for several reasons. In the first place, in the domestic economy the factors of production as well as goods and services are free to move throughout the market area. In the international economy the movement of labour is certainly subject to serious barriers created by national immigration policies (and in some cases restraints on emigration as well), and the freedom of movement of capital is also restricted by barriers created by national laws. The freedom of movement of goods is also restricted by tariffs and other barriers to trade. It is true that there are certain kinds of artificial barriers to the movement of goods and factors internally to a national economy (apart from natural barriers created by distance and cultural differences) created sometimes by national policy (e.g., regional development policies) and sometimes by the existence of state or provincial governments with protective policies of their own. But these are probably negligible by comparison with the barriers to the international mobility of goods and factors of production. The existence of these barriers means that the fixed exchange rate system does not really establish the equivalent of a

single international money, in the sense of a currency whose purchasing power and whose usefulness tends to equality throughout the market area. A more important point, to be discussed later, is that if the fixity of exchange rates is maintained, not by appropriate adjustments of the relative purchasing power of the various national currencies, but by variations in the national barriers to trade and payments, it is in contradiction with the basic argument for fixed rates as a means of attaining the advantages internationally that are provided domestically by a single currency.

B. Concern Over Regional Imbalance

In the second place, as is well known from the prevalence of regional development policies in the various countries, acceptance of a single currency and its implications is not necessarily beneficial to particular regions within a nation. The pressures of competition in the product and factor markets facilitated by the common currency instead frequently result in prolonged regional distress, in spite of the apparent full freedom of labour and capital to migate to more remunerative locations. On the national scale, the solution usually applied, rightly or wrongly, is to relieve regional distress by transfers from the rest of the country, effected through the central government. On the international scale, the probability of regional (national in this context) distress is substantially greater because of the barriers to both factors and goods mobility mentioned previously; yet there is no international government, nor any effective substitute through international co-operation, to compensate and assist nations or regions of nations suffering through the effects of economic change occurring in the environment of a single currency. (It should be noted that existing arrangements for financing balance-of-payments deficits by credit from the surplus countries in no sense fulfill this function, since deficits and surpluses do not necessarily reflect respectively distress in the relevant sense, and its absence.)

C. Lack of Central Control of Currencies

Thirdly, the beneficent effects of a single national currency on economic integration and growth depend on the maintenance of reasonable stability of its real value; the adjective "reasonable" is meant to allow for mild inflationary or deflationary trends of prices over time. Stability in turn is provided under contemporary institutional arrangements through centralization of control of the money supply and monetary conditions in the hands of the central bank, which is responsible for using its powers of control for this purpose. (Formerly, it was provided by the use of precious metals, the quantity of which normally changed very slowly.) The system of fixed rates of international exchange, in contrast to a single national money, provides no centralized control of the overall quantity of international money and international monetary conditions. Under the ideal old-fashioned gold standard, in theory at least, overall international monetary control was exercised automatically by the available quantity of monetary gold and its rate of growth, neither of which could be readily influenced by national governments, operating on national money supplies through the obligation incumbent on each country to maintain a gold reserve adequate to guarantee the convertibility of its currency under all circumstances at the fixed exchange rate. That system has come to be regarded as barbarous, because it required domestic employment objectives to be subordinated to the requirements of international balance; and nations have come to insist on their right to use

interventions in international trade and payments, and in the last resort to devalue their currencies, rather than proceed farther than they find politically tolerable with deflationary adjustment policies.

The result is that the automatic mechanisms of overall monetary control in the international system implicit in the gold standard have been abandoned, without those mechanisms being replaced by a discretionary mechanism of international control comparable to the national central bank in the domestic economic system, to the dictates of which the national central banks, as providers of the currency of the "regions" of the international economy, are obliged to conform. Instead, what control remains is the outcome on the one hand of the jostling among surplus and deficit countries, each of which has appreciable discretion with respect to how far it will accept or evade pressures on its domestic policies mediated through pressures on its balance of payments, and on the other hand of the ability of the system as a system to free itself from the remnants of the constraint formerly exercised by gold as the ultimate international reserve, by using national currencies and various kinds of international credit arrangements as substitutes for gold in international reserves.

In consequence, the present international monetary system of fixed exchange rates fails to conform to the analogy with a single national currency in two important respects. Regions of the system are able to resist the integrative pressures of the single currency by varying the barriers to international transactions and hence the usefulness of the local variant of that currency, and in the last resort by changing the terms of conversion of the local variant into other variants; moreover, they have reason to do so in the absence of an international mechanism for compensating excessively distressed regions and a mechanism for providing centralized and responsible control of overall monetary conditions. Second, in contrast to a national monetary system, there is no responsible centralized institutional arrangement for monetary control of the system.

This latter point can be rephrased in terms of the commonly held belief that the fixed rate system exercises "discipline" over the nations involved in it, and prevents them from pursuing "irresponsible" domestic policies. This belief might have been tenable with respect to the historical gold standard, under which nations were permanently committed to maintaining their exchange rates and had not yet developed the battery of interventions in trade and payments that are now commonly employed. But it is a myth when nations have the option of evading discipline by using interventions or devaluation. It becomes an even more pernicious myth when it is recognized that abiding by the discipline may entail hardships for the nation that the nation will not tolerate being applied to particular regions within itself, but will attempt to relieve by interregional transfer payments; and that the discipline is not discipline to conform to rational and internationally accepted principles of good behavior, but discipline to conform to the average of what other nations are seeking to get away with. Specifically, there might be something to be said for an international monetary system that disciplined individual nations into conducting their policies so as to achieve price stability and permit liberal international economic policies. But there is little to be said for a system that on the one hand obliges nations to accept whatever rate of world price inflation or deflation emerges from the policies of the other nations in the world economy, and on the other hand obliges or permits them

to employ whatever policies of intervention in international trade and payments are considered by themselves and their neighbours not to infringe the letter of the rules of international liberalism.

D. "Harmonization" and "Surveillance"

The defenders of the present fixed rate system, if pressed, will generally accept these points but argue the need for a solution along two complementary lines: "harmonization" of national economic policies in accordance with the requirements of a single world currency system, and progressive evolution towards international control of the growth of international liquidity combined with "surveillance" of national economic policies. The problem with both is that they demand a surrender of national sovereignty in domestic economic policy which countries have shown themselves extremely reluctant to accept. The reasons for this have already been mentioned; the most important are that there is no international mechanism for compensating those who suffer from adhering to the rules of the single currency game, and that the nations differ sharply in their views on priorities among policy objectives, most notably on the relative undesirability of unemployment on the one hand and price inflation on the other. The main argument for flexible exchange rates at the present time is that they would make this surrender of sovereignty unnecessary, while at the same time making unnecessary the progressive extension of interventions in international trade and payments that failure to resolve this issue necessarily entails.

The case for fixed exchange rates, while seriously defective as a defense of the present system of international monetary organization, does have one important implication for the case for flexible exchange rates. One is accustomed to thinking of national moneys in terms of the currencies of the major countries, which currencies derive their usefulness from the great diversity of goods, services and assets available in the national economy, into which they can be directly converted. But in the contemporary world there are many small and relatively narrowly specialized countries, whose national currencies lack usefulness in this sense, but instead derive their usefulness from their rigid convertibility at a fixed price into the currency of some major country with which the small country trades extensively or on which it depends for capital or investment. For such countries, the advantages of rigid convertibility in giving the currency usefulness and facilitating international trade and investment outweigh the relatively small advantages that might be derived from exchange rate flexibility. (In a banana republic, for example, the currency will be more useful if it is stable in terms of command over foreign goods than if it is stable in terms of command over bananas; and exchange rate flexibility would give little scope for autonomous domestic policy.) These countries, which probably constitute a substantial numerical majority of existing countries, would therefore probably choose, if given a free choice, to keep the value of their currency pegged to that of some major country or currency bloc. In other words, the case for flexible exchange rates is a case for flexibility of rates among the currencies of countries that are large enough to have a currency whose usefulness derives primarily from its domestic purchasing power, and for which significant autonomy of domestic policy is both possible and desired.

III. THE CASE FOR FLEXIBLE EXCHANGE RATES

The case for flexible exchange rates derives fundamentally from the laws of demand and supply—in particular, from the principle that, left to itself, the competitive market will establish the price that equates quantity demanded with quantity supplied and hence clears the market. If the price rises temporarily above the competitive level, an excess of quantity supplied over quantity demanded will drive it back downwards to the equilibrium level; conversely, if the price falls temporarily below the competitive level, an excess of quantity demanded over quantity supplied will force the price upwards towards the equilibrium level. Application of this principle to governmental efforts to control or to support particular prices indicates that, unless the price happens to be fixed at the equilibrium level—in which case governmental intervention is superfluous—such efforts will predictably generate economic problems. If the price is fixed above the equilibrium level, the government will be faced with the necessity of absorbing a surplus of production over consumption. To solve this problem, it will eventually have to either reduce its support price, or devise ways either of limiting production (through quotas, taxes, etc.) or of increasing consumption (through propaganda, or distribution of surpluses on concessionary terms). If the price is fixed below the equilibrium level, the government will be faced with the necessity of meeting the excess of consumption over production out of its own stocks. Since these must be limited in extent, it must eventually either raise its control price, or devise ways either to limit consumption by rationing, or reduce the costs of production (e.g., by producer subsidies, or by investments in increasing productivity).

A. Effects of Fixed-Rate Disequilibrium

Exactly the same problems arise when the government chooses to fix the price of foreign exchange in terms of the national currency, and for one reason or another that price ceases to correspond to the equilibrium price. If that price is too high, i.e., if the domestic currency is undervalued, a balance-of-payments surplus develops and the country is obliged to accumulate foreign exchange. If this accumulation is unwelcome, the government's alternatives are to restrict exports and encourage imports either by alloting or promoting domestic inflation (which in a sense subsidizes imports and taxes exports) or by imposing increased taxes or controls on exports and reducing taxes or controls on imports; or to appreciate its currency to the equilibrium level. If the price of foreign exchange is too low, the domestic currency being overvalued, a balance-of-payments deficit develops and the country is obliged to run down its stocks of foreign exchange and borrow from other countries. Since its ability to do this is necessarily limited, it ultimately has to choose among the following alternatives: imposing restrictions on imports and/or promoting exports (including imports and exports of assets, i.e., control of international capital movements); deflating the economy to reduce the demand for imports and increase the supply of exports; deflating the economy to restrain wages and prices and/or attempting to control wages and prices directly, in order to make exports more and imports less profitable; and devaluing the currency.

In either event, a deliberate choice is necessary among alternatives which are unpleasant for various reasons. Hence the choice is likely to be deferred until the disequilibrium has reached crisis proportions; and decisions taken under crisis conditions are both unlikely to be carefully thought out, and likely to have seriously disruptive economic effects.

All of this would be unnecessary if, instead of taking a view on what the value of the currency in terms of foreign exchange should be, and being therefore obliged to defend this view by its policies or in the last resort surrender it, the government were to allow the price of foreign exchange to be determined by the interplay of demand and supply in the foreign exchange market. A freely flexible exchange rate would tend to remain constant so long as underlying economic conditions (including governmental policies) remained constant; random deviations from the equilibrium level would be limited by the activities of private speculators, who would step in to buy foreign exchange when its price fell (the currency appreciated in terms of other currencies) and to sell it when its price rose (the currency depreciated in terms of foreign currencies).

On the other hand, if economic changes or policy changes occurred that under a fixed exchange rate would produce a balance-of-payments surplus or deficit, and ultimately a need for policy changes, the flexible exchange rate would gradually either appreciate or depreciate as required to preserve equilibrium. The movement of the rate would be facilitated and smoothed by the actions of private speculators, on the basis of their reading of current and prospective economic and policy developments. If the government regarded the trend of the exchange rate as undesirable, it could take counter-active measures in the form of inflationary or deflationary policies. It would never be forced to take such measures by a balance-of-payments crisis and the pressure of foreign opinion, contrary to its own policy objectives. The balance-of-payments rationale for interventions in international trade and capital movements, and for such substitutes for exchange rate change as changes in border tax adjustments or the imposition of futile "incomes policies," would disappear.

If the government had reason to believe that private speculators were not performing efficiently their function of stabilizing the exchange market and smoothing the movement of the rate over time, or that their speculations were based on faulty information or prediction, it could establish its own agency for speculation, in the form of an exchange stabilization fund. This possibility, however, raises the questions of whether an official agency risking the public's money is likely to be a smarter speculator than private individuals risking their own money, whether if the assumed superiority of official speculation rests on access to inside information it would not be preferable to publish the information for the benefit of the public rather than use it to make profits for the agency at the expense of unnecessarily ill-informed private citizens, and whether such an agency would in fact confine itself to stabilizing speculation or would try to enforce an official view of what the exchange rate should be—that is, whether the agency would not retrogress into *de facto* restoration of the adjustable peg system.

B.   Freeing Domestic Economic Management

The adoption of flexible exchange rates would have the great advantage of freeing governments to use their instruments of domestic policy for the pursuit of domestic objectives, while at the same time removing the pressures to intervene in international trade and payments for balance-of-payments reasons. Both of these advantages are important in contemporary circumstances. On the one hand, there exists a great rift between nations like the United Kingdom and the United States, which are anxious to maintain high levels of employment and are prepared to pay a price for it in terms of domestic inflation, and other nations, notably Western Germany, which are strongly adverse to inflation. Under the present fixed exchange rate system, these na-

tions are pitched against each other in a battle over the rate of inflation which is to prevail in the world economy, since the fixed rate system diffuses that rate of inflation to all the countries involved in it. Flexible rates would allow each country to pursue the mixture of unemployment and price trend objectives it prefers, consistent with international equilibrium, equilibrium being secured by appreciation of the currencies of "price stability" countries relative to the currencies of "full employment" countries.

On the other hand, the maximum possible freedom of trade is not only desirable for the prosperity and growth of the major developed countries, but essential for the integration of the developing countries into the world economy and the promotion of efficient economic development of those countries. While the postwar period has been characterized by the progressive reduction of the conventional barriers to international trade and payments— tariffs and quotas, inconvertibility and exchange controls—the recurrent balance-of-payments and international monetary crises under the fixed rates system have fostered the erection of barriers to international economic integration in new forms—aid-tying, preferential governmental procurement policies, controls on direct and portfolio international investment—which are in many ways more subtly damaging to effiicency and growth than the conventional barriers.

The removal of the balance-of-payments motive for restrictions on international trade and payments is an important positive contribution that the adoption of flexible exchange rates could make to the achievement of the liberal objective of an integrated international economy, which must be set against any additional barriers to international commerce and finance, in the form of increased uncertainty, that might follow from the adoption of flexible exchange rates. That such additional uncertainty would be so great as to seriously reduce the flows of international trade and investment is one of the objections to flexible rates to be discussed in the next section.

C. The Mechanics of Flexible Exchange Rates

At this point, it is sufficient to make the following observations. First, as pointed out in the preceding section, under a flexible rate system most countries would probably peg their currencies to one or another major currency, so that much international trade and investment would in fact be conducted under fixed rate conditions, and uncertainty would attach only to changes in the exchange rates among a few major currencies or currency blocs (most probably, a U.S. dollar bloc, a European bloc, and sterling, though possibly sterling might be included in one of the other blocs). For the same reason—because few blocs would imply that their economic domains would be large and diversified—the exchange rates between the flexible currencies would be likely to change rather slowly and steadily. This would mean that traders and investors would be able normally to predict the domestic value of their foreign currency proceeds without much difficulty.

But, secondly, traders would be able to hedge foreign receipts or payments through the forward exchange markets, if they wished to avoid uncertainty; if there were a demand for more extensive forward market and hedging facilities than now exist, the competitive profit motive bring them into existence.

Third, for longer-range transactions, the economics of the situation would provide a substantial amount of automatic hedging, through the fact that long-run trends towards appreciation or depreciation of a currency are likely to be dominated by divergence of the trend of prices inside the currency area

from the trend of prices elsewhere. For direct foreign investments, for example, any loss of value of foreign currency earnings in terms of domestic currency due to depreciation of the foreign currency is likely to be roughly balanced by an increase in the amount of such earnings consequent on the relative inflation associated with the depreciation. Similarly, if a particular country is undergoing steady inflation and its currency is depreciating steadily in consequence, money interest rates there are likely to rise sufficiently to compensate domestic investors for the inflation, and hence sufficiently to compensate foreign portfolio investors for their losses from the depreciation.

Finally, it should be noted that the same sort of political and economic developments that would impose unexpected losses on traders and investors through depreciation under a flexible exchange rate system, would equally impose losses in the form of devaluation, or the imposition of restrictions on trade and capital movements, under the present fixed rate system.

IV. THE CASE AGAINST FLEXIBLE EXCHANGE RATES

The case against flexible exchange rates, like the case for fixed exchange rates, is rarely if ever stated in a reasoned fashion. Instead, it typically consists of a series of unfounded assertions and allegations, which derive their plausibility from two fundamentally irrelevant facts. The first is that, in the modern European economic history with which most people are familiar, flexible exchange rates are associated either with the acute monetary disorders that followed the First World War, or with the collapse of the international monetary system in the 1930's; instead of being credited with their capacity to function when the fixed exchange rate system could not, they are debited with the disorders of national economic policies that made the fixed exchange rate unworkable or led to its collapse. The second, and more important at this historical distance from the disastrous experiences just mentioned, is that most people are accustomed to the fixed exchange rate system, and are prone to assume without thinking that a flexible rate system would simply display in an exaggerated fashion the worst features of the present fixed rate system, rather than remedy them.

The historical record is too large a topic to be discussed adequately in a brief essay. Suffice it to say that the inter-war European experience was clouded by the strong belief, based on pre-First World War conditions, that fixed exchange rates at historical parity values constituted a natural order of things to which governments would seek eventually to return, and that scholarly interpretation of that experience leaned excessively and unjustifiably towards endorsement of the official view that any private speculation on the exchanges based on distrust of the ability of the authorities to hold an established parity under changing circumstances was necessarily "destabilizing" and anti-social. It should further be remarked that European inter-war experience does not constitute the whole of the historical record, and that both previously (as in the case of the United States dollar from 1862 to 1879) and subsequently (as in the case of the Canadian dollar from 1950 to 1962) there have been cases of a major trading country maintaining a flexible exchange rate without any of the disastrous consequences commonly forecast by the opponents of flexible rates.

The *penchant* for attributing to the flexible rate system the problems of the fixed rate system can be illustrated by a closer examination of some of the arguments commonly advanced against floating exchange rates, most of which allege either that flexible rates will seriously increase uncertainty in international transactions, or that they will foster inflation.

A. Flexible Rates and Uncertainty

1. INSTABILITY OF THE EXCHANGE RATE

One of the common arguments under the heading of uncertainty is that flexible rates would be extremely unstable rates, jumping wildly about from day to day. This allegation ignores the crucial point that a rate that is free to move under the influence of changes in demand and supply is not forced to move erratically, but will instead move only in response to such changes in demand and supply—including changes induced by changes in governmental policies—and normally will move only slowly and fairly predictably. Abnormally rapid and erratic movements will occur only in response to sharp and unexpected changes in circumstances; and such changes in a fixed exchange rate system would produce equally or more uncertainty-creating policy changes in the form of devaluation, deflation, or the imposition of new controls on trade and payments. The fallacy of this argument lies in its assumption that exchange rate changes occur exogenously and without apparent economic reason; that assumption reflects the mentality of the fixed rate system, in which the exchange rate is held fixed by official intervention in the face of demand and supply pressures for change, and occasionally changed arbitrarily and at one stroke by governmental decisions whose timing and magnitude is a matter of severe uncertainty.

2. REDUCTION OF FOREIGN TRADE

A related argument is that uncertainty about the domestic currency equivalent of foreign receipts or payments would seriously inhibit international transactions of all kinds. As

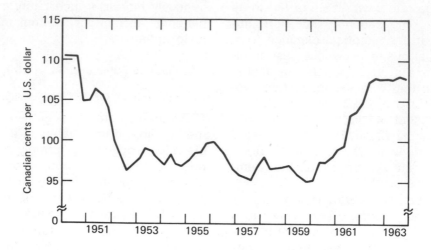

Chart 1. Canadian foreign exchange rate.

NOTE: Canada was on a floating exchange rate from late 1950 to mid-1962. The sharp movements of both ends of the period represent the transition from fixed rates to flexible rates. Once the free market equillibrium rate was established, it movd in a relatively narrow quarter-to-quarter range.

Source: Bank of Canada.

argued in the preceding section, trends in exchange rates should normally be fairly slow and predictable, and their causes such as to provide more or less automatic compensation to traders and investors. Moreover, traders averse to uncertainty would be able to hedge their transactions through forward exchange markets, which would, if necessary, develop in response to demand. It is commonly argued at present, by foreign exchange dealers and others engaged in the foreign exchange market, that hedging facilities would be completely inadequate or that the cost of forward cover would be prohibitive. Both arguments seek to deny the economic principle that a competitive system will tend to provide any good or service demanded, at a price that yields no more than a fair profit. They derive, moreover, from the experience of recent crises under the fixed rate system. When exchange rates are rigidly fixed by official intervention, businessmen normally do not consider the cost of

forward cover worth their while; but when everyone expects the currency to be devalued, everyone seeks to hedge his risks by selling it forward, the normal balancing of forward demands and supplies ceases to prevail, the forward rate drops to a heavy discount, and the cost of forward cover becomes "prohibitive." Under a flexible exchange rate system, where the spot rate is also free to move, arbitrage between the spot and forward markets, as well as speculation, would ensure that the expectation of depreciation was reflected in depreciation of the spot as well as the forward rate, and hence tend to keep the cost of forward cover within reasonable bounds.

3.   INCENTIVE TO "DESTABILIZING SPECULATION"

A further argument under the heading of uncertainty is that it will encourage "destabilizing speculation." The historical record provides no convincing supporting evidence for this claim, unless "destabilizing speculation" is erroneously defined to include any speculation against an officially pegged exchange rate, regardless of how unrealistic that rate was under the prevailing circumstances. A counter-consideration is that speculators who engage in genuinely destabilizing speculation—that is, whose speculations move the exchange rate away from rather than towards its equilibrium level—will consistently lose money, because they will consistently be buying when the rate is "high" and selling when it is "low" by comparison with its equilibrium value; this consideration does not however exclude the possibility that clever professional speculators may be able to profit by leading amateur speculators into destabilizing speculation, buying near the trough and selling near the peak, the amateurs' losses being borne out of their (or their shareholders') regular income. A further counter-consideration is that under flexible rates, speculation will itself move the spot rate, thus generating uncertainty in the minds of the speculators about the magnitude of prospective profits, which will depend on the relation between the spot rate and the expected future rate of exchange, neither of which will be fixed and independent of the magnitude of the speculators' transactions. By contrast, the adjustable peg system gives the speculator a "one-way option": in circumstances giving rise to speculation on a change in the rate, the rate can only move one way if it moves at all, and if it moves it is certain to be changed by a significant amount—and possibly by more, the stronger is the speculation on a change. The fixed exchange rate system courts "destabilizing speculation," in the economically incorrect sense of speculation against

the permanence of the official parity, by providing this one-way option; in so doing it places the monetary authorities in the position of speculating on their own ability to maintain the parity. It is obviously fallacious to assume that private speculators would speculate in the same way and on the same scale under the flexible rate system, which offers them no such easy mark to speculate against.

B. Flexible Rates and Inflation

The argument that the flexible exchange rate system would promote inflation comes in two major versions. The first is that under the flexible rate system governments would no longer be subject to the "discipline" against inflationary policies exerted by the fixity of the exchange rate. This argument in large part reflects circular reasoning on the part of the fixed rate exponents: discipline against inflationary policies, if necessary for international reasons, is necessary only because rates are fixed, and domestic inflation both leads to balance-of-payments problems and imposes inflation on other countries. Neither consequence would follow under the flexible exchange rate system. Apart from its external repercussions, inflation may be regarded as undesirable for domestic reasons; but the fixed rate system imposes, not the need to maintain domestic price stability, but the obligation to conform to the average world trend of prices, which may be either inflationary or deflationary rather than stable.[2] Moreover, under the adjustable peg system actually existing, countries can evade the discipline against excessively rapid inflation by drawing down reserves and borrowing, by imposing restrictions on international trade and payments, and in the last resort by de-

---

[2] A good example is Germany, which is suffering from balance-of-payments surpluses, because its price increases have been less than the average world trend.

valuing their currencies. The record since the Second World War speaks poorly for the anti-inflationary discipline of fixed exchange rates. The reason is that the signal to governments of the need for anti-inflationary discipline comes through a loss of exchange reserves, the implications of which are understood by only a few and can be disregarded or temporized with until a crisis descends—and the crisis justifies all sorts of policy expedients other than the domestic deflation which the logic of adjustment under the fixed rate system demands. Under a flexible rate system, the consequences of inflationary governmental policies would be much more readily apparent to the general population, in the form of a declining foreign value of the currency and an upward trend in domestic prices; and proper policies to correct the situation, if it were desired to correct it, could be argued about in freedom from an atmosphere of crisis.

The second argument to the effect that a flexible exchange rate would be "inflationary" asserts that any random depreciation would, by raising the cost of living, provoke wage and price increases that would make the initially temporarily lower foreign value of the currency the new equilibrium exchange rate. This argument clearly derives from confusion of a flexible with a fixed exchange rate. It is under a fixed exchange rate that wages and prices are determined in the expectation of constancy of the domestic currency cost of foreign exchange, and that abrupt devaluations occur that are substantial enough in their effects on the prices of imports and of exportable goods to require compensatory revision of wage bargains and price-determination calculations. Under a flexible rate system, exchange rate adjustments would occur gradually, and would be less likely to require drastic revisions of wage- and price-setting decisions,

especially as any general trend of the exchange rate and prices would tend to be taken into account in the accompanying calculations of unions and employers. Apart from this, it is erroneous to assume that increases in the cost of living inevitably produce fully compensatory wage increases; while such increases in the cost of living will be advanced as part of the workers' case for higher wages, whether they will in fact result in compensatory or in less than compensatory actual wage increases will depend on the economic climate set by the government's fiscal and monetary policies. It is conceivable that a government pledged to maintain full employment would maintain an economic climate in which any money wage increase workers chose to press for would be sanctioned by sufficient inflation of monetary demand and the money supply to prevent it from resulting in an increase in unemployment. But in that case there would be no restraint on wage increases and hence on wage and price inflation, unless the government somehow had arrived at an understanding with the unions and employers that only wage increases compensatory of previous cost of living increases (or justified by increases in productivity) would be sanctioned by easier fiscal and monetary policy. That is an improbable situation, given the difficulties that governments have encountered with establishing and implementing an "incomes policy" under the fixed rate system; and it is under the fixed rate system, not the flexible rate system, that governments have a strong incentive to insist on relating increases in money incomes to increases in productivity and hence are led on equity grounds to make exceptions for increases in the cost of living. It should be noted in conclusion that one version of the argument under discussion, which reasons from the allegation of a persistent tendency to cost-push inflation to the prediction of a persistent tendency towards depreciation of the currency, must be fallacious: it is logically impossible for all currencies to be persistently depreciating against each other.

V. CONTEMPORARY PROPOSALS FOR GREATER EXCHANGE RATE FLEXIBILITY

A. Increased Flexibility in the IMF System

The extreme difficulties that have been encountered in recent years in achieving appropriate adjustments of the parity values of certain major currencies within the present "adjustable peg" system of fixed exchange rates, as exemplified particularly in the prolonged agony of sterling from 1964 to 1967 and the failure of the "Bonn crisis" of November 1968 to induce the German and French governments to accept the revaluations of the franc and the mark agreed on as necessary by the officials and experts concerned with the international monetary system, have generated serious interest, especially in the United States Administration, in proposals for reforming the present I M F system so as to provide for more flexibility of exchange rates. It has been realized that under the present system, a devaluation has become a symbol of political defeat by, and a revaluation (appreciation) a symbol of political surrender to, other countries, both of which the government in power will resist to the last ditch; and that this political symbolism prevents adjustments of exchange rates that otherwise would or should be accepted as necessary to the proper functioning of the international monetary system. The aim therefore is to reduce or remove the political element in exchange rate adjustment under the present sys-

tem, by changing the system so as to allow the autonomous competitive foreign exchange market to make automatic adjustments of exchange rates within a limited range.

The two major proposals to this end are the "wider band" proposal and the "crawling peg" proposal. Under the "wider band" proposal, the present freedom of countries to allow the market value of their currencies to fluctuate within one per cent (in practice usually less) of their par values would be extended to permit variation within a much wider range (usually put at five per cent for argument's sake). Under the "crawling peg" proposal, daily fluctuations about the par value would be confined within the present or somewhat wider limits, but the parity itself would be determined by a moving average of the rates actually set in the market over some fixed period of the immediate past, and so would gradually adjust itself upwards or downwards over time to the market pressures of excess supply of or excess demand for the currency (pressures for depreciation or appreciation, rise or fall in the par value, respectively).

Both of these proposals, while welcomed by advocates of the flexible exchange rate system to the extent that they recognize the case for flexible rates and the virtues of market determination as contrasted with political determination of exchange rates, are subject to the criticism that they accept the principle of market determination of exchange rates only within politically predetermined limits, and hence abjure use of the prime virtue of the competitive market, its capacity to absorb and deal with unexpected economic developments.[3] The criticism is that *either* economic developments will not be such as to make the equilibrium ex-

---

[3] It is quite likely that a crawling peg would not have provided an equilibrium exchange rate in France after the events of May 1968.

change rate fall outside the permitted range of variation, in which case the restriction on the permitted range of variation will prove unnecessary, or economic change will require more change in the exchange rate than the remaining restriction on exchange rate variation will permit, in which case the problems of the present system will recur (though obviously less frequently). Specifically, sooner or later the exchange rate of a major country will reach the limit of permitted variation, and the speculation-generating possibility will arise that the par value of that currency will have to be changed by a finite and substantial percentage, as a result of lack of sufficient international reserves for the monetary authorities of the country concerned to defend the par value of the currency.

In this respect, there is a crucial difference between the wider band proposal and the crawling peg proposal. The wider band system would provide only a once-for-all increase in the degree of freedom of exchange rates to adjust to changing circumstances. A country that followed a less inflationary policy than other nations would find its exchange rate drifting towards the ceiling on its par value, and a country that followed a more inflationary policy than its neighbours would find its exchange rate sinking towards the floor under its par value. Once one or the other fixed limit was reached, the country would to all intents and purposes be back on a rigidly fixed exchange rate. The crawling peg proposal, on the other hand, would permit a country's policy, with respect to the relative rate of inflation it preferred, to diverge permanently from that of its neighbours, but only within the limits set by the permitted range of daily variation about the daily par value and the period of averaging of past actual exchange rates specified for the determination of the par value itself. For those persuaded of the case for flexible exchange rates, the crawling peg is thus definitely to be preferred. The only question is the empirical one of whether the permitted degree of exchange rate flexibility would be adequate to eliminate the likelihood in practice of a situation in which an exchange rate was so far out of equilibrium as to make it impossible for the monetary authorities to finance the period of adjustment of the rate to equilibrium by use of their international reserves and international borrowing power. This is an extremely difficult empirical question, because it involves not only the likely magnitude of disequilibrating disturbances in relation to the permitted degree of exchange rate adjustment, but also the effects of the knowledge by government of the availability of increased possibilities of exchange rate flexibility on the speed of governmental policy response to disequilibrating developments, and the effects of the knowledge by private speculators that the effects on the exchange rate of current speculation will determine the range within which the exchange rate will be in the future, on the assumption that the crawling peg formula continues to hold.

Evaluation of how both the wider band and the crawling peg proposals should work in practice requires a great deal of empirical study, which has not yet been carried out on any adequate scale. In the meantime, those persuaded of the case for flexible exchange rates would probably be better advised to advocate experimentation with limited rate flexibility, in the hope that the results will dispel the fears of the supporters of the fixed rate system, than to emphasize the dangers inherent in the residual fixity of exchange rates under either of the contemporary popular proposals for increasing the flexibility of rates under the existing fixed rate systems.

B.   A Floating Pound?

The argument of the preceding sections strongly suggests the advisability of a change in British exchange rate policy from a fixed exchange rate to a market-determined flexible exchange rate. The main arguments for this change are that a flexible exchange rate would free British economic policy from the apparent necessity to pursue otherwise irrational and difficult policy objectives for the sake of improving the balance of payments, and that it would release the country from the vicious circle of "stop-go" policies of control of aggregate demand.

A flexible exchange rate is not of course a panacea; it simply provides an extra degree of freedom, by removing the balance-of-payments constraints on policy formation. In so doing, it does not and cannot remove the constraint on policy imposed by the limitation of total available national resources and the consequent necessity of choice among available alternatives; it simply brings this choice, rather than the external consequences of choices made, to the forefront of the policy debate.

The British economy is at present riddled with inefficiencies consequential on, and politically justified by, decisions based on the aim of improving the balance of payments. In this connection, one can cite as only some among many examples the heavy protection of domestic agriculture, the protection of domestic fuel resources by the taxation of imported oil, the subsidization of manufacturing as against the service trades through the Selective Employment Tax, and various other subsidies to manufacturing effected through tax credits. One can also cite the politically arduous effort to implement an incomes policy, which amounts to an effort to avoid by political pressure on individual wage- and price-setting decisions the need for an adjustment that would be effected automatically by a flexible exchange rate. A flexible exchange rate would make an incomes policy unnecessary. It would also permit policy towards industry, agriculture, and the service trades to concentrate on the achievement of greater economic efficiency, without the biases imparted by the basically economically irrelevant objectives of increasing exports or substituting for imports.

The adoption of flexible exchange rates would also make unnecessary, or at least less harmful, the disruptive cycle of "stop-go" aggregate demand policies which has characterized British economic policy for many years. British Governments are under a persistently strong incentive to try to break out of the limitations of available resources and relatively slow economic growth by policies of demand expansion. This incentive is reinforced, before elections, by the temptation to expand demand in order to win votes, in the knowledge that international reserves and international borrowing power can be drawn down to finance the purchase of votes without the electorate knowing that it is being bribed with its own money—until after the election the successful party is obliged to clean up the mess so created by introducing deflationary policies, with political safety if it is a returned government, and with political embarrassment if it is an opposition party newly come to power. If the country were on a flexible exchange rate, the generation of the "political cycle" would be inhibited by the fact that the effort to buy votes by pre-election inflationary policies could soon be reflected in a depreciation of the exchange rate and a rise in the cost of living. Even if this were avoided by use of the Government's control of the country's international reserves and borrowing powers to stabilize the exchange rate, a newly elected Government of either complexion would not be faced with the absolute necessity of introducing deflationary economic policies to restore its international reserves. It could instead allow the exchange rate to depreciate while it made up its mind what to do. Apart from the question of winning elections, Governments that believed in demand expansion as a means of promoting growth could pursue this policy *a outrance,* without being forced to reverse it by a balance-of-payments crisis, so long as they and the public were prepared to accept the consequential depreciation of the currency; Governments that believed instead in other kinds of policies would have to argue for and defend them on their merits, without being able to pass them off as imposed on the country by the need to secure equilibrium in the balance of payments.

C.   The Feasibility of Floating

While these and other elements of the case for a floating pound have frequently been recognized and advocated, it has been much more common to argue that a flexible exchange rate for sterling is "impossible," either because the position of sterling as an international reserve currency precludes it, or because the International Monetary Fund would not permit it. But most of the arguments for the presumed international importance of a fixed international value of sterling have been rendered irrelevant by the deterioration of sterling's international position subsequent to the 1967 devaluation, and in particular by the Basle Facility and the sterling area agreements concluded in the autumn of 1968, which by giving a gold guarantee on most of the overseas sterling area holdings of sterling have freed the British authorities to change the foreign exchange value of sterling without fear of recrimination from its official holders. Moreover, the relative decline in the international role of sterling, and in the relative importance of Britain in world trade, finance and investments that have characterized the post-war period, has made it both possible and necessary to think of Britain as a relatively small component of the international monetary system, more a country whose difficulties require special treatment than a lynch-pin of the system, the fixed value of whose currency must be supported by other countries in the interests of survival of the system as a whole.

Under the present circumstances, adoption of a floating exchange rate for the pound would constitute, not a definitive reversal of the essential nature of the I M F system of predominantly fixed exchange rates, but recognition of and accommodation to a situation in which the chronic weakness of the pound is a major source of tension within the established system. The International Monetary Fund is commonly depicted in Britain as an ignorantly dogmatic but politically powerful opponent of sensible changes that have the drawback of conflicting with the ideology written into its Charter. But there is no reason to believe that the Fund, as the dispassionate administrator of an international monetary system established nearly a quarter of a century ago to serve the needs of the international economy, is insensitive to the tensions of the contemporary situation and blindly hostile to reforms that would permit the system as a whole to survive and function more effectively.

READING 42

FLUCTUATING EXCHANGE RATES: THE FUND'S APPROACH

Margaret G. de Vries

There has been a great deal of mis-conception about the International Monetary Fund's approaches to fluc-tuating exchange rates, or as they are often called, "floating rates." Critics of the Fund frequently suggest that it has been too uncompromising in its sup-port of the present world-wide system of fixed exchange rates. The implica-tion is that the Fund's attitude stems primarily from the requirements of its Articles of Agreement, or that its eco-nomic reasoning is too rigid. It is worthwhile, therefore, to take a deeper look at what the Fund policies have been, and their underlying rationale.

The Fund has, of course, consistently and strongly supported the system of institutionally agreed par values. How-ever, this stand has only in part re-flected the requirements of its Articles; it owes far more to the Fund's own widening experiences with deviations from that system. Furthermore—and this is much less generally realized—

while the pursuit of fixed exchange rates has remained the underpinning of its philosophy, the Fund has also, *tem-porarily and in carefully delineated cir-cumstances,* supported what it regards as less than ideal types of exchange rate adjustments; the latter have in-cluded fluctuating rates.

I. MODERATIONS OF POLICY OVER TIME

From 1946 to 1968, it is possible to discern almost step-by-step move-ments in the Fund's policies on fluc-tuating rates. In its very early days the Fund put primary stress on the fact that fluctuating rates were inconsistent with its Articles. Concern with the for-mal position of a country with a fluc-tuating rate was exemplified by the Fund's first encounter with such a rate: In July 1948 Mexico suspended trans-actions at its par value and let the market set the exchange rate. The Mex-

Source: Reprinted from *Finance and Development,* No. 2, 1969, International Monetary Fund, Washington, pp. 44–48.

ican authorities did not wish to resort to exchange controls on capital movements—the source of the deficit—and believed more time was required to determine an appropriate new par value.

For the newly formed International Monetary Fund this posed a serious problem. Accordingly, the Mexican Government and the Fund were in continuous consultation with a view to establishing a new par value for the peso; this was done in July 1949, one year after the suspension of the initial parity.

II. THE "EXCEPTIONAL" SITUATION

Very soon pragmatic considerations began to overshadow the more technical ones. Hoping that a few exceptions would not cause a return to the rate instability of the pre-Fund era, the Fund recognized the possibility that certain unusual circumstances might arise.

This change in attitude was evidenced in November 1949 when Peru suspended transactions at its par value. Peru had had an exchange system consisting of three separate markets, the rates in one of which were fixed on the basis of the par value. Now the market with fixed rates was to be abolished and all transactions were to be conducted in two markets, both of which would have fluctuating rates. The rates in the two markets were expected to follow each other closely.

This time the Fund recognized the exigencies of the situation that had made Peru unable both to maintain its old par value and immediately to select a new one. There was possibly even something to praise in the Peruvian exchange system. It was essentially unified and the new rates seemed realistic; this represented substantial progress compared with the complex multiple rates of many other countries. Therefore, with the understanding that the purpose of Peru's action was the establishment of a unitary exchange sys-

tem on a more appropriate level, the Fund did not object to the use of the fluctuating rate as a temporary measure.

As of March 1, 1969, Peru still had not set a new par value. Meanwhile, in the intervening years, the Fund had permitted Peru to draw on the Fund's resources and to assume the obligations of Article VIII—that is, to be regarded as a country which is relatively free of restrictions and which has a convertible currency.

III. THE INSTANCE OF CANADA

A second example of the Fund's acceptance of toleration of a fluctuating rate in exceptional circumstances is, of course, that of Canada, which had a fluctuating rate from September 1950 to May 1962. This rate was introduced in order to dampen a heavy inflow of capital, mainly from the United States. This inflow, which had become especially great in 1950, added to the money supply and tended to depress interest rates, thus augmenting inflationary pressures. The object of this exchange rate change was thus in contrast to most other exchange rate adjustments that are intended to rectify an unfavorable balance of trade and to check an outflow of capital. Because of the speculative nature of much of the capital inflow, the Canadian Government felt unable to foresee the end of the capital movement so long as a fixed exchange rate was maintained. As, in the view of the Canadian Government, it was impossible to determine in advance with any reasonable assurance what new level would be appropriate, it announced that the rate of exchange should be left to be determined by market forces.

After discussion of possible alternative courses of action that Canada might follow, the Fund again decided to recognize the exigencies of the situation as well as to take note of the intention of the Canadian Government to remain in consultation with the Fund and to reestablish an effective par value as soon as circumstances warranted.

By 1956, the Fund regarded Canada's relative success with a fluctuating rate as reflecting the uniqueness of Canada's circumstances. Canada had not only a trade deficit but a substantial capital inflow. There was confidence in the Canadian dollar because of the fiscal and credit policies being followed. Canada was relatively free of restrictions and had a convertible currency. Moreover, the institutional background led many persons to regard as natural a parity for the Canadian dollar somewhere near that of the U.S. dollar, and close interdependence between short-term capital movements and movements of the exchange rate had caused capital flows on the whole to be equilibrating rather than disturbing. Finally, the exchange rate had fluctuated only about 3–5 per cent, despite the absence of intervention by the authorities except for the purpose of maintaining an orderly exchange market. For all these reasons, Canadian trade and normal capital transactions had not lost the important benefits commonly associated with exchange rate stability. The Canadian example was not a precedent for the circumstances of other countries.

By mid-1961 disenchantment with the way the Canadian rate had been operating since the late 1950's began to be discernible both among Canadian authorities and in the Fund. A very large deficit on current account had emerged, the rate of economic growth had decreased, and unemployment had risen. The Canadian authorities attributed these economic reverses in large part to the then unduly high exchange rate; the inflow of capital had caused the rate to reach a point at which it

acted as a stimulus to imports and as some deterrent to exports. And the Fund itself, observing the adverse developments, had entered into active consultation with Canada concerning the circumstances in which the establishment of a new par value would be appropriate. On May 2, 1962, in the midst of exchange difficulties, Canada finally gave up its fluctuating rate and declared a new par value to the Fund.

In addition to Peru and Canada, other Fund members which have had fluctuating exchange rates for relatively long periods include Lebanon, the Syrian Arab Republic, and Thailand. In 1954, in order to facilitate Fund transactions in currencies where fluctuating rates prevail—such as Fund drawings in these currencies or payment of additional local currency in order to preserve the value of Fund assets—the Fund set up special rules for computing exchange rates of those countries with fluctuating rates. Computations were to be based on the midpoint between the highest and lowest rates for the U.S. dollar quoted for cable transfers for spot delivery in the main financial center of the country of the fluctuating currency on specified days. Computations under this decision have been made only for those countries for which transactions no longer take place at their par values. As of August 15, 1968, for example, computed effective rates applied only to Argentina, Bolivia, Brazil, Chile, Colombia, Indonesia, Korea, Paraguay, Peru, and Venezuela.

IV. FLUCTUATING RATES AND EXCHANGE REFORM

In a second set of circumstances, the Fund has gone somewhat further: in conjunction with exchange reform and stabilization, the Fund has supported programs which have included a fluctuating rate. To some extent Peru's fluctuating rate, described above, had been introduced as part of an exchange reform. But even before reform Peru's exchange system had been fairly simple, inflation had not been massive, and the devaluation involved was modest. In the late 1950's the technique of using a fluctuating exchange rate to effect reform of very complex exchange systems, with a multiplicity of rates, became more widely used. Bolivia and Thailand were among the first, in 1955–56, to take this type of action. They were followed in the next few years by Chile, Paraguay, and Argentina. Similarly, in 1962, the Philippines resorted to a fluctuating rate as a means of devaluation and decontrol of restrictions; this rate lasted until November 1965.

At the time of stabilization after a prolonged period of inflation, these countries have devalued, but not necessarily to new fixed rates. Fluctuating rates were used for a time as a means of finding the point at which the rate could ultimately be maintained. In the circumstances that prevailed in those countries it was impossible to determine the appropriate level for the exchange rate in advance. Where a combination of restrictions and multiple rates existed, this was true because even the level of the rate currently in effect would not readily be determined. As well, it was uncertain how effective the new anti-inflationary measures would be. Movements in prices and wages following the adoption of measures designed to eliminate distortions in the economy are difficult to estimate. In still other instances, a new par value could not be determined until after a new tariff system had been established. For these reasons, as exchange reforms have been undertaken, several countries have instituted a single fluctuating rate.

Although problems have arisen, experiences with these temporary fluctuating rates have often proved to be quite successful. Several of them have eventually been stabilized and have furnished the basis for new par values (see Margaret G. de Vries, "The Decline of Multiple Rates, 1947–67," *Finance and Development,* Vol. IV, No. 4, December 1967). The Fund, by 1962–63, therefore, turned to positive support of this means of exchange reform.

Even more significant is that a fluctuating rate adopted in these circumstances has carried with it an understanding between the country and the Fund that the fluctuating rate will be allowed to move in accordance with market forces; the authorities are to intervene only to maintain orderly market conditions. Even when the need for rate flexibility is recognized, the authorities often find it difficult to maintain a flexible rate; in the absence of clear criteria for exchange rate action, the tendency is to peg the rate at a level which soon becomes out of line with developments in the economy. Accordingly, in some countries where a flexible rate policy is considered essential because of continuing inflation, a test has been set up as a means of assuring that a rate will be maintained which conforms to the basic market trends. Such a test usually consists of a prescribed minimum level at which the foreign exchange reserves of the country are to be maintained during a stated period, with exchange rate action taken whenever that level is threatened. Even so, inasmuch as most countries have been reluctant to see their rates depreciate excessively, the Fund has frequently had to call upon countries with flexible rates not to stabilize prematurely.

V. STABILITY THE ULTIMATE OBJECTIVE —FIXED RATES FOR THE GENERAL SYSTEM

The Fund's ultimate objective, nonetheless, even in cases of exchange reform, has been to create the conditions for the restoration of a stable and unified exchange rate. The fluctuating rate has been regarded as a temporary means to an end. Moreover, the Fund has also continued to regard a general system of fixed rates and institutionally agreed par values as decidedly superior to a system of fluctuating rates. These positions have been held primarily because, in the Fund's view, experience has revealed several weaknesses of fluctuating rates.

First, to those who advocate allowing rates to find their "natural" level, the Fund has stated that there is no such thing as a natural level for the rate of exchange of a currency. The proper rate, in each case, depends upon the economic, financial, and monetary policies followed by the country concerned, and by other countries with whom it has important economic relationships. In addition, whether a given exchange rate is at the "correct" level can be determined only after there has been time to observe the course of the balance of payments in response to that rate.

Second, movements in fluctuating rates have been significantly affected by large speculative transfers of capital. Consequently, countries have preferred to make adjustments in their exchange rates in a manner that would minimize distortions through speculation. And fluctuating rates are often inappropriate where excessive outflows of capital, or underinvoicing and smuggling, have been troublesome. Additional capital inflows that are speculative on exchange rate movements may be induced.

Third, in circumstances of continuous inflation, fluctuating rates give rise to a vicious circle of devaluation and inflation. On the one hand, so long as internal prices are not stabilized, flexible rates are necessary to prevent overvaluation. Yet under conditions of internal price instability, the rate depreciates regularly, which in turn contributes to even greater inflation. Furthermore, if a country does not clearly and quickly adopt a monetary policy aimed at general stability, the movements of its fluctuating rate are likely to be oscillations not around a stable value but around a declining trend.

In this regard, the Fund has concluded that it is an illusion to expect a fluctuating rate to ease the problems facing the monetary authorities. On the contrary, by eliminating the rallying point of the defense of a fixed par value, a fluctuating rate makes it necessary for the authorities to exercise greater caution in determining monetary policy. When fluctuations in the rate become of significant amplitude, these fluctuations may themselves contribute to the forces leading to depreciation. Depreciation may create inflationary pressures. Indeed, depreciation of the exchange rate often proceeds more rapidly than the accompanying or ensuing price inflation.

Consequently, experience with fluctuating rates has suggested that the countries using this device had not, on the whole, been able to protect thereby their economies from pressures arising abroad. Moreover, should they pursue expansionary domestic policies, countries might still lose reserves, unless the authorities are prepared to let the rate depreciate continuously. And, the Fund observed, orderly exchange arrangements and exchange stability had been recognized by most countries to be important and generally accepted objectives of economic policy. Even in countries where the authorities were not prepared formally to stabilize the exchange rate on the basis of a realistic parity, *de facto* stable rates were often maintained for long periods of time. For all these reasons, the Fund has retained exchange rate stability as the ultimate goal even for those countries which have temporarily resorted to a fluctuating rate.

Finally, the Fund has had still another reason for preferring a general system of institutionally agreed parities. As a body for international consultation on exchange rate changes, the Fund has feared that, under a system of flexible rates, exchange rate policy would tend to become much more a matter of unilateral action and thus make the process of international collaboration in financial matters far more difficult.

The debates over the relative merits of fixed and fluctuating exchange rates, such as have been going on among economists in the last several years, may never end. Certainly similar discussions of this issue have also occurred in the past. In the early 1950's, for example, interest in a possible fluctuating rate system, even in some official quarters, was sufficiently intense that the Fund felt obliged to explain its position. However, as time has gone on, two major developments in Fund policy stand out. First, Fund policy has evolved in a direction of accepting, indeed supporting, flexible rate regimes as temporary expedients where carefully defined exceptional circumstances seem to warrant such flexibility; by no means has the Fund categorically opposed all such schemes. Second, Fund policy in favor of fixed and stable rates has increasingly been based on its own widening unsatisfactory experiences with deviations from the par value system and because, in its view, a general flexible rate system would make international monetary cooperation extremely troublesome; Fund policy has gone beyond a mere reiteration of the requirements of its Articles.

READING 43
THE BRAVE NEW WORLD OF SDR'S

Otmar Emminger

I

As these lines are being written it has become nearly certain that the "activation"; i.e., the putting into effect, of the Special Drawing Rights Scheme will be decided upon at the next Annual Meeting of the International Monetary Fund. The amount to be allocated to participants in the Scheme in proportion to their IMF quotas, is likely to be 3½ billion dollars in 1970 and 3 billion dollars each in the two subsequent years.* This, at least, has been the recent consensus among the Group of Ten countries. It is known that this reflects also pretty well the thought of the Managing Director of the IMF who has to make the official proposal to the members of the Scheme.

The new SDR Scheme has often been haled as a "landmark in monetary evolution," and Mr. Edward M. Bernstein, one of the founding fathers of the International Monetary Fund at the Bretton Woods Conference of 1944, re-

cently called it "the most important development in the international monetary system since Bretton Woods." We should, however, harbour no illusions. In looking at the new Scheme, I am reminded of the words of Lord Keynes when he moved the adoption of the Final Act on the IMF at the Bretton Woods Conference: "How much better," he said, "that our projects should begin in disillusion than that they should end in it!"

Let us face it: the first allocation of SDR's is not likely to visibly and profoundly change the face of the world economy. A 4 per cent annual addition to present global world reserves of about 75 billion dollars is no earth-shaking affair. As this amount is going to be spread over a hundred or more countries, the actual sums allotted to individual countries are in most cases relatively small. It may take quite some time before any tangible effects of the

Source: Reprinted from *International Currency Review*, August 1969, pp. 5–14.

* These were essentially the terms agreed upon at the subsequent meeting.

new Scheme will be felt—or to put it more correctly; if the Scheme succeeds, the effects may not even become outwardly visible at all. For the main purpose of the Scheme is not to achieve, but to avert something tangible, namely, the possibly disruptive effects of a shortage of world reserves. It would also be illusory to believe that the putting into effect of the SDR Scheme could be a cure-all for the present acute problems in the international payments field.

However, with all these reservations it can fairly be claimed that the establishment of the new reserve instruments as such signals fundamental progress. The principle has now been accepted that there should be a deliberate control over the world's supply of reserves by the creation of fiduciary reserves through a permanent new system.[1] The progress towards deliberate reserve creation must be viewed in the perspective of historical evolution. On the national plane, the completely free issuing of bank-notes and creation of book money by unsupervised private banks have in the course of the past hundred years gradually been transformed into a system under which money creation is controlled by the central bank with the aim of attaining greater economic stability. Now we are beginning to extend this deliberate control over money to the international sphere. The recent convulsions of the international monetary system have clearly shown how necessary it is that "the great free nations of the world take control of our monetary problems if these problems are not to take control of us" (President Kennedy in Frankfurt, July 1963).

II

There are several reasons why reserve creation through a new fiduciary asset has become unavoidable. The *first reason* is that *supply mechanism of reserves* in the present system has very nearly come to a dead end. The stock of *monetary gold* in the world may be regarded as virtually fixed at its present level. During the last two years before the "Gold Pool" of the seven major control banks collapsed in March 1968, national gold reserves were depleted by nearly 3 billion dollars due to speculative private demand. Since the establishment of the two-tier gold price system in spring 1968, a large part of the newly-mined gold seems to have been absorbed by private demand at higher prices than the official gold price of $35 an ounce.

As concerns *reserve currencies,* especially U.S. dollars, signs have been increasing since about 1965 that this kind of reserve creation may be approaching saturation point. Over the last 18 months no new official dollars reserves have been created on a net basis (although there have been violent ups and downs in the meantime). The creation of reserves through official holdings of a reserve currency must of necessity sooner or later come to an end—either voluntarily or through a crisis. There is a limit to the external short-term indebtedness which the reserve currency country can safely build upon a given amount of its own reserves. Its international liquidity position cannot deteriorate beyond a certain point without provoking a crisis of confidence. Already in July 1966, the Deputies of the Group of Ten in their

[1] There have been forerunners as far as creation of fiduciary reserves is concerned. The most important one was the European Payments Union (EPU) of 1950 which provided automatic credit lines to participants with the express purpose (laid down in the Preamble of the EPU Agreement) of "providing them with resources to play in part the role of gold and foreign currency reserves." These reserves were, however, limited to settlements inside a regional group and clearly designed as temporary, and not permanent, reserve assets.

report which prepared the groundwork for the SDR Scheme noted: "For a variety of reasons, further substantial increases of dollar reserves are unlikely to occur and in our view it would indeed be undesirable that the increase in the external short-term indebtedness of the U.S. should continue as in the recent past." Over the past four years, reserves stemming from "traditional" sources declined by about four billion dollars. The increase in total world reserves which nevertheless took place, was attributable to abnormal factors, mainly to balance-of-payments credit extended by the IMF and by central banks on a temporary basis to major deficit countries, like the United Kingdom and France. This, however, is not a sustainable basis for a steadily growing supply of world reserves—and it is, at the same time, potentially the most inflationary kind of reserve creation.

The second reason behind the search for a new reserve asset lies in the unsatisfactory quality of the "traditional" reserve assets. *Foreign exchange holdings* are not a final reserve asset; for they are, and must be, convertible into other currencies or into gold (directly or indirectly). They suffer from the fact that they serve in the dual role of international reserves and national currencies. This makes the world reserve system vulnerable to every weakening of confidence in the monetary or political stability of the reserve currency country. *Gold* suffers from the disadvantage of serving at the same time as an official reserve asset and as a speculative commodity. Its supply for monetary purposes is dependent on the vagaries of gold production, Russian gold sales, use as a material for industry and jewellery and—not least—on private speculative demand. Pegging the price for the private use of gold to its official price makes the world's official gold stock dependent on all sorts of non-monetary developments.

Both gold and foreign exchange pose problems of *co-existence;* in the case of gold, it is the co-existence between official gold reserves and the private demand for gold. In the case of foreign exchange, it is the co-existence between the different national currencies serving as reserve assets and between them and gold.

III

When the planners of the Group of Ten worked, from 1965 to 1967, on a reform of the reserve system, they had these drawbacks and shortcomings of the "traditional" reserve instruments before their eyes. They knew any rational new reserve asset would have to conform to the following prerequisites and qualities:

First, it should be used purely for international reserve purposes and not serve at the same time as a national currency. Any extension of the present system into a multiple currency standard had to be discarded because it would multiply the potential dangers of confidence crises and disruptive shifts from one currency to another.

Second, the new reserve asset should not, like dollar or sterling reserves, "bear the mark of one particular country"—to use an expression of General de Gaulle. It should not arise out of, nor its amount be determined by, the balance-of-payments deficits of one particular country, and it should not be used to finance this country's deficit, thus conferring a special privilege on it. It should also not be dependent for its standing and acceptability on the confidence in this particular country's evolution and policies.

Third, the new reserve asset should instead be a claim against the whole community of countries, and its full usability assured by a clear acceptance obligation on the part of all countries with strong currencies.

Fourth, The new reserve instrument should be a final reserve asset, that is to say, not be convertible into gold, although it should have a full gold guarantee so as to facilitate its co-existence with gold reserves. Altogether it should be made as much "gold-like" as possible so as to grow over time into a fully accepted supplement to the world's scarce gold reserve.

Fifth, the new reserve asset should be usable as a truly "owned reserve" without any conditions attached to it. However, it should not be used for disequilibrating shifts from one kind of reserves to another but only to procure intervention currency for genuine balance-of-payments needs; and there should be provisions both for its use alongside other (traditional) kinds of reserves and for a reasonable reconstitution after a period of time so as to promote the re-adjustment of balance-of-payments disequilibria.

Sixth, the volume of reserve creation should not arbitrarily be determined by the ups and downs in the U.S. balance of payments, nor by the blind forces working in the gold market; it should be governed by deliberate decisions of the community of nations and be adjusted to the slowly growing collective need of the world economy for reserves.

These are, indeed, the main prerequisites which the system of Special Drawing Rights is intended to fulfill.

IV

A number of questions have been raised in connection with the new SDR Scheme. Why such an elaborate scheme at all? Why not solve the problem of providing new world reserves in a seemingly simpler way by an *increase in the official price of gold?* Some academic economists appear to believe that the main arguments against such a course stem either from American pride in not wanting to concede a formal "devaluation of the dollar" against gold, or from idiosyncrasies of old-fashioned central bankers. There are, however, other and better economic arguments. *First,* one would probably have to raise the official price of gold in a rather massive way, in order to make the increase credible and prevent speculation for further price increases from re-appearing rather soon thereafter. This would inevitably create a large inflationary potential, even if the paper profits in national currencies were sterilized; for the excessive reserve creation as such would remain and would exert its damaging effect on balance-of-payments discipline. *Secondly,* the benefits of such reserve creation would be very inequitably and very inappropriately distributed among the various countries and groups of countries. Nearly nine-tenths of the total amount of gold reserves plus hoarded gold are in the hands of about a dozen rich countries; they would therefore benefit quite disproportionately from a reserve distribution through a gold price increase. A redistribution of such reserve gains over the countries of the world—as has sometimes been proposed by Prof. Rueff/France—would be more complicated and more difficult to achieve than to start afresh with the allocation of new reserve assets according to a better formula. *Third,* not even a rather massive increase in the gold price, say by 50 per cent (equal to a reserve creation of 20 billion dollars plus unknown quantities of dishoarded gold) would safely prevent the possibility of new crises arising, perhaps after a lapse of a few years, out of the uneasy co-existence of gold as a reserve in-strument and a speculative commodity; thus the present separation of official gold from the private gold market could hardly be abolished, at least not for any length of time. *Fourth,* it should at least be mentioned that a massive increase in the official price of gold would expose the U.S. to an awkward situ-ation in view of the oft-repeated pledges of several U.S. Administrations concerning the present gold value of the dollar—pledges which have formed the basis on which other countries have built up and held a large part of their reserves in dollars.

V

Deliberate reserve creation on a world-wide scale, and SDR's as its in-strument, are novel concepts. It is therefore not surprising that they are surrounded by a lot of misunderstand-ings. Both the proponents of an early and massive application of the SDR Scheme and its most vehement critics have often based their cases on wrong or misleading arguments.

In Anglo-Saxon countries, in partic-ular, the view is widely held that sup-plementary reserves have to be created "in order to finance expanding world trade." In reality, reserves are not needed to "finance world trade," but to finance deficits and and surpluses of balances of payments. Tentative calcu-lations for the period 1954–68 show that average balance of payments dis-equilibria have increased a little less than world trade turnover. World re-serves have increased much less still. For the whole period from 1950 through 1968, world trade has increased by an impressive annual average of about 7½ per cent, world reserves by only about 2½ per cent annually. Certainly some particular features of this period, espe-cially the redistribution of the reserves

of the U.S. cannot be projected into the future. It is, however, noteworthy that during recent official discussions in the Group of Ten, no one suggested that in the coming year world reserves should necessarily be increased pari passu with the expected growth rate of world trade of about 8 per cent (this would imply an increase in world reserves of about 6 billion dollars annually).

Another view has been that creation of reserves through SDR's should alle-viate the position of major deficit coun-tries like the U.S. or the U.K., by help-ing them finance part of their present deficits. One is tempted to say: the reverse would be correct. For the whole purpose of the Scheme has been to provide supplementary reserves for the time when U.S. deficits will have largely disappeared and thus a major source of "traditional" reserves will have dried up. Adequate supplies of reserves for the rest of the world should help the U.S. not to continue but to end its chronic deficit. Another misunder-standing is the assumption that the present international wave of high interest rates indicates a "lack of inter-national money" which should be rem-edied by large injections of new reserves. In reality—as a recent report of Working Part 3 of OECD has pointed out—these high interest rates "should principally be regarded as symptoms of inflationary pressures or payments im-balances rather than as reflecting re-serve shortage, though a desire to minimize reserve losses has also, in some cases, been evident."

VI

The critics of the very notion of de-liberate reserve creation have main-tained that this is "artificial," that it is "monetary alchemy," inflationary by its very principle, and that allocation of SDR's to the participants is "mannah from heaven" or a "free gift." Prof. Rueff in a recent article very much harps on this theme, and adds: "Gold is 'earned' whereas special drawing rights are 'allocated.' " This is a strange argument in the mouth of someone who is known for supporting a doubling of the official gold price. Doubling the gold price would indeed be a completely "free" and "unearned" gift to holders. In contrast, allocation of SDR's is not a free gift: the beneficiaries have to assume an obligation for repayment at the time of an eventual winding up of the scheme and—more importantly —a commitment to accept from other participants and convert into usable convertible currency an amount of SDR's which is double their own allocation. Allocation of SDR's is no more artificial than the allocation of an automatic credit line on the basis of mutuality.

Whether the creation of SDR's has an inflationary impact on the world economy or not depends on its effect on the participants' economic policies. The initial distribution of SDR's in itself, which will be counted as a statistical increase in world reserves, has probably a lesser inflationary impact than an equivalent accumulation of gold and dollar reserves; an increase in the latter, in particular, has over the last few years usually been associated with inflationary demand in the U.S. spilling over into the rest of the world. The intention of SDR creation has been to offset the potential shortfall of reserve creation from "traditional" sources and to prevent insufficient reserves from causing disruptive trade and payments restrictions.

VII

In this context the criticism has been made, especially in the German-speaking press, that the recent discussions inside the Group of Ten seem to have completely disregarded the provision laid down in the SDR Scheme, i.e. that "the first decision to allocate special drawing rights shall take into account, as special considerations, a collective judgment that there is a global need to supplement reserves, and the attainment of a better balance of payments equilibrium, as well as the likelihood of a better working of the adjustment process in the future."

As a matter of fact, several recent meetings of Working Party 3 of the OECD, which specializes in balance-of-payments questions, were devoted to assessing the appropriateness of allocating SDR's from 1970 onwards, in view of their possible effects on balance-of-payments adjustment in the world.

It is true that there were some serious doubts whether better balance of payments equilibrium had already been reached in the two reserve-currency countries. The present surpluses on an official settlements basis of both the U.S. and the U.K. were discounted as being due in large part to exceptional and temporary factors, although it was conceded that they had contributed to some reserve destruction.

The main conclusion of the discussions was that at present there are two conflicting risks; on the one hand, a premature allocation of SDR's could cause the large deficit countries to drag their feet in adjusting their disequilibria. On the other hand, *once the adjustment of the U.S. and the British balance of payments in the direction of better equilibrium had been set in motion* it could be impeded and partly frustrated, if other countries should take premature defensive measures because of an inadequate level of their reserves. In this connection, a number of delegates stated flatly that their countries could not accept any significant reserve losses, and several of them indicated that their countries definitely intended to raise their reserves to a permanently higher level. Under these circumstances, the likelihood of a global need for additional reserves during the next few years had to be acknowledged.

In assessing the probable effect of SDR allocation on balance-of-payments discipline in the world, Working Party 3 was prepared to give the present American and British stabilization efforts the benefit of the doubt. It was evident that the present fight against inflation in the U.S. was so imperative for a number of domestic reasons that an SDR allocation from next year onwards was not likely to weaken the determination of the U.S. authorities. Equally credible was the formal assurance of the British representatives that—since the possible SDR allocation would be small compared with the large debt obligations falling due over the next few years and with the need to rebuild reserves— it would not provide scope for any relaxation of British policies to strengthen the external position of sterling. These statements of intent on the part of the reserve currency countries were held by other delegates to be one of the bases on which to justify a favourable vote for SDR activation in 1970.

Weighing all the pros and cons, the final judgment of Working Party 3 was: "There is a general consensus that, from the point of view of the adjustment process and of balance-of-payments equilibrium, it would not be inappropriate to proceed with an early allocation of special drawing rights."

VIII

Will the new SDR system win general acceptance and credibility in the near future? There have been doubts expressed on that score. Some of these doubts have found their way into a prominent publication, namely the Annual Reports of the Bank for International Settlements (BIS). Doubt has been expressed whether the execution of the new Scheme would not be too *timid* to attain full credibility; it was feared that the strong position of creditor countries in the Scheme (by the veto power conferred on countries having 15 per cent or more of the vote) would prevent the allocation of adequately large amounts of SDR's. The functioning and the credibility of the Scheme can indeed be endangered both by too much and by too little reserve creation. I believe that the present agreement on the amount to be allocated—9½ billion dollars for the next three years—represents a reasonable compromise.

The BIS experts have also expressed some doubt whether gold, dollars and SDR's will be able to co-exist usefully and without upsets. They keep their fingers crossed over whether *Gresham's Law* will not begin to work, and if so, what bad money will drive out what good. Indeed, it cannot be excluded that SDR's, being in effect an interest-bearing gold certificate secured by an acceptance obligation of all strong countries, will look so good to hold that it will not be very much used for settlements. In any case, care has been taken to put the co-existence of SDR's with other reserve assets on a safe footing: their acceptability is fully secured under any circumstances and they cannot be used for disequilibrating shifts between different reserve instruments. Thus, *Gresham's Law* appears to have been foiled by the provisions of the Scheme.

SDR's are, however, no cure-all for all the problems of the international monetary system. What is left unsolved is, for instance, the problem of co-existence between gold and dollar reserves, especially in the longer run. And even that problem looks minor in comparison with the most acute of the present problems, i.e., the unsolved problem of smoother balance-of-payments adjustment between chronic deficit and surplus countries. Here the SDR Scheme may make some contribution by providing a better environment for the necessary shifts in countries' reserve and payments positions (as has been pointed out by Working Party 3 of the OECD). But the main task in this field still lies before us.